THE CONVICT SHIPS

Mitchell Library, Sydney, N.S.W.

Pencil sketches of the first "SURREY", probably by Edward Dobson

THE
CONVICT SHIPS

1787-1868

BY

CHARLES BATESON

GLASGOW
BROWN, SON & FERGUSON, LTD., PUBLISHERS
4-10 DARNLEY STREET

First Edition - 1959
Second Edition- 1969
Reprinted- - 1985

ISBN 0 85174 195 9

Made and Printed in Great Britain

PREFACE TO FIRST EDITION

THIS book tells the dramatic story of a single phase of the convict transportation system—that of the actual conveyance of the prisoners to Australia from England and Ireland between the years 1787 and 1868. It is the history of the convict ships, of the officials and merchants who despatched them, of the men of the navy, the army and the mercantile marine who manned them, and of the hapless convicts who peopled their dank and gloomy prisons below decks. It is a history which has many dark and sombre hues—a story of hardship and human suffering, of disease and callous brutality, of mutiny and shipwreck, of cowardice and courage.

The scope of the work has been confined to those vessels which conveyed prisoners from England and Ireland. These were the convict ships proper. India, the Cape of Good Hope, Mauritius, Bermuda, Canada, and other places also shipped unwanted felons to the Australian colonies, but such prisoners arrived in relatively small numbers, generally in passenger and cargo vessels which had not been expressly chartered to carry convicts.

I have to thank particularly the librarian and staff of the Mitchell Library, Sydney, without whose help this book could not have been written, the staff of the Archives section of the State Library of Tasmania, who mainly compiled the appendix of the Tasmanian convict ships, and the staff of the Archives Branch of the Public Library, Museum and Art Gallery of Western Australia, who assisted in the compilation of the West Australian appendix.

The Trustees of the Public Library of New South Wales kindly gave me permission to consult and quote from the following manuscripts and original documents in the Mitchell and Dixson collections:

Despatches to and from the Governors of N.S.W.

Journals of Lieut. William Bradley, R.N., Lieut. Philip Gidley King, R.N., Lieut. Ralph Clark, R.N., Surgeon Arthur Bowes, the

Missionaries in the *Royal Admiral*, 1800 (Haweis Papers), Surgeon Joseph Arnold in the *Northampton*, 1815, and William S. Edwardson in the *Surrey*, 1816.

Diary of Rev. Walter Lawry in the *Lady Castlereagh*, 1817–18.

James Downie's log of the *Coromandel*, 1819.

Official Journal of Surgeon William Elyard, R.N., in the *John Bull*, 1821.

Convict Ships, Van Dieman's Land, 3 vols.

Landing Certificates, 1827–1853, 4 vols.

Indent Papers (Bound).

Indents, Assignments, etc. (Loose), 1788–1842.

Charters of Affreightment.

Bonwick's Transcripts, especially Minutes of the Directors of the East India Company, Log Books of the First Fleet and Biographical.

Colonial Secretary's Papers, 1815–1841. (Ships' musters, reports and letters from masters and surgeons, shipping returns, judgments of magistrates and minutes of evidence of courts of inquiry, etc., are to be found in the as yet unsorted and unindexed portions of this valuable collection).

Shipping Arrivals, Port Jackson, 1826–1841.

Supreme Court Papers (especially the bundles of ships' protests and Vice-Admiralty Court proceedings).

Diary of William Noah in the *Hillsborough*, 1798–9 (Dixson Collection).

Diary of Sergeant James Scott in the *Prince of Wales*, 1787–8. (Dixson Collection).

Professor Michael E. Lewis, of the Royal Naval College, Greenwich, generously gave advice on naval matters and found time to read and comment on several of the early chapters, making many valuable suggestions.

Others to whom my thanks are due include: Miss Rose Kelsall, of Perth, W.A., for the loan of Surgeon Henry Kelsall's diary of the loss of the *Waterloo* and of certain printed official documents relating to the wreck of that ship; Lloyd's Register of Shipping, London; the Librarian of H.M. Customs and Excise, London; the Register-General of Shipping and Seamen, Cardiff; the officials of the Public Records Office, the British Museum, South African Public Library (Cape Town), the Department of the U.S. Navy, Division of Naval History (Washington); Mr. H. Sargeant, City Librarian and Curator of the City of Portsmouth Libraries and Museums department; the Commonwealth Relations Office, London, for making it possible to obtain mirofilms of convict ship log-books; the Librarian and staff of the National Maritime Museum, Greenwich, for giving my daughter every assistance in obtaining information for me. Miss Jean March also helped greatly by compiling many records from the library of Lloyd's Shipping Register.

The account by Captain A. J. A. Mann on the voyage of the *Racehorse* is quoted from an article by Commander B. Wemyss-Gorman in *Blackwood's Magazine*, and I have to thank the author and the proprietor of that magazine for their permission to use this material. The extracts from the diary of Charles Picknell relating to the voyage of the *Kains* are taken from *Blue Peter*, which later was incorporated in the now defunct *Trident*. I regret that my efforts to trace the holder of the copyright of this material have proved fruitless. *Trident* did not own the copyright, and owing to the destruction of many of its records during the war, could not tell me who did. Whoever he or she may be, I trust my apologies will be accepted for being unable to make full acknowledgement of my indebtedness.

For the illustrations my thanks are due to Miss Rose Kelsall, of Perth, W.A., for those of Surgeon Henry Kelsall and the *John Calvin*; to Mr. R. W. Glassford, of Chatswood, N.S.W., for that of the *Edwin Fox*; to the trustees of the Public Library of N.S.W., for the sketches of the *Surrey*, the chart of the *Neva's* wreck and the poster advertising the *Success* (all from the Mitchell Library); to the Nautical Photo Agency, Beccles, for the photographs of the *Vimeira* and the *Success*; and to the National Maritime Museum, Greenwich, for the remainder.

Lastly, but above all, my thanks are due to both my wife and daughter, who have helped me at all stages of the preparation of this book . . . from note-taking to proof-reading.

In a history of this magnitude, covering a period of eighty years and for which the records are so scattered and often incomplete, it is inevitable that some events should have been overlooked and some inaccuracies perpetrated, despite all efforts to prevent them. These shortcomings lie at my door alone, and I apologise for them. I shall, however, welcome correspondence drawing my attention to them or making available fresh material, and such correspondence should be addressed to me care of Box 4922, G.P.O., Sydney, Australia.

CHARLES BATESON.

PREFACE TO SECOND EDITION

SINCE its first publication this book has stood the test of critical examination well, and in this second edition it has been necessary to correct only two or three major and a number of minor errors. However, the microfilming of the journals of surgeons-superintendent (Adm. 104 in the P.R.O.) has enabled me to examine something like 600 of these for the first time, with the result that I have been able to revise the appendices in respect of sailing dates, ports of departure, surgeons' names, and the statistics of embarkations, deaths and landings. It has also been possible to incorporate additional material in the text, particularly in regard to the West Australian transports. I have cited authorities for the statements made in the text, but in the interval of more than a dozen years since the main research was completed some of these have been lost or mislaid and I am conscious that the documentation is not as complete as it should be. For this I apologise.

I thank all those who have helped in the book's revision, but, in particular, Miss Dawn Morgan, now Mrs. Troy, whose intimate knowledge of the convict material in the N.S.W. Archives was invaluable and much simplified my task, and my wife, Ann, who at all stages gave encouragement and aid.

JULY 15, 1969. CHARLES BATESON.

CONTENTS

ILLUSTRATIONS

CHAPTER ONE

"FOR THEIR COUNTRY'S GOOD"

THE first of the English adventurers to sail beneath the Southern Cross, those hardy seamen who left the narrow confines and comparative safety of their own northern oceans to meet the challenge of the unknown and uncharted Pacific, did so as much for knowledge as for gain. The existence of a vast southern continent—the half-legendary Isles of Spice which beckoned Magellan, the fabled Tierra Australis of Pedro de Quiros and Luis Torres—served for more than two centuries as the magnet which, in turn, drew Spanish, Portugese, Dutch, English and French navigators into the immense extent of the rolling blue Pacific.

Geographers were emphatic that this continent, stretching perhaps right away to the shores of South America, must exist; for they believed that only by such a counterweight at the opposite end of the world was the northern land mass anchored in position. So the intrepid seamen of the Old World steered their frail, crank ships out into the vastness of the Pacific, where, while the *terra incognita* of the New World eluded them, they found and lost islands in curiously prodigal style.

Each daring navigator, at some stage or other of his journeyings, imagined that he had discovered the great southern land which all were certain existed, but no sooner had he returned home to announce his success than some other voyager disproved his claim by showing that the so-called continent was just another of the hundreds of islands dotting the Pacific. The great southern continent proved obstinately elusive, a mysterious El Dorado that served perpetually as a challenge to seafaring mankind. Relentlessly the quest continued, as the seamen of the maritime nations strove to extend the borders of their country's territory on the faint outskirts of their maps, to discover what hitherto had escaped all, and to gain knowledge, fame and riches in one epoch-making voyage.

"Whereas the making discoveries of countries hitherto unknown," ran Captain James Cook's secret instructions for his first voyage,[1] "and the attaining a knowledge of distant parts which though formerly discovered have yet been but imperfectly explored, will redound greatly to the honour of this nation as a Maritime Power, as well as to the dignity of the Crown of Great Britain, and may tend greatly to the advancement of the trade and navigation thereof; and whereas there is reason to imagine that a continent, or land of great extent, may be found to the southward of the tract lately made by Captain Wallis in His Majesty's ship the *Dolphin* . . . or of the tract of any former navigators in pursuits of the like kind; you are therefore in pursuance of His Majesty's pleasure hereby required and directed to put to sea with the bark you command, so soon as the observation of the transit of the planet Venus shall be finished, and . . . proceed to the southward in order to make discovery of the continent above-mentioned . . ."

When he returned to England in the *Endeavour* in 1771, Cook, who had circumnavigated New Zealand and faithfully delineated on the map the eastern coast of Australia, was almost convinced that no vast southern continent existed, and on his second voyage, begun in the following year, he finally exploded the long-cherished myth. "Terra Australis Nondum Cognita," the enormous tract of country, the size of Europe and Asia combined, which was shown on the maps as lying athwart the Pacific from the tip of South America, had no reality outside the imaginations of the men who had so patiently sought it.

No navigator explored the Pacific as thoroughly as did Cook, nor made discoveries as momentous and important. In a ceremony, arresting in its simplicity, he had taken possession in the name of His Britannic Majesty of the largest land mass in the Southern Hemisphere, the island continent of Australia, the shadowy outlines of which were etched on the maps of the day under the name of New Holland. Its colonisation was the rich reward garnered from Cook's voyagings, but its settlement was not effected in the tradition and spirit which had inspired the great navigator. The circumstances of the founding of Australia are divorced entirely from those of its discovery and exploration by Cook. The mainspring was very different, and in the conditions of the day, and the state of man's thoughts and outlook at the time, it was perhaps inevitable that it should be so.

Never in history were a country's beginnings laid by such unhappy and unenthusiastic pioneers as the seven hundred and fifty-nine convicts of Australia's first fleet and the thousands of prisoners who followed them into an unwanted exile. In the words of Henry Carter's poem—the so-called Barrington Prologue[2] that was said to have been spoken by that celebrated pickpocket at the opening of the first Australian theatre in 1796:

> "From distant climes, o'er wide spread seas we come,
> (Though not with much éclat, or beat of drum)
> True patriots all; for be it understood,
> We left our country for our country's good."

Yet time has proven that these bewildered prisoners were men and women of destiny and of history. Not until many years after the arrival of the First Fleet did Australia's essential character of a penal settlement change: the first influx of free immigrants did not occur until the 1820's, and for at least a decade it was a mere trickle. The truth is that Australia, which to-day stands as a symbol of the New World and the Old Freedoms, was pioneered, during the first thirty years of its existence, solely through the labour of those who had left their country for their country's good.

Australia, of course, served for much longer than thirty years as a dumping-ground for the surplus criminal population of England and Ireland. The first penal settlement within its borders was established by Captain Arthur Phillip, R.N., on the wooded shores of Port Jackson in 1788; the last convict ship discharged her human freight at Swan River, Western Australia, in 1868. During that span of eighty years 158,702 male and female prisoners were landed in Australia from the Mother Country. In addition, prisoners reached Australia from India, Canada, the Cape of Good Hope, Bermuda, Mauritius and other places, many of these arrivals being soldiers sentenced to transportation for mutiny, desertion or other military crimes. The conveyance of these prisoners to Australia lies outside the scope of this work, but roughly 1321 arrived from places other than Great Britain and Ireland, and have to be added to the above total, making a grand total of 160,023. This figure, however, does not represent the total of Australia's convict population, since individuals locally convicted or convicted elsewhere in Australia were transported to New South Wales or Tasmania. The history of the conveyance of the prisoners from

British and Irish ports is absorbingly interesting, full of the rich drama of human suffering and human endeavour, a story in which tales of mutiny and shipwreck are intermingled with the more prosaic record of the conquest of disease at sea and of the gradual shortening of the length of the passage from England and Ireland to Australia by sailing ship.

The number of prisoners embarked aboard the convict ships was substantially greater than the number landed at their destination. Disease took by far the heaviest toll. Scurvy, dysentery, typhoid fever, smallpox and other diseases were commonplace, especially in the earlier years of transportation, and effective measures to combat them were introduced but tardily.

For long no real effort was made to ensure that the convicts embarked were physically fit to withstand the rigors of the long voyage through varying climatic conditions. The medical examination prior to embarkation was perfunctory, and, indeed, was for many years a useless formality. The magistrates, gaolers, hulk officials and departmental officers were less concerned with the well-being of the prisoners on the passage than with ridding the gaols and hulks of as many of their inmates as was possible, so that the constant stream of new prisoners might be accommodated. The result was that many convicts, having already spent months in the insanitary, fever-ridden gaols or in the noisome hulks, were sent aboard the transports in a sickly and emaciated state and, often enough, suffering from an infectious or contagious complaint.

Conditions aboard the convict ships, more particularly in the early years, were not such as were calculated to prevent or check disease. The prisons in the 'tween decks were gloomy, dank and insanitary, and frequently the prisoners, generally handcuffed and leg-ironed, were confined in them for long periods. As gross overcrowding was common, it is not surprising that the prisons were fertile breeding-places for diseases of all kinds.

The British authorities were not insensible to these dangers, and regulations designed to protect the health of the convicts were framed with care and foresight. It was stipulated that the prisons should be cleaned and fumigated regularly, that they should be adequately ventilated, and that the prisoners should be given access to the deck daily for fresh air and exercise. These precautions, however, were too frequently neglected because of laxity, inefficiency or ignorance on the part of the officers of the convict ships. The provisions were generally of good quality, but the convicts received less, and sometimes considerably less, than their due because the rations were not always truly served.

The great defect in the organisation of transportation was the absence, until a comparatively late date, of any effective supervision during the voyage. Departmental and inter-service rivalry, and petty jealousy among the various officers in the convict ships, delayed the solution of this problem, and not until many years after the sailing of the First Fleet was over-riding responsibility entrusted to a single official, the surgeon-superintendent. The beneficial results were immediately apparent in a sharp fall in the mortality rate.

The traditional conservatism of officialdom was responsible for delays in the introduction of other reforms. Suggestions that the convict ships should not be despatched in the height of the winter, and that the responsibilities of the different officers should be clearly defined, were at first obstinately ignored. At the same time proposals for remunerating the contractors, not according to the number of convicts embarked, but according to the number landed in good health, were rejected. Recommendations regarding the type of clothing provided for the voyage, the quality, quantity and nature of the rations, and the provision of medicines, anti-scorbutics and fumigants in adequate quantities were likewise adopted only after long delay.

The essential difference between the system of transportation to the American colonies prior to the War of Independence and that to the Australian colonies was well understood by the British Government, but its implications were not clearly appreciated by the departmental officials charged with the direction and supervision of the shipment of prisoners to Australia. They failed to realise that safeguards which had been present in the American system were absent from the Australian.[3]

The contractors who had shipped convicts across the Atlantic had possessed a proprietary interest in their charges. The services of the prisoners, for the terms of their respective sentences, had been assigned to the contractors. The latter were at liberty to sell their interest in each convict to the highest bidder, and the steady demand for labour among the American colonists ensured that the convicts' services could be disposed of profitably. Moreover, during the later stages of transportation to America, and especially after the passing of the Act of 1718 (6 Anne c. 9), the contractors received a subsidy, which within a few years was stabilized at £5 per head. This payment by the British Government, added to the sale price, ensured a good profit to the shipper. So high was the demand for convict labour in the plantations, however, that in 1772 the subsidy was discontinued, although for a time contractors were able to secure its payment from the local authorities. Financial considerations alone provided a powerful incentive to the contractors to land their prisoners in as healthy a state as possible[4].

This incentive of financial gain was absent from the Australian system. The contractors had no proprietary interest in the convicts. The services of the prisoners were asssigned to them, but this was a legal formality: the contractors on landing their charges were bound to transfer the assignments to the local governor or his deputy. Prohibited from selling the convicts' services, the contractors derived no financial benefit from landing them in a physically sound and healthy state. Indeed, dead convicts were more profitable than the living, since every prisoner who died on the passage represented a saving in the expenditure on provisions.

Next to disease and ill-treatment, marine disaster exacted the heaviest toll of life, but by comparison the mortality from this cause was trifling. From the outset the naval authorities exercised considerable care in the chartering of vessels as transports, and with few exceptions those chosen were staunch and well-found. Between 1787 and the middle of 1833 only one vessel carrying convicts was lost on the outward passage, and she was not a transport proper, but a vessel of the Royal Navy. H.M.S. *Guardian*, officially designated a storeship, was carrying a few specially-selected convict artificers when she struck an iceberg after leaving the Cape of Good Hope towards the end of 1789, but the lives of most of these prisoners were saved. The first major disaster to a convict ship, involving heavy loss of life, did not occur until August, 1833. In fact, during the eighty years of transportation to Australia fewer than 550 convicts lost their lives as a result of shipwreck—a total barely double the number who died of disease during the voyage of the Second Fleet alone.

The losses from other causes were insignificant. A handful of prisoners were executed for attempts at mutiny or were killed in the suppression of these revolts. The only convict ship captured by mutineers was seized, not by the prisoners, but by the military guard, assisted by some of the crew. Similarly, only one transport was lost by enemy action: she was captured by an American privateer during the war of 1812. A few convicts contrived to escape after embarkation, either before sailing or at a port of call en route to their destination, but the total was very small.

Of the convicts who reached Australia, the majority were landed in New South Wales. Transportation to that colony was abolished by an Order-in-Council of May 22, 1840. Towards the end of 1844, however, a public meeting at Melbourne decided that "exiles" —prisoners who had served a probationary period in England and had been pardoned on condition of deportation—might with benefit be received in the Port Phillip district. At that time, and, indeed, until separation was formally proclaimed on July 1, 1851, the Port Phillip district, of which Melbourne was the headquarters, was officially included within the boundaries of New South Wales. Later, in 1847, a proposal was advanced that, on certain conditions, 2000 exiles should be imported in each of three successive years.

Several hundred exiles reached Melbourne and Sydney without any opposition to their landing being expressed, and this fact induced Earl Grey to attempt to revive transportation to New South Wales on a modified basis. In 1848 he revoked the Order-in-Council abolishing transportation to that Colony. His action at once aroused the distrust and hostility of the colonists, and when two vessels with exiles reached Melbourne in the middle of 1849 they were refused permission to land their passengers. Both vessels went on to Sydney, where the exiles, despite largely-attended meetings of protest, were allowed to disembark.

The arrival of these vessels hardened public opinion against Earl Grey's scheme, and the following year forty petitions, bearing the signatures of 36,589 residents of the Sydney district and praying that transportation should be totally abolished, were presented against eight, signed in the aggregate by a mere 525 persons, supporting a continuance of transportation on a modified basis. This clearcut expression of public opinion was decisive. On October 1, 1850, the New South Wales Legislative Council resolved that no more prisoners should be received under any conditions, and the following April Earl Grey's revocation of the Order-in-Council of 1840 was rescinded[5].

With the cessation of transportation to New South Wales, the flow of convicts was diverted to Tasmania, which until January 1, 1856, was officially known as Van Diemen's Land. The first convict ship to reach Tasmania direct from England had arrived at Hobart on October 19, 1812, but the earlier practice of transhipping prisoners from Sydney was then reverted to, and it was not until 1818 that the shipment of convicts direct from England was resumed. From then until 1840 the convict ships sailed either to Port Jackson or Hobart, although a few disembarked their prisoners at both places. After 1840 all transports, except those carrying the exiles landed at Melbourne, Geelong, Sydney or Brisbane between 1844 and 1850, and a few which called first at the penal settlement of Norfolk Island, made Hobart their destination until the introduction of transportation to Western Australia in 1850.

During the decade from 1840 to 1849, the anti-transportation movement in Van Diemen's Land gathered momentum, and when a transport freighted with Irish convicts reached Hobart in April, 1850, its arrival provoked vigorous protests against a continuance of transportation. This vessel had been precipitately despatched to the Cape of Good Hope by Earl Grey, but so bitter had been the outcry of the Cape colonists that the local governor declined to allow the prisoners to land until he had consulted the Home authorities. Eventually the transport was sent on to Hobart, but it was decided, in view of the protests of the Tasmanians, to pardon her convicts. On previous occasions Pentonville and Millbank exiles had been landed at Hobart without opposition, and the authorities no doubt hoped that the action of converting the prisoners' status from that of convicts to that of exiles would mollify the Tasmanians. It had, however, a contrary effect, incensing the colonists, who fully realised that the decision made a mockery of the principle of the exile system, since the prisoners had not undergone any probationary period before shipment.

The storm evoked by this vessel's arrival was an important factor in the formation of the Anti-Transportation League the following year. Van Diemen's Land was now aligned with the mainland in opposition to transportation. The British Government had no option but to bow to the will of the colonists, and in 1853 the abolition of transportation to Van Diemen's Land was formally announced[6].

The only Australian colony to which convicts might now be despatched was Western Australia. It had been founded, ironically enough, as a free colony, with a stipulation that no prisoners should be shipped to it, but free immigration had failed to satisfy the colonists' demand for labour. As early as 1831 suggestions had been made that it would be advisable to import convicts. Nothing had come of these proposals, but in 1843 inmates of the Parkhurst Penitentiary in England had been despatched to Western Australia. Indentured to the colonists, they had been euphemistically termed "government juvenile immigrants" and had not been considered convicts[7].

In 1849, however, the settlers of Western Australia petitioned the British Government to "erect the colony into a regular penal settlement," and the invitation was accepted with alacrity. In May of that year the necessary Order-in-Council was issued, and on June 1, 1850, the first convict ship arrived. Male prisoners, though in small numbers, continued to be shipped to Western Australia until 1868, when transportation was finally abolished[8].

Rather more than half the total number of convicts to reach Australia from England and Ireland was disembarked in New South Wales, but a considerable number of these was subsequently transhipped to Van Diemen's land or Norfolk Island. In round figures, excluding those prisoners from within Australia and from places other than England and Ireland, some 84,000 convicts, including about 11,500 women, reached New South Wales. The total landed in Van Diemen's Land, including those sent direct to Norfolk Island from England, exceeded 67,000, of whom between 11,000 and 12,000 were women. The number disembarked in Western Australia, whither no women were sent, was a mere 9,720, while only a few hundred landed at Moreton Bay.

CHAPTER TWO

THE CONTRACTORS

THE fitting out, assembling, provisioning and despatch of the First Fleet, which sailed for Botany Bay from Spithead on May 13, 1787, was the work of many government departments and private contractors, but predominantly of the Royal Navy. Once the Home Department and the Treasury had set the machinery in motion, the main task of organising the expedition and getting it to sea fell to the Admiralty and the Navy Board.

The Lords Commissioners of the Admiralty provided the convoying warships and their crews, furnished a detachment of marines to guard the convicts and to protect the new settlement against the incursions of the natives, and advertised for vessels to convey the prisoners and stores[1].

The Commissioners of the Navy, who collectively were styled the Navy Board, undertook the direction and supervision of the detailed preparations. The tenders received in response to the Admiralty's advertisement were submitted to the Board, whose officers inspected and surveyed the proffered vessels. On the reports and recommendations of these officers, the Board selected those vessels which appeared best qualified to undertake the long and hazardous voyage to Australia, and concluded the charter-parties for their hire. To the Board and its officers also fell the responsibility of seeing that the chartered vessels were adequately found and equipped and properly fitted up for the conveyance of convicts, and, when all was in readiness, of arranging for the embarkation of the prisoners.

The provisioning of the expedition, both for the voyage and for a period of two years after its landing, was entrusted to the victualling department of the Navy. The Commissioner of Victualling, who was a member of the Navy Board, determined the scale of rationing and let the contracts for the supply of provisions to private contractors[2].

For the most part, the charter-parties were made with William Richards, a prominent Walworth shipbroker, who acted as agent for the owners and masters. The transports were chartered at a flat rate of ten shillings per register ton per month. Payment for three of them was to be made until the date each returned to England, but the remaining three were to be discharged from government employ as soon as they had disembarked their passengers and discharged their stores in New South Wales. These vessels were then to commence a new contract with the East India Company, which had chartered them to proceed to China to load tea for the London market[3].

The government's firm adherence to the principle of direct naval responsibility was a novel but wise departure from previous practice. Until the War of Independence had ended transportation to the American colonies, convicts had been shipped across the Atlantic under private contract. Nine months before the First Fleet sailed, and ten days before the Admiralty was instructed to furnish a convoying warship and tender, a proposal was made to the government that transportation to Australia should likewise be undertaken by private contract. On August 21, 1786, two merchants, Turnbull Macaulay and T. Gregory, offered to provide the necessary vessels and provisions at the rate of 28 guineas for each convict embarked, and as an inducement to the acceptance of this offer expressed their willingness to permit the vessels to remain at Botany Bay for two months after arrival without any charge being imposed for demurrage.

The offer was rejected. Rightly, the British Government decided that the foundation of a new settlement in an unknown land 13,000 miles away should not be entrusted to private contractors whose sole interest in the venture would be limited to the successful completion of the voyage and to the unloading of their vessels after arrival. At the same time it must not be imagined that the rejection of the offer was a repudiation of the principle of private contract. The government had no objection to the employment of private contractors once the initial step of founding the penal settlement had been accomplished. Not only did it adopt the system of private contract, but on the ground of economy, and possibly under pressure from vested interests, it adhered steadfastly to it even when its inherent defects became only too obvious[4].

Apart possibly from its cheapness, which may well be debatable, this retrograde step had only its administrative simplicity to recommend it. It did away with the need of a multiplicity of contracts with individual shipowners and merchants through a number of government departments, all of whose activities required to be co-ordinated. Instead, a single agreement with a single contractor sufficed. All responsibility was virtually shifted to his shoulders. He furnished vessels, crews, provisions, clothing and even, in some instances, the prisoners' guards, making the best terms he could with a host of sub-contractors.

The contract system relieved departmental officials of a mass of detailed work. They exercised no more than a general oversight of the arrangements. Had the officials been overburdened with the details of wartime administration, as later certainly was the case, there might have been some excuse for the adoption of private contract, but as Britain was at peace when private contract was instituted, and the system was continued after the Napoleonic wars ended, pre-occupation with the conduct of a great war cannot be advanced in extenuation of the government's decision.

Nearly all the evils associated with the actual conveyance of the convicts had their origin in the contract system. It was responsible for incalculable human misery, suffering and loss of life. The authorities were aware of the dangers, but although they genuinely strove to avoid them, the precautions taken to ensure the humane treatment of the prisoners on the voyage were at first inadequate.

From the outset the contracts were drawn up with meticulous care. Here the Navy Board's long experience in the transportation of troops to all parts of the world proved invaluable. Its charter-parties stipulated that the convicts' quarters should be adequately ventilated and regularly cleansed and fumigated, the prisoners properly clothed and furnished with beds and bedding, space set apart as a hospital, and an approved surgeon carried in each transport. The conditions on which the prisoners were to be admitted to the deck for fresh air and exercise were laid down, as also was the scale of rations. Provision also was made for the supply by the Government of medicines and anti-scorbutics, though, as experience was to show, on an insufficient scale.

From time to time, as the need for them became apparent, new conditions were introduced; for as practical experience revealed defects and deficiencies, the authorities endeavoured to render the contracts more stringent and comprehensive. The contract of December 31, 1801, with Brown, Welbank & Petyt, agents for the owners of the transports *Coromandel* and *Perseus*, is typical of the form which the charter-parties had assumed within little more than a decade of the First Fleet's departure, and it is significant of the determination to take every precaution and to provide for every contingency, at least on paper, that little alteration subsequently had to be made in the form of the charter-parties. Except for a few minor amendments, those of the 1830's are identical with that of 1801[5].

The contractors covenanted that the ships should be tight, strong and substantial, above and below water, and manned by qualified seamen on the scale, in 1801, of six men and a boy and, at a later date, of seven men and a boy to every hundred tons register measurement. The contractors were to fit the ship with masts, sails, yards, anchors, cables, ropes, cords, apparel and other furniture, and to furnish coals, wood, fire-hearths and furnaces for cooking and dressing the provisions, as well as with bowls, spoons, platters and other necessaries for the convicts and their guards. Water casks and fresh water were to be provided at the rate of one butt for each person. Sufficient scrapers, brooms, swabs and other articles for cleaning the prisoners' quarters were to be furnished, and the contractors agreed to employ these in accordance with the directions of the surgeon or surgeon's mate.

It was stipulated also that each ship should carry not less than three proper boats, that wholesome provisions and a sufficiency of water should be furnished to the seamen, and that two windsails for ventilation purposes and an Osbridge's machine for sweetening water should be in each vessel. This machine consisted "of a hand pump which is inserted in a scuttle made at the top of a cask, and by means of it the water, being raised a few feet, falls through several sheets of tin pierced-like cullenders and placed in a half-cylinder of the same metal. The purpose of it is to reduce the water into numberless drops, which being exposed in this form to the open air is deprived of its offensive quality. It is a machine very deservedly in common use . . ."[6]

The contractors also covenanted that the ships' masters would obey all orders given by the Transport Commissioners, their agents, and the officers in command, and that the masters would proceed to their destination without delay, touching at such ports only as might be necessary to obtain refreshments on account of the health of the convicts. They were prohibited from remaining at ports of call for their private concerns or for longer than was necessary for taking in provisions and water.

"And the said Brown, Welbank & Petyt do covenant," continued the charter-party of 1801, "that during the passage the master of each ship and his men shall use all the means in their power for ventilating and cleaning the parts of the ships in which the convicts are, and shall as much as possible consistent with safety admit the convicts on deck, particularly those whose health may most require it, taking care to admit a proper number at a time, and in the several respects, the said masters shall attend to the application of the surgeon or surgeon's mate."

The detailed nature of the provisions of the charter-parties is revealed in the clauses relating to the keeping of log-books. Each master was to keep a log-book in duplicate, recording, not only the details of the weather, the ship's position and the steering orders, but also "all remarkable occurrences, particularly births, deaths, sickness and behaviour of the convicts, the number from time to time admitted on deck, or reasons why they were not admitted on deck; all requests from the surgeon or his mates touching the convicts to be entered, and details of the daily expenditure of provisions and water." One log-book was to be handed to the governor on arrival in New South Wales; the other, along with all orders and instructions issued by the Transport Commissioners, their agents or the officers in chief, was to be lodged at the Transport Office on the ship's return to England.

While the Transport Commissioners agreed to furnish the necessary medicines for the voyage, the contractors undertook to supply a qualified surgeon and to provide him with a complete set of instruments. The surgeon was obliged to keep a diary in duplicate, recording in it all particulars relating to the sick, the medicines issued, the number of prisoners admitted on deck daily, details of the fumigating, ventilating and scraping of the convict's quarters, and "all other circumstances which may immediately or remotely affect the health of the convicts". As with the ship's log-book, one copy of the surgeon's diary was to be handed to the colonial governor on the ship's arrival at her destination, and the other lodged with the Transport Board on the surgeon's return to England.

Additional clauses dealt with the rates of payment, the provision and payment of a guard, the number of working or, as they were termed, lay days allowed for fitting up the transports and for the embarkation and disembarkation of the prisoners, and with the rate of demurrage payable for detention beyond these periods. A space equal to one-fifth or one-sixth the ship's registered tonnage was to be reserved for the government's sole use and was to be paid for at the rate of £2 per ton. This space, which was to be separated from the rest of the ship by the erection of a bulkhead, was additional to the space required for the carriage of baggage and provisions, including rations for victualling the prisoners for nine months after their arrival, and presumably was used for the conveyance of stores and supplies, particularly for the colony's garrison. The contractors also undertook not to land spirits or other commodities contrary to the port regulations or without the requisite permit, and not to carry away any person from the Australian colonies without the governor's order in writing.

As security for the performance of the terms of the charter-party, the contractors were obliged to lodge a bond in the sum of £1000. As an additional safeguard, it was provided that part of the payment stipulated should be withheld until the governor had issued "certificates of the true and just delivery of all the provisions, cabins, wood and iron work, medicines, and other stores belonging to the government . . . and of the proper conduct of the masters and surgeons".

As we shall presently see, the provisions of the charter-parties were reinforced by the issue of instructions to the masters and surgeons and, later, to the surgeons-superintendent. These dealt with the treatment to be accorded the prisoners, and were of a detailed nature.

Drafted with skill and comprehensive in scope, the charter-parties were admirable, and from the first would probably have proved satisfactory and effective had the means for the enforcement of the provisions been provided. For many years, however, the authorities failed to realise that stringent supervision of the contractors was essential, and in the absence of such supervision the safeguards incorporated in the charter-parties were too frequently ignored or evaded.

The responsibility of the Navy Board under the contract system was strictly limited. At an early date this responsibility was delegated to the Commissioners of His Majesty's Transport Service, who, for brevity's sake, were styled the Transport Commissioners or the Transport Board. The Board's history had been chequered. It had been instituted first in 1689, when, in consequence of William III's war with France, the Navy Board had represented its inability to undertake, in addition to its many other responsibilities, the provision of transports. A separate board had therefore been set up to deal solely with the transporting of troops in vessels other than men-of-war. In 1724, however, the Transport Board had been abolished and its duties had reverted to the Navy Board. With the outbreak of war in 1793 the position which had existed in 1689 had again arisen, and the following year it had led to the revival of the Transport Board.

The Board continued in existence until 1817, when it was finally abolished and the control of the business of transports once again devolved upon the Navy Board. When the latter was itself abolished in 1832 the Admiralty assumed responsibility for the provision of transports, one of its five principal officers being styled the Comptroller of Victualling and Transport Services[7].

The Transport Commissioners concluded the charter-parties, inspected and passed the vessels hired by the contractors, and, when the supervision of naval surgeons was transferred in 1806 from the old-established Sick and Hurt Board to the Transport Board, issued instructions to the masters and surgeons. The fitting out of the transports was supervised by the Transport Commissioners and with rare exceptions was carried out at Deptford. Some of the West Australian transports were fitted out in the West India Docks[8] and in 1838 the *Clyde* was altered at Liverpool[9], but these were exceptional and normally even the Irish transports fitted out at Deptford and then crossed to Cork or Dublin. The work was usually executed by the contractors and the cost refunded by the Treasury, but sometimes the necessary alterations were made by the workmen employed in the Deptford naval dockyard. In either case the material used remained the property of the government and was landed when the transport reached its destination; and much of it was shipped back to England for re-use, although, somewhat belatedly, the Navy Board in 1831 decided that the return of the prison doors and bulkheads was not worth the expense of the freight from Australia and issued orders that in future these articles were not to be returned. The time allowed for the construction of the prison quarters and for the embarkation of the convicts was 30 working days, 10 days longer than was allowed for disembarkation[10].

The Transport Commissioners also appointed the Naval Agent, when one was despatched with a transport or group of transports, but it would seem that the approval of the Admiralty had first to be obtained for these appointments. Later, when the Transport Board assumed control of the naval surgeons, it examined and approved the surgeons engaged by the contractors, and perused and examined the duplicate log-books and surgeons' journals[11].

All these duties, of course, were discharged by the Navy Board prior to the revival of the Transport Commissioners in 1794 and after their abolition in 1817, and when the Navy Board was itself abolished in 1832 they were performed by the Admiralty. There was, however, one curious exception. When the Transport Board went out of existence, the surgeons were placed, oddly enough, under the control of the Victualling Commissioners, who then became responsible for the examination of the surgeons' journals[12].

Apart from the preparatory supervision, confined to the inspection and fitting out of the transports and the embarkation of the prisoners, the only check on the contractors was through the Naval Agent and, after 1814, the surgeon-superintendent, and the examination of the ships' log-books and surgeons' journals months after the completion of the voyage. The latter check was of little practical value, except as a means of suggesting improvements for the future, of enabling incompetent or undesirable surgeons to be weeded out, and of debarring brutal or inefficient masters from future employment in the convict service. Even this limited effectiveness depended upon the thoroughness of the examination, and there is little doubt that it was not always carried out with care and judgment. Moreover, falsification might be practised and might go undetected, however painstaking the scrutiny of log-books and journals.

To some extent, however, these defects were offset by vigilance at the Australian end. It became the practice, when the prisoners were mustered on their arrival, to inquire if there were any complaints, and when charges were made against the master or surgeon a Board of Inquiry was appointed to investigate them. Its report and the minutes of the evidence were transmitted to England for appropriate action, and this system seems to have worked, on the whole, satisfactorily. Many convicts with just grounds for complaint, no doubt, remained silent for fear of meeting with harsh treatment, but a sufficient number spoke up boldly, and, in one way and another, the colonial authorities learnt of at least the most flagrant cases of neglect and ill-treatment. The number of inquiries held is impressive, and the invitation to the prisoners to state their complaints does not seem to have been accompanied by any attempt to prevent them speaking out. The writer is aware of only one instance where an effort was made to gag criticism, a surgeon-superintendent attempting to prevent convicts from lodging a complaint at the muster, and failing in his object.

The work of the Naval Agent is examined in the next chapter. All that need be said here is, firstly, that he was often given a physically impossible task and, secondly, that his powers were so ill-defined that he was unable to enforce obedience to his orders or compliance with the terms of the charter-party. The appointment of Naval Agents was discontinued at an early date, and from the closing years of the 18th century until 1814, when the surgeon-superintendent came into being, the contractors and their agents were subject to no direct supervision during the passage to Australia.

When the prisoners had been subjected to ill-treatment, or the conditions of the charter-parties had been flagrantly contravened, it was virtually impossible to bring the offenders to justice. Legal opinion secured by the Transport Commissioners in response to a request by Governor King in 1802 revealed that infringements of the charter-parties were not cognisable before the courts of judicature in New South Wales. The only action open to the governor was to order an inquiry and to forward the evidence and findings to England. Such action enabled the Transport Commissioners to mulct the contractors by withholding or refusing payments due under the charter-parties on the ground that the conditions of the latter had not been fulfilled or to decline to further employ the offenders in the convict service, but it did not allow criminal prosecutions to be launched in the English courts. If the culprits were to be prosecuted on their return to England, the witnesses had to be sent home. Governor Macquarie adopted this course in 1817, when criminal charges were preferred against the master, surgeon-superintendent and certain members of the military guard of the transport *Chapman*. All were acquitted, however, at an Admiralty Sessions at the Old Bailey without being called upon for the defence, and Macquarie was reprimanded by the British authorities for the expense he had incurred by his action![13]

Thus, for many years the contractors were subject to no more than an extremely loose and ineffective supervision and were virtually immune from prosecution for criminal acts. Once a transport had sailed the convicts were entirely at the mercy of the ship's officers and the contractors' agents. A few masters and surgeons were debarred from further employment, but in only one instance was similar action taken against a firm of contractors. Efficient and effective supervision during the voyage was only secured with the introduction of the practice of placing a naval surgeon, amenable to naval discipline and answerable for any neglect of duty, in each convict ship as surgeon-superintendent.

Once introduced, private contract remained the standard method by which convicts were shipped to the Australian colonies. The system, especially in the earlier years, was bitterly criticised, but only one half-hearted attempt was made to replace it.

In 1801 the then Home Secretary, Lord Pelham, proposed that naval vessels alone should be employed as convict transports, and that they should be despatched, not at the height of the inclement winter season, but regularly twice a year, at the latter end of May and at the beginning of September. After some delay, the suggestion was adopted, and in 1803 H.M.S. *Glatton* and H.M.S. *Calcutta* sailed with convicts, the latter vessel carrying an expedition despatched to found a new penal settlement at Port Phillip[14].

Although successful, the experiment was not repeated. The necessities of war, which prevented the detachment of warships on the long round voyage to Australia, and the natural repugnance of naval officers to being employed on such a service, compelled its abandonment, and when the Napoleonic wars ended the plan was not revived. By then, with the improvements which had been introduced in the interval, the contract system was at last working more satisfactorily. However, in later years convicts were occasionally sent out aboard a warship, most probably for reasons of economy.

Among the improvements must be included the alteration effected in the basis of remunerating the contractors. Private contract was instituted with the despatch from England on July 29, 1789, of the *Lady Juliana*, the first convict ship to sail after the departure of Phillip's fleet. The contract with William Richards, jun., provided that he should receive payment at the rate of nine shillings and sixpence per register ton per month from the time the *Lady Juliana* was taken up until six weeks after her discharge in New South Wales, with an allowance of 40 shillings per head for the clothing of each prisoner during the voyage and a victualling allowance of sixpence a day for each convict embarked. The latter payment was to be increased to ninepence a day so long as fresh provisions were served before sailing and to a shilling a day when fresh rations were supplied at foreign ports of call. In addition, Richards was to be paid, so long as the prisoners were aboard, seven shillings a day towards the salary of a surgeon[15].

The contract of August 27, 1789, with George Whitlock, agent for the owners of the Second Fleet transports *Neptune*, *Scarborough* and *Surprize*, however, adopted a *per capita* system of payment. The convicts were to be transported, clothed and fed for an all-inclusive payment of £17 7s. 6d. per head. The fearful death-roll in these vessels led to a modification of this method of payment with the object of preventing an excessive mortality. Thus, the contract made with William Richards, jun., in 1792 for the transportation of convicts from Ireland provided for a payment of £17 for each convict embarked and for a further payment of £5 for each prisoner landed in satisfactory health. James Duncan's contract of 1798 for the *Hillsborough*, and that of 1801 with Brown, Welbank & Petyt for the *Coromandel* and the *Perseus*, were on a similar basis. Duncan was to receive £18 for each convict embarked and an additional £4 10s. 6d. for every prisoner landed, while the payments for the convicts shipped in the *Coromandel* and the *Perseus* were £10 and £5 respectively, with an allowance of 14d. per head per lunar month for necessary money[16].

This latter payment was an innovation. Its purpose was to

remunerate the contractors for fitting up the ships and for providing the necessary water casks, brooms, scrapers, windsails, cooking and eating utensils and other articles. In addition, of course, the contractors were paid freight on such government stores as were shipped, the rate for the *Hillsborough* being £8 per ton and for the other two vessels £2 per ton.

This method of remunerating the contractors was certainly preferable to the flat *per capita* payment for each convict embarked. It provided the contractors with a financial incentive to treat the convicts humanely. The embarkation payment may have been too high and the disembarkation payment too low, but at least dead convicts no longer were more profitable than the living.

At the same time that this alteration was effected bonus payments were introduced, though at first, apparently, they were not universally granted. In 1794 the superintendent of convicts, who was a minor civilian official going out to take up a superintendent's post in the colony, the surgeon and the master of the *Surprise* were promised a guinea each for every convict landed at Port Jackson, "as an inducement to them to take every possible care for their preservation", while in other instances the masters were rewarded with a gratuity of £50 for careful supervision, and the surgeons were paid 10s. for each prisoner disembarked in good health. There was no regularity about these payments, however, until much later, when masters and surgeons-superintendent, on production of a certificate from the colonial authorities that they had faithfully discharged their duties, received a gratuity of £50 each on their return home. Smaller bonus payments were also made to the mates of transports which carried women prisoners[7].

Eventually the system of *per capita* payments was abandoned in favour of contracts on a tonnage basis—a reversion to the practice adopted in the case of the *Lady Juliana*. The advantage of this method, at least in theory, was that large vessels might be chartered, enabling civilian and military officials, free settlers and government stores to be shipped economically. As in practice shipowners preferred to tender their smaller vessels, it may be doubted if the convicts derived much benefit from the change. Overcrowding was not lessened, and, as a general rule, larger numbers could not be admitted to the deck simultaneously for exercise and fresh air.

The contractors now received a flat rate per register ton and the allowance of fourteenpence per convict per lunar month for necessary money, less a deduction at the rate of £12 per centum. When the master was required to keep a suitable table for any officer or official on the passsage, the contractors received £78 for each such passenger. Payment was made in two stages. One-third of the freight, and £20 for each passenger, was paid when the ship had sailed, and the balance due on both accounts on receipt of certificates from Australia that the contract had been satisfactorily completed. Demurrage, in the event of detention beyond the period stipulated, was at the rate of 10s. per register ton a calendar month.

The adoption of the tonnage method of payment was accompanied by an alteration in the system of clothing and victualling the convicts. Their rations and clothing were supplied under separate contracts concluded by the Victualling Commissioners, and there seems little doubt that the convicts benefited through this change. The provisions improved in quality and possibly in quantity, and the clothing supplied was not only more suitable but also of better manufacture[8].

On the whole, private contract worked well after 1815. The appearance on the scene of the surgeon-superintendent ensured that the rations were truly served, that the regulations in regard to hygiene and sanitation were observed, and that the contractors and their agents discharged their responsibilities in accordance with the terms of the charter-parties. Instances of neglect and ill-treatment were not unknown, but they were rare, and although complaints were numerous, particularly against ships' officers, the majority were of a trivial nature. The gross abuses earlier practised by the contractors were almost entirely eliminated.

CHAPTER THREE

THE NAVAL AGENT AND THE GUARD

THE duties of the naval agent were, firstly, the oversight of the preparatory arrangements and, secondly, the supervision of the contractor's agent during the voyage, primarily to ensure that the terms of the charter-party were faithfully observed and that the passage was completed with a minimum of delay.

The preparatory supervision demanded specialised knowledge and previous experience in the conveyance of large numbers of men by sea, but presented few difficulties to officers who had been employed for some years in the transport service or who had risen to lieutenant's rank. The second duty, however, was more difficult and exacting, and, while requiring some expert knowledge, demanded for its efficient performance qualities of tact and commonsense above the average.

In addition to directing the fitting out of the transport, the naval agent had to co-ordinate the arrangements for assembling the prisoners from the gaols or hulks, see that they were put aboard the convict ship, and supervise the shipment of provisions, water, clothing, and other stores. He was responsible for directing the stowage of the cargo, and had to see that the conditions of the charter were complied with generally before sailing. He discharged these duties in person, visiting the ship daily to inspect the progress of the work and to issue his instructions. The prison quarters were constructed to a standardised pattern, and their erection, in both English and Irish transports, was with rare exceptions carried out at Deptford, where a naval dockyard was situated. In England the embarkation of the prisoners was always carried out at one of the naval ports—in the Thames or at Portsmouth or Plymouth.

Thus, if unexpected difficulties arose, such as in the procuring of materials or the provision of labour for the construction of the prison or the furnishing of boats for the embarkation of the convicts and the shipment of stores, the naval agent was readily able to seek the advice or enlist the assistance of his fellow officers or the dockyard officials. If the contractors or their agents proved contumacious, he could always call upon superior authority to enforce compliance with his orders.

When, as sometimes happened, the naval agent's appointment was delayed, the work of preparatory supervision was entrusted to another officer attached to the transport service. In the late 1790's, when the transport officers had been divided into two categories, "Resident Agents" attached to bases and "Agents Afloat" serving in the ships, the former performed the work, and when the appointment of naval agents in the convict ships was discontinued, it came to form part of the resident agents' regular duties. Thus, at the beginning of the 19th century the fitting out of the transports and the embarkation of prisoners shipped at London was supervised by Captain Stephen Rains, the resident agent of the Transport Board for the Thames. His counterparts at Portsmouth and Plymouth attended to the embarkation of the prisoners taken aboard at those ports, while in Ireland this work was performed by Lieutenant Richard Sainthill, the agent of the Irish Government. The latter was also responsible for the transmission to the colonial authorities of the indents of the convicts, in which the details of their sentences were recorded, and the invoices for goods shipped, a duty which, probably because of the negligence of the Irish officials, he was unable to perform efficiently[1].

On the whole, the preparatory supervision was competently executed. It is true, of course, that overcrowding, even by the standards of the day, was not prevented, but this was not the fault of the naval agent. He was obliged to receive the number of prisoners ordered to be embarked. If he considered the number excessive, he was expected to report the fact; but he was not empowered to disembark surplus prisoners without an order to do so from his superiors. Possibly the naval agents were backward in representing that vessels were overcrowded, but in the absence of the necessary data it is impossible to reach a conclusion on this point. Instances of the cargo being badly stowed, of the terms of the charter-parties being flagrantly flouted, and of the ship's officers being allowed to ship articles of private trade were, however, comparatively rare, which indicates that neglect or lack of vigilance on the part of agents was unusual.

Supervision during the passage was exercised in very different circumstances. When the naval agent was responsible for a group of transports, it was physically impossible for him to efficiently discharge his duties. Except before sailing and when the convict ships were anchored together at a port of call, he could exercise authority only aboard the vessel in which he himself had embarked. An energetic and conscientious officer might seize every opportunity presented by favourable weather at sea to visit his other charges by ship's boat, but such visits could be made only at irregular and infrequent intervals and necessarily were of short duration. They did not provide an effective check upon unscrupulous masters or incompetent surgeons.

But it was exceptional for convict ships to remain in company at sea for any length of time. Since their sailing qualities were seldom uniform, and in thick or heavy weather they would quickly become separated, they usually made their way individually to their destination. Freed of all surveillance by the naval agent, the ship's officers and the contractor's agent might then treat, or ill-treat, the convicts as they chose. In these circumstances they were free at ports of call to bring aboard articles of private trade, the shipping of which, by cluttering up the 'tween decks, reduced the space available for the prisoners and prevented the free circulation of air, to the detriment of the convicts' health.

The futility of entrusting a group of convict ships to the supervision of a single naval agent was well illustrated in the case of the Third Fleet. The Portsmouth division of five vessels was in charge of Lieutenant Robert Parry Young, but one vessel parted company the first night at sea, two others shortly afterwards, and the fourth four nights later. Thus, Lieutenant Young, when scarcely out of sight of the English coast, had lost contact with all his charges except the vessel in which he had embarked, and he did not sight them again until he reached Port Jackson. The naval agent for the Plymouth division, Lieutenant Richard Bowen, was more fortunate, as his three vessels successfully kept company until nearing the Equator, when one parted company, to rejoin the others at Rio de Janeiro. After leaving that port, however, and when still five weeks' sail from Sydney, all three vessels were separated in a heavy gale and did not again meet until all had arrived at Port Jackson.

But even aboard his own ship the naval agent was seldom able to exercise effective supervision. His status and powers were ill-defined; for no attempt was made by the Navy Board or the Transport Commissioners to settle the respective spheres of responsibility of the master, the commander of the guard, the surgeon, and the naval agent. Inevitably there were sharp and sometimes violent differences of opinion[2].

In the First Fleet marines were furnished by the Admiralty to guard the convicts, and had this system continued a degree of mutual co-operation between the naval agent and the commander of the guard might have been achieved. But the provision of the guard became a War Office instead of a naval responsibility, and the element of inter-service rivalry was thus introduced.

The military guards furnished by the War Office were obtained either from drafts ordered to join their regiments in India or from regiments detailed for service in the Australian colonies. The usual detachment was one or two officers and about 30 other ranks, although in the later convict ships the guard sometimes had a strength of about 50, officers and men. The officer in command was generally a captain or lieutenant, but occasionally might be an ensign or sergeant. In at least one instance, owing to the desertion of a sergeant before sailing, the guard was commanded by a corporal. The wives and children of officers and men accompanied the detachment in the proportions permitted by War Office regulations. Often enough, especially when formed of drafts bound for India, the guard might be drawn from as many as four or five different regiments and be commanded by an officer belonging to a regiment not represented in the ranks. After a detachment of the New South Wales Corps had seized the female transport *Lady Shore* in 1797, guards were not placed aboard ships conveying women convicts only[3].

During the long struggle against Napoleon the man-power shortage sometimes prevented the War Office furnishing the guard, and the contractors were then called upon to supply additional men to serve as guards. Indeed, the Transport Commissioners, after the loss of the *Lady Shore*, placed such little trust in a military guard that, with the government's sanction, they for a time ignored the War Office and made their own arrangements. James Duncan's contract for the *Hillsborough* in 1798 provided that he should engage 30 men, over and above the 48 men forming the ship's company, to serve as guards, and in a report of June 11, 1800, the Transport Commissioners declared that they had taken this action "on account of the loss of the *Lady Shore* and the little trust we found in the military guard on board that ship, as well as the difficulty of procuring a proper one at the time." The additional men furnished by the contractor were paid at the rate of £5 each per calendar month from the date the convicts were embarked until their disembarkation in New South Wales. In 1801 the contractors provided a guard of 20 men for the *Coromandel* and 16 for the *Perseus*, receiving a flat rate of £75 for each man in payment. A guard furnished by the contractor was not commanded by a military officer, but was considered as forming part of the crew, and the master was responsible for its direction, conduct and discipline.

A change in the method of providing the guard was made when transportation to Western Australia began. Instead of employing drafts destined for India or detachments of regiments detailed for service in Australia, pensioners willing to become servants or settlers on arrival at their destination were engaged. In effect, they undertook the duty in return for a free passage to Western Australia for themselves and their families. This employment of pensioners had been tried in some of the Tasmanian ships, but, not proving satisfactory, had been discontinued[4].

There was, of course, ample room for disagreement among the various officers in a convict ship. For example, the charter-parties obliged the contractors to admit the convicts to the deck as far as was consistent with their security and the safety of the ship, and the surgeon and naval agent were both enjoined to pay attention to the carrying out of this regulation. But it was not specified who was to be the judge of the factors involved in giving effect to this regulation. Did the decision lie with the master, the commander of the guard, the surgeon or the naval agent? Each might with justice claim that it was his responsibility to say when and in what numbers the prisoners should be admitted to the deck, or, for that matter, whether they should be allowed on deck at all. What if the surgeon declared that it was essential for the prisoners' health that they should be freely admitted to the deck, but the master asserted that the safety of the ship would be imperilled or the commander of the guard maintained that the security of the convicts would be endangered?

Again, the master might legitimately assert that it was his prerogative to determine the length of stay at ports of call, and when at sea, the amount of sail to be carried. If the guard's commander could claim no direct interest in these matters, they certainly concerned both the surgeon and the naval agent. The former was responsible for the health of the convicts, and the checking of an outbreak of scurvy or other disease might well depend upon the time allowed the prisoners for recuperation at a port of call; or their health might be endangered by too prolonged a stay at a tropical port at the wrong season of the year. The carrying of too much sail at sea might jeopardise the prisoners' health through the ship becoming extremely wet, so that it was impossible to dry the prison quarters or to allow the convicts on deck, while if too little sail were carried the voyage might be unduly prolonged and scurvy make its appearance. The naval agent, besides being to some extent responsible for the convicts' health, was charged with seeing that the voyage was completed with a minimum of delay, so that he also possessed a direct interest in the amount of sail carried and the time spent in ports of call *en route*.

Problems such as these arose on every voyage, and led to misunderstandings and quarrels. These genuine differences of opinion were accentuated by the natural irritations and clashes of personality inevitable among individuals of diverse temperament, education and interests in a small vessel on so long a voyage. Cooped up for months in cramped quarters, deprived of all privacy, and engaged on a voyage which all must have regarded with some measure of repugnance, the officers found it difficult and often impossible to live together harmoniously. Trifles were magnified out of all proportion to their importance, and frequently led, particularly among officers jealous of their own authority and dignity, to bitter and sometimes violent quarrels.

The British authorities can scarcely have been unaware of these disagreements or of their harmful results, but they took no action. As late as 1819, long after the appointment of naval agents had been discontinued and when the system of surgeons-superintendent had been in existence for five years, Governor Macquarie drew attention to the omission to define the powers and responsibilities of the various officers. Reporting that "very unpleasant disagreements and altercations" had occurred between the masters and the commanders of the guard aboard some convict ships, he expressed the opinion that these had arisen "chiefly from the relative powers and duties of those persons not being sufficiently understood and properly explained to them previously to the commencement of the voyage, and which might have been obviated had they been furnished with distinct written instructions for their mutual guidance". He deemed the matter so important that he penned a separate despatch on the subject, and in this suggested the points to be dealt with in the written instructions he advocated[5].

In his dealings with the other officers, the naval agent was at a decided disadvantage. The commander of the guard could rely, as a rule, upon his non-commissioned officers and men to enforce his orders, as the master could rely upon the ship's officers and crew. If the guard had been furnished by the contractors, the master's authority was strengthened by reason of the fact that he commanded the guard as well as the crew. The ship's surgeon was engaged and paid by the contractors, and unless a man of unusual probity and strength of character (which seldom was the case), he tended, from motives of self-interest, to side with the ship's captain in any dispute with the naval agent or the commander of the guard.

The naval agent, on the other hand, stood alone. There was nobody he could call upon to back up his authority or to enforce obedience to his orders. He and the commander of the guard were both officers in His Majesty's service, but they belonged to different services and each generally was jealous of his own authority. Mutual co-operation between them usually proved impracticable, primarily, perhaps, because of the instructions which came to be issued to the military officers by the War Office. In the First Fleet the officers commanding the marine detachments in each transport were charged with inspecting the quality of the rations served, and with seeing that each convict received his just proportion. This practice, according to Captain Watkin Tench, was discontinued with the sailing of the Second Fleet, and the military officers instructed not to interfere in any matters relating to the convicts, except to prevent their escape. Consequently the guard commanders did not feel themselves obliged to support or assist the naval agent or to interest themselves in any matter which did not directly involve the security of the prisoners. What the military officers regarded as the strict performance of their duty in accordance with their orders, the naval agent, naturally enough, viewed as apathy or neglect, if not as downright obstruction, and this divergence of outlook was the cause of many quarrels[6].

A further complication arose from the character and personality of the average naval agent. Although agents of transports possibly originated when the Transport Office was established in 1689, probably were employed in ships conveying troops during the Seven Years' War, and certainly were on the scene during the War of American Independence, they were not governed, apparently, by any definite rules and regulations until 1794 or 1795. Before that, the personnel of the transport service was obtained by sporadic drafting. The service was unpopular; for it presented few opportunities for promotion or prize money and was something of a blind alley. After the reinstitution of the Transport Commissioners in 1794, the transport service was organised as a separate branch, but this did not render it more attractive to naval officers. Those who served in it did so only because they had no means of getting out of it. The ambitious and the capable, and those officers who were backed by influential patrons, if they chanced to be drafted into the transport service, pulled every string they could command and got out of it as quickly as they could. The failures and the nonentities, those who lacked ambition, ability, and interest, alone remained in it; for they could hope for no better employment[7].

Even if the naval agent assigned to the convict service was competent and efficient in his own particular sphere, the chances were that he was embittered and disgruntled. Years spent in shifting troops from one part of the world to another, seldom gaining promotion and rarely, if ever, being the recipient of prize money, had blunted his ambition and soured his temperament. Such a man was unlikely to be the most tactful of individuals, and tact was the one quality most needed in a convict ship. There can be little doubt, indeed, that many of the quarrels among the officers of convict ships originated in the defects of the naval agent's character, although the entire blame is not to be laid at his door. The truth is, of course, that the naval agent was seldom equipped, save in a narrow technical sense, to perform the duties he was called upon to discharge, and when he was inefficient or incompetent or dishonest, the result might well be disastrous for the unfortunate convicts.

The voyage of the Second Fleet emphasises this point. The three vessels of this fleet, the transports *Neptune, Scarborough* and *Surprize,* were in charge of Lieutenant John Shapcote as naval agent. He had been commissioned as a lieutenant on January 12, 1778, so that when he sailed with the Second Fleet on January 19, 1790, he had already served 12 years in this rank. The mortality in the three transports during the passage was the highest in the history of transportation, no fewer than 273 men and 11 women dying and upwards of 500 sick being landed on arrival at Port Jackson. It is significant that the heaviest mortality occurred in the *Neptune,* the vessel in which Shapcote sailed, and although there is no proof that he was a party to the rapacity and brutality of the *Neptune's* master, there is abundant evidence that Shapcote was lax, incompetent, and irresolute.

The *Neptune* lost 150 men and 11 women, of whom 46 died between England and the Cape of Good Hope. Yet in his report from the Cape, Shapcote declared, "I met nothing material on the passage." He made no adverse comment on the conduct of the ship's officers, but reported that the soldiers and convicts, to a large number, were "exceeding ill" with scurvy on reaching the Cape, and that, in consequence of the representations of the surgeon's mate of the troops and the surgeons of the convict ships, "and as our stay here will be short," he had ordered the masters to issue fresh meat daily, with a sufficient quantity of vegetables. The transports remained 16 days at the Cape, and there is nothing to indicate that it occurred to Shapcote that a longer stay was desirable if the ravages of scurvy were to be checked.

Shapcote died on the passage from the Cape to Port Jackson, but although the death-roll among the convicts was heaviest on this leg of the journey it is inconceivable that their ill-treatment took place only after Shapcote's death. The evidence proves that the prisoners were starved, kept heavily ironed, and refused access to the deck except in inadequate numbers and at long intervals. Their ill-treatment certainly was worse after leaving than before arriving at the Cape, but the death-roll of 46 between England and the Cape, exactly double the combined mortality of the other two transports, proves that the prisoners were not ill-treated only during the final stages of the passage, and is a sufficient indication of Shapcote's incapacity[8].

When Governor Phillip's reports reached England, the conduct of the masters of the three transports was investigated, and Phillip was officially informed that the *Neptune's* master, Donald Trail, could not be prosecuted because he had absconded. It is difficult to reconcile this statement with the fact that Trail and his first mate, William Ellington, were acquitted at the Old Bailey on June 8, 1792, on a privately-preferred charge of wilful murder. As the inquiry into his conduct had begun in the previous December, it is unlikely that the authorities moved so tardily that they were not ready to act until after June, especially as the frightful mortality had aroused public opinion and the government had shown itself anxious to placate its critics. It seems more probable that the authorities did not wish to prosecute Trail because of Shapcote's laxity and the discredit which would be brought on penal transportation and on the system of naval agents by revelations regarding his inaction and incompetency.

A statement regarding the *Neptune's* voyage was published two years after Shapcote's death. It sought to exonerate Trail and to lay the whole blame on Shapcote, and, obviously drawn up by Trail's friends, if not at the instigation of the Second Fleet contractors, Messrs. Camden, Calvert and King, it necessarily has to be accepted with caution. It is of interest, however, because of the light which it throws on what were regarded as the naval agent's duties.

It asserted that the convicts were ironed under Shapcote's inspection, and that whenever a prisoner was reported as being in ill-health, he saw to it that he was released from his irons. At the first embarkation the convicts were searched on Shapcote's orders, and he himself inspected their luggage, confiscating 70 to 100 knives, a number of tin-pots and many chests fitted with iron hinges and clasps—all articles from which mutinously-inclined prisoners might have manufactured weapons. It was claimed that the rations had been served by the ship's steward under Shapcote's supervision, and that he had made no complaint to Trail concerning either the quality or quantity of the provisions. It was also alleged that when, after leaving the Cape, an epidemical fever had broken out, Shapcote had refused to authorise Trail to serve porter to the prisoners[9].

The *Surprize* and the *Scarborough* lost 38 and 85 men respectively on the passage. In a letter written after his arrival at Sydney, Captain Hill, the commander of the guard in the *Surprize*, stressed that the naval agent was aware only of what transpired in his own vessel. "It therefore concerns government," Hill wrote, "to lodge in future a controlling power in each ship over those low-lifed, barbarous masters, to keep them honest instead of giving it to one man (an agent) who can see only what is going forward in his own ship. As there will be, generally, officers of the navy coming out, men disinterested and, it is to be hoped, possessing humanity, and that point of honour which is expected from the profession, that power can nowhere be better lodged than in them"[10].

The majority of the naval agents of the convict ships were as undistinguished, though hardly as incompetent, as Shapcote. With three exceptions, all appear to have failed to secure promotion above the rank of lieutenant, and most of them, having drifted into the transport service, lacked the initiative or the influence to get out of it.

The most brilliant was Lieutenant Richard Bowen, who was naval agent of the Plymouth division of the Third Fleet. Nelson wrote of him that "a more enterprising, able and gallant officer does not grace His Majesty's service," and St. Vincent spoke of him as one "whose brilliant services far surpass those of any other captain in His Majesty's navy." Bowen had both ability and influence, and his brief but meteoric career—he was killed at the disastrous attack on Santa Cruz, Teneriffe, on July 24, 1797—emphasises the gulf separating him from the average naval agent. He was the younger brother of James Bowen, who, as master of the flagship *Queen Charlotte* at the battle of the June 1 in 1794, was the protégé of the great Howe and a man with influential friends at the Transport Office. Through his brother's prestige and influence, Richard Bowen obtained his lieutenant's commission into the transport service on September 21, 1790. He went out to Australia with the Third Fleet, and after his arrival at Sydney was employed by Phillip to procure provisions from India. He did not long remain in the transport service, however, and on April 2, 1794, was promoted direct to Captain's rank[11].

The slowness or lack of promotion of other naval agents employed in the convict ships reveals how differently situated they were to Richard Bowen. The most efficient of the nonentities was probably

Lieutenant John Shortland, who, lacking influence and realising probably that he could not obtain other employment, made the best of a bad job and grew to like, perhaps even to love, the transport service. About 16 when he joined the navy, Shortland saw eight years' service as a midshipman before being promoted lieutenant on December 12, 1763. He then joined the transport service, and for the next 25 years was employed almost continuously in supervising the conveyance of troops, principally to and from the American colonies, but including the landing of reinforcements at Gibraltar during the siege of 1782. After serving as a lieutenant for 27 years, he was commissioned as commander and master on September 21, 1790, and was not again promoted. He seems to have ended his naval career in command of the Impress service at the Yorkshire port of Whitby, a post to which he was appointed in February, 1794, and which he still held in June, 1797.

Shortland's appointment by the Commissioners of the Navy as Agent of Transports in the First Fleet earned them a gentle reproof from the Lords Commissioners of the Admiralty for their failure to first refer his appointment to their lordships, but perhaps a better choice could not have been made. Possessed of unusual zeal and energy, and thoroughly experienced in transport work, Shortland carried out his duties with diligence and forethought, as Phillip's letters prior to the departure of the expedition testify, and he contributed materially to the success of the First Fleet's passage[12].

Lieutenant Daniel Woodriff, who arrived at Port Jackson in 1792 as naval agent of the transport *Kitty*, spent most of his career in the transport service, in one form or another, and was more successful in gaining promotion than most of his fellow naval agents. Commissioned as lieutenant on April 1, 1783, he gained his first promotion a little more than 12 years later, being made a commander on September 18, 1795, and after less than five years in that rank was promoted captain on April 28, 1802. The following year he commanded H.M.S. *Calcutta* in Lieutenant-Governor David Collins's expedition to found a penal settlement at Port Phillip. In 1805, when on convoy duty to St. Helena in the *Calcutta*, he engaged, and was captured by, a French squadron of one three-decker, three 74-gun ships, three frigates and two brigs, but saved almost all his convoy. He remained a prisoner until released on exchange in 1807. Seven years later Woodriff secured a snug post as Resident Commissioner at Jamaica Dockyard, but this put him out of the running for further promotion, and when, on January 10, 1837, his turn came for promotion to rear-admiral, he had to accept retirement as a captain. He died in 1842[13].

Following the mortality in the Second Fleet, and, no doubt, as a result of the inquiry into that disaster, the employment of officers of the transport service as naval agents of convict ships seems to have been discontinued in favour of placing a naval surgeon aboard each transport, an experiment dealt with in the next chapter. The *Kitty*, which sailed in March, 1792, carried Woodriff as naval agent, but the next four convict ships to leave—the *Royal Admiral* and the *Bellona* in 1792 and the *Boddingtons* and the *Sugar Cane* the following year—were in charge of naval surgeons. Although not employed in the transport service, these surgeons were, to all intents and purposes, naval agents, but the demands of the war with France prevented the new system being continued or the old one revived. The navy could spare neither surgeons nor naval agents for the convict ships, and after 1795 until the appointment of surgeon-superintendents in 1814 the masters of the transports were under no surveillance during the passage. The appointment of Lieutenant James Marshall as naval agent of the convict ship *Earl Cornwallis*, which sailed from England towards the end of 1800, was an isolated exception for which there is, apparently, no logical explanation.

The guards in the First Fleet were marines, and being accustomed to shipboard life they were admirably fitted to perform their duties. It was a retrograde but inevitable step when they were replaced by soldiers. The military detachment occasionally was composed of raw recruits, but generally consisted of veterans, frequently dissolute, ill-disciplined and in poor health. It was, of course, the cheapest way to send regiments out to Australia and probably also of getting small drafts of reinforcements to India, but in proportion to their numbers the guards required greater medical attention *en route* and frequently caused much trouble by their drunkenness and unruly conduct. Often they were much more severely punished than the convicts, who probably regarded their own plight, dire though it was, as better than the lot of their gaolers.

"The conduct of the guard generally, with very few exceptions, is becoming every day so bad as to threaten the worst consequences as well as to require the most vigorous and active reprehension," wrote John William Hallion, surgeon-superintendent of the *Isabella*, after a private, ordered into handcuffs for "insolent and contemptuous behaviour", had committed suicide by jumping overboard. The *Isabella* was then only eleven days out from Spithead, from where she had sailed on April 3, 1818. Two years later the surgeon of the *Elizabeth*, A. Montgomery, tells us under date August 29, that the conduct of the guard "is becoming every day more disorderly and occasionally amounting to mutiny." Three weeks later he records that for rioting, fighting and being drunk—the ship was then well out in the Atlantic—three members of the guard each received 36 lashes and afterwards were ironed on the poop, where a corporal, reduced to the ranks, lay handcuffed in charge of a sentry. Less than a fortnight later a private received 36 lashes for striking another when the latter was on sentry duty. Frequently during this voyage the sentries were found asleep at their posts[14].

The punishments inflicted in the *Elizabeth* were light. A court-martial held on board the *Hadlow* when she lay at Cork in 1820, found a private of the 28th Regiment guilty of desertion and two others of having aided and assisted his escape and sentenced all three to 300 lashes each. However, the punishment was reduced respectively to 150, 200 and 100 lashes, which were inflicted before the convicts were embarked. In the same year a private of the Royal Scots in the *Lord Sidmouth*, also then lying at Cork, received 275 lashes for "insubordinate conduct and disrespect to the officer commanding the detachment", and a member of the same regiment who had absented himself from the guard in the *Prince Regent* without leave was given 150 lashes aboard the *Lord Sidmouth*. He later apparently committed suicide by jumping overboard from the latter vessel as she neared her destination, Port Jackson. A member of the guard in the *Castle Forbes* received 300 lashes while the ship lay at Cork in 1820 and another 75 lashes. According to James Scott, the surgeon, the guard during the voyage was "almost in a state of mutiny, acting with the greatest disrespect to the officer on board, leaving their posts when stationed as sentinels and fighting amongst themselves, corporals challenging the privates, and the whole of them acting in the most irritating manner to the sailors."[15]

It will be observed, however, that these examples of flagrant

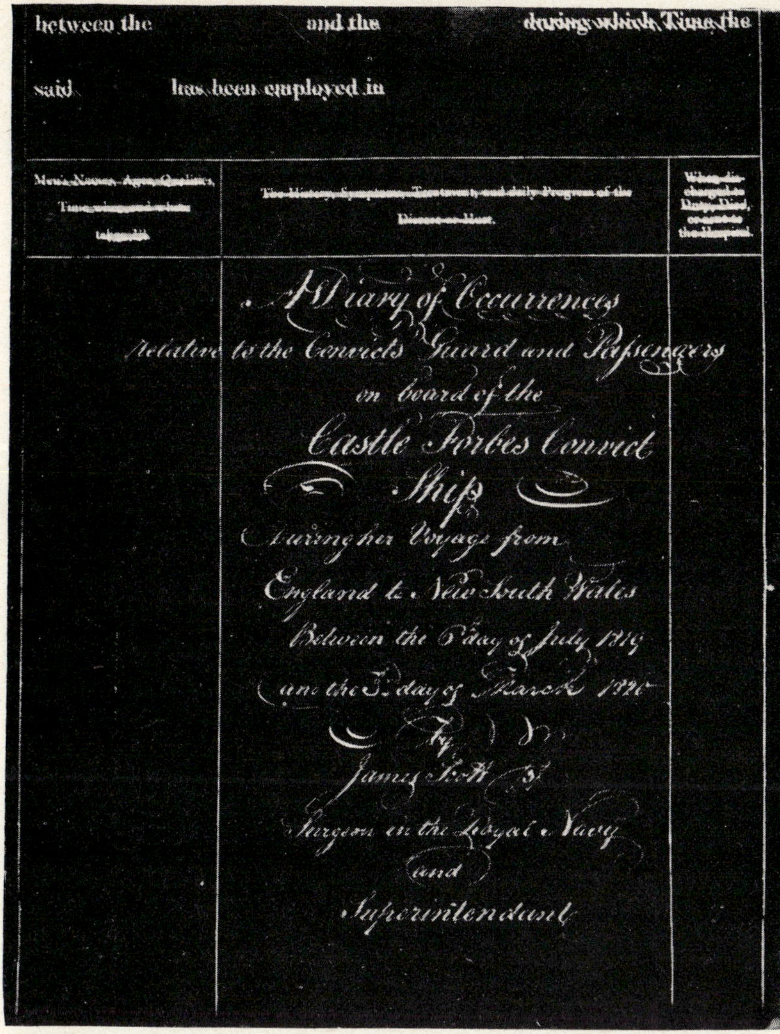

between the and the during which Time the

said has been employed in

A Diary of Occurrences

Relative to the Convicts Guard and Passengers

on board of the

Castle Forbes Convict

Ship

during her Voyage from

England to New South Wales

Between the 6th day of July 1819

and the 5th day of March 1820

By

James Scott

Surgeon in the Royal Navy

and

Superintendant

Mitchell Library, Sydney, N.S.W.

Title page of Diary of Occurrences by James Scott, "CASTLE FORBES"

Oil painting by T. Whitcombe *National Maritime Museum, Greenwich*

The "PROVIDENCE", 1807

misconduct and heavy punishments occurred about the same time, and in other years the military guards in convict ships were less unruly, although always inclined to drunkenness. Judging, however, from the sick lists filed with the surgeons' journals their health was never good. The mortality among the soldiers was not excessive, but frequently they were constantly on the sick list. Although the surgeons of several ships in which scurvy occurred among the convicts comment on the apparent immunity of the guard from this disease, the experience of the *Lord Auckland*, from Dublin to Hobart in 1846, seems to have been typical rather than exceptional. Of her guard of 50 men no fewer than 39 were on the sick list at some stage of her voyage, although none died; three of the six wives of the soldiers and four of their six children also required medical attention. Among the convicts, four of whom died, 90 out of 180 were admitted at some stage to the sick list[16].

CHAPTER FOUR

THE SURGEONS AND SURGEONS-SUPERINTENDENT

THE medical care of the convicts in the First Fleet was entrusted to the surgeons going out with the expedition to form the medical establishment of the colony on arrival, and the shipowners from whom the transports had been chartered were not obliged to furnish an approved surgeon for each vessel. As there were only five surgeons, a convict bred to surgery, John Irving, was placed on the sixth vessel, the *Prince of Wales*, to care as best he could for the prisoners in that transport.

The Principal Surgeon of the new colony was John White, who had received his first warrant in the navy in 1780, and he had charge of the medical arrangements during the voyage. He embarked in the *Charlotte*, and his three assistants—William Balmain, Thomas Arndell and Dennis Conssiden—went out in the *Alexander*, the *Friendship* and the *Scarborough* respectively. A surgeon volunteer, John Turnpenny Altree, was in the *Lady Penrhyn*, but he proved unequal to the task and, as this vessel had a doctor aboard, he was superseded at Teneriffe by the ship's surgeon, Arthur Bowes.

The practice thus instituted was followed in later years, and surgeons going out in convict ships to join the colonial medical establishment were placed in charge of the prisoners' health during the voyage. As such appointments were few, and made at irregular intervals, the medical care of the convicts was normally entrusted to surgeons engaged by the contractors in accordance with the provisions of the charter-parties. The applicants selected by the contractors had to be officially approved. They were first examined at Surgeons' Hall, presumably as to their professional qualifications, and afterwards by the Sick and Hurt Commissioners, and after their abolition at the end of 1805, at the Transport Office, the latter examinations, no doubt, being directed at establishing their general fitness for the post. How thorough these examinations were cannot now be determined with certainty. They may have been perfunctory, a mere formality, and certainly there is some evidence to suggest that no real attempt was made to investigate either the qualifications or the character of the surgeons.

When transportation to Australia was introduced, the management of the medical arrangements and the direction and supervision of the surgeons were in the hands of the Commissioners of Sick and Wounded, an old-established branch of the navy whose history may be traced back to 1653. In 1775 the number of commissioners was increased from two to five, but its administration was in a state of chaos, and although in 1796 the care of prisoners of war was transferred to the Transport Board no improvement in efficiency resulted. Under Sir Gilbert Blane important innovations were made at the instigation of the Board, but absenteeism on the part of the Commissioners was so frequent that the Board was virtually run by the clerks. In 1805, when the unsettled accounts of the Sick and Hurt Board totalled two and a half million pounds, some being of forty years' standing, it was officially reported that "the disorder into which the office has fallen is the best proof that can be adduced of its being totally inadequate to the duty with which it is charged." In these circumstances, and since the commissioners' responsibilities had been greatly increased by the outbreak of war, it may be doubted whether they paid much attention to the medical arrangements in the convict ships or to the selection of surgeons by the contractors[1].

From January, 1806, the management of the medical side of the navy was transferred to the Transport Board, whose personnel was augmented by the addition of a physician. The Transport Board itself was not beyond reproach, and its administration had been the target of much criticism, on the score of corruption as well as of inefficiency. The forthright St. Vincent had denounced it in 1797, as "of no use whatever". This verdict was altogether too sweeping and, so far as the convict service is concerned, the Transport Commissioners, despite their many other preoccupations, did a remarkably fine job[2].

The transference of the medical administration of the navy from the Sick and Hurt Board to the Transport Board may not have resulted in a more rigorous examination of the applicants for posts as surgeons, but in other directions it certainly was beneficial to the convict service. The Transport Commissioners paid greater attention to the medical needs of the prisoners than had their predecessors, and it was an advantage that the taking up and fitting out of the transports, and the medical arrangements for the voyage, were centred in the same hands. Even before the transfer took place, the Transport Commissioners had revealed interest in the medical arrangements aboard the convict ships, and in 1801 they had issued instructions for the care of the prisoners both to the masters and the surgeons. After they assumed control, the Commissioners promptly and, as far as we can tell, thoroughly investigated complaints, and if they were slow to introduce reforms, the credit for adopting the system of surgeons-superintendent belongs to them[3].

On the abolition of the Transport Commissioners in 1817, the medical administration was handed over to the Commissioners of Victualling. Why they should have been given control of the naval surgeons is not very clear, but they continued the system of surgeons-superintendent and the convict service did not suffer from this administrative change. The introduction of further reforms and the attainment of greater efficiency, however, had to await the abolition of the outmoded Navy Board, with its innumerable commissioners and many scattered offices. This overdue step was taken in 1832, and the direction of the medical service was then transferred to the Admiralty and vested in the newly-created post of Physician of the Navy, whose title was altered in 1841 to Inspector-General of Naval Hospitals and Fleets and in 1843 to Director-General of the Medical Department of the Navy. No major innovations followed, so far as the convict service was concerned, but many minor improvements were effected and for the remaining years of transportation the medical arrangements in the convict ships were satisfactory. Endorsements on the surgeons' journals show they were regularly referred to and read by Sir William Burnett, both when he was one of the Medical Commissioners on the Transport Board and later when he became the first medical officer to have a seat on the Board of Admiralty[4].

As might be expected, surgeons found employment in the convict service unattractive. The work was exacting, the conditions unpleasant, and the pay poor. With more lucrative and congenial opportunities offering ashore, and with an increasing demand for surgeons by both the army and the navy, it is not surprising that the qualifications and characters of the applicants for posts in the convict ships were of a low standard. With rare exceptions, those who proffered their services were either novices fresh from the lecture-room or embittered failures in the profession. The former, as Assistant-Surgeon William Redfern, of the Colonial Medical Establishment, stressed in 1814, were "but ill-qualified to take charge of 200 or 300 men about to undertake a long voyage, through various climates and under peculiarly distressing circumstances," while the latter, too frequently, were "devoted to inebriety[5]."

The treatment of the surgeons was often humiliating. "They are employed by the owners of the ships," reported Redfern, "and placed immediately under the command of the masters of the transports, who, with few exceptions, having little claim to education, refined feeling, or even common decency, generally treat their surgeons, as they do their apprentices and men, with rudeness and brutality. Incapable of appreciating the value of learning, and despising all knowledge beyond what they themselves possess, they avail themselves of every opportunity to insult and mortify their surgeons. Under this species of treatment, with no means of redress during a long voyage, the mind becomes paralysed, they view their situation with disgust, and, if they have the means, should they not have been so before, they soon become confirmed drunkards. Hence their duty is neglected, and the poor convicts become the unhappy victims of the captain's brutality and the surgeon's weakness, want of skill or drunkenness. That this picture is not surcharged, the records of the colony will furnish but too many proofs. Yet, at the same time, it is but fair and just to observe that, although this is by much too frequent, it is not so general but there is now and then an exception."

Redfern's official position afforded him peculiar opportunities for judging the characters and difficulties of the surgeons, but, as a surgeon and an emancipated prisoner, his sympathies naturally were with the surgeons and the convicts. A naval surgeon, he had played a minor part in the mutiny of the Nore, and for this had been sentenced to death by a court-martial. He had been reprieved on account of his youth, however, and in 1801 had been transported to New South Wales. The following year he had received an absolute pardon, and thereafter had been constantly employed in the Colonial Medical Establishment[6].

Redfern's condemnation of the transport surgeons, and his description of their treatment aboard ship, is in many instances fully justified, but it is questionable whether the percentage of competent and conscientious surgeons and of understanding masters was not considerably higher than he indicates. Brutal as were many of the masters, and incompetent and drunken as were many of the surgeons, the proportion who treated the convicts humanely and co-operated harmoniously with one another was relatively high, as is evidenced by the number of convict ships which arrived without a heavy death-roll to report.

The difficulties confronting the contractors in engaging surgeons were, of course, great. Outside those employed in the navy, there were few surgeons with sea experience. East Indiamen, possibly from as early as 1613, always carried a surgeon, but under British law only certain types of vessels were obliged to do so. As early as 1629 ships sailing from the Port of London were required to number a surgeon in the crew, and in 1771 every Arctic whaler of 200 tons was obliged to carry a surgeon, although from earliest times it seems to have been the whaler's practice to embark a medical man. In 1789 it was made obligatory for slavers to have a surgeon, but not until 1803 was a statute passed compelling every vessel carrying 50 persons to carry a surgeon. Thus, it was not until about 1804 that the larger British merchantmen invariably had a surgeon aboard. In times of peace, of course, naval surgeons on half-pay were available to shipowners, but when Great Britain was at war this source of supply was not available. It was well-nigh impossible for the owners of convict ships to successfully compete with the owners of passenger ships and slavers for experienced surgeons, since the rewards in the convict service were so much lower, the round voyage generally longer, and the work more disagreeable, and it is not altogether surprising that they were compelled to accept surgeons who had just taken their degrees or men who had failed in their profession[7].

The decision of the British authorities to replace the naval agents in the convict ships by naval surgeons was made in consequence of the reports concerning the Second Fleet's voyage, but it was probably also influenced by the known difficulties of the contractors in procuring satisfactory surgeons. It is not clear who originated the scheme, but probably it was the sequel to discussions between the Home Department and the Navy Board. It is perhaps significant that while the surgeons were appointed by the Commissioners of the Navy, presumably on the recommendation of the Sick and Hurt Board, their instructions were signed by Evan Nepean, who was then Under-Secretary for Home Affairs and who did not succeed Philip Stephens as Principal Secretary for Marine Affairs until March 3, 1795[8].

The new system was inaugurated with the despatch of the *Royal Admiral* from England on May 30, 1792. Richard Alley, who had received his first warrant as a surgeon of the navy in 1783 and who had served as surgeon in the convict ship *Lady Juliana* in 1789-90, was appointed, as the Commissioners of the Navy informed Phillip, "to superintend the convicts and assist the surgeon on board the *Royal Admiral*". Alley was the first surgeon to make a second voyage to Australia with convicts, but his status in the *Royal Admiral* was very different to what it had been in the *Lady Juliana*. In the latter ship he had been simply the surgeon, engaged and paid by the contractors and amenable to the master's orders; for the Commissioners' representative in the *Lady Juliana* had been Lieutenant Thomas Edgar, the naval agent. In the *Royal Admiral*, however, Alley was the government's representative, paid by and answerable to the Home Department, and his medical duties were subsidiary to his other responsibilities. He was, in fact, a surgeon serving as a naval agent. The *Bellona*, which sailed less than three months after the *Royal Admiral*, and the Irish convict ships *Boddingtons* and *Sugar Cane*, which left for New South Wales in the earlier months of 1793, also carried naval surgeons serving as naval agents[9].

The experiment was eminently successful; for out of a total of 670 prisoners, of whom 534 were men and 136 women, only twelve men and two women died on the passage. With the exception of the *Royal Admiral*, in which 12 of the 14 deaths occurred, all the ships arrived in a healthy state and with few sick aboard[10].

These naval surgeons were officially styled superintendents, but not surgeons-superintendent, and were granted leave of absence by the Navy Board to accept their appointments. Thus, they did not serve in their official capacity, but as volunteers. They were paid twelve shillings a day from the time they took up duty until their return to England. Nepean's instructions make it clear that the naval surgeon's responsibilities were greater than those with which the naval agents had been charged; for, in addition to seeing that the terms of the charter-parties were obeyed, they had to assist the contractors' surgeons in the medical attendance on the prisoners. They had to see that a proper proportion of medicines and necessaries were shipped and to ensure that these were issued, and they had to supervise the serving of the rations. They were required to submit reports and returns to the governor and to the Home Department, furnishing the latter, on their return to England, with a general statement of their proceedings and their opinions as to how far the contractors had properly fulfilled their engagements[11].

As with the naval agent, no attempt was made to define the navy surgeon's powers or to invest him with the requisite authority, and in this respect he was at an even greater disadvantage than his predecessor. The latter had been at least a lieutenant, who was a commissioned officer, but the navy surgeon was a warrant officer and was destined not to attain commissioned rank until 1843. Nor did he acquire a distinctive uniform until 1805, in which year he was given relative rank with medical officers in the army and allowed to rank with, but subordinate to, lieutenants in the navy. His lowly position increased his difficulties with the commissioned officers in command of the guard and with the masters. Many of the latter were masters in the navy, but even those unconnected with the navy were averse to taking orders from one whom they regarded as very much an inferior[12].

The Report forwarded to the Home Department in 1793 by Richard Kent, the navy surgeon in the *Boddingtons*, makes this clear. "I must say," he wrote, "that it would be right to bind down the captains of ships carrying convicts under the direction of an agent, that he might comply with the orders given him for the preservation of the lives and health of the convicts; for, if I had not persevered and got everything done myself on the *Boddingtons*, for the cleanliness and comfort of the convicts, I do believe there might be a great mortality amongst them; for my orders respecting them were never attended to, and Captain Chalmers told me he only came in the ship to navigate her. After which I contrived to get the convicts themselves to preserve order, cleanliness and regularity among one another, and I am happy to say that the trouble I took in keeping them in order was amply compensated in the little trouble there was with them in the medical department."

Kent's suggestion went unheeded. Whether this was because of the neglect or conservatism of the authorities, or because the appointment of both naval agents and naval surgeons was shortly discontinued, it is impossible to say. After the *Sugar Cane*, the first convict ship to sail with any considerable number of prisoners was the *Surprize*, and aboard her the general supervision of the convicts was entrusted to William Baker, who had been appointed to the colony as a superintendent of convicts and was going out in the *Surprize* to take up his appointment. The care of the prisoners' health was left to James Thomson, who had served as a contractors' surgeon in the *Atlantic* in 1791 and who was going out in the *Surprize* to join the Colonial Medical Service as an assistant-surgeon. However, the *Marquis Cornwallis* carried a navy surgeon when she sailed from Cork on August 9, 1795, as probably also did the *Indispensable*, which left England two months later. Thereafter, except for Lieutenant James Marshall's appointment as naval agent in the *Earl Cornwallis* in 1800, neither navy surgeons nor navy agents went out in the convict ships, and, as Alexander Macleay, secretary of the Transport Board, told the Select Committee on Transportation in 1812, "the master has the sole management of the convicts in the passage".[13]

The discontinuance of supervision resulted in a sharp rise in the number of deaths on the voyage and in the number of sick landed on arrival. Excluding the *William* and the *Sovereign*, each of which carried but a single privileged convict, 18 transports sailed from England or Ireland between the beginning of 1792 and May, 1800. Six of these—the *Royal Admiral*, *Kitty*, *Bellona*, *Boddingtons*, *Sugar Cane* and *Surprize*—sailed at intervals during the 24 months from May, 1792, to May, 1794, each carrying an agent of some kind. They embarked 567 men and 226 women, of whom 11 men and 5 women died on the passage. Of the next six ships to sail—the *Marquis Cornwallis*, *Indispensable*, *Britannia*, *Ganges*, *Barwell* and a second *Britannia*—only the first two carried an agent. The death-roll in these six ships was 43 men and 5 women out of 806 men and 343 women embarked. The last six transports to sail in this period were the *Hillsborough*, *Minerva*, *Friendship*, *Luz St. Ann* or, as she came to be called on arrival, the *Anne*, *Speedy* and

Royal Admiral, none of which carried a naval surgeon or a naval agent. They embarked 1040 men and 103 women, and the deaths during the passage totalled 175 men and 3 women.

Thus, the deaths among male convicts in the first six vessels averaged one to every 55 embarked, but in the second group one to every 19, and in the third one to every six. The mortality rate among the women convicts was more constant, being respectively one to every 45, one to every 68, and one to every 34[14].

Startling as are the figures for the male convicts, they do not tell the full story; for while the majority of the prisoners in the first six ships were landed in good health, those in the later ships were sickly and emaciated when disembarked. Yet it would be wrong to lay the entire blame on the absence of supervision in the last two groups of ships. The heavy death-roll on the *Hillsborough*—95 out of 300 men embarked—was due to an outbreak of typhus which no amount of supervision could have checked, although the British authorities might have prevented it. In other transports also disease was carried aboard from the gaols and hulks. Still the fact that, excluding the *Hillsborough*, the mortality rate of the remaining five transports of the unsupervised group was one to every nine men embarked is sufficient proof that the absence of supervision was an important, perhaps the primary, factor in the high death-roll.

The combination of a brutal master and an incompetent surgeon made the voyage of the first *Britannia* a frightful one. The magistrates who inquired into the conditions aboard her reported that the master had exhibited excessive severity in punishing the convicts, and that the surgeon, Augustus Jacob Beyer, who had been the surgeon of the *Scarborough* in the ill-fated Second Fleet "was beyond all other bystanders particularly culpable in not steadfastly protesting against the cruelties—and was therefore inexcusably negligent in the performing of his duty and consequently in an eminent degree, accessory to the inhumanity, he complains of." The remedy, the magistrates suggested, lay in placing a government officer aboard each convict ship. "All ships coming to this port with convicts," they declared, "should have on board an officer of the Crown, who should be invested with proper power and authority, as well for the conducting of the ship as the particular inspection and direction of the management of the convicts on board." Governor Hunter, a naval officer himself, warmly endorsed this proposal, but the British authorities chose to ignore it, and the plan of placing a navy surgeon in each convict ship was not reintroduced[15].

The rising mortality rate, however, could not be wholly disregarded, but instead of striking at the root of the trouble the measures taken were mere palliatives. Bonus payments, first introduced in 1794, were extended. At first this inducement to good conduct was not dangled before the eyes of every master and surgeon, but after 1800 the bonuses were paid in most instances and ultimately in all. More detailed instructions were issued to both masters and surgeons, and it is probable that at the same time steps were taken to reduce overcrowding and to make the medical examination prior to embarkation more rigorous[16].

The issuing of detailed instructions to the masters and surgeons was instituted by the Transport Commissioners prior to the sailing of the transports *Canada*, *Minorca* and *Nile* in 1801. The need of cleanliness and proper ventilation was emphasised, and the surgeon was directed to see that the 'tween-decks, sleeping quarters and the hospital were swept and scraped daily, that at least twice weekly the bottom boards of the berths were carried on deck, washed with salt water, and thoroughly dried before being replaced, and that all bedding was aired on deck daily. He was enjoined also to properly trim the windsails, to keep open the air scuttles and to have the air machines working. He was to see that the sick were given free access to the deck, and was to report to the master when prisoners, because of illness or debility, should have their irons removed. He was to issue medicines and comforts to the sick, to see that the hospital was kept neat and clean, and on no account to return a discharged patient to the prison without first having thoroughly fumigated his clothes "with the vapour of burning brimstone and the oxygenec gas". The surgeon was also directed to see that each prisoner was admitted to the deck at least twice in every 24 hours, that no washing and drying of clothes took place in the 'tween-decks, and that this part of the ship was regularly fumigated in the manner specifically detailed in his instructions. Lastly, the surgeon was advised to issue lemon-juice, sugar, sago, rice, oatmeal, peas and bread, with a proportion of wine and tea, to any persons showing signs of scurvy or other disease.

But on the vexed questions of the respective spheres of responsibility of the various officers, the instructions were silent. Nothing was said as to who was to exercise the decisive authority when a conflict of opinion arose. Their instructions merely informed the surgeon that "in all and every of which" matters "the master and his officers are hereby required and obliged to assist and support you."[17]

Curiously enough, there was, after 1801, an improvement in the conditions in the convict ships. The prisoners were more humanely treated, and there was a fall in the death rate and in the number of sick landed. It seemed, indeed, that at least the more glaring defects had been eradicated. There were, of course, a few exceptions, notably in the two Irish transports *Atlas* and *Hercules* in 1801-2. Conditions aboard those vessels were shocking and deplorable, but in the majority of the convict ships there was little sickness, few deaths and scarcely any complaints of ill-treatment. The system seemed to be working so satisfactorily, indeed, that the authorities were lulled into a sense of false security.

Their complacency, however, was rudely shattered in 1814. In rapid succession, three transports—the *General Hewart*, the *Three Bees* and the *Surrey*—reached Port Jackson with their convicts sickly and emaciated, the majority suffering from the ravages of scurvy or typhus. The deaths in the *General Hewart* and the *Surrey* were exceptionally heavy. Governor Macquarie, besides ordering a thorough inquiry, obtained from Surgeon Redfern a detailed report on the conditions in each ship.

In his report, Redfern strongly urged the appointment of naval surgeons to the transports, stressing that they were accustomed to sea practice and proposing that they should not be subject to the control of the masters, but should combine the functions of principal medical officer and agent. He also recommended that each ship should carry an assistant surgeon, expressing the opinion that attendance on 200 or 300 convicts was too exacting a duty for one man to perform and that such an appointment was a necessary precaution against the contingency of the surgeon dying on the passage. Dealing with his recommendation regarding the employment of naval surgeons, he declared: "An appointment of this nature, filled by a person duly qualified, promises to be attended with incalculable advantage, and that, too, at a trifling increase of expense."[18]

There was, of course, nothing novel about this proposal: it had been adopted briefly 20 years earlier. Whether Redfern's report led to the appointment of a naval surgeon, Joseph Arnold, as surgeon-superintendent of the transport *Northampton*, which sailed from England on January 2, 1815, is doubtful. Copies of Redfern's report were forwarded by Macquarie to the Transport Commissioners and the Home Department, and these despatches left Sydney aboard the *Seringapatam* when she sailed for London direct on October 16. To have reached London by the end of the year she would have had to make a passage of 76 days or better, and even with the most favourable weather it is unlikely she was capable of that. The Home Department did not acknowledge Macquarie's despatch until December 4, 1815, which gives no indication as to when it was received[19].

The appointment of Arnold to the *Northampton* was probably decided upon in consequence of unofficial reports concerning the mortality on the *General Hewart* and *Surrey*, the latter of which, the last to arrive, reached Sydney more than two months before Macquarie penned his first despatch. But if Redfern's report was not responsible for Arnold's appointment, it undoubtedly influenced the Transport Commissioners to adopt the system of surgeons-superintendent promptly on a permanent basis, and for that they are entitled to credit.

The efficacy of the system of surgeons-superintendent was proved quickly. Macquarie in 1816 warmly praised its "good and beneficial effects," and again alluded to it in favourable terms the following year. Its principal defect was the failure to invest the surgeon-superintendent with adequate authority. We have seen that Macquarie drew attention to this aspect in 1819. The draft set of regulations which he proposed laid it down that the convicts should not be confined or punished without the surgeon-superintendent's authority, and that the master and officer commanding the guard should be obliged to obey the surgeon-superintendent's orders, "so far as they respect the convicts, in like manner as the commands of a civil magistrate when given in order to suppress riots or to enforce the laws". This, however, was carrying the matter too far, and Macquarie's proposed regulations were not adopted[20].

But within a short time the wisdom of the principle he had

advocated was realised. It is not clear when regulations placing the primary responsibility upon the surgeon-superintendent were introduced, but by the mid-1820's his was the chief voice, and the master and the commander of the guard were expected to heed his requests. He was not empowered, however, to act alone in all matters. The power of punishment, for instance, was, probably in 1823, entrusted conjointly to the surgeon-superintendent and the master, and this was a wise and just precaution.

When the transport *Pilot* arrived at Port Jackson on July 28, 1817, her surgeon-superintendent, Charles Queade, forwarded to the Governor of New South Wales a copy of the instructions which he had issued to the master and the commander of the guard, and these have been preserved. Queade may have been an exceptionally careful and conscientious surgeon but it is possible that similar instructions were also issued by other surgeons. It is important to note, however, that Queade's instructions were issued as requests, and the preamble which he deemed it necessary to pen indicates that he was doubtful of his authority to issue such definite and detailed orders as he did.

"As I am placed here as surgeon Royal Navy and superintendent of the prisoners about to be embarked aboard the *Pilot*," he wrote the guard's commander, "and as their sole management and treatment is placed under my direction by the instructions furnished me by the Honourable the Commissioners of His Majesty's Transport Board, I request that you may be pleased to direct that the following rules may be strictly attended to by the soldiers under your command for the security of the said prisoners, and that you may be pleased to attend to any suggestions I may hereafter offer to your consideration for their better security during the voyage to New South Wales." A similar paragraph prefaced his instructions to the master.

Queade's instructions concerned all aspects of the care of the convicts, and he evidently considered himself primarily responsible for their security. He "recommended" to the commander of the guard that, night and day, three sentries should be constantly kept on deck under arms at stations which he designated, and, in additional orders issued to the master after the *Pilot* had sailed, he directed him to keep the ship's firearms in good order, to have the two after guns on the quarter deck charged with round and grape shot, inspecting them regularly to see that the powder was dry, to order each officer to keep in his cabin a brace of pistols, with ball ammunition, and a cutlass, and to place a blunderbuss or two muskets in both the main and mizen tops, detailing two trustworthy seamen to make their way aloft immediately the alarm should be given.

He forbade the soldiers and seamen using "abusive, insulting or irritating" language towards the convicts, and prohibited trafficking, especially in spirits, frankly telling the guard's commander that if any soldiers were detected in this offence he would see that they were prosecuted by military law. He dealt also with such matters as the locking of the prison at night, the stowing of the prisoners' beds at daylight, the inspecting of the sentries at night, the issuing of the rations, and the maintenance of ventilation and sanitation. Queade also drew up a set of rules and regulations for the prisoners, and had a copy of these hung up in the 'tween decks for their guidance[21].

In the early 1820's the steps taken by Queade were rendered unnecessary. Not only were more explicit and comprehensive instructions issued to the surgeon-superintendent and other officers, but detailed regulations for the management of the prisoners were drawn up. At first written copies of these were displayed for the guidance of the prisoners, and eventually the regulations were printed. Thus, not only was the status of the surgeon-superintendent established, but the various officers were told precisely the nature of their duties and responsibilities, and the convicts were aware of what was expected of them[22].

The great advance made in the framing of the instructions and regulations is at once apparent when those issued in 1832 are examined. The surgeon-superintendent, who was warned that he must not leave his ship once the guard had been embarked, was furnished with a copy of the charter-party and with lists showing the proportion of stores allowed for every hundred convicts, male or female. He was advised that it was his duty to see that the master complied with the terms of the charter-party and that neither the master nor any other person shipped articles of private trade. He was instructed not to interfere with the navigation of the ship, but that, when necessary, he was to attend the crew in a professional capacity. Article seven of his instructions ordered him not to receive on board any convicts whose state of health was such that their lives would be endangered by the voyage or who were suffering from an infectious disorder. He was to examine each prisoner in the presence of the medical officer of the hulk from which the convicts were being embarked, but was warned not to reject any prisoner merely because of old age or bodily infirmity.

The surgeon-superintendent was made solely responsible for the rations. He had to see that each convict received his due share, without any deduction, that the food was properly cooked, and that it was served at the appointed meal hours. If the ration of any particular article was greater than some of the convicts were able to consume, as frequently occurred with the salt provisions when in the tropics, he was to order the master to reduce the issue. Every cask of provisions was to be opened on deck in his presence, and, having noted the state, mark, number and contents of each cask in his journal, he was to see the beef and pork placed in the padlocked harness casks and was to hand the keys to the mates.

He had also to inspect the convicts daily and to visit the sick at least twice daily, and to see that each man received an ounce of lemon-juice and sugar daily. The cleanliness of the prisoners, and the cleansing and ventilating of their quarters, were among his specific responsibilities. The detail to which his instructions descended may be judged from the fact that he was ordered to see that two lanterns were kept burning in the fore and main hatchways during the night. He had to keep a great number of returns and, of course, his journal, and he was instructed to use his best endeavours to establish schools, particularly for boys, who were to be kept apart from the men, and to read divine service every Sunday.

The Admiralty's instructions advised the surgeon-superintendent to "secure the cordial co-operation of the officer of the guard and the master in the execution of the duties entrusted to you, in order that your united exertions in the service may be performed in the most efficient manner possible". The need for tact on so long and unpleasant a voyage was at last officially recognised! But if tact and goodwill failed, the surgeon-superintendent might call upon the senior naval officer at any port of call for assistance, "showing him these instructions". The master's instructions, besides making clear the surgeon-superintendent's authority, required him to comply with the latter's regulations regarding the management of the prisoners and to admit them to the deck as ordered. He was also enjoined to make all information available to the surgeon-superintendent.

The regulations of the War Office were included in the Queen's Army Regulations; they dealt with details relating to the security of the convicts and enjoined co-operation by the guard with the surgeon-superintendent and the master[23].

The naval surgeons selected as superintendents of the convict ships were probably selected by the Admiralty from a roster, as they certainly were for similar posts in the early emigrant ships. The roster, no doubt, contained the names, in order of seniority in the service, of all surgeons in receipt of half-pay. When his turn came to be offered a post, the surgeon might refuse if he chose, but if he accepted and discharged his duties satisfactorily, he was given the opportunity, apparently, of continuing in the convict service. A surprisingly large number of surgeons made repeated voyages to New South Wales or Van Diemen's Land, and, with short intervals ashore in the colonies and in England, were engaged in the service over a period of years. Sometimes they were accompanied by their wives and occasionally also by their children, the surgeons in such cases paying the passages or at least the messing of their family out of their own pockets. Several finally took up permanent residence in the colonies, becoming settlers or private practitioners or obtaining employment in the colonial service, and a number died on the voyage to Australia.

At first the surgeons were treated somewhat shabbily by the colonial authorities because no instructions had been issued from England regarding their return passages. "I trust my conduct will meet your approbation," wrote Richard Kent, the naval surgeon of the *Boddingtons*, to Evan Nepean in 1793, "tho' it is a line I should have no ambition to embark in again, as I now feel my situation, in being left on shore here, and the great uncertainty with respect to my return, very disagreeable, for there is no mode of subsisting comfortably here but by raising stock, which cannot be done by one whose time is so precarious." Kent eventually got home by paying £80 for his passage out of his own pocket, and in 1795 he was seeking a refund of this expenditure[24].

Kent's complaint was echoed 20 years later by the first surgeon-superintendent, Joseph Arnold. Writing from Batavia in 1815, he informed the Transport Commissioners that he had been refused rations and a passage home by Macquarie, and he urged that unless surgeons were victualled and lodged in the colonies, and received a passage home at government expense, they must be "totally ruined". "I was obliged to leave the colony even before I had recovered from the effects of the preceding long voyage," he informed the Transport Board. "I paid nearly £100 as part only of my passage money home, and, having arrived at Batavia, the *Indefatigable* was totally burnt by accident, and I have lost clothes, instruments, and books, to the amount of £200, and, what will be still more detrimental to me, the masters of the ships here ask 3000 and even 5000 rupees for a passage to England."

The fact that naval surgeons were warrant, and not commissioned, officers may have had something to do with the attitude of the colonial authorities, but the Transport Board took up the cudgels on their behalf, and the Home Department was induced to issue explicit instructions regarding their treatment. Eventually each naval surgeon was empowered to draw bills on the Admiralty for £100 to defray his passage home[25].

A few years later, however, it was the surgeons who were causing trouble. As they were in receipt of pay until their return to England, they were not always anxious to return home immediately or to travel by the most direct route. Moreover, an astute surgeon, able to wait a favourable opportunity, could make his return passage quite profitable. If he was unable to secure a post in medical charge of troops being despatched from Australia to India, he could at least usually secure employment on a homeward-bound ship carrying passengers or at least obtain a free passage from the master in return for his professional services during the voyage. So many surgeons delayed their return home that eventually the colonial authorities received instructions from England that the surgeons-superintendent must return home by the first available direct ship after their arrival. This regulation, however, was so frequently disregarded that it became necessary to list in the surgeon's certificate the number of direct ships which had sailed between his arrival and ultimate departure[26].

The most frequent excuse advanced for failure to leave Australia promptly was ill-health, and the frequency with which certificates were produced from one of the Colonial Surgeons suggests either that the health of the surgeons was greatly impaired during a voyage in charge of convicts or that there was collusion on the part of the local surgeons to defeat the Transport Commissioners' regulation. Occasionally the Harbourmaster at Port Jackson certified that all accommodation on the earlier vessels had been booked out or that particular vessels possessed no suitable accommodation. In 1830 the governor endorsed as correct George Fairfowl's explanation that one vessel had all her accommodation booked, a second was too small to provide accommodation, and a third so deeply laden as to be unsafe for a voyage home round Cape Horn. In one way and another the surgeons usually got their way and escaped with no more than a severe admonition from the Transport Board concerning their conduct, but repeatedly the local authorities were rejecting requests from surgeons to be permitted to return home by way of New Zealand, China or India[27].

A ludicrous situation arose in 1831 through the manoeuvres of three surgeons who were anxious, apparently, to return home via India. Believing that the *Georgiana* was being taken up to convey troops to India, Surgeons John Tarn, William Conborough Watt and James Osborne all applied for the post in medical charge of the detachment, and their consternation was great when they learnt that the *Georgiana* was to take troops, not to India, but to Mauritius. All three immediately sought to withdraw their applications. The military commander-in-chief, Colonel Snodgrass, declined to decide the matter. "It appears that none of the surgeons in Sydney have any wish to undertake the passage," he wrote the Colonial Secretary, "and as it is no affair of mine to make the selection, will you let me know who you appoint." So the Colonial Secretary referred the matter to the governor, who selected Tarn on three grounds—firstly, because he had arrived as surgeon-superintendent of the *Georgiana*, secondly, because he had been longer in the colony than either of the other two surgeons, and, thirdly, because he was the junior in seniority. As Tarn was out of town, an express was at once despatched to him by a mounted trooper announcing this decision, but he promptly pleaded "an inflammatory sore throat and rheumatism," and, in addition, triumphantly pointed out that he was not the junior surgeon. This latter claim was correct, and in the end all three surgeons successfully avoided making the voyage to Mauritius, the exasperated governor, on the eve of the *Georgiana's* sailing, being compelled to agree to the appointment of a fourth surgeon[28].

It is impossible to determine the standard of professional ability of the naval surgeons who accepted employment as superintendents in convict ships. The probability, however, is that those of outstanding ability were exceptional. The more able and ambitious naval surgeons, particularly if they possessed influential friends, had little difficulty in obtaining more congenial and lucrative employment ashore, either in private practice or official posts, when placed on half-pay. The majority who drifted more or less permanently into the convict service did so because it was the only employment they could find. In this respect, their position was not unlike that of the earlier naval agents, and some of them proved incompetent or drunkards. But the naval surgeons were, undoubtedly, much superior, both in character and professional ability, to the general run of the contractors' surgeons whom Surgeon Redfern had so roundly condemned.

With the appointment of the surgeons-superintendent, the ships' surgeons fall very much into the background, and, in most cases, we do not know even their names. It is doubtful if the contractors now had to furnish surgeons, as they are seldom found in the ships' musters on arrival and in many cases, when a convict ship left on the return passage, we find the name of a surgeon-superintendent recorded as the ship's surgeon for the voyage to England. When a surgeon was carried as a member of the crew on the outward voyage, he merely served as the assistant surgeon that Redfern had advocated should be appointed in all convict ships, a recommendation which was never adopted.

When the work of the surgeons and surgeons-superintendent of the convict ships is considered, the state of medical knowledge at the time must not be overlooked. The only infectious disease which could be controlled, thanks to Jenner, was smallpox, but the quality of the lymph issued was often poor or deteriorated at sea; for when the surgeons vaccinated those who had not previously been vaccinated they repeatedly reported failure. Very little was known about the transmission of infectious diseases, and the causes of such diseases as dysentery, typhus and cholera had not been discovered. Although it had been suggested as early as 1689 that consumption was contagious, there was no general acceptance by medical men of this theory, and although it had been proved that scurvy could be prevented, there was still astonishing ignorance on this subject and scurvy remained a common complaint in convict ships until a late date[29].

CHAPTER FIVE

THE CONVICTS

In England the convicts were embarked in the Thames and at Portsmouth and Plymouth from the nearby gaols or the hulks, or were put aboard in batches as they arrived at the seaports from the inland prisons. The women prisoners were conveyed in carts or coaches, and when the journey was made in winter often arrived wet and miserable. "When first the women came on board from the different country gaols," wrote Thomas Prosser, surgeon of the *Maria*, in 1818, "a great number of them, through exposure to cold by travelling, became affected with rheumatisms, coughs, colds, etc." Harman Cochrane records that one woman had a painful journey from Worcester to London to board the *Mary* in 1823 and says had the weather permitted he would have sent her back immediately with the officer who brought her. As it did not and he considered her unfit to make the voyage, he sent her to the hospital ship at Woolwich. The women embarked in the *Roslin Castle* in 1830 arrived in late January and early February in a pitiable condition, several having travelled upwards of 150 miles on the outside of coaches in very inclement weather. "It was not without experiencing a feeling of disgust to the persons who had them in charge," wrote the surgeon, W. C. Watt, "that I discovered that many of the poor wretches had been heavily ironed during the whole of the journey and that in consequence several were afflicted with chilblains and that one woman had both her feet partially frost-bitten." The women prisoners who boarded the *Edward* at Woolwich in 1834 arrived in small numbers and at different times, some having travelled considerable distances, such as from York. "Often they were much fatigued and not infrequently with catarrahs," wrote Joseph Steret[1].

We may deduce from the absence of references in the surgeons' journals that the men, who usually trudged on foot from the inland gaols, never embarked immediately, but were first sent to one of the hulks or a nearby prison. There they might remain for several weeks or months before being transported.

In Ireland the prisoners, both men and women, were collected from the country and city gaols and placed aboard small vessels at Dublin or Cork or to voyage to one of those ports. Sometimes they remained for weeks in the small, crowded brigs, awaiting the arrival of a convict ship, but more often the convict ship had to await its passengers. It was seldom that the British and Irish authorities synchronised their arrangements so as to save the convicts as much misery and suffering as possible. In 1819 the *Castle Forbes* arrived at Cork on July 31, but did not embark her first convicts until September 16, and in 1820 the *Prince Regent*, arriving on July 8, received her first prisoners on August 20. The same year the brigs carrying the men for the *Almorah* became wind-bound at Waterford when journeying from Dublin to Cork. They had sailed from Dublin on July 23, the day the *Almorah* reached Cork, and the convicts were not embarked until the *Almorah* put into Waterford on August 12. The *Portland* reached Cork in 1833 on January 11, but did not receive the last of her prisoners until February 9. Even when the convicts were at last aboard, the ships were often held up by contrary winds or the dilatory manner in which the Irish authorities forwarded the assignment lists and the ship's sailing orders[2].

Both in England and Ireland many of the convicts had been in custody in the fever-ridden gaols or hulks for months and were in a wretched state of health. At first the lax medical examination led to the rejection only of those who were so obviously ill that they could not be moved, and many were embarked suffering from a contagious or infectious disease or in such a debilitated condition that their chances of surviving the rigors of the long voyage were slight. This was an important contributory factor in the high mortality rate in the early convict ships. Later, when the instructions to surgeons-superintendent ordered them not to embark any convict suffering an infectious or contagious disease or who was unfit to undertake the voyage, there was some improvement.

However, the gaol authorities, as well as the convicts, often conspired to defeat the surgeon's utmost vigilance. The surgeons were subject to pressure as well as deceit. At the medical examination the prisoners were made to appear at their best. They were washed and dressed in new clothes and warned to appear smart and cheerful before the doctor. As most of the convicts, sickened by their imprisonment in the crowded and unhealthy gaols and hulks, were only too eager to get away they concealed their disabilities and cheerfully lied about the state of their health. For their part, the hulk and prison authorities suppressed the health records of their charges and sometimes deliberately misled the surgeon as to a particular man's record or illness.

The circumstances under which the medical examination was carried out rendered it anything but thorough, even under the best conditions. The men were paraded in large numbers, so that there was no opportunity to examine each thoroughly and at leisure, and all the surgeon could do was to reject those who appeared obviously ill. Harvey Morris, surgeon of the *Bangalore*, was forced to carry out his examination of Irish prisoners in 1848 "almost in the open air on excessively cold days", so that it was impossible to ask the men to remove their clothing. In 1847 the surgeon of the *Cadet*, owing to the miscarriage of a letter, did not see his charges at all until they filed by him as they came aboard. In 1840, C. A. Browning was compelled to examine the *Margaret's* prisoners in the absence of the gaol surgeon, who did not put in an appearance until the examination had been completed. In his absence Browning had to rely, apart from his own observation, on what little the matron and governor could, or would, tell him, and he seems to have believed the gaol surgeon had deliberately absented himself so as to avoid answering awkward questions. "A disposition to impose upon me prisoners whose age and state of health rendered them unfit for subjection to the influences which generally obtain during a long voyage," he wrote, "was, as usual, manifested, though perhaps in a somewhat less degree than on former occasions." Charles Smith remarked in 1850 that had he known the prison histories of some of his charges in the *Duke of Cornwall* he would have selected others more healthy[3].

All prisoners for embarkation were obliged to have a medical certificate from the shore authorities, and this precaution was very necessary in the case of convicts from the inland gaols. Yet, as we have seen, many of the women when they arrived aboard were in a poor state of health and often had to be relanded as unfit to make the voyage to Australia. As James Rutherford, surgeon of the

Pyramus in 1831-2, wrote: "Considering that prison surgeons would naturally wish the more speedy removal of those likely to be the more troublesome inmates the actual state of health of the prisoners corresponded as much as could be expected with the certificates, which, it must be confessed, however, seemed in some few instances to prove the correctness of an opinion very generally received in the world that poor judgment must sometimes yield when opposed by the powerful arguments of self-interest." In the *Aurora* in 1851 the surgeon had one woman "unhandsomely pawned" upon him direct from the Millbank Prison Infirmary, where she had been under medical treatment, and many others were less healthy than represented, "which I think highly derogatory to those in authority." Much earlier, in 1832, Joseph Steret reported: "I found that my friends at the hulks contrived to palm off several old ulcers notwithstanding my utmost care. Their irons were placed on the diseased leg when they came on board, which proved a good excuse for not taking the stocking completely off." The same year Thomas Galloway found he had been sent an infirm old man whose hearing and sight failed within a few days of sailing and whose helplessness in the face of the rolling and pitching of the ship left no alternative but to admit him to the hospital for the entire voyage. In the *Layton* in 1839, Isaac Noott found four prisoners who had been "conditioned to conceal their complaints", having been told by their keepers that if they were rejected by the surgeon they would be placed in the "black hole". Another convict certified as being in good health Noott found to be an idiot, and on this voyage three of the four men who died, in Noott's opinion, should not have been embarked. Alexander Cross claimed that at least a quarter of the 61 convicts sent to the *Equestrian* from Dartmoor prison in 1852 were "old and worn out men", while he believed that probably more than 30 of the original number had been sent to Dartmoor as invalids from other prisons. He asserted he would have objected to 30 or 40, but he thought it unlikely his objection would have been sustained[4].

The desire of the gaol and hulk authorities to get rid of as many of their charges as possible, and in particular those who were most troublesome, was aided by the general wish of the convicts to be transported. The surgeons' journals record many instances of both men and women concealing illness or injury for fear they would be left to rot in prison or aboard the hulks[5]. Some prisoners told George Birnie they would rather take their chance of dying at sea than remain longer in the hulks, and a chimney-sweep confessed to A. D. Wilson that he had concealed his disability to ensure being shipped, "hoping to better his condition, not having experienced any of the comforts of life in England". Convicts in the *Arab* in 1834 told C. A. Browning that it was a common practice aboard the hulk *York* at Portsmouth to bribe subordinate officers so that their names would be included in the list of those to be transported. However, there were some prisoners who so dreaded transportation that they feigned illness to avoid shipment, and some succeeded on two or three occasions in avoiding being sent to Australia. One malingerer became suddenly well when threatened with a flogging[6].

The surgeons did their duty as best they could. They often rejected men and women as unfit for the voyage, and in 1832 we find Andrew Henderson refusing to take no fewer than 23[7]. However, their objections were sometimes ignored or overruled, in at least one instance even when the surgeon had the support of the Director-General of the Medical Department of the Navy[8]. In other instances the shore surgeons by gross misrepresentations induced a withdrawal of the objections. Thus, George Fairfowl rejected in 1833 a stone-cutter, a man of 18 who was 6 ft. 4 in. tall, who had "a meagre, attenuated person, evidently of consumptive and scrofulous habit", but agreed to accept him when the shore surgeon gave an assurance that the man had never been on the sick-list and had no complaint. The man died of phthisis during the passage. David Deas, after rejecting a man suffering ophthalmia, consented to take him when the hulk authorities explained that on the morning of the medical examination the convict's eye had been irritated while he was working as a hewer near where lime was being slaked and that no outbreak of ophthalmia had occurred in the hulk. The inclusion of this man led to an outbreak among the prisoners in the *Lord Petre* and caused "much suffering".

Pressure also was brought to bear by higher authorities. T. Clarke received a note from the Secretary of State's office that the removal of an old woman, whose age and appearance had led the surgeon to conclude she had little hope of ever reaching Australia, was very desirable, and P. Jones, who had objected to a number on the ground of unfitness, was informed by the Inspector-

General that it was a particular request from the Dublin authorities that he would not press his objections on account of age, as the prisoners "had given the magistrates much trouble and it was most desirable they should be sent out of the country." Both surgeons withdrew their objections. The woman in the first case died on the passage, as also did two of those Jones had at first refused to accept. In 1834, Joseph Steret received a letter from the prison medical officer suggesting that a woman who had been confined to bed for nearly three years was feigning illness. However, Steret would have refused to take her but he was informed officially that it was considered advisable to send her, her temper and habits in prison being so vile that her removal was thought necessary. She reached Australia although she was confined to bed for most of the voyage[9]. In view of the callousness of the authorities and of subordinate officers in shipping aged and unfit prisoners, it is not surprising that it was common for deaths to occur before sailing.

From the middle of 1795 those convict ships which called at Portsmouth were inspected by Sir John Fitzpatrick, the Home Department's Inspector-General of Health, who was stationed at that port. His principal duty seems to have been to see that the ships were reasonably hygienic, but he also inspected the convicts after embarkation. He was empowered to order bulkheads to be removed, the location of privies to be altered, and other structural alterations to be carried out with a view to improving ventilation and sanitation, and he had a free hand in effecting such changes as he deemed necessary in the internal arrangements for the housing and caring of the prisoners. He was also invested with authority to order convicts to be disembarked if he considered they were unfit to make the voyage or constituted a threat to the health of the other prisoners. It is clear that he was active and zealous in the performance of these duties, and he did not hesitate to exercise the authority he possessed.

His advice, however, was not always heeded, and the tragedy of the *Hillsborough*, which sailed from England in October, 1798, and lost 95 men on the passage, would not have occurred if his representations had been heeded. He urged the authorities not to embark prisoners from Langstone Harbour, where the gaol fever had been raging with much virulence, but his recommendation was disregarded. The result was an outbreak of typhus during the passage.

The inspection of convict ships did not form part of Sir John's routine duties, and in 1802 he put in a claim for extra remuneration for having inspected 15 convict ships between June 27, 1795, and January 1, 1802[10].

The prisoners were thoroughly washed and issued with new clothing before being embarked, but occasionally were put aboard in a filthy state. The regulation dress for the men comprised jackets and waistcoats of blue cloth or kersey, duck trousers, check or coarse linen shirts, yarn stockings and woollen caps. These clothes were suitable for a summer voyage, but were altogether too light for winter. The naval authorities objected on hygienic grounds, however, to flannel and woollen garments, contending that these materials harboured disease. In consequence, the lightly-clad convicts, whose bed-clothing was limited to a single blanket, suffered acutely from cold in the winter months and in the high southern latitudes. In the hulks they wore woollen clothing and the substitution of lighter clothing when they were sent to the convict ship in cold weather often led to sickness[11].

However, the provision of suitable clothing and the attainment of uniformity took time. In 1820 the men who embarked in the *Elizabeth* wore a woollen cap, a guernsey frock, a check shirt, raven duck trousers, a neckerchief, and shoes and stockings, and Patrick McTernan, without giving details, records that between his visits in 1827 and 1828 the clothing was altered, "much to the advantage and comfort of the convicts". Yet a few years later, in 1835, when a party of boys from the Chatham hulk *Euryalus* embarked in the *Aurora* wearing knee-breeches while others came aboard in duck-trousers, we find Andrew Henderson plaintively inquiring: "Has there not been sufficient time to make up our minds in what uniform convicts ought to be sent out in?" As early as 1832 he had recommended the adoption of cloth trousers, which he still favoured three years later. It is clear that alterations suggested in the scale and type of clothing were adopted but tardily, but whether because of conservatism or lack of finance, cannot be determined. Before 1820, however, the prisoners were furnished with three shirts, two pairs of trousers, a pair of shoes, and other warm clothing, and a decade later the clothing for the voyage included flannel underclothes and raven duck overalls. As the clothing was generally of poor quality, it was usually worn out by the time Australia was reached, and additional clothing was shipped in each convict ship and the prisoners completely outfitted before being landed at their destination[12].

Yet complaints of the inadequacy of the prisoners' clothing to combat the cold of the high southern latitudes when the ships were running down their easting were being made as late as the early 1840's. Campbell France reported that old and feeble convicts complained much of the severe cold, their clothes having worn very thin and being insufficient to protect them. Another surgeon asserted that each man should have two flannel shirts, a wise precaution since at this stage of the journey, with strong gales, high seas and heavy rain, the drying of laundry or sodden garments was often a long process. In 1849, Alexander Kilroy was urging that women prisoners should be supplied with thicker and stronger shoes, since those supplied were so thin that they were damp for most of the voyage and caused much catarrhal illness. Spare clothing to replace items worn out during the voyage or lost overboard in squalls when drying on the rigging had never been supplied, and as late as 1843 David Deas was complaining of this omission. Surgeons had to cut up sheets and blankets to make extra shirts, trousers and caps. Clothing was not supplied to children embarked in female convict ships and often they came aboard in rags, so that they suffered greatly from the cold. The surgeons did what they could to improvise clothing from sheets and blankets[13].

We possess less information regarding the clothing of the women. They were issued with a regulation dress of some kind, but the clothing of the female convicts in the First Fleet was so defective that it fell to pieces in a few weeks. By the late 1820's, however, the item of "clothing for use during the voyage" had been eliminated from the stores list of female convict ships, which suggests that they were outfitted before leaving the gaols or were permitted to take with them such clothing as they might possess. Before being disembarked, however, each woman was given a brown serge jacket and petticoat, a couple of linen shifts, a linen cap, a neck handkerchief, a pair of worsted stockings, and a pair of shoes. When the Quaker heroine, Elizabeth Fry, aroused interest in the female convict ships, ladies' committees were formed, and gifts were given to each woman prisoner before her ship sailed. The parcel included a Hessian apron and another of black stuff, as well as a cotton cap and a Hessian bag in which to keep her clothes, and by 1842 the women were supplied with white jackets and checked aprons for use in the tropics[14].

The scale of rations was adequate and, rather surprisingly, the food was generally of good quality, being better than that furnished either in the army or the navy. Indeed, complaints regarding the quality of the provisions were relatively few. The reverse was the case with the serving of the rations. The convicts were often cheated of their due proportion and sometimes half-starved. Rascally masters and their stewards did not hesitate to employ false weights and measures, and more than one ship's captain was accused of having set up store on arrival and retailed, at an exorbitant profit, the rations withheld from the convicts.

The purchase, often enough by the ship's master, of the prisoners' salt rations while the ship was in the tropics constituted another abuse. Medical opinion was not unanimous that their health suffered in consequence of no substitute being provided for the salt beef or pork they sold, but the purchaser made a very handsome profit at the convict's expense. They never received a fair price for their meat. They were paid in tea, coffee, tobacco and similar articles, and these were charged to them at prices which showed an enormous profit on prime cost, so that actually they received very little in return for the food they thus sold.

These abuses, which were, of course, the result of the absence of supervision, were gradually checked and eventually stamped out with the appointment of the surgeons-superintendent. But at a comparatively late date, through fraud or negligence, the prisoners were sometimes cheated of their just share of provisions, and in 1820 it was officially announced that, on application to the Principal Superintendent of Convicts, prisoners by two ships would receive trifling sums—tenpence halfpenny in one case and two shillings and twopence in the other—to compensate them for rations short-served during the voyage[15].

From the outset the scale of rations was based on the allowance in the Royal Navy, the convicts receiving two-thirds the naval ration. In the Second Fleet each mess of six convicts should have received 16 lb. of bread, 12 lb. of flour, 14 lb. of beef, 8 lb. of pork, 12 pints of pease, 1½ lb. of butter, and 2 lb. of rice weekly. This remained the standard ration for some years, but by 1812 each mess received 20 lb. of bread, 12 lb. of flour, 16 lb. of beef, 6 lb. of pork, 12 pints of pease, 1 lb. of butter, 8 oz. of rice, $1\frac{1}{2}$ lb. of suet, 3 lb. of raisins, 6 pints of oatmeal, and 4 oz. of sugar. Thus, while the quantity of bread and beef had been slightly increased, and raisins, suet, oatmeal and sugar had been added to the ration, a reduction had been effected in the quantity of pork, butter and rice.

From time to time alterations were made in the dietary scale principally as a result of the recommendations of the surgeons and surgeons-superintendent. Before sailing, and at ports of call, fresh meat and vegetables were served, a necessary precaution against scurvy. Tea and sugar formed part of the regular rations of female prisoners, and aboard both male and female convict ships a few delicacies were provided for the sick. Later, preserved meat was introduced and with preserved potatoes was given once a week in lieu of salt provisions. The effects were considered beneficial, but in 1844 we find J. Clarke pointing out that the allowance of 1 lb. for each female convict for the whole voyage was absurd and in 1850 R. W. Clarke found that while the small tins of preserved meat were good and useful the large tins when opened were often bad. Even at this late date the salt meat was sometimes old and subject to great shrinkage in boiling, so that when cooked it seldom weighed more than three or three-and-a-half ounces free of bone. C. H. Fuller proposed that if the dressed beef or pork weighed less than half its weight when raw, an extra quantity should be served as compensation for the loss sustained and the meat's poor quality. There is no evidence that his suggestion was adopted[16].

"The rations are both good and abundant," declared Surgeon Peter Cunningham, writing of the convict ships of the 1820's, "three-quarters of a pound of biscuit being the daily allowance of bread, while each day the convict sits down to dinner of either beef, pork or plum-pudding, having pea soup four times a week, and a pot of gruel every morning, with sugar or butter in it. Vinegar is issued to the messes weekly; and as soon as the ship has been three weeks at sea, each man is served with an ounce of lime-juice and the same of sugar daily, to guard against scurvy, while two gallons of good Spanish red wine and 140 gallons of water are put on board for issuing to each likewise—three to four gills of wine weekly, and three quarts of water daily, being the general allowance."[17]

Water was always a problem, particularly when the casks were filled from the Thames. The regulations governing the filling of the casks required the water to be properly filtered and prohibited the work being performed at certain stages of the tide. Often, however, the water went bad long before the Cape of Good Hope, becoming very offensive in smell as well as taste and depositing a copious, dark, peat-like sediment on the bottom of the cask. Thames water was so unreliable that many masters and surgeons preferred to call at Teneriffe to complete their water.[18]

On embarkation the prisoners were allotted numbers and divided into messes, usually six to a mess. They were then issued with their bedding and cooking and eating utensils. Each man received a bed and pillow and a single blanket, with two wooden bowls and a wooden spoon. Each mess was given a keg and a horn tumbler, a kettle for tea-making being added in female transports. Each morning the convict had to roll his bedding and secure it with two pieces of sennit, but the space on deck for storing the bedding during the day was often insufficient and the canvas hammock cloths so worn as to be useless for protecting the bedding from rain and spray. After the 1840's hammocks were sometimes supplied instead of beds and in the *Anson* in 1843-4 Andrew Millar considered them more suitable "both for health and morality".[19]

The prisoners generally elected their own mess captain, who, besides drawing the ration, was responsible for the maintenance of tidiness and for the orderly conduct of his messmates. The other appointments seem to have been made by the surgeons, who might select half-a-dozen of the more deserving mess captains as captains of the deck or appoint a single convict to serve in this capacity, possibly on the recommendation of the hulk or gaol officials. They also chose those to serve as hospital attendants, cooks, water-closet attendants, barbers and so on. Each surgeon followed his own inclinations in the number and nature of the appointments he made. George Thomson, in 1826, appointed two captains for the prison deck and another two for the upper deck as well as a captain for each division of 25 into which he divided the prisoners. On the other hand, S. Alexander preferred a single captain of the deck, with several petty officers and a barber for each division. Sometimes the captain of the deck was designated a superintendent or boatswain. Constables were also selected among the convicts. On his first voyage with prisoners, Thomas Dunn formed seven ex-soldiers, all of whom had been sentenced to transportation by court-martial for military offences, into a constabulary and found them of the greatest use in promoting cleanliness and good order. He entrusted them with a great deal of authority over their fellow prisoners. In four ships, George Fairfowl found a night patrol of six men, who were relieved every four hours, effective in preventing petty thefts and disturbances. In female convict ships the women given similar responsibilities to the captains of the deck in male ships were known as matrons.[20]

The prison was situated in the 'tween decks. In the Second Fleet transport *Neptune* it occupied the orlop or third deck, and was confined to a space some 75 feet long and, at its widest, 35 feet broad, with a height of 6½ feet between the beams and 5 feet 7 inches below the beams. There were four rows of one-storey high cabins, each about 6 feet square, two rows on either side of the ship from the mainmast forwards and two shorter rows amidships. Stout bulkheads, studded with nails and loopholed, cut off the prison quarters from the main and fore hatchways[21].

In 1817 the Navy Board altered the standard design of the prison by dividing it into three distinct apartments, separated by open iron railings. The object was to segregate the juvenile from the more hardened offenders and at the same time to permit a freer circulation of air. The first transport fitted out to this plan was the *Lady Castlereagh*, which arrived at Port Jackson on April 30, 1818, and, according to Macquarie, the new design was a marked improvement. He reported that the prison was better lighted and better ventilated than previously had been the case.

Peter Cunningham has left us a description of this type of prison as constructed in the 1820's. "Two rows of sleeping-berths, one above the other," he says, "extend on each side of the between-decks, each berth being 6 feet square, and calculated to hold four convicts, every one thus possessing 18 inches space to sleep in—and ample space, too! The hospital is in the fore-part of the ship, with a bulkhead across, separating it from the prison, having two doors with locks to keep out intruders; while a separate prison is built for the boys, to cut off all intercourse between them and the men. Strong wooden stanchions, thickly studded with nails, are fixed round the fore and main hatchways, between decks, in each of which is a door with three padlocks, to let the convicts out and in, and secure them at night. The convicts by these means have no access to the hold through the prison, a ladder being placed in each hatchway for them to go up and down by, which is pulled on deck at night."

In December, 1839, the United States surveying and exploring expedition commanded by Commodore Charles Wilkes, U.S.M., called at Sydney to refit and refresh, and Wilkes was shown over a convict ship. His description clearly shows that the prison quarters at this time were very similar in design to those of half-a-century earlier. "Between decks a strong grated barricade, spiked with iron, is built across the ship at the steerage bulkhead," he wrote. "This gives the officers a free view of all that goes on among the prisoners. Bunks for sleeping are placed on each side all the way to the bows. Each of these will accommodate five persons. There is no outlet but through a door in the steerage bulkhead, and this is always guarded by a sentry. Light and air are admitted through the hatches, which are strongly grated . . . The quarter-deck is barricaded near the mainmast, abaft which the arms of the guard are kept."[22]

The new design introduced in 1817 was evidently not retained. Wooden stanchions replaced the lighter and less massive iron bars, and we find surgeons over the years suggesting, apparently quite unaware of the experiment of 1817, that bar iron should be employed instead of wood. In 1831 George Birnie stressed that the change would effect a great saving in labour and materials and improve ventilation. Seven years later, arguing the same case, J. G. Stewart pointed out that the wooden stanchions measured between 5½–6 inches, with only 2½– 3 inches between each stanchion, so that only about a third of the hatchway was open to the free access of air. He urged the substitution of half-inch bars set three inches apart, and pointed out that a great increase in ventilation would result. However, as late as 1850 the use of iron in place of the heavy wooden stanchions was still being suggested without avail.[23]

The fact is that the prison quarters were always dark and gloomy, and utterly foul. The ventilation, particularly in the earlier convict ships, was bad. Ships' officers for long had little faith in the air and ventilating machines or even in the windsails and despite the clauses relating to their use in the charter-parties, they frequently refused to permit them to be employed or neglected to attend to them, so that they soon became useless. In stormy weather, of course, it was necessary to keep the air scuttles closed, and aboard a vessel that laboured a good deal they often could not be kept open even in moderate weather. Thus, the air in the prison usually hung heavy and lifeless, and when the ship was passing through the tropics it was stifling and oppressive. J. G. Stewart, surgeon of the *Nautilus*, described the heat in the prison at night as "really dreadful", and the records kept by surgeons prove that often the temperature at night below was between 90° and 100°, although the daytime temperature at noon in the shade was commonly between 76° and 82° and seldom exceeded 86°. In the *Isabella* in 1832 the prison temperature at night did not fall below 92° for many nights, and in 1843 the surgeon of the *Maitland*, A. McLaren, considered that whereas the temperature on deck and in the prison was identical during the daytime when the latter was unoccupied, the prison was 10° hotter when all the prisoners were crowded into it at night. In the *Hive*, in 1834, the prison temperature reached the century and her surgeon, George Fairfowl, allowed sixty men to sleep on deck at a time, changing them every four hours. He estimated that when this number of men went on deck the temperature below fell by from 5° to 8°. Morgan Price, surgeon of the *Almorah* in 1824, found that the excessive heat caused many of the women convicts to faint, so that he was continuously employed reviving them, and to relieve their sufferings allowed them to remain on deck until 10 p.m. That no improvement occurred over the years is proved by the fact that in the West Australian transport *Clyde*, in 1863, the temperature reached 88° in the hospital and 92° in the prison.[24]

Many of the transports were wet ships, and in these the prison was always damp and dank. The water seeped through the ship's seams, and the convicts' bunks and bedding could not be kept dry. In very heavy seas the hatches had to be battened down, but it was not uncommon for the prisoners to find themselves washed from their bunks by a swirling mass of water. The surgeons of the day, who did not appreciate that scurvy was the result of a vitamin deficiency, attributed the outbreaks of this disease to the dampness of the prison when ships were running down their easting in the high southern latitudes.

The stench of the prison, crowded with perspiring humanity, was indescribable, and even to prisoners inured to the fetid atmosphere of the insanitary gaols and hulks it must have been well-nigh unbearable, particularly in the tropics. The acrid smell of stale bilge water and of mouldy, rotting timber mingled in the still air with the foul odours of closely-packed humanity, and the wonder is that so many prisoners survived the experience, not that so many died under such appalling conditions.

In rough weather, when the prisoners had to be kept below beneath battened hatches, and when, following an attempt at mutiny or because of a suspected plot to seize the ship, the convicts were refused admittance to the deck for several days, the thick, rank atmosphere of their quarters bred disease of all kinds. The sufferings of the prisoners under these conditions defy description, but the worst horrors in the floating hell that was a convict ship's prison occurred when the ship was passing through the tropics. Perhaps, the most graphic pen-picture of the scene then witnessed is contained in the pages of a novel written by the Irish political prisoner, John Boyle O'Reilly. He was transported to Western Australia in the *Hougoumont*, the last convict ship to Australia, but subsequently escaped to the United States.

"When the ship was becalmed in the tropics," O'Reilly wrote, "the suffering of the imprisoned wretches in the steaming and crowded hold was piteous to see. They were so packed that free movement was impossible. The best thing to do was to sit each on his or her berth, and suffer in patience. The air was stifling and oppressive. There was no draught through the barred hatches The deck above them was blazing hot. The pitch dropped from the seams, and burned their flesh as it fell. There was only one word spoken or thought—one yearning idea in every mind—water, cool water to slake the parching thirst. Two pints of water a day were served out to each convict—a quart of half-putrid and blood-warm liquid. It was a woeful sight to see the thirsty souls devour this allowance as soon as their hot hands seized the vessel. Day in and day out, the terrible calm held the ship, and the consuming heat sapped the lives of the pent-up convicts . . . Hideous incidents filled the days and nights as the convict ship sailed southward with her burden of disease and death. The mortality among the convicts was frightful. Weakened and depressed by the long drought, the continuous heat, and the poisonous atmosphere, they succumbed to the fever in its first stages.''[25]

However, some changes were made in the fitting up of the prisons which, while they may not have improved ventilation, did give the inmates some slight comforts. Perhaps the most important of these gave each convict a separate sleeping-berth place which could be converted in the daytime into seats and tables. This innovation seems to have been introduced about 1844 and was considered by the surgeons a great improvement, especially as the moveable part of the wooden framing could be taken down and cleaned on deck. According to John Inches, the *Lady Harewood* in 1832 was the first vessel fitted up with midship berths having hammocks, which allowed him to keep a clear space in the daytime that assisted the free circulation of air. Whatever the exact change made, it evidently was not universally adopted, since Alexander Nisbet, surgeon of the *Earl Grey*, records in 1838 that 234 prisoners were accommodated in standing berths and fifty-six were placed in hammocks in the middle of the prison. In 1843 the *Equestrian* had no standing-bed places. Upright stanchions were erected in rows along the deck and connected by transverse bars on which hammocks were suspended in two tiers, one above the other. The prisoners found some difficulty in getting in and out of them. Oliver Sproule tells us that a new and improved method of fitting up the prison enabled the *Isabella* in 1833 to carry about a hundred more convicts than formerly without overcrowding, but he gives no details.

It is evident, however, that the attempts to segregate the prisoners by dividing the prison into several apartments were hardly successful. In the *Emma Eugenia* in 1850 the prison was fitted up in the usual way, but at the last moment it was decided to divide the prison into three distinct apartments. However, the two apartments on the starboard side had to be virtually thrown into one, since the door between them had to be kept open to allow access to the water closets. Moreover, apart from separating the boys from the men, there was little point in trying to graduate the prisoners and keeping each section apart, as when ill they had to intermingle and during school hours all classes were brought together. The need, at least in female ships, for three or four berths being railed off from the rest of the prison, so they could be used as a place of confinement for convicts under punishment, was emphasised, but although individual surgeons may have had the ship's carpenter adopt this idea it seems never to have been generally accepted by the naval authorities responsible for fitting out the transports. Yet the confinement boxes furnished for the punishment of unruly convicts were so small that only one person could fit into them at a time, and in the tropics and whenever it was hot, no prisoner could be confined in the box for more than four hours.[26]

Apparently, only one set of keys to the prison doors was furnished. In the *Eliza* in 1822 the second mate, having just locked up the prison, was swept overboard and the keys went with him. The only way in which the prison could be unlocked was by picking the lock[27].

When exercising on deck, the prisoners presented a degrading sight. Ironed to one another by clanking chains, they shuffled dispiritedly round and round the deck to the jingle of their irons, with the scarlet-coated sentries, posted on the poop, watching them closely. The Second Fleet contractors, having been engaged previously in the slave trade, supplied irons that had been used aboard the slavers, and these were barbarous. Captain Hill, the commander of the guard in the *Surprize*, described these shackles as made "with a short bolt, instead of chains that drop between the legs and fasten with a bandage about the waist, like those at the different gaols; these bolts were not more than three-quarters of a foot in length, so that they could not extend either leg from the other more than an inch or two at most; thus fettered, it was impossible for them to move but at a risk of both their legs being broken". Such irons, however, were not usual, and in the later convict ships ordinary handcuffs and leg-irons were used, through which chains might be run to loop the prisoners together in batches. These leg-irons were officially described as "bazzels with chains". Ultimately the "articles of security" were furnished by the British authorities, and were shipped back to England for re-use. In addition to the handcuffs and leg-irons, they included two oak blocks with plates and rings, and a similar number of stakes, for stapling offenders to the deck, a recognised method of punishment[28].

In the prison the convicts were ironed to ringbolts, but under a humane captain and surgeon-superintendent, the irons were struck off early in the voyage. In the early days of transportation the prisoners might be ironed throughout the voyage, but it was only occasionally in the later convict ships that a suspected mutineer or an habitual offender was kept ironed throughout the passage.

The punishments were brutal and harsh, and until their infliction was made the joint responsibility of the master and the surgeon-superintendent, they were frequently vicarious and unjust. From about 1823 onwards the punishments awarded were much milder and less injurious to health than earlier had been the case. Certainly they were less severe aboard the convict ships than at such penal hells in Australia as Norfolk Island and Macquarie Harbour.

A few prisoners were executed for attempts at mutiny, and many others, for the same offence, were severely flogged with the cat-o'-nine-tails. In the 18th and early part of the 19th century the lash was regarded as indispensable to the maintenance of discipline, and it was commonly employed in the army and navy a well as in the gaols and penal settlements. The shipboard floggings, at least in the first years of transportation, were often brutal and excessive, and timid masters, fearing for the safety of their ships, resorted to the lash often at the mere rumour of a mutiny attempt. Later, the floggings were milder, usually from half-a-dozen to two dozen lashes, but in the *John Barry*, in 1819, one man was given seventy-two lashes and another forty and in the *Minerva* in 1821 Charles Queade imposed punishments of seventy-two, forty-eight and thirty-six lashes. Even as late as the 1860's, in the West Australian ships, quite severe floggings by modern standards were administered. In the *Merchantman* in 1864 punishments of forty-eight and thirty-six lashes were awarded and at least one man received thirty-six lashes in the *Racehorse* in 1865. The floggings were not always carried out at the gangway on deck or with a cat-o'-nine-tails. In the *Grenada* in 1821, Peter Cunningham ordered one man to be given twenty-four cobs with a rope's end by his messmates for stealing, and in the *England* in 1826 George Thomson sanctioned up to forty-eight cobs with a leather thong. In this form of punishment the culprit received the blows across the buttocks. Many surgeons, however, found it unnecessary to resort to flogging in any form[29].

Next to flogging, the most common punishment was ironing. Prisoners were placed in single or double irons—that is, they were simply handcuffed or both handcuffed and leg-ironed—and sometimes, especially at night, they might be linked together with a chain passed through their irons and secured to a ringbolt at either end. The ironing might last for many days, sometimes even for the entire duration of the passage, but more commonly the prisoners were released after from twenty-four to forty-eight hours. Eventually, as with flogging, ironing was largely laid aside, and instead offenders were made to stand erect in a narrow box on the deck. Commodore Wilkes declares that this punishment was effective in reducing the worst male culprits to order, but that the women wailed so loudly, and used their tongues so freely, that it was found necessary to place a cistern of water on top of the box. "This was turned over upon those who persisted in using their tongues," he states, "and was always efficacious." In the West Australian ships the men might be confined in the box on bread and water for from one to four days, the punishment forming a species of solitary confinement[30].

Women were occasionally flogged or caned, and in the *Elizabeth* in 1836 Robert Espie, finding that solitary confinement and more lenient punishments failed, whipped the women over their arms, legs and backs with a stout piece of rope, apparently escaping an official reprimand. Women might have their heads shaven, a punishment they much disliked, although at least one surgeon found this mode of punishment ineffective. J. Ellis, surgeon of the *Diana* in 1833, thought shaving the head the only punishment the women dreaded, "but when this is once done, in place of it bringing about a better conduct it renders them still more incorrigible, fancying, as they do, that they have suffered the last and worst degradation, to bring all others to the same level with them is among the first things they set about . . ." Women sometimes were made to wear a scold's bridle or to parade the deck in a tub, but more commonly were confined on bread and water in the coal-hole, one of the darkest and gloomiest parts of the ship. However, the use of the coal hole and a confinement box in female transports seems to have been discontinued, and at a later date we find surgeons representing that a cell for purposes of solitary confinement was much needed.[31]

The voyage to Australia was long and tedious, and it was no easy problem to keep the prisoners occupied. Indeed, in the early

Miss Rose Kelsall, Perth, W.A.

Aboard the "JOHN CALVIN" in the N.E. trades near Madeira, from an original painting by Kanute Bull, a convict

Oil painting by W. A. Knell — *National Maritime Museum, Greenwich*

The "MOUNT STEWART ELPHINSTONE"

convict ships little effort was made to help them pass the time, except to keep them endlessly scrubbing, scraping, swabbing and dry-holystoning the decks, according to the state of the weather. The women were left very much to their own devices. The beneficial effects of keeping the prisoners out of mischief by occupying their time was soon realised, however, and within a few years a marked improvement was effected. The men were made to pick oakum, to sew trousers and jackets, to knit socks and sometimes were allowed to assist in the navigation of the ship. The women were supplied, at first by charitable organisations such as that formed by Elizabeth Fry and later by the government, with needles, thread and cloth, and those who conducted themselves well were in some, but not all, cases permitted to sell such articles as they made for their own profit on their arrival in Australia. Dancing and singing were encouraged, and eventually small libraries were shipped, although these were mainly confined to works of a religious, devotional and moral nature. Schools were formed, and on the voyage many convicts learnt to read or write. The reports of the prisoner-schoolmasters on their pupils, with specimens of the latter's writing to indicate the progress they had made, are among the historical curiosities in Australian libraries and archives.[32]

"From the commencement of the voyage to its termination," wrote the earnest but narrow-minded Surgeon Colin Arrott Browning, who served as surgeon-superintendent in several convict ships between 1831 and 1847, "the prisoners breathe a moral and spiritual atmosphere." The results of religious instruction, however, were scarcely what Browning claimed; for it seems clear that the majority of the convicts found it simpler and more profitable to play the hypocrite than to stand out against well-meaning religious fanatics. "Gambling is a prevailing vice," declared the more sensible Surgeon Peter Cunningham, "and requires great exertion to keep it under; dice, cards, pitch and toss, and various other speculations, soon becoming general, unless checked; and to such a height of infatuation will this vice be carried, that I have known a country simpleton go three whole days without food, having gambled away all his rations for that period. Until gambling is stopped, thieving will be carried on, because the fellow who loses his own dinner will always insure one out of some other person's mess, unless he is a very sorry thief indeed." Cunningham, who was one of the surgeons who encouraged dancing every afternoon and singing at all times, added: "As they have but little to amuse themselves with, endeavours must be made to find amusement for them, and this can be no ways better accomplished than by giving them something to work at."[33]

Most convicts were generally tired of the hulk and anxious for removal and a change of scene, but it was noticeable from their letters, which the surgeon had to censor, that there was also a marked and general despondency. Their friends and relatives were allowed aboard to say good-bye before the ship sailed and the knowledge that they were unlikely to meet again probably led to depression. Among those who had experienced the silent system, serving periods of solitary confinement in the penitentiaries, as was the case with many of the exiles, hysterical and epileptic fits were common during the first forty-eight hours aboard. When a steamer took the *Marion* in tow to take her to sea in 1847 "the noise and confusion of this operation had a severe effect on many of the Pentonville exiles. They were seized suddenly and fell in a complete state of insensibility, which lasted from ten to thirty minutes. It resembled a deep sleep. There was large snoring, but an undisturbed countenance and a placid, tranquil pulse." Other surgeons noted the same phenomena and all attributed it to the sudden change from long continued solitary confinement to the bustle of a crowded ship, with all its attendant noise. Women convicts in the *Mariner* in 1824 had suffered similar attacks, although they had not been in solitary confinement[34].

The women convicts seem to have given the most trouble and to have been the most difficult to manage. "If there ever was a hell afloat," wrote T. Clarke, surgeon of the *Kains* in 1830–1, "it must have been in the shape of a female convict ship—quarrelling, fighting, thieving, destroying in private each other's property from a mere spirit of devilishness, conversation with each other most abandoned, without feeling or shame." Small wonder that when the *Lord Sidmouth* reached Sydney in 1823 Robert Espie wrote: "I cannot but express my great joy at having got rid of so troublesome a charge." The English authorities, however, showed utter callousness to those women convicts who were mothers. In the gaols they were forced to wean their babies prematurely, so that both might be shipped out of the country at the earliest minute, and as in those days suitable food for young infants was not to be had in the convict ships many young children died on the voyage. One surgeon suggested women convicts should not be transported until their children were eighteen months old, but his humane proposal was ignored.[35]

The juveniles always presented a problem. At first no attempt was made to segregate them, and, as happened in the gaols, many were corrupted by the older and hardened offenders. Later, they were separated from the men in the prison below, being housed in a separate apartment, but were allowed to mingle with the older prisoners on the deck, and in many instances their downfall naturally followed. Many youths and young girls were among the prisoners transported, and a total of 1116 convicts under 21 years of age arrived aboard 26 transports between 1812 and 1817. The smallest number in a single transport was 12, the largest, 82. The average number for each convict ship was almost 43. Of the total, 349 were 17 years of age or under, including 5 boys aged 11, 6 boys and one girl aged 12, and 19 boys and one girl aged 13.[36]

It was not until the late 1830's that the experiment of sending out the juvenile offenders in separate ships was tried, but, of course, this could apply only to the boys. A few specially-selected adult male convicts accompanied these ships as petty officers, and an effort was made to educate the youths. Examinations were held and prizes awarded. "While one-third of the boys were at school," wrote Alexander Nisbet, surgeon-superintendent of the Tasmanian transport *Frances Charlotte* in 1836, "the remainder were on deck, where they were allowed and encouraged to amuse themselves with all sorts of games, and as we had a violin-player on board, dancing was permitted after school hours. On leaving England, some of the seamen being mutinous and refusing to work, I allowed a watch of eight boys to be kept during the night, and it was continued during fine weather; it was an object of great ambition to be enrolled in the watch."[37]

As in the case of boys, it was not at first considered necessary to segregate men and women prisoners by transporting them in separate vessels. In 1786 Sir Charles Middleton, the Comptroller of the Navy, could see no force in the objection to placing men and women aboard the same transport, because "it is done continually in all the African (Negro) cargoes that are carried to the West

Indies." Incredible as it may seem, Middleton was not alone in holding this opinion, and for some years, although women were often shipped in separate ships, transports continued to reach Australia with both men and women aboard. Fortunately, wiser counsels in the end prevailed, and ultimately women were never shipped in the same vessels as male prisoners. In the female convict ships prostitution to the crew always presented a problem, and every effort to stamp it out failed.[38]

The daily routine aboard ship began early. The convicts selected as cooks were the first admitted to the deck, being sent up in some ships as early as 4.30, in others not until half-an-hour or an hour later. At sunrise the prison doors were thrown open for all, and both in male and female ships the bathing tub was placed in position on deck, water being thrown over each prisoner from buckets. At six o'clock rations were served out to the messmen, and while the rest were below volunteers swabbed the deck, all beds then being brought up and stowed. At eight breakfast was served, and afterwards the prison deck was cleaned, usually being dry-holystoned. School assembled during the morning, those not attending being kept on deck picking oakum or working at their trades or, in female ships, doing needlework. The lime or lemon juice, mixed with sugar and water to make a half pint of what was termed sherbert, was in some ships served just before the noon dinner, but in others the wine allowance was served before, and the lime juice after, the meal. Most surgeons insisted upon the prisoners passing the tub in rotation and required them to drink their allowance before moving on, thus preventing trafficking. School met again in the afternoon, and supper, usually served at four o'clock, was followed by dancing, singing, and games, such as leapfrog, for exercise. The men were shaved twice a week and their hair was cut fortnightly, and two days weekly were designated laundry days, when both men and women were required to wash their own clothes, although in some ships a few prisoners were appointed to do this work for all. The beds were taken below before or after supper, and at sunset all were mustered below and the prison locked. The routine was varied only by wet or stormy weather or by the working of the ship, but individual surgeons had their own ideas as to the best way of carrying out the necessary duties and passing the time and there was some variation between shipboard life on individual ships. The general pattern, both in male and female ships, however, was similar.[39]

At Port Jackson the convicts, except those requiring hospital treatment, were kept aboard on arrival for at least a week or ten days, and sometimes for longer, but at Hobart, under regulations framed by Governor Arthur, they were generally landed within two or three days. On arrival the transports were inspected by a colonial surgeon and, at a later date, the Port Health Officer, and as soon as he had issued a clean bill of health, the Principal Superintendent of Convicts and other officials went aboard. They inspected both the ship and its human cargo, and mustered the prisoners and crew. Commissariat officials arranged for a supply of fresh meat and vegetables to be sent aboard daily, and, as soon as the prisoners had been disembarked, took steps to land the unexpended government stores and, until orders were issued from England that they were to be shipped back home by the ship in which they had arrived, the irons and other prison equipment. The initial shipboard inspections gave the prisoners an opportunity to lodge complaints concerning their treatment during the voyage, and another opportunity was presented when they were put ashore and inspected by the governor or his deputy.[40]

While the convict ship was anchored with her prisoners aboard much time was consumed in ascertaining full particulars of the prisoners. The indent papers forwarded by the British authorities were at first little more than lists recording the names and sentences of the convicts, while the Irish officials were so incredibly lax that the indent papers of Irish transports were not received in Australia until months, and sometimes years, later. Lists of the convicts were forwarded by Lieutenant Sainthill, but these gave only scanty particulars, and sometimes the Australian authorities lacked such essential information concerning Irish convicts as the terms of their sentences and the dates of their conviction, upon which, of course, the date of their ultimate release depended. It was many years before the indent papers recorded all relevant particulars—the names, offences, sentences, date and place of conviction, trades, and personal descriptions of the prisoners. Only at a relatively late date was any effort made to grade the prisoners, and even then it was generally confined to a separate list designating those prisoners who were to be sent to Norfolk Island or who were to be kept at labour in the road gangs. Until the indent papers were properly prepared the Australian authorities had to rely upon particulars, furnished by the convicts themselves and on the reports of their conduct during the voyage supplied by the masters and surgeons or surgeons-superintendent.[41]

So far as the actual voyage was concerned, the worst horrors of the convict system had ended by the dawn of the 19th century. There were some disastrous voyages after 1800, but, on the whole, conditions steadily improved, and from the 1820's onwards there were comparatively few grave complaints. In fact, conditions in the later convict ships, probably because discipline could be maintained aboard them, were better, or at least no worse, than in the early emigrant ships, and the convict ships had a better health record and were freer of marine disaster.

CHAPTER SIX

THE TRANSPORTS

THE vessels which conveyed the convicts to the Australian colonies were ordinary British merchantmen, such as might be seen in ports the world over. No vessel was specially designed and built as a convict ship, and although many made numerous voyages with prisoners, none remained exclusively in the convict service. A vessel might make several successive voyages as a transport and then not be seen again in the role of a convict ship for several years, if at all; or she might carry prisoners one year and the next turn up in Australian waters with cargo and passengers or immigrants, or simply as a freighter.

The vessels chartered for the convict service were all square-rigged, and, except for a few brigs, all were ships or barques, the majority of small or moderate tonnage. For many years, they were mostly vessels of from 200 to 400 register tons, and later they were generally under 600 tons. The largest merchant vessels employed in the convict service to New South Wales and Tasmania were just under 1000 tons and they were few in number. Four of the ships to Western Australia, however, exceeded 1000 tons, the largest being the second *Clyde*, of 1151 tons[1].

It was the practice to charter the vessel that could be hired at the lowest rate per ton, provided she was certified as seaworthy. If her burthen was greater than actually required, two tons being the normal allowance for each convict, the surplus tonnage was utilised for the despatch of civilian or military personnel and for the shipment of provisions and stores. Shipowners, however, seldom tendered any but their smaller vessels; for they could more profitably employ their larger vessels elsewhere. Since the voyage to Australia involved great navigational hazards, commonly occupied many months, and for a long time return cargoes were unobtainable in the colonies, the reluctance of the shipowners to tender their larger vessels is understandable.

So well-known a writer about the sea and ships as the late Frank C. Bowen has asserted that "the highest charter price which the State would pay for the convict ships was usually so low that they only got the worst and most decrepit tonnage". Other writers, almost without an exception, have advanced a similar opinion, but such assertions are false[2].

In the first place, the chartering of convict ships was always by tender. It was not the State but the shipowners who determined the hiring rates, and there is little doubt that these reflected the general fluctuations in freight rates and the availability of shipping. There is no evidence to suggest that the tenders were not competitive, or that the government employed coercion to secure ships at a low rate. Admittedly, pressure was brought to bear upon the East India Company to charter the convict ships for the return voyage, but this merely made the convict service more attractive and, by ensuring a profitable return passage, enabled vessels to be hired at the lowest possible rate. Secondly, no tender was accepted unless the vessel had been inspected by the naval authorities and had been certified as being seaworthy and well-found.

The charter rates varied considerably, even in the same year. The fact that there was no fixed rate is itself proof that the tenders were competitive, and that they were determined by prevailing freights and the shortage or surplus of available shipping. So far as can be judged at this distance of time, they appear to have been fair and reasonable to both parties.

According to a Parliamentary return, the highest rate paid in 1816, for instance, was £7 19s. 5d. per register ton for the *Atlas* (501 tons), and the lowest, £4 19s. 6d. for the *Sir William Bensley* (584 tons). The average rate for nine ships taken up in this year was £6 1s. 9d. The rate for the *Atlas*, however, was unusually high, and on two occasions only between 1816 and 1821 inclusive was it exceeded, £8 5s. 6d. being paid for the *Hadlow* (372 tons) in 1818 and £8 10s. for the *Isabella* (579 tons) in 1821. The lowest rate paid in the same period was £4 18s. 3d. for the *Caledonia* (412 tons) in 1820. Within a few years, however, charter rates had fallen substantially. In 1828 the highest rate was £5 4s. 9d. for the *Fergusson* (554 tons) and the lowest, £4 6s. 4d., except that one vessel, the *Bengal Merchant* (503 tons) was hired for Van Diemen's

Land at £4 5s. The highest rate paid in 1829 was £5 19s. for the *Lady of the Lake* (243 tons), and the lowest, £4 6s. 4d., as in the previous year.* The average rate for 16 ships in 1828 was £4 15s. 10d. and for 22 vessels in 1829 it was £5 2s. 6d. These were vessels taken up for New South Wales. For vessels chartered for Van Diemen's Land the average rates were slightly higher in 1829—£4 7s. 5d. for eight ships in 1828 and £5 7s. 7d. for nine ships in 1829.

Of 94 vessels chartered between 1816 and 1821 inclusive, two were taken up at over £8 per register ton, 13 at £7 or over, 31 at £6 or over, 42 at £5 or over, and six at under £5. In 1828, out of 24 vessels, only one was chartered at over £5 and 17 were engaged at £4 10s. or less, while the following year no fewer than 24 out of 31 ships were chartered at £5 or over and only three at £4 10s. or under[3].

Until 1847, when the Marine Department of the Board of Trade was established, the British Merchant Marine was in a deplorable state, although some improvement had been effected in 1834 by the adoption of a system of proper survey and classification of merchant ships. The restrictive tonnage laws, which, in the computation of tonnage for the payment of harbour and other dues assumed that the depth was equal to the half beam, led to the building of thoroughly unseaworthy vessels and greatly hampered the development of more practicable ship designs. To reduce the dues payable to a minimum, ships were built as narrow and as deep as possible, and this policy persisted until 1835, when the adoption of "New Measurement" as the basis of tonnage computation established the depth of the hold as an essential factor. Moreover, since the influence of naval architecture predominated, merchantmen, like the ships of the Royal Navy, were built of massive timbers which, having been seasoned in salt water for many years, were as hard and almost as heavy as iron, and as their spars, rigging and blocks were in keeping, they were also heavy aloft.

The merchant ships were not built on fine lines until the advent of the clipper ship in the middle of the 19th century, and qualities of speed were subordinated to securing the maximum carrying capacity. Narrow and deep, flat-sided and flat-bottomed, the convict ships often required, even when loaded, a considerable

---

* The rate of £3 9s. given for the *Larkins* in the return is a typographical error for £5 9s.

quantity of ballast to stop them from capsizing. In 1828, for instance, the *City of Edinburgh*, a ship of 366 tons register, which brought out female convicts and a number of prisoners' wives and children from Cork, obtained permission from the Navy Commissioners to ship 100 tons of iron in lieu of an equal quantity of shingle ballast[4].

The East Indiamen, the largest class of merchantmen, were strong, fine ships. No expense was spared in their building, and only the finest materials were used. They were full in the bilge and very nearly wall-sided, with less tumblehome than the warships of the period, though very similar in design and appearance to the men-of-war. Another distinctive class among the ocean-going merchantmen was the West Indiaman, a smaller edition of the East Indiaman, except for some slight difference in deck design. The East and West Indiamen were well cared for, but the rest of the merchantmen, due to the lack of government supervision, were often neglected and ill-found, and many were so utterly rotten in their timbers and rigging as to be unseaworthy vessels that should never have been permitted to put to sea.

The East Indiamen were capably officered and well manned. They maintained a discipline that, in its use of the lash, was as pitiless as that of the Royal Navy, and they were as smart in appearance, and as smartly handled, as the men-of-war. The personnel of the rest of the merchant marine, however, was drawn from the very dregs of society. With hardly an exception, the officers had worked their way up from the fo'c'sle, and were men of little education or refinement. They were hard-drinking, hard-swearing and brutal, often so illiterate that they could barely scrawl their own signatures. They were wholly unskilled in the higher branches of navigation and seamanship. The men, recruited from the waterside taverns by unscrupulous crimps and living aboard ship under conditions of squalor and hardship, were tough and quarrelsome. Their indiscipline was notorious, and desertions were frequent. Extant muster lists of incoming convict ships indicate that many arrived with two or three short of their proper complement of men and boys, due to deaths by disease or accident during the passage and to desertions before sailing or at ports of call. In time of war, when the man-power shortage was acute, and the press-gangs were particularly active, under-manning, no doubt, was more common and more serious, but an examination of 22 muster lists of vessels which reached Australia in 1829-30, when seamen were easier to procure, shows that nine were deficient one or more men. Of the remaining 13 ships, nine had their correct complement and four carried more men than required by their charter-parties. The largest deficiency was eight men in the *Guildford,* from which one man had been discharged sick, one had been drowned, and three had run. The average age of men and officers, if the few muster lists recording this information are any criterion, was around 25, and in some instances the second and third mates were youngsters of about 21.

The majority of the convict ships carried three officers in addition to the master, and a few had a fourth mate as well. The carpenter seems to have been regarded as more important than the boatswain: he is nearly always listed ahead of the boatswain in the muster and in many instances he had a mate, whereas hardly any ship carried a boatswain's mate. Indeed, every ship carried a carpenter, but three out of 25 whose musters are extant did not carry a boatswain, although all three were vessels of around 400 tons or over. A number of ships carried a sailmaker, but fewer had a caulker, armourer or joiner, and only one or two carried a man specially designated as the butcher or baker. All except two had a cook, and some carried two men in the galley. Pursers and clerks were rare. One of the best-manned ships was the *Sophia,* which arrived at Port Jackson from Dublin on January 17, 1829. A vessel of 537 tons, she was officered by a master and four mates, and her crew of 40 men included two quartermasters, a carpenter, carpenter's mate, boatswain, two boatswain's mates, cook, ship's cook, steward, sailmaker, armourer, and midshipman, with 13 able seamen, six ordinary seamen, four apprentices and four natives. At the other end of the scale we have the Leith-built barque *Forth,* of 369 tons, which was manned by a master, three mates, carpenter, sailmaker, cook, 18 seamen and two boys[5].

If the naval authorities could do little to ensure the maintenance of a high standard among the officers and men, they at least saw to it that only the better class of vessel was hired for the convict service. Their examinations were thorough, and they insisted upon a reasonably high standard of seaworthiness. Occasionally a ship rotten in hull and equipment was chartered but these vessels were few in number. The fact that during the continuance of transportation, when losses in other trades were heavy, no convict ship foundered on the passage to Australia is a sufficient refutation of the claim that the most decrepit tonnage was employed in the convict service, and it is also proof of the thoroughness with which the naval authorities performed the task of selection.

When the navy estimates were under discussion in the House of Commons in 1836, the government explained that considerations of economy prevented the Admiralty from chartering vessels of an A1 classification. Yet a careful analysis of the vessels employed as convict ships reveals that a surprisingly large number of vessels ranking in the first-class were chartered prior to 1834, when Lloyds' Register came into existence and a proper system of survey and classification was instituted, and that the proportion of A1 vessels engaged after 1834 was higher than has hitherto been realised. A study of the information contained in the appendices will make this clear.

This does not mean very much, so far as the period prior to 1834 is concerned. Toward the close of the 18th century, when the Underwriters' Green Book was established, the system of classification depended upon the place of build and the age of the vessel. It was a loose and inequitable system, and as proper surveys were not carried out, it was also unreliable. Thames-built vessels were admitted to the first-class—designated at this period by the letter M—for 13 years, but vessels of the same description and size were eligible for admission for but eight years when built at one of the northern ports. With the establishment of the rival Shipowners' Red Book in 1799, the number of classes was reduced from five to four, and the older character designations of A, E, I and O for the four classes in that order were reintroduced. Thames-built ships, if entirely of British oak and well fastened, were classed A1 for 12 years. Vessels built at other British ports received an A1 classification for 10 years on the same conditions. The system, although fairer, was still discriminatory. Second-class ships, those awarded an E rating, were thus classed when on survey no defects were revealed and they were deemed capable of carrying a dry cargo safely. The Underwriters' Green Book, faced with the competition of the Red Book, promptly adopted the same classification system and symbols, but neither register made any provision for continuing or restoring a vessel's original classification. No matter how thoroughly she might be repaired or strengthened, she automatically lapsed into an inferior grade upon the expiration of her original class. The two lower classes—the I vessels deemed seaworthy for carrying only goods not liable to sea damage and the O vessels regarded as unfit for making foreign voyages—do not concern us. The convict transports invariably belonged either to the A or E class, and always were classed as A1 or E1, the numeral signifying that they were well-found in equipment. No vessel indifferently found, and therefore classed as A2 or E2, was chartered.

Between 1801 and 1815 inclusive it has been possible to identify the class of 48 convict ships. Thirty-two were classed A1 and 16 E1, so that the number of first-class vessels chartered was exactly double the number of second-class ships. From 1815 to 1823 inclusive, however, the number in each class was almost equal—52 with an A1 rating against 48 classed E1. Many of the latter were old vessels, but having been built in Indian shipyards of the best teak, a very durable timber, and having in many instances undergone extensive repairs, they were generally equal in seaworthiness to most of the A1 vessels, and had lapsed into the E1 class only by virtue of age.

With the establishment of Lloyd's Register in 1834, proper surveys were instituted, and provision was made for continuing or restoring a vessel's original rating when she had undergone the necessary repairs. A1 vessels were those which had not passed a prescribed age, had complied with the standard laid down for this class, and had been kept in the highest state of repair and equipment. No longer was there discrimination against vessels built at ports other than the Thames. AE1 vessels formed a second description of those in the first-class: they had passed the prescribed age and had not been sufficiently repaired to secure a continuation or restoration of their A1 certificate, but were well-found in equipment. Only vessels with an A1 or AE1 rating were chartered; those of the second and third-class, distinguished by the symbols E and I respectively, were never chartered.

Of the transports which went to Port Jackson between 1835 and 1837 respectively, 13 were classed A1 as against 23 rated AE1 among those ships whose classification can be established, but from 1838 to 1840 inclusive, the position was reversed, and 20 vessels classed A1 were employed as against 11 in the AE1 class[6].

It is clear that the convict service, while it did not secure the best tonnage, certainly did not obtain the worst. It chartered the best vessels tendered, and these, with but few exceptions, were seaworthy and well-found.

Following the inquiry into the Second Fleet's voyage, a proposal was made that the prisoners should be shipped solely in vessels owned or chartered by the East India Company. The East Indiamen, of course, were the finest ships of the merchant marine, but it was not because of the superior quality of the vessels themselves that the suggestion was made. It was advanced because the officers in the East India Company's employ were of superior education and character. The plan, in fact, originated in a genuine humanitarian desire to improve the conditions of transportation and to ensure that the convicts would be humanely treated. "I trust," wrote the Home Secretary to Phillip, in announcing the adoption of the proposal in 1792, "that by this means the evils which have hitherto subsisted will be put an end to."

His optimism might have been justified had the original proposal not been nullified by the pressure of vested interests and considerations of economy. The contractors stressed that they could transport the convicts at a lower rate per head if the East India Company would charter their vessels for the homeward passage or would waive its trading monopoly to permit them to load cargoes in India or China on their own account. Their contention, of course, was perfectly sound. The government therefore brought pressure to bear on the Company, which, fearful of losing its profitable monopoly, reluctantly acquiesced. But it sought to insist that it should be obliged to charter only those vessels which met its rather exacting standards by passing surveys carried out by the Company's own officers. In this, however, it was unsuccessful. In 1798 the Company refused to charter the *Minerva* on what its directors considered "the most substantial grounds", but the ship's owners induced the government to intervene, and the Company reluctantly reversed its decision and waived the need for the vessel to pass its surveys[7].

Thus, instead of hiring the East Indiamen as convict transports, the government compelled the Company to charter the vessels engaged as convict ships—a reversal of the plan as originally propounded. Naturally the object of the proposal was not achieved.

although some improvement did result from the mere fact of the ships being also chartered by the Company.

In 1801, as a result of the heavy mortality in the convict ships in the closing years of the 18th century, it was suggested that the conveyance of convicts should be entrusted exclusively to the ships of the Royal Navy. With hopeful optimism, it was calculated that by this means the cost of transportation would be halved, and that a further reduction might be effected, and a national service performed, if the men-of-war loaded return cargoes of timber in Australia or New Zealand, masts and spars being much required by the navy. The proposal was adopted, and simultaneously it was decided that the prisoners should be shipped regularly twice a year—in May and September.

The necessary instructions were issued to the Admiralty on March 9, 1802, and in September, 1802, H.M.S. *Glatton* sailed. But although eminently successful from a health point of view, the experiment was quickly discontinued. The war against Napoleon rendered it impracticable, no doubt, to detach naval vessels for the convict service, but the natural repugnance of naval officers to being employed in such a service was also an important factor in effecting its abandonment. It is significant that when peace came the proposal to employ the king's ships was not revived[8].

Nor was the decision to despatch convict ships only at favourable seasons of the year implemented. This matter was often raised, but the transports were not despatched with any regularity, and frequently they sailed in the middle of winter. In 1836 the government blandly informed the House of Commons that "it had decided to avoid sending out convicts at that period of the year when they were more liable to disease on the voyage from cold". It did not add, though it might well have done so, that, periodically, that decision had been announced during the previous 35 years! The failure to adhere to twice-yearly sailings was due, of course, to the fact that the determining factor in the despatch of the convict ships was the state of the gaols and hulks. If they were overcrowded with prisoners awaiting transportation, ships were taken up, no matter what the season of the year. The well-being of the convicts on the voyage was a secondary consideration; what mattered was the emptying of the gaols and hulks to make room for the never-ending stream of new prisoners[9].

The plans to exclusively employ, firstly, East Indiamen and, secondly, men-of-war having fallen through, the government was compelled to rely upon the humble, ocean-going merchantmen. We know broadly what these vessels looked like both above and below decks; but we possess little detailed information regarding their design and rigging, and few authentic models of them exist. They sailed badly and incredibly slowly, but speed was not considered essential, their masters were not great sail carriers, and the vessels were often snugged down at night. The convict ships made leisurely passages, especially in the earlier years, when they normally called at two or three ports *en route*. Only when direct passages became increasingly common was the length of the voyage to Australia notably shortened, and even then only a handful of vessels were able to record passages of under 110 days.

Contemporary descriptions of the convict ships as ships, barques and brigs can be misleading; for the practice of rigidly defining a vessel by the number of her masts and the precise nature of her rig was largely an innovation of the last half of the 19th century, when the convict ship had all but passed away. In the first half of the century the now universally accepted definitions had still to be evolved. Vessels were described according to the build and shape of their hulls, and classification by a vessel's rig was introduced only gradually. There was naturally a transition period during which the various rigs were loosely defined. Thus, a vessel which might be regarded by one observer as a barque might be classed by another as a ship, and even official records are not unanimous. Consequently, we can never be certain precisely what sails a particular ship carried, much to the regret of the nautical-minded, anxious to assess sailing performances or to trace the evolution and development of the different rigs and sails.

A similar lack of precision, though for different reasons, characterises contemporary records of the convict ships' tonnages. Until 1786 British law required only certain classes of vessels to be registered, but in that year registration of "all ships having a deck or being of the burthen of 15 tons or upwards" was made compulsory. The method of computing tonnage was by builders', or, as it was later termed, old, measurement. Under this system the actual depth of the hold was not measured, but for the purpose of calculating tonnage was assumed to be equal to the half beam. This rule produced many absurdities in tonnage measurement. A vessel, for example, might be cut down from a three- to a two-decker, but although obviously a much smaller ship, its tonnage would remain the same, or a two-decker, having an inch or so more beam, would be computed to be of a greater tonnage than a three-decker of the same length.

Nevertheless, builders' measurement remained in force until January 1, 1836, when new measurement was introduced and established the depth of the hold as a necessary factor for the calculation of tonnage. The result was still an approximation, but, broadly speaking, new measurement gave a smaller tonnage than builders' measurement, and for this reason, anxious to attract passengers or freight, ships' masters often recorded in official documents and newspaper advertisements their ship's tonnage by old instead of new measurement, although usually they were careful to give the smaller figure when it came to calculating harbour and other dues! Apart from this, there was a good deal of carelessness in recording, and possibly in computing tonnages, with the result that even official records frequently give different figures for the same transport.

Finally, on May 1, 1855, new measurement was replaced by the present basic system of tonnage measurement, sometimes known as "Moorsom's Law" or "new new measurement", naturally a much more exact method of computing tonnage[10].

CHAPTER SEVEN

THE VOYAGE OF THE FIRST FLEET, 1787-8

A LETTER of August 18, 1786, from the Home Secretary, Lord Sydney, to the Lords Commissioners of the Treasury set in motion the machinery to implement the British Government's decision to found a penal settlement at Botany Bay. No immediate flurry of excitement or of bustling activity followed on the despatch and receipt of this directive, and not until August 31 was the decision conveyed to the Admiralty. The various departmental officials set to work in leisurely and rather dilatory fashion, and during the remaining months of the year the personnel and vessels for the expedition were slowly assembled.

From the vessels proffered in response to an Admiralty advertisement posted up in the coffee-houses frequented by shipowners, shipbrokers and merchants, the Navy Board chartered five transports—the *Alexander, Charlotte, Friendship, Lady Penrhyn* and *Scarborough*—and three store-ships—the *Borrowdale, Fishburn* and *Golden Grove*. It soon became obvious, however, that these eight vessels and the two warships, the *Sirius* and the *Supply*, would be inadequate, and a sixth transport, the *Prince of Wales*, was added to the expedition[1].

These merchantmen were comparatively new vessels, and, with the exception of the *Friendship*, all had three masts and were fully square-rigged. They were classed in the Underwriters' Green Book as ships, but at least two, the transports *Alexander* and *Charlotte*, were described in their official registers as "barque-built". The *Friendship* was sometimes referred to in contemporary records as a snow, but was described in the Green Book as a brig. Unfortunately, as with the *Scarborough* and the three storeships, she was registered just a year before the collection of transcripts in the General Register and Record Office of Shipping and Seamen begins, and the transcripts of registry of these five vessels are consequently not extant. That she had two masts, both square-rigged, is shown, however, by a drawing in the manuscript journal of Lieutenant William Bradley, first lieutenant of H.M.S. *Sirius*. This sketch, the nautical detail of which may be accepted as accurate, depicts the seven vessels which reached Botany Bay on January 20, 1788, entering the harbour under full sail, while the four earlier arrivals, with sails furled, lie moored close to the shore at the head of the bay. Two of the latter vessels each have two masts. Obviously they are the *Supply*, a brig-rigged sloop, and the *Friendship* but the detail is insufficient to enable us to determine whether the *Friendship* had, immediately abaft the main lower-mast, the small trysail-mast for her spanker which would make her rig that of a snow.

Of the six transports, the *Scarborough* was built at the port from which she derived her name in 1782, the *Alexander* at Hull in 1783, the *Charlotte* and the *Friendship* the following year, the former on the Thames and the latter at Scarborough, and the *Lady Penrhyn* and the *Prince of Wales*, both the products of Thames yards, in 1786. The latter vessel is said to have been built at Sidmouth in 1779 and previously to have been named the *Hannibal*. She was owned by J. Mather, and her master had been John Mason, but she was not the vessel which sailed in the Botany Bay fleet. It was the later *Prince of Wales*, built on the Thames by Christopher Watson & Co. and launched on August 12, 1786, that was taken up as a convict ship. She also was owned by the Cornhill merchant, James Mather, and was commanded by John Mason, which explains the wrong identification of the earlier vessel as having been the *Prince of Wales* of the First Fleet. The three storeships were all owned by Leighton: the *Fishburn* and the *Golden Grove* had been built at Whitby in 1780, the *Borrowdale* at Sunderland in 1785.

The transcripts of registry of five of the transports have survived and these furnish invaluable information concerning the size and appearance of the convict ships of the First Fleet.

The largest was the *Alexander*, which had a length of 114 3/10 feet, and a breadth of 31 feet. She was a three-master of two decks, without galleries or figurehead, and was described as a "barque-built ship with a quarter deck". She was owned by Walton & Co., whose senior partner was a Southwark master mariner, William

Walton. The *Scarborough* was slightly smaller, having an extreme length of 111 feet 6 inches, an extreme breadth of 30 feet 2 inches, and a height between decks of 4 feet 5 inches. She was a two-decked, three-masted vessel, rigged as a barque, and was owned by three Scarborough merchants, Thomas, George and John Hopper. The *Charlotte* was still smaller, with a length of 105 feet and a breadth of 28 3/10 feet. She was a three-masted two-decker, with neither galleries nor figurehead, and was owned by Mathews. She was described as "barque-built, with quarter badges"—that is, she had small windows set flat in her quarters—but when re-registered a few years later, in 1794, she was described as "a square-sterned ship, with quarter badges".

The newest transports were almost identical in size. The *Lady Penrhyn* had a length of 103 9/10 feet and a beam of 27 5/10 feet; the *Prince of Wales* was 103 feet long, with a breadth of 29 3/10 feet. Both, of course, were three-masted two-deckers, and each was a square-sterned ship. While the *Lady Penrhyn* had a round house and quarter badges, with a woman as figurehead, the *Prince of Wales* had a poop deck, quarter galleries—that is, projecting covered balconies on either side of the ship toward the stern, probably decorated with small pilasters framing a single tier of windows—and a fiddle head, a scroll which curved upwards and outwards.[2]

Blunt-nosed and round-bodied, the transports were extremely small by modern standards. The length measurements given above were the extreme measurements aloft; the upper deck length would in each case be slightly smaller. The breadths were the extreme breadth in the broadest part of each ship, above the main wales. Contemporary records give different figures for the tonnages of the convict ships, but hitherto the figures recorded in his journal by Lieutenant Philip Gidley King, second lieutenant of H.M.S. *Sirius*, generally have been accepted. His combined total of 3202 tons for the transports and storeships, however, is slightly too high. The most accurate figures probably are those given in a "Register of Transports, 1774-1794", but although presumably the tonnages as computed by Admiralty surveys, they do not tally with those in the five registers which have survived. These different sets of figures compare as follows:—[3]

Vessel	*Registers*	*Admiralty*		*King*	
Alexander	445	452 85/94		452	
Charlotte	338	345 53/94		335	
Friendship	—	278 1/94		274	
Lady Penrhyn	322	338 13/94		333	
Prince of Wales	318	333 67/94		350	
Scarborough	411	418 36/94	2166 67/94	430	2174
Borrowdale	—	272 26/94		275	
Fishburn	—	378 26/94		378	
Golden Grove	—	331 30/94	981 82/94	375	1028
			3148 55/94		3202

The statements of the tonnage of the *Sirius* are also conflicting. King states she was of 612 tons, but Collins, who, except for a misprint in his figure for the *Friendship*, gives the tonnage of the merchantmen accurately, records her as being of 520 tons, and in the papers of the late Commander J. A. Rupert-Jones her burthen is stated to have been 540 tons. King alone gives the *Supply's* tonnage, recording it as 170 tons. Assuming that King's figures are correct, the men-of-war had a combined tonnage of 782, or, if Collins's lower figure for the *Siri s* be accepted, of 690 tons. The total tonnage of the First Fleet, accepting the Admiralty's figures for the transports and storeships, was therefore either 3930 or 3838 tons.[4]

In other words, the combined tonnage of the 11 sail was, roughly, one-twentieth of the tonnage of the British liner *Queen Elizabeth*, so familiar to tens of thousands of Allied servicemen during World War II, and greater by either 430 or 338 tons than the 3500 gross tons of the auxiliary steamer *Great Britain*, which conveyed 630 passengers and a ship's company of 130 from Liverpool to Australia in 1852.[5]

When the First Fleet left England the 11 vessels carried, in addition to provisions and stores, almost 1500 persons, including the naval and merchant seamen who manned them. The returns of the prisoners are contradictory, but the best evidence indicates that the six convict ships sailed with 568 male and 191 female prisoners—a total of 759 convicts, one fewer than the number of persons aboard the *Great Britain* in 1852. Yet the combined tonnage of the six transports was rather more than 1300 tons less than the gross tonnage of the *Great Britain*, and, of course, in addition to the prisoners, the transports carried the marine guards, with their families, the convicts' children, certain officials, and their crews. Since the decks of the convict ships were cluttered up with water casks and with pens of animals and birds, and below decks provisions and stores were stowed in considerable quantities, it is obvious that the transports were very crowded. By modern standards, but not those of the 18th century, the ships were woefully overcrowded.[6]

The transports were fitted out at Deptford under the supervision, firstly, of Captain George Teer, the Agent for Transports in the Thames, and, later, of Lieutenant John Shortland, who, on returning with troops from Halifax, was appointed naval agent in the First Fleet. The first convicts were embarked at Woolwich by the *Alexander* and the *Lady Penrhyn* on January 6, 1787. The *Charlotte* and the *Friendship* embarked their prisoners at Plymouth, and the *Prince of Wales* and the *Scarborough* at Portsmouth, where a few late arrivals were also put aboard the *Alexander* and the *Lady Penrhyn*.

Gales and thick weather, inevitable at this season, delayed the assembling of the fleet at the Motherbank, and interrupted the embarkation of the prisoners and the loading of provisions and stores, which had to be taken out to the fleet in lighters. One party of 210 convicts, travelling, ironed together, on waggons under a guard of light horse, reached Portsmouth on March 2, but as it was blowing a gale, five days passed before they could be embarked. It was not until March 16 that all 11 sail anchored at the Motherbank, and another two months elapsed before the fleet was ready to put to sea.

There was trouble with the prisoners from the outset. Many were in indifferent health when embarked, and their confinement in the prisons below deck, "handcuffed together from the time of their embarkation", as Lieutenant King informs us, led to outbreaks of illness, despite the fact that they were receiving fresh provisions. By April 15, 11 men had died in the *Alexander*. A fever aboard the *Lady Penrhyn* was less virulent, causing the death of only one woman. While lighters took off some of the *Alexander's* prisoners, the ship was thoroughly cleaned, smoked, sponged with oil of tar, and white-washed. These measures were only partially effective; for although it is stated that the prisoners began to recover, a further five deaths occurred before sailing. In the *Lady Penrhyn* the state in which the women had been embarked had contributed to, if it had not caused, their illness. They were so naked and filthy when sent aboard that their condition, in the words of the forthright Philip, stamped the magistrates "with infamy", and "nothing but clothing them could have prevented them from perishing".[7]

The women proved difficult to control, and prostitution could not be prevented. On April 19 five of the *Lady Penrhyn's* prisoners were put in irons for this offence, and the second mate was dismissed the ship. But it was found impossible to keep the women and the seamen apart. There was similar trouble in the *Friendship* and, doubtless, in the *Prince of Wales* also[8].

At last, however, all was ready. True, the women's clothing, despite Phillip's appeals, had not arrived, and the Ordnance Office, notorious for its inefficiency, had failed to deliver the expedition's small-arms ammunition, a fact which was not discovered until the fleet was at sea and which was then kept a close secret for fear that it might encourage the prisoners to mutiny. Phillip, who had spent most of his time in London attending to innumerable details connected with the expedition, joined the *Sirius* on May 7, 1787, and on the 12th, when H.M.S. *Hyaena* (which was to escort the expedition to sea) had arrived, he made the signal to sail.

The seamen in some of the merchantmen, however, refused to man the yards, demanding their wages and the right to go ashore for one final visit. Principal Surgeon White considered the trouble arose "more from intoxication than from nautical causes", but Lieutenant King took a more charitable view cf the seamen's action. "I think the seamen had a little reason on their sides," he wrote in his private journal. "They had been in employ upwards of seven months, during which time they had received no pay except their river pay and one month's advance. The great length of the voyage rendered it necessary that they should have more money to furnish themselves with such necessaries as were really indispensable; but it became the masters' interest to withhold their pay from them, that they might be obliged to purchase those necessaries from them on the course of the voyage at a very exorbitant rate."[9]

The fleet had no alternative but to anchor again. On Phillip's order, some of the recalcitrant seamen were removed from their ships, and the rest then returned to their duty. However, it was too late for the fleet to sail that day, but at three o'clock next morning—Sunday, May 13—with a fresh breeze from the south-east, the fleet weighed, and by 10 a.m. had cleared the Isle of Wight. The distribution of the convicts aboard the transports at the time of sailing was as follows:—

Vessel	*Master*	*Surgeon*	*Convicts*	
			M.	*F.*
Alexander	Duncan Sinclair	William Balmain	195	—
Charlotte	Thomas Gilbert	John White	88	20
Friendship	Francis Walton	Thomas Arndell	76	21
Lady Penrhyn	Wm. Cropton Sever	(i) John Turnpenny Altree,		
		(ii) Arthur Bowes	—	101
Prince of Wales	John Mason	———	1	49
Scarborough	John Marshall	Denis Considen	208	
		Total:	568	191

The number of convicts embarked had been 586 men and 192 women, but two men had later received pardons and had been re-landed. In the *Alexander* 16 men died before sailing and in the *Lady Penrhyn* one woman, but the rest of the transports sailed with the complements of prisoners they had originally embarked[10].

The run down Channel occupied three days. The *Charlotte* which on the day of the fleet's departure fell several miles astern, and the *Lady Penrhyn*, whose master, since she was a new ship, probably had not yet learnt her peculiarities, sailed very ill. On May 20, the fleet hove to some 200 miles to the west of the Scilly Isles, and Phillip ordered the *Hyaena* to return to Plymouth. The weather was fine, but such a high sea was running that the expedition's commander, experienced seaman though he was, found it very difficult to sit at table, and it prevented the boats of the *Sirius* being despatched to the transports to collect the returns relating to the prisoners. Phillip had sealed his despatches when word reached him of trouble aboard the *Scarborough*. He hastily penned a short report of the occurrence, the despatches were placed aboard the *Hyaena*, and, having exchanged three cheers with Phillip's fleet, she parted company.

Coloured aquatint by E. Duncan after W. J. Huggins.
Published by Huggins

National Maritime Museum, Greenwich

The "LADY KENNAWAY" off Margate—Homeward bound

Line engraving by T. Medland after R. Cleveley
Published by J. Stockdale, 1789

National Maritime Museum, Greenwich

The "SIRIUS" and the "SUPPLY", in Botany Bay

The *Scarborough's* master, John Marshall, believed that a serious plot had been formed among the convicts to seize his ship, but it is perhaps doubtful if there was any real attempt at mutiny. An informer alleged that a rising was planned, and he named the ring-leaders. As Phillip had earlier directed that the irons of the convicts except those under punishment, should be removed, the report was naturally taken seriously, and the alleged ringleaders, Philip Farrell and Thomas Griffiths, were transferred to the *Sirius*. Each was given 24 lashes, and they were then sent, heavily ironed, aboard the *Prince of Wales*.

Although the majority of the prisoners suffered acute seasickness during the early part of the voyage, their health generally improved once the fleet got to sea. The weather was fine and moderate, and the convicts, freed of their irons, were admitted constantly to the decks. On June 3 the fleet reached Teneriffe and anchored in the Santa Cruz roads. A return dated the following day reported that 74 prisoners were sick or convalescent, of whom 30 were suffering from debility and 20 from intermittent fever, and that seven men and one woman had died between the Motherbank and Teneriffe. Despite the cleaning and smoking she had undergone before sailing, the *Alexander* was still the unhealthiest vessel of the fleet. There had been a further five deaths among her convicts, bringing the total to 21 since embarkation, and she had 21 prisoners on the sick-list. The *Charlotte* had 15 sick. One man had died in this transport, and a second death occurred on June 10, the day the fleet sailed from Teneriffe. The *Friendship* had lost one man and had 12 prisoners on the sick-list, while another woman had died in the *Lady Penrhyn*, whose sick numbered ten. Thus, up to June 10 there had been nine deaths at sea—eight men and one woman—and 16 men and 1 woman before sailing, making 24 men and 2 women dead since embarkation. Fresh provisions were served the prisoners at Teneriffe, where the only excitement was an unsuccessful attempt at escape by a man in the *Alexander*. He got clear of the ship in the jolly-boat, but was recaptured next day.

When the fleet weighed on June 10, the light nor'-nor'-wester lasted only long enough to give the vessels an offing, and the north-east trade was not picked up until three days later. The weather was extremely hot, with stifling calms and frequent rain squalls. Living conditions, especially for the prisoners, were thoroughly disagreeable. The ships were infested with rats, cockroaches, bugs and other vermin, and William Faddy, the junior lieutenant of marines in the *Friendship*, who slept in a "small place", spent the Sunday morning of July 22 in killing "above 100 bugs with oil and tar". If such were the conditions in the officers' quarters, how much worse must they have been in the over-crowded prisons? Windsails were rigged, gunpowder was exploded in the 'tween decks, and the ships were sweetened by a liberal use of oil of tar and lime, but the air in the prisons remained heavy and still, and the atmosphere was foul with the acrid stench of stale bilge water, the odours of perspiring and unwashed humanity, and the smells from mouldering provisions and rotting ship's timbers[11].

The women convicts suffered worse than the men; for at night they had to be battened down in the fetid prisons. "... the hatches over the place where they were confined could not be suffered to lay off, during the night, without a promiscuous intercourse immediately taking place between them and marines," wrote White. "... In some of the other ships, the desire of the women to be with the men was so uncontrollable, that neither shame (but indeed of this they had long lost sight), nor the fear of punishment could deter them from making their way through the bulkheads to the apartments assigned the seamen."[12]

On the run from Spithead to Teneriffe, the convicts, apart from the alleged mutiny in the *Scarborough*, gave little trouble. For the first week they were kept ironed, but once their irons were struck off, the novelty of their surroundings, with the sightings of strange fish and birds and of an occasional sail, kept them fully occupied. The weather generally was fine and moderate, but there were days when a strong wind blew, bringing squalls or drizzling rain, and a heavy swell ran, causing the heavily-laden vessels, lying low in the water, to pitch, toss, and wallow. The majority of the prisoners were then too low-spirited and dejected from seasickness to cause any trouble, but by the time Teneriffe was left behind they had nearly all found their sea-legs and the first novelty of their strange surroundings had worn off.

Thieving and quarrelling earned floggings for some of the men, but the women were the worst behaved and gave the most trouble. In the *Friendship* a handful of prisoners were the offenders, fighting and quarrelling among themselves, abusing the officers and surgeon, and repeatedly finding their way into the crew's quarters.

The day before the fleet sailed from Teneriffe, Clark ordered four women—Elizabeth Dudgeon, Margaret Hall, Elizabeth Pully and Charlotte Ware—to be put in irons for fighting, and they were not released until June 19, ten days later. In view of the heat the punishment was a severe one, but the day the four women were freed of their irons, Clark wrote: "I am convinced they will not be long out of them. They are a disgrace to their whole sex, b——s that they are. I wish all the women were out of the ships." His gloomy prognostications were soon realised. On the night of July 2 the *Friendship's* master, Francis Walton, called the marine officers because his seamen had broken through the bulkhead into the prison, and he had found four women in their quarters. Two of "these d——d troublesome whores," as Clark called them, were Elizabeth Dudgeon and Elizabeth Pully who had been among those ironed for ten days on leaving Teneriffe, but the other pair, Elizabeth Hackley and Sarah McCormick, had not been implicated in the fight at that port. When the incident was reported to the flagship, orders were issued for the carpenter, boatswain, steward and one seaman to be sent across to the *Sirius*, where all, except the carpenter, were flogged. The four women were put in irons. "If I had been the commander," wrote Clark, with virtuous indignation, "I should have flogged the four whores also."

A few days later Elizabeth Dudgeon gave the commander of the guard in the *Friendship*, Captain James Meredith, a taste of her spiced tongue, and he promptly ordered her a flogging. "The corporal did not play with her," Clark recorded, with grim satisfaction, "but laid it home, which I was very glad to see. Then he ordered her to be tied to the pump. She has been long fishing for it, which she has at last got until her heart's content."

On July 18 a new offender, Elizabeth Barber, entered the lists with an accusation of impropriety against the surgeon, Thomas Arndell, calling "him all the names she could think of". Under Captain Meredith's questioning, she insisted upon the truth of her charge, but, as an interesting commentary on conditions in the *Friendship*, Clark declares she "was very much in liquor". When she was placed in irons, "she began to abuse Captain Meredith in a much worse manner than she had done the doctor; she called him everything but a gentleman. She then began and abused Lieutenant

Faddy, and I wonder how she came to forget me among the number," Clark wrote. "In all the course of my days I never heard such expressions come from the mouth of a human being." The woman's hands were tied behind her back, and she was gagged. Clark states that Elizabeth Barber "remained in that position that she was left in until six o'clock" next morning, but presumably he refers only to the tying of her hands; for had the gag not been removed she must inevitably have died during the night. No sooner had she been released than she was again tied up, and this punishment was repeated the following day.

During the next fortnight other women were ironed. They were mostly the old offenders. In the tropical weather their health immediately suffered as a result of their close confinement, and Surgeon Arndell ordered first one woman and then another to be released. By August 1, however, he had reported that all except Sarah McCormick had recovered sufficiently for their punishment to be resumed. Elizabeth Barber was handcuffed to Elizabeth Hackley, and Elizabeth Dudgeon to Elizabeth Pully. "The damned whores the moment that they got below fell a-fighting amongst one another," Clark wrote, "and Captain Meredith ordered the sergeant not to part them, but to let them fight it out, which I think is very wrong in letting them do so."

Apart, however, from the ten or twelve who always were in trouble, the women aboard the *Friendship* conducted themselves well. The marine officers experienced no difficulty in finding women to do their washing and mending or to make clothes and other articles, and when, while at Rio, some of the *Friendship's* women prisoners were exchanged into the *Charlotte*, Clark declares they were the best behaved aboard. So, clearly, all the women prisoners were not trouble-makers![13]

On the run from Teneriffe to Rio, Phillip had planned to anchor for 24 hours at Port Praya, in the Cape Verde Islands, to procure water and fresh vegetables. On June 15, five days after leaving Teneriffe, the fleet crossed the tropic of Cancer, and, as was usual in those days, the ceremonies now kept when crossing the Equator were staged aboard some of the vessels among the sailors and marines. Indeed, the members of the *Lady Penrhyn's* crew were so busily engaged in paying tribute to King Neptune that there was nearly a collision between that ship and the *Charlotte*. Three days later, on June 18, the fleet was off Port Praya, but on hauling round the reef off the eastern point of the bay the *Sirius* was taken aback and soon after was becalmed, with the rest of the fleet clustered about her. "No true wind was blowing," wrote Bradley, "but catspaws from every point of the compass and a heavy swell setting in upon the shore, which circumstances altogether rendered our getting in with the convoy very hazardous from the danger of falling on board each other in such a swell as well that of being near the eastern reef." Some of the convict ships, according to King, were within half-a-mile of the reef, and, rather than court disaster, Phillip prudently signalled the fleet to get an offing. In the calms and catspaws, it was two hours before the fleet found the true wind and proceeded on its way.[14]

A few days later the north-east trade was lost, and variable winds, accompanied by heavy rain, thunder and lightning, compelled Phillip to keep on to the eastward. On July 5, anticipating a tedious passage, he reduced the water ration to three pints per person per day, but two days later the south-east trade was picked up and the fleet was able to get to the westward. On the 14th the Equator was crossed and, progress being better than had been anticipated, the water ration was increased to two quarts daily per person. On August 2 Cape Frio was sighted, and on the 5th the fleet reached Rio de Janeiro.

The voyage so far had been more successful than most people had dared to hope. Despite the heat and the rain of the tropics, the fleet was still remarkably healthy. Five men and one woman had died since leaving Teneriffe, bringing the total dead since embarkation to 29 male and three female prisoners. The number of sick—marines, seamen and convicts—was less than 100, and the fresh provisions served at Rio soon improved the health of all. By August 30 only 81 marines and convicts were on the sick-list, and of these 30 were convalescent.

On the whole, the weather had been exceptionally favourable, and the fleet had kept company without great difficulty. The *Lady Penrhyn* had consistently proved the worst sailer, and usually had been some miles astern. "Lay to, to let the *Lady Penrhyn* come up, she is sailing so exceedingly bad," recorded Clark on July 20, and on August 1 he wrote: "The *Lady Penrhyn* a good way astern.

She sails very bad, for she was up with the fleet last night." It was not always the vessel's fault that she lagged; for her crew gave Captain Sever trouble. On July 13, according to Bradley, Sever brought on board the *Sirius* "three of his people who had been guilty of mutiny in refusing to steer the ship as directed by the master, by which means she was brought far to leeward out of her station". Phillip kept them aboard the flagship, replacing them aboard the *Lady Penrhyn* with three of his own seamen.

The tiny *Supply* was the swiftest sailer in the fleet and a handy vessel, but she was so small and lay so low in the water that in a gale she laboured a great deal and could carry little canvas. When Phillip expected to make a landfall, she was always sent ahead, and she was constantly employed rounding up the stragglers and relaying the commodore's signals, which sometimes were unobserved or ignored. There was always work for her to do.

There had, of course, been the mishaps and accidents inevitable in the days of sail and of small vessels. In a heavy squall the *Sirius* had carried away her main topsail yard in the slings; the *Friendship* one night had split her jib and main topgallant sail and the next had lost her fore topgallant sail; the *Golden Grove* had carried away her fore topgallant mast on three occasions, and a similar mishap had occurred in the *Borrowdale*. In heavy seas on the night of July 28 the women's caboose—a cooking house on the deck—had been swept overboard from the *Friendship*. The previous day, when shortening sail, the *Alexander* had lost a man overboard, and although the *Supply* and the transport searched for half-an-hour he was not recovered. In the *Lady Penrhyn* a woman convict drank "a solution of mercury sublimat. corrosive" in mistake for water, and a 60-year-old woman had broken two ribs through falling down the steerage, but both women had recovered. Incidents such as these were of almost daily occurrence.

The passage to Rio, of course, had been slow, due to the sailing of the deeply-laden transports and storeships, especially the *Lady Penrhyn*, and to the necessity of the vessels keeping company, no matter what the state of the weather. Under these handicaps, however, some excellent 24-hour runs had been recorded. The best had been 174 miles from noon on June 16 to noon the following day, which, as Clark remarks, had not been "bad going for a transport deeply loaded". The *Sirius* that day had logged 163 miles, the best day's run the flagship had recorded between England and Rio de Janeiro. From noon on 12th June to noon on June 21—a period of nine days—the *Friendship* had covered 1128 miles. Her worst runs had been 28 miles on June 28, which may have been an error on Clark's part, and 29 miles on June 26, under which date he remarks ungrammatically "gone 10 miles back again from where we was yesterday".

The *Friendship's* daily runs, as recorded by Clark, who omits this information after July 4, and the log-book figures of the *Sirius* as far as Rio, are as follows, the mileage in both cases being that for the 24 hours ended at noon on the date given:

	Friendship	*Sirius*		*Friendship*	*Sirius*
May 15	—	37	June 22	77	68
,, 16	101	92	,, 23	60	56
,, 17	73	58	,, 24	51	47
,, 18	65	50	,, 25	43	35
,, 19	—	84	,, 26	29	25
,, 20	65	40	,, 27	48	36
,, 21	48	19	,, 28	28	45
,, 22	44	32	,, 29	63	50
,, 23	90	75	,, 30	43	28
,, 24	83	85	July 1	57	45
,, 25	109	118	,, 2	80	42
,, 26	—	108	,, 3	54	56
,, 27	125½	125	,, 4	47	40
,, 28	131	159	,, 5	—	37
,, 29	155	150	,, 6	—	57
,, 30	99	—	,, 7	—	44
,, 31	90	95	,, 8	—	60
June 1	58	38	,, 9	—	56
,, 2	—	17	,, 10	—	47
,, 12	—	39	,, 11	—	52
,, 13	95	82	,, 12	—	54
,, 14	95	104	,, 13	—	74
,, 15	130	123	,, 14	—	64
,, 16	157	142	,, 15	—	44
,, 17	174	163	,, 16	—	60
,, 18	166	—	,, 17	—	85
,, 19	104	—	,, 18	—	90
,, 20	99	86	,, 19	—	106
,, 21	108	97	,, 20	—	54

	Friendship	*Sirius*		*Friendship*	*Sirius*
July 21	—	67	July 28	—	106
,, 22	—	63	,, 29	—	133
,, 23	—	58	,, 30	—	92
,, 24	—	100	,, 31	—	104
,, 25	—	94	Aug. 1	—	94
,, 26	—	106	,, 2	—	132
,, 27	—	94			

The fleet recuperated at Rio de Janeiro until September 4 when the voyage was resumed. The weather in the South Atlantic was stormier than it had been during the first stage of the voyage. The winds, although favourable, were much stronger, and a heavy sea was generally running. However, the fleet kept company, although the *Lady Penrhyn* was often a great way astern and on September 29, when the wind had swung round from the south-west to the south-east, all the fleet except the two men-of-war and the *Scarborough* and the *Friendship* got a great way to leeward, so that next morning the 11 sail were very scattered. The convict ships rolled and pitched a great deal, and they shipped much water. On September 23 the *Friendship's* hatches had to be battened down because of the seas breaking over her, and on the 25th, Clark recorded in quaint language, that a great deal of water "went between decks and washed the marines out of their beds, and the convict women". On the run to the Cape, indeed, the prisons could hardly have been dry for any length of time, and the seasick convicts, compelled to remain below, must have suffered acutely. Yet the health of the entire fleet remained extraordinarily good.

The sailing performance of the 11 sail was excellent. On October 10 the *Sirius* logged 190 miles, her best 24-hour run of the whole voyage. The *Friendship* also proved her worth in a good stiff wind, and at noon on September 28 her log showed a run of 188 miles for the preceding 24 hours. In four successive days, from noon on September 24 to noon on September 28, she covered 641 miles; the *Sirius*, in the same period, logged 642 miles. The flagship's log shows that in the seven days ending at noon on September 29 she had travelled 1136 miles. It is obvious that even the laggards of the fleet must have performed well on the strong, favourable gales which were encountered for the greater part of the passage from Rio to the Cape.

The prisoners, doubtless because of the boisterous weather, were less troublesome. Two women only seem to have been put in irons aboard the *Friendship*, one for fighting and the other for theft, while in the *Prince of Wales*, according to the diary of a marine non-commissioned officer, Sergeant James Scott, one woman received six lashes for theft—the first woman to be flogged in that ship[15]. The only serious trouble occurred in the *Alexander*, a plot between the prisoners and some of the seamen being discovered. With the assistance of the seamen, who had furnished them with an iron crowbar and other instruments, the convicts planned to attempt to escape at the Cape. The ringleader in this madcap scheme was John Powers, the man who had tried to escape at Teneriffe. He was sent aboard the flagship, where he was heavily ironed and stapled to the deck, and three of the *Alexander's* seamen were exchanged into the *Sirius*. The convict informer who had revealed the plot, being in danger of his life, was transferred to the *Scarborough*.

If, on the whole, the convicts were well-behaved, those in charge of them were not. The marines had given a certain amount of trouble throughout the voyage. A marine sergeant got drunk aboard the *Prince of Wales* on July 14, and after abusing a number of his shipmates had jumped down the main hatchway, landing on the wife of the diarist Scott. One marine in the *Prince of Wales* received 175 lashes for insolence and disobedience of orders and another the same number for abusing an officer when drunk. At Rio a marine was punished with 100 lashes for being found with the women convicts, a second was sentenced to 300 lashes for attempting to suborn a sentinel to allow him to go among the women, a sentence which was remitted, and a third received 200 lashes for attempting to pass a spurious dollar which he had obtained from a convict. Before the fleet sailed on its voyage, a marine, sentenced by court-martial to 200 lashes for unsoldierlike behaviour, received 150 lashes on board the *Charlotte*, a sergeant, corporal and six privates from each of the other ships being required to witness the punishment. Other marines on the *Scarborough* received from 50 to 150 lashes for different offences. Compared with these penalties, the one and two dozen lashes given convicts were mild[16].

Now, after leaving Rio, it was the officers who caused Phillip most concern. Their long association with one another in cramped quarters produced bickerings and quarrels, and drove many to excessive drinking. The traditional Saturday night toasts in the cuddy to sweethearts and wives were made an excuse for rowdy carousals. In the *Friendship*, where conditions were not exceptional, Captain Meredith and Surgeon Arndell, who hitherto had been friendly, came to words over a small piece of wood. "The doctor told the captain that he did not behave like a gentleman," stated Clark, "on which the captain struck him, which the doctor did not return. I ordered them both to be quiet or I would confine them both, so there the matter stands." Meredith and his second lieutenant, William Faddy, had also quarrelled; but all three men were soon again on sufficiently good terms to sing and drink together until the small hours. "The doctor, Captain Meredith and Mr. Faddy kept it up last night" is a refrain which runs through Clark's journal all the way from Rio to the Cape. Marines and convicts alike suffered, no doubt, from the surly tempers which their carousals developed in the officers.

At the Cape drinking parties were held aboard the different ships. One night Lieutenant Faddy visited the *Scarborough*, and, drunk when he returned to the *Friendship*, he grossly abused the abstemious Clark. The latter promptly demanded that his junior should be hailed before a general court-martial, but Major Ross, in command of the detachment of marines, was not anxious to have to transmit to his superiors the minutes of a general court-martial: it might lead to much unpleasantness and the asking of a number of awkward questions. He therefore suggested that Faddy's conduct should be inquired into by a number of officers, and eventually Clark agreed to this course. Captain Meredith and Dr. Arndell had again quarrelled in a drunken moment, but Ross and Surgeon White intervened and effected a reconciliation without the necessity of having to report to London. Meredith received a dressing-down from Ross in public which, however much it may have been deserved, was hardly conducive to the maintenance of discipline by him among the *Friendship's* guard[17].

The fleet anchored in Table Bay on the evening of October 13. "Have had no very bad and a good deal of good weather," was the summing-up of Daniel Southwell, a midshipman in the *Sirius*, in a letter to his mother, "so there is no reason to complain of our passage, which was indeed a fine one, and tolerably expeditious, considering we had to keep company with a convoy of vessels, and that tho' some sail but indifferently we must not leave them behind." There were now 20 marines and 93 convicts on the sick-list, and although none required hospital treatment ashore, the total reflected the wet conditions which had persisted on the run from Rio to the Cape[18].

Some difficulty was experienced in procuring fresh provisions from the polite but unhelpful Dutch, but soft bread, vegetables and fresh meat were eventually forthcoming. The fleet, or at least the marines and convicts in the *Friendship*, had to go hungry on one occasion through official stupidity. It blew so hard on November 8 that the boats could not be sent ashore to pick up the fresh provisions, and as no order had been issued to substitute salt rations, no food was served that day to either the marines or the convicts, according to Clark.

Phillip purchased such livestock and fodder as was offered, and this example was followed by the officers. The animals were accommodated principally in the flagship and the three storeships, but the *Friendship's* women convicts were transferred to the *Lady Penrhyn*, the *Charlotte* and the *Prince of Wales*, and their places taken by a number of sheep. "I am very glad of it," wrote Clark, "for they were a great trouble, much more so than the men," and when the sheep came aboard a week later, he expressed the opinion that "we will find them much more agreeable shipmates than the women".[19]

The fleet was ready to sail on November 11, but the wind was foul, and it was not until the 13th that it weighed. For nearly a week southerlies and sou'-easterlies drove it to the westward, but on the 19th the wind dropped and the fleet lay becalmed. Phillip, who planned to go ahead in the *Supply*, followed closely by the fastest-sailing convict ships, so as to prepare for the landing of the main body of the expedition, seized the opportunity to transfer baggage, tools, and personnel to the vessels which were to form the van. Next day, when the water allowance was reduced to three pints daily per person, a breeze sprang up from the nor'-nor'-east. The fleet ran down its easting in 39 degrees south. The wind was fair and blowing hard, and there was a high following sea. The little *Supply* was at her worst in such conditions, and as she could not keep up the fleet had to shorten sail. However, in the 24 hours to noon on November 22 the *Sirius* logged 160 miles and the *Friendship* 166.

By the 25th the weather had moderated, and that day Phillip transferred to the *Supply*, and, accompanied by the *Alexander*, the *Friendship* and the *Scarborough*, crowded on sail. Next morning the *Supply* was a long way ahead of the three transports and by early afternoon was out of sight, while from the transports the *Sirius* and the main body were hull down a long way astern and soon dropped below the horizon.

The three transparts in the van were under Lieutenant John Shortland's command, and had been ordered by Phillip to follow as closely as possible in the *Supply's* wake. The convicts aboard them must have been thoroughly miserable; for it grew much colder and a succession of gales and heavy seas were encountered. The vessels, pitching and rolling, shipped water continuously, and the prisoners were only momentarily diverted from their sufferings by the schools of whales and grampusses which were sighted and the many albatrosses, black and blue petrels, gannets, gulls and other birds which followed the ships.

"The ship rolled her sides under the water and the sea broke over us almost every moment," Clark recorded in his journal on November 29. "I never was in a ship that rolled as much as this one does." When the wind dropped there was little relief for the *Friendship*; for when there was no breeze to steady her, the brig rolled almost as badly as when in a gale. On December 3 she logged 164 miles and next day 168. The larger *Alexander* and *Scarborough* were in little better plight, though they shipped less water than their tiny consort. On the 6th the three vessels were close together shrouded in a thick fog—an eerie experience for the sodden convicts as, huddled below in the damp, foul prisons, they listened apprehensively to the booming of the ships' guns and the ringing of their bells. On the 16th the *Friendship* logged 172 miles, which was, as Clark commented in his journal, "delightful going". Four days later, on the 20th, the *Alexander* carried away her fore top sail yard in the slings, and while another was being got up the other two vessels had to proceed under easy sail. It was a bitterly cold day, with hail and snow, and Clark relates that he was obliged "to put on a flannel waistcoat and in the place of one pair of stockings two pairs, and obliged to keep my greatcoat on constantly all day". With no clothes but their regulation dress and but a single blanket, the prisoners must have been frozen.

On the 22nd there was a fine, fair wind, but Shortland, if Clark is to be believed, refused to order sail to be crowded on. "The old agent," he wrote, "will not make the most of it by setting more sail." However, at this period the three transports were making some excellent 24-hour runs, as the *Friendship's* log proves: December 25, 160 miles; 26th, 172; 28th, 152; 29th, 181; 31st, 170; January 1, 1788, 168; 3rd, 156; and 4th, 191.

On January 5 the coast of Van Diemen's Land was sighted. A gale was still blowing, and the three transports were constantly losing sails and yards as they wallowed in the high seas. The heavy weather, and the failure of the fodder supply, took toll of the sheep in the *Friendship*, and a shortage of fuel restricted, if it did not prevent the cooking of meals. But on the 19th the three transports entered Botany Bay, where the *Supply* had anchored the previous afternoon.

The *Sirius* and the main body, following a day's sail behind the advanced transports, encountered much the same weather conditions, and the prisoners in the *Charlotte*, the *Lady Penrhyn* and the *Prince of Wales* suffered to the same extent from the strong gales, heavy seas and bitter cold. They, too, were washed from their berths when heavy seas were shipped. Surgeon Bowes, in the *Lady Penrhyn*, records that during a fierce storm on January, 10 "the convict women . . . were so terrified that most of them were down on their knees at prayers, and in less than one hour after it had abated they were uttering the most horrid oaths and imprecations that could proceed out of the mouths of such abandoned prostitutes as they are". In the *Prince of Wales* the flour and butter furnished by the contractor was exhausted by December 17, and it became necessary to broach some of the stores which had been shipped in her. By this means flour and oatmeal were obtained, and on the first calm day butter was procured from the *Fishburn*. The fodder could not be replaced, however, and the mortality among the livestock was heavy in every ship[20].

The log-book of the *Sirius* shows that the main body sailed remarkably well in the strong, favourable winds. In a period of 23 days—from noon on December 15 to noon on January 7—

the flagship logged 3318 miles, an average of 144 miles a day. Her best day's run was 185 miles, and in the seven days from December 24 to December 31 she covered 1121 miles. That the sluggards of the fleet, the *Lady Penrhyn* and the *Charlotte*, were able to keep up proves that they both sailed well in a strong wind. The main body sighted the coast of Van Diemen's Land on January 6, but in a heavy squall, accompanied by thunder and lightning, four days later—the same storm that set the *Lady Penrhyn's* women praying—the *Prince of Wales* carried away her main yard and split her main topsail and main topstaysail, and the *Golden Grove* split her topsails.

Midshipman Southwell, in one of his letters to his mother, gives a vivid little picture of the difference between the seamanship of the navy and that of the merchant captains on this day. "We luff'd up in a hard squall," he wrote, "and shook it out, as we term it, but were in luck that it did not shake or blow all the sails from the y'ds or the masts over the side; 'twas some time before we could take the canvas in, and being of long continuance it press'd her down in good faith to her best bearings, and she look'd for some time as though she did not mean to right. Our ship perhaps was a little crank; however, we sustained but trifling damage. Some of the convoy split their topsails, some their courses, and some both; others were seen with staysails blown away. Our main staysail was the only thing of consequence that gave way, and it was recover'd, tho' something the worse for wear and tear. . . . The merchantmen, as is their usual way, wore round or put before it; but we, as I said, shook it out or, in other words, presented her ship's head to the wind; 'tis a point much contested among seamen which is best." Years later, when the wool clippers were racing home from Australia, the relative merits of the two methods were still a subject of frequent debate[21].

The *Sirius* and her convoy anchored in Botany Bay on January 20,1788, barely 48 hours after the *Supply*. The voyage of 15,063 miles from England had been accomplished, without serious loss of any kind, in between 250 and 252 days, of which 68 had been spent in ports *en route*. It was a magnificent feat of navigation and seamanship. The fleet had reached Teneriffe 21 days out from the Motherbank, had made the passage from Teneriffe to Rio de Janeiro in 56 days, and had run from Rio to the Cape in 39 days.

The *Supply* had been 66, the *Alexander*, the *Friendship* and the *Scarborough* 67, and the rest of the fleet 68 days on the passage from the Cape to Botany Bay. The actual sailing times of the three divisions were 182, 183 and 184 days respectively. This gives an average daily run of about 82 miles, and an average speed of slightly over three knots an hour. As in the most favourable winds the *Sirius* was incapable of exceeding eight knots, the First Fleet hampered by the poor sailing qualities of the *Supply* in heavy weather and of the *Charlotte* and the *Lady Penrhyn* in light winds, put up a splendid sailing achievement. Of its 68 days in port, seven were spent at Teneriffe, 30 at Rio and 31 at the Cape.

On January 26, in consequence of Phillip's wise selection of Sydney Cove as the site for the new settlement, the entire fleet went round to Port Jackson. At this late hour disaster was narrowly averted. In getting out of the narrow entrance to Botany Bay with the wind against them, the *Prince of Wales* and the *Friendship* fouled one another, and the latter lost her jib-boom. "I was afraid that we should both have been driven on shore, as the wind blew fresh," Clark wrote. "Soon after the *Charlotte* ran foul of us and shook us very much. I was more frightened than I was when the *Prince of Wales* was foul of us. If it had not been by the greatest good luck we should have both been on shore or the rocks, and the ships must have all been lost and the greater part, if not the whole, on board drowned, for we should have gone to pieces in less than half-an-hour." However, the fleet brought to in Port Jackson without further incident.

Even more remarkable than its navigational feat was the fleet's health record. Its mortality rate had been far lower than the most sanguine had dared to hope. According to Surgeon White's return of June 30, 1788, 36 male and four female prisoners had died between embarkation and landing, and in the same period there had been eight other deaths—a marine, a marine's wife, a marine's child and five convicts' children. The total deaths, therefore, were 48. Of the 568 male and 191 female prisoners who actually sailed, 548 men and 188 women were landed, 20 men and three women having died on the actual passage. On June 30, 66 convicts were under medical treatment, of whom 24 were in hospital, and between landing and that date 20 men and eight women had died among the prisoners[22]. The deaths among the convicts up to landing had occurred as follows:—

	Men	Women
Between embarkation and sailing - - -	16	1
Between the Motherbank and Teneriffe - -	7	1
At Teneriffe - - - - - - - -	1	0
Between Teneriffe and Rio de Janeiro - -	5	1
Between Rio and Port Jackson - - -	7	1
Total - - - - - - - - -	36	4

"It is pretty extraordinary," wrote Surgeon Bowes, "how very healthy the convicts on board this ship in particular and the fleet in general have been during so long a passage and where there was a necessity of stowing them thick together, if I except the *Alexander*, where many of the convicts were embarked from the different gaols with malignant disorders among them, and consequently made many die on board, not less than 30. The *Scarborough*, where they were embarked in a healthy state, had not lost a single person during the passage. But this phenomenon will not appear so strange when I inform my readers how very well government have provided for the accommodation of the convicts. I believe I may venture to say few marines going out of England upon service were ever so amply provided for as these convicts are, and the surgeons and officers of the different ships pay such strict attention to their keeping themselves and their berths well aired and perfectly clean, together with the remarkably fine weather we have experienced during the whole of the voyage. Therefore, I must again repeat that (had the convicts been all embarked in the perfectly healthy state which government meant they should have been and believed were) I firmly believe very few, if any, would have died hitherto. In the *Lady Penrhyn* only two women have died since leaving England: one 82 years of age of a dropsy which had long rained upon her, and the other of a consumption, sent on board the *Lady Penrhyn* in the last stages thereof from the *Friendship* whilst we were at the Cape of Good Hope."[23]

Clark also testified to the care taken of the prisoners. Writing to a friend in England from the Cape, he declared: "Never was prisoners so much taken care of than they have been by the

Commodore, since his first taking charge of them. . . . They have been treated more like children than prisoners."

In his journal, as we have seen, Clark had characterised the female prisoners as a villainous and demoralised lot, and on December 23 he recorded of the men that "never were such d——d rascals collected together as there is on board this ship". However, in the letter just quoted, Clark asserted that the prisoners "have behaved very well and quiet".[24]

"I believe I may venture to say," wrote Surgeon Bowes, "there was never a more abandoned set of wretches collected in one place at any period than are now to be met with in this ship in particular, and I am credibly informed the comparison holds with regard to all convicts in the fleet. The greater part of them are so totally abandoned and calloused to all sense of shame and even common decency that it frequently becomes indispensably necessary to inflict corporal punishment upon them, and sorry I am to say that this rigid mode of proceeding has not the desired effect, since every day furnishes proofs of their being more hardened in their wickedness, nor do I conceive it possible in their present situation to adopt any plan to induce them to behave like rational or even human beings. Perpetually thieving the clothes from each other, nay almost from their backs, may be ranked amongst the least of their crimes. . . . The oaths and imprecations they daily make use of in their common conversation and little disputes with each other far exceed anything of the kind to be met with amongst the most profligate wretches in London. Nor can their matchless hypocrisy be equalled except by their base ingratitude, many of them plundering the sailors (who have at every port they arrived at spent almost the whole of the wages due to them in purchasing different articles of wearing apparel and other things for their accommodation) of their necessary clothes and cutting them up for some purpose of their own."

In the *Lady Penrhyn*, according to Bowes, the women were punished for thieving, fighting and abusive language by having thumb-screws or iron fetters put on their wrists. Sometimes they had their hair cut off and their heads shaven, a punishment they disliked above all others. At first one or two were flogged, but the cat-o'-nine-tails was later laid wholly aside. The women were generally so abusive when undergoing punishment that they had invariably to be gagged.[25]

The convicts having been disembarked and the provisions and stores landed, the three transports under charter to the East India Company—the *Charlotte, Lady Penrhyn* and *Scarborough*—sailed early in May for China and eventually reached England with their cargoes of tea. The *Charlotte* was then sold to Bond & Co., a firm of Walbrook merchants, and was put on the London-Jamaica run. After further changes of ownership, she was eventually sold to a Quebec merchant, John Jones, junior, and in 1818 her registry was transferred to Quebec. She was lost off Newfoundland in November of that year. The *Lady Penrhyn*, purchased by the London firm of Wedderburns, was also put on the London-Jamaica run. She had several changes of ownership, and, according to *Lloyd's List* of September 3, 1811, was captured in the West Indies in that year. The *Scarborough*, as we shall see, went out to Port Jackson again with the Second Fleet, and was broken up in 1798.

The other three transports—the *Alexander, Friendship* and *Prince of Wales*—left Port Jackson with the storeship *Borrowdale* for England on July 13 or 14. Scurvy soon decimated the crews of the *Alexander* and the *Friendship*, and as insufficient able men were left to work both vessels, the brig was scuttled in the Straits of Macassar on October 28 and her survivors transferred to the *Alexander*. The latter, having called at Batavia and the Cape, arrived off the Isle of Wight on May 28, 1789. On March 31, 1792, her London registry having been cancelled, she was registered at Hull, and eventually disappeared from the records after 1808. The *Prince of Wales* went home by way of Cape Horn, and reached Rio de Janeiro in great distress owing to scurvy. Her master, John Mason, died on 9th October, and was succeeded by Samuel Moore. Fourteen of her hands were so stricken with scurvy at that time as to be incapable of duty, and when she arrived at Rio, men from the boats which boarded her were compelled to bring her to an anchor. She eventually reached Falmouth on March 22, 1789, and Deptford on 30th April. She continued to sail out of London for some years, but on July 5, 1797, she was registered anew at Fort Royal, Martinique, which had been captured from the French three years before. Her ultimate fate is not known.

Of the three storeships, to complete the story of the merchantmen of the First Fleet, the *Borrowdale* and the *Fishburn* disappeared from the records after their return to England. The *Golden Grove* was registered in Newcastle in 1793 and on January 12, 1799, her registry was transferred to Liverpool. She possibly was put on the Liverpool-Jamaica run, but disappeared from the records after being re-registered at Liverpool in 1804.[26]

CHAPTER EIGHT

THE VOYAGES, 1789-1800

"The Lady Juliana."

THE first convict ship to leave England after the First Fleet was the *Lady Juliana*. A ship of 401 tons, she was chartered by William Richards, jun., who had contracted to transport women prisoners to Botany Bay on a *per capita* basis. The East India Company agreed to charter her for the return voyage, provided she arrived at Canton before January 15, 1791, and was in a fit state to receive a cargo of tea.[1]

For one reason and another, the *Lady Juliana's* departure was long delayed, and she lay for six months in the Thames before sailing. John Nicol, her steward, wrote a colourful account of her voyage in his reminiscences, but his statements are not always accurate. He declares, for instance, that the naval agent first appointed to her, an old lieutenant, was discharged because of his cruelty to the women. "He had even begun to flog them in the river," says Nicol. But official records prove that the first officer selected, Lieutenant Samuel Edward Marshall, declined the appointment, and Lieutenant Thomas Edgar was then given the post.[2]

Edgar was a picturesque character. He had been master of the *Discovery* on Captain Cook's last voyage, and had been promoted lieutenant in 1781. From the racy recollections of James Anthony Gardner, who served with Edgar in the *Gorgon*, 44, in 1794, we learn that this elderly lieutenant was known to his shipmates as "Little Bassey", because, unable to say "blast ye", he invariably used the expression, "God bass 'e!" Nicol describes him as a "kind, humane man", very good to the women convicts. "He had it in his power," Nicol recalls, "to throw overboard all their clothes when he gave them the convict dress, but he gave them to me to stow in the after hold, saying they would be of use to the poor creatures when they arrived at Port Jackson."[3]

The *Lady Juliana's* surgeon was Richard Alley, whose first

warrant as a naval surgeon was dated 1783. He made a second voyage with convicts in the *Royal Admiral* in 1792, and apparently was a competent medical officer by the standards of the day, although, bowing perhaps to the inevitable, he made little effort to maintain discipline aboard the *Lady Juliana.*

As was not uncommon with female transports, the *Lady Juliana's* voyage was protracted. She left Plymouth on July 29, 1789, with two hundred and twenty-six female convicts, although Nicol asserts she carried two hundred and forty-five. She arrived at Port Jackson on June 3, 1790, three hundred and nine days out from Plymouth. She called at Teneriffe and St. Jago, and was a hundred and twenty days out when she arrived at Rio de Janeiro, where she remained for forty-five days. From Rio she ran out to the Cape in fifty days, arriving at Table Bay on March 1, 1790. H.M.S. *Guardian,* which had left England six weeks after the *Lady Juliana,* arrived at the Cape more than three months before her. The *Lady Juliana* remained nineteen days at the Cape, and took seventy-five days for the passage from the Cape to Port Jackson[4].

Her convicts were as troublesome as the women in the First Fleet, and Nicol gives an illuminating pen-picture of them enlivened with many personal touches. The majority were London prostitutes, but there was a sprinkling of hardened offenders—thieves, receivers, and shoplifters. They were embarked in the Thames from Newgate prison and the county gaols, those from the latter coming aboard in irons which were rivetted, not locked. Nicol claims the gaolers paid him a fee of 2s. 6d. each for knocking off the irons.

Mrs. Barnsley, a noted sharper and shoplift, boasted that for a century her family had been swindlers and highwaymen, and her brother, a knight of the road "as well dressed and genteel in his appearance as any gentleman", often visited her on board before sailing. In the same category came Mrs. Davis, a swindler and fence, and Mary Williams, a receiver, who, with eight others, had long been inmates of Newgate, where, according to Nicol, they had been supported by Lord George Gordon. "I went once a week to him," says Nicol, who performed errands for the women ashore, "and got their allowance from his own hand all the time we lay in the river". Yet another of the prisoners was Mrs. Nelly Kerwin, "a female of daring habits, banished for life for forging seamen's powers of attorney and impersonating their relations."[5]

All the women, however, were not hardened offenders. A young Scottish girl felt her position so keenly that she died of a broken heart before the ship sailed from the Thames. "The young Scottish girl, I have never yet got out of my mind," declares Nicol. "She was young and beautiful, even in the convict dress, but pale as death and her eyes red with weeping. She never spoke to any of the women or came on deck. She was constantly seen sitting in the same corner from morning to night; even the time of meals roused her not. . . . At length she sunk into the grave of no disease but a broken heart."

Cast in somewhat the same mould was "young and pretty', Sarah Dorset, but her story, if Nicol is to be believed, had a far happier ending. She had been deserted by her lover and forced by want upon the streets. Her parents, "decent-looking people", visited her before she sailed, and on the voyage one of the crew, William Power, fell in love with her. He returned to New South Wales when she had served her sentence, married her, and took her back to England! Another, "a pretty girl, well behaved", was reputed to be an illegitimate daughter of Pitt, to whom she bore, in Nicol's words, "a most striking likeness . . . in every feature, and could scarcely be known from him as to looks".

On the passage to Port Jackson the *Lady Juliana* was nothing more than a floating brothel. "When we were fairly out at sea". recalls Nicol, "every man on board took a wife from among the convicts, they nothing loath." At the various ports of call seamen from every vessel in harbour were freely entertained, and there seems to have been no lack of either gaiety or liquor. The officers, including Edgar and Alley, made no attempt, apparently, to suppress prostitution[6].

In other directions, the women proved "a troublesome cargo, yet not dangerous or very mischievious; as I may say, more noise than danger". They fought among themselves, chiefly, it would seem, so that they would be ordered below into the prison; for they had found means, probably with the connivance of the seamen, of breaking into the hold and broaching the porter stowed there. When Edgar realized that confining the women below was simply presenting them with an opportunity for a carousal, he ordered Nicol "to take a flour barrel, and cut a hole in the top for their heads and one on each side for their arms". Placed in this wooden jacket, the offenders "could only walk or stand in it; they could not lie or sit down with it". Thus confined, one woman, Nance Ferrel, strutted about smoking a pipe and even walking a minuet, turning her head from side to side like a turtle, but eventually fatigue compelled her to beg release. A few days later she was again unruly, but this time was tied up and given a dozen lashes.

Having thoughtfully brought some linen aboard, the ship's master, Captain Aitken, kept a score of the women at work throughout the passage making shirts. Naturally, he paid the women very little for their labour, but sold the shirts to great advantage at Port Jackson. It was an evil of the transportation system that women convicts could be thus exploited by the ship's officers, but it had not yet occurred to the British authorities to place materials aboard so that the female convicts might practise handicrafts, and themselves reap the profit of their labour on arrival at their destination[7].

At the Cape disaster almost overtook the *Lady Juliana*. The carpenter carelessly allowed the pitch-pot to boil over on deck, and as flames and smoke arose, the frightened women ran screaming about the deck, creating a great deal of confusion. Nicol says he was able to keep the fire under control until the seamen extinguished it with water, and the ship was saved from burning. She had another narrow escape when standing into Port Jackson in a strong southerly. She got close into North Head, and only the set of the tide saved her from going ashore. As it was, she was unable to make her way up harbour, and eventually had to be towed into Sydney Cove on June 6, three days after she had entered the heads.

Despite her protracted voyage, only five women died during the passage. Edgar saw that the rations were properly issued and insisted upon the ship being kept clean and properly fumigated, but the low mortality rate was primarily due to the women being given free access to the deck and to the long sojourns in ports *en route*, at all of which fresh provisions were plentifully supplied.

Her long but leisurely voyage strained the *Lady Juliana's* timbers, and on arriving at Port Jackson she was not deemed sufficiently seaworthy to make a trip to Norfolk Island, where a penal settlement had already been established. With the help of some convict carpenters, however, she was patched up, and on

July 25, 1790, she sailed for China. She reached Table Bay again on June 26, 1791. Assuredly the *Lady Juliana* was no passage-maker![8]

The Wreck of the "Guardian".

Strictly speaking, H.M.S. *Guardian* was not a convict ship. She was taken up as a storeship, but as she embarked twenty-five specially selected prisoners, and was the first vessel carrying convicts to be wrecked on the passage to Australia, her story may be briefly recapitulated here[9].

Designed as a 44-gun frigate, she was armed *en flute*, her lower tier of guns being removed, when, commanded by Lieutenant Edward Riou, R.N., she sailed from Spithead on September 12, 1789. The *Guardian* carried 1003 tons of cargo, and had as passengers the Rev. John Crowther, who had been appointed assistant chaplain at Sydney, a number of superintendents being despatched to the penal settlement, Elizabeth Schafer the ten-years-old daughter of one of the superintendents, and the twenty-five convicts.

At Santa Cruz, where she remained four days, the *Guardian* shipped 2000 gallons of wine, and on November 24 she anchored in Table Bay. Having loaded some cattle and horses, she resumed her voyage on December 11. On the 22nd, when the temperature had dropped to 49°, she sighted her first ice, and two days later, with the wisps of fog showing every sign of clearing, she fell in with a huge iceberg. As the cattle were consuming prodigious quantities of water, Riou decided to replenish the supply by collecting some of the loose ice which had floated away from the berg. The *Guardian* was then 1300 miles from the Cape, in Lat. 44° S. and Long. 41° E.

The jolly-boat and the cutter were hoisted out and began to pick up the loose ice, but the fog, instead of clearing, suddenly came so thick that from the *Guardian's* decks the berg could scarcely be discerned three-quarters of a mile away. An hour was occupied in emptying the boats and hoisting them on board, and then, with Riou directing the steering, the *Guardian* tacked. Soon she was making six or seven knots. Riou remained on deck for fifteen or twenty minutes, when, believing the ship was clear of the berg, he went below. Half-an-hour later she struck, her bows crashing on to a projecting ledge of ice under the water. She got free, but was apparently in a sinking condition, and as she swung round her stern struck violently, severely damaging the false and main keels and sternpost, and knocking away the rudder.

Water at once poured into the *Guardian*, and, despite the manning of her four pumps, it gained steadily. Cattle, guns and cargo were jettisoned to lighten the ship, and she remained afloat. During the night the wind freshened until it was blowing a gale. The main topsail and fore topgallant sail were ripped to shreds. The work of pumping and lightening the ship continued throughout the night, and an attempt was made to fother her, a lower studding sail, filled with rolls of oakum, being passed under her bottom forward, carried aft and there made fast. When day dawned, the *Guardian*, with six or seven feet of water in her hold, was still afloat, but she was labouring and pitching heavily in the rough sea. Late in the afternoon a second attempt was made to fother her, but every effort to locate the leak failed.

On the 25th the five boats were hoisted out. Worn out by their exertions at the pumps and in lightening the ship, and believing she must sink at any moment, many of the officers, seamen and convicts had broached the liquor aboard and were hopelessly drunk. A quarrel between two drunken sailors led to the swamping of one boat, but the other four got clear. One man, dressed in Riou's new gold-laced hat and two of his uniform coats, and carrying his sword, drunkenly told the commander that an officer had drowned the surgeon. One boat, filled principally with drunken seamen, returned to the ship. While its occupants were demanding a sail to replace the one they had lost overboard, at least twenty men jumped from the *Guardian* into the sea and tried to clamber into the already overcrowded boat.

"It seems that they had not a single thing in this boat either to eat or drink," wrote Riou, in his narrative of the disaster, "and she was loaded as full of men as she could hold. If these men lived out the day it was the utmost; indeed, I am inclined to think they could but have survived a few minutes."

With the departure of the boats, about sixty-two persons were left with Riou in the *Guardian*. Twenty-one of these were convicts, the other four prisoners having leapt overboard into one of the boats. In cold, tempestuous weather, the fight to keep the *Guardian* afloat continued. By January 7 the water was above the lower deck, and the ship, so deep that she scarcely moved through the water, was shipping whole seas. The survivors pumped until they fell from sheer exhaustion or, having, in their despair, broached a puncheon of rum or a cask of wine, they were incapable of any labour. The attempts to fother the ship were renewed, and an effort was made to steer her, first by the construction of a steering machine, which was unsuccessful, then by the use of a cable, which proved uncertain, and, finally, by the making of a rudder, which it was found impossible to place in position.

The pumps alternately gained and lost, but the *Guardian* miraculously remained afloat. She staggered drunkenly across the Indian Ocean almost to Cape St. Mary, Madagascar, and then made her uncertain way back to the coast of Africa, which was sighted on February 21. Boats came to her assistance and she anchored in False Bay, where the salvaging of such of her provisions as had not been jettisoned was put in hand. On April 12, however, a fierce gale drove her from her moorings and on to the beach, where she became a total wreck.

Of her boats, only the launch, commanded by her master, Thomas Clements, was rescued, being picked up by the French merchantman *Viscountess of Brittany* on January 3. The ten survivors, who included the Rev. John Crowther, were landed at Table Bay eight days later, although some accounts assert that fifteen persons were aboard when she was picked up. The remaining boats were never heard of again. The twenty-one convicts who had remained aboard the *Guardian* were saved, but one subsequently died at the Cape. The remaining twenty eventually reached New South Wales, and fourteen of them, in consequence of Riou's report of their good conduct, received conditional pardons from Phillip[10].

THE SECOND FLEET

Arrival 1790	*Vessel*	*Rig*	*Tons*	*Master*	*Surgeon*
26 June	*Surprize* (1)	Ship	400	Nicholas Anstis	Wm. Waters
28 June	*Neptune*	Ship	809	Donald Trail	Wm. Gray
28 June	*Scarborough* (2)	Ship	418	John Marshall	Augustus Jacob Beyer

The three ships of the Second Fleet embarked their convicts in December, 1789, and sailed from England in charge of Lieutenant John Shapcote, as Agent of Transports, on January 19, 1790. The

Scarborough was making her second voyage with convicts, having previously gone out with the First Fleet. The *Surprize*, by reason of her size and build, was an unsuitable vessel for so long a voyage and proved a wet ship even in moderate weather. In the rough seas, and heavy gales encountered after leaving the Cape the convicts, according to Captain William Hill who commanded the guard in her, "were considerably above their waists in water, and the men of my company, whose berths were not so far forward, were nearly up to the middles". The *Scarborough* and the *Surprize*, however, had been chartered by the East India Company to load tea at Canton on the return passage, but for some reason the *Neptune*, built in the Thames in 1779 and the largest vessel so far employed in the convict service, was rejected, and the Company refused to waive its exclusive charter to permit her to load home a cargo of cotton wool at Bombay[11].

The three transports arrived at the Cape in company on April 13, 1790, after a passage of 84 days from Portsmouth. They refreshed at the Cape for 16 days, and sailed again on April 29. The *Surprize* having parted from her consorts in heavy weather, was in sight of the entrance to Port Jackson on June 23, but was blown out to sea by contrary winds and did not make port until the 26th, 158 days out from England and 58 days from the Cape. The *Neptune* and the *Scarborough* arrived two days later, on the 28th.

Although the Second Fleet made a relatively fast passage, especially on the run from the Cape, the voyage was disastrous, and the mortality rate was the highest in the history of transportation to Australia. The three ships had embarked 1017 prisoners, of whom 939 were men and 78 women, but 11 men had been disembarked before sailing. At the Cape the 20 convict survivors of the *Guardian* had been embarked, 12 in the *Neptune* and eight in the *Scarborough*. Between embarkation and arrival, 256 men and 11 women, a total of 267, had died, the details being as follows:[12]

Vessel	*Embarked*		*Relanded*		*Embarked at Cape*		*Deaths*		*Disembarked*	
	M.	*F.*	*M.*	*F.*	*M.*	*F.*	*M.*	*F.*	*M.*	*F.*
Surprize –	256	0	2	0	0	0	36	0	218	0
Neptune –	424	78	3	0	12	0	147	11	286	67
Scarborough	259	0	6	0	8	0	73	0	188	0
Totals:	939	78	11	0	20	0	256	11	692	67

Aboard all three ships, but particularly in the *Neptune*, the prisoners were treated with savage brutality. We have already seen that Lieutenant Shapcote, while perhaps not a party to the rapacity of the *Neptune's* master, the avaricious and unscrupulous Donald Trail, was inexcusably lax and incompetent, and that after his death the prisoners were treated with incredible severity. They were shamefully starved, kept heavily ironed, and, except in inadequate numbers and at long intervals, refused access to the deck. There was no excuse for Trail's callousness, as at no stage of the voyage was there any suspicion of attempted mutiny.

In the smaller *Surprize*, owing to the great quantities of water shipped, the convicts lived in a state of perpetual misery and discomfort, and as the decks were swept continuously by seas in heavy weather, they necessarily had to remain confined for long periods in the damp, unhealthy prison. Scurvy and other diseases appeared and could not be checked, but there seems little doubt that, as in the *Neptune*, the prisoners were deliberately starved by the ship's master, Nicholas Anstis, who had been chief mate of the *Lady Penrhyn* in the First Fleet.

"The slave trade," declared Captain Hill, in a letter written after his arrival, "is merciful compared with what I have seen in this fleet; in that it is in the interests of the masters to preserve the health and lives of their captives, they having a joint benefit with the owners; in this, the more they can withhold from the unhappy wretches the more provisions they have to dispose of at a foreign market, and the earlier in the voyage they die, the longer they can draw the deceased's allowance to themselves; for I fear few of them are honest enough to make a just return of the dates of their deaths to their employers. . . . My feelings never have been so wounded as in this voyage, so much so, that I shall never recover my accustomed vivacity and spirits; and had I been empowered, it would have been the most grateful task of my life to have prevented so many of my fellow creatures so much misery and death."[13]

The rations of the prisoners in the *Scarborough* were not deliberately withheld, but owing to a reported attempt at mutiny the convicts were very closely confined. On February 12, when the *Surprize* was out of sight and the *Neptune* a long way ahead, a plot to seize the ship and murder the officers was formed by some of the prisoners. Their intentions were disclosed by a forger, Samuel Burt, and the plotters were secured without difficulty. The ringleaders were flogged, and the more dangerous of them stapled to the deck. Although Judge-Advocate David Collins declares that the master's humanity "considerably lessened the severity which the insurgents might naturally have expected", the prisoners were kept closely confined and given insufficient access to the deck. It was to this fact that the high death rate was directly due.[14]

The three ships presented a pitiful and sickening sight when they arrived at Port Jackson. "...I beheld a sight truly shocking to the feelings of humanity," wrote the settlement's chaplain, Rev. Richard Johnson, describing his visit to the *Surprize*, "a great number of them laying, some half and others nearly quite naked, without either bed or bedding, unable to turn or help themselves. Spoke to them as I passed along, but the smell was so offensive that I could scarcely bear it." Johnson was persuaded not to venture into the *Scarborough's* prison, and of the *Neptune* he wrote that she "was still more wretched and intolerable, and therefore never attempted it."

Johnson, however, watched the prisoners being disembarked. "The landing of these people was truly affecting and shocking," he wrote, "great numbers were not able to walk, nor to move hand or foot; such were slung over the ship's side in the same manner as they would sling a cask, a box or anything of that nature. Upon being brought up to the open air some fainted, some died upon the deck, and others in the boat before they reached the shore. When come on shore many were not able to walk, to stand, or to stir themselves in the least, hence some were led by others. Some creeped upon their hands and knees, and some were carried upon the backs of others." All were in an indescribably filthy state, "covered", as Johnson said, "almost with their own nastiness, their heads, bodies, cloths, blankets, all full of filth and lice".[15]

At least 486 sick were landed—269 from the *Neptune*, 121 from the *Surprize*, and 96 from the *Scarborough*. Those who did not require medical treatment were described as "lean and emaciated" by Collins, who added that both the living and the dead exhibited "more horrid spectacles than had ever been witnessed in this country".

Governor Phillip informed the British Government that the mortality had been caused "by the contractors having crowded too many on board" and "from their being too much confined during the passage" . . . "I believe," he added, "while the masters of transports think their own safety depends on admitting few convicts on deck at a time, and most of them with irons on, which prevent any kind of exercise, numbers must always perish on so long a voyage." Collins was of the same opinion, saying the convicts' condition was due "to confinement, and that of the worst species, confinement in a small space and in irons, not put on singly, but many of them chained together". "The usage they met on board, according to their own story, was truly shocking," the Rev. Johnson declared. "Sometimes for days, nay, for a considerable time together, they have been to the middle in water chained together, hand and leg, even the sick not exempted—nay, many died with the chains upon them. Promises, entreaties, were all in vain, and it was not till a very few days before they made the harbour that they were released out of irons. The greatest complaints by far were from those persons who had come in the *Neptune*."[16]

When the reports eventually reached England, both public and official opinion was astounded, and the colonial office described the occurrence as a "shocking calamity". The strictest inquiry was promised, and towards the end of November, 1791, the depositions of some of the *Neptune's* crew and of several marines were taken before Alderman Clark at the Guildhall in London. These witnesses testified that Trail and his first mate, William Ellington, had kept the convicts short in their provisions and that on arrival at Sydney they had opened a warehouse and sold the rations thus unjustly detained.

A despatch of January 10, 1792, informed Phillip that Trail had absconded to avoid prosecution, but in May the Secretary of State wrote that he had taken the necessary steps "to bring forward the conduct of the parties concerned". By then, of course, the public outcry had subsided, and no real effort was made to bring the offenders to justice. Trail and Ellington were indicted at the Old Bailey on June 8, 1792, on a private prosecution for the wilful murder of one of the convicts, but were acquitted after a three hours' trial. No attempt was made at this time to arrest Trail or to bring a public prosecution against him. He was a master in the Royal Navy, having served in that capacity under Nelson in H.M.S. *Albemarle* from August 16, 1781, until July 3, 1783, and his misconduct in the *Neptune* did not prevent him from being appointed Master Attendant at the Cape, a post he was holding in 1795 and 1796, when Captain George Elphinstone, the future Lord Keith, declared he was "very active, attentive and able".[17]

The Second Fleet contractors, Messrs. Camden, Calvert & King, also escaped prosecution. A further contract, covering the transportation of the prisoners in the Third Fleet, had been signed with them on November 18, 1790, before the reports of the Second Fleet's passage reached England. This contract they completed, but they were not again employed in the convict service.

The "Mary Ann" and H.M.S. "Gorgon".

In 1791 two vessels carrying convicts sailed independently for Port Jackson. The first, the *Mary Ann*, a ship of 298 tons, was an old vessel, built in France in 1772. Commanded by her part-owner, Mark Munroe, she embarked 150 female convicts, and sailed from England on February 16. She touched only at St. Jago, where she remained ten days, and anchored in Port Jackson on July 9 after an uneventful passage of 143 days. This was the fastest passage yet made by a convict ship, but, possibly because she called at only one port *en route* to refresh her prisoners with fresh provisions, there were nine deaths on the passage—a high mortality rate for a female transport.[18]

Like the ill-fated *Guardian*, the second vessel, H.M.S. *Gorgon*, was a 44-gun frigate converted into a storeship. She embarked 31 male convicts and leaving England on March 15, called at Teneriffe, St. Jago and the Cape. She remained six weeks at the latter port to embark livestock, and arrived at Port Jackson, with the loss of one prisoner, on September 21, after an uneventful passage of 190 days.[19]

The Third Fleet.

The remaining convict ships to leave England in 1791 formed the Third Fleet proper, and sailed in two divisions. Possibly because of the reluctance of shipowners to tender their ships in the face of the storm clouds gathering over Europe, the vessels taken up were mostly old, and the Navy Board's officers were less vigilant than usual or had no alternative but to accept vessels that were in poor repair and ill-found. The oldest were the *William and Ann*, built in one of the King's yards as early as 1759, and the brig *Active*, launched at Shoreham in 1764. The Georgia-built *Queen*, dated from 1773, the *Salamander* had been turned out by a Thames yard in 1776 and the *Atlantic* had been built in Wales in 1784. The *Matilda*, the *Admiral Barrington* and the *Albemarle* were the products of French yards; the former had been built in 1779 and the *Admiral Barrington* in 1781, but the date of the *Albemarle's* launch is not recorded. Of the *Britannia*, no record has been found.[20]

Arrival	*Vessel*	*Rig*	*Tons*	*Master*	*Surgeon*
1791					
1 Aug.	*Matilda*	Ship	460	Matthew Weatherhead	
20 Aug.	*Atlantic*	Ship	422	Archibald Armstrong	James Thomson
21 Aug.	*Salamander*	Ship	320	?J. Nichol	
28 Aug.	*William and Ann*	Ship	370	?E. Bunker	
26 Sept.	*Active*	Brig	350	John Mitchinson	
26 Sept.	*Queen*	Ship	400	Richard Owen	
13 Oct.	*Albermarle*	Ship	530	George Bowen	
14 Oct.	*Britannia*	Ship	520	Thomas Melville	
16 Oct.	*Admiral Barrington*	Ship	527	Robert Abbon Marsh	Peter Gossam

The *Atlantic*, the *Salamander* and the *William and Ann*, in charge of Lieutenant Richard Bowen as naval agent, sailed from Plymouth on March 27, and the same day the *Albemarle*, the *Active*, the *Admiral Barrington*, the *Britannia* and the *Matilda*, with Lieutenant Robert Parry Young as naval agent, left Portsmouth. The *Queen*, although belonging to the Portsmouth division, embarked her convicts at Cork and had her own naval agent, Lieutenant Samuel Blow. She sailed from Cork at the beginning of April, apparently with orders to rendezvous with the rest of the division at St. Jago. She was the first vessel to convey Irish prisoners to Australia.

Lieutenant Bowen's Plymouth division had an uneventful passage. Late in April, when approaching the Equator, the *Salamander* parted company one dark, squally night, but she rejoined at Rio de Janeiro, and the three ships sailed from there together. However, they almost at once ran into bad weather and became separated in a heavy gale. All three made the passage from Rio to Port Jackson direct, being the first convict ships to do so. They independently worked their way down to the latitude of the Cape, and then, without calling at Table Bay or False Bay, ran down their easting in about 40° S. The *Atlantic* arrived at Port Jackson on August 20, 146 days out from England, and the *Salamander* anchored the following day, but the ancient *William and Ann* was 154 days out from Plymouth when she reached Sydney.

There had been 30 deaths among the prisoners in the three transports during the passage—18 in the *Atlantic*, five in the *Salamander* and seven in the *William and Ann*. Responsibility for the high death-roll in the first-named ship rested with the British authorities. She had embarked her convicts at Woolwich and Plymouth, and those taken aboard from the *Dunkirk* hulk at the latter port had been in bad health. At least a dozen had been so ill that they had been unable to scramble up the ship's side, and they had had to be hoisted aboard in a chair. Surgeon James Thomson had wished to exchange them for men physically better able to withstand the rigours of the voyage, but had failed to obtain the necessary authority. The callousness of the authorities in compelling these sick men to make the voyage is incredible. Six had died before sailing, and another 12, of whom all but one had been numbered among the 50 on the sick-list when the *Atlantic* had sailed, had died on the passage. However, there were only nine men on the sick-list when the *Atlantic* arrived, and the *Salamander* had but one man sick. The decrepit *William and Ann* was the least healthy, and although only five of her prisoners required hospital treatment, Collins states that her convicts on arrival were very ill. As her master was fined for assaulting and beating some of the soldiers during the passage, it is probable that conditions aboard the *William and Ann* were unsatisfactory and that her prisoners were not as humanely treated as they might have been.[21]

The Portsmouth division was quickly scattered by heavy weather. The *Matilda* parted company off Dunnoze the first night at sea, the *Active* and the *Britannia* during the night of April 3, and the *Admiral Barrington* during a hard gale on the 7th. The *Albemarle*, in which Lieutenant Young had embarked, was thus alone on the 9th when some of the convicts attempted her capture. At seven-thirty that morning the first batch of prisoners was admitted to the deck, the watch at the time being aloft trimming the sails. Led by William Siney and Owen Lyons, the convicts knocked the sentinels to the deck and seized their arms. Brandishing a cutlass, Siney led a rush aft toward the quarter-deck. The *Albemarle's* master, George Bowen, ran into the cabin, picked up a blunderbuss, and returned to the deck to find Siney aiming a blow with his cutlass at the helmsman. Bowen, firing hastily, wounded the mutineer in the right shoulder, and Siney, dropping his cutlass, fled toward the forehold, closely followed by the rest of the prisoners. Left in possession of the deck, Bowen summoned the guard and the ship's company, and an armed party was sent below to round up the mutineers.

The first man brought up, Thomas Pratt, on threat of instant hanging, confessed that a plan had been formed to seize the ship and sail her to America, and named Siney and Lyons as the ringleaders. Consulted by Lieutenant Young, Bowen, the ship's officers, the surgeon, and the sergeant of the guard concurred that the safety of the ship demanded an immediate example being made, and Siney and Lyons were promptly hanged at the fore-yard arm. Several other prisoners were severely flogged. These measures proved effective, and the prisoners gave no further trouble.

After the excitement had died down, the convicts handed Bowen a letter in which, after praying forgiveness, they asserted the mutiny had been instigated by two seamen, Thomas Haynes and John Bennet. It was claimed that the seamen had supplied the prisoners with knives. These had been converted into files, enabling the convicts to get rid of their irons. Haynes and Bennet were heavily ironed and placed on the quarter-deck under guard. On April 23, after a boisterous passage of 25 days from the Lizard, the *Albemarle* put into Madeira, and Haynes and Bennet were landed. They were kept in custody until the arrival of a British warship enabled them to be shipped back to England.[22]

The *Matilda,* the first of the Portsmouth division to arrive at Port Jackson, made a remarkable passage, being 127 days out when she anchored on August 1. This bettered the *Mary Ann's* record by 16 days. The *Matilda's* master, Matthew Weatherhead, evidently drove her hard; for she was very leaky on arrival and required extensive repairs. She had been detained two days by anchoring in a bay of Schouten Island, off Freycinet Peninsula, Tasmania, but probably Weatherhead had been obliged to put in for shelter or because the *Matilda* was so leaky.

There were 25 deaths during the passage, and on arrival 20 of her prisoners required hospital treatment. Many aged and infirm had been embarked, and some of these men had been unfit to make the voyage. But the primary causes of the high death-roll were probably the leakiness of the ship, and Weatherhead's hard driving. The *Matilda* must have been a wet, as well as a damp ship, and scurvy, no doubt, was the result. The fact that while ten convicts died between England and the Cape, 15 were buried at sea between the Cape and Port Jackson seems to bear this out.[23]

The *Active* and the *Queen* both entered Port Jackson on September 26. The date of the latter ship's departure from Cork is not recorded, but the *Active* made a passage of 183 days from Portsmouth. She evidently struck very bad weather after leaving the Cape, as she took 91 days from that port to Sydney—a particularly long passage. Twenty-one of her prisoners died between embarkation and landing, while the *Queen* lost seven men. The survivors in both vessels, but especially in the *Active*, were in a feeble and emaciated state, and complained bitterly of not having received their proper allowance of provisions.

A magisterial inquiry revealed that gross abuses had been practised in the *Queen*. The second mate, Robert Stott, who usually supervised the issuing of the rations, had ordered the leaden weights to be scraped, and when the convict employed in this work protested that too much had been scraped off, Stott's only reply was to order him to scrape them again. The 4-lb. weight was proved to be six ounces under weight, and the 2-lb. weight almost three ounces. The use of false weights, however, was the least of the abuses. The convicts had been flagrantly cheated by the use of a 4-lb. weight in place of a 5-lb. weight and the substitution of a 3-lb. weight for a 4-lb. one. Where 132 lb. of beef should have been served, only 60 lb. were issued, and 68 lb. of fish had been handed out instead of 120 lb. No wonder the cook had frequently been at a loss to know how to divide the meat between the different messes!

Lieutenant Blow's attitude toward the convicts' complaints is inexplicable. He made no attempt to himself supervise the issuing of the rations, but caused the prisoners to elect one of their own number to assist Stott, and merely furnished this man with a schedule of the rations to be issued. The convict, not unnaturally, was frightened to disclose the short-serving of the provisions, particularly as Stott did not fix him to a ration, but allowed him to help himself. When the prisoners complained to Ensign William Cummings, who commanded the guard, he advised them to see Blow, but they said it was useless, as they got no redress. Cummings spoke to the naval agent about the complaints, but Blow blandly asked, "My dear fellow, what can I do?"

A fortnight or three weeks before the *Queen* reached Sydney there was a quarrel between Stott and the master, Richard Owen. Stott thereupon told Ensign Cummings, according to the latter's evidence at the inquiry, that he had defrauded the convicts against his conscience. He blamed Owen, saying that had he taken the whole of the prisoners' rations he still could not have given Owen satisfaction, and he went on to abuse Lieutenant Blow as an old rascal, saying that he would not believe but that Blow was privy to the fraud.

The magistrates found that the rations stipulated in the contract with Messrs. Camden, Calvert & King had not been supplied, that frauds had been committed, and that those who should have seen the full ration served had failed to take proper steps when complaints of deficiencies had been made. They were unable, however, to determine with any precision the extent of the deficiencies, so as to enable redress to be made to the prisoners and the punishment of Owen and Stott to be fixed. They therefore submitted the evidence to Phillip, and left it to him to decide what action should be taken. "I doubt if I have the power of inflicting a punishment adequate to the crime," declared the governor in his despatch to the Secretary of State.

The abuses in the *Active* had been less flagrant, but her prisoners had been at least partially starved.

No action, however, appears to have been taken by the British authorities in the case either of the *Queen* or of the *Active*. The contractors and the ships' officers went unpunished, and, except possibly for a reprimand from the Navy Board, so also did Lieutenant Blow. The government's refusal to institute public prosecutions seems to have been the result of deliberate policy, and the conclusion is inescapable that it feared the consequences, believing that revelations in court would so discredit the transportation system that a public demand for its abolition might result. The government wished to avoid such an agitation at all cost[24].

The *Albemarle* and the *Britannia* arrived within a day of one another, after passages of 200 and 201 days respectively. There had been 32 deaths among the *Albemarle's* prisoners, including the two men executed, and 21 among those in the *Britannia*. Lieutenant Young's return from the Cape shows that each ship had lost nine men between March 27, the date of sailing, and August 9, so that in each the majority of the deaths occurred after leaving the Cape. This in itself tends to indicate that the convicts had not been embarked in a sickly state, and as the survivors, on arrival, had no complaints of ill-treatment, it seems probable that the mortality in each ship was due to the cumulative effects of scurvy or to the outbreak of some kind of epidemic after leaving the Cape.

Last of the Third Fleet transports to reach Port Jackson was the *Admiral Barrington*. She had been in the London-Copenhagen trade before being taken up as a convict ship, but although a relatively new ship was scarcely seaworthy. Lieutenant Philip Gidley King, who was at the Cape when she arrived there, reported that she was in a very leaky state and "infamously found in standing and running rigging". He seriously doubted whether she would reach her destination. The *Active*, the *Queen* and the *Britannia*, in charge of Lieutenant Blow, left the Cape together, and about a week later the *Albemarle* and the *Admiral Barrington* sailed in company under Lieutenant Young's command, which suggests that the last-named vessel had been detained by the necessity of undergoing repairs. If this is so, they could not have been very efficiently carried out, as she sailed with a crippled mainmast.

On her arrival off the New South Wales coast, the *Admiral Barrington* was driven out to sea by a gale, and for a time fears were entertained for her safety. However, she made port on October 16, 203 days out from Portsmouth. There had been 36 deaths among her prisoners, 11 of which occurred before she reached the Cape. The prisoners apparently had not been ill-treated, and the mortality among them probably was due to overcrowding, her unseaworthy state, and the length of her passage.[25]

Despite the irregularities which occurred in the *Queen* and the *Active*, the convicts who reached Port Jackson in 1791 had been more humanely treated than those in the Second Fleet, and the mortality rate among them had been lower. The number of deaths, however, had been excessive, and the precautions against illness in the passage inedequate. "Although the convicts landed from these ships were not so sickly as those brought out last year," reported Phillip, "the greatest part of them are so emaciated, so worn away by long confinement, or want of food, or from both these causes, that it will be long before they will recover their strength, and which many of them never will recover." On November 5, 1791, 626 convicts were under medical treatment, of whom no fewer than 576 had arrived in the Third Fleet.

Details for these transports are as follows:

Vessel	*Embarked*		*Deaths*		*Disembarked*	
	M.	*F.*	*M.*	*F.*	*M.*	*F.*
Mary Ann	0	150	0	9	0	141
H.M.S. *Gorgon*	31	0	1	0	30	0
Matilda	230	0	25	0	205	0
Atlantic	220	0	18	0	202	0
Salamander	160	0	5	0	155	0
William and Ann	188	0	7	0	181	0
Active	175	0	21	0	154	0
Queen	133	22	7	0	126	22
Albemarle	282	0	32*	0	250	6†
Britannia	150	0	21	0	129	0
Admiral Barrington	300	0	36	0	264	0
Totals:	1869	172	173	9	1696	169

Having regard to the build and size of some of the Third Fleet transports, it is clear that gross overcrowding occurred in several of the ships, notably in the *Admiral Barrington* and to a less extent in the *Albemarle*. These two ships and the *Britannia* were all vessels of approximately the same tonnage, and yet while the *Britannia* embarked only 150 male convicts, the *Albemarle* carried 282 and the *Admiral Barrington* 300. It is reasonable to assume that overcrowding was at least a contributing factor to the heavy death-roll[26].

* Includes two men executed.

† The arrival of six women in the *Albemarle* is unexplained, but possibly they had been transferred from the *Mary Ann*. If so, the latter presumably landed 135 women, reducing the total of women landed from 169 to 163. It does not appear that the number of women embarked exceeded 172.

Five of the Third Fleet transports were the first convict ships to go whaling off the Australian coast. This trade was included in the monopoly enjoyed by the East India Company, and before the convict ships sailed from England their owners had to secure the Company's permission for them to engage in whaling. This permission was granted, but the convict ships met with little success, and soon departed Australian waters. The *Matilda*, when bound for the coast of Peru, was wrecked on a shoal, but her crew reached Tahiti in the ship's boats, and there 21 survivors, including a convict stowaway, were picked up by H.M.S. *Daedalus*. The *Atlantic*, being chartered by Phillip, made a voyage to Calcutta for provisions, and on her return sailed for England, Phillip, who had resigned because of ill-health, being a passenger in her. The remaining four merchantmen—the *Active, Albemarle, Queen* and *Admiral Barrington*—proceeded to India, the Third Fleet contractors having obtained the East India Company's sanction to load them home with cotton on private account and having transmitted £30,000 in specie from England with which to purchase their cargoes.

The *Admiral Barrington* reached India safely, but in a heavy gale was driven from her anchorage at Bombay and was totally wrecked, on Malwan Island. As the shipwrecked mariners reached shore they were slain by natives. Observing the fate of their shipmates, the master, the chief mate and the surgeon swam to a ship and were taken aboard. They were the only survivors[27].

The Arrivals in 1792.

Arrival	*Vessel*	Rig	*Tons*	*Master*	*Surgeon*
1792					
14 Feb.	*Pitt*	Ship	775	Edward Manning	Jameson
7 Oct.	*Royal Admiral*	Ship	914	Essex Henry Bond	Richard Alley
18 Nov.	*Kitty*	Ship	363	George Ramsay	J. P. Niebuhr

At the time she was taken up, the *Pitt* was the largest vessel so far employed in the convict service and the first regular East Indiaman to carry prisoners to Australia. Her ship's husband, as the owner of a vessel taken up by the Company for six or more voyages was styled, was George Mackenzie Macaulay, an alderman of the city of London. After she had sailed for Port Jackson he offered to charter her to the Company to load home tea from China, but although previously she had been chartered by the Company, his offer was declined by the Court of Directors on September 21, 1791. Presumably the *Pitt* was rejected because, being already on the high seas, she could not be examined by the Company's officers in dry dock, an examination insisted upon under the Company's regulations. However, after disembarking her prisoners at Port Jackson, she sailed for India and, apparently, was freighted home by the Company; certainly she was later chartered by the Company for other voyages.

The *Royal Admiral*, belonging to Thomas Larkins, a member of perhaps the most prominent family associated with the Company's shipping, was a larger vessel than the *Pitt* by 139 tons. She had a length of 120 ft. 2 ins. and a beam of 37 ft. 10 ins. Both the *Royal Admiral* and the *Pitt* had been built in the Thames, the former in 1777 and the latter in 1780.

The third convict ship to reach Port Jackson in 1792, the *Kitty*, was an ordinary merchantman. She had been built at Sunderland in 1787, and was, of course, a much smaller ship than the two East Indiamen.[28]

The *Pitt* originally embarked 443 men and women, but in consequence of an anonymous complaint that she was overcrowded, an inquiry was ordered by the Commissioners of the Navy. Three officers inspected her and reported that she was incapable of accommodating more than 410 prisoners. "In the prison," they stated, in a report of June 25, 1791, "the space of a cube of six feet is all that is allowed to eight men, and should the 391 men be placed in the prison every berth or space of 18 inches would be occupied; if a sickness should happen, a sick and a person in health must touch each other."

The officers added that on the gundeck three separate places before the Great Cabin had been set apart for the women's quarters. Two of these measured 6 ft. 7 ins. in length by 7 ft. 10 ins. in width, and were intended to each accommodate ten women. The third space, designed for 27 women, was 13 ft. 7 ins. long by 8 ft. 4 ins. wide.

On both sides, the *Pitt* was full of casks and cases. She was, in fact, as full as she could be stowed. The officers were obliged to keep their baggage in the Great Cabin, where they barely had room to hang their cots.

As a result of this report, 33 sick or diseased male prisoners were re-landed. Actually, when she sailed from Yarmouth Roads on July 17, 1791, she seems to have carried 344 male and 58 female convicts, a total of 402 prisoners. It is not clear, however, whether her complement of convicts was reduced from 410 to 402 by additional re-landings or whether eight deaths occurred between embarkation and sailing. Nor can we tell whether the 58 women were crammed into the three cabins originally designed to accommodate 47, or whether another cabin was erected on the gundeck to house the 11 surplus women.

Lieutenant Richard Nairne was appointed naval agent in the *Pitt*, an appointment which the Treasury confirmed on May 20. Presumably he sailed in her, but, oddly enough, he is not mentioned in contemporary Australian documents relating to the *Pitt's* voyage. If he protested against the overcrowding, his protests were ineffective; for had it not been for the anonymous complaint to the Home department no inquiry would have been held and the number of prisoners originally embarked would not have been reduced.[29]

The *Pitt's* passage was protracted, as she did not reach Port Jackson until February 14, 1792, 212 days out from Yarmouth Roads. Smallpox, which presumably had been carried aboard, made its appearance shortly after her departure, and before she touched at St. Jago there had been 15 deaths among the prisoners. It was an unhealthy season for calling at the Cape Verde Islands, but despite this both the sailors and soldiers were allowed ashore. She resumed the voyage about August 20, and in the Doldrums, experienced calms and incessant rain for a month, during which time she made scarcely any headway. The prisoners developed ulcers on their bodies and legs and showed symptoms of scurvy, but otherwise remained comparatively healthy. Among the seamen and military guards, and the families of the latter, however, a malignant fever appeared, and is said to have caused 27 deaths in a fortnight. Her crew was so depleted, indeed, that when the *Pitt* left the calms behind and ran into heavy gales, some of the convicts had to be recruited to help navigate her.

By the time she reached Rio de Janeiro, probably in the middle of October, 13 soldiers, five soldiers' wives and seven seamen had died, although Major Francis Grose, going out in the *Pitt* to assume command of the newly-raised New South Wales Corps, reported from Rio on October 22 that there had been eleven deaths among the seamen. Seven soldiers' and convicts' children had also died. Thus, the death-roll between St. Jago and Rio was at least 32 men, women and children, but not a single prisoner had died. Grose asserted that the mortality was due to defects in the arrangements aboard ship, but the *Pitt's* master, Edward Manning, blamed the call at St. Jago, and the evidence supports his contention.

At Rio the sick were sent to hospital and the convicts landed on an island from which four escaped, although it was believed that they were drowned in the attempt. The serving of fresh provisions and the spell ashore did much to restore the health of all.

The *Pitt* resumed her voyage on November 1, and if Captain William Bligh, then at the Cape with the *Providence* and the *Assistant*, recorded the date of her arrival at Table Bay correctly, she made a very favourable passage of 24 days from Rio to the Cape. Here another prisoner escaped, and when the voyage was resumed sickness again broke out. When she arrived at Port Jackson, 20 male and nine female prisoners had died on the passage, and 120 men were landed sick, many of whom died in the weeks following their landing. Counting deaths among the survivors after disembarkation, the *Pitt's* death-roll was heavy, but the statement that at the end of the year only 29 of her prisoners were still alive is unquestionably a gross exaggeration.[30]

The *Royal Admiral*, a particularly smart and well-kept ship, was larger and roomier than the *Pitt*, but she embarked 62 fewer prisoners. Yet on her arrival Phillip reported that too many convicts had been crowded aboard her. Her master and officers, in conformity with the practice of the East India Company, possessed regulated rights of private trade, and as Collins records that they sold £4,350 worth of goods at Sydney from their private speculations, there seems little doubt that the overcrowding of which Phillip complained arose from the quantity of trade goods they shipped.

The treatment of the prisoners in the *Royal Admiral* was excellent and a marked improvement on that in other transports. Both the master, Essex Henry Bond, a careful and experienced seaman, and the ship's surgeon, John Syme, gave every support and assistance to Richard Alley, the first navy surgeon to be employed as a naval agent. The prison was regularly cleansed and fumigated, and the convicts were well fed and admitted freely to the deck. A conspiracy of some kind—it is not clear if it was a plot to seize the ship—was detected when the *Royal Admiral* had been three weeks at sea but was considered sufficiently punished by giving one prisoner three dozen and seven others two dozen lashes each—comparatively mild punishments for those days.

The *Royal Admiral* made a fast passage of 130 days from Torbay, where she had taken shelter after embarking her last convicts at Portsmouth. Leaving Torbay on May 30, she was 72 days to Simon's Bay, at the Cape, where she anchored at noon on August 10. Sailing again on August 31, she made a splendid passage of 37 days to Port Jackson. That these sturdily-built East Indiamen given the right winds and well handled, could sail smartly is shown by the fact that in the 16 days from September 17 to October 2 inclusive, the *Royal Admiral* logged 3,131 miles. Her best seven days' run was 1,459 miles from September 17 to September 23 inclusive.

Her log records the deaths of eight male and one female convict on the passage, and of a man and a woman after arrival. Official returns, however, assert that ten men and two women died, evidently including another death after arrival. Seventy-two men and 11 women were on the sick-list on the ship's arrival. A convict escaped at the Cape, but as his place was taken by the *Pitt's* escapee, who had been recaptured, the number of prisoners in the *Royal Admiral* remained unaltered.[31]

The *Kitty's* voyage started inauspiciously. She left England in March, 1792, with ten male and 30 female convicts, but sprang a leak and had to put back to Spithead for repairs. While these were being effected, eight of the men escaped, and had not been recaptured when the *Kitty* resumed her voyage. Her passage from Portsmouth on April 6 was marred by continuous bad weather and by frequent disputes between the naval agent, Lieutenant Daniel Woodriff, and the master, George Ramsay. Woodriff, on reaching Port Jackson, reported that Ramsay had deliberately prolonged the passage. At Rio, where the *Kitty*, arriving in a leaky state, had remained five weeks, the master had refused to speed up the work of effecting repairs by hiring men to assist the carpenters to caulk her. She was still defective and leaky when she sailed from Rio on July 31, and some of the bolts in the main wales were loose. In consequence Ramsay was compelled to put into the Cape, where further repairs in a great measure stopped the leak.

Sailing from the Cape on September 10, the *Kitty* made a very leisurely run to Port Jackson. Woodriff claimed that his frequent requests for more sail were ignored, and, indeed, asserted that whenever he demanded that more canvas should be carried, Ramsay's reply was to reduce sail. The master was also alleged to have hove to when the wind was fair, and to have laid to longer than was necessary when there was a moderate blow. The *Kitty* was 69 days out from the Cape, and 231 from England, when, three of the women convicts having died, she reached Port Jackson on November 18.[32]

The statistics of the prisoners in these three transports are as follows:

Vessel	*Embarked*		*Escaped*		*Emb'd Cape*		*Deaths*		*Disembarked*	
	M.	*F.*	*M.*	*F.*	*M.*	*F.*	*M.*	*F.*	*M.*	*F.*
Pitt - - -	352	58	5	0	0	0	20	9	319	49*
Royal Admiral -	299	49	1	0	1	0	10	2	289	47
Kitty - -	10	30	8	0	0	0	0	3	2	27
	661	137	14	0	1	0	30	14	610	123

The table reflects the greater care taken of the convicts. Although the prisoners in the *Pitt* and the *Royal Admiral* were crowded, the number embarked in the three ships fell short by 219 of the total herded into the three Second Fleet transports. Yet the combined tonnage of the latter was less by 425 tons than the combined tonnage of the *Pitt*, the *Royal Admiral* and the *Kitty*. The deaths in the last-named ships totalled 44—223 fewer than in the Second Fleet.

The decline in the mortality rate is strikingly illustrated by the following comparison for the individual convict ships:

* The discrepancy of eight between the total of escaped, deaths and disembarked, and the number embarked, is probably accounted for by prisoners relanded before sailing and after embarkation, or possibly by deaths before sailing, if the logbook is in error in not recording any such deaths.

Year of Arrival:	*Vessel*								
1790	*Neptune* – –	One	death	to	every	3·1	convicts	embarked
1790	*Scarborough* –	,,	,,	,,	,,	3·5	,,	,,
1790	*Surprize* – –	,,	,,	,,	,,	7·1	,,	,,
1791	*Britannia* – –	,,	,,	,,	,,	7·1	,,	,,
1791	*Active* – –	,,	,,	,,	,,	8·3	,,	,,
1791	*Admiral Barrington*	,,	,,	,,	,,	8·3	,,	,,
1791	*Matilda* – –	,,	,,	,,	,,	9·2	,,	,,
1791	*Albemarle* – –	,,	,,	,,	,,	9·4	,,	,,
1792	*Pitt* – – –	,,	,,	,,	,,	11·0	,,	,,
1791	*Atlantic* – –	,,	,,	,,	,,	12·2	,,	,,
1791	*Mary Ann* – –	,,	,,	,,	,,	16·4	,,	,,
1791	*Queen* – –	,,	,,	,,	,,	22·1	,,	,,
1791	*William and Ann*	,,	,,	,,	,,	26·8	,,	,,
1792	*Royal Admiral* –	,,	,,	,,	,,	29·0	,,	,,
1791	*Salamander* – –	,,	,,	,,	,,	32·0	,,	,,

The *Kitty* and H.M.S. *Gorgon* have been omitted because of the small number of prisoners they carried.

The Arrivals in 1793.

Arrival 1793	*Vessel*	*Rig*	*Ton*	*Master*	*Surgeon*
16 Jan.	*Bellona*	Ship	472	Matthew Boyd	Richard Clarke
7 Aug.	*Boddingtons*	Ship	331	Robert Chalmers	Richard Kent
17 Sept.	*Sugar Cane*	Ship	403	Thomas Musgrave	David Wake Bell

Although three vessels—a storeship and two transports—conveyed convicts to Port Jackson in 1793, the number of prisoners despatched was much smaller than in previous years, a mere 320 men and women being landed. In consequence of the calamitous voyage of the Second Fleet, greater precautions were taken to protect the lives and health of the convicts. Each vessel carried a naval surgeon as Agent of Transports; care was taken to avoid overcrowding; the basis of payment was altered, so that five pounds of the *per capita* payment became due only in respect of the prisoners landed at their destination in good health, and the contracts were no longer concluded with Messrs. Camden, Calvert & King. These measures were effective. Of 235 men and 87 women embarked, only one died on the passage, and the prisoners were landed in a very healthy condition.

The *Bellona*, taken up as a storeship, carried 17 women convicts. A comparatively large ship, built at London in 1782, she was heavily overloaded with cargo and, experiencing a boisterous, rainy passage and being very deep in the water, proved very wet. Much of her cargo was damaged, but after a passage of 163 days from Gravesend she landed all 17 prisoners in good health.[33]

The *Boddingtons* and the *Sugar Cane*, which carried Irish convicts, were also Thames-built vessels, launched respectively in 1781 and 1786. The first-named ship was delayed in reaching Cork, and her prisoners, having been cooped up for seven weeks in another vessel awaiting the *Boddingtons'* arrival, were sickly when embarked. The naval surgeon, Richard Kent, and the ship's surgeon, Augustus Jacob Beyer, who had been surgeon of the *Scarborough* in the Second Fleet, restored them to reasonable health, however, before the ship sailed on February 15, 1793. She embarked five men in excess of her appointed complement, and, according to Kent, could not have carried another prisoner. A smaller vessel than the *Sugar Cane* by 72 tons, she carried only five fewer convicts, and on her arrival, Collins thought it worth remarking that every prisoner had a bed to himself. If there was overcrowding, it was not productive of the usual consequences. She ran out to Rio de Janeiro in 54 days, arriving there on April 10, and made the passage from Cork to Port Jackson in 173 days. Only one prisoner, who had been ill when embarked, died on the voyage, and but one man was on the sick-list when she arrived at her destination.

Throughout the *Boddingtons'* voyage there were frequent alarms of mutiny and conspiracy among the convicts and the guard of the New South Wales Corps, but no attempt to seize the ship actually occurred. In the *Sugar Cane*, which sailed on April 12, an informer reported on May 25 that some of the prisoners planned to gain possession of the ship and to kill all the officers, except the surgeon and second mate. He asserted that some prisoners had already freed themselves of their irons, and that several members of the crew and of the guard had agreed to join them. Surgeon Bell acted promptly. That night one prisoner who had been found out of his irons was executed, and next day several others were flogged. These measures put an end to the talk of mutiny.

The *Sugar Cane* made the passage from Cork to Port Jackson in 157 days, running out from Rio in 65. Except for the man executed, there had been no deaths among her prisoners, and on arrival she had scarcely any sick.[34]

Details of the prisoners in these three ships are as follows:

Vessel	*Embarked* *M.*	*Embarked* *F.*	*Deaths* *M.*	*Deaths* *F.*	*Disembarked* *M.*	*Disembarked* *F.*
Bellona	0	17	0	0	0	17
Boddingtons	125	20	1	0	124	20
Sugar Cane	110	50	1*	0	109	50
Totals:	235	87	2	0	233	87

The Arrivals, 1794-1796.

Arrival	*Vessel*	*Rig*	*Ton*	*Master*	*Surgeon*
1794					
10 Mar.	*William*	Ship	305	William Folger	
25 Oct.	*Surprize* (2)	Ship	400	Patrick Campbell	James Thomson
1795					
5 Nov.	*Sovereign*	Ship	362	George Storey	
1796					
11 Feb.	*Marquis Cornwallis*	Ship	654	Michael Hogan	Matthew Austin
30 Apr.	*Indispensable*	Ship	351	Wilkinson	

From 1794, owing to Great Britain's preoccupation with the war against France, the flow of convicts to Port Jackson dwindled to a mere trickle. Eighty-four convicts arrived in 1794, one the following year, and 353 in 1796, a total of 438 for the three years.

The *William* and the *Sovereign*, both storeships, each carried a single privileged prisoner, and, touching at Rio, made uneventful passages of 171 and 165 days respectively. The former carried a female prisoner, and the latter, Joseph Gerrald, one of the Scottish martyrs. The *William* was an old vessel, built in France in 1770, and was owned by Samuel Enderby, the pioneer of South Sea whaling.

The *Surprize* was the same vessel as had made the voyage with the Second Fleet, but whereas she had embarked 256 male convicts in 1790, she carried only 23 men and 60 women when she left England on May 2, 1794. Her surgeon, James Thomson, had been surgeon of the *Atlantic* in 1791, and was going out to New South Wales to take up an appointment as an assistant surgeon on the Colonial Medical Establishment. Touching only at Rio de Janeiro,

* Executed.

the *Surprize* made the passage in 176 days, and landed her prisoners without loss. Her convicts included the Rev. Thomas Fyshe Palmer, Thomas Muir, William Skirving and Maurice Margarot, four of the Scottish Martyrs. On arrival her master, Patrick Campbell, alleged that Palmer and Skirving had plotted to seize the *Surprize* and sail her to France, a charge which the two men, to use Palmer's phrase, heard with "astonishment, indignation and horror". They claimed that Margarot had prompted the accusation and that Campbell had attempted to extort evidence against them by means of promises, bribes, threats and tortures, but their demand for an inquiry was refused.

The *Indispensable*, a French-built ship launched in 1791, carried female prisoners, and, touching at Rio, was about six months on the passage. Two of her 133 prisoners died during the voyage.[35]

The "Marquis Cornwallis" Mutiny.

The convict ship which had the most eventful passage in these years was the *Marquis Cornwallis*. Built in India in 1789, she was owned by Hogan & Co., so that her master, Michael Hogan, was presumably a part-owner. Having embarked 163 men and 70 women, she sailed from Cork on August 9, 1795. Her guard, a detachment of the New South Wales Corps, was commanded by Ensigns John Brabyn and William More, and as with so many other detachments of this corps, proved unreliable and mutinous. When the guard embarked at Portsmouth before the *Marquis Cornwallis* sailed for Cork, the officer who had conducted the detachment from Chatham reported that the men were very mutinous and that the worst among them was Sergeant Ellis. Despite this warning, however, Ensign Brabyn took no special precautions.

On September 9, when the *Marquis Cornwallis* had been a month at sea, her master received a note from the prison that two prisoners wished to see him. He interviewed them next morning. They disclosed that a plot to seize the ship had been formed by the prisoners and some of the soldiers, and named Sergeant Ellis as the ringleader, asserting that he had undertaken to furnish the convicts with knives so that they might rid themselves of their irons.

Hogan, having returned the informers to the prison, asked

Brabyn to inspect the soldiers' kits. The guard's commander then disclosed that at the beginning of the voyage he had issued four knives to Ellis, and that the previous day, as Ellis had claimed to have lost these, he had handed him a further two. All six knives were found when Ellis's baggage was examined. Two days later, on September 12, the gunner overheard Ellis using inflammatory and mutinous language to the other soldiers, particularly the sentinels at the prison door. He had been telling them that they were much worse off than the convicts, since while the latter were being transported for seven years, they were being sent out for life.

Brabyn, however, refused to take any action against Ellis, presumably fearing that if he did so, the whole detachment might mutiny, but had he acted with promptitude and determination the tragedy that followed might have been avoided. In view of his attitude, Hogan could do no more than add a seaman to the two military sentinels at the prison door and to warn his officers and men to be constantly on their guard.

Another prisoner now turned informer. He substantiated the earlier disclosure of a plot between Ellis and the convicts, and added that the women prisoners were to convey knives into the prison and to put pounded glass into the crew's food. Hogan instructed the informer to gain further information regarding the plot, and sent him back to the prison. About this time it was discovered that Ellis had spiked the touchholes of six muskets and had disabled two pistols he had been given to clean by one of the officers, but Brabyn still refused to act.

The prisoners' plan was to seize the master when he was making one of his weekly inspections of the prison. He was accompanied on these visits by some of his officers and by one of the surgeons, either Matthew Austin, who had been appointed by the government, or John Hogan, the ship's doctor. They were to be killed with their own swords. At the same time as the rising in the prison, Ellis and his fellow conspirators among the soldiers were to attack the officers remaining on deck and be ready to serve out arms to the convicts as they ran up from below.

Hogan, however, decided to forestall this plan. He took the opinion of all the officers, and as they supported his decision to immediately punish the conspirators, he gave orders for their apprehension. It is interesting that this action was not instituted by Brabyn, who as commander of the guard was responsible for the security of the prisoners, but, possibly because of inexperience, his conduct throughout was weak and pusillanimous. Forty-two of the male convicts were flogged and six of the women prisoners punished, while Ellis was confined to the poop and his head shaven. He was then handcuffed, thumb-screwed, and leg-bolted to one of his supporters, Private Lawrence Gaffney, and the two men transferred to the prison.

The prisoners, realising that their plans had gone astray, strangled one of the informers on September 22 and, swarming round the fore hatchway, attempted to smash down the barriers and force their way on deck. Hogan and his officers, each armed with a pair of pistols and a cutlass, took up positions at the prison door, fired into the milling prisoners and eventually drove them back. No prisoner was killed outright in the fracas, but several were badly wounded and seven later died of their wounds. Nine days later Ellis, still ironed to Gaffney, also died, possibly having been wounded during the indiscriminate firing.

The prisoners gave no further trouble, and, having called at St. Helena and the Cape, the *Marquis Cornwallis* arrived at Port Jackson on February 11, 1796, after a passage of 186 days from Cork. There had been 11 deaths among her prisoners, including the seven men who had died of gunshot wounds. Surgeon Austin certified that Hogan had paid due attention to the health of both convicts and soldiers, and a magisterial inquiry exonerated him of having employed undue harshness. The magistrates reported that his actions had been justified by the necessity of ensuring the ship's safety and of protecting the lives of those aboard, and added that he had not improperly interfered with the military guard.

The voyage had a curious sequel. Austin charged the master, the ship's surgeon, and the Port Jackson pilot, Henry Hacking, with assault. The circumstances which prompted his action remain unknown, but the court acquitted John Hogan and Hacking. Michael Hogan, however, was convicted and fined fifty pounds.[36]

Details of the prisoners carried by these five transports are as follows:

Vessel	*Embarked*		*Deaths*		*Disembarked*	
	M.	*F.*	*M.*	*F.*	*M.*	*F.*
William – –	0	1	0	0	0	1
Surprize (2) –	23	60	0	0	23	60
Sovereign – –	1	0	0	0	1	0
Marquis Cornwallis	163	70	11	0	152	70
Indispensable –	0	133	0	2	0	131
Totals: –	187	264	11	2	176	262

The Carrying-off of the "Lady Shore".

The first, and only, successful mutiny in a convict ship occurred in 1797, when the *Lady Shore* was seized by her military guard and sailed to a South American port. A ship-rigged vessel of 316 tons, she had been built at Hull in 1793, and previous to being taken up as a convict ship early in 1797 had been chartered by the East India Company. She had left the Cape, homeward bound, in July, 1796, but when only a few miles to the westward had been captured by the French corvette *Le Moineau*. After her cargo had been pillaged, she was released and returned to the Cape, arriving there on July 21. Her master, James Willcocks, who also was her owner or part-owner, claimed that her release had been due to his exertions, and on February 8, 1797, the Court of Directors of the East India Company voted Willcocks and his crew salvage money at the rate of ten per cent. of the net value of the sugar saved in her.[37]

On being chartered as a transport, the *Lady Shore* embarked at Gravesend a detachment of the New South Wales Corps under Ensign William Minchin. When the second mate, Simon Murchison, was showing the guard's commander the soldiers' quarters, Minchin remarked that they would have to look sharp at the soldiers, as some of them were French and Irish deserters. He added that one Frenchman had informed General Fox, the commandant at Chatham Barracks, that if they could not take the *Lady Shore* they would set her on fire; for to Botany Bay they would not go. A French report indicates that some of the Frenchmen had belonged to the crew of *La Bonne Citoyenne*, a corvette which had been dismasted going to the West Indies in Rear-Admiral Sercey's fleet, and taken off Finisterre by some English ships. Delis, the chief helmsman, and Thierry, the second coast-pilot, were two of the prisoners from *La Bonne Citoyenne* placed aboard the *Lady Shore*. The detachment was brought aboard under a heavy guard, and a few days later, despite his warning to Murchison, Minchin issued the men with muskets, bayonets, cartridge-boxes and ammunition, and they took up duty as sentinels in different parts of the ship.

The *Lady Shore* embarked one male and 66 women convicts. The man was the notorious adventurer and swindler, Major Semple, who called himself Major Semple Lisle and who had served, not without distinction, in the British, Russian and Austrian armies. A second male prisoner, Knowles, the pardon-vendor, is also said to have been transported in the *Lady Shore*, but his name does not figure in the indent.

While the ship lay at Portsmouth, the soldiers proved troublesome. On one occasion the non-commissioned officers lined both sides of the quarter-deck, and when ordered forward by Lambert, the first officer, they refused to move, declaring that they had a better right to walk the quarter-deck, or any other part of the ship, than he. Lambert called Minchin, who, from the top of the companion, informed his men they had no right to walk the quarter-deck. Some of them made their way forward, but one, Sergeant Hughs, refused to leave the quarter-deck. Lambert summoned Murchison, and bade the second mate arm himself. Hughs, swearing he would cut a limb off the first man to oppose his walking the quarter-deck, went down the main hatchway to fetch his sword. He was stopped, however, by Major Semple, who, picking up a carpenter's broad axe, bluntly told the sergeant he would split open his head if he lifted a sword or any other weapon against one of the officers. This was language that Hughs understood, and he turned back. When Willcocks returned to his ship that evening he insisted that Hughs should be punished. Minchin at first refused, but after a long argument agreed to order Hughs into irons.

As the soldiers became more mutinous and Minchin seemed unable to control them, Willcocks lodged an official complaint, and Lieutenant-Colonel Francis Grose, who had returned from New South Wales, was sent down to hold an inquiry on the spot. According to Murchison, Grose remained aboard the *Lady Shore* for only a few minutes. In his report, a copy of which was forwarded to Willcocks at Falmouth by the Transport Board, Grose described the master as a passionate, overbearing man and, with strange prescience, suggested that the *Lady Shore* would never reach her destination. It is inexplicable that no action was taken by the War Office. The guard's unreliability must have been obvious to the meanest intelligence. Six of its members had been embarked from the Savoy military prison, having been condemned for various offences to service for life in a New South Wales regiment, and the Irish and French deserters, several of whom could not speak English, had been virtually impressed. Moreover, apart from the fact that there was no need of a military guard in a female transport, the mutinous disposition of the detachment had clearly shown itself at Chatham Barracks in the open threats to capture or fire the ship.[38]

The *Lady Shore* sailed in May, 1797, and at 4 a.m. on August 1, when the ship was four days' sail from Rio de Janeiro, the guard and several of the sailors mutinied. They quickly carried the ship. Instead of at once giving the alarm when he saw the men coming aft, Lambert, the chief mate, ran to his cabin to load his pistols, and was closely pursued by the mutineers. They fired several shots at him through the cabin windows. Lambert answered this fire, killing a Frenchman, Delahay, but the others broke down the cabin door and attacked him with their bayonets. Although wounded in several places, Lambert succeeded in bursting open the door between his cabin and that of the purser, John Black. Under fire from the mutineers, Lambert and Black tried to force the door into the captain's stateroom, but failed, and Lambert was again wounded this time by a shot in the back. Black, however, tore down the canvas screen separating his cabin from the cuddy, and the two men stumbled through the opening, Lambert being again wounded.

At this instant Willcocks, aroused by the shouting and firing, ran from his cabin, but was bayoneted at the cuddy door and fell to the deck. He regained his feet and sprang toward the after hatchway, down which he tumbled. He received another wound in the neck, but a shot which was fired at him missed its mark. Minchin, remaining in his cabin, demanded to know what was the trouble, and in a faint voice Willcocks informed him that the men had seized the ship.

Meanwhile, Lambert had stumbled into the captain's empty cabin, through the windows of which he called to Minchin that the men were murdering the officers. A soldier, following Lambert into the cabin, shot him, and a few minutes later the chief mate died.

Murchison, Gerrard Drummond, the third mate, and Black tried to make their way on deck, but they found four of the mutineers guarding the after hatchway with fixed bayonets. Other soldiers were pointing one of the great guns down the hatchway, and two other guns were being trained toward the round-house.

Major Semple was called in to act as interpreter, and through him Minchin was ordered to surrender his pistols and to call upon those soldiers who had remained loyal to throw down their arms. Willcocks, having struggled into the great cabin, called out for them to give up the ship. Minchin, standing at the cabin door, repeated this order several times, at which the mutineers began cheering. All in the 'tween decks were then informed through Major Semple that if there was any further resistance, a general massacre would take place.

The officers were herded into the Great Cabin, and two sentries mounted at the door, one inside and the other outside. The soldiers who had not participated in the mutiny were kept amidships. Fyfe, the ship's surgeon, attended to the wounded. At first he was hopeful the captain would recover, but in the early hours of August 3 Willcocks died. His body was committed to the sea that morning, the officers being allowed on deck under the watchful eyes of two sentinels carrying cocked pistols. After the ceremony the mutineers were drawn up under arms on either side of the quarterdeck, with the seamen in the centre. Mounting the arms chest, one of the ringleaders then read the regulations which the mutineers had established, and Major Semple translated them. It was announced that Dubois, alias Delis, had been appointed captain with Thomeo, alias Thierry, as his lieutenant, and that the *Lady Shore* was to be sailed to the Rio de la Plata. A promise was made that, as soon as the ship had passed the latitude of Rio de Janeiro, the officers and such of the soldiers as wished to leave the ship would be set adrift in the ship's boats. The seamen were informed that they would receive a gratuity on reaching the Rio de la Plata, but were warned that any found conversing with the officers would be shot, along with the officer concerned.

Documents in French diplomatic archives indicate that the mutiny was carefully planned. Individual mutineers were assigned particular posts—one to guard the hatch leading to the prison, two to prevent the remainder of the guard ascending to the deck, two to take care of the helmsman and the watch on deck, two towards the officers' quarters, two to the captain's cabin, two to secure the officer of the watch, and the twelfth man to break open the ammunition box and start distributing cartridges. The signal for the attack was the cry of "Vive la Republique", and, after Willcocks had been wounded, according to this account, both he and Minchin cried out, "Give up the ship to the French", which ended resistance. One of the mutineers, Le Maillot, an ex-sergeant of the 3rd Regiment of Hussars, who fell out with Delis and Thierry and in a letter of September 24, 1798, charged them with having pillaged the *Lady Shore* for their own profit, claimed that the mutiny had been planned for an earlier night than the morning of August 1, so that the ship might be carried into Bordeaux. He asserted that Thierry's cowardice prevented the attack and that his mistress—presumably one of the convicts—gave warning to the ship's officers next day of what was afoot.

On the evening of August 7, when it was blowing hard from the north-east, the *Lady Shore* was taken aback. Getting sternway, a high sea pooped her. The cabin windows were stove in and the cabin flooded, so that its occupants found themselves up to their knees in water. As the ship appeared to be settling fast by the stern, all was confusion on deck. The alarmed helmsman, not knowing what to do, let go the tiller, which flew wildly from side to side, and a babel of voices called out confusing orders in French, German and English. The mutineers believed the ship was going down, but the officers, with the assistance of two seamen, got up the deadlights before the *Lady Shore's* stern was struck by two heavy seas. The pumps on the upper deck could not be cleared for an hour, and the water was baled out with buckets.

Next day the mutineers compelled the officers to sign documents undertaking not to serve against the French and their allies for a year and a day, and certifying, firstly, that the *Lady Shore* had been surrendered to the mutineers acting in the name of the French Republic, and, secondly, that the surgeon, carpenter, boatswain and seamen had been detained against their inclination in order to navigate the ship. In return the captain, lieutenant and secretary of the mutineers signed a certificate that "Lieutenant-Colonel Grose is, through fraud, force and ill-treatment, together with our purest Republicanism, the material cause of the capture of the vessel the

Lady Shore". The mutineers said the death of Willcocks had been unintentional, and they were sorry for it, but that the killing of Lambert had been determined upon.

During the afternoon of August 14 the longboat was hoisted out and rigged. She was provisioned with three small casks of water and four bags of flour, but the steward contrived to heave into the boat two cheeses, two hams, some pieces of boiled beef, and a keg containing five gallons of rum. After much entreaty, the mutineers handed over a quadrant, but refused to part with a compass, and when the boat was cast off about 6.30 p.m. the officers in it had only a small pocket-compass belonging to Drummond. There were 29 persons—men, women and children—in the boat. Surgeon Fyfe wished to go in her, but the mutineers refused to let him leave the *Lady Shore.*

It was a stormy night, with thunder, lightning and rain, and the sea was rough. Some of the baggage and provisions had to be thrown overboard to lighten the boat and keep her afloat, but at 4 p.m. on August 17, 46 hours after having left the *Lady Shore,* she made Rio Grande, on the coast of Brazil. The boat's occupants were hospitably received, and eventually were found passages to Rio de Janeiro. Major Semple was among them.

After the longboat had been cast off, the *Lady Shore* continued to sail toward the Rio de la Plata. On August 28 she entered Montevideo, where she was at once condemned as a Spanish prize. The mutineers were made prisoners of war, but the convict women were distributed as servants among the Spanish ladies. While the *Lady Shore* lay dismantled at Montevideo, she was reputedly sold for forty thousand dollars. Her subsequent career remains unknown, although in 1801 a newsletter reported that she had been captured and carried into the Cape by H.M.S. *Tremendous.*

Major Semple, who made his way from Brazil to Barbary and entered the Moroccan service, surrendered to the British authorities in 1799. He was returned to England, where, at a later date, he is stated to have been again sentenced to transportation, on this occasion reaching Australia and serving his sentence. The mutineers seem to have received little sympathy from the authorities at Montevideo and existed there in a miserable condition while the French Republic made representations for their return to France. All we know of their fate is that Jean Baptist Prevot, a Frenchman, was executed for the murder of Willcocks, in Execution Dock, London, on December 23, 1799.[39]

The Arrivals, 1797-1800.

Arrival	*Vessel*	*Rig*	*Ton*	*Master*	*Surgeon*
1797					
27 May	*Britannia*	Ship	500	Thomas Dennott	Augustus Jacob Beyer
2 June	*Ganges*	Ship	700	Thomas Patrickson	James Mileham
1798					
18 May	*Barwell*	Ship	796	John Cameron	John Thos. Sharpe
18 July	*Britannia*	Ship	301	Robert Turnbull	
1799					
26 July	*Hillsborough*	Ship	764	William Hingston	John Justice Wm. Kunst
1800					
11 Jan.	*Minerva*	Ship	558	Joseph Salkeld	
16 Feb.	*Friendship*	Ship	430	Hugh Reed	
15 Apr.	*Speedy*	Ship	313	George Quested	
20 Nov.	*Royal Admiral* (2)	Ship	914	William Wilson	Samuel Turner*

Of the vessels which reached Port Jackson between 1797 and 1800, only the *Royal Admiral* was making her second voyage in the convict service. The rest formed a somewhat miscellaneous collection. The *Speedy*, built in the Thames in 1779, and the second *Britannia*, launched at Bridport in 1783, were both whalers belonging to the fleet of Samuel Enderby & Co. Each carried a small number of prisoners, and made uneventful voyages. The *Speedy*, after running out to the Cape in seventy-two days, took a hundred and forty-three days for the passage from England to Port Jackson. The Thames-built *Barwell* was an East Indiaman, built in 1782, and was reputedly a fast sailer. The *Minerva* and the *Ganges* had been built in India, and the first *Britannia* was registered as having been built in East India in 1774. She was the oldest of the nine vessels chartered, having been launched three years before the *Royal Admiral* and five years before the *Speedy*. The newest ship was the *Friendship*. Owned by John and James Mangles, the prominent London shipowners, she had been launched in the Thames in 1793, a year before the building of the *Ganges* in India. Particulars of the

* Died on the voyage.

Hillsborough have not been found, and the only record of the *Minerva* indicates that she was built at Bombay, but the year is not given.

The fastest passage was recorded by the *Minerva*. She was detained in the Thames for many weeks by a dispute between her owner, Robert Charnock, and the East India Company regarding her homeward charter. On her previous voyage, when returning from India with a cargo for the Company, she had gone ashore in Ramsgate harbour through stress of weather. For this reason and because she had been half laden when again proffered to the Company, rendering impracticable the dry-dock survey which the Company's regulations demanded, she had been refused a charter. Charnock, unwilling to accept this decision, induced the Home Secretary, the Duke of Portland, and the Secretary of War and Treasurer of the Navy, Henry Dundas, to bring pressure to bear on the Company. Since the latter feared for its exclusive monopoly of eastern trade, these representations were successful. On July 18 the Court of Directors, lamenting at being obliged to waive its regulations "to conform to the wishes of those right honorable characters", agreed to freight the *Minerva* homeward from India.

On August 6 she sailed for Cork, but was then further detained by the outbreak of the Irish rebellion. To Charnock's disgust, the first convicts were not embarked until February 12, 1799, and the last prisoner not until August 19. The *Minerva* had then received two hundred and six prisoners, of whom nine had been relanded and six had died. She sailed with a hundred and sixty-five male and twenty-six female prisoners. A number of Irish rebels, having been summarily tried by court-martial and sentenced to death, but reprieved on agreeing to leave the country, were shipped, without any legal warrant, in the *Minerva*. They included General Joseph Holt, Father James Harold, the Rev. Henry Fulton, an Episcopalian minister, and two British Army officers, Captains Alcock and St. Leger.

The *Minerva* left Cork with the *Friendship* in a small convoy on August 24, and went out to Port Jackson via Rio in a hundred and forty days. In the early part of the passage she had often to lie to for the sternmost ship of the convoy, which probably was the *Friendship*, to come up, and no sooner had the convoy's commodore, in H.M.S. *Dryad*, turned back on September 14 than the *Minerva's* master, Joseph Salkeld, signalled that she could not keep the *Friendship* company any longer, as the latter sailed so badly. The *Minerva* parted that day, and was alone on October 1, when chased and fired on by two ships flying Portugese colours. Logging three and four knots, however, she soon left them behind.

Anchoring at Rio de Janeiro on October 20, the *Minerva* remained there until November 8th. Like many East Indiamen, she had a good turn of speed, and, favoured by fresh to strong breezes, she sometimes logged eleven or twelve knots for several hours at a time. Her best twenty-four hours' run was two hundred and seventy-two miles on December 23, an abstract of her log for that day reading:

"Fresh breezes and cloudy weather with increasing gales of wind. At 10 p.m. wind shifted to the N.W., with strong gales and hard squalls, with showers of hail and rain, and a very high confused sea. Battened down all the hatchways. At daylight found the starboard lower quarter gallery washed away. The ship rolling deep and shipping much water. At 10 a.m. the sea broke into the jolly-boat on the larboard quarter and broke the boat in two. Continued strong gales and hard squalls, with hail. Lat. 42° 5, S., long. 122° E."

Running down her easting the *Minerva* logged 6,433 miles in thirty-three days, November 29 to December 31 inclusive, an average of almost a hundred and ninety-five miles a day. Her best seven days' run—December 20 to 26 inclusive—was 1,575 miles, and in the sixteen days from the 12 to the 27 she logged 3,468 miles—three hundred and thirty-seven miles more than the *Royal Admiral* in the same period in 1792. The *Minerva's* log for November 29 gives her position as lat. 29·38 S., long. 19·57 E., and for December 31 as lat. 43·18 S., long. 144·24 E. She anchored in Port Jackson on January 11, 1800, sixty-four days out from Rio. Although many of her prisoners had been aboard for six months before sailing, only three had died on the passage[40].

The "Friendship" and the "Ganges."

The *Friendship*, from which the *Minerva* had parted at sea on September 14, arrived at Sydney thirty-six days after the East Indiaman, having buried nineteen of her hundred and thirty-three prisoners—a mortality rate of one death to every seven men embarked. As there were no complaints of harsh treatment, and the survivors were in good health, the high death-rate probably was due to the state in which the convicts had been embarked and the fact that several were aged.

The *Ganges* was one of the first convict ships inspected at Portsmouth by Sir James Fitzpatrick, the Home Department's surgeon-general. He ordered certain structural alterations, and placed aboard ventilators, water purifiers, fumigants and medicines. The *Ganges* embarked 203 men, but her master and part-owner, Thomas Patrickson, asked that her complement should be raised to 300. Fortunately, his request was refused, and as she was a ship of 700 tons, she was not overcrowded when she sailed. Thirteen convicts died on the passage, and many of the survivors were suffering from scurvy on arrival. Her surgeon, James Mileham, who was going out to join the Colonial Medical Establishment, probably was inexperienced in the management of a large body of men at sea, and if another 100 men had been embarked, it seems certain that the death roll in the *Ganges* would have been much heavier[41].

The Hell-ship "Britannia".

As in the Second Fleet transport *Neptune*, the combination of a callous and brutal master and a weak, incompetent surgeon made the voyage of the first *Britannia* one of the worst in the history of transportation. There was one death to every 17 prisoners embarked, 10 men and one woman dying out of 144 men and 44 women; but the convicts were brutally mistreated and the survivors were landed in a wretched and emaciated state. Had she carried English prisoners, the deaths would have been far more numerous, but the ability of Irish convicts to withstand the hardships of the voyage to Australia under the most distressing circumstances was remarkable.

The *Britannia's* master, Thomas Dennott, was a sadist who, in consequence, as Governor Hunter declared, "of some conjecture of mutiny", kept the prisoners confined in irons and flogged them unmercifully. Even the women received three or four dozen cuts from a cane for the most trivial offences.

Dennott's orders to the mate, John Thomas Ricketts, before sailing from Cork on December 10, 1796, left no doubt of his determination to maintain discipline or of the methods by which it was to be enforced. The convicts were never to be admitted to the deck in batches of more than 30 at a time or for longer than two hours at a stretch, and when on deck were always to be chained to the ship's side. Their irons were to be inspected twice daily, and a prisoner found out of his irons was to receive, for a first offence, six dozen lashes, with a right and left cat. Ricketts, not the surgeon, was to judge whether or not a culprit could physically bear such punishment. A convict found in possession of any instrument was to receive four dozen lashes; when found in a berth all the occupants were to be thus punished unless they named the culprit. The prisoners were to be locked up at night and, if Ricketts deemed it necessary, during the day also. Thus, Dennott transferred from the surgeon to the chief mate responsibility for deciding if the convicts should be admitted to the deck.

The surgeon first engaged for the *Britannia* declined at the last moment to sail, and was replaced by Augustus Jacob Beyer. As Beyer previously had been surgeon of the *Scarborough* in the Second Fleet and of the *Boddingtons*, he became the first surgeon to make a third voyage in a convict ship to Australia.

On the discovery of the supposed mutiny, Dennott immediately ordered the most savage punishments. For example, he directed that James Brannon should receive 300 lashes the first day and 500 the second, but it is uncertain whether Brannon received the full 800 lashes. Another man, John Burke, was also flogged twice, while Patrick Garnley was given 400 lashes without Beyer being consulted as to his fitness to bear such excessive punishment, and died next morning. Francis Cox, John Rutlidge, and James Brady each received 300 lashes, and the latter was informed he would be given another 300 next day, but the second flogging was not administered. These punishments, typical of those ordered by Dennott, were by far the most severe ever to be administered in a convict ship during the entire history of transportation to Australia.

Nor did the women escape lightly. Several, after their heads had been shaven, were placed in the neck-yoke or publicly whipped at the bulkhead with a cane, and they were heavily ironed. Dennott personally cut off Jenny Blake's hair and beat her over the face, back and shoulders with a cane, after which he ordered her to be ironed on both legs as well as chained. Her only offence, apparently, was that she had attempted to commit suicide. Mary Cogan, who was mentally deranged and had twice attempted suicide when in Dublin Gaol, took her own life because, it was claimed, Dennott threatened to punish her next morning.

When Brannon was about to receive a second flogging, Dennott observed that the cat did not have sufficient tails to open his skin. The master obtained a piece of horseskin and the boatswain a second, and both were added to the cat and the leather knotted. "Damn your eyes, this will open your carcase," Dennott cried, and ordered the floggers grog before they began their cruel work. On another occasion, when some prisoners were about to be punished, Dennott told them: "I will not hang you; it is too gentle a death, but I will cut you to pieces." In the middle of his flogging, James Brady begged for water, saying he would die if he did not get it, but Dennott told him: "Die and be damned!"

It is not surprising that several prisoners should have died shortly after being flogged. Patrick Garnley died the morning after he had received 400 lashes. Beyer attributed his death to his punishment, although it was stated that he had expressed the opinion at the time that Garnley had died of thirst. Another convict, Stapleton, lived three or four days after he had been flogged, and James Brannon, although flogged on successive days, lingered longer. When he was let down after having been flogged, Patrick Garodby lay in the prison on his back, handcuffed to another prisoner, calling out for water or an orange. A fellow convict gave him some wine during the night, but he died at seven o'clock next morning. Many of the convicts were crying out for water, but none was sent down to them until Garodby's death. Naturally there was a scramble when a bucket containing seven or eight gallons was taken into the prison, and the master despatched the third mate, Isaac Frome, accompanied by two of the crew, to find out what the noise was about. Dennott ordered Frome to knock down any convict he found out of his berth, and the third mate struck a man named Connor across the loins as he was stooping to get a drink. Connor, who was one of those who had been flogged, died the following morning.

Beyer, ignored and intimidated by Dennott, lacked the moral courage to oppose the master. He did not always attend when punishments were inflicted, apparently because Dennott did not order him to be present and he did not consider it his duty to attend. The commander of the guard, Lieutenant William Burn, of the New South Wales Corps, remonstrated with Dennott for placing a woman convict, who bore a good reputation, in the neck-yoke for two hours, but was curtly told by the master that he had no right to interfere with the convicts, and after this rebuff Burn seems to have made no further protest regarding the brutality with which the prisoners were treated.

The surgeon shamefully neglected his duties throughout the passage. Afraid of the convicts and fearful that they would cut his throat, he always carried a stick and seldom descended into the prison. It was alleged, indeed, that during a period of nine weeks he made only three or four visits. Convicts in need of medical treatment had to be brought to him on deck, but many were so afraid of him, or of his methods of treatment, that they refused to consult him. One sailor asserted that he was asked by convicts who had been flogged to procure plasters for their lacerated backs, but when he approached Beyer the latter refused the requests. When the women asked for medicines, Beyer was said to have simply damned them, and it was claimed that he had misapplied the wine and other comforts supplied for the sick.

Neglect of his duties, however, was not the only charge brought against Beyer. The chief mate asserted that the surgeon had beaten some of the women, and the boatswain declared that when John Burke received his second flogging, Dennott had expressed the opinion that he was not able to bear it, but that Beyer had said he was. As he was being flogged, Burke called to the doctor to let him down. "You be damned, you——!" Beyer was alleged to have cried. "You are yet able to bear it." Burke said that when Dennott had ordered him to be untied, Beyer had directed that he should be given another eight lashes.

Governor Hunter ordered an inquiry after the *Britannia's* arrival at Port Jackson, and two charges were preferred against Dennott. Firstly, he was accused of having caused the deaths of six convicts by the severity of the punishments he had ordered, and secondly, he was charged that his general conduct had not been conducive to the carrying out of the government's intention that the prisoners should be conveyed to Sydney in health and safety.

Beyer, called as a witness, told the court that in only two

instances had he been consulted regarding the punishments. He admitted that he had not interfered with the floggings or advised the master that the convicts under punishment were not able to bear further punishment, but explained that, as his frequent reports to Dennott had been ignored, he regarded himself as being under restraint. He gave it as his opinion that Garnley and some of the other prisoners had died in consequence of their floggings.

On the question of the general treatment of the convicts, the evidence disclosed that the *Britannia* had been very leaky. When he had inspected her, Sir John Fitzpatrick had stated that some improvement in the prisoners' accommodation was absolutely necessary. These alterations were not made while the ship was at Portsmouth, and Sir John had urged that they should not be omitted at Cork. It is improbable, however, that they were carried out, and as a result a great deal of water entered the prison during the passage. At first some effort was made to dry out the convicts' quarters, but later, presumably because of the discovery of the suspected mutiny, these measures were neglected. The second mate, however, claimed that they were discontinued because no swabs were left. Whatever the correct explanation for the neglect, the fact remains that several beds were destroyed and the convicts to whom they had belonged were compelled to sit up at night, while, from want of brooms and swabs, the prison became extremely filthy.

Isaac Frome claimed that the prisoners had frequently complained of the badness of their bread and the smallness of their allowance of wheat. He told the court that Dennott had embezzled government stores, and that at Rio de Janeiro many water-casks had been broken up so that Dennott's private trade goods might be stowed aboard. It is likely enough that the provisions were short-served, but as the third mate had quarrelled with Dennott his evidence has to be treated with caution.

The court was unanimous that Dennott's punishment of the convicts had been imprudent and ill-judged by reason of his failure to individually consult the other officers, and that his conduct had bordered on too great a degree of severity. It held that Beyer, beyond all other bystanders, was particularly culpable in not steadfastly protesting against the cruelties with which he charged Dennott, and that the surgeon therefore had been inexcusably negligent and indifferent in the performance of his duty to such an extent that, in an eminent degree, he was accessory to the master's inhumanity. The court's verdict was, to put it mildly, inexcusably lenient. Dennott's guilt was clear and obvious, and there was no excuse for the severe punishments he had ordered. He should have been convicted of manslaughter, if not of murder. As for Beyer, he had failed completely in the discharge of his duty and had utterly disgraced the profession of which he was a member.

To the everlasting shame of the British authorities, neither Dennott nor Beyer were punished, except that they were not again employed in the convict service. Governor Hunter sent a transcript of the court proceedings to England, but, as in other instances of a similar nature, no prosecutions were instituted. Admittedly the legal difficulties were great. Proceedings could not be taken in Australia, and for a prosecution to be launched in England it would have been necessary for the witnesses to be sent home, but these difficulties were not insurmountable. Indeed, if the British Government had really wished to punish such men as Dennott and Beyer, it could have set up a competent court in Australia by Act of Parliament.[42]

The Plot on the "Barwell".

The *Barwell*, having embarked 296 prisoners, sailed from Portsmouth on November 7, 1797, and although detained for a fortnight by calms and adverse winds, ran out to the Cape in 74 days. She was detained there until March 19 because her officers, fearing they would not find a profitable market at Port Jackson, desired to dispose of their European trade goods, and she did not reach Sydney until May 18, 1798, 192 days out from England and 60 from the Cape.

Soon after leaving the Cape a plot was allegedly hatched between the convicts and the soldiers to combine to seize the ship. Ensign George Bond, of the New South Wales Corps, was named as one of the ringleaders, and the *Barwell's* master, John Cameron, having consulted the ship's officers and Ensign Bayly, Bond's superior officer, ordered Bond to be confined in irons. Several of the soldiers of the detachment were also thrown into irons, and at least one received three dozen lashes. Many of the convicts were flogged, one or two being given eight dozen lashes as principal ringleaders, but the majority being given three dozen. In all, about a score were punished for having their irons off or as being implicated in the alleged mutiny. This was, apparently, the second conspiracy in the *Barwell*. Although the ship's log is silent on the matter, a private letter written from the Cape by Richard Dore, who was proceeding to Sydney to take up his appointment as judge-advocate, states that on the passage to the Cape 25 prisoners had planned to seize the cuddy arms while the sailors were aloft and murder the officers. The plot was disclosed by an informer the night before the attempt was to be made, and next morning, as the convicts reached the deck, the conspirators were seized, double-ironed and chained together.

When the *Barwell* reached Sydney, Ensign Bayly charged Bond with drunkenness and other offences, but the commanding officer of the New South Wales Corps, Major Foveaux, supported, apparently by his officers, represented to Governor Hunter that Bond should be permitted to resign his commission rather than face a court-martial, and to this course Hunter agreed. On reflection, however, he regretted his too ready acquiescence to this request. "Coming here thus degraded (i.e. under arrest) and charged with offences of so serious a description," wrote the governor in a despatch of September 12, 1798, "I may have reason to regret that I listened to Major Foveaux's interposition in behalf of a man whom I am sorry to say has not answered my expectations." In acknowledging this despatch, the Duke of Portland bluntly declared that Bond's resignation "should not have been accepted, as it was evidently given in with a view to defeat his being tried by a court-martial".

While the authorities were prepared to hush up Bond's actions, Captain Cameron was not. The court-martial for the ensign's trial had been summoned to meet on June 7, but this order was cancelled when Bond resigned. Cameron soon learnt that he had been liberated, and on the 11th swore an information before Judge Advocate Richard Dore in which he stated that "he hath good and sufficient grounds from the testimony of various persons to believe that the said George Bond was not only an accessory to but the principal ringleader and projector of the dreadful conspiracy" to seize the *Barwell* and, having murdered her officers, to carry her to Mauritius. He, therefore, prayed the governor to bring Bond to justice.

As a result of Cameron's insistence a Vice-Admiralty Court was assembled for the first time in the colony's history. Its members were drawn, of course, from the naval and military officers at the settlement, and there is little doubt that they had determined in advance to acquit the prisoners. Five privates were first arraigned, but one was promptly discharged on a legal technicality, the indictment being found defective because it wrongly recorded his Christian name. The case against the remaining four was weak, since it rested principally on the testimony of convicts, and they were acquitted.

Bond's trial followed, apparently on a private prosecution launched by Cameron. The *Barwell's* master, however, expected an acquittal, as he made clear in his address to the court. Bond was charged that "with force and arms upon the high seas . . . he piratically and feloniously did endeavour to stir up, excite and make . . . a revolt and mutiny" in the *Barwell.* The principal witness was the ship's surgeon, John Thomas Sharpe, but, as in the earlier cases, the evidence was weak and unconvincing and Bond was acquitted without being called upon for his defence. He later announced his intention of bringing a civil suit against Cameron for false imprisonment, and estimated the damage he had suffered at £10,000, but did not proceed with the action.

The full story of what transpired in the *Barwell* was never told, but whether or not Bond was implicated in a plot to take the ship, his conduct was in some way reprehensible. This seems evident, but the military coterie at the infant settlement succeeded in hushing up the affair.[43]

The Fever Ship "Hillsborough."

From the point of view of the number of deaths on the passage, the most disastrous voyage was that of the *Hillsborough.* Typhoid, carried aboard by convicts from the fever-ridden hulks at Langstone Harbour, Portsmouth, caused the deaths of 95 of the 300 prisoners embarked, and several others died shortly after their arrival at Sydney.

The *Hillsborough* was a large and roomy ship, and, according to the Transport Commissioners, had been fitted out on an improved plan, the bars of the prison being built far apart to admit the air more freely. She embarked 152 prisoners at Gravesend, and when she arrived at the Motherbank on November 17, 1798, her master William Hingston, reported to the Transport Board's agent at

Portsmouth, Captain Charles Patton, that one convict had died and several others were sick. Sir John Fitzpatrick, who had inspected the ship in the Thames, ordered the sick to be transferred to a hospital ship, and urged most strongly that the ship's complement of convicts should not be made up from the prisoners in the Langstone Harbour hulks, aboard which the gaol fever, or typhoid, had raged in a malignant form for some time. His advice was disregarded, as were his further protests after the Langstone convicts had been embarked. He insisted, however, that five prisoners, all in an advanced stage of the disease, should be disembarked, and all five died within a few days.

The *Hillsborough* sailed in a convoy from Portland Roads on December 23, and at once ran into heavy weather. As her decks required caulking, and the sea was breaking over her continuously, the convicts' quarters were deluged and their bedding soaked. When the weather moderated a few days later, a youthful informer told the captain that many of the convicts were out of their irons and intended to murder the officers. Those found out of their irons were flogged, receiving from one to six dozen lashes each, and were shackled and handcuffed, some with iron collars round their neck. Their allowance of rations and water was also reduced, so that for several days the prisoners were half starved.

In all the circumstances it is not surprising that the disease carried aboard by the Langstone convicts spread rapidly, and from the beginning of January deaths became alarmingly frequent. Yet the convicts were kept closely confined and double-ironed, were short of water, and were half starved. "It was, one would think," wrote William Noah, a convict who left a moving account of the prisoners' sufferings in his diary of the voyage, "enough to soften the heart of the most inhuman being to see us ironed, handcuffed and shackled in a dark, nasty, dismal deck, without the least wholesome air, but all this did not penetrate the breasts of our inhuman captain, and I can assure you that the doctor was keep at such a distance, and so strict was he look after, that I have known him sit up till opportunity would suit to steal a little water to quench the thirst of those who were bad, he being on a very small allowance for them."

According to Noah, thirty convicts had died when the *Hillsborough* anchored in Table Bay on April 13. There were then about

100 prisoners very ill, and although fresh provisions were served, deaths became so frequent that the authorities were alarmed, and the ship was ordered to move to False Bay. Noah alleges that to avoid further interrogation, the master buried some of the convicts at the harbour entrance, but within a few days the bodies were washed ashore. On May 5, by which time at least 28 convicts had died since the ship's arrival at Table Bay, the surgeon, J. J. W. Kunst, returned from Capetown with an order permitting the sick to be landed. Why this step was so long delayed is incomprehensible but it was useless because no provision was made for the proper accommodation of the patients ashore. When 146 were landed on May 6 they found that their miserable hospital had previously been a stables and was without a fireplace, windows and lavatory accommodation, and next morning 56 of the prisoners were returned to the ship. When the *Hillsborough* sailed on May 29 at least 50 of the convicts had been buried at the Cape.

Governor Hunter, when the *Hillsborough* reached Sydney, described the survivors as "the most wretched and miserable convicts I have ever beheld, in the most sickly and wretched state". Almost every prisoner required hospital treatment. The frightful mortality was due primarily to the embarkation of the Langstone prisoners, but also partly to the harsh treatment of the convicts on the voyage. Noah's diary proves that they were kept double-ironed, and when on deck were chained together, so that they could not walk about at all, but had either to stand up or lie down on the deck. They were inadequately fed, and, especially between the Cape and Port Jackson, the weather was so stormy that the prison was continuously damp and the convicts' bedding seldom dry.[44]

Fever on the "Royal Admiral".

The gaol fever was also carried aboard the *Royal Admiral*, which sailed from England on May 23, 1800, but it raged less malignantly. She had embarked 300 convicts, 48 fewer than on her previous voyage, when Philip had considered her overcrowded, and 43 of her prisoners died on the passage. The *Royal Admiral* also carried 11 missionaries, having been chartered to convey them, after delivering her convicts, to the South Sea Islands. The surgeon was Samuel Turner, who previously had been surgeon of the missionary ship *Duff*, but he became ill of the fever and died on June 2.

On June 23 a reported plot to seize the ship threw the missionaries into something very like a panic. Dividing themselves into watches, they stood guard in the steerage from 8 p.m. until 7 a.m. each night. But no rising took place.

Four strange sail were sighted on August 4. The *Royal Admiral's* decks were cleared for action as she made all sail, and about five o'clock the boom of gunfire could be heard—a novelty, though doubtless an unpleasant one, for the convicts crowded in the stifling prison. The commodore of the convoy, Captain Rowley Bulteel, in the *Belliqueux*, 64, and the East Indiaman *Dorsetshire* compelled the French 40-gun frigate *La Concorde* to strike, while after a running fight lasting several hours another French frigate, the *Médée*, 36, surrendered to the East Indiamen *Bombay Castle* and *Exeter*. Next day fifty-nine prisoners from *La Concorde* were transferred to the *Royal Admiral*, and were soon complaining that the convicts had robbed them.

On August 12 the *Royal Admiral* arrived at Rio de Janeiro, after a passage of 81 days from England. Twenty-three convicts had died, and there were a further five deaths by August 25. In addition to Surgeon Turner, four seamen, a convict's wife and a convict's child had also died, bringing the total death-roll to 35 persons. The *Royal Admiral* did not sail from Rio until September 15, and when she reached Port Jackson on November 20, after a passage from England of 181 days, the deaths among the prisoners had risen to 43. Almost all the survivors required medical treatment. The state in which the convicts had been embarked alone had been responsible for the large number of deaths and the great amount of sickness. On March 10, 1801, Governor King reported that the prisoners were still very weak, and later still, on October 30, 1802, he declared that many remained in a state of debility and would never recover the strength of men.[45]

From the sailing of the First Fleet in 1787 until the end of 1800, 43 convict ships, including the wrecked *Guardian* and pirated *Lady Shore*, had sailed from England or Ireland for Port Jackson. Between them they embarked 7,486 prisoners—6,040 men and 1,441 women—of whom 705 men and 51 women died, a total of 756 deaths. The number landed at Port Jackson was 6,634, of whom 5,304 were men and 1,330 women. Thus, in this period one man died out of every 8·57 convicts embarked and one woman out of every 28·2 female prisoners put aboard in England or Ireland.

Statistics for the prisoners in these vessels are as follows:

Vessel	*Embarked*		*Deaths*		*Disembarked*	
	M.	*F.*	*M.*	*F.*	*M.*	*F.*
Britannia (1797)	144	44	10	1	134	43
Ganges – –	203	0	13	0	190	0
Barwell – –	296	0	9	0	287	0
Britannia (1798)	0	96	0	2	0	94
Hillsborough (1799)	300	0	95	0	205	0
Minerva (1800) –	165	26	3	0	162	26
Friendship –	133	0	19	0	114	0
Speedy – –	0	53	0	3	0	50
Royal Admiral (2)	300	0	43	0	257	0
Totals: –	1541	219	192	6	1349	213

CHAPTER NINE

THE VOYAGES, 1801-1820

AFTER 1800 the vessels employed as convict ships were of only slightly larger tonnage than those previously chartered. The Transport Board, as its secretary, Alexander Macleay, informed the Select Committee on Transportation in 1812, preferred to charter large vessels and engaged them even though they cost more. But the number of large vessels tendered was disappointingly small. No merchantman of a thousand tons or over was taken up, the largest being the *General Hewart*, of 973 tons, and comparatively few of those chartered exceeded a burthen of 600 tons.[1]

Perhaps it would be more accurate to say that between 1801 and 1820 fewer small vessels were hired, and that the majority of the convict transports were of moderate tonnage. The number under 400 tons was relatively few, while after 1815 vessels of a greater burthen than 600 tons seldom carried convicts to Australia. During the last four years of this period most convict ships belonged to the 400 to 550 tons category.

The *Surrey*, or, as her name was generally spelt, the *Surry*, was a typical convict ship of the period. She had such a long career, principally in the convict service but also as a trader, that she became one of the best-known vessels to visit Australia, being familiarly known, in later years, as the old *Surrey*. By then, of course, she had been so extensively rebuilt as to be almost a new vessel. She paid Port Jackson her first visit as a convict ship in 1814, and she was still voyaging to Australia with prisoners in the 1830's.

Built at Harwich in 1811, she was owned by the well-known London firm of Mangles. She was a fully square-rigged ship of 443 72/94 tons, with an overall length of 117 ft. 6 ins. and a breadth above the wales of 29 ft. 6 ins. Her draught when loaded was 18 ft., but when carrying prisoners and stores in 1816 she drew 16 ft. 3 ins. forward and 17 ft. 2 ins. aft, being down by the stern eleven inches.

She was copper-sheathed, and had quarter galleries, with a Minerva bust for a figurehead. As originally built, the *Surrey* had two decks with a height between decks of 5 ft. 8 ins., but was rebuilt about 1818 and from the following year is shown in the registers as having three decks. She rated for many years as a first-class ship built of first-class materials.

Probably half the convict ships to reach Australia between 1801 and 1820 were of the first class. An overwhelming majority were two-deckers, but about a score had three decks and possibly half-a-dozen a single deck with beams.[2]

The Armament of Convict Ships.

From the outset, of course, all the convict ships had been armed, but, except for the East Indiamen, the number and calibre of the guns each carried had depended upon the judgment of the owners rather than the size of the vessel. Perhaps, also, the future employment of the ship was a determining factor: presumably she would be more heavily armed if she were to sail in waters likely to be infested with pirates or did not expect to return to England in convoy.

The *General Hewart*, with a crew of eighty men, was armed with 14 guns, the same number as carried by the *Surrey*, a vessel of half her tonnage and manned by but thirty men. The *Earl Spencer*, whose burthen was 300 tons less than that of the *General Hewart*, and whose crew numbered 56, had 16 guns, while the *Marquess of Wellington*, a ship of comparable tonnage, mounted but 12. Moreover, the number of guns carried varied from voyage to voyage. The *Canada*, of 403 tons, was armed with eight, 10 and 12 guns respectively on three successive voyages. The tiny, 146-ton *Experiment*, with a crew of 12 men, mounted eight guns, but the *Francis and Eliza*, a vessel of almost thrice her tonnage and a crew twice as strong, carried only four guns.

There is little information until the 1820's about the type and calibre of the guns mounted. Only the largest, best-manned vessels, notably the East Indiamen, were capable of putting up any sort of resistance against a small enemy man-of-war or a heavily-gunned privateer. Because of the space occupied by the prisoners' quarters, the guns were almost certainly carried only on the upper deck. The East Indiamen mainly mounted eight-feet long 18-pounders, although their armament may also have included a few

24-pounder guns and 32-pounder carronades. The carronade was a short range weapon, unsatisfactory except in close action. The smaller convict ships did not often mount heavier weapons than 12-pounder carronades and 6-pounder long guns, which seem to have been the most popular weapons, but a proportion of their armament was probably of still smaller calibre.

To carry the story of armament beyond the period with which we are immediately dealing, the end of the Napoleonic wars led to a considerable reduction in the number of guns carried, and in the 1820's it was unusual for a ship to carry more than four guns. Protection was required only against pirates and hostile natives, and to intimidate the convicts against mutiny.

Of 83 convict ships employed between 1823 and 1830 for which it has been possible to compile records, and it should be remembered that there is some duplication of individual vessels in this total as several were chartered for more than one voyage, only 13 carried six guns, whereas 29 mounted four guns and 38 but two. Of the remaining three vessels, one carried five guns and two were armed with three guns.[3]

The nature of their armament may be seen from the following table:

	Carronades						*Long Guns*				*Mixed*			
No. Guns	18	18 & 12	12	12 & 9	9	6	9	9 & 6	6	6 & 4	18*C* 9*L*	12*C* 9*L*	12*C* 6*L*	*Total Ships*
Six	2	1	5	1					2		1		1	13
Five									1					1
Four	4		14		2		1	1	3	1		2	1	29
Three			1				1							2
Two	2		14		2	2	2		16					38
Totals	8	1	34	1	4	2	4	1	22	1	1	2	2	83

C=Carronades. *L*=Long guns.

The Routes of the Convict Ships.

The choice of a convict ship's route was left, apparently, to the owners and the master, but, of course, during the war years it was influenced by that of the convoy in which she sailed. Almost invariably the convict ships accompanied large convoys of West or East Indiamen, or were escorted through the danger zone by British warships bound for the Spanish coast or the Mediterranean. The

Transport Commissioners issued directions as to the convoy which the convict transport was to join, but gave no further orders in respect of her route, and merely stipulated that she should proceed to her destination without unnecessary delay.

At first the circuitous route pioneered by the First Fleet was followed, calls being made at Teneriffe, Rio de Janeiro and the Cape. The *Lady Juliana*, on her leisurely 309 days' passage, touched at St. Jago as well. Later, however, some masters eliminated the call at either Rio or the Cape. Those who elected to call only at the first-named port sailed direct to Port Jackson from South America, working their way down to the latitude of the Cape of Good Hope and then running down their easting in the same way as those vessels which had called at the Cape.

From 1800 onwards there was a wider choice of routes and ports of call, dictated, to some extent at least, by the routes of the outward-bound convoys. An increasing number of convict ships made the passage direct without touching anywhere *en route*, although, owing to the unsatisfactory nature of Thames water later ships often called briefly at Teneriffe to complete their fresh water. Other masters who called at one port only might choose to touch at Maderia, Rio de Janeiro, the Cape of Good Hope or, occasionally, St. Helena in preference to Teneriffe. After 1818 few ships followed the First Fleet's example by calling at Teneriffe, Rio and the Cape.

The reasons underlying these changes are not difficult to understand. Until the turn of the century provisions and stores had to be shipped to the colony in substantial quantities, since it had not yet become self-dependent, and, although storeships were chartered, a great deal of the necessary food was despatched in the convict ships. The usual practice was for them to carry sufficient provisions to victual the prisoners for the voyage and for nine months thereafter. This meant that the ships were so fully loaded that they could carry sufficient wood and water for a passage of only 60 or 70 days, and the convicts were so crowded together that it was desirable, if not essential, in the interests of their health that they should be given some period of recuperation at a port of call during the voyage.

As the colony became self-sufficient, and as traders began voyaging to Port Jackson in increasing numbers, it became unnecessary for the convict ships to ship a larger quantity of provisions than would be required for the voyage, and there was also a reduction in the quantity of stores, such as tools and agricultural implements, shipped for the settlement's use by these ships. This enabled larger quantities of wood and water to be stowed, and enabled some, if not all, ports of call to be eliminated.

Naturally, there was a reduction in the length of the passage to Australia. Between 1801 and 1811 few passages of under 155 days were recorded, but after 1812 many convict ships went out to Australia in under 150 days, and between 1818 and 1820 passages of under 130 days became comparatively common. Even vessels which called at one or two ports *en route* frequently made a passage of under 140 days from England or Ireland to Port Jackson, indicating that the length of stay in foreign ports was being reduced.

Some surgeons considered that direct voyages increased sickness among the convicts, particularly causing scurvy, and advocated that ships should call at one port *en route* at least. David Reid, surgeon of the *Baring* in 1819, recommended that unless the passage from England to the southern tropic was quick, a ship should touch at Rio, "which is preferable to the Cape for refreshment, as vegetables and fruit are plentiful and very cheap". Other surgeons preferred the Cape, not only because after its capture from the Dutch it was a British possession, but also because it gave the convicts some respite and fresh food before they were subjected to the cold and boisterousness of the high southern latitudes. Samuel Sinclair, surgeon of the *Mary* in 1831, considered the voyage too long for convict ships to go direct and thought that in the interests of the convicts' health they should call at the Cape or Rio. "This is opposed by shipowners and masters," he wrote, "on account of the expense and delay (self-interest and gain, of course, being their ruling maxim)." He admitted the surgeon had the right of decision, but considered he rarely used it except in extreme cases of distress, "scarcely if ever as a precautionary measure"[4].

Since the voyages of many of the convict ships were now uneventful, details of the vessels and the statistics for their prisoners are summarised in the appendices, and the text is confined to those voyages which, for one reason or another, possess more than average interest.

The Mutiny on the "Anne".

The first convict ship to reach Port Jackson in 1801 was the *Anne.* A foreign-built ship, presumably French or, more probably, Spanish, she was taken prize by the *Dover* and the *Cecilia* in circumstances which have now been forgotten, and originally had been named *Luz St. Ann* or *Luz St. Anna.* She was licensed at London on April 9, 1799, and when chartered for the convict service was taken up under her original name. The missionary diarist of the *Royal Admiral,* which was still at Rio when the *Luz St. Anna* arrived there, refers to her as the *St. Ann*, but official shipping returns for Port Jackson and the lists of her prisoners compiled after her arrival style her the *Anne.* She was a vessel of 384 tons and 12 guns, and, commanded by James Stewart, was manned by 42 men, additional seamen having been engaged by the contractors to guard the prisoners as the War Office had been unable to spare a military detachment for her[5].

Although taken up in March, 1799, the *Anne* did not sail from Cork, where she embarked male and female prisoners, until June 26, 1800. After her arrival at Port Jackson, Governor King, a man of strong prejudices, described her convicts as "the most desperate and diabolical characters that could be selected"—a statement which may have been applicable to a small minority of the prisoners, but certainly was an exaggeration so far as the majority were concerned.

The *Anne* joined a convoy as far as the Canary Islands, but on July 29, when about three weeks' sail from Rio de Janeiro, she was alone, with no sail in sight. Stewart, accompanied by the mate and the gunner, was below, supervising the fumigation of the prison. It was the moment for which the convicts had been waiting. As the smoke began to rise from the first explosion of gunpowder, a prisoner, with a loud cry of "Death or Liberty", seized Stewart by the throat, and his comrades milled round the three officers, desperately seeking to gain possession of their arms. The sounds of the scrimmage penetrated to the deck, and thirty prisoners at exercise rushed the sentinels, some of them drawing iron bars which they had concealed on their persons. One guard, a negro, was knocked over and his cutlass seized, but the *Anne's* well-disciplined crew responded instantly to the threat of danger. The seamen armed themselves and, led by the other officers, vigorously attacked the convicts, who were hampered by their clanking irons. The fight was fierce but short, the prisoners on deck being overpowered before their companions below could reinforce them.

Meanwhile, the three officers in the prison succeeded in breaking loose from their would-be captors, and, aided by two prisoners, reached the deck. They were bruised, but otherwise unhurt. The mutiny, although planned with skill and, for once, not prematurely disclosed by an informer, had failed. Within a few minutes order had been restored and the convicts locked up in the prison. One prisoner had been shot dead.

Stewart summoned a meeting of the officers, and it was decided that a ringleader in the rising should be at once executed. The choice fell on Marcus Sheehy, who had led the attack on the officers in the prison. Participants in previous convict ship mutinies, when adjudged to death, had been hanged at the yard's arm, but Sheehy, in the presence of all the prisoners, was executed by being shot to death by a firing squad. He has the dubious distinction of being the only prisoner thus executed in a convict ship. The leader of the deck rising, Christopher Grogan, received a flogging of 250 lashes. According to the *Royal Admiral's* diarist, three prisoners, besides the man shot dead, had been wounded during the short-lived fight, one of them dangerously, but there were no casualties, apparently, among the seamen[6].

The *Anne* made a passage of 58 days from Cork to Rio, where she arrived on August 23. Before resuming her voyage she embarked for the Cape six seamen from a British warship, two of whom were described as being "daring, mutinous and infamous". The wisdom of placing these men in a convict ship in which a mutiny had just been suppressed, and aboard which there was no military guard, was questionable, but the prisoners had learnt their lesson, and if the six seamen tried to incite the convicts to further mutiny, they failed. However, the Cape authorities refused to permit the two seamen mentioned to be landed with their fellows and they were carried on to Port Jackson, where they were deemed too incorrigible even for admittance to the ranks of the infamous New South Wales Corps.

The *Anne's* passage from Cork to Port Jackson occupied 240 days. She made a faster passage to Rio than the *Royal Admiral*—58 days as against 81—but took 59 days longer for the entire voyage.

She does not appear to have been detained unduly at the Cape, so it would seem that after leaving Rio she encountered exceptionally adverse weather. As an interesting sidelight on the laxity of the Irish authorities, her indent papers, the official record of the prisoners' sentences which determined the dates of their release, were not forwarded to New South Wales until 1819—almost 19 years after the ship and her convicts had arrived![7]

The "Coromandel's" Fast Passage.

Of the five convict ships to reach Port Jackson in 1802, the *Coromandel* and the *Perseus*, both owned by Reeve & Green, sailed from England in company on February 12, 1802. The former, a teak-built ship of 522 tons, built in India in 1793, made much the faster passage. She was the first convict ship to make a direct passage, and took only 121 days. This was six days shorter than the previous record passage via the Cape of the *Matilda* in 1791. The older and smaller *Perseus*—she was of 364 tons and had been built at Stockton in 1789—was incapable of making a direct passage, and was 173 days out when she reached Port Jackson, having touched at both Rio and the Cape *en route*.

Although her direct passage denied her convicts fresh provisions on the voyage, their health did not suffer in consequence, and the *Coromandel* lost only one man. Her surgeon, Charles Throsby, was one of the first surgeons of the convict ships to become a permanent settler in Australia. He secured an appointment as a colonial surgeon four months after his arrival, and later became a magistrate and prominent landowner, achieving some distinction for his work of exploration[8].

The Bloodshed on the "Hercules".

The *Hercules* and the *Atlas*, two square-rigged two-deckers of just over 400 tons, were taken up together and sailed in company from Cork on November 29, 1801, but soon separated. Built at Shields that year, each probably was making its maiden voyage.

By December 29 the *Hercules* was in the vicinity of the Cape Verdes. A fortnight or three weeks earlier an informer had disclosed to her master, Luckyn Betts, that a plot to seize the ship was afoot. However, the convicts gave no trouble, and as the voyage continued peacefully and uneventfully, with no hint of a brewing storm, his story was dismissed as having been concocted in the hope of gaining indulgences.

Shortly after half past two on the afternoon of December 29 luncheon was drawing to a close in the cabin. Betts was dining with his chief mate, Aiken, the commander of the guard, Captain Ralph Wilson of the New South Wales Corps, the purser, John Carr, the surgeon, J. J. W. Kunst, and two women passengers, presumably the wives of the military officers aboard. On the quarter-deck two sentinels, seeking what shelter they could from the sun, kept a lazy eye on the convicts at exercise. With the exception of the mate whose watch it was and the helmsman, the rest of the soldiers and seamen were below.

Suddenly the attention of the cabin occupants was attracted by shrill cries from the female prisoners in the roundhouse and the noise of shuffling feet moving quickly across the deck. Betts and Wilson, followed closely by Aiken, Carr, and Kunst, ran from the cabin to find the sentinels overpowered and the prisoners in possession of the quarter-deck. A convict snapped a blunderbuss at Betts and Wilson, but it failed to go off, and the man was shot down instantly by Wilson. Aroused by the sound of the shot, the soldiers and seamen swarmed on deck and opened a general fire at the convicts. For ten to fifteen minutes, the mutineers retained possession of the quarter-deck, but gradually the guard and the ship's company, using their cutlasses and the butts of their muskets, and occasionally firing a shot, drove the convicts down the ladders into the prison. After 45 minutes they had secured the deck, and all the prisoners were below. Thirteen convicts had been killed, some on the quarter-deck, others on the main deck and yet others in the prison, whose inmates, when the firing had commenced, had unsuccessfully attempted to break out of the 'tween decks.

On Aiken's orders, two convicts who had freed themselves of their irons were held on the quarter-deck. One of these men, Jeremiah Prendergass, had been named by the informer as the ring-leader who, if the first attempt to capture the ship failed, was to head a second rising. Although the ship was now secure, Prendergass was shot dead by Betts as he knelt on the deck, protesting his innocence.

It was the bloodiest mutiny attempt which had occurred in a convict ship, and during the remainder of the voyage Betts kept the

Coloured aquatint by E. Duncan after W. J. Huggins *National Maritime Museum, Greenwich*

The "MELLISH", entering Sydney Harbour, 1820

prisoners closely confined. The ship called at Rio and the Cape, but when she arrived at Port Jackson, after a passage of 209 days, the convicts showed only too obviously the effects of their rigorous confinement. They were filthy and dreadfully emaciated. Including the fourteen men killed in consequence of the mutiny, among whom, ironically, was the convict who had first warned Betts of the plot, there had been 44 deaths—a mortality rate of one death to every 3·8 convicts embarked—and 43 prisoners, rather less than half the survivors, required medical treatment.

At Sydney, Betts was tried before a Vice-Admiralty Court, firstly, for the shooting of the thirteen convicts killed in the suppression of the mutiny and, secondly, for the killing of Prendergass. On the first charge he was, quite rightly, acquitted. On the second, he was convicted of manslaughter and fined £500, the court ordering that he should be imprisoned until the fine was paid. Governor King, who doubted the court's power to sentence Betts, granted him a conditional pardon, remitting the sentence until the question could be submitted to the British authorities for decision, but obliging Betts to surrender to justice within four days of his return to England. No action, however, was taken against him, and he seems to have escaped punishment.

But Betts deserved severe punishment. The shooting of Prendergass was carried out in cold blood at a considerable time, perhaps as long as an hour, after the mutiny had been put down and all danger to the safety of the ship and to those aboard had passed. It was without justification. Betts maintained that Captain Wilson had approved his action and had advised "Shoot the rascal!" but Wilson, although frankly admitting that he had said that Prendergass had deserved his fate, denied having made use of the expression attributed to him by Betts.

Following the trial of Betts, five seamen of the *Hercules* were arraigned before the Vice-Admiralty Court as being implicated as principals in the mutiny. The evidence against them, however, was unconvincing, and all were acquitted.

In addition to the investigations before the Vice-Admiralty Court, the conduct of Betts was inquired into by a committee comprising a lieutenant of H.M.S. *Investigator*, the Naval Officer at Port Jackson—a post which combined the duties of harbourmaster and collector of customs—and the master of a whaler. Governor King requested this committee to determine whether Betts had complied with that condition of his charter-party which obliged him to prosecute his voyage without undue delay. He was adjudged guilty of this technical offence, the committee holding that as he had been under no necessity to call at either Rio de Janeiro or the Cape he had unduly prolonged his voyage. But had he not called at these ports, the death-roll from disease in the *Hercules* would almost certainly have been far higher than it was. Betts, in fact, was probably justified in calling at Rio and the Cape because of the adverse effect of their close confinement upon the prisoners' health, but whether he was justified in confining them to the extent he did following the mutiny is another question[9].

The Inhumanity of Captain Brooks.

The voyage of the *Atlas* was even more disastrous than that of the *Hercules*, but the circumstances were very different. Firstly, the Irish authorities permitted the prisoners to be embarked in a deplorable state of health, and, secondly, the avariciousness, neglect and inhumanity of the master of the *Atlas*, Richard Brooks, turned the voyage into one of the worst in the history of transportation.

The *Atlas* embarked her first prisoners at Dublin. They were brought out to her in three brigs, and all were more or less unhealthy. Many of those transhipped from the *Henrietta* were suffering from typhus or dysentery, and should never have been embarked. The *Atlas* completed her complement of convicts at Cork, where a number were convalescents from recent illnesses. Surgeon Elphinstone Walker viewed the embarkation of these prisoners with alarm, but he did not feel empowered to refuse to accept them. He did, however, order one old man to be returned ashore, and the man died before regaining the land. Two of the *Henrietta's* convicts died before the *Atlas* sailed.

On leaving Cork the *Atlas* ran into heavy weather. She was so deeply laden that generally the air scuttles had to be kept closed and the deadlights shut in. Under these circumstances, and as every available inch of space was utilized for the stowage of the master's private trade, not a breath of air reached the prison. The needs of the convicts had been utterly disregarded in cramming merchandise aboard wherever room could be found for it. On the upper deck the spars on either side of the waist had been raised three or four feet and the longboat placed in the centre; half the hospital had been appropriated as a sail room; the main hatchway was stowed so full of casks, and the stanchions of the after hatchway boarded up so close, that all air was shut out of the prison, and the prison itself was lumbered with goods of all kinds, principally the master's private property. That the ship was permitted to sail in such an incredibly cluttered state indicates that the *Atlas* either was not properly inspected prior to departure or that the officer responsible was grossly negligent.

After a stormy passage, during which she sprung her mizen mast and carried away her bowsprit bitts, the *Atlas* arrived at Rio on February 2, 1802. Fifteen prisoners had died since embarkation, and upwards of 70 were sick. As the *Atlas* required repairs, the convicts were landed on an island, and, with the serving of fresh provisions, the sickness began to abate. In agreeing to the landing of the prisoners, however, Brooks had been motivated by self-interest rather than by the dictates of humanity, and while the ship was free of her human freight he seized the opportunity to restow her less perishable cargo, so that more private trade goods might be crammed into the already over-burdened vessel. Surgeon Walker had hoped to thoroughly cleanse and fumigate the *Atlas*, but he was largely defeated by the piles of merchandise which littered the prison.

One convict aboard the *Atlas* suffered no privations, but, on the contrary, enjoyed a rare measure of liberty. The privileged Sir Henry Brown Hayes, a wealthy Irish knight, once sheriff of Cork, had been sentenced to transportation for the abduction of a Quaker heiress, and for a substantial bribe Brooks permitted him to travel and mess in the cabin. Surgeon Thomas Jamison, who had been on leave in England and was shortly to be appointed Principal Surgeon in the Colony, was returning to New South Wales as a passenger in the *Atlas*, and he was outraged at the preferential treatment accorded Hayes. As he made no attempt to conceal his feelings, he was openly insulted by Hayes, and the atmosphere in the cabin became so strained that at Rio, Jamison transferred to the *Hercules*. On arrival at Port Jackson he brought various civil actions against both Brooks and Hayes.

The *Atlas* sailed from Rio on February 26 and arrived at the Cape on April 12. In his report to the Transport Commissioners from the latter port, Brooks, justified his action in calling there by declaring that in the early hours of March 3 the convicts had mutinied. He added that, at about the same time, the prisoners had attempted to poison the soldiers, causing the deaths of a sergeant and a soldier's wife, and he inferred that Surgeon Walker had also been poisoned. "I determined to shape my course for the Cape to obtain some medical assistance," he wrote the Transport Board, "and to give the sick troops a few days on shore, and at the same time to procure a supply of bread, as we began to grow short owing to the quantity damaged by the very bad weather we experienced on our first sailing from Ireland."

There is no evidence, beyond the master's own statement, that the prisoners had attempted to seize the *Atlas*, and Governor King certainly considered that there had been no attempt at mutiny. We are justified, in fact, in concluding that Brooks invented the story of a mutiny and of the poisoning of the soldiers' coffee so as to have an excuse for calling at the Cape. At Rio he had learnt that European goods were a glut on the Sydney market, and his motive for calling at the Cape was to try and find an alternative market for his private trade. In this he may have been disappointed, as the *Atlas* remained at the Cape for only a week.

On the run from Rio the number of sick had diminished, but the death-roll had risen to 24 men and one woman by the time the *Atlas* sailed from the Cape on April 19. Two men and a woman had died at Rio, six men between Rio and the Cape, and another man at the latter port. The weather on quitting the Cape was very bad, and the prisoners were kept closely confined. Their quarters were by now noisome and verminous, and the air so devoid of oxygen that the candles in the cabin went out. Scurvy made its appearance, and the hapless convicts fell victims to its ravages. As his supply of anti-scorbutics was almost exhausted, Surgeon Walker could do little to check the disease.

The ship was in a thoroughly filthy and objectionable condition. Brooks neglected every precaution. The convicts' hammocks and bedding, partly, it is true, because of the bad weather, were rarely aired on deck, and the prison was seldom cleaned or fumigated. The windsails, never having been attended to or repaired, were without hoops to expand the canvas of which they were made. In addition to being closely confined, the convicts were constantly ironed, and were compelled to carry two heavy irons on their legs and a third around their necks, with a large padlock weighing at least one and a half pounds. Moreover, they were defrauded of their rations by the use of false weights and measures, and their water ration, which, according to Surgeon Jamison, had been reduced to three pints daily before the ship's arrival at Rio, was inadequate.

The *Atlas* was 220 days on the passage, and 63 men and two women had died between embarkation and arrival at Port Jackson. Another four men died shortly after she made port. Twenty prisoners were so ill that they could not be removed ashore. The remainder, in the words of Governor King, were "in a dreadfully emaciated and dying state".

The same committee which had investigated Betts's compliance with the terms of his charter-party inquired into the conduct of Brooks. These three officers were asked by King to determine whether Brooks had been compelled to call at Rio and the Cape, whether he had used every exertion to expedite the voyage, and whether the ship's detention at the two ports of call had caused the mortality among the prisoners. He also directed the committee to ascertain how far "the circumstances of a part of the hospital and prison being filled with a part of the ship's stores and the master's private trade, and a quantity of lead being stowed in the 'tween decks, contributed to prevent the circulation of air and keeping the place where the convicts were in a clean and wholesome state, from which causes it is alleged the mortality on board has been occasioned".

The committee reported that Brooks had been justified in putting into Rio for repairs, but that he had been under no necessity to call at the Cape, and that after leaving that port he had not used every exertion to expedite the voyage. The mortality had not been caused, in the committee's opinion, by disease carried aboard when the convicts had been embarked, but had resulted from "the want of proper attention to cleanliness, the want of free circulation of air, and the lumbered state of the prison and hospital".

In his despatch dealing with the arrival of the *Hercules* and the *Atlas*, King wrote: "Although there was no mutiny aboard the *Atlas* Brooks's conduct appears as much, if not more, reprehensible than that of the master of the *Hercules*. The survivors of both ships were in a miserable state, being filthy beyond description, some of the convicts lying dead with heavy irons on; many of them died as they were coming from the ship to the hospital." On the ground that the quantity of spirits and the master's bulky trade goods in the *Atlas* had contributed greatly to the mortality among the convicts, King refused Brooks permission to land and sell 2,166 gallons of spirits and 120 gallons of wine, allowing him to dispose of only 800 gallons to the French exploring expedition under Baudin, then lying in Port Jackson.

As with other callous masters who had shamefully maltreated the prisoners entrusted to their care, Brooks escaped punishment. On November 14, 1803, the Transport Commissioners advised King that they had instructed their solicitor to prosecute Brooks for the penalty of the contract, that a charge against him of having embezzled some of the provisions had been referred to the Commissioners of Victualling and that payment to the owner of the *Atlas* was being withheld meanwhile. If Brooks was mulcted for his failure to comply with the conditions of his charter-party he was neither prosecuted for his maltreatment of the prisoners nor debarred from further employment in the convict service. The official memory was surprisingly short; for in 1806 he arrived at Port Jackson in command of the convict ship *Alexander*. On this occasion no complaints were made against him, and he landed his prisoners in good health. Later he was master of various merchantmen trading to New South Wales, and ultimately settled in the colony, residing at Denham Court, near Liverpool, Sydney, and becoming a justice of the peace[10].

The First Convicts at Port Phillip.

The first prisoners to land at Port Phillip were despatched from England in 1803 in H.M.S. *Calcutta*, which with the storeship *Ocean*, conveyed the expedition under Lieutenant-Colonel David Collins detailed to found a new penal settlement. Collins, after serving as Phillip's judge-advocate in the First Fleet, had returned to England in 1797. The *Calcutta's* sister-ship, H.M.S. *Glatton*, a 56-gun ship armed *en flute*, with only eighteen guns on her upper deck, had arrived at Port Jackson with prisoners on March 11, 1803. Touching at Madeira and Rio de Janeiro, the *Glatton* had made a passage of 169 days.

The *Calcutta*, having embarked 307 male convicts, with 30 of their wives and children, sailed from Spithead on April 24, 1803.

Three days later she and the *Ocean* left Yarmouth Roads. They made the passage to Teneriffe in 19 days, and, after a stay of four days, resumed their voyage on May 20. They ran from Teneriffe to Rio in 40 days, arriving there on June 29. They sailed again on July 19, but on the 31st, the two ships separated in thick weather. The *Ocean* sailed direct to Port Phillip, and arrived there on October 7. The *Calcutta* arrived two days later. She had run from Rio to the Cape in 24 days and from the Cape to Port Phillip in 45. The voyage from Spithead had occupied 168 days, on 109 of which the *Calcutta* had been at sea.

Including a prisoner drowned in attempting to swim ashore at the Cape, eight convicts died on the passage, but as five deaths had occurred before the *Calcutta* left Teneriffe, it is evident that some of the prisoners had been embarked in poor health. Regarding Port Phillip as an unsuitable site for the settlement, Collins early in 1804 transferred the expedition to Sullivan's Bay, on the banks of the Derwent River, in Tasmania, thus becoming the founder of Hobart instead of Melbourne[11].

The Two "Experiments".

On June 25, 1809, the *Experiment* arrived at Port Jackson with women prisoners. She is an interesting ship because she was the smallest vessel ever employed in the convict service. A prize, built at Georgia in 1802 of live oak, cedar and pine, she was a brig of only 146 tons, and had a single deck with beams. She belonged to Peter Evet Mestaers, a Dutchman who was a prominent London shipowner; his firm was a small one, but built East Indiamen in a yard at Rotherhithe. Commanded by Joseph Dodds, the *Experiment* carried a crew of 12 men and mounted eight guns, presumably of small calibre.

She was evidently a splendid sea boat and a good sailer; for, sailing in a West India convoy after embarking her prisoners at Cork, she ran out to Rio in 47 days. Few convict ships accomplished this passage in less than 55 days. She then made the passage from Rio to Port Jackson in either 98 or 99 days, having taken 155 days from Cork. She landed her 60 prisoners in good health and without loss.

Almost five years earlier to the day another *Experiment* had reached Port Jackson with prisoners, all but two of whom were women. She was a much larger vessel than the little brig, a three-decker of 568 tons, built at Stockton in 1798. She sailed from England on December 4, 1803, but ran into a violent gale in the Bay of Biscay and sustained considerable damage, springing her bowsprit and carrying away her main topgallant mast. In no condition to continue her voyage, she limped back to Cowes to repair the damage. Sailing again on January 2, 1804, with a convoy of 150 West Indiamen, from whom she parted in the Western Ocean, she encountered favourable weather, except for adverse winds which prevented her entering Port Jackson for three days. She was 65 days on the passage to Rio, and dropped anchor in Port Jackson 173 days out from Cowes. She had several deaths to report and landed 21 prisoners sick[12].

The record of the two *Experiments* illustrates that the fastest passages were not always made by the larger vessels, and that a small ship might have a better health record than a much larger and roomier vessel.

The Female Transports.

The rigid segregation of male and female convicts into separate transports was not yet a feature of the transportation system. Between the beginning of 1801 and the end of 1811 nine convict ships to reach Port Jackson—not quite a quarter of the total arrivals in that period—carried both men and women, while eight ships conveyed only women. After 1811, however, segregation became the rule, and between 1812 and the end of 1820 only two vessels, both from Ireland, carried men as well as women—the *Archduke Charles* in 1813 and the *Francis and Eliza* two years later. The protracted passages of the female transports were largely a thing of the past, and those ships which carried women only were now making passages which compared favourably with those of the male transports.

The *William Pitt*, however, was an exception. This extra East Indiaman, in the same ownership as the brig *Experiment*, left England on September 1, 1805, and did not reach Port Jackson until 222 days later. Hers was the longest passage of any female transport between 1801 and 1820. A first-class ship of 604 tons, she was a comparatively new vessel, having been built at Liverpool in 1804. She was larger than most of the vessels which carried women prisoners; for few of the female transports exceeded a burthen of 500 tons and the majority were of 400 tons or under.

The *William Pitt* sailed from Falmouth on August 10, and from Cork on the 31st, with the expedition under Commodore Sir Home Riggs Popham intended for the reduction of the Dutch settlements at the Cape of Good Hope. The fleet called at Madeira and San Salvadore, reaching the latter port after having lost the *Britannia* and the transport *King George* on Las Rocas, a group of sandy hummocks between the Brazilian coast and the island of Fernando Noronha. The fleet reached the Cape on January 4, 1806, and the *William Pitt's* longboat helped ferry the troops ashore. "This morning," runs the ship's log for January 8, "heard a constant firing of cannon and musketry, the English and Dutch armies engaging." She was the only convict transport to participate in an overseas expedition. The *William Pitt* sailed from the Cape on February 9th in convoy. Smallpox raged aboard for two months, but only one of the two convicts who died on the passage succumbed to it[13].

The female transports *Duke of Portland* and *Speke* also made protracted passages. The former, a Bordeaux-built vessel, launched in 1790, arrived in Port Jackson on her first voyage in 1807 and on her second, when she took 185 days from Portsmouth, in 1809. The previous year the *Speke*, which was to visit Australia again as a convict ship many years later, had made the passage from Falmouth in 185 days. She was 67 days from Falmouth to Rio, 30 days from Rio to the Cape, and 47 days from the Cape to Port Jackson. Among the convict ships, only the East Indiaman *Pitt* and H.M.S. *Calcutta* had at this time recorded faster passages from Rio to the Cape, each having taken 24 days, while the *Royal Admiral* alone had bettered the *Speke's* time from the Cape to Port Jackson. In 1792 she had completed this passage in 37 days, but H.M.S. *Calcutta* had made the shorter passage to Port Phillip in 45 days in 1803.

The smartest passages by female transports were those of the *Minstrel* and the little *Sydney Cove*. The latter, a Rotterdam-built ship of only 282 tons, made a direct passage from Falmouth in 1807 of 158 days, and after her arrival became a successful sealer. The *Minstrel* was a square-sterned flush deck vessel of 351 tons, with an extreme length of 104·5 ft., a breadth of 28·9 ft. and a height between decks of 6·9 ft. A three-master of one and a half decks, she had a quarter gallery and a man's figure as a figurehead. She had been built at Hull in 1810, and two years later went out to Port Jackson in 143 days, taking 54 or 55 days from England to Rio and making a direct passage from Rio to her destination of 75 days[14].

At this time, so far as available records reveal, only four convict ships, excluding the *Minstrel*, had made the passage from England or Ireland to Rio in better than 60 days. The little *Experiment's* 46 days from Cork in 1809 was easily a record, but the *Boddingtons*, in 1793, *Admiral Gambier* (1811) and *Anne* (1800) had taken 54, 57 and 58 days respectively. The *Admiral Gambier* had made the fastest passage direct from Rio to Port Jackson, having taken 62 days in 1811. Only two other convict ships had bettered the *Minstrel's* run of 75 days, the female transport *Friends* having taken 72 days in 1811 and the *Sugar Cane* 65 days in 1793.

Transports Lost.

The first transport lost on the homeward voyage during this period was the 467-ton *Tellicherry*, belonging to the prominent London merchant and shipowner, J. St. Barbe. Having touched only at Madeira, she arrived at Port Jackson from Cork in 1806, 168 days out. On April 6 she sailed for China, where she was to load tea for London, but was wrecked in the Straits of Apo, in the Philippines. Her crew reached Manila in the boats, and, obtaining a passage to China, arrived at Canton on August 1[15].

The ship *Boyd*, a Thames-built three-decker of 392 tons, launched in 1793, was lost in more dramatic circumstances and with heavy loss of life in 1809. She arrived at Port Jackson on August 14, 1809, from Cork, having made a passage of 157 days by way of the Cape, and on her discharge from Government employ was chartered by Simeon Lord, an emancipist who had become one of Sydney's most prominent merchants and shipowners. Lord loaded her with a cargo of timber, coal, seal-skins and sperm oil, and on November 8 she sailed for the Cape of Good Hope via New Zealand, it being the intention of her master, John Thompson, to procure some spars in New Zealand to complete her lading.

With this object, Thompson entered Whangaroa Harbour early the following month, but three days later the *Boyd* was attacked by the Maoris. Although contemporary accounts differ as to the reason for the attack, it seems probable that it was in revenge for floggings administered to two Maori chiefs who were passengers by the *Boyd* from Sydney. The crew was taken by surprise and the ship quickly carried, almost all aboard—some 60 or 70 persons—being massacred. As the Maoris were plundering the *Boyd* some powder was accidentally ignited. Five natives were killed in the explosion and the *Boyd* was set on fire, burning to her wales.

On news of the tragedy reaching the Bay of Islands, a favourite rendezvous of whalers, several well-armed boats set out for Whangaroa. They found the *Boyd* lying in shoal water, burnt down to her copper sheathing. Aided by a friendly Maori chieftain, the only survivors of the massacre—a woman, Mrs. Morley, her young daughter, another girl, Betsy Broughton, and a boy, Thomas Davis—were rescued[16].

The Capture of the "Emu".

In 1812, the *Emu*, the only convict ship lost by enemy action, was captured by the New York privateer *Holkar*. The *Emu*, which had been purchased expressly for the colonial service, was an armed brig mounting ten guns and fitted with a patent defence surmounting her bulwarks, composed of spring bayonets, to prevent boarding. She was commanded by Lieutenant Alexander Bissett, R.N., and carried a crew of 22.

Having embarked her women convicts, the *Emu* sailed from England for Hobart with the *James Hay* on November 11, 1812. The two vessels soon parted company, and the *Emu* was alone when she encountered the *Holkar* on November 30. The American privateer, an 18-gun brig manned by 150 men and commanded by Captain J. Rowland, was built on fine lines, thin planked but prodigious of mast and spar. Bissett realised that he had no chance of escape; for the sturdily-built *Emu* was both outgunned and outsailed. If he seriously contemplated trying to disable the *Holkar* aloft, so as to attempt his escape, his crew's desertion speedily put an end to the plan. Only a gunner and a landsman stood by him; the rest of the crew refused to fight. Bissett, after throwing overboard his despatches and the ship's papers, had no alternative but to surrender.

When the Americans boarded their prize, they found that she was carrying a great quantity of ammunition and had forty-nine women convicts aboard. On January 17, 1813, Bissett and the women convicts were landed on the island of St. Vincent, one of the Cape Verde Islands. The fate of the prisoners is not recorded. The *Emu*, however, was sent into New York by the *Holkar*, and presumably was sold there as a prize[17].

Detention of the "Francis and Eliza".

Three years later, at the beginning of 1815, the *Francis and Eliza*, carrying male and female prisoners, was taken by the New York privateer *Warrior* in Long Island Sound, but after being detained for 24 hours she was allowed to proceed on her voyage. Although neither participant in this incident was aware of the fact at the time, the Treaty of Paris, terminating hostilities between England and America, had already been signed.

The *Francis and Eliza* sailed from Cork in convoy on December 5, 1814. She was an old vessel, a two-decker built on the Thames 32 years before, and was a second-class ship of 345 tons, mounting four guns and carrying a crew, when she reached Sydney, of 24 men. In American records, however, she is listed as of 377 tons and 10 guns, with a crew of 35. The *Warrior* was a brig of 430 tons, mounting 21 guns and manned by 150 men, and was commanded by Captain G. Champlin. She captured the *Francis and Eliza* on January 4, 1815. The convict ship's guns, ammunition, and much of her cargo were removed into her captor, her papers were confiscated, and several members of her crew, expressing a wish to desert to the Americans, were allowed to remain aboard the *Warrior*. Her convicts were not interfered with, and the *Francis and Eliza* resumed her interrupted voyage.

The position of her master, William Harrison, was unenviable. Not only was he short-handed as a result of the desertions, but the rest of his crew were mutinous and discontended. They broached the liquor aboard, and, according to a contemporary account, "the most dreadful scene of riot and intemperance prevailed". Harrison probably feared a conspiracy between his insubordinate seamen and the prisoners, but, fortunately, the latter, only about half of whom were men, behaved well. They threw off the normal restraints of a convict ship, but made no attempt to capture the ship, which, in the absence of a military guard and with many of the seamen mutinous, might not have been difficult. Indeed, the prisoners, dividing themselves into watches, assisted the depleted crew to navigate the ship.

On January 10 the *Francis and Eliza* put into Teneriffe, and Harrison availed himself of the presence of a British man-of-war at Santa Cruz to ship back to England his chief mate and four seamen on account of their unruly conduct. He engaged such men as were offering under verbal agreements, since he had lost his ship's papers, but was still short-handed. At later ports of call, however, he was able to pick up a few additional men.

Harrison sailed from Santa Cruz in company with the *Canada*, a convict ship which originally had left Cork in the same convoy as the *Francis and Eliza*. They were escorted to Senegal by a British frigate, H.M.S. *Ulysses*, whose captain arranged for a military guard to be put aboard the *Francis and Eliza* at Sierra Leone. This detachment was drawn from the 1st Regiment and the Royal African Corps, under the command of Ensign Daniel Alt, of the latter corps: it was the only occasion on which the Royal Africans furnished the guard of a convict ship. From Sierra Leone the two ships continued in company to the Cape, where they arrived on May 2, 148 days out from Cork. They remained some time at the Cape and sailed together, but parted company at sea, the *Canada* completing her voyage in 243 days and the *Francis and Eliza* taking three days longer[18].

Regular Visitors.

Already some shipowners were finding it profitable to keep certain of their vessels more or less permanently employed in the convict service, and by 1820 a number of ships were regular visitors to Port Jackson. The *Canada* was one of the best-known, but the *Guildford*, the *Shipley*, the *Surrey*, the *Morley* and the *Elizabeth*, by the end of 1820, had each made three or more voyages with convicts.

The *Canada* held the record with five voyages. Built at Shields in 1800, she was a new vessel, possibly making her maiden voyage, when she first carried male convicts to Port Jackson in 1801. For the next few years, however, she was employed elsewhere, and not until 1810, when she had passed from the ownership of F. & T. Hurry to that of Reeve & Co., did she return to the convict service. A two-decker of 403 tons, she was a popular ship, if any convict ship can be said to have been popular, and being well managed and run she had an enviable health record. Only five prisoners died aboard her, and her convicts were always landed in good health, except that in 1815, due to the length of her passage, a number were suffering slightly from scorbutic complaints. It was the *Canada*, incidentally, which brought to the colony the news of Napoleon's escape from Elba. After parting company with the *Francis and Eliza*, she picked up this titbit of information when, three weeks sail from Sydney she spoke the merchantman *Hebe*, and then beat her into Port Jackson with the news by six days.

The *Canada's* last two voyages, when she had been relegated to the second class, were both excellent. In 1817, carrying female convicts, she made the passage from Cork in 138 days, running out to Rio in the good time of 46 days and taking 70 days from Rio. In 1819, following the same route on her last voyage as a convict ship, she made the passage from London in 131 days.

The *Elizabeth's* three voyages, on each of which she was commanded by William Ostler, were made in 1816, 1818 and 1820. Built at Chepstow in 1809, she was a ship of 481 tons, and before entering the convict service had been employed on the Bristol to Nevis and St. Christopher run. In 1814, on being purchased by J. Birch & Co., she went out to Batavia, being one of the first two East Indiamen ever to sail from Bristol. She was owned by Ward & Co. when she became a convict ship, and recorded her best passage on her first voyage, reaching Port Jackson in 123 days from England.

Built at Whitby in 1805, the *Shipley* was a second class ship of 381 tons and two decks. She reached Sydney as a convict ship in 1817, 1818, 1820, and 1822, and on all four of her voyages was commanded by Lewis William Moncrief. On her first voyage she made the passage from England in 127 days, and came through Bass Strait. All her passages were direct, and she proved a consistent sailer; for she went out from Woolwich in 1818 in 123 days, from the Downs in 1820 in 113, and on her last voyage in 1822 made the passage from London in 124 days.

The careers of the *Guildford* and the *Morley* in the convict service are dealt with in the next chapter, as both continued in the trade until the late 1820's, but mention must be made here of the latter's record passages, to Port Jackson in 1816-17 and to Hobart in 1820. On her first voyage as a convict ship she left England on December 18, 1816, and ran out to the Cape in 62 days. After spending a week at that port, she made the passage from the Cape to Port

Jackson in 41 days. The entire voyage occupied only 113 days, which beat by eight days the previous record of 121 days for a direct passage, made by the *Coromandel* in 1802. On her second voyage with convicts she came out from the Downs to Port Jackson in 112 days. On her third voyage, in 1820, she carried female prisoners for both Hobart and Sydney, and made a direct passage to the first-named port of 99 days. After disembarking the Tasmanian section of her convicts, she continued her voyage and reached Port Jackson 113 days out from England[19].

The "Surrey's" Nightmare Voyage.

Of what may be termed the regular convict ships the *Surrey* experienced the most disastrous voyage when she first conveyed convicts to Port Jackson in 1814. Carrying 200 male convicts, she left England on February 22, 1814, in company with the *Broxbornebury*, a large, Thames-built ship of 720 tons.

On March 7 the first well-defined case of typhus made its appearance. The prison was regularly cleansed and fumigated, but for some reason her master, James Patterson, kept the prisoners closely confined, and, except for fourteen men who were assigned various duties and more or less enjoyed the run of the ship, not more than about 20 convicts were admitted to the deck at a time. The manner in which the overwhelming majority of the prisoners were kept constantly in the prison contributed to the spread of the disease. The *Surrey* put into Rio, but remained only ten days, and after she sailed on April 21 the outbreak of typhus became more virulent than ever.

It literally decimated the convicts, seamen, and guards. After June 2 the deaths, as Surgeon Redfern stated in his report to Governor Macquarie, became "awfully frequent". By July 26, when she was off the New South Wales coast, the *Surrey* was in a perilous position. Her master, two of her mates, her surgeon, 12 seamen, six soldiers, and 16 prisoners were lying dangerously ill, and before nightfall that day her master died. There was now nobody to navigate the ship and but few men to work her. Fortunately, when off Shoalhaven, the *Surrey* fell in with the *Broxbornebury*, from which she had parted company much earlier in the voyage, and a volunteer was sent aboard from the latter vessel to navigate the stricken ship to port.

After a passage of 156 days from England, the *Surrey* arrived at Port Jackson on July 28. Her death-roll since embarkation stood at 51—36 convicts, her master, the first and second mates, the boatswain, six seamen, the surgeon, and four soldiers. Typhus was still raging aboard, and the surviving seamen and convicts were in a deplorable state of health. The *Surrey* was at once quarantined, and those aboard were landed on Sydney's North Shore, where tents were erected for their reception and surgeons sent to attend them. "It is only to be wondered at that so few died," was Redfern's summing-up of the *Surrey's* voyage, after he had completed his inquiry.

Typhus may or may not have been carried aboard the *Surrey* when her convicts were embarked, but the spread of the disease was due to the close confinement of the prisoners and the neglect of ordinary precautions during the voyage. Redfern calculated that almost 165 convicts were locked up in the prison and hospital at all times, and said that ventilation was utterly neglected and that the bedding was not once aired on deck. He added that there was an utter want of personal cleanliness among the prisoners, due principally to soap having been withheld from them so that it might be sold on arrival to enrich the purser or steward. Without explanation, the ship's journal disclosed a deficiency of 240 gallons in the quantity of wine issued, which meant, of course, that the convicts were defrauded to that extent.

"I have much reason," wrote Macquarie, in reporting the *Surrey's* arrival, "to apprehend that this destructive disease originated in the mismanagement of the master and surgeon," but as both had fallen victims of their own neglect, they were beyond the reach of human punishment[20].

Through the deaths of his superiors, a junior officer, Thomas Raine, succeeded to the command of the *Surrey* and was confirmed as her master on reaching England. He commanded her on her second and third voyages in 1816 and 1818-19. A manuscript log of her 1816 voyage, kept by her chief mate, William S. Edwardson, testifies to Raine's extreme care in the management of her prisoners.

Evidently retaining harrowing memories of her first voyage as a convict ship, he was determined that the scenes he had then witnessed should not be repeated. Meticulous attention was paid to the removal of the hatches, to the opening of the air scuttles and to the setting of the windsails whenever the weather permitted, and to the cleaning of all parts of the ship. The convicts were admitted to the deck in double divisions, so that half of them were on deck at once. Wine was issued regularly as an anti-scorbutic, and care was exercised to see the prison was cleaned and fumigated. Classes in reading, writing and other subjects were organized, and the prisoners were kept employed picking oakum. Raine regularly inspected the ship at a fixed hour each day, and when his daily inspection could not be carried out until later because the crew was engaged aloft, the delay is carefully noted in the log.

Raine was evidently a man of advanced humanitarian outlook. He relied upon rewards rather than punishments in his management of the prisoners. They were released from their irons for good conduct, and toward the end of the voyage, on December 6, the log notes that only eight convicts remained in single irons. As the *Surrey* neared her destination, the prisoners were not locked up for the night until 9.30 or 10 p.m., being allowed on deck to that hour "to recreate with music for their general good conduct" or "dancing and music for their general good conduct and as an anti-scorbutic". The floggings administered for theft, disorderly conduct and other offences were few and lenient, on no occasion exceeding 18 lashes.

On this voyage the *Surrey* recorded a passage of 159 days from Cork. She called at Rio, and when leaving that port, as sometimes happened, she was fired on by the guns of an island fort near the harbour entrance. Through the negligence of the local officials, the fort's commander had not been advised that the *Surrey* had been cleared. As soon as fire was opened, Raine brought the ship to, but one shot penetrated a timber on the starboard side below the main crosstree and had to be plugged.

On several occasions after leaving Rio, the *Surrey* logged over 1,000 miles in seven consecutive days, her best week's run being from November 25 to December 1 inclusive, when the log recorded 1,246 miles. She logged over 200 miles on each of two consecutive days—209 miles on November 29 and 206 the following day. Her best day's run, however, was made on November 14, when, having sighted the island of St. Paul the previous day through mizzling rain, she ran 230 miles by the log.

The *Surrey* on this occasion landed all her convicts in good health and without loss, and the prisoners seem to have responded well to

O

Raine's humane treatment. It is not surprising that the log records that, when being disembarked, the convicts "cheered repeatedly and expressed the liveliest gratitude for their good treatment".[21]

The Mortality on the "General Hewart".

Prior to the *Surrey's* arrival in 1814, the *General Hewart* and the *Three Bees* had reached Port Jackson with their prisoners in a shocking state. Aboard four of the ships to arrive that year the mortality rate was one death to every 89·5 prisoners embarked, but in the *General Hewart*, the *Three Bees* and the *Surrey* the rate was one death to every 9·1 convicts embarked. After the excellent health record of the transports in the immediate preceding years, this high mortality surprised and shocked both official and public opinion, and, as we have seen, led to the decision to appoint a surgeon-superintendent in charge of each convict ship.

The *General Hewart* was built at Calcutta in 1812, and was a first-class ship of 973 tons. She was a three-decker, with a crew, according to Redfern of 104 or, by the Naval Officer's records, of 80. She had a remarkably long life, as she was still voyaging to Australia in the 1840's. Her name is also recorded as *General Hewitt.*

She began embarking her prisoners at Woolwich on July 28, 1813, when 24 men were put aboard, and completed her complement of 300 at Portsmouth on August 23. Until she sailed three days later, they were not admitted to the deck. Her surgeon, Richard Hughes, who had been surgeon of the *Aeolus* in 1808 and of the *Providence* in 1811, objected to 15 or 16 of the convicts, claiming they were in a state of debility. The prison hulk surgeons, however, had certified that all the prisoners were in good health, and although he did not in every instance concur with these certificates, Hughes was compelled to accept the convicts. On his own statement, none was suffering from an infectious complaint.

The *General Hewart* called first at Madeira, where throughout her nine days' stay the convicts were kept closely confined below. The weather was hot and humid, and the atmosphere of the prison was stifling. When the voyage was resumed, the *General Hewart* ran into heavy and almost continuous tropical rain which denied the convicts access to the deck and saturated their bedding when it was being aired. Dysentery broke out, and when she arrived at Rio on November 17th, after a passage of 83 days from Portsmouth, there had been about 19 deaths and there was a heavy sick-list. She remained 15 days at Rio, and Hughes did not feel himself empowered to suggest that she should remain longer, so as to afford the prisoners an opportunity to recuperate. They were still very sickly when the voyage was resumed.

The prisoners were now allowed free access to the deck, but this action, of course, came too late. The dysentery, which, it must be remembered, medical opinion at that time did not regard as contagious, could not be checked, and when the *General Hewart* arrived at Port Jackson after a passage of 165 days, 34 men had been buried at sea.

The three surgeons appointed by Macquarie to inquire into the circumstances of her voyage reported that wet weather had been the primary cause of the mortality. The saturated bedding had been thrown together till heated and afterwards slept on, and it had not been possible to allow the prisoners on deck because of the incessant rain. The surgeons also expressed the opinion that Hughes should have maintained his objection to the embarkation of the debilitated prisoners, and branded as highly censurable the master's action in withholding portion of the convicts' rations of salt beef while in the tropics, even though Hughes had sanctioned his action.

As a member of the court of inquiry, Redfern subscribed to the finding that the prisoners had been humanely treated and the prison and hospital carefully cleansed, fumigated and ventilated. But in a special report to Macquarie he stated that these precautions had been neglected during the latter stages of the passage. He also disclosed that the damp bedding had been thrown overboard three weeks before the *General Hewart* had reached Rio, and declared that when colder weather was encountered, the lack of the bedding was acutely felt. A passenger, Surgeon John Harris, of the New South Wales Corps, testified to the attention shown the prisoners by Hughes. "I very frequently visited the prison," he asserted, "and never saw any place better fitted up, nor kept in a more cleanly state, and the prisoners had frequent and, indeed, almost constant access to the deck." To some extent, then, the evidence was contradictory, and it would seem that Redfern, being an emancipist, accepted too readily the stories told him by the prisoners.[22]

The "Three Bees".

Three months after the *General Hewart's* arrival the *Three Bees* anchored in Port Jackson. There had been only nine deaths among her male prisoners, but no fewer than 55 of the survivors required hospital treatment, the majority for scurvy.

The *Three Bees*, a first-class ship of 459 tons, built at Bridgwater in 1813, had embarked her first convicts at the Canal Docks, Dublin, on August 26, 1813, and had completed her complement at Cork, where she had anchored on September 22. The weather had been sultry and at night the closely crowded prison had been suffocating. The embarkation of the prisoners at Cork had not been completed until October 2, and it was the 27th before she had sailed for Falmouth to pick up a convoy. The weather when she had arrived had been exceedingly cold, the reverse of what it had been at Cork. She had been detained five weeks at Falmouth and the prisoners had suffered severely.

Yet such was the hardihood of the Irish convicts that despite the sudden extremes of temperature, and the fact that some of them had been confined aboard for three months, there were few sick when the *Three Bees* eventually sailed on December 8. She ran into stormy weather, and the convicts could not always be admitted to the deck. The prison, however, was cleaned and fumigated regularly. At Rio the weather was very hot, but the prisoners were admitted freely to the deck, the temperature in the prison falling six or eight degrees when all had left it. One man died of fever, but there was no hint that the voyage was to be an unhealthy one, and when she sailed on February 17 the number of sick was small.

On February 27, however, a strange sail was sighted-. Believing her to be an enemy, orders were issued for the convicts' bedding to be brought on deck and made into a barricade. It remained on deck throughout the night and was drenched by heavy rain. Efforts to dry it failed, and it was returned to the prison, the convicts being warned not to use it. However, they disregarded this injunction, and scurvy broke out, causing seven of the nine deaths. It was fortunate that the *Three Bees* made a passage of 149 days from Falmouth, as had she made a longer passage there is little doubt that other deaths would have taken place. Many of the convicts who required hospital treatment were very badly affected by scurvy.

Fourteen days after her arrival, on May 20, the *Three Bees* caught fire at her anchorage near the Government Wharf in Sydney Cove. An officer, accompanied by a boy carrying a candle and lanthorn, had entered the after hold during the morning, and presumably the boy had dropped an unextinguished candle snuff among some oakum or other combustible material—a frequent cause of fire in the days of sail. Nothing was noticed at the time, and it was not until about 4.30 p.m. that it was realised the ship was on fire. As columns of suffocating black smoke spiralled into the air, there was almost a panic among the residents of Sydney; for rumour magnified the thirty casks of powder aboard into 130.

The fire had a good hold when first discovered, and soon the standing rigging was ablaze and the flames were leaping to the masthead. The crew had no chance of fighting the flames, and the *Three Bees* was cast adrift and abandoned, it being thought that the southerly wind would carry her out into the open harour. Vessels anchored nearby hurriedly weighed and moved to positions of greater safety, while ashore huge crowds gathered to watch the blazing vessel. The feelings of the spectators, no doubt, were faithfully expressed by the *Sydney Gazette's* reporter, who wrote: "A ship of nearly five hundred tons, set loose, it may almost be said, in the middle of a town, unmanageable, and pouring forth columns of smoke and fire, threatening desolation all around her, with her guns all loaded, first pointed upon one object and then upon another, and every instant expected, by her explosion, to throw down or cover with the dreadful blast all the buildings around or near her."

The first gun went off about 5.30 p.m., and the explosion of 13 others quickly followed. One swivel ball, entering the parlour window of the residence of the Naval Officer, Captain John Piper, smashed the corner off a portable writing desk, but did no other damage. Nobody was injured in this involuntary bombardment of Sydney, and there was little damage to property. By 7.30 p.m. the *Three Bees* had drifted on to the rocks at Bennelong Point, and 15 minutes later her magazine exploded. "It was not as awful as had been expected," stated the *Gazette*, with a hint of disappointment. The *Three Bees* blazed throughout the night, and by morning was a total wreck, burnt to the water's edge.[23]

The First Transport to Tasmania.

The first transport to reach Tasmania direct from England was the *Indefatigable,* which arrived at Hobart on October 19, 1812. She had been preparing to sail for Port Jackson when a despatch was received in London from Macquarie urging that a convict ship should be despatched direct to Tasmania. Hitherto, with the exception of the prisoners transferred from Port Phillip by Collins in 1804 all the convicts to reach Tasmania had been transhipped from Sydney. Usually they were despatched in small batches in the brigs and schooners owned by the colonial government or in locally-owned traders hired for the purpose. This system, however, was uneconomical, and, in addition, prevented the convict population in Tasmania being built up rapidly. Macquarie's suggestion had been prompted by these considerations, and, the British authorities concurring with it, the *Indefatigable's* destination was altered.

The *Indefatigable,* having embarked 200 prisoners, sailed from London on June 4 in company with the *Minstrel,* bound for New South Wales and making her second voyage as a convict ship. Built at Whitby in 1799 by Ing. Eskdale, the *Indefatigable,* a first-class ship of 549 tons, was owned by the well-known shipping firm of James Atty & Co. She was a square-rigged three-master, with a length of 127 ft. and a beam of 31 ft. 8 ins., and had three decks. The two ships made a passage to Rio of 54 or 55 days, and sailed again in company on August 11. From Rio the *Indefatigable* took 69 days to Hobart, where she anchored, 137 days out from London, with the loss of one man. The *Minstrel* made Port Jackson on October 25, 75 days out from Rio and 143 from London.[24]

For some reason, it was decided not to adopt Macquarie's proposal permanently, and the experiment of despatching a convict ship direct to Tasmania was not immediately repeated. In 1818, therefore, Macquarie hit upon the plan of chartering transports arriving at Port Jackson to carry their convicts on to Hobart without disembarking them at Sydney. On April 30, the *Minerva,* from Ireland, and the *Lady Castlereagh,* from England, arrived at Port Jackson, and Macquarie hired both ships to proceed to Hobart at the rate of two pounds per convict, with the government victualling the prisoners. With no knowledge of Macquarie's action, the authorities in England had decided to introduce direct sailings to Tasmania, and on December 18, 1818, the *Lord Melville* arrived at Hobart direct from England. She was followed by the *Hibernia* the following year, and from 1820 onwards convict ships regularly reached Hobart direct from England and Ireland.

After delivering her convicts at Hobart, the *Lady Castlereagh* was chartered by Macquarie to take troops to India, and there she was wrecked. The *Indefatigable* had previously ended her days. In 1815 she had made a second voyage as a convict ship, and, having delivered her prisoners, had sailed for Java. On October 23 she caught fire at Batavia, and became a total loss.[25]

Mutiny on the "Chapman".

The scene in the *Chapman* when she reached Port Jackson on July 26, 1817, was reminiscent of the horrors which had characterised some of the voyages of the earlier convict ships. She was a particularly interesting vessel, and was destined to have a remarkably long career, during the course of which she made two other voyages as a convict ship.

Built at Whitby in 1777, she had been named for her original owner, Abel Chapman. Her builder was Thomas Fishburn, who probably also built the First Fleet storeship *Fishburn*. In 1818 the *Chapman* ranked as a second-class ship. She was a two-decker of 558 tons, with a length of 116 ft. and a beam of 33 ft. She was still afloat in 1851, when she was owned by King & Co., of London, but she had by then, 74 years after her launching, been several times rebuilt. In fact, when she arrived at Hobart as a convict ship in 1826 it was said of her that she had been rebuilt about 1798, and that on that occasion only one sound plank of her original timbers had been left to perpetuate her name and identity.

The *Chapman*, commanded by John Drake, embarked 198 convicts at Cork. Those put aboard from the brig *Atlas* were described by the latter's master as a turbulent, desperate and dangerous set of men, and he warned Drake that they would need watching with extreme care. This seems to have convinced Drake, who had not previously commanded a convict ship, that his prisoners were certain to give trouble, and he determined to adopt extreme precautions from the outset. The surgeon-superintendent,

Alexander Dewar, either agreed with Drake or was powerless to influence the master's decision.

While the *Chapman* was still anchored in the Cove of Cork, Drake would permit no more than 12 convicts on deck at the same time, and after she sailed on March 14, 1817, he continued to enforce this regulation. Each batch of 12 prisoners was allowed to remain on deck for an hour. The nervous Drake would not permit the prisoners' irons to be knocked off at sea, except in the case of those employed as hospital attendants or certified as sick by the surgeon. When wine was due to be issued, the heavily-ironed prisoners were brought up on deck by the main hatchway, handed their ration, and hurriedly passed down the fore hatchway into the prison again. A similar procedure was followed when their irons were examined. The guard and crew were drawn up under arms, and the convicts were then passed up the main hatchway and down the fore hatchway as on wine days.

Rumours of mutiny were in the air from the day the *Chapman* sailed, and at 10 p.m. on March 22, when the ship had been a week at sea, the first alarm was raised. Rightly or wrongly, the sentinel at the prison door reported that an attempt was being made to pick the locks. Drake and Dewar at once went below, and, whatever the nature of the disturbance in the prison, they restored order, but about midnight a second, and this time unquestionably false, alarm was given. Matters seem to have then been tranquil until 7 p.m. on April 12, when there was another false alarm.

Four days later an informer, Michael Collins, disclosed that a plot was afoot to seize the ship and carry her to America. Drake at once ordered the chain cable to be passed over the fore-and-aft hatchways for greater security. The arms chest was placed on the poop, all firearms were brought up from below, and the capstan was rigged with cutlasses, so that, if the need arose, they might be seized by the seamen without a moment's delay. These precautions taken, the convicts were passed round the deck and their irons examined, many being found to be defective. Next morning another inspection was made.

Throughout that day, April 17, the atmosphere in the *Chapman* was tense with a brooding expectancy. The guard, a detachment of the 46th Regiment commanded by Lieutenant Christopher Busteed, of the 69th Regiment, and the crew were convinced that the prisoners were about to rise, and both the soldiers and the seamen, nervously apprehensive, were on the verge of panic. Suddenly, at 8 p.m., cries were raised that the prisoners were breaking out. No attempt was made to verify the truth of the alarm. Drake, Busteed, Dewar, and the rest of the officers jumped at once to the conclusion that the long-expected mutiny had begun: they were the victims of their own nervous fears. Without a moment's delay, the loopholes in the prison bulkheads were manned, and a general and indiscriminate fire was opened on the unfortunate convicts. The firing lasted for from thirty to forty-five minutes before the soldiers and seamen withdrew to the deck, where they remained, nervously alert, throughout the night.

The moans of the wounded could be plainly heard, but no attempt was made that night to visit the prison. "It was not deemed safe to open the prison that night," was Dewar's explanation, "and if I myself had been willing to take the risk, I could have found no one hardy enough to have accompanied or assisted me." Next morning when the prison door was at last opened, it was found that three convicts had been killed and twenty-two wounded.

The alleged ringleaders of the mutiny, who, no doubt, were the men named by the informer, Michael Collins, were severely flogged, and an uneasy peace settled on the *Chapman*. It was broken on April 28 by a further alarm. Firing again broke out, one prisoner, Bryan Kelly, being shot dead on the poop and four others wounded. A seaman, who died on May 24, probably was wounded at this time, most likely by a panic-stricken member of the guard or crew. On this occasion, however, the prison was visited later in the evening, so that we must presume the wounded men received medical attention.

In the punishment of the prisoners, Drake was merciless. The floggings were most severe, and confinement in the prison rigorous. A chain cable was carried along the prison and passed through the prisoners' irons, at first 50 or 60, and later 100, men being fastened to it throughout the night. Indeed, frequently they were shackled to it for 14 or 15 hours at a stretch, during which time it was impossible for them to rest. As rumours of mutiny continued to circulate, Drake refused to relax his precautions, and the rigorous confinement and ironing of the prisoners continued until the

Chapman, without further serious incident, arrived at Port Jackson, where she anchored on July 26. There had by then been 14 deaths among the prisoners. Five men had been killed outright during the firings, seven had died of wounds, and two others had succumbed to dysentery. Two seamen had also been killed or had died of wounds. Although the surviving convicts were suffering from starvation and the effects of close confinement, only ten required hospital treatment, five of whom were suffering from gunshot wounds.

An immediate investigation was made by a court of inquiry comprising Judge-Advocate Wylde, D'Arcy Wentworth, the colony's Principal Surgeon and Superintendent of Police, and J. T. Campbell, Governor Macquarie's secretary. The two members first-named reported that there was no evidence that the convicts had attempted to break prison, but that at the time of the shooting on April 17 the ship's officers, the guard and the crew had probable grounds for apprehending and did in fact apprehend, that the prisoners were attempting to break out of the prison. They added that the general firing on April 28 began because of "the weak suspicions of a sentry, or one or more other persons, but the reasonableness of this apprehension is questionable because the party or parties commencing the firing could not be particularised and indentified, but the position of those who joined in the firing would be similar to that on the first occasion." They stated, in respect of both occasions, that personal responsibility could not be fixed upon any individual or individuals, and that the firing had ceased as soon as the guard and crew had realised that no probable or sufficient cause for alarm existed. In the opinion of Wylde and Wentworth, the ship's officers and the members of the guard and crew, in their treatment of the convicts, were guilty of misdemeanour only.

Campbell, however, disagreed with these findings. He considered that the firings, the excessive corporal punishments, which, he stated, amounted to upwards of four thousand lashes, and the "neglects, privations and cruelties, exercised in a variety of forms towards unoffending men loaded with irons, closely confined and strictly guarded", amounted to such systematic criminality that the culprits should be brought to trial before a competent tribunal. He recommended that Drake, Dewar, Busteed, the three mates, and three soldiers should be sent home to England for trial.

The liberal-minded Macquarie adopted Campbell's recommendations. Dewar, Busteed, and Privates James Clements, John Hogan, and John Jordan, were placed under arrest and, along with certain witnesses, were sent to England, while steps were taken to ensure that Drake would surrender to the British authorities on his return to England. The accused were tried at an Admiralty Sessions at the Old Bailey on January 11, 1819, and were acquitted without being called upon for their defence. "It appeared to the court and jury," Lord Bathurst advised Macquarie, in a despatch of April 12, "that upon the evidence the conduct of the convicts aboard the *Chapman* was of a nature to excite in the minds of the officers and crew such an apprehension of danger . . . as could excuse at least, if not justify, the several acts of homicide laid to their charge." All that Macquarie got for his zeal was a reprimand about the serious inconvenience of sending parties to England for trial when the charges against them were not supported by a body of evidence worthy of credit![26]

Posterity will not agree with the court's acquittal of the prisoners, at least so far as Drake, Dewar and Busteed are concerned. The mutiny was very much of their making, and their nervousness and apprehension communicated itself to those under their command. There can be no question but that more resolute and enlightened officers, acting with firmness and caution, would have prevented the bloodshed that occurred.

Some Female Transports.

The slaughter in the *Chapman*, however, was an isolated incident: it was not the system that was at fault, but the individuals. On the whole, the surgeons-superintendent were discharging their duties capably and faithfully, and as a result of their direction and management of the prisoners a marked improvement in the standard of treatment of the convicts had resulted. But there was one grave problem which they were unable to solve. In female transports prostitution was rife, and all efforts to stamp it out failed.

Aboard the *Friendship*, for example, the master, Andrew Armet, and the surgeon-superintendent, Peter Cosgreave, made every effort to stop the prostitution of the women to the crew, but failed. This ship, which sailed from England on July 3, 1817, south-west of Madeira picked up an open boat containing six Spaniards and an

American, who had converted their shirts into a sail. For six days they had eaten no food except for a little raw turtle, and they were in an exhausted state. They were hoisted aboard the *Friendship*, and seven days later, on August 4, were transferred at sea to an American ship. The *Friendship* then went on to St. Helena. Here the conscientious Cosgreave applied to the admiral in command for assistance in preventing cohabitation between the seamen and the women. Two post-captains held an inquiry, but their report was not handed to Armet or Cosgreave. Presumably the problem was also beyond the ingenuity of the post-captains to solve.

The *Friendship* made a protracted passage to Port Jackson of 195 days, and when she arrived Cosgreave reported that prostitution had begun before the ship had left England and had continued throughout the voyage. Three magistrates held an inquiry at Macquarie's direction, and reported that the charges were "most fully proved", but that Armet and Cosgreave had done everything possible to prevent the intimacy which had taken place between the women and some of the officers and seamen[27].

In 1820 the voyage of another female transport, the *Janus*, also formed the subject of an inquiry. Significantly both the *Friendship* and the *Janus* carried passengers who were members of the church, a missionary being aboard the former and two Roman Catholic priests in the latter, and the inquiries may have been instituted because of their representations or to forestall public criticism by them.

The *Janus*, which really was a whaler, embarked her prisoners at Cork, and, running out to Rio in 64 days, completed the passage to Port Jackson in 150 days. Her master, Thomas J. Mowat, had been ordered to call at Hobart, but when the surgeon-superintendent, James Creagh, died off the Tasmanian coast, Mowat chose to disregard his orders. The magistrates reported that prostitution had prevailed "in a great degree" throughout the voyage, and that charges that Mowat and the officers had not made due exertions to prevent it were "true and well founded in fact."[28]

The impossibility of preventing prostitution in the female convict ships was stressed by Mr. Justice Barron Field, who arrived at Sydney in 1817 in the *Lord Melville* to take up his judical appointment. Field claimed that Daniel McNamara, who had joined the ship as surgeon-superintendent after the women had been embarked.

the previous surgeon having been dismissed or having declined to continue in the post, "might have reformed the practice; but to prevent connection between the women and the seamen would (I am convinced) be quite impossible, even if the hatches had been battened down every night. Upon the whole, I think there was as little immorality on board the *Lord Melville* as it is possible should prevail among such a ship's company of different sexes, so brought into contact. Of this, I am sure, that a decent exterior was presented." The judge, whenever the weather had permitted, had read prayers to the prisoners on Sundays, and afterwards had taken occasion "to give them some moral or religious exhortation adapted to their circumstances", and he flattered himself that his presence aboard had acted as some moral check on the women and the seamen.[29]

Whether or not the judge's prayer-reading and moral addresses helped or influenced the prisoners, his presence in the *Lord Melville* must have acted as a spur to the officers to exert themselves to stamp out prostitution. They would have realised that Field was bound to report on their conduct on his arrival. If, in these circumstances, prostitution could not be prevented, it is only reasonable to assume that it prevailed to a much greater extent, and that less determined efforts to check it were made in female convict ships which carried no distinguished passengers.

A stormy Voyage.

Apart from the *Chapman*, there was only one convict ship between 1814 and 1820 in which the number of deaths on the passage reached double figures. This vessel was the *Tottenham*, which had been built at Stockton in 1802 by Thomas Haw for the London shipowner, Robert Wigram. Exclusive of her equipment, she cost fourteen pounds per ton, her builder receiving a payment of £7,238. She measured 102 ft. 6 ins. on the keel and 31 ft. in breadth. Her tonnage when built was 517 tons, but when she arrived at Port Jackson in 1818 she was officially recorded as being of 557 tons, and paid harbour dues on this tonnage. She was then a three-decker of the second class, and ship-rigged.

The *Tottenham* left Spithead, where apparently she had taken shelter, on March 27, 1818, but three days later it was found that the upper pintle of her rudder was broken off and she put into

Plymouth for repairs. She sailed from there on April 17. When she put into Rio on June 24 there had been 36 cases of scurvy, of which 16 were still under treatment. She remained at Rio until July 16, but when she arrived at Sydney on October 14, ten deaths had occurred among the prisoners since embarkation.

Rumours of mutiny were as rife in the *Tottenham* as in the *Chapman*, but were viewed in a commonsense light and caused no panic. On June 1 a prisoner reported that an attempt to gain possession of the ship was planned and named the ringleaders, and similar reports were made on several occasions later that month. "Their liberty not in the least abridged and their conduct orderly," wrote the surgeon, Robert Armstrong, after recording one of these reports. There was no mutiny, but on the evening of July 26 the sentry at the fore hatchway, after the prisoners attempted to put out the light in the prison despite his repeated warnings, fired a shot. The two balls which were in the piece lodged in one of the stanchions without injuring any convict.[30]

Scurvy on the "Baring".

Another vessel to experience a long and tedious passage when most of the convict ships were arriving in under 130 days was the *Baring*, which sailed from England on January 27, 1819. She had made a previous voyage as a convict ship in 1815, and was an East Indiaman, launched at Barnard's yard at Deptford on November 21, 1801. A ship of 830 tons, she was classed in the second-class in 1819, and, next to the 842-ton *Lady Castlereagh*, was the largest convict ship employed between 1815 and 1820.

The *Baring* sailed from Sheerness on December 18, 1818, but going into the Downs the pilot ran her aground and when she got off she had to go into dock at Chatham. She did not sail finally from the Downs until January 27 and was detained near the Equator by light winds. As she neared Australia she met a series of light easterly winds which greatly retarded her progress, and on June 14 she was compelled to put into Hobart for water and fresh provisions. Scurvy had made its appearance some time earlier, and five convicts suffering from the disease were landed, one of them dying next day. At sea she had buried five men. She went on to Port Jackson, which she reached after a passage of 150 days, on June 26. In 1822 it was claimed that on putting into Hobart

50 or 60 of her convicts had been exceedingly ill from scurvy, but this seems to be an exaggeration, as at the time of her arrival at Sydney Macquarie reported that her prisoners were in good health[31].

The "Eliza's" Fast Passage.

A new record for a convict ship from England to Port Jackson was established when the *Eliza* entered Sydney Heads on January 21, 1820. She had sailed from England on October 15 or 16 of the previous year, and had made a direct passage of 97 or 98 days—a remarkable performance for a vessel of her build. Her time clipped 14 or 15 days off the previous record of 112 days for a direct passage. The *Eliza*, which was to make further voyages as a convict ship, was a second-class two-decker of 511 tons, and had been built in India in 1806.

Several of the convict ships which arrived in 1820 made fast passages. It was a favourable year so far as the weather and winds were concerned, as it had been also the previous year. In 1819 the *Minerva*, on her second voyage as a convict ship, made the passage from Cork in 113 days, the *Daphne*, touching only at Teneriffe, in 116, and the *Bencoolen* and the *Mary*, which left Cork on successive days, each in 123 days. The *Atlas*, which was to be wrecked on Poulicat Sands on May 9, 1820, when homeward bound, with the loss of five men, came out from England by way of the Cape in 131 days.

Next to that of the *Eliza*, the fastest passage in 1820 was the *Morley's* 99 days from London to Hobart. The *Shipley* took 113 days from the Downs to Sydney, the *Neptune* a day longer, the *Asia* 116 days and the *Mangles*, from Falmouth, 118. The smartest passages from Cork to Sydney were made by the *Castle Forbes*, 116 days, the *Almorah*, which actually sailed from Waterford, 122, and the *Hadlow*, 125. The *Juliana* took 116 days from England to Hobart and the storeship *Dromedary*, 121.[32]

The "Castle Forbes" Plot.

As we have seen, many attempts to seize convict ships on their passages from England or Ireland had been made, but in 1820 there occurred the first and only plot to seize a convict ship after she had disembarked her prisoners.

The *Castle Forbes* arrived at Port Jackson from Ireland on January 27, 1820. She was a new vessel, having been launched at Aberdeen in 1818. Macquarie chartered her to carry her prisoners on to Hobart. Four aged men from her complement were landed at Sydney and their places taken by four prisoners transferred from the *Prince Regent*, which had arrived at the same time as the *Castle Forbes*. Another 40 men were also transferred to her from the *Prince Regent*, and on February 15 the *Castle Forbes* sailed for Hobart, where, having disembarked her prisoners, she began to load spars for India.

Twenty-eight convicts at Hobart formed a daring plan to capture her as she lay at anchor and to sail her out of Australian waters. They proposed to gain possession of three boats in which they would drop down the Derwent River under cover of darkness to the *Castle Forbes*. The prisoners believed they stood a good chance of getting aboard the ship without raising suspicion. As precautions aboard the *Castle Forbes* had been relaxed when her convicts had been disembarked, it is certainly probable that an inefficient watch was maintained, and if the pirates could carry the ship swiftly, so as to get her under weigh smartly, and the wind was right, the scheme stood a good prospect of proving successful.

Its weakness lay, of course, in the number of men who had to be admitted to a knowledge of the plan. The ring-leaders had to recruit sufficient men to ensure being able to work the ship and get her to sea, and this involved acceptance of the risk of one of the men turning informer. This is precisely what happened. One of the conspirators went to the authorities, and when 14 of the would-be pirates were arrested, the remainder abandoned the plan[33].

The Surgeons-Superintendent.

By 1820, although the system of surgeons-superintendent was only six years old, quite a number of naval surgeons had already found more or less permanent employment in the convict service. The conclusion of peace in 1815 had led, of course, to the demobilisation of many army and naval surgeons, the majority of whom found it difficult to establish themselves in civilian practice or to obtain suitable employment. To the naval surgeons who lacked money or influence employment in the convict service, however uncongenial such work may have been, at least offered the prospect of some security. There thus was no lack of applicants, and those who secured appointments were in many instances unwilling, or could not afford, to leave the service on their return to England.

James Bowman, who had entered the navy in 1804 and had been placed on half-pay in 1814, obtained his first appointment to a convict ship in 1815 when he became surgeon-superintendent of the *Mary Anne*. He served in a similar capacity in the *Lord Eldon* in 1817 and in the *John Barry* two years later. Bowman was a shrewd, pushing type, with a keen eye to the main chance, and on his various visits he was careful to ingratiate himself with Governor Macquarie. The result was that on his third visit he was appointed the Principal Surgeon of the colony. Four years later, by his marriage to the second daughter of John Macarthur, the founder of the Australian wool industry, he acquired 2,000 Merino sheep and over 200 head of cattle. He was one naval surgeon who certainly did very well for himself by way of the convict service.

Edward Ford Bromley was another who utilised service in convict ships as a stepping-stone to more congenial and more lucrative employment. He was surgeon-superintendent of the *Ocean* in 1816, of the *Almorah* in 1817 and of the *Lord Wellington* in 1820. On his first visit he was recommended for appointment as colonial surgeon at Port Dalrymple, in Tasmania, a post which had been held for a good many years by Jacob Mountgarrett, who had arrived in Australia as surgeon of H.M.S. *Glatton* in 1803. By the time his appointment had been tentatively approved by the British authorities, however, Bromley was back in England, and he had lost his chance. In 1820, however, he obtained the post of Naval Officer at Hobart, but was later removed when defalcations in the accounts were discovered[34].

Robert Espie also made three voyages—in the *Morley* in 1817, the *Shipley* the following year, and the *Dorothy* in 1820. On the latter voyage he was accompanied by his wife and three children and shortly after his arrival secured the appointment which Bromley had originally but unsuccessfully sought. Espie succeeded Mountgarrett as surgeon at Port Dalrymple, but resigned within a few months and returned to England to find employment again in the convict service in the 1820's.

Major West and James Scott, surgeons-superintendent of the *Francis and Eliza* in 1815 and of the *Castle Forbes* in 1820 respectively, also found employment in the colony. West was appointed an assistant surgeon in Sydney, but, becoming interested in extensive farming ventures, attended irregularly to his medical duties at the hospitals at Windsor and Emu Plains, and was suspended from duty in 1826. Scott set up in private practice in Sydney at No. 1 Macquarie Street, now the Harley Street of Sydney, but, apparently, without success. Early in 1821 he accepted a post as colonial surgeon and controller of medical services in the southern part of Tasmania. His appointment was made permanent in 1824 and he held it until 1835, being also a magistrate and landowner[35].

Among those who had twice visited Australia as surgeons-superintendent of convict ships by 1820 were Charles Queade, George Clayton, Daniel McNamara, Robert Armstrong, Patrick Hill, David Reid, Henry Ryan, Morgan Price, Matthew Anderson, Thomas Reid, William Evans and William Macdonald, and the majority of these naval surgeons continued in the service after 1820, some finally settling in the colony.

CHAPTER TEN

THE VOYAGES, 1821-1840

A Shortage of Ships.

IF there was any period when the convict service was compelled to accept decrepit tonnage it was in the late 1830's and early 1840's. The emigration boom, particularly to America, but also to Australia, began in the mid-1830's, and steadily gathered momentum. It did not reach its zenith in the case of America until between 1846 and 1854, when almost two and a half million persons sailed from British ports, or, in Australia's case, until after the discovery of gold in the early 1850's, but the shortage of shipping became acute from 1835 onwards and lasted until the builders had been able to catch up with the demand.

In the early years of the boom every vessel that could be made to serve as an emigrant ship was pressed into service. The convict service, of course, could not meet this competition; for in the emigration trade the shipowners found quick and substantial profits. The only vessels offering for the conveyance of prisoners to Australia were those which were so old and slow as to be unable to find employment in the emigrant trade. The Admiralty in these years had very little from which to choose. It had to relax its standards and accept the best of the vessels proffered.

About two-fifths of the convict ships to reach Australia between 1836 and 1840 were vessels which had been built in 1820 or earlier. Among these were a number of Indian-built vessels which still had many years of useful life in their durable hulls, but although still seaworthy they were not of modern design and, dark, evil-smelling and poorly ventilated, they were in many respects unsuitable for employment as convict ships. But the older English-built vessels were infinitely worse, and some of them were only just seaworthy.

The Crews and Officers.

Perhaps of more serious consequence than the standard of the vessels employed as convict ships was the decline in the standard of the men who manned them. The personnel of the British Mercantile Marine, as we have seen, had never been high, but it reached its lowest ebb in the 1820's and 1830's. The seamen, rebelling at last against their atrocious living conditions aboard ship as well as against the methods under which they were engaged, were restive and mutinous. Not only were desertions common, but the masters of convict ships found it difficult to enforce discipline and often had more to fear from their unruly seamen than from a possible rising among their prisoners.

The deep current of dissatisfaction among the seamen is understandable, but the explanation of the serious deterioration in the standard of seamanship of the officers is not so readily apparent. Yet it is undoubtedly a fact that in the 1830's a large proportion of the officers of the merchant ships were incompetent. There was a sharp rise in the toll of marine disaster, and in many instances the losses were directly attributable to drunkenness or incompetency. The convict ships in this respect, as we shall see, were no exception.

Instances of trouble with the crews were of frequent occurrence throughout the period under review, and repeatedly the masters of convict ships were compelled, on reaching Sydney or Hobart, to proceed against their men for mutiny or insubordination. Generally the sailors, on appearing before a police magistrate, agreed, albeit reluctantly, to return to their duty, but occasionally the more determined or recalcitrant were sentenced to imprisonment.

The trouble in the female transport *John Bull* in 1821 seems to have arisen from the efforts of the master, William Corlett, and the surgeon-superintendent, William Elyard, to prevent prostitution between the female convicts and the members of the crew. It began with the steward being flogged by Corlett's order for having roundly abused Elyard. Then the second mate, who had encouraged the unruly prisoners in their defiance of the surgeon and in whose cabin one of the women was found to have secreted herself throughout one Sunday, was thrown into irons and, having been under arrest for five days, was disrated and sent forward to bunk with the seamen in the fo'c'sle.

Later the chief mate and two seamen were wounded in a fracas on deck, and in consequence the latter, after Elyard had dressed their wounds, were placed in irons. An attempt by the crew to take the ship was evidently feared; for that night Corlett and Elyard, both armed, sat up until 2 a.m. and only turned in to be on watch again at 4.30 a.m. No further trouble developed with the crew. The women, although Elyard threatened them with the cat, were only punished by being confined in the coal-hole or hospital, one woman having the additional indignity of a neck-collar being placed on her[1].

Throughout the *Burrell's* voyage in 1832 the crew was insubordinate, threatening the master, John Metcalf, with violence and breaking into the spirit room, but they did not refuse duty until after the ship's arrival at Port Jackson. Seven of the seamen were then charged in the police court, but, faced with the certainty of punishment, agreed to return to their duty. Three, however, were sent for trial, and ultimately convicted and sentenced for having broken into the spirit room.

The trouble in the *Isabella* in the same year was a good deal more serious. Carrying male convicts, the ship left Plymouth on November 27, 1831, and on February 6 a seaman, Jacob Anderson, refused to obey the second mate's order to rig some clothes-lines. He was ordered to the poop as a punishment, but instead went forward, and when again ordered to the poop a number of his shipmates announced that they would not touch another rope in the ship unless his punishment was remitted. Despite this threat, the master, William Wiseman, and his mates placed Anderson in irons, and more than twenty of the men then refused duty, one leaving the wheel that night without being relieved. When some of them were also placed in irons, eight seamen resumed duty, but fourteen remained recalcitrant, and were still under arrest when the *Isabella* arrived at Port Jackson. They were convicted of mutiny and sentenced to imprisonment.

The ship was navigated to port by the officers, carpenter, boatswain, joiner, eight seamen, and the apprentices, assisted by members of the military guard and occasionally by the convicts. Fortunately the prisoners, despite a rumour of mutiny at the beginning of the voyage, were well behaved; if they had not been, the consequences of the crew's defection might have been serious[2].

Mutiny Rumours.

Few convict ships reached their destination in these years without having to report a suspected mutiny among the prisoners during the passage. It is doubtful, however, if in any single instance the danger of a rising was really serious. There was, undoubtedly, much loose talk of mutiny among the prisoners, but it seems to have been mostly in the nature of idle bragging. The officers of the convict ships, probably because of the mutinous disposition of the seamen, were too readily inclined to listen to these threats and to the tales of the informers who were to be found in every ship.

In their reports the surgeons-superintendent, almost without an exception, asserted the truth of these plots, but the incidents which they described in support of their contention merely indicate that the mutinies were very half-hearted affairs. Yet men were freely punished for their alleged participation in them on the word of an informer who had poured an alarmist story into the ears of the credulous officers, although the punishments awarded were certainly much milder than had been the case a few years earlier.

The Trouble on the "Ocean".

In the *Ocean* in 1823 the first informer came forward when the ship was five days out from Portsmouth. He declared that the prisoners planned to seize the ship the first day on which all were admitted to the deck, and he named five men as the ringleaders. Half the *Ocean's* convicts had been embarked at Portsmouth from the *York* hulk, in which they had been closely confined because of attempts to escape, and James McTernan, who was making his first voyage as a surgeon-superintendent and who had joined the ship only the day before she sailed, regarded these men as being of infamous character and of turbulent disposition. In his report he stated that before sailing they had "declared an intention to take possession of the *Ocean*".

However, the informer was a man of ill-repute, and McTernan received his revelations with considerable suspicion. Nevertheless he augmented the guard and gave each post a number, which the sentry was ordered to proclaim at half-hourly intervals throughout the night. Finally, on May 4, he placed the five ringleaders in double irons.

At 2 a.m. on May 7 the alarm was given. At that hour, according to McTernan, a violent rush was made by the convicts against the stanchions of the fore hatchway, and simultaneously a diversionary assault was delivered against the main hatchway. The guard and crew turned out under arms within a few minutes, and the prisoners were heard returning to their beds. The incident was over almost as soon as it had begun, but the officers believed that a rising had been intended, and as a second informer named the same five men as the ringleaders, the latter were flogged and other prisoners ironed at night.

The other half of the *Ocean's* convicts had been embarked from the *Leviathan* hulk, and as these men had not participated in the demonstration, and were considered to be "of good conduct and fair character", McTernan selected 12 men from their ranks to form a prison night guard. He divided them into three watches, with instructions to challenge any noise in the prison and to report all who left their bunks or resisted their authority, and ordered the sentries to co-operate with them. The appointment of convict constables was a common practice in the convict ships, but they can hardly have been very useful, although McTernan reported of those in the *Ocean* that, with a few exceptions, they had faithfully performed their duties. At any rate, the remainder of the voyage was tranquil[3].

The "Mangles" Mutiny.

The mutiny in the *Mangles* in 1824 was as tame and half-hearted an affair as that in the *Ocean*. Sailing from Portsmouth on July 13 with male convicts, the *Mangles* touched at Teneriffe, and after leaving the latter port an informer disclosed that the prisoners, assisted by some members of the crew, intended to rise and take the ship. Some credence was lent to this story by the fact that the seamen had been grumbling openly because the master, John Cogill, had made a search of their chests in consequence of some paltry thefts. The sentinels were therefore increased from four to six, and a rack was built on the poop for the guard's muskets, which were now kept loaded.

"The convicts have lately been observed talking in bodies in whispers together," the commander of the guard, Lieutenant Dalrymple, wrote in a report on August 19, "and making remarks to the men and sentinels of the 40th, such as, 'We cannot all be hanged and they can but transport us again if we are caught,' 'If we had you ashore,' and 'We could easily break through the stanchions of the prison if we chose.'" The convicts, no doubt, got a lot of quiet satisfaction out of ribbing their guards, but the effect of their threats and boasting was to induce the officers to accept the story told by the informer. According to him, the rising was planned to take place when the hatches were opened at 6 a.m. one morning and most of the soldiers were below. The convicts were to rush the cabin, seize what arms they could find, and block the hatchway leading to the guard's sleeping quarters, where, until the erection of the rack on the poop, the arms had been kept.

The reality proved very different. A sentry gave the alarm about 7 p.m. on August 15, and the guard and crew at once mustered under arms. "The sentinel had heard a noise, as if the prisoners were rushing to the hatchway," stated Dalrymple, in his report. "As they had been quiet just before, he thought they were making good their escape." This incident, which existed probably only in the overwrought imagination of the sentry, constituted the only attempt at mutiny aboard the *Mangles*![4]

The Plot on the "Isabella".

"A dangerous mutiny which was on the eve of breaking out among the prisoners was discovered on the voyage," declared Surgeon William Rae, in reporting the *Isabella's* arrival at Port Jackson in December, 1823, "and but for timely prevention would certainly have ended in much bloodshed."

Rae's "dangerous mutiny", however, amounted to no more than a blood-curdling story told by an informer, who asserted that it was being hatched by seven of the worst characters aboard. There was no actual attempt to break out of the prison or to seize the ship, but this did not stop Rae from declaring that the ringleaders "poisoned the minds of their perhaps less desperate associates with the idea of money being on board, which was to be distributed amongst those who should most distinguish themselves." Specie for the use of the colony was often shipped aboard the convict ships, but none was being carried by the *Isabella*[5].

The "Royal Charlotte".

Surgeon George Fairfowl's assessment of the alleged plot in the *Royal Charlotte*, which arrived at Port Jackson on April 29, 1825, exhibits a much saner outlook than was usual among the officers, and his resolute and sensible action indicates how simply these plots, whether real or imagined, might be defeated. Fairfowl, however, was making his third voyage in charge of prisoners, and was destined to become one of the best known of the surgeons-superintendent.

"The plan," wrote Fairfowl, after stating that on March 8 an informer had disclosed that 43 prisoners planned to murder the officers and seize the ship, "was sufficiently feasible and well digested to inspire them with sanguine hopes of success, although too contemptible, in my opinion, to give me a moment's anxiety about the fate of the ship had it been put into execution. As, however, it was to have begun in the murder of one or two soldiers and must have terminated in a horrible slaughter of the convicts, it became my duty to guard against the occurrence of an incident so revolting to the feelings of humanity."

Fairfowl achieved this merely by separating the ringleaders. Ten of them, secured in triple irons and fed on bread and water, were placed under the forecastle, 18 were confined in double irons in the boys' room, and another 10 double-ironed in the main prison. He imposed no other punishments, not because he did not think punishment was deserved, but because he believed that no flogging he could order would be adequate to the nature of the offence! The justice of his measures are perhaps open to question, but their effectiveness is beyond challenge. There was no further trouble in the *Royal Charlotte*[6].

The Attempt to Burn the "John".

The history of these nebulous plots at mutiny might be prolonged indefinitely; for the officers of almost every convict ship had stories of alarming plots to relate, and they lost nothing in the telling. The incidents already related, however, have been selected from a great number, and are typical. They sufficiently indicate the general nature of the alleged mutiny plots of the '20's and '30's. Even when, as happened in the *England* in 1826, the plot was branded by a magisterial inquiry as "fully proved", and regret expressed that the "very mutinous and turbulent disposition" shown by the prisoners early in the voyage had not been "at once and promptly" punished by corporal punishment, the evidence indicates that there was no serious attempt at mutiny.

But occasionally there was an incident of a more serious nature or one which had an unfortunate sequel. The attempt to burn the

John in 1832 belongs to the latter category; for although she was an old ship, built at Chester in 1810, the foolish action of some of the convicts in trying to start a fire in the prison did not seriously endanger her.

Carrying male prisoners from London to Port Jackson, she had not been long at sea when the inevitable informer announced that a rising was being planned. Surgeon James Lawrence, who previously had served as surgeon-superintendent of the *Ann and Amelia* in 1825, apparently accepted the story unreservedly and, after consulting the master, Samuel John Lowe, and the officers of the guard, placed the alleged ringleaders in double irons.

On the night of March 25, when the *John* was in the South Atlantic in the latitude of the Tropic of Capricornia, two prisoners attempted to kindle a fire in the prison, "for the purpose it is supposed," reported Lawrence, "of setting fire to the prison, which several of the prisoners had threatened to do." The two men, Samuel Dodds and William Buosey, secretly smuggled a live coal into the prison and with it ignited a small pile of oakum and chips close to the foremast. The alarm was given when smoke penetrated into the hospital and rose through the fore hatchway, and the fire was promptly extinguished, having done no damage beyond charring the prison floor. Dodds and Buosey were punished, and there the incident might have ended had not another convict, John Clifton, been heard to remark that he wished the ship was on fire from stem to stern. Rightly or wrongly, Lawrence believed that Clifton had been concerned in the kindling of the fire, and, as a punishment for his remark, ordered him next morning to walk the deck with a bed on his back for two hours.

This curious punishment took place in the port waist under the supervision of two convicts told off for that purpose by Lawrence. Clifton was leg-ironed, although the ship's master thought he had on only one leg iron. When the punishment started at 10 a.m., Clifton's bed had not been brought up from below, and Lawrence ordered him to walk at a quick pace. Whether he or the two cnnvicts misinterpreted the surgeon's order is not clear, but when Lawrence observed Clifton about three-quarters of an hour later the unfortunate man was running, not walking, the deck. It was a hot day, with the thermometer in the shade of the cuddy registering 80 degrees, and Lawrence immediately told Clifton, in the hearing of the supervising convicts, that he was to walk and not run. There is some doubt as to when Clifton's bed was brought on deck, but, according to Lawrence, Clifton lugged it around on his back only during the final fifteen minutes of his punishment.

When his ordeal finished at noon, Clifton was perspiring freely and was much fatigued. He sat down on the deck, and later in the afternoon the surgeon found him there, cold and shivering. Clifton was at once carried below, but he died about four o'clock.

In reporting Clifton's death after the *John's* arrival at Sydney, Lawrence admitted that Clifton had been "exhausted a good deal" by his punishment, and asserted that "while in that state he drank, unknown to me, about two quarts of cold water, which caused his death". The evidence at the magisterial inquiry revealed that Clifton had been freely supplied with water, and even with some wine by his fellow convicts while he was in a distressed condition from the exertion of his punishment.

"I am decidedly of opinion," reported the magistrate, "that no blame can attach to any person on account of the sudden death of the prisoner, the testimony being unanimous in stating that the punishment sustained by Clifton was very light and that the conduct of the surgeon-superintendent towards him and all the prisoners under his charge was characterised by the greatest kindness and humanity." The legality of Clifton's punishment, which certainly was unorthodox, was not questioned, nor was it satisfactorily explained how he came to run instead of walk the deck. There can be little doubt that Lawrence was negligent in not more closely supervising Clifton's punishment in the tropical heat and in failing to examine him immediately on its conclusion to ensure that he had suffered no ill effects. With a little more care on the surgeon's part, the tragedy of Clifton's death might have been prevented[7].

Convicts Shot.

In all the alarms of mutiny bloodshed occurred rarely. The inevitable informer came forward in the *John Barry* in 1821 with the familiar story of an attempt to seize the ship being planned, and although the surgeon, Daniel McNamara, placed no credence in the report he took the precaution of handcuffiing the five men named as the ringleaders. "At about half past seven this evening," he wrote in his journal under date August 18, when the ship was in Lat. 22° 47′ S., Long. 40° 55′ W., "while we were sitting round the table in the cabin under the poop we were alarmed by the discharge of a musket on deck, immediately followed by a second and a third. All was confusion in a moment. Each person seized arms and before we could reach the deck and ascertain the cause of the alarm a fire of musquetry took place from the soldiers' apartments into the prison.

"I first made my way to the larboard gangway and, finding all quiet there, called to cease firing. At this time the master and officer of the guard, seeing that the alarm was groundless, exerted themselves to stop the firing. The latter ran down into the guard-room, but before his endeavours could avail about ten or a dozen shots were fired thence into the prison."

The prison door was opened and three prisoners were found to have been wounded, two of them severely, although both recovered. The trouble had been started by a nervous sentry, whose "manner and tone of voice seemed to be affected by liquor". He claimed that he had called in vain for the convicts to cease the noise in the prison and when he was not obeyed he fired, "with the cool indifference," according to McNamara, "that a man would feel on firing into a flock of wildfowl." The surgeon said that if a number of the prisoners had been out of their beds they could not have returned to them without the clank of their irons having been heard or without more than three being wounded, and he accepted the convicts' assurance that the only men out of bed were the watchmen. The sentry was arrested, but what punishment he received is not disclosed[8].

Details of the mutiny plot in the *Florentina* in 1830 are scanty, but, as in the *John Barry*, the military guard became apprehensive. On September 17, when the *Florentia* had been just a month at sea, an alarm was given that the prisoners were about to take possession of the ship, and a nervous sentry began firing in the resultant confusion. One of the prisoners was killed outright, but he was the only casualty, the position being brought quickly under control and order restored[9].

Women Attack a Surgeon.

Aboard the female transports the prevention of prostitution was still proving an insoluble problem, and repeatedly the local authorities at Sydney and Hobart found it necessary to report that masters and surgeons-superintendent had not sufficiently exerted themselves to prevent this practice. When the officers endeavoured to enforce the regulations, they were, on the whole, unsuccessful in preventing prostitution, and found themselves powerless in face of the unruliness of the women prisoners and the insubordination of the seamen.

Events in the *Brothers*, which arrived at Hobart from England on April 15, 1824, illustrate, not only the difficulties of this problem, but also the need of tact on the part of the surgeon-superintendent. This officer aboard the *Brothers* was James Hall, who previously had made voyages in charge of convicts in the *Agamemnon* in 1820 and the *Mary Anne* in 1822 and who was a zealous, meddlesome and litigious individual. The manner in which he sought to suppress prostitution in the *Brothers* quickly earned him the enmity of the worst of the women prisoners and of a section of the crew. The result was that on December 12, 1823, when the ship had been but a week at sea, he was assaulted in the prison.

"Six women conspired to murder me," Hall declared, in his official report, "and did actually form a mutiny of an alarming nature, in which I was knocked down in the prison, beaten, and kicked." Hall claimed that the assault had been instigated by the chief mate, James Thompson Meach, who, he asserted, had offered the women a bottle of rum if they would knock him down. Hall also asserted that Meach had struck him at the time and had rescued one of his assailants from the master, Charles Motley, the second mate and Hall.

By Hall's orders, the six women concerned in the assault were confined for a week in the coal-hole on bread and water, but were allowed on deck daily. Meach, who was alleged by Motley to have opened the prison by means of duplicate keys and to have encouraged and connived at an association between the crew and the women prisoners, was eventually suspended from duty. Hall said his suspension was for the part he had played in the assault, but Motley declared it was for striking a woman prisoner.

Hall insisted that Meach should be prosecuted, but when the matter was referred to the attorney-general, the latter reported that the case against Meach appeared to be "one only of aggravated assault and conspiracy, not mutiny or attempted murder". With the crown's refusal to move in the matter, a series of court actions between the various officers of the *Brothers* followed. Hall brought a civil action against Meach, but the magistrates found that he had not proved his charges of mutiny and conspiracy of assault, and gave costs against him. He at first refused to pay these, but after a distress warrant had been issued against him, he paid up and promptly applied to the Supreme Court for a refund, with what result it has not been possible to discover. Motley, who had treated his chief mate in arbitrary fashion, having had him gaoled at Hobart without adequate cause, now found himself sued by Meach, who won a verdict against him for £172 15s. damages on one day and another for £20 the following day.

Whatever Meach's part in the events in the *Brothers*, there seems little doubt that Hall's lack of tact was the primary cause of the trouble. Temperamentally he was unfitted for a post as surgeon-superintendent. When he expressed a wish to become a settler, the Governor, Sir Thomas Brisbane, advised the British authorities not to consider his application. He recalled that on Hall's previous visit in the *Mary Anne*, the surgeon had become involved in a local faction fight, had allegedly challenged an official to a duel, and had been the defendant in a libel suit. On that occasion Hall's interference in local affairs had earned him the severe censure of the colonial office, and when the reports concerning the voyage of the *Brothers* reached England, it was decided not to again employ him in the convict service. However, he seems to be identical with the James Hall, described as for long surgeon of the Ordinary at Sheerness, who was surgeon-superintendent of the *Georgiana* to Tasmania in 1833. The latter's journal mentions his four voyages with convicts, which would tally with Hall's record[10].

Surgeon Burnside's Dismissal.

Other surgeons besides Hall found themselves in trouble. The offence of Matthew Burnside, for instance, was serious, and he deserved the punishment he received. He arrived at Hobart as surgeon-superintendent of the female transport *Providence* on May 16, 1826, and at the inquiry into his conduct was proved to have cohabited for the greater part of the voyage with one of the female prisoners entrusted to his care and to have invited other convicts to his cabin for a drink. Instead of remonstrating against these irregularities, the ship's master, John Wauchope, had been a party to them.

The governor of Tasmania, Sir George Arthur, refused both men certificates of good conduct, and recommended to the British authorities that their gratuities should be withheld and that they should be dismissed the convict service. Both recommendations were adopted.[11]

Another surgeon-superintendent, William McDowell, who arrived at Hobart on April 9, 1825, in charge of male convicts by the *Lady East*, was also called upon to face an inquiry. When the prisoners were mustered, many of them complained of gross ill-treatment and excessive punishment at McDowell's hands.

The magistrate, however, exonerated McDowell, reporting that the prisoners had conducted themselves with great insubordination during the voyage, and that McDowell had inflicted no punishment beyond what was necessary for the preservation of order and discipline. An incomplete punishment return shows that while the *Lady East* was at Falmouth 15 convicts were punished for having filed through their irons with an intention to escape. Five were given 36 lashes each, one 30, seven 24, one 18 and another 12, and by the standards of the day these punishments cannot be regarded as excessive.[12]

A few years later McDowell appeared as the complainant. As surgeon-superintendent of the *Harmony*, which arrived at Sydney on September 27th, 1827, with women convicts, he alleged that the master, R. D. Middleton, had short-served the convicts' rations. The minutes of the inquiry, apparently, have not survived but the governor, Sir Ralph Darling, wrote that he was strongly disposed to concur with the report of one member of the board of inquiry, who had asserted that although McDowell's conduct had been irritating, the master's proceedings had been "most unbecoming and improper".

The Commissioners of the Navy promised to take notice of "the improper conduct of the master", and as Middleton did not again command a convict ship, we must presume that he was debarred the service.[13]

An Antipathy Toward Clergymen.

The trouble with Surgeon Charles Carter was that he had a deep-seated antipathy to clergymen, and in the end it was his undoing. He was one of the best-known of the early surgeons-superintendent. He first left England in charge of convicts in the *Hibernia* in November, 1818, and during the next seven and a half years he spent most of his time in convict ships or in returning to England after having delivered his charges. He arrived at Hobart in the *Hibernia* in May, 1819, came to Sydney the following year in the *Hebe*, returned to Hobart in the *Arab* in 1822, made a third passage to Tasmania in the *Sir Godfrey Webster* the following year, and in 1825 again reached Sydney in the Irish transport *Henry Porcher*.

On the last-named vessel's arrival the Rev. John Espie Kean, who had come out in her with his family, complained of Carter's conduct, but the deliberations of the court of inquiry were brought to an abrupt conclusion when Carter refused to appear before it. He maintained that, having delivered his prisoners, he was not amenable to an investigation of his conduct towards a passenger.

It was not the first occasion on which his conduct had been called in question by a clergyman. In the *Hibernia* in 1818-19 he had been involved in disputes with the Rev. Richard Hill, who had complained that Carter had prohibited him visiting the ship's sick-bay without his sanction and had ridiculed his efforts at the moral instruction of the prisoners. Carter had admitted having refused Hill permission to visit the hospital quarters without his permission, but had justified his action on the ground that "nothing more tends to depress the spirits of the sick than such untimely visits", and had charged Hill with constant and extreme officiousness in respect of all matters relating to the management of the prisoners. No charges had been brought against Carter regarding his conduct in the *Hebe*, the *Arab* or the *Sir Godfrey Webster*, but these ships had carried no clergymen passengers.

Carter's refusal to appear before the court of inquiry appointed to investigate his conduct in the *Henry Porcher* caused the church authorities to recall to the governor the earlier complaints of the Rev. Hill, and Sir Ralph Darling recommended that Carter should not again be employed. The convict service thus lost an experienced and capable surgeon-superintendent merely because of his lack of tact when dealing with clergymen, who, it must be confessed, were themselves not always the most diplomatic individuals among a convict ship's complement.[14]

Convicts' Rations Stolen.

Yet despite such incidents as those quoted, which, while trivial and unimportant in themselves, serve to illustrate the conditions in the convict ships at this time, the management of the prisoners generally was satisfactory. There were no gross abuses, as had earlier been the case, and serious complaints of ill-treatment or brutality were rare.

Occasionally, however, the prisoners might be starved as happened in the *Adamant* in 1821. This ship reached Port Jackson from England on September 8, but the convicts, so far as extant records reveal, had no complaints, although the surgeon-superintendent, James Hamilton, refused to sign the master's accounts until the latter had agreed to credit the government with the value of medical comforts that were deficient. On October 24, however, when the ship had almost cleared Sydney Heads on her return voyage, police officers boarded her and seized 386 lb. of sugar, 752 lb. of beef, 35 lb. of soap, and varying quantities of wine, vinegar, pepper, ginger, chocolate, suet, oatmeal, bread, preserved meat and portable soup alleged to have been stolen from the provisions and medical comforts supplied for the prisoners on the outward passage.

The seizure followed a quarrel between the *Adamant's* master, William Ebsworthy, and the ship's steward, George Farris. The latter had sold some wine to a woman innkeeper and had collected payment, but Ebsworthy had insisted that the money should be paid to him and had threatened to seize the wine. When a constable arrived in response to Ebsworthy's summons, Farris swore that he had sold the wine on the master's instructions and that it had been embezzled, along with other goods secreted in the ship, from the convicts' provisions. "Just before we crossed the Line," asserted Farris, in a sworn statement, "the captain had a scuttle cut in the after hold for the purpose of adulterating the king's stores, and by his order I drew off twelve or fourteen gallons from each puncheon and made up the deficiency with water."

The evidence is contradictory as to whether Ebsworthy or Farris was the instigator, but there is no doubt that the prisoners received watered wine and that portion of their rations was embezzled. Ebsworthy, when the matter came before the magistrates, refused to submit a written defence, and the evidence was forwarded to the Commissioners of the Navy without comment. What action they took does not transpire, but although there were other, and later, instances of the prisoners' rations being short-served, the largest deficiency seems to have been that which occurred on the *Adamant*[15].

The "Phoenix" becomes a Convict Hulk.

Appropriately, Australia's first prison hulk was a condemned convict ship. Many years before, after she had been found unseaworthy, H.M.S. *Supply* had been converted into a hulk at Sydney and used for the storage of provisions and as a receiving depot for newly-arrived prisoners. She had never served, however, as a floating gaol. The dubious distinction of being the colony's first prison hulk belongs to the ship *Phoenix*.

Commanded by Robert White and carrying male prisoners, she arrived at Hobart from England on July 21, 1824, having made a passage of 114 days from Portsmouth by way of Teneriffe. She was a ship of 589 tons, but I have not been able to trace her history. Apparently she was a different vessel to the *Phoenix*, a two-decker built at Topsham in 1810, which had arrived at Hobart as a convict ship in 1822, as that vessel's tonnage is recorded as 493 tons. The *Phoenix*, after disembarking her convicts at Hobart, sailed for Sydney, and early in August arrived off the entrance to Port Jackson. She picked up a pilot, John M. Gray, but after passing safely through the Heads struck on the Sow and Pigs, a group of rocks a short distance inside the harbour entrance.

The following evening, after having been considerably lightened, she was refloated with the assistance of a boat from H.M.S. *Tamar*, but on being hove down it was discovered that she had sustained greater damage than had been thought, and she was condemned. Put up for sale, she was purchased by the colonial authorities for a thousand pounds, and was fitted up as a prison hulk, aboard which were held prisoners awaiting transportation to Moreton Bay, Norfolk Island and other penal settlements. For many years she was a familiar sight as she swung at her moorings in Lavender Bay, which was at first called Hulk or Phoenix Bay, but later was renamed for one, George Lavender, who was the hulk's boatswain[16].

The "Guildford's" Smart Passage.

The smartest passage from England to Port Jackson in the early 1820's was made by the *Guildford* in 1822. This twelve-years-old, Thames-built two-decker was making her fifth voyage with prisoners under the command of Magnus Johnson. She left London on April 7, touched briefly at Teneriffe, and anchored in Port Jackson on July 15, 99 days out. Her passage was the more meritorious because it was not a particularly good year for fast passages. The *Asia*, a ship of 533 tons, launched at Aberdeen in 1819, left England three days before the *Guildford*, but arrived at Port Jackson nine days after the latter ship, recording a direct passage of 111 days. The only other convict ship to leave England in April was the *Prince of Orange*, a two-decker of 363 tons, built at Sunderland in 1813. She made the best direct passage of the year from England to Hobart, but took 113 days.

The best passage from Cork to Port Jackson this year was the *Countess of Harcourt's* 109 days, but she did not sail from Ireland until September 3. However, she was a particularly smart ship, and her master, George Bunn, who later became one of the best-known shipping agents at Sydney, was something of a sail-carrier. She was built in India in 1811 and was a two-decker of 517 tons. On her maiden voyage as a convict ship in 1821, Bunn took her out to Hobart from Portsmouth in 99 days, and if contrary winds had not held her up for two days after entering the Derwent she would have anchored off Hobart 97 days after leaving England. At that time only one other convict ship had gone out to Hobart from England in under 100 days, and not until 1837 was the record of 99 days bettered.

The *Guildford* was one of the best-known convict ships. She was a slightly larger vessel than the old *Surrey*, being of 521 register tons against the *Surrey's* 443 tons, but, being built within a year of one another, they were probably very similar in other respects. In eight voyages as a convict ship the *Guildford* conveyed over 1,500 male prisoners to Australia for the loss of about a dozen men on the passage, the record of her passages being as follows:

1812	London to Port Jackson - -	137 days
1816	Ireland to Sydney - - -	Not Recorded
1818	Cork to Sydney - - -	138 days
1820	Portsmouth to Sydney - -	139 days
1822	London to Sydney - - -	99 days
1824	England to Sydney - - -	190 days
1827	Plymouth to Sydney - -	116 days
1829	Dublin to Sydney - - -	115 days

Her master on her first seven voyages was Magnus Johnson, but, as the Sydney *Monitor* phrased it, after having the sea as his mistress for so many years, Johnson married at last, and on returning to England from his 1827 voyage he relinquished the command to Robert Harrison. Johnson was a prudent and conscientious master, and he treated the convicts humanely. Various charges were brought against him by Surgeon Charles Linton after the *Guildford's* arrival at Port Jackson in 1827, but Linton was piqued by Johnson having failed to consult him when an informer had disclosed an alleged plot at mutiny, and there seems no doubt that the charges were groundless. In an affidavit, the commander of the guard, Captain J. D. Forbes, of the 39th Regiment, declared: "During the greater part of the voyage the prisoners were, with very few exceptions, out of irons, and, whenever the weather permitted, on deck, far more, indeed, than appeared to me either consistent with prudence or warranted by necessity, and generally the whole of them (190) at once." In another affidavit, the third mate, George Lynch Cotton, disclosed that he had been appointed by Johnson to assist Linton and had been relieved "from every other duty relative to the ship".[17]

On her sixth passage, which was her slowest, the *Guildford* sprang a leak after leaving Teneriffe and was compelled to put into Rio for repairs. Probably she was fortunate to make the South American port, as the leak necessitated continuous pumping. She was hove down and rendered watertight, the guard and convicts being transferred to a hulk lent for the purpose by the Brazilian government. Her two months' sojourn at Rio caused considerable sickness among the convicts, but the only man to die on the passage was accidentally killed when, in the high southern latitudes, he was flung into the hold and pitched on his head.

On her return to England after this voyage the *Guildford* passed into the ownership of James Mangles and Magnus Johnson, and was given a thorough repair. When she was registered anew, she was described as carvel-built and square-rigged, with a standing bowsprit. Except that her depth was reduced by two inches to 5 ft. 8 ins., her dimensions remained unaltered, and she retained her square stern, quarter galleries, and shield bust figurehead. Her register tonnage, however, was increased from 521 51/94 to 533 62/94 tons. When she next reached Port Jackson, in 1827, it was reported that twenty thousand pounds had been spent on her and as she had obtained a charter from the East India Company, fulfilling the company's requirements of a dry-dock survey, it is evident that she had received a very thorough overhaul.

On her last voyage as a convict ship she arrived at Port Jackson from Dublin on November 4, 1829. Early the following year she sailed from Hobart with a detachment of troops for India, arriving at Bombay on April 14, 1830. Harrison then took her out to Singapore, from which port she sailed for England. She was never heard of again and presumably foundered[18].

Faster Passages.

Compared with a few years earlier, the convict ships were now making faster passages, primarily because the majority were making direct passages, but also, no doubt, because their masters were gaining experience in finding the most favourable winds.

From the beginning of 1821 to the end of 1828 we have the records of 100 passages of convict ships from England or Ireland to Port Jackson, of which no fewer than 67 were of 130 days or under as against 33 of 131 days and over. There were 43 passages of 120 days or better and 20 of 141 days or over, five vessels which called first at Hobart being included in the latter total. Naturally, however, the number of ships capable of bettering 110 days for the passage was small, and in the eight years, there were but 13 passages to Port Jackson of 109 days or under. They were made by 10 ships, both the *Mangles* and the *Marquis of Hastings* each recording two passages of less than 110 days. When it is recalled that it was not uncommon for the hard-driven clippers, including some of the most famous, to make passages to Australia of over a hundred days, the performances of these ten convict ships were remarkable. They were not built for speed, and they were not sailed with the object of making record passages, but when favourable weather was encountered and they found the right winds, they were capable of making very good passages. Admittedly they were not consistent passage-makers, but neither were the clippers.

Details of the twelve fast passages between 1821 and 1828 are as follows:

Arrival		*Vessel*	*Date of Sailing*	*From*	*Days*
15 July	1822	*Guildford*	7-4-22	London	99
2 June	1828	*Mangles*	23-2-28	Dublin	100
3 Dec.	1827	*Louisa*	24-8-27	Woolwich	101
31 July	1827	*Marquis of Hastings*	18-4-27	Portsmouth	104
12 Oct.	1828	*Marquis of Hastings*	30-6-28	London	104
27 Oct.	1824	*Mangles*	13-7-24	Portsmouth	106
19 Feb.	1821	*Lord Sidmouth*	4-11-20	Cork	107
22 Apr.	1825	*Hooghly*	5-1-25	Cork	107
17 Sept.	1827	*Cambridge*	2-6-27	Dublin	107
27 Sept.	1827	*Prince Regent*	11-6-27	Deal	108
21 Dec.	1822	*Countess of Harcourt*	3-9-22	Cork	109
15 Jan.	1824	*Castle Forbes*	28-9-23	Cork	109

The most favourable year for fast passages was 1827. Of the 17 convict ships to arrive at Port Jackson that year, 13 made passages of 130 days or better, and only four took 131 days or over, the longest passage being the *Grenada's* 137 days by way of Hobart. Eight ships bettered 121 days, four of these vessels making passages of under 110 days. Another favourable year was 1825. All but two of the 14 ships to arrive made passages of 130 days or better, but although nine of them took 120 days or less, only one bettered 110 days.

On his arrival in Australia the master of a convict ship normally reported as his date of sailing from England or Ireland the day he left his last port of call or even the day on which Land's End vanished from sight. This gave him the fastest passage he could claim. Often, however, his ship might have been tossing about in the Channel for days, been driven back to port by heavy weather or lain wind-bound in the Downs or a Channel port. In 1821, for example, the *Phoenix* embarked her prisoners at Portsmouth on November 10, but she was then detained by westerly winds until December 20. She was forced to anchor at Dungeness on the 22nd and sailed from there on the 30th, but the bad weather continuing, she sought shelter at Portsmouth next day and did not finally sail from the Motherbank until January 5, almost two months after her convicts had embarked. In the appendices the date of sailing, whenever it has been possible to establish it, is the day on which the ship left port with all her convicts embarked, even though she may later have been driven into another port and taken her final departure days or even weeks later.[19]

The "Mangles" as a Passage-maker.

It was appropriate that two of the fastest passages in these years should have been made by the *Mangles*; for she was a regular visitor to Australia as a convict ship and was as well known as the *Guildford* and the *Surrey*. Moreover, she was a vessel with a particularly interesting history.

The *Mangles* was built at Calcutta for the London firm whose name she bore, and was initially registered at Calcutta on March 1, 1803. Built of teak, she was a vessel of 574 58/94 register tons, and was pierced for 22 guns. She was a three-master, ship-rigged, and had two decks, with poop and forecastle. Her stern was square, but when her registry was transferred to London on May 16, 1804, it was not stated whether she had quarter galleries. Her registered owners were then John and James Mangles, the part-owners of the *Guildford*, John Bannister Hudson, of St. Helen's, Bishopsgate-street, esquire, Thomas Reid, of Wapping, gentleman, and Hugh Reid, of Wellclose-square, the latter also being her master. The dimensions of the *Mangles* were: length, 121 ft. 2 ins., breadth, 32 ft. 3 ins., and depth, 5 ft. 6 ins. She was thus two and a half feet shorter than the *Guildford*, but the beam was greater by 15 inches. In 1806, when rice cargoes were plentiful and freights good, the *Mangles* was employed in the Bengal rice trade to China, and in September of the following year she was the second rice-ship captured by the famous French privateer, Robert Surcouf, who, evading the British squadron blockading Mauritius, had entered Port Louis the previous June in his 18-gun ship, the *Revenant*. The *Mangles* remained in the possession of the French until recaptured in 1813, when she was registered *de novo* at London by order of the Commissioners of the East India Company, dated October 8, 1813.

Her 1813 registry gives her dimensions as: Length, 121 ft. 2 ins., breadth, 32 ft. 11 ins., and depth, 5 ft. 5 ins. She was recorded as being of 560 58/94 register tons, and was still a three-masted, ship-rigged vessel, with two decks and poop and forecastle decks. She was now shown, however, as having quarter galleries and a woman as figurehead. Her new owners were Thomas Watkin Court, a mariner of Union Court, Broad-street, London, and two Calcutta merchants, Thomas Askin and Shaik Gollaum Hassen, but the latter became her sole owner in 1814 and within a few days of purchasing her had again sold her. She was owned in Calcutta until 1816, when she was purchased by Thomas Henry Buckle, Henry Mole Bagster, Walter Buchanan, and John William Buckle, all merchants of Mark-lane, London, and another London merchant, William Parker, of John-street, America-square. Buckle, Buckle, Bagster, and Buchanan were a well-known firm of London shipowners, and many of their vessels found employment in the convict service. On April 5, 1816, the firm sold a quarter of its interest in the *Mangles* to the ship's master, George Bunn, but he sold these rights back again the same day. The reason for this transaction is not apparent, but a similar incident occurred in 1818, when the firm, on the same day, first sold a sixth and then a fifth of their interest in the *Mangles* to Benjamin Bunn the younger, of Hackney, and next day he sold back to them all his interest in a quarter share. When Buckle & Company registered the *Mangles* anew at London in 1816, she was recorded as being of 594 38/94 register tons. The vessel's description was unaltered, but her dimensions were given as: length, 123 ft. 2 ins., breadth, 33 ft., and depth, 5 ft. 5 ins.

The *Mangles* made her first visit to Australia with convicts in 1820, when she arrived at Port Jackson on August 7. She was still owned by Buckle & Co., and her master was John Cogill, whose name, in English records, is spelt Coghill. She continued to be regularly employed as a convict ship until 1828. The following year she was put into the China tea trade. She was now owned by Buckle, Bagster & Buckle and McGhie, Hawkes & Carr, the last-mentioned partner in the latter firm being her master, William Carr of Waterloo-terrace, Commercial-road, London. Carr took her from London to Capsing-Moon, some miles to the north of Macao, during the south-west monsoon in the remarkable time of 94 days, running from Anjer to her destination in nine days. She returned to the convict service in 1832 and made her last voyage with prisoners in 1840.

As her outward passage to China in 1829 indicates, the *Mangles* possessed a turn of speed unusual in a vessel of her build, and, next to the *Morley*, she was probably the most consistent passage-maker among the regular convict ships, as the following details of her passages prove:

1820	Falmouth to Sydney – –	118 days
1822	Cork to Sydney – – –	140 days
1824	Portsmouth to Sydney – –	106 days
1826	Cork to Sydney – – –	118 days
1828	Dublin to Sydney – – –	100 days
1833	London to Sydney – –	126 days
1835	London to Hobart – –	102 days
1837	Portsmouth to Sydney – –	109 days
1840	Portsmouth to Sydney – –	150 days

On the first four of these passages she was commanded by John Cogill, and averaged 120½ days. She was very nearly lost when leaving Sydney, homeward bound with passengers and colonial produce, on February 12, 1825, being becalmed as she was clearing Port Jackson Heads. A strong current and swell threatened to put her on shore, but with the assistance of a number of boats which answered her distress signals she was kept off the land, and, after having been in danger for seven hours, a favourable breeze sprang up in the evening and she was able to bear away to sea. On her arrival at Sydney in 1826, Cogill left her to become a settler and was succeeded in the command by the chief mate, William Carr, who on September 9, 1839, became the sole owner of the *Mangles*.

Carr was probably a more intrepid sail-carrier than Cogill, or perhaps more fortunate in the weather he encountered. At any-rate, it was under his command that the *Mangles* really showed her capabilities. In 1828 she ran out to Sydney from Dublin in 100 days, and the following year made her smart passage to China. On her five passages as a convict ship under Carr's command, four of which were to Sydney and one to Hobart, she averaged 117 days, and on the first four of these her average was 109 days. Her second voyage under Carr, in 1833, began inauspiciously. Sailing from London on December 16, 1832, she struck a winter gale in the Channel and was forced to seek shelter at the Scilly Isles. She did not sail from there until January 1. Thus, although she was 126 days out from London when she arrived at Port Jackson, the

Mangles made the passage from St. Marys' Sound, in the Scillies, to Port Jackson in 100 days.

Her slowest passages were made in 1822, under Cogill, and in 1840, under Carr. On the first, she called at Rio, from which port she recorded a passage of 68 days to Port Jackson, which was rather better than average. In 1840 she put into the Cape, presumably because of an outbreak of scurvy among her prisoners, and her passage of 57 days from the Cape to Port Jackson was only fair. By then, however, her bottom was probably foul, and she was nearing the end of her long career. Carr died in 1841, and the *Mangles* passed into the ownership of the Ratcliffe shipowner, Thomas Ward. He transferred her to a Kingston-upon-Hull shipbuilder, Thomas Humphrey the elder, the following year, and when the latter went bankrupt the same year, the *Mangles* passed into the hands of a firm of Hull bankers, Pease and Liddells, in 1845. She was broken up that year.[20]

Another Fast Passage.

In 1829 the *Eliza's* record passage of 97 or 98 days from England to Port Jackson was equalled or bettered. The *Norfolk*, commanded by Alexander Greig, left Spithead on May 22, 1829, and dropped anchor in Port Jackson on August 27, after a passage of 97 days. The *Norfolk* was a barque of 537 tons, and, built at Littlehampton in 1814, was partly constructed of fir plank. She made five voyages with convicts, averaging 109 days. Her four passages to Sydney were made in 123, 97, 117 and 104 days, and on her only voyage to Hobart she took 106 days from Sheerness. The *Norfolk* disappeared from the register in 1838.

The "Chapman's" Last Voyage.

In 1824 the *Chapman* ran out to Hobart from England in 112 days, calling *en route* at St. Jago. Although this was by no means a record, it was nevertheless a good passage; for the *Chapman* was the ancient, Whitby-built ship which had been the scene of the bloody mutiny in 1817. She had of course, been substantially rebuilt since her launching in 1776, but was nearing her end when she made her second voyage as a convict ship in 1824. She was commanded by John Milbank, who was also her master when she made her third and final passage with prisoners two years later.

On the latter occasion this 50-years-old vessel was fortunate to reach her destination. She sailed from London for Hobart on April 10, 1826, and touched at St. Jago, resuming her voyage on May 10. In the South Atlantic, when in Lat. 32° 45, S., Long 28° 40, W., she encountered a severe gale on June 20, and suffered considerable damage. She lost her mainmast and mizentopmast, had her port bulwarks stove in, and her port quarter boats and davits carried away. For the convicts, battened down in the prison, it was a terrifying ordeal, and they must have expected the *Chapman* to sink at any moment. When the storm blew itself out, the crippled vessel lay wallowing in heavy seas, but fortunately the wind remained steady at south-east and she was able to bear up for Rio de Janeiro, where she arrived on the 28th.

Her repairs were not completed until the second week in August. Two prisoners succeeded in escaping while she was refitting and had not been recaptured when the *Chapman* sailed on August 9. She had an uneventful passage of 59 days from Rio to Hobart, where she arrived on October 7, 180 days out from London. She was not again employed as a convict ship, but she was still afloat in 1851, being then owned by King & Co., of London.[21]

The "Morley's" Fine Record.

In 1829 the *Morley*, which, like the *Chapman*, had first arrived at Port Jackson with prisoners in 1817, ended her career as a convict ship. Today she is usually remembered because of her introduction of whooping-cough into Sydney, but she has a better claim to rememberance; for she was a particularly smart sailer and she had an excellent health record.

The whooping-cough episode occurred in 1828, on her fifth passage with prisoners. When she anchored in Port Jackson from Dublin on March 3 of that year, neither her master, Henry Williams, nor her surgeon, Peter Cunningham, disclosed immediately that whooping-cough had occurred during the passage, among the soldiers' children. Consequently she was not at once quarantined, and it was only after communication with the shore had taken place that the local authorities learned of the outbreak. They acted promptly, placing the *Morley* and all aboard her in quarantine, but the damage had already been done, and for several weeks whooping-cough swept through Sydney, causing the deaths of several children.

The *Morley* was a Thames-built vessel, launched in 1811. On her first four voyages as a convict ship she was described as a ship of 480 tons, but subsequent to 1823 she underwent an extensive repair, and when she returned to Port Jackson in 1828 she was of 492 register tons. The *Morley*, of course, was not built for speed, but speed always was an elusive quality with sailing ships. Many vessels deliberately built for speed proved merely average and even slow passage-makers, while others not designed for speed unexpectedly earned themselves a reputation for quick passages. It was to this latter group that the *Morley* belonged, as is indicated by the following record of her passsages as a convict transport:

1817	England to Port Jackson, via the Cape	113 days
1818	The Downs to Port Jackson - - -	112 days
1820	London to Hobart - - - -	99 days
1823	The Downs to Hobart - - - -	108 days
1828	Dublin to Port Jackson, via Teneriffe -	121 days
1829	London to Port Jackson - - -	114 days

Her average for her six passages—four to Port Jackson and two to Hobart—was 111 days. On her two Tasmanian passages she averaged 103 days, and on her four New South Wales passages 115 days. As her 1817 and 1828 passages at least were not made direct, and her longest passage occupied 121 days, her record was a fine one, and she was remarkably consistent. Her health record, despite the whooping-cough episode, was also excellent. She conveyed over a thousand male and female convicts to Australia for the loss of only six men, and on three of her passages she arrived with no deaths to report among her prisoners.[22]

Tasmanian Passages.

The *Morley's* passage of 99 days from London to Hobart in 1820 stood as the record for a convict ship for many years. It was equalled in 1821 by the *Countess of Harcourt*, which sailed from Portsmouth, but it was not bettered until 1837, and in the intervening years the only transport to make the passage in less than 101 days was the *Moffatt*. In 1834 this 27-years-old, Bengal-built vessel, a ship of 820 tons, ran out from Plymouth to Hobart in 100 days.

Although a number of convict ships went out from England or Ireland in under 110 days, the passages to Hobart right up to the end of 1840 were very ordinary. The one exception was the passage of the *Sarah,* which left Spithead on December 22, 1836, and anchored off Hobart 97 days later, on March 29, 1837. A ship of 488 tons, built at London in 1819, she was making her second voyage as a convict ship, and she seems to have been especially fortunate in the weather she encountered. On her first passage with convicts in 1829, she ran out from London to Port Jackson in 100 days despite short calls at Tristan d'Acunha and St. Paul's Island. The *Claudine,* which left London five days before the *Sarah,* took 104 days for the passage from London to Port Jackson, but the *Larkins,* an old East Indiaman, left Cork 13 days before the *Sarah* sailed from London and did not make Port Jackson until 15 days after the *Sarah* had arrived. The latter's surgeon was the well-known Alick Osborne, who earlier in the year, on January 17, had arrived at Sydney as surgeon-superintendent of the *Sophia.* He was the first, and possibly throughout the history of transportation, the only, surgeon to arrive in Australia with prisoners twice in the same year. The *Sarah,* incidentally, made only these two voyages as a convict ship.

The Unlucky "Kains".

If the *Sarah* may be regarded as a lucky ship, although there were nine deaths among her prisoners on her Tasmanian passage, the *Kains* certainly was not. Built in 1816 for the Shields firm of shipowners, Kains & Co., she was a ship of 353 tons register, and her first voyage as a convict ship was also her last. One of her able seamen was Charles Picknell, whose illiterate diary affords one of the most interesting and vivid accounts of a convict ship's voyage. Picknell, having served a four years' apprenticeship, signed on the *Kains* on June 27, 1830, "for," as he put it, "sidney, new holland, vandemons land, to hell or elsewhere."

The voyage of the *Kains* began unhappily. On July 3, when she was lying at Woolwich taking her prisoners on board, a Sunderland brig drove athwart her, and carried away her maintopsail yard in two pieces. Next day, however, she continued to embark her prisoners, and after they had been visited by Quakers, who gave the prisoners many useful presents, the *Kains* sailed on July 8, only to lie windbound in the Downs before being able to proceed to Spithead, from where she sailed on the 17th. The weather in the Channel was fair, except for some fog, and when visitors came aboard off Exmouth on the 24th, Picknell cheered them so heartily that he lost his cap overboard. By the 27th the *Kains* was off Plymouth, and the following day, when in company with the convict ship *Burrell*, the shores of England disappeared below the horizon. "women was downhearted to leave old england," records Picknell, with a fine disregard for grammar and capital letters. "We run the *Burrell* out of sight."

Next day there was trouble with the crew. "Captain said 6 A.B. seamen wanted to rise a mutiny," is Picknell's laconic description of the incident. "it was for talking to the women. put in irons. lashed down to poop deck 2 days. 1 night as mutineers. put 4 from larbert (larboard). 2 starbert (starboard) watches. fire arms over our heads. 2 guns upon the poop levelled into the main deck. 2 hundred miles from old england in the west ocearn. then he (the master, William Lushington Goodwin) began to ill use us. prentice fredrick smith lashed up to larbert main rigging. flog 6 dosen lashes for saying you and i cant ist (hoist) this punchin of wine alone. gard over im. soards. daggers. captain struck several. women crying."

However, the trouble blew over, the seamen being released at 6 p.m. on the 30th amid the crew's rejoicings. The *Kains* spoke a number of vessels as she made her way down the Bay of Biscay at, according to Picknell, eight or ten "nots", but with the death of a little girl of three, on August 3, the ship was evidently thrown into gloom; for that evening Goodwin "gave larbert (watch) bottle rum for singing to cheer the women up". However, on the 7th when Picknell got the guns ready for a pirate, there was more trouble. The chief mate was confined for getting drunk and encouraging his watch to sing saucy songs, and the boatswain was promoted to take charge of the mate's watch. The mate was not released until the *Kains* arrived at Teneriffe on the 11th.

After watering, the *Kains* resumed her voyage on the 14th, and two days later the water was rationed to a gallon a day per man, half a gallon for each pig, a pint for each goose, half a gallon for a dozen ducks, and a pint for a dozen chickens. Next day the chief mate was again confined, for having sent letters to London from Teneriffe and for other misconduct, but on the 18th Picknell records: "chief mate let loos to walk the decks. He broke, to have no command nor say whatever no more on board."

The first death among the convict women occurred on the 22nd, and caused "crying all over the ship". Sharks were caught, the "tails and wings" of one being put at the end of the jibboom and the spritsail yard arm's end, presumably for good luck, much as a householder might hang a horseshoe on his dwelling. The same day a boat was sent across to a Portuguese brig, whose master presented the *Kains* with "thoussands of segars". On September 7, according to Picknell, there was an encounter with a pirate. "a beautiful brig, a pirate, spanish, bore down upon us," he wrote, "and came up under lee. ask us in spanish where from. ask us in english were bound. told him east india. we opened ports, loaded up all our guns with 2 balls ready for action." But evidently the Spaniard did not consider a convict ship worth the trouble of taking, and the *Kains* continued on her way unmolested. On the 17th, when a heavy sea was running, she ran into a fierce tropical storm, with heavy claps of thunder and vivid lightning. "we choaked our pumps up with swobs," Picknell says. "our ship chafed her rigging all to peases and (it) laid about decks like hoakum." On the 21st the fore topsail was blown away, and when a new one was bent, the old one was thrown out of the fore top and cut the cook's head open. "stunersail fell down upon my starbert second toe," Picknell records, on the same day, "and brake two plases. very painful."

There was still trouble with the crew. Goodwin accused Picknell and other seamen of having given their rum ration to the women convicts, and struck several of the men. "I got out of his way," Picknell remarks. The men's grog ration was stopped. The second mate, who apparently had been a prisoner for six weeks, although Picknell had not previously mentioned the fact, was released and allowed to return to duty. On September 25 an American ship and a London cutter were boarded, tobacco being purchased from the former. Two days later Picknell's curious diary contains this entry: "Macollum flogged boy ramsden for dishonesty. ramsden flogged boy macollum for laziness. 6 dosen each. lashed up to main rigging the first time." The equinoctial line was crossed on the 28th, but because of the women convicts Goodwin would not allow the usual homage to be paid to King Neptune. But, oddly enough, he permitted the men as much grog as they wanted, and

Picknell says: "grog came to us in horse buckets. captain, doctor, and all the ofisers drank with us. we sung and played habrem wackets and parson parrish (two sailors' games). quite merry and drunk. P.M. 6 aclock. i begun to throw wauter about all hands, wauter flew in all directions over all hands. P.M. 8 aclock. gave three cheers and drop it . . . prisoners singing well below. i kept myself sober and had all the sport."

With the wind mostly foul, the *Kains* made slow progress. The seamen complained of their food. "our bread mouldy and magoty," says Picknell. "our beef like oakwood. our water stink and magoty. Oour peas all goan (gone). 1 more cask of flour. we must now eat what the hogs want or starve quite." The *Kains* had crossed the equinoctial line for the second time on October 5, and she crossed it again on the 19th. A week later, with still no sign of a fair wind, Goodwin accused the chief mate and three seamen of trying to raise a mutiny. They were all four put in irons and secured to the chain cable before the windlass, but next day the mate was confined to his cabin. The water ration was further reduced, being cut by half a gallon for both the convicts and the sailors. On November 1, according to Picknell, the *Kains* was only 15° south of the equinoctial line, but that day the wind swung round to the south-west, and stunsails were set alow and aloft. "going 8 nots," says Picknell. "thank god for it. different climate. cold." On November 5, when Picknell tells us he thought of the fireworks in England and wished to be there, the second death among the prisoners occurred, the victim being the oldest woman aboard, aged 81. Two days later the last of the mutinous seamen was released from his irons, but the chief mate's punishment continued and he was not returned to duty until November 11.

On the night of the 13th, if we are to believe Picknell, the phantom Flying Dutchman was sighted at ten o'clock. "broat her into action," he records. "fired 1 gun. set all the women acrying, praying, and confessing of there sins. plenty of fun and grog that night." The *Kain's* ill-luck was still holding. Foul wind alternated with light, fair breezes, and because of the bad provisions and her protracted passage through the tropics, scurvy had made its appearance, several of the seamen being confined to their bunks. Even when the ship at last entered Table Bay bad luck dogged her; for her topsail sheets carried away. The previous day she had lost

Oil painting by W. A. Knell *National Maritime Museum, Greenwich*

The "MORLEY", off the Lizard, 1823

Water-colour by Neve *National Maritime Museum, Greenwich*

The "FLORENTIA" passing through Tellicherry Roads, 1825

her stream anchor, and a day or two later the gig's stem was damaged when, secured astern and rising on a sea, the boat struck the ship's counter or side. The seamen went on strike, but Goodwin, apparently, drove them back to their duty with a mallet, and then had four of them gaoled, each being later sentenced to 15 days' imprisonment. While necessary repairs were carried out to the ship's rigging, and sheep, goats, kids, a bull, geese, ducks, and fowls were shipped, three of the seamen deserted, taking the cutter with them. The boat was recovered at a cost of 100 Cape dollars, but the men, apparently, were not picked up. On December 26 the *Kains* got under weigh, but she was becalmed and could not get out of Table Bay until the following day. She was still off the Cape of Good Hope, with a foul wind, on the 31st, when Picknell's diary ends[23].

The *Kains* eventually arrived at Port Jackson on March 11, 1831, 246 days out from London. The *Burrell,* which she had so quickly outsailed the day both lost sight of England, had arrived at Sydney on December 19, after a passage from Plymouth of 145 days. The *Kains* had had more than her share of mishaps, but more were still to come. After disembarking her women convicts, she left Sydney on June 5 for Launceston, in Tasmania, with passengers and a miscellaneous cargo, but ran into a storm and took a terrible battering, losing her main topgallant mast, her foretopmast and foretopgallantmast. Two of her seamen were lost overboard and not recovered. On July 21 she limped back to Sydney.

She sailed again for Launceston on September 11, but evidently again encountered adverse weather. On October 20 she entered Whirlpool Reach of the Tamar River, on the shores of which Launceston stands, with a good breeze, but no sooner was she within the Reach than the wind suddenly dropped and she lay becalmed. Within a few minutes she struck her keel on a sunken rock, and her sternpost and rudder were carried away. She was run ashore in North Harbour, which was more commonly called the Devil's Elbow, and within 10 minutes there was five feet of water in her hold. The *Kains* was hard and fast, in 15 feet of water at high tide, but dry when the tide was out. The wreck was sold for £330, and after much effort her hull was got off and brought up the Tamar, where, after repairs, it was converted into a floating store. The unlucky *Kains* had sailed her last voyage.

R

The Wreck of the ''Amphitrite''.

The first convict ship proper to be lost on the outward passage to Australia was the *Amphitrite,* which went ashore on the French coast with heavy loss of life during a fierce gale in 1833. Owned by her master, 33-years-old John Hunter, who had commanded her for eight years, the *Amphitrite* had been chartered as a convict ship through the prominent London shipbroker, Joseph Lauchlan. After her loss it was alleged that she had been unseaworthy, it being asserted that her timbers were rotten and not properly fastened. These charges, of course, were denied, and there seems little doubt that, whether seaworthy or not, her condition had nothing to do with her wreck. Five months earlier she had undergone a thorough repair at Deptford under the supervision of the naval authorities, by whom she was employed at the time as a transport, and before being taken up for the convict service she underwent the usual naval examination, being certified as seaworthy and well-found.

The *Amphitrite* sailed from London on August 25. She had embarked 106 female prisoners and 12 of their children, and, in addition, carried Surgeon-superintendent James Forrester, his wife, and a crew of 16. There were therefore 136 persons aboard. It was Forrester's third voyage in charge of convicts. He had arrived at Port Jackson as surgeon-superintendent of the *Brothers* in 1827 and of the *Southworth* in 1832, but apparently on neither occasion had he been accompanied by his wife.

The day after she sailed the *Amphitrite* ran into a violent storm off Dungeness. On the morning of the 30th she hove to, and about noon that day, when she first sighted the French coast, she was lying three miles to the east of Boulogne Harbour. It was blowing very hard, with poor visibility and a mountainous sea. During the afternoon, in an attempt to keep her off the land, Hunter set the fore and main topsails, but she continued to drift towards the coast and by three o'clock was in sight of Boulogne. An hour and a half later, the tide having carried her round into the harbour, she grounded on the sands. It was low tide, and Hunter let go the anchor, hoping that the *Amphitrite* would swing round with the turn of the tide.

As soon as her plight was observed, thousands of people assembled on the beach to watch the stricken vessel. A pilot-boat, commanded by Francis Heuret, set out for the *Amphitrite*, and by five o'clock was under her bows. There is little doubt that at this stage all aboard might have been saved with little difficulty, but Hunter refused the pilot-boat's offer of help. He does not seem to have realized that the *Amphitrite's* position was critical, believing she would float off when the tide turned, but the primary reason for his rejection of the pilot-boat's proffered assistance was, apparently, Forrester's insistence that the women prisoners should not be landed, as there would be no means of keeping the women together and many of them would seize the opportunity to escape. Hunter concurred with this view, and the obstinacy of the two men led to the tragedy which now occurred.

A French sailor, Pierre Henin, did not share the master's sanquine hopes. Knowing Boulogne Harbour intimately, he foresaw that when the sea began to come in, the *Amphitrite's* position would be hopeless. About six o'clock, when the pilot-boat had left the stranded vessel, Henin stripped off his clothes, secured a light line to his body, and plunged into the surf. The *Amphitrite* lay three-quarters of a mile from the shore, and Henin was about an hour swimming out to her. He told those aboard that unless they got speedily ashore, they would be lost, and he urged them to throw him a line. Two lines were thrown over by members of the crew, one from the stern and the other from the bow, and Henin succeeded in taking hold of the latter. He began to swim toward shore, but after a few minutes the line was not paid out, and Henin returned to the ship, calling out to those aboard to give him more rope. Both Hunter and Forrester refused, as the line had been flung overboard without the master's orders, and he and Forrester were equally determined not to abandon ship. In the face of both men's obstinacy, there was nothing more that Henin could do. He was by now utterly exhausted, and he was hauled ashore.

Whether the convicts and their children were battened down below or were already on deck is uncertain. They had been below when the ship had struck, but at some time during the evening they broke down the half deck hatch and rushed frantically on deck. Their piteous cries carried clearly on the rising wind to those on shore, who now helplessly watched the final tragedy.

When the flood-tide began, the *Amphitrite* started to pound heavily on the sands. Around eleven o'clock a heavy sea struck her, and immediately she broke in two amidships. She went to pieces in a few minutes. Only three seamen reached shore alive, floating in on pieces of wreckage until they were close enough to be hauled through the breakers on to the beach by those watching the grim drama from the shore. They were the only survivors, the remaining 133 persons aboard being drowned.

Driven on a lee shore in a fierce Channel gale, the wreck of the *Amphitrite* was inevitable, particularly as Hunter was unacquainted with Boulogne Harbour and there was no pilot on board. Had a pilot-boat put out to her as soon as she was observed in distress, she possibly might have been saved and have been brought safely to an anchorage within the harbour, but, when no boat put out to her until after she had struck, her doom was certain. Yet her passengers and crew might have been saved had Hunter accepted the offers of assistance, firstly, from the pilot-boat and, secondly, from Henin. It was the master's lack of judgment—whether or no he was swayed by Forrester's arguments, as the survivors asserted—that was the real cause of the tragedy of the *Amphitrite*[24].

The Tragedy of the ''Neva''.

Almost two years later, but some 13,000 miles away from the scene of the *Amphitrite's* wreck, another female convict ship was lost with an even heavier toll of life. Bound for Port Jackson, the barque *Neva* sailed from Cork on January 8, 1835. A Hull-built vessel of 331 tons, she had been launched either in 1813 or 1818, and was classed AE1 by Lloyds. There was no question that she was thoroughly seaworthy and well-found. From January, 1828, until May, 1832, she had been in the transport service, and had made voyages to North America, the West Indies, the Mediterranean, and elsewhere. On her discharge from the transport service she had been given a thorough repair at a cost of £2,800 in St. Ive's dock at Deptford, and had then been taken up for the convict service. She had reached Sydney with male convicts on November 21, 1833, making a direct passage from Plymouth of 115 days. From Sydney she had gone to Manilla and then to Singapore, where she had loaded a valuable cargo for London. On her return from this first voyage as a convict ship, she had gone into Dowson's dock at Limehouse, and, after upwards of five hundred pounds had been spent on her, had again been accepted for the convict service.

Her master on both her voyages as a convict ship was Benjamin Hutchins Peck. He had been master of the transport *Silvia* from July, 1829, until his appointment as master of the *Neva* in March, 1833, and had made voyages to Bermuda, North America, the Mediterranean, the Brazils and South America.

On her second voyage, the *Neva* left Cork on January 8, 1835, bound for Port Jackson. She had 150 women convicts, 55 children, and nine free women aboard under the superintendence of Surgeon John Stephenson, who was making his fifth voyage in charge of prisoners. He had first arrived at Port Jackson as surgeon-superintendent of the *Guildford* in 1829, and had returned there in the *Eleanor* in 1831 and the *Waterloo* in 1833. His third passage in a convict ship had been to Hobart in 1832, in the *Katherine Stewart Forbes*.

The *Neva*, 125 days out from Cork, was in Bass Strait on May 13. At 2 a.m., when under double-reefed topsails and courses, King Island was sighted, and, with the wind freshening from west-nor'-west, Peck at once hauled the *Neva* to the wind on the port tack to clear the Harbinger Reefs. The wind was blowing strongly, but it was moonlight, with occasional clouds, and the master felt quite certain of his position and of the ship's safety. "The northern extremity of the island was from two to three points open to the lee bow," he later told a court of inquiry, "and appeared to be distant about three or four leagues." The *Neva* stood on the larboard, or, as we should now say, the port, tack for about three hours, but suddenly, about 5 a.m., the lookout reported breakers ahead.

Peck instantly ordered the helm hard a-starboard. As the *Neva* came head to wind, her keel struck a rock under her stern, unshipping her rudder. She payed off, came back again, and filled. The head sheets were let fly, and the head yards shivered, to bring her to the wind again, but she gathered way before this could be accomplished, and, striking the reef on the port bow, swung broadside on, the sea making a fair breach over her. The mainsail was hauled up and the yards braced a box to keep the *Neva* steady on the rock, but she bilged and filled with water. The foremast and all the topmasts were cut away, leaving only the mainmast and mizenmast standing, but the stanchions of the prison fell down from the pounding on the reef, and the prisoners rushed on deck and flocked aft to the cabin and poop.

An effort was now made to launch the boats. The gig, however, was dashed to pieces when one of the iron davits broke, and although the pinnace was launched over the gunwale by cutting the bulwarks, she sank when she was rushed by the women prisoners. Peck, Stephenson, who had been for some days extremely ill with scorbutic dysentery, some of the women, and several members of the crew had got into the pinnace, but when she was swamped only Peck and two seamen were able to regain the wreck. The remainder, including Stephenson, were drowned. The longboat was next launched. Every precaution was taken to prevent her being rushed by the frenzied women, but almost at once she was capsized by the sea, all in her except the master and the chief mate, Joseph Bennett, being drowned. The cutter had been got in upon the poop, but it was either found impossible to launch her or, like the longboat, she was capsized by the seas breaking over the *Neva*.

In about four hours after striking, the barque went to pieces. She parted in four places, and the poop deck fell in upon the women crowded in the cabin below, killing or injuring many of them. According to the testimony of two of the women who were saved, some of those who had taken refuge in the cuddy had broached some liquor, and were so hopelessly drunk when the *Neva* finally went to pieces that they were incapable of helping themselves.

Twenty-two survivors drifted ashore on pieces of wreckage. In addition to Peck and Bennett, 12 of the women prisoners and eight of the crew reached shore. The piece of wreckage on which Peck took refuge was eight hours drifting ashore. Originally about 21 persons had been clinging to it, but with the seas breaking over it continuously all but Peck and two others were swept to their deaths before the shore was reached. After they had landed, the survivors found a partly filled puncheon of rum which had drifted ashore from the wreck, and Peck served a dram to each person.

The survivors slept that night in the bush, but when Peck wakened the following morning he found, ten or twelve yards away, three of the women lying dead with their faces to the sand. On the beach, near to the rum puncheon, two others were also dead, and a third was dying. A boy also died after reaching shore, reducing the number of survivors to 15. Some flour and pork drifted ashore from the wreck, and the next few days were spent in collecting what provisions could be found washed up on the beach. Peck and two of the seamen then set off along the beach in one direction and the mate and another two seamen in the opposite direction, and in two days the six men buried 95 bodies which had been washed ashore.

When they had been a fortnight on the island, the survivors were found by two other shipwrecked mariners. These men came from the cutter *Tartar,* which had been wrecked on King Island about the same time as the *Neva.* They told Peck of a sealer living on the island, and a search party located him. The sealer, whose name was Scott, had a number of dogs, and the survivors of the *Neva* and the crew of the *Tartar* lived on wallabys which the dogs cornered and killed. Shortly after Peck's party had found Scott, Charles Friend, the owner of the *Tartar,* reached King Island in a small vessel named the *Sarah* or *Sarah Ann* in search of his missing cutter. He located her crew and, learning from them of the *Neva's* loss, tramped 35 miles to Peck's camp. Friend embarked 12 of the convict ship's survivors, and landed them at George Town, on the Tamar River below Launceston, on June 26. He had been unable to pick up two women and a man who were on another part of the island, but they were rescued in due course by a small government vessel despatched to King Island for the purpose.

A court of inquiry consisting of Major George Deare, the commandant at Launceston, Mr. W. Lyttleton, the police magistrate at the settlement, and Lieutenant Matthew Curling Friend, R.N., the Port Officer, exonerated the master, surgeon, officers and crew of the *Neva* from all blame for her loss. In his evidence, Peck had attributed the barque's loss to the set of the current, which he claimed had carried the *Neva* 25 miles to the southward, and to the position of the Harbinger Reef having been laid down in his chart too far to the eastward. The court decided that the *Neva's* loss was due to the extraordinary strength of the tide, "the reef being improperly laid down or an erroneous opinion formed by the master and crew of their distance from the land when the ship hauled to the wind, or more probably the concurrent influence of several minute errors". The court reported that the seven survivors who died on King Island during their first night ashore were the victims of cold and fatigue, "aided if not caused by the inordinate use of rum".

There is some conflict of evidence as to the number of persons drowned when the *Neva* went down. Peck told the court that 239 persons were on board when she struck, there having been three deaths—a seaman, a woman convict and a child—and one birth up to that time. If Peck did not include himself in his total, there were actually 240 persons on board at the time of the wreck. An official report sent to Sydney from Hobart on July 4 stated that the surgeon, 17 seamen, nine free women, 138 female prisoners and 59 children had been drowned. With the 22 survivors, including the seven who died after landing, this gives a total of 246 or, after making allowance for the three earlier deaths and one birth, of 244. However, evidence at the court of inquiry mentions only 55 children as being aboard, and if this is correct the total is reduced to 240 persons, thus agreeing with Peck's figure if he had not counted himself. It would therefore seem that 218 persons were drowned, of whom 138 were convicts, and to this death-roll has to be added the seven survivors who died on King Island, six of whom were prisoners, making the total of deaths in the disaster 225, 144 of whom were convicts.[25]

The Wreck of the "George III".

The *Neva* was the second convict ship lost off Tasmania with heavy loss of life in 1835. A month earlier the *George III* had struck a sunken and uncharted rock in D'Entrecasteaux Channel when bound for Hobart.

A ship of 394 tons, built at a Thames yard in 1810, the *George III* was commanded by William Hall Moxey, and had embarked 220 male prisoners at Woolwich. Her surgeon-superintendent was David Wyse, whose only previous voyage in charge of prisoners had been to Hobart in 1833 in the old *Surrey*, then making her seventh voyage as a convict ship. The *George III* left the Downs on December 12, 1834. Scurvy, which Wyse attributed to the scantiness of the provisions and the substitution of cocoa for oatmeal in the prisoners' diet, made its appearance among the convicts. When the *George III* sighted the Tasmanian coast about Port Davey on the morning of April 12, 1835, 121 days out from England, 12 prisoners had died of scurvy, and there were 60 on the sick-list, 50 of whom were confined to bed with scurvy and quite unable to help themselves.

Wyse regarded it as of paramount importance for the health of

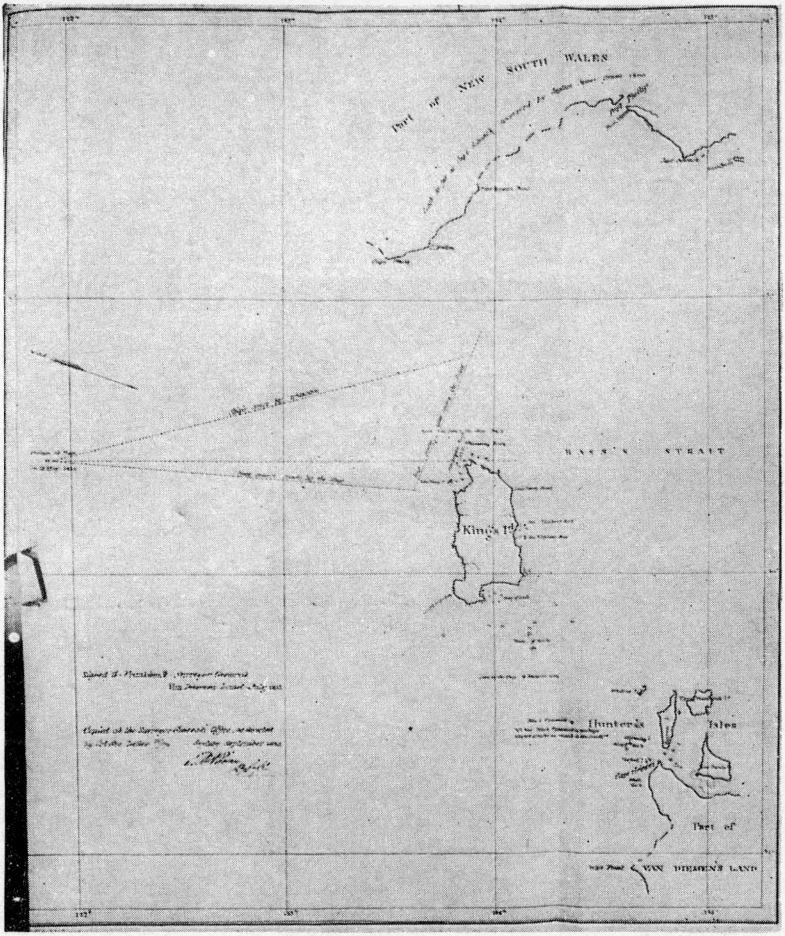

Mitchell Library, Sydney, N.S.W.

Official chart illustrating the wreck of the "NEVA". The top line shows the ship's course by estimation from her position at noon on May 12, 1835; the bottom line her true course, including her turn to port on sighting land

Coloured Lithograph by J. Grieves after Colonel Light. *National Maritime Museum, Greenwich*

From left to right: "HENRY PORCHER", "GOSHAWK", "EDEN" and "EMERALD ISLE", lying in Port Adelaide. The last two and the "HENRY PORCHER" carried convicts to Australia the prisoners that the *George III* should make port with the least possible delay. On his previous voyage the *Surrey* had entered the Derwent by the Storm Bay passage, but there was a shorter approach to Hobart through D'Entrecasteaux Channel, lying between North and South Bruni Islands and the coast of the Tasmanian mainland. It was not favoured by sailing ships because of the violent squalls which suddenly rushed down from the hills and prevented vessels from carrying sail, but Wyse suggested it should be used by the *George III.* Having consulted his charts and the sailing directions of Captain John Horsburgh, the recognised authority of the day, Moxey agreed to take D'Entrecasteaux Channel, stating that, as there was good anchoring ground in the channel, he would immediately let go the anchor should the weather prove unfavourable.

The *George III* sighted the high land in the vicinity of Port Davey at eleven o'clock on the morning of April 12, and, rounding South West and South Capes, entered D'Entrecasteaux Channel in the evening. The weather was mild, and visibility was good, the land standing out distinctly under the bright moonlight. A leadsman was stationed in the chains, and the ship made her way cautiously up the channel under easy sail, moving at from one and a half to two knots. She passed between the Actaeon Reefs with seven and a half fathoms beneath her, and Moxey and his officers were satisfied that every danger had been negotiated and that it was safe to proceed. The soundings were kept going, and the *George III*, two or three miles from the land, was kept under double-reefed topsails, with the foresail hauled up, ready to come immediately to anchor should danger threaten or the moon vanish behind clouds.

At about 9.30 p.m., some 15 minutes after passing between the Actaeon and Black reefs, the leadsman suddenly cried: "Quarter less four." Moxey, who was on the weather side of the poop, at once ordered the helm to be put hard a-port, but almost at the same instance the ship struck, though not violently. She grazed along the sunken, and until then unknown, rock (which today is marked in the charts as the King George Rock) and brought up. The sea was smooth, and a boat was lowered to sound round the ship, finding two fathoms ahead, two and a half fathoms abreast the starboard gangway, three and a half fathoms on the port quarter and four and a half fathoms on the starboard quarter.

A swell now commenced and the water began to break, causing the ship to strike so violently that those on deck were flung from their feet. After about five shocks, the mainmast crashed over the starboard side, carrying away the mizentopmast and breaking the weather bulwarks down to the deck. The lee bulwarks were cut away so that the gig might be lowered, but she went down stern foremost and was swamped. Moxey ordered the jolly-boat, in which the third mate, Field, had been sounding round the ship, to come alongside, but Field replied that the sea was too rough and the boat already crowded, having picked up some of those thrown into the water from the gig when it was swamped in lowering. Field was therefore ordered to find a landing-place, disembark the 11 persons aboard, and return at once. The third mate, however, believing that he was only 15 miles from Hobart, decided to make for that port to report the wreck and procure help. Actually the jolly-boat was 60 miles from Hobart. The 10 persons in the boat with him were more than the boat could safely hold, and he landed four at Three Hut Point to lighten her, but it was not until 8 p.m. on April 13 that the jolly-boat reached Hobart.

Meanwhile, amid a scene of indescribable confusion aboard the *Geroge III*, efforts were made to launch the longboat. The foremast had followed the mainmast and mizentopmast over the side, and although it was only 15 or 20 minutes since the ship had struck, the water was already swirling over the main deck. The longboat, already filled with survivors, according to the captain, was floating from one side of the deck to the other, in imminent danger of being stove in. However, in some way she was got outside the ship, but then lay on the heaving sea, entangled in the fallen spars and the debris of the wrecked rigging. Moxey, trying to push the foreyard under the water to enable the boat to pass over it, became jammed between it and the boat, but was dragged into the boat before he was seriously injured. The boat was at last got free of the wreckage, and Surgeon Wyse, according to his own story, rushed forward and clambered into her.

At this time the *George III* had canted to starboard, and those still aboard were clinging to the port side, which was the only part of the ship now above the seas. They cheered loudly as the longboat, in which there were 42 persons, pulled clear, and set out for the shore. The *George III* was on her beam ends and gradually sinking, with the survivors huddled together on the port side or clinging to the shattered stumps of the fore and main masts and to the spars floating in a tangled mass around the ship. About four o'clock the mizen-mast snapped off and fell overboard, the ship righting slightly, so that only half the deck was now under water.

Moxey, in the longboat, experienced difficulty in finding a landing-place owing to the rocky shore and high surf, but eventually located Southport Beach. Here 36 of those in the boat were landed, wading to the shore through the surf almost up to their necks. Surgeon Wyse was among those landed, being asked by the master to take charge of the party set ashore. With five men, Moxey then returned to the wreck in the longboat, reaching the *George III* about six o'clock and being greeted with cheers. She took aboard between 40 and 50 persons, including the three military officers in charge of the convict ship's guard, and landed this party on the beach around eight o'clock.

Once more the longboat set out for the wreck, but as she again approached it a passing schooner, the *Louisa,* was seen heading for the *George III.* She picked up the remaining survivors, and then headed for Southport Beach, where Moxey had returned in the longboat. He found that Assistant Surgeon McGregor, of the 50th Regiment, had wandered into the bush and, apparently, had become lost. Moxey ferried out the survivors he had earlier landed to the *Louisa,* but left seven men behind with the longboat to try and locate McGregor.

On news of the disaster reaching Hobart at eight o'clock that night, the Colonial Government's brigs *Tamar* and *Isabella,* and the tiny paddle-wheel steamer *Governor Arthur,* the first steamship built on the Derwent, were ordered to the scene. All three vessels left Hobart within two hours of the jolly-boat's arrival, and at 4 a.m. on April 14, the *Governor Arthur* met the *Louisa* 30 miles from Hobart. Having supplied the schooner with provisions, the *Governor Arthur* proceeded to Southport Beach, where Surgeon McGregor and the seven men left behind by Moxey were picked up. All were suffering from cold and exposure, and the Colonial Surgeon considered that had he not been rescued, McGregor must have died within two hours. The paddle-wheeler then went on to the wreck in case any survivor was still aboard, but the party which boarded the *George III* found only the body of an elderly convict, John Roberts, who, being unable to swim, had lashed himself to a ringbolt in the surgeon's cabin in the hope of being washed ashore, and had been drowned.

The *George III* had left England with 308 persons aboard, of whom 220 were male prisoners. Allowing for two children born on the passage, and the deaths of a soldier's wife, three children, and 12 convicts, there were 294 persons aboard when she was wrecked. Of this total, 161 were saved, and 133 drowned, although some accounts place the figure of drowned at 134. The whole of the military guard, consisting of three officers and 29 other ranks, were saved, together with six of the soldiers' wives and 11 of their children, and all but two members of the crew were among the survivors. The death-roll was confined almost exclusively to the prisoners, of whom only 81 were saved and 127 perished, with a soldiers's wife, three children and the two seamen. The reason why so few prisoners were saved was never satisfactorily explained, and it constitutes the blackest feature of the story of the *George III's* loss. So confusing and contradictory is the testimony as to what happened aboard the ship after she struck, however, that a clear picture of the events cannot be drawn.

When the *George III* crashed on to the sunken rock the prisoners were, of course, below deck, having been locked up in the prison some hours earlier. At the first shock, and especially after the ship began to pound violently on the rocks, they begged to be released, and tried to break out of the prison, using saws and hammers which they had secreted. The sentries on duty at the main hatchway leading to the prison were in charge of Corporal Deverell. Certainly two, and probably three, shots were fired, one of which may have been intended as a signal of distress when it had been found impossible to fire one of the ship's guns. But some of the convict survivors declared that the prisoners had been fired on to prevent them breaking out of the prison and reaching the deck, and it was claimed that two men, Robert Luker and William Yates, were killed. In consequence of these reports, and persistent rumours that the convicts had been fired on within a few minutes of the *George III* being wrecked, the bodies of some of the prisoners who had perished were exhumed, but a coroner's jury reported that they could find no sign of gunshot or cutlass wounds on them. This evidence, however, is of little value, since the bodies were very decomposed, and those of Luker and Yates were not identified.

The evidence of Surgeon Wyse before the court of inquiry shows that when the ship began to strike violently the prisoners were screaming out to be released. He went down to the prison doors, and the convicts, putting their hands through the grating, seized hold of him, saying, "You promised to stand by us." "So I will," Wyse said he replied. "I shall remain here with you." Two of the stanchions had fallen down, and some of the convicts were trying to clamber through the opening.

"A considerable body of the military," Wyse told the court, "formed a compact guard round the hatchway, with their muskets levelled, I conceive, in intimidation. Two of the most deserving convicts in the ship came through the opening to me and clung to my knees. Corporal Bell ordered them back, but the men cried out, 'The water is already up to our knees.' The crashing of the rocks through the ship's bottom whilst I was in the hatchway was dreadful."

Wyse left the hatchway, and at his order Bell allowed the two convicts to follow him. A few minutes later the mainmast fell. "Someone," said Wyse, "suggested the propriety of firing a gun, but it was impossible. This was not more than five minutes after the first shock. Major Ryan said he would fire some muskets as a signal, and I heard a report of two or three shots, but did not see on what part of the ship they took place." At this time Wyse expected the ship to go to pieces in a few minutes, and thought his only chance of saving his life would be to fasten himself to a spar.

Major Thomas Ryan, of the 50th Regiment, the commander of the guard, had been confined to his bunk for three weeks suffering from severe ophthalmia. He ran at once to the quarter deck, where he was met by his second-in-command, Lieutenant Minton of the 6th Regiment, and Corporal Deverell. Minton reported that the prisoners were breaking out of the prison, and as he did so a sea broke over the vessel, sweeping everything before it. Ryan called for Wyse, and several of the soldiers came to him, saying that the prisoners had broken out of the prison and were rushing on deck. "Good God," said Ryan, "what is to be done? Where is the doctor?"

"The mainmast then fell," Ryan told the court, "and at this moment I believe that nearly all who were drowned met their melancholy fate, as the ship filled nearly to the upper deck. Mr.

Matson (the chief mate) tried in vain to fire off one of the large guns, and I desired one of the soldiers to fire his musket over the side of the ship as a signal of distress, which was done. A great number of the prisoners were then on deck. The guard was nearly up to the middle in water surrounding the hatchways, and trying to prevent the prisoners from coming up. The foremast then fell, tearing away everything with it. . . . I got on the poop. . . . The captain was amidships, trying to launch the longboat, where an immense crowd were rushing. The doctor was on the poop, with his coat off, perfectly cool and collected.

"I said, 'Good God, what is to be done? The longboat will be stove to pieces. Where are the prisoners?'' He replied, 'I fear they are all drowned.' He grasped my hand and said, 'Major, God bless you; in five minutes we shall all be in eternity.' He then rushed to the longboat, which was then cleared of the ship. From the first moment of the ship's striking till the total wreck could not have exceeded six minutes. Previous to this, a great number of convicts rushed to the poop, saying, 'May we come up, sir?' I said, 'Yes, save your lives if you can.' Every individual who was drowned must have perished within the first three or four minutes."

Ryan, who was taken off the wreck on the longboat's second trip, was emphatic that only one musket was fired from the quarter deck, and asserted that this was the only shot he heard at the time of the wreck. "I never myself gave orders to fire upon the convicts nor did I hear any other person do so," declared Ryan, "but I did hear in the course of the night that a prisoner had been shot."

According to Lieutenant Minton, Corporal Deverell came aft when the ship struck and asked him for orders, as the convicts were breaking out of the prison. Minton said he then went to Ryan for orders, and the latter said the convicts must be kept below. "I then went forward," Minton said, "and entreated the convicts to be quiet, assuring them that if there was any danger they would be allowed to come up. The mast had not then fallen. Some of the soldiers who guarded the hatchways pointed their muskets down and threatened to fire if the prisoners came forward. I reported to Major Ryan the state of the prisoners, and Dr. Wyse and myself again went forward.

"On returning aft, I fell from the striking of the ship and was much stunned. On recovering, I saw a shot fired on the quarter deck in the air, and heard one fired afterwards, after which the convicts began to make their appearance on deck in great numbers. A third shot may have been fired, but I can speak positively only to two. I never ordered a shot to be fired. I was of opinion that if the convicts got on deck, and rushed the launch, which was our only resource, not a soul would be saved. When the convicts broke the prison gate, all opposition from the soldiers ceased."

Deverell's story was that Minton had told him that if the convicts forced the hatchways, the military would be obliged to fire, and that Ryan had told him to do his duty. "I returned to the hatchway," said Deverell, "and saw one convict with a saw and others with hammers, endeavouring to break through the barricade. I saw one bar broken and some of the prisoners trying to get through. At this time no officer was present at the main hatchway, and I desired one of the soldiers to fire down by way of intimidation."

The corporal claimed that this shot was fired, not in the direction of the prisoners, but towards the port side of the lower deck. It was after Wyse had been down the hatchway. Deverell was positive, firstly, that only one shot was fired, and, secondly, that no convict was hit. "For three or four minutes after the shot was fired the convicts were quiet and held back," he said. "I heard no cries from below of any person being wounded. I heard cries for mercy." Deverell added that soon after the shot was fired, the water blew up the main hatchway. The prisoners were up to their middles in water, and then came up. This, according to Deverell, was at the time the bulwarks were being cut away to get the gig launched. He then left the hatchway with the rest.

In bed when the *George III* struck, Corporal David Bell, also of the 50th Regiment, found the prisoners trying to break out, and went on deck to reinforce the guard at the hatchways. "When the mainmast fell," stated Bell, "I heard several men call out, 'Mr. Minton, shall we fire?' Mr. Minton said, 'No, no, keep them down with your firelocks.' Notwithstanding this, two shots were fired by some of the soldiers. I never heard any orders again to fire on the prisoners by any military or other officer in the ship. There was an order to fire as a signal. I saw two shots fired by the soldiers down the main hatchway, at short intervals, and I heard some voices cry out, 'A man is shot.' About ten minutes after the last shot, the launch was got off. The order for firing down the hatchway was given by the corporal of the guard."

Several convicts told of the guard's threat to shoot, and they agreed that only two or three shots were fired. One man said there was an interval of ten minutes between the first and second shots, but a second placed it at from three to four minutes, and a third at five minutes. One convict saw Robert Luker fall after the first shot, and two others observed both Luker and Yates fall. There was, however, no suggestion by any of the prisoners that any other convict had been killed or wounded.

The evidence of Moxey and Wyse further confuses the critical question as to when the prisoners flocked on deck. "I kept the prisoners below until the boat could be launched," asserted Wyse, "for if I had not, I do not think a soul would have been saved. The moment the boat was launched, the guard was withdrawn." On the other hand, Moxey told the court: "As soon as the ship struck, the prisons between decks broke down, and the prisoners came out as fast as they could, all hands trying to save themselves; many were washed off."

All the officers concurred that it was necessary to keep the convicts below to prevent them rushing the boats, but in actual fact the prisoners' conduct, on gaining the deck, was exemplary. Moxey, who had not seen any shots fired at the convicts, said he had received all possible support and assistance from everybody on board, and that some of the prisoners made themselves particularly useful, several going with him to and from the shore in the longboat. Wyse described their conduct from the vessel's striking as most meritorious, assisting the officers rather than looking to their own safety. Ryan said he could not speak too highly of the conduct of the prisoners throughout the voyage, and disclosed that after the longboat had left on the first trip to the shore, a keg of spirits was handed up to the survivors huddled on the port deck, but was cheerfully and readily thrown overboard at his order.

We shall never know the true facts of what happened during the first 10 or 15 minutes after the *George III* struck, or whether the convicts who perished were drowned in the prison like rats or were swept overboard by the waves as they reached the deck. But it does seem certain that the members of the guard and of the crew were more concerned with saving themselves than with getting the convicts safely ashore. The evidence of Major Ryan and of Wyse himself shows that the surgeon thrust himself into the longboat as soon as she was launched. He had promised to remain with the prisoners, but he did not do so, although everybody agreed that during the voyage he had treated them with the greatest care and had won their regard and affection. He seems to have entirely forgotten his duty to his 60 patients in the hospital, 50 of whom, as he stated, were confined to their beds. Only two of these 60 men were saved. It was Ryan who, according to the report of the court of inquiry, suggested on the longboat's return to the wreck from the shore, that the women, children and invalids should be removed first, and this was done. But the three miliary officers all went ashore with this boatload, although in justice to Ryan it must be said that, if the story of one of his men is to be believed, he got into the boat only because his men insisted that he should go. Nor do any of the ship's officers appear to have remained with the 50 or 60 survivors who clung to the wrecked ship after the longboat left on her second trip to the shore.

The court of inquiry exonerated the master and all the officers of all blame for the tragedy, and there can be no question that Moxey's navigation of the ship was not at fault. He took every possible precaution on entering D'Entrecasteaux Channel. The *George III* was wrecked on an uncharted rock, and Moxey was in no way to blame for her loss. Moreover, he did everything possible to save those aboard after the ship had struck, but the roll of those saved and those drowned tells its own story. The fact that only two seamen were lost, and that the whole of the guard reached shore, clearly indicates that no real attempt was made to save the convicts. If, as Ryan asserted, all those who perished were drowned in the first few minutes after the ship struck, how was it that no soldier and only two seamen were among the number?[26]

The "Hive" Runs Ashore.

If the loss of the *George III* was unavoidable in the circumstances, that of the *Hive* later in the year was inexcusable. On a dark, cloudy night with a fresh breeze and a smooth sea, she ran aground in a bight to the south-west of Cape St. George with all sails set, but, with the exception of the boatswain, who was drowned, all aboard got safely ashore.

The *Hive* was making her second voyage as a convict ship, having reached Sydney the previous year, and was commanded by John Thomas Nutting. About noon on December 10 the *Hive* was ten or 12 miles off Montague Island, to the north of Bermagui, on the New South Wales coast, and shortly before eight o'clock that night sighted the mainland on the beam, eight or nine miles off, according to the chief mate, Edward Kenny, but 12 or 14 miles distant, according to Nutting. The ship was steering north by east, but her course was now altered to north by east half east.

Kenny, who had just handed over the watch to the third officer, Thomas Morgan, advised the master that the course was shaped to carry the ship too close in, saying that it might do for a day, but not for a night, course. Nutting retorted that one man was sufficient to navigate the ship, and retired to his cabin, but the snubbed Kenny, fearful of danger, did not follow the master's example and go to bed.

About nine-thirty he suggested to Morgan that the main topmast and lower studding sails should be taken in, but as Nutting had ordered him to carry all sail, Morgan did not act on the chief mate's suggestion. About 10 o'clock, Morgan came to Kenny's cabin and told him there was something white on the port bow, like breakers. Kenny immediately ran on deck, and seeing breakers ordered the helm to be put hard a-port. But the ship struck, running aground on a flat, sandy beach.

Kenny ordered the yards to be thrown back, but Nutting, appearing on deck, ordered them to be braced up and the studding sails to be taken in. When he asked Nutting for orders, the master told Kenny to do what he thought best, and the mate ordered all sails furled, hove over the spars and cleared the longboat for launching. Nutting then intervened, saying that he would not have the longboat hoisted out and insisting that the weather quarter boat should be launched. Kenny strongly objected, but at the master's insistence hoisted out the boat and, as he had feared, she was swamped the instant she touched the water. The boatswain was drowned, but Kenny caught a rope from the ship and clambered back on board the *Hive*, while one of the seamen, clinging to the upturned boat, drifted on shore through the surf.

It was then decided to get a warp on shore, which was done by means of a small line. Kenny swam ashore to help draw the warp high and dry and make it fast. Nutting now consented to the longboat being launched, and the women and children, with part of the military guard, were landed, the remainder of the guard and the prisoners then being ferried safely ashore.

According to the surgeon-superintendent, Anthony Donoghoe, however, it was due to Kenny, and not to Nutting, that the longboat was launched. The master had appeared so confused and unequal to giving the necessary orders when the ship ran aground that, with the approval of the commander of the guard, Lieutenant Edward Lugard, of the 31st Regiment, Donoghoe deposed Nutting in the command. For the remainder of the night while Kenny gave the orders, Nutting stood silent on the poop, but with daylight he ordered the jolly-boat to be launched on the weather quarter, with the result, as we have seen, that she was immediately capsized.

Whatever the actual sequence of events, and whether or not Nutting was deposed in the command—he himself emphatically denied at the subsequent inquiry that he had been deposed, although he admitted that Donoghoe and Lugard had attempted to relieve him of the command—the wreck of the *Hive* was due to the master's obstinacy and incapacity. Donoghoe, Lugard, and Ensign Kelly, the second officer of the guard, all gave evidence that Nutting had been out in his longitude on several occasions. He had been eight or nine degrees out in making Cape Otway, and was so inefficient in taking sights that Kenny had often to take them for him. When Donoghoe was asked if he thought Nutting was a competent person to command the ship, the surgeon-superintendent declared that he considered him unfit from his repeated mistakes in the reckoning.

The court of inquiry, whose members comprised the harbour-master and master attendant at Sydney, John Nicholson, the senior lieutenant and the master of H.M.S. *Zebra*, respectively W. Lefebre and L. C. Bailey, and two convict ship captains, John Robson of the *John Barry*, and John Moncrief of the *Royal Sovereign*, delivered their report on February 11, 1836. They reported that the course steered by the *Hive* would have taken the ship clear of Cape St. George but for a strong indraught, of which Nutting had been ignorant. They censured the master for the inefficient manner in which he had conducted the *Hive* after leaving Montague Island, and especially for having retired to bed when Kenny had suggested that the ship was too close in. They also found that Nutting had not used any exertions to extricate the *Hive* after she had struck, and that in consequence he had been deprived of the command, not issuing any further orders until daylight.

The survivors from the *Hive* were brought to Sydney by H.M.S. *Zebra*, the schooner *Edward* and the cutter *Prince George*. She was carrying Irish convicts, one of whom had died of illness before the ship struck, and another, a convalescent, on shore after the wreck. The *Hive's* stores and ten thousand pounds in specie for the military chest were saved and brought to Sydney in the three vessels mentioned, but all efforts to refloat the ship failed[27].

Two Fast Passages.

Between 1829, when the *Norfolk* made her passage of 97 days from Spithead to Port Jackson, and 1840, when the last convict ship proper, the *Eden*, reached Sydney, there were surprisingly few outstanding passages. There were, however, two exceptions.

In 1831, the *Hooghly* made a direct passage from Cork to Port Jackson in 95 days. This Thames-built ship of 466 tons, launched in 1819, was making her third voyage in the convict service. On her first, she had reached Sydney in 1825, running out from Cork by way of Rio de Janeiro, in the really excellent time of 107 days. Three years later, in 1828, she again entered Port Jackson with prisoners, having made a passage of 111 days from London. On her 1831 voyage she left Cork on June 24, and anchored in Port Jackson on September 27. She was the only convict ship to leave England or Ireland in May or June that year, and consequently there is no other ship with which her performance can be compared, but no other vessel arriving in 1831 made a fast passage. The best were those of the Quebec-built *Georgiana*, which, leaving London on April 1, made a passage of 117 days, and the Calcutta-built *Asia*, then 17 years old, which left Cork on August 6 and arrived at Sydney 118 days later. On all three of her passages the *Hooghly* was commanded by Peter John Reeves, but on her fourth and last voyage as a convict ship her master was George Bayly. Under his command she arrived at Port Jackson in 1834, 113 days out from Portsmouth.

Although her 1831 passage was exceptional, due, no doubt, to particularly favourable weather, the *Hooghly* made consistently good passages, and as she could not have always met exceptionally good weather, she must have possessed an unusual turn of speed for a vessel of her description. Her average for her four passages as a convict ship was just over 106 days.

The *Emma Eugenia*, on the other hand, made only rather worse than average passages, with one exception. A barque of 383 tons, she was built at Whitby in 1833, and had first been named the *Colonist*. She became one of the large fleet of the London shipowner, Joseph Somes, many of whose vessels found employment in the convict service.

The *Emma Eugenia* was five years old, and classed A1 at Lloyds, when she arrived at Port Jackson on February 9, 1838, 95 days out from Portsmouth, thus equalling the *Hooghly's* passage from Cork. Her master on this occasion was Giles Wade, who was well known in the Australian trade and who commanded a number of other convict ships. After this voyage the *Emma Eugenia* did not return to the convict service until 1842, when she arrived at Hobart from Woolwich by way of the Cape, making a passage of 136 days. She made three further visits to Hobart as a convict ship, arriving in 1844, 1846 and 1851, sailing on each occasion from London and, apparently, making a direct passage in each instance. She took 124 days in 1844, 115 in 1846, and 128 in 1851, so she cannot be considered as noted for speed.

The Fight Against Disease.

Throughout this period the fight against disease continued, and, on the whole, successfully. From time to time changes were made in the dietary scale, not always with the approval of the surgeons, We have already seen, for example, that the outbreak of scurvy on the ill-fated *George III*, which caused the deaths of 12 men and rendered 50 others seriously ill, was attributed by Surgeon David Wyse to the substitution of cocoa for oatmeal and to the scantiness of the provisions generally. The prisoners did not take kindly to the cocoa, and no fewer than 115 of the men aboard consistently refused to drink it throughout the voyage. "They loathed it so much," reported Wyse, "that it invariably made them sick."

The convicts on the *George III*, however, were particularly unfortunate. On January 27, 1835, when the ship was six weeks out from London and in the vicinity of the Line, the *George III* caught fire through carelessness when spirits were being drawn off.

The flames spread rapidly and soon threatened to ignite two casks of gunpowder, which, according to a recent direction, were packed in copper. If the powder had blown up, the *George III* almost certainly must have been lost there and then, but two of the prisoners, William Nelson and David Jones, courageously seized the two casks, and although their hands were scorched by the hot copper, succeeded in carrying them clear of the fire. Aided by a gang of prisoners, the seamen and soldiers gradually got the fire under control and eventually extinguished it, but a good deal of damage had been done to the ship and a large quantity of provisions had been consumed.

In consequence of this mishap, and since Moxey, presumably with Wyse's approval, refused to put into either Rio or the Cape to replenish supplies, the prisoners were half-starved for the remainder of the voyage[28].

In the majority of the convict ships, however, the rations, if not always the most suitable, were certainly adequate. The quality perhaps showed a deterioration compared with the period prior to 1820, but the provisions furnished for the convicts were no worse, and probably better, than those aboard most men-of-war, and certainly were superior, in quantity as well as quality, to those on many of the early emigrant ships. Apart from the case of the *Adamant*, there were few complaints regarding the serving of the rations. The convicts who arrived at Hobart in 1830 by the *Southworth* complained of inadequate victualling, and when the *Emperor Alexander* reached the same port in 1833 there was an inquiry into allegations that the master, John Hurst, had short-served the rations of both the prisoners and the soldiers. But such complaints were unusual, and the gross abuses practised in the earlier convict ships were not repeated[29].

Nevertheless, scurvy remained a grave problem. The methods by which it could be successfully combatted were known, but many misconceptions persisted regarding its prevention and treatment. Both in the convict ships and British merchantmen generally reliance was placed in lime juice as an effective anti-scorbutic; it was this fact which earned British merchant ships the generic name of "Lime-juicers". Yet, years before, it had been proved that lime juice was relatively ineffective, but either on grounds of economy, or through pig-headed conservatism, British shipowners and officials clung tenaciously to lime juice. This fact, coupled with the lowering of the scale of rations in 1833, was responsible for scurvy continuing to appear constantly in the convict ships, although the frightful scenes which had been witnessed aboard the *Surrey* in 1814 were never repeated.

Dysentery took a heavier and more consistent toll of life in the convict ships than did scurvy; for when deaths occurred on the passage, some at least were always due to this disease. The medical profession at that period knew very little about its causes, and its contagious nature was not recognised until many years later. In the then state of medical knowledge, there was a similar ignorance about other diseases, and to some extent this was responsible for convicts being embarked when suffering from a contagious or infectious complaint.

Yet a large number of convict ships reached Australia without any deaths having occurred on the passage, and the number in which the deaths on the passage exceeded two or three was comparatively small.

Some Scurvy Ships.

The first transport to arrive with a considerable number of prisoners suffering from scurvy was the *Minerva*, which reached Port Jackson towards the end of 1821, after a passage of 137 days from London. Three prisoners had died of the disease during the passage and 25 required hospital treatment on arrival.

James Bowman, formerly a convict ship surgeon, but now the colony's Principal Surgeon, laid the blame for the outbreak on the *Minerva's* surgeon-superintendent, Charles Queade. The latter had served in the Royal Navy for eighteen years, and had made two previous passages with prisoners—in the *Pilot* in 1817 and in the *Minerva* on her first voyage in 1819.

Bowman reported that scurvy had made its appearance early in the voyage, but that although lemon juice, wine, and other anti-scorbutics had been liberally furnished, they had not been issued with any regularity. Each prisoner, under the regulations, was supposed to receive an ounce of lemon juice daily, but Bowman claimed that none was issued from October 30 to December 3, and that the first issue of wine had not been made until the *Minerva* had been six weeks at sea. Bowman also criticised Queade for having permitted a passenger to purchase the convicts' ration of salt beef when in the tropics, without a substitute being provided, and said that in consequence of under-nourishment the prisoners had fallen ready victims to the disease. He also stressed that many prisoners had been kept in irons, that only one division had been admitted to the deck at a time for two hours, and that with so many prisoners always below it had been impossible to properly cleanse and ventilate the prison.

Queade vigorously denied Bowman's charges, asserting that his report was "partial and unsatisfactory". He claimed that in the *Pilot* in 1817 he had expended 100 lb. of lemon juice and in the *Minerva* in 1819 double that quantity, but that the expenditure on the latter ship in 1821 had been no less than 964 lb. No deaths had occurred in the *Pilot*, although she had called at Rio, or in the *Minerva* on her direct passage of 113 days in 1819, when she had sailed from Cork. He did not specifically deny Bowman's statement that lemon juice had been issued irregularly, but declared he had given instructions for it to be issued daily, "unless at any time it be improper or prejudicial for them to be supplied therewith", and added that when issued to prisoners who had not received it while suffering from dysentery, their sickness had returned with "increased violence".

On the question of the salt beef, Queade said that it had been issued to the convicts, but because of the hot weather they had left it uncooked about the deck. He had then permitted the passenger to purchase it for a fortnight, but asserted that during that period the prisoners had continued to receive their ration of salt pork, and denied they had been under-nourished. He added, as an interesting aside on the question of diet, that many prisoners did not consume 10 lb. of salt beef or pork during the passage, but lived principally on pudding, pea soup, bread and tea, for which they exchanged their meat. The men who adhered to such a diet, he said, were always the healthiest aboard. "Any experienced medical seafaring man who takes the effect of diet in all its bearings on the human frame," wrote Queade, "will agree with me that the more farinaceous and less animal food convicts have, the greater will be their security from inflammatory or other disease."[30]

Despite Bowman's report, the authorities did not blame Queade; for he reached Hobart in 1824 as surgeon-superintendent of the

Phoenix, and the following year had medical charge of troops being sent from Australia to India in another well-known convict ship the *Grenada*.

A more serious outbreak of scurvy occurred in the *Ocean* in 1823, six convicts dying on the passage and 40 being admitted to hospital on the ship's arrival. Bowman in this case reported that he had been unable to determine how the disease originated, and he brought no charges against the surgeon-superintendent, James McTernan. The latter claimed that those who developed scurvy "consisted for the most part of men who by repeated acts of misconduct in their hulks had forfeited any claim to indulgence, had formed a resolution to take whatever ship they should be sent out in, had actually attempted to possess themselves of the *Ocean* and concerted measures to repeat their attempt". McTernan suggested the scurvy resulted from their despondency at the failure of their mutiny attempts and the ship's quick transition from the tropics to the high southern latitudes[31].

The worst outbreak, however, occurred in the *Lord Lyndoch*, which arrived at Port Jackson from London on August 8, 1838 This 23-years-old, Calcutta-built ship of 638 tons, which had made three previous passages with prisoners, carried her normal complement of 330 convicts when she sailed. Scurvy made its appearance when she was a little to the eastward of the Cape and no fewer than 160 men, almost half the prisoners aboard, were afflicted with it in greater or less degree. There were 19 deaths on the passage, eight of them from scurvy and the remainder from other causes, and on her arrival 113 or 114 men suffering from scurvy had to be taken straight from the ship to hospital.

On March 8, 1839, seven months after her arrival, the governor, Sir George Gipps, reported that only 89 of her prisoners had escaped the disease. By then the total death-roll had risen to 39. In addition to the eight men who had died of scurvy and the 11 of other diseases on the passage, another 20 men had died of scurvy after the *Lord Lyndoch's* arrival. Fifteen of these latter deaths occurred before September 24, 1838, and the other five between then and the date of the governor's report.

An inquiry was held, but its findings, apparently, have not been preserved. The *Lord Lyndoch's* surgeon-superintendent was Obediah Pineo. He had made previous voyages to Sydney in the *England* in

1835 and the *Pyramus* in 1836, but after the *Lord Lyndoch's* disastrous passage he did not receive another appointment in the convict service. Whether this was because he was held to have been responsible for the outbreak on that ship must remain a matter for conjecture[32].

There were many other outbreaks of this disease, but deaths were few. In the *Earl St. Vincent* in 1823 there were 192 cases, only one of which was fatal. The disease appeared early and the surgeon, Robert Tainsh, ordered the master to put into Rio de Janeiro, where fresh provisions were obtained. Tainsh had no idea the disease was due to a vitamin deficiency, but considered it resulted from the Irish convicts having been put aboard in cold and stormy weather. By ordering the ship into Rio, however, he may well have prevented a heavy death-roll. The *Medina*, which sailed from England in late April, 1825, had 58 convicts under treatment by the end of August and sent 24 to hospital on arrival at Hobart. In the *Burrell* in 1830, although there were no deaths from scurvy, almost every prisoner showed some symptoms of the disease, but the military guard escaped scot free. "They had provisions of the same nature and quality as the prisoners," reported the surgeon, William West. "We must then attribute the difference to greater exercise and occupation of mind." In the *Bengal Merchant* in 1834-5 scurvy made its appearance on reaching the meridian of the Cape of Good Hope and increased so rapidly that there were 77 cases before reaching Sydney after a direct passage of 121 days from London. Eight men were sent to hospital, but there were no deaths from scurvy while at sea[33].

The Toll of Dysentery.

Despite such virulent outbreaks of scurvy as occurred in the *George III* and the *Lord Lyndoch*, however, dysentery took a more consistent toll of life during this period, and the total of deaths from this cause was higher. Even in those ships which had only two or three deaths during the passage at least one or two were usually the result of dysentery, and in some instances all the deaths were due to this disease. The outbreaks sometimes occurred in the tropics, but often took place when the prisoners had been on board only two or three days or did not appear until the ship had entered the cold southern latitudes.

In the *Eliza* in 1828, for instance, there were forty-two cases of dysentery out of sixty-seven on the sick-list during the passage, and seven of them terminated fatally. Her surgeon, James Patton, attributed the dysentery to the convicts having been long on salt provisions, since the voyage was protracted, and to the cold, damp and rain experienced in running down her easting in 40° South. The outbreak, which did not occur until the ship had been 120 days at sea, was confined to the convicts, only one soldier among the guard and seamen suffering dysentery. In the *America* the following year, however, it persisted right up to the time of her arrival at Sydney. Fifty men, almost a third of her complement of prisoners, were stricken with the disease during the passage, seven dying before Port Jackson was reached and two others succumbing in hospital after arrival. As illustrating the extent of medical knowledge at the time, the Inspector of Hospitals at Sydney reported on the *America's* arrival that the dysentery had "not in any case evidenced a contagious nature", and he saw no reason why the convicts should not be immediately disembarked[34].

This view was in accordance with medical opinion of the day. As with cholera and other diseases, the infective nature of dysentery was denied by the medical profession, and naval surgeons and their fellow practitioners ashore held firmly to the miasmatic or atmospheric theory of the causation of disease. Occasionally, however, a surgeon more observant than his fellows might form another conclusion and in 1830, when an outbreak of dysentery occurred in the convict ship *Persian*, bound for Hobart, her surgeon, Thomas Galloway, cautiously wrote that the disease "at one period was infectious, I had not the least hesitation in believing, as it was confined to particular berths for a short period".[35]

The *America's* surgeon nearly reached a similar conclusion, but could not quite convince himself. Having received the last of her prisoners on March 30, she sailed from Woolwich on April 8, but encountered foul winds and could not get down the Channel, being forced back to the Downs and not finally sailing from there until the 21st. Measles had broken out among the members of the guard before sailing and a few days after embarkation dysentery, which had been very prevalent in the *Justitia* hulk, appeared among the convicts. "There are some circumstances," wrote Alexander

Stewart, her surgeon-superintendent, "that might lead one to suppose this disease to have been contagious, but on the other hand all were exposed equally to the exciting cause, whatever that might have been, without any reference to contagion." The vessel was quarantined for a week on arrival because of the outbreak of measles[36].

In the *Middlesex*, which arrived at Port Jackson on January 24, 1840, the disease did not make its appearance until the last six weeks of the passage. A barque of 418 tons new measurement, classed A1 at Lloyds for 11 years, the *Middlesex* had been launched at Sunderland the previous year, and she was on her maiden voyage. Soon after sailing, she ran into a succession of gales, in which, besides losing a man overboard, she had her fore and main topmasts carried away and suffered other damage. The bad weather greatly retarded her passage and she put into the Cape having up to that stage only one death among her prisoners, the result of dropsy. By some oversight her lower tier of water casks were not filled and after leaving the Cape a shortage of water compelled her to bear up for Mauritius. She entered Port Louis on November 25 and remained there until December 14.

It was while she was at Mauritius that dysentery made its appearance and eight of the 32 men affected died, the last death occurring a few days before she made port[37].

There were 86 cases of dysentery in the *Andromeda* in 1830, four terminating in death. Her surgeon, George Fairfowl, attributed the outbreak to the replacement of the water closets, which, having "a constant supply of water, could be kept clean and wholesome all the 24 hours", by large iron buckets with "covers loosely fitted which could not be emptied and cleaned out during the whole night" and consequently were "most offensive to the person coming in from the fresh air". In the *Asia* in 1831, George Birnie found his Irish convicts "pale, emaciated and feeble", and several of them "did not exhibit any degree of good spirits on the voyage, but continued at all times thoughtful and silent or, when sick and conscious of external sympathy, they spoke about home, their mothers and being reprieved". Of the eleven deaths on the passage, seven were the result of dysentery[38].

Cholera and Smallpox.

More serious diseases seem to have been combatted more successfully, but the British authorities took serious risks in allowing some convict ships to sail when cholera, smallpox, or some other disease had revealed itself aboard before sailing. It may be doubted whether the risks were worth taking, but fortunately luck was on the side of the authorities and no serious consequences resulted.

When the *Norfolk* was beaten back thrice in 1834 her prisoners were transferred to the *Lady Kennaway*. The latter ship embarked 100 men at Woolwich early in June, 1834, and before the end of the month took aboard 180 men at Portsmouth. Leaving the latter port on June 30, she proceeded to Cork and there embarked a further 31 military offenders, who were not Irish convicts. There was a great deal of sickness aboard, and the prisoners from the *Norfolk* were in a shocking state of health. There were 17 deaths at Cork, and 18 others were landed sick at Haulbowline Island. Nevertheless, the *Lady Kennaway* was allowed to sail, and finally left Cork on October 27, more than four months after she had embarked her first prisoners at Woolwich. Yet there were only two deaths on the passage, making the total death-roll 19 from the time of embarkation to the ship's arrival at Hobart[39].

In the *Fanny*, cholera made its appearance before she sailed from London for Port Jackson on July 29, 1832, and six of her female convicts died as a result between July 4 and 21 out of ten cases. Her surgeon, Francis Logan, reported that it was difficult to say how cholera was brought on the ship, but attributed it to a sailor who came aboard drunk late the night before the ship sailed down the Thames and three days later, on July 1, was in a state of collapse with cholera. "There being only a few stanchions between the sailors and the women," he wrote, "causes me to think this might be the way it came amongst the women." Fearing the outbreak might prove virulent on the passage, the authorities placed an additional surgeon, William Marshall of H.M.S. *India*, aboard to assist Logan. Fortunately their fears were not realised, and no cases of cholera appeared during the passage. Thirty women, however, developed scurvy, but, at the insistence of the surgeons, the *Fanny* put into the Cape, where fresh provisions were procured and the prisoners given an opportunity to recuperate. These measures were effective. There were only two deaths on the passage, and neither was due to either cholera or scurvy, while when the *Fanny* arrived at Port Jackson on February 2, 1833, after a passage of 188 days from the Downs, her convicts were in good health[40].

Another female transport, the *Frances Charlotte*, to Hobart, was the scene of an outbreak of cholera before sailing. The disease was of a malignant type and caused eight deaths—four among the convicts, two among the children and two among the crew—but the disease did not reappear during the voyage. In the *Isabella* in 1833 there were ten deaths, six of convicts and four of soldiers. As these all occurred before sailing, they delayed her departure A new method of fitting up the prison enabled this ship to carry a hundred more convicts than previously, but her surgeon, Oliver Sproule, did not consider there was overcrowding or that the manner in which the prisoners were packed in contributed to the spread of the disease. Cholera also broke out in the *Asia* before she sailed in 1833. There were 24 cases, in five of which death resulted. She was hauled alongside the *Tremendous*, to which her convicts were transferred during the day, so that they might enjoy a pure atmosphere and obtain exercise. The disease had disappeared before the *Asia* sailed and did not recur.[41]

The worst outbreak of cholera occurred on the *Katherine Stewart Forbes* in 1832. The disease appeared on February 27, the day the ship sailed from Woolwich with 222 male convicts, and her surgeon, John Stephenson, ordered the master to bear up for Plymouth Sound, where the ship anchored on the evening of March 2. There were then five cases of very malignant cholera. "Here," records Stephenson, "we were not allowed to remain, but obliged by the positive orders of the Port Admiral to proceed to sea the next day, being with difficulty allowed to receive a small supply of medicine from the hospital and an assistant surgeon from the *San Josef*. On the night of the 3rd and all the 4th it blew very hard. We attempted to reach Milford, but the wind being foul, we were obliged to bear up for Stangate Creek. The 5th was tolerably fair, but on the 6th we had a heavy gale, during which the hospital was quite dark and wet. Every bed was occupied. There were only two attendants with myself able to hold up their heads, and on the lower deck, just outside the hospital, were upwards of 200 seasick convicts." In February there were four cases, with one patient dying, and in March twenty-one fresh cases occurred, seven of which terminated fatally. The last cholera deaths, however, took place on March 5, but the *Katherine Stewart Forbes* remained at Stangate Creek until March 25, when she was permitted to resume her voyage. No further deaths from cholera occurred, but, including the deaths before she finally sailed, there were 13 deaths by the time she arrived at Hobart on July 16, although the surgeon's journal records only twelve. The *Hydery* put into Stangate Creek some ten days after the *Katherine Stewart Forbes* had sailed. She also had cholera aboard, but in a less virulent form, and only one woman convict died of the disease.[42]

Smallpox was not of frequent occurrence in the convict ships, as, thanks to Jenner, it was one infectious disease that could be controlled. However, it appeared in the *Bussorah Merchant* before she sailed from England in 1828, and a negro seaman was removed to the hospital ship at Chatham. Presumably the crew and convicts were, or already had been, vaccinated, and the ship was permitted to sail. Four cases of smallpox occurred during the passage, two of the patients being convicts, but all recovered. There were four deaths from other causes. The smallpox outbreak was not reported when the *Bussorah Merchant* arrived at Port Jackson on July 26, presumably because there had been no sign of the disease since early in May, and when the port authorities learnt accidentally of the outbreak, they were thrown into a mild panic. The ship and all aboard her were hurriedly placed in quarantine, and a small colonial vessel, the *Alligator*, was converted into a hospital ship. Her only patients, however, were a few men suffering from minor ailments. The *Bussorah Merchant's* surgeon-superintendent, Robert Dunn, regarded the precautions as unnecessary, but despite a favourable medical report on August 21, the ship was not released from quarantine until the following month.[43]

A Favourable Comparison.

The success achieved in the fight against disease is shown, firstly, by the number of transports which had no deaths on the passage or in which only one or two prisoners died, and, secondly, by the much lower mortality rate in those ships in which outbreaks of scurvy, dysentery, cholera and other diseases occurred compared with the earlier years of transportation. A number of convicts, both male and female, died on the voyage of complaints, such as phthisis, heart disease, blood pressure, senile decay and the like, which would have caused death before long had they remained in England or Ireland, and at the worst the rigours of the voyage merely accelerated death.

Almost 440 shiploads of male and female convicts reached Sydney and Hobart from the beginning of 1821 until the end of 1840, but in only nine ships did the deaths from disease equal one death to every 20 prisoners embarked, or less, and in no case did the deaths exceed one to every 16·3 prisoners embarked. The following table strikingly illustrates the improvement in the mortality rate, the deaths from drowning in the *George III*, of course, being excluded:

Year	*Vessel*	*One death to every*
1802	*Atlas*	2·7 convicts embarked
1790	*Neptune*	3·1 ,, ,,
1798	*Hillsborough*	3·1 ,, ,,
1790	*Scarborough*	3·5 ,, ,,
1802	*Hercules*	3·8 ,, ,,
1814	*Surrey*	5·5 ,, ,,
1814	*General Hewart*	8·8 ,, ,,
1835	*Lady Kennaway*	16·3 ,, ,,
1832	*Katherine Stewart Forbes*	17·0 ,, ,,
1838	*Lord Lyndoch*	17·3 ,, ,,
1829	*Vittoria*	17·7 ,, ,,
1833	*William Bryan*	18·5 ,, ,,
1835	*George III*	18·5 ,, ,,
1828	*Eliza*	18·7 ,, ,,
1833	*Waterloo*	19·4 ,, ,,
1833	*Frances Charlotte*	20·0 ,, ,,

The Surgeons-Superintendent.

The improvement, unquestionably, was due primarily to the adoption of the system of appointing surgeons-superintendent, and to the policy of employing the same naval surgeons again and again; for those who were regularly employed in the convict service, as the majority were, quickly gained experience in the handling of prisoners on the passage to Australia, and the prisoners benefited greatly in consequence.

The surgeon who made only one or two voyages in charge of prisoners was the exception, not the rule. James McTernan and

Thomas Braidwood Wilson each made at least nine voyages between 1821 and 1840, and George Fairfowl, Campbell France, and Andrew Henderson each visited Australia on at least seven occasions. Those who made six voyages included such well-known surgeons as George Shaw Rutherford, William Evans, Alexander Nisbet, Alick Osborne, Thomas Bell, Henry Gordon Brock, Robert Epsie, and William Bell Carlyle. Joseph Cook, Peter Cunningham, William Rae, Alexander Neill, Morgan Price, William Conborough Watt, Oliver Sproule, George Ellery Forman, Joseph Steret, William McDowell, Gilbert King, Anthony Donoghoe and many others made four or five passages.

It is not always possible to compute the number of voyages made by individual surgeons; for several had the same surname, and occasionally their Christian names are not recorded. These men seem usually to have been relatives. Alick, James and John Osborne were brothers, as also were George Shaw and James Rutherford and probably John and Charles Inches. Then there were the three Wilsons—James, Andrew Douglas and Thomas Braidwood, the first and third of whom were brothers. The second suffered from rheumatism and when he reached Sydney in the *Asia* in 1832 he had to be hoisted out of the ship in a chair. James and Thomas Braidwood Wilson, with a third brother, settled in Tasmania, but Thomas Braidwood subsequently moved to New South Wales, where he named his land-grant Braidwood, a name which was transferred to the town which was later founded there[44].

Last N.S.W. Convict Ship.

It has frequently been stated that the last convicts, as distinct from the "exiles", reached Sydney in 1841, and even such a standard work as the *Australian Encyclopaedia* perpetuates this error. Actually, the last convict ship to New South Wales was the *Eden*, and she arrived at Port Jackson on November 18, 1840, after an uneventful passage from Sheerness, via Teneriffe, of 131 days. One of her 270 male prisoners died on the passage. Her surgeon-superintendent was George Ellery Forman. The *Eden* had been launched at Bristol in 1829, and originally had been classed A1 for ten years[45].

CHAPTER ELEVEN

THE VOYAGES, 1841-1868

Long-lived Indian Ships.

ALMOST from the inception of transportation to the Australian colonies Indian-built ships were extensively employed as transports, and the period after 1840 was no exception. Of a total of rather over 150 passages to Hobart between the beginning of 1841 and the end of 1853, just over 40—nearly a third—were made by vessels built in India. Many of these were old ships, launched many years before, and practically all had performed years of useful service in the Indian Country trade, plying between Indian ports and voyaging to China, before they entered the convict service. After 1843, however, an increasing number of comparatively new Indian-built vessels, classed A1 at Lloyd's, were chartered to carry prisoners. The majority of both types had been built at Calcutta, which, despite its dependence upon imported timber, was a thriving centre of Indian shipbuilding, but the convict ships also included vessels built at Moulmein, Cochin, Bombay, Cringa, and other Indian ports.

In many respects, the Indian ships made ideal convict transports. The Country traders were larger and roomier than the contemporary British vessels, and they were staunchly built. After years of arduous service, the Indian vessels, particularly those built of the finest teak, were still thoroughly seaworthy and capable of making good passages, and in these respects they compared more than favourably with British-built vessels. They simply refused to be worn out, and many of them ultimately were scrapped merely because they had become out-moded. The older Indian vessels employed in this period were inferior in design to later British and Indian ships, but although gloomy and ill-ventilated below decks, the health of their prisoners did not appreciably suffer in consequence.

Their durability is almost incredible. Two barques—the large *Cornwall*, of 872 tons register, and the smaller *Fairlie*, of 756 tons—

were each 40 years old when they arrived at Hobart with prisoners in 1851 and 1852 respectively. Both had been built at Calcutta, the *Cornwall* in 1811 and the *Fairlie* a year later, and as Country traders each had repaid its original cost many times over before entering the convict service. The Cochin-built *Navarino*, launched in 1808, was 33 years old when she made her first voyage as a convict ship in 1841, and she returned to Hobart with prisoners again two years later. The *Maitland* and the *Neptune*, both the products of Calcutta shipyards, were each 36 years old when they made their last voyages as convict ships in 1846 and 1850 respectively. Long after they had left the convict service, some of these vessels continued to sail the seas, and after their days of usefulness as sea-going ships had ended, their durable hulls served as hulks for many years.

Some Smart Passages.

The traditional view of these Indian-built ships is that they were large, massive vessels, and exceptionally heavy-working. In actual fact, the Country traders were better designed and constructed, as well as speedier and more seaworthy, than the contemporary East Indiamen, the finest British-built ships afloat. They were capable of making excellent passages, as the records of those employed in the convict service indicate.

The *Cornwall* and the *Fairlie*, which, as we have seen, were forty years old at the time, made passages of 107 and 114 days respectively in 1851 and 1852. The former went out to Hobart from Portsmouth by way of Gibraltar, the latter from Plymouth. The *Moffat*, built at Bengal in 1807 and therefore thirty-five years old when she made her fourth voyage as a convict ship in 1842, recorded a direct passage of 106 days from Portsmouth to Hobart, and the *Lady Kennaway*, built at Calcutta in 1817, performed the same passage in 1851 in 112 days. The most remarkable passage of the older Indian vessels, however, was the *Susan's* 92 days from Plymouth to Hobart in 1842, when she was twenty-nine years old, having been launched at Calcutta in 1813.

The new Indian vessels, as sturdily constructed but more modern in design, accomplished even faster passages, although only one bettered the *Susan's* 92 days. This was the *Anna Maria*, a barque of 421 tons, built at Calcutta in 1836. She was twelve years old when she made the passage from Woolwich to Hobart in 90 days in 1848. She was apparently only 86 days from the Downs to Hobart.

The best passages in this period by Indian-built convict ships to Hobart were as follows:

Year of Arrival	*Vessel*	*Age*	*From*	*Days*
1848	*Anna Maria* - - -	12	London - -	90
1842	*Susan* - - - -	29	Plymouth - -	92
1845	*Theresa* - - - -	11	London - -	93
1845	*Marion* - - - -	11	London - -	94
1850	*Eliza* - - - -	35	London - -	100
1849	*Lord Auckland* - -	13	Dublin - - -	101
1845	*Mount Stewart Elphinstone*	19	London - -	102
1848	*Marion* - - - -	14	London - -	102
1850	*Baretto Junior* - -	32	Downs - - -	103
1843	*Emerald Isle* - - -	7	Sheerness - -	104
1849	*Adelaide* - - -	17	London - -	104
1842	*Moffatt* - - - -	35	Portsmouth - -	106
1851	*Cornwall* - - -	40	Portsmouth via Gib.	107
1841	*Navarino* - - -	33	London - -	107
1843	*Forfarshire* - - -	3	Spithead - -	107
1846	*Sea Queen* - - -	5	Woolwich - -	109
1843	*Navarino* - - -	35	Ireland - -	110

The Story of the ''Success''.

Of all the Indian vessels associated with the transportation of prisoners to Australia the most famous is the *Success*. A wealth of myth and legend clings to her name, and thousands of people who visited her when she was a floating museum continue to regard her as the last and most famous of the convict ships. She was still on show in America, complete with cat-o'-nine-tails, handcuffs, leg-irons, the waxen figures of prisoners, and all the rest of the paraphenalia, in the 1930's. Billed as "the last of England's Infamous Felon Fleet", the *Success* was claimed to have been "the commodore or principal devil-ship" of the fleet, and was stated to have been built at Pegu, as Moulmein was originally named, in 1790. Even such an authority on Indian-built ships as Commander W. H. Coates accepted the *Success* as having been built at Pegu in 1787.

The truth, of course, is that the *Success* was not built at Moulmein until 1840, and she was never a convict ship. Her original owners were Phillips, Shaw & Lowther, of the Exchange

Buildings, London, and for six or seven years they employed her as a Country ship and in the United Kingdom–East Indies trade. They then put her into the Australian emigrant trade, and on September 29, 1847, she sailed from Plymouth on her first voyage to Australia. On that occasion she conveyed 245 emigrants to Adelaide, where she arrived on January 27, 1848. The following year she carried emigrants to Melbourne, and she made a third voyage, also with emigrants, in 1852, arriving at Melbourne on May 31, after a passage of 123 days from Plymouth.

While lying at Corio Bay, Geelong, her crew deserted her to try their luck on the goldfields, and the *Success* was then purchased by the Victorian Government. In August the work of converting her into a prison hulk began, and early the following year she commenced duty as a floating prison. With four other similar hulks—the *President*, the *Sacramento*, the *Lysander* and the *Deborah*—she was moored in Hobson's Bay, off the Strand, Williamstown. The *Success* continued to be used as a prison hulk until 1858, and later served as a women's prison, a reformatory and dormitory for boys, and an explosives hulk.

In the 1870's she was sold. Her new owners were speculators who fitted her up as a convict ship and exhibited her as a grim relic of the convict days. In 1890 a former bushranger, Harry Power, joined her as compère, and the following year she was towed to Sydney by the tug *Eagle*. She arrived on November 6 and remained on exhibition for some months. She then again changed hands, and it was announced that she would be taken to England to serve as a floating museum. The residents of Sydney, however, had no desire to see her taken overseas, and she was quietly scuttled when lying in Kerosene Bay. Six months later she was raised, but her owners were refused a Customs clearance on the ground that she was unseaworthy. She left Port Jackson surreptitiously, however, and reached England safely. She was exhibited in English waters until 1912, when she was purchased by an American company and crossed the Atlantic in 98 days. She remained on display at various American ports until the shortage of shipping during World War I caused her to be equipped with a Diesel engine and converted into a cargo ship in 1917. She was sunk when she got caught in ice at the junction of the Ohio and Kentucky rivers, but she was again raised and once more resumed her old job as an exhibition ship. The *Success* was one of the star attractions of the Chicago World Fair in 1933, and she was still afloat five years later. I have been told that she eventually came into the possession of the United States Coastguard and was destroyed by fire, but I have been unable to check the authenticity of this statement[1].

In 1930 it was claimed that 21 million people had visited her during her long career as a museum ship, and even if this total is a gross exaggeration, it is certain that very few of her visitors realised that she was not the convict ship she claimed to be. For a convict ship the *Success* never was!

The Old "Surrey's" Record.

The old *Surrey*, one of the most famous of the genuine convict ships, has drifted in and out of these pages. She had one of the longest careers as a convict transport, but when she reached Hobart on August 11, 1842, she had made her last passage with prisoners. It was her eleventh voyage in the convict service.

The *Surrey's* career as a convict ship extended over 28 years. After her disastrous first voyage under James Patterson in 1814, she was a particularly well-run ship under his successor, Thomas Raine, who commanded her for her next three voyages. Charles Kemp then became her master for four voyages; he was succeeded by George Sinclair, who was her master on her ninth and tenth voyages, and on her last voyage she was commanded by Henry Innott Naylor. The *Surrey* landed 2,173 male and female prisoners in Australia on her 11 visits, and lost 50 men and one woman during her passages, 36 of the men dying during her disastrous first passage.

The *Surrey* was a slow ship, but on her tenth voyage, in 1840, she made a direct passage from the Downs to Sydney of 102 days. This was an exceptional passage for her; her previous best had been 129 days from Cork to Port Jackson in 1836. Her first four passages all took 150 days or over. Her smartest passage to Hobart was in 1833, 124 days from the Downs.

She was the only transport to make 11 passages to Australia with convicts. Next to her came the *Mangles* and the Aberdeen-built *Asia*, each of which made nine passages with prisoners. The latter vessel was built in 1819, and made her first voyage in the convict service the following year. Her last passage was to Hobart in 1840

Miss Rose Kelsall, Perth, W.A.

SURGEON HENRY KELSALL, from an original painting

Mitchell Library, Sydney, N.S.W.

A poster advertising the "SUCCESS" when on exhibition in New York

when Thomas Fisher Stead, her master on her previous six voyages, had left her.

The Wreck of the "Waterloo".

Another well-known convict ship, the *Waterloo*, also made her last voyage in 1842, but she did not reach her destination, being wrecked at the Cape on the outward passage. A ship of 414 tons, she had been built at Bristol in 1815 by Hillhouse & Co., and eventually had passed into the ownership of Thomas Brocklebank. She had first reached Port Jackson with prisoners in 1829, and had then become a regular visitor, arriving at Sydney in 1831, 1833, 1836 and 1838 and at Hobart in 1835.

On her return to England from her 1838 voyage her master, John Cow, who had commanded her since 1833, left her, and when she was again taken up for the convict service, early in 1842, her master was Henry Ager. He had made three previous voyages in command of convict ships. In 1827 he had reached Hobart in the Calcutta-built *Asia*, and he still commanded that vessel when she arrived at Sydney in 1831 on her second voyage in the convict service. Three years later he had returned to Port Jackson as master of the *Fairlie*.

The *Waterloo*, under Ager's command, left London on her seventh voyage with prisoners on June 1, 1842. Her surgeon-superintendent was Henry Kelsall, an experienced naval surgeon who had visited Sydney in that capacity in the *Andromeda* in 1834 and in the *Margaret* three years later. Kelsall, when he joined the *Waterloo* on May 6, was not at all impressed by her. "The ship was perfectly rotten, as were also many other ships taken into government employ, probably through interest or jobbery of some kind," he wrote in an unpublished narrative of her voyage. "I visited the ship and was very dissatisfied with her. I told the chief mate so, but he ridiculed the idea, and said the vessel was going to be renovated and cased. I knew nothing about nautical matters, and had therefore to be content with the mate's word." When Kelsall boarded the ship at Deptford prior to sailing, he wrote that he "liked the vessel then as little as ever". This was the period when, as previously pointed out in these pages, the convict service was getting a good deal of decrepit tonnage.

The *Waterloo* was classed AE1 at Lloyd's. In 1833 she had been given new decks and large repairs, and six years later she had been doubled from keel to wale with three-inch American elm below water, and three-inch Dantzig deal above. On being taken up for the convict service in 1842 she was caulked from the copper up, including both decks, and received some minor repairs. In April she was surveyed by Lloyd's surveyors, who reported that she was "in a good, sound, wholesome state, fit for the safe conveyance of dry and perishable goods to and from all parts of the world". Her AE1 classification was continued, but the sequel was to raise grave doubts as to her seaworthiness when she sailed.

Kelsall records that when she encountered the fierce rain squalls of the Equator, "the crazy vessel let the water through her decks like a sieve". Much pumping became necessary, and the *Waterloo* was such a wet ship that scurvy made its appearance among the prisoners. It caused no deaths, but Kelsall ordered Ager to put into the Cape, so that fresh meat and vegetables might be procured and the convicts given a period for recuperation. On the evening of August 23, six days after Kelsall had issued his instruction to the master, the land about the Cape was sighted at a distance of 25 miles. At this stage the only death which had occurred among the prisoners was that of a man who had been suffering from consumption, but many convicts were ill of scurvy. Kelsall wanted Ager to enter Simon's Bay, but although the wind was fair, Ager hove to that night, and the ship drifted to leeward of Cape Point. Ager's action seems to have been deliberate: he had resolved to enter Table Bay in preference to Simon's Bay, although he could hardly have been unaware that at that season Table Bay was an unsafe anchorage.

The *Waterloo* anchored in Table Bay on the 24th, and that evening Ager went ashore and remained there, leaving the ship in charge of the chief mate, Jackson. Neither Ager nor Kelsall reported the ship's arrival to Vice-Admiral Sir E. D. King, the Commander-in-Chief of the Cape station, but the latter could hardly have been unaware of the arrival of the *Waterloo* and of a troop transport belonging to Duncan Dunbar, the *Abercrombie Robinson*, and his statement, after both vessels had been wrecked, that had he known they were in Table Bay he would have instantly ordered them to Simon's Bay, seems to have been a specious excuse. Twenty-three other vessels were also anchored in Table Bay!

On the 26th the weather became dark and cloudy and that night a strong northerly gale sprang up, accompanied by heavy rain. The ship drove that morning, but the starboard bower and port anchors were let go, and she rode out the storm. Ager did not go out to her, and although her top-gallant masts had been brought down on deck, her topmasts were not struck. Next morning the wind fell, but toward evening it rose again, and by midnight a violent northerly gale, with heavy rain squalls, was blowing and a high sea was running.

"About 10 p.m. I began to be apprehensive," declares Kelsall, recording the events of the 27th in his narrative, "and consulted the second mate, as I did in every difficulty. The first mate was a stupid, obstinate fellow, who would do nothing and suggest nothing, and would take no advice. I got to bed at 11 p.m., but could not sleep. Soon there was a loud rattling and a violent vibration, which nearly threw me out of my cabin. I now became aware that the worst had happened and that we had parted from both anchors, and the ship was drifting in the trough of the sea. I ordered Ensign Leigh to fire some muskets as signals of distress, but only two or three would go off. It was pitch dark and my lamp had gone out. I asked for rockets or blue lights. Only four could be found in the ship, and these were burnt on the quarter deck till they burnt out, one after the other."

By four o'clock on the morning of the 28th the wind was at hurricane strength, and there was vivid lightning, loud thunder and heavy rain. Before daylight the *Abercrombie Robinson*, whose cables had also parted, was ashore at the mouth of the Salt River. Her master, when her cables parted, hoisted the jib, and, steering for the beach, drove her ashore on an even keel. The firing of her guns as a signal of distress brought surf boats and waggons from Cape Town, and her troops and crew, numbering about 700 men, were safely landed without loss of life.

According to the reports of those ashore, the *Waterloo* at this stage did not appear to be in immediate danger. The wind had moderated and had veered more to the west, and to those on the beach she seemed to be riding safely at anchor. Kelsall tells a rather different story, but the fact that no action was being taken aboard the *Waterloo* may have induced those ashore to believe she was not in imminent danger. Her topmasts still had not been struck; no attempt had been made to lighten the vessel by cutting away her masts or by jettisoning her cargo, and no effort had been made to launch her boats. In fact, although those on the beach could not have observed this, the longboat was lumbered with spars and no attempt had been made to clear her, and the port quarter-boat was still stowed bottom up.

"By 4.20 a.m.," says Kelsall, "the ship was going fast towards land, distant little more than three miles. The crew were either panic-stricken or else too sleepy or lazy, and sticks had to be used to induce them to come on deck and attend their duties. Leigh and I continued to fire muskets to attract those on shore. The chief mate came lounging in. 'What have you done?' I asked. 'Nothing,' replied the officer. 'What can I do?' 'Have you got another anchor?' I asked. 'Yes,' replied the other, 'but the stream chain would not hold a ship in such a storm.' 'Why not cut away the mast, and then perhaps it would hold?' 'Oh, I could not take that responsibility upon me,' and he rolled out of the cuddy.

"The cabin was now afloat with water and soaking gunpowder. Daylight was now coming on and I ordered the irons to be taken off the convicts who were manacled. Angry breakers in twelve or fourteen tiers could now be seen breaking about fifty yards distant. At 8 a.m. I contrived a primitive sort of rocket apparatus by firing a chord from a musket, to establish communication with the shore. This, however, proved to be unfeasible. Pumping was resorted to, but the rate of leakage made it useless; it was too late for that now. The ship was grinding on the bottom with her keel. The planks of the deck moved backwards and forwards, and felt like blows of a mallet on the feet. The ship was now entering the surf. The chain cable had not been cut, so that the sail which was now hoisted was useless!"

The women, collected in the cuddy with their children, "bestowed all their attention on their parcels, bandboxes and garments," but when tremendous seas, striking the bow, made the vessel stagger from stem to stern, they fell to praying. The prisoners had not yet been released, and were still below. About ten o'clock the wind backed to the northward, and the *Waterloo* was half hidden from those ashore in driving rain squalls. Her foretopmast staysail was hoisted, but, as Kelsall says, it was too late. Her bow did not swing round into the wind, for her small bower cable could not be slipped owing to the shackle-bolt being corroded, and she was driven on to the beach on her port quarter.

"Provision cases broke loose," states Kelsall, "and threatened to crush the people to death. The cuddy cabin was demolished, and the ship's sides gaped and closed alternately as the waves assaulted and retreated. I saw that the mainmast had gone, broken close to the deck, and would presently fall. At the first glance on the quarter deck I also perceived to my satisfaction that the convicts were apparently all on deck, many of them ascending the fore rigging, and great numbers jumping overboard. After a few more rolls the mainmast fell over into the water among the crowd of men struggling in the surf, and I suppose many of them were killed. The mizzen-mast immediately followed the mainmast, breaking off about six feet above the poop-deck.

"As soon as the mast fell, the ship laid over on her broadside, with her deck facing the beach, which was now distant about 250 yards. The mainmast, however, did not go clear overboard; it was poised across the bulwarks for several minutes, nearly half of it being inboard, the broken heel of the mast projecting into the cuddy towards the starboard side, against the bulkhead of which it was propelled by the rise and fall of the surf. During the whole of this time the crashing of timbers, the shrieks, the crying of young children, the prayer of Holy Mary, may well be imagined to have formed a horrible concert. The dissolving ship seemed to me like the dissolving of the world; for it was the world so far as all on board were concerned.

"At length the mainmast went clear over the side, and the wreck turned completely over, so that the deck was nearly perpendicular to the water. The foremast yet stood, the fore topsail yard dipping in the water, and the fore yard immersed almost to half its length."

The *Waterloo* pounded heavily in the boiling surf. In fifteen minutes her upper works parted from her hull, and within two hours she went to pieces. Help was slow in coming from the shore. "I anxiously looked towards the shore," says Kelsall, who, clambering across some spars, had found a precarious perch on the floating mainmast, "hoping to see a boat launched, but there was no appearance of anything of the kind. There were thousands of people on the beach—ladies, female servants and children, carriages, gentlemen on horseback, and one fisherman's boat, some twenty yards above the water-mark, round which there was a crowd, and the boat's crew were standing on each side of the gunwale, leaning on it with their elbows, apparently in consultation with the bystanders as to the propriety of launching it. They seemed an awful long time in making up their minds."

The boat was at length launched, but fearing that it would be swamped by survivors trying to clamber into it, the fishermen approached to within only thirty yards of the wreck. However, Ensign Leigh swam to the boat and was pulled aboard, and a convict was also picked up. The boat returned again from the beach, and this time secured a rope from the shore to the forepart of the ship. Yet at this time, according to Kelsall, two surf boats were conveying troops ashore from the *Abercrombie Robinson*, the hull of which was still intact. One of these boats was eventually diverted to help the *Waterloo's* survivors, but the second continued to ferry baggage ashore from the troopship.

The *Waterloo's* death-roll was heavy, and, as in other convict ship disasters, the loss fell heaviest on the prisoners. A hundred and forty-three convicts were drowned, with 14 of the crew, 15 of the guard of the 99th Regiment, four soldiers' wives and 14 soldiers' children. The three mates and the two officers of the guard, Lieutenant Hext and Ensign Leigh, were saved, as also was Kelsall. The latter owed his life to a convict, William Gardner, whose irons the surgeon had knocked off that morning. Kelsall had been clinging to a small plank when he had been dragged under by another survivor grasping hold of him. "We sank together, but only for an instant," recalls Kelsall, "for finding himself under water, the fellow let go his hold, and I found my head above water, but so completely exhausted that I had not power even to move my hand; my natural corpulency, I suppose, buoyed me up. I fully expected I should shortly sink, as others had, and again abandoned all hope, when all at once I felt someone pulling me by the collar of my coat, with a strong hand. It was that of the convict, William Gardner, whose irons I had placed on him as a punishment, and which I had directed to be removed at daybreak. This man's exertions did not cease until he had dragged me, almost inanimate, to a place of comparative safety, close to where he was holding on to part of the submerged poop. Here I got my legs between some of the prostrate mizzen shrouds and Gardner held up my head for some minutes till some inspirations of air somewhat restored me, and I had a return of power sufficient to clamber on to some solid planks which yet remained of the poop. The poor convict seemed much delighted with having been the means of rescuing me, and said: 'God bless you, sir; if you had forgotten this morning that my irons were on, I should have been dead before now. You saved my life by taking them off, and now I would freely give my life if it would save yours.' " Gardner also was among those saved.

The officers who inquired into the cause of the *Waterloo's* loss rightly censured Ager for having remained ashore, and criticised strongly the failure of the chief mate, Jackson, a young man, to take effective measures to save the ship and those aboard her. There is little doubt that Jackson was incompetent; for had he accepted the responsibility of ordering the topmasts down, had the masts cut away and lightened the ship by jettisoning stores and spars, she would in all probability have been saved. The Board of Inquiry also reported that an examination of the wreckage revealed that the *Waterloo's* timbers had been decayed and rotten, and that she had not been properly fastened. The opinion was expressed that she had been unseaworthy when she sailed, and it was suggested that an inquiry should be held into the system of classification of ships at Lloyd's. Lloyd's Committee denied that the *Waterloo* had been unseaworthy, and produced for the Admiralty the record of her various surveys.

Although the *Waterloo* might have been saved had Ager remained aboard in command, or Jackson taken effective measures for the preservation of the ship in time, there seems little doubt that she was decayed. No instructions had been issued, apparently, to the Transport Officers at Deptford in regard to the survey of ships since 1810, and these instructions were of a very general nature. It is significant that, in consequence of the wreck of the *Waterloo*, more detailed instructions respecting the survey of ships were issued by the Admiralty on December 22, 1842.[2]

Seventy-two of the survivors among the *Waterloo's* convicts were later embarked on the Sunderland-built barque *Cape Packet*, which sailed from the Cape for Hobart on October 14. She also carried three prisoners sentenced at the Cape to transportation. The *Cape Packet*, after a 40 days' passage, arrived at Hobart, with the loss of one prisoner, on November 23. Kelsall completed his voyage in her as surgeon-superintendent. The *Waterloo's* original complement of prisoners had been 219, so that with the 143 drowned, the convict who had died of consumption prior to the Cape, and the 72 forwarded by the *Cape Packet*, there is a discrepancy of three prisoners. Presumably these men died after reaching shore from the wreck, or were still in hospital when the *Cape Packet* sailed and were later forwarded to Hobart by another convict ship[3].

The Mutiny on the "Somersetshire".

Five months before the *Waterloo's* wreck, another convict ship had arrived at the Cape with a remarkable story to relate of an attempted mutiny. The plot to seize the *Somersetshire* seems to have been the most serious attempt at mutiny for a quarter of a century.

Like the *Waterloo*, the *Somersetshire* was an old ship. She had been launched at London in 1810, and had carried convicts to Port Jackson four years later. On her second voyage in the convict service, she cleared Plymouth on December 20, 1841. Commanded by Charles Motley, and with Thomas Gibson as her surgeon-superintendent, she had 219 male prisoners. A plot to seize the ship, murder the officers and, after setting adrift in the ship's boats those who would not join the mutineers, to sail the *Somersetshire* to South America was formed at an early stage of the voyage. The plan was concocted by a number of the prisoners in association with several members of the military guard, composed of two officers and fifty other ranks of the 57th and 99th Regiments, and for this reason it was serious.

Whether the plot was disclosed by an informer or whether an attempt to take the ship was actually made is not known, but the position was regarded so seriously by Motley and the other officers that it was decided to put into the Cape. The *Somersetshire* arrived at Table Bay in March. Four members of the guard were tried by court-martial, and three of them, belonging to the 99th Regiment, convicted on the evidence of the fourth, who had been admitted as Queen's evidence. The court-martial, which was held aboard the *Somersetshire*, lasted a fortnight. Private John Agnew, who was adjudged the ringleader, was sentenced to death, and his two companions were ordered to be transported for life. Agnew was presumably executed by a firing-squad, and the other two men forwarded to Tasmania later in the year, probably in the *Surrey*, which embarked six prisoners when she called at the Cape. The *Somersetshire* sailed from the Cape on April 12 and arrived at Hobart without any further trouble on May 30.[4]

Some Excellent Passages.

When John Cow left the *Waterloo* on her return to England from her 1838 voyage, he was appointed to the command of the *British Sovereign*, a new Sunderland-built barque of 493 tons. She was making her maiden voyage when she sailed from Dublin with prisoners on December 16, 1840. She made a passage of 92 days to Hobart—a new record for a convict ship. It bettered by no less than five days the previous record, standing to the credit of the *Sarah*.

In the previous 22 years only four vessels had carried prisoners out to Hobart from England or Ireland in under 100 days—the *Morley* (1820), *Countess of Harcourt* (1821) and *Runnymede* (1840), each taking 99 days, and the *Sarah* (1837), 97. British shipbuilders, emulating the Americans, were now turning out ships of better design, built on finer lines and more efficiently rigged. Several of these new vessels found their way into the convict service. They were not clippers, of course, but British builders were striving to attain speed, which previously they had ignored, and they were launching sharper models. As a result, passages of under 100 days to Hobart became increasingly common during the period now under review.

In 1842, when the 29-year-old Calcutta-built *Susan* equalled the *British Sovereign's* record passage of the previous year another new ship, the *Isabella Watson*, launched at Leith in 1840, ran out to Hobart from Dublin in 94 days. From the beginning of 1844 until the end of 1853 there were no fewer than 24 passages of under 100 days by convict ships, and seven of these were passages of 90 days or under.

The Indian-built *Anna Maria* made a passage of 90 days from Woolwich to Hobart in 1848 and two years later the *Nile*, a new Sunderland-built ship, also recorded 90 days. In 1851 the *London*, which had been built in 1833, became the first ship to better 90 days, taking 89 days from Dublin. Towards the end of the year the *Rodney* arrived from Queenstown by way of Gibraltar in 87 days, and in 1853 she made the passage in 80 days, on this occasion having embarked her convicts at Cork. The *Aboukir*, which, like the *Rodney*, had come from a Sunderland shipyard, took 83 days from Plymouth in 1852 and the Greenock-built *Martin Luther* arrived from Dublin the same year in 85 days.

The *Aboukir* made only the one voyage in the convict service, but the *Rodney*, which should not be confused, of course, with Devitt & Moore's crack passenger ship of the same name, was on her third passage with prisoners when she arrived at Hobart in 1853. She had made her first voyage in 1850, the year of her launch, running out to Hobart from Portland in 97 days, and the following year took 87 days from Queenstown to Hobart, with a call *en route* at Gibraltar. Her career was a short one, as she and a Dutch barque, the *Oliver van Noord*, were totally wrecked on Kenn Reef in 1858, when bound from Melbourne to India in company with two other vessels.

The *Rodney's* quick passage was due, not only to the fact that she was a fast weatherly ship, one of the new frigate-built merchantmen, but also to the greater knowledge now possessed of the best routes for traversing the Pacific. Lieutenant Maury, the great American student of the winds and currents, did not publish his *Physical Geography of the Sea* until two years after the *Rodney's* record-breaking passage, but for years he had corresponded with ships' masters all over the world, and his work and conclusions had become widely known. He had shown that Cape San Roque, with its dreaded leeward currents, was no longer the menace it had formerly been, and he had advocated the adoption of a Great Circle course from San Roque so as to get into the high latitudes as soon as possible. There is little doubt that the *Rodney's* master, Alexander Maclean, who had commanded her since her first voyage, was well aware of the results of Maury's investigations, and knew that in 1850 the *Constance*, sailing on a Great Circle track, had run out to Adelaide from Plymouth in 76 days. Although the records are silent on the point, there seems little doubt that Maclean likewise followed a Great Circle track, and that this made possible her 80 days' passage. The only other vessel to reach Hobart in 1853 in under 100 days was the barque *Midlothian*, which arrived 12 days after the *Rodney*, 99 days out from Dublin. The remainder of the convict ships to arrive this year made longer passages.

Sunderland-built Vessels.

The domination of Sunderland-built vessels in the convict service during the final years of transportation to Tasmania is remarkable. Almost all the newer vessels after 1841 came from the shipyards of this Durham port, and they proved excellent frigate-built vessels. They were fast and seaworthy, and their more modern design made conditions for the prisoners far more pleasant than previously had been the case or was still the case in the older vessels.

In addition to the *British Sovereign*, the *Aboukir* and the *Rodney*, new Sunderland-built vessels which came into the convict service in these years included the ships *Cressy* (built in 1843), *Sir Robert Peel* (1841), *Hyderabad* (1841), *Nile* (1849) and *Lord Dalhousie* (1847), and the barques *East London* (1839), *Asiatic* (1841), *Orator* (1841), *Emily* (1841), *Tasmania* (1841), *Phoebe* (1842), *Elizabeth and Henry* (1845), *Tory* (1842), *Stately* (1847), *Australasia* (1847), *Blackfriar* (1848), and *Aurora* (1843). The majority made only the one passage in the convict service, but the *Elizabeth and Henry*, the *Tory* and the *Hyderabad* made several voyages.

Most of the other new vessels were the products of Indian shipyards. Of the other vessels built in 1840 or later, Whitby furnished the barques *Lord Petre* (1843) and *Samuel Boddington* (1841) and the ship *Ratcliffe* (1842). The first-named made a passage of 100 days from London in the year of her launch, while the *Ratcliffe* recorded 103 days from Woolwich in 1845 and 106 days from Spithead in 1848. The ship *Blenheim* (1845), which, on her third voyage in the convict service, ran out from Cork in 94 days, and the barque *Candahar* (1840) were the only new Shields-built ships. Hull also provided only two new vessels—the ship *Equestrian* (1842) and the barque *Angelina* (1842). The latter made only one passage with prisoners, but the *Equestrian* made three voyages to Hobart. Her smartest passage was her 95 days from Woolwich on her first voyage in 1844. Other new vessels were the *Isabella Watson* (Leith, 1840), *Duke of Richmond* (Dysart, 1842), *Maria Somes* (Yarmouth, 1841), *Cadet* (Isle of Man, 1841), *Duke of Cornwall* (Bristol, 1843), *Martin Luther* (Greenock, 1840), *Oriental Queen* (Cork, 1842), and *Richard Webb* (Redbridge, 1840). Of these latter vessels, only the *Martin Luther*, with a passage of 85 days from Dublin in 1852, the *Isabella Watson*, which took 94 days from the same port in 1842, and the *Maria Somes*, which first ran out from London in 1844 in 96 days and took a day less from Portsmouth on her second voyage in 1850, went out to Hobart in under 100 days. The appendices record other new ships and details of good passages.

The Norfolk Island Ships.

In 1843 the direct shipment of prisoners to Norfolk Island was instituted. Previously convicts sent there had been transhipped from Sydney, mostly in small colonial vessels, and for a time this penal settlement had been reserved for colonially-convicted prisoners and for convicts specially marked by the British and Irish authorities for transfer there. After the island was transferred from the administration of the New South Wales authorities to that of the Tasmanian officials, however, ships were despatched direct to Norfolk Island, although they occasionally first called at Hobart for orders.

The first direct ship was the Calcutta-built *Maitland*, and this 34-years-old vessel arrived on February 7, 1844. She called both at the Cape and Sydney, but unlike the vessels which had preceeded her to Norfolk Island in 1840—the *Nautilus*, *Augusta Jessie* and *Mangles*—she did not disembark any of her prisoners at Sydney. Two new ships, the *Blundell* and the *Agincourt*, followed her to Norfolk Island before the end of the year, and three ships arrived in each of the years 1845 and 1846. The records of the Norfolk Island ships are scanty, but the last direct ship seems to have been the *Eliza* in 1850, although she possibly landed five of her convicts at Hobart. She was proceeded by the *Tory* in 1847. Orders to abandon the island as a penal settlement were not issued until 1854, and by May 7, 1856, all the prisoners had been removed, except for three left behind as caretakers[5].

Except for the ships to Norfolk Island, the only convict ships which did not land their prisoners, including the so-called "exiles", at Hobart, Melbourne, Geelong, situated on Corio Bay, an arm of Port Phillip, or Sydney were the *Pestonjee Bomanjee* in 1847 and the *Mount Stewart Elphinstone* and the *Bangalore*, the former in 1849 and the latter in 1850. The two last-named vessels put into Sydney for orders, and were sent on to Moreton Bay to land their prisoners there. They were the only vessels throughout the history of transportation which carried convicts direct to Moreton Bay. The *Pestonjee Bomanjee*, a Dumbarton-built barque which made four voyages in the convict service, arrived at Hobart for the second time on February 17, 1847, and received orders to disembark her male prisoners at Maria Island[6].

Few Deaths on Passage.

The health record of the later Tasmanian convict ships was excellent, and in no case do the deaths during the passage seem to have reached double figures in the male transports. The highest mortality rate was aboard the *Cadet* in 1849. Seven of the 150 male prisoners died on the passage from Plymouth—a mortality rate of one death to every 21·7 convicts embarked. This was an unusually high rate for this period.

The female transports did not have such a good record. In the earlier period of transportation, as we have seen, deaths among the women prisoners were less numerous than among the men, but several of the female transports after 1841 had a relatively high mortality rate. In 1843 there were 17 deaths among the women in the new Sunderland-built *East London*, which arrived at Hobart on September 21, after a passage of 133 days from Dublin. She also carried a number of children, and deaths among them brought the total death-roll to 31. She presumably embarked 133 women, 116 of whom were landed at Hobart, so that her mortality rate was one death to every 7·8 prisoners embarked, and is reminiscent of the worst death ships among the early convict ships. The journal of the *East London's* surgeon, Edward Caldwell, was endorsed by the Director-General: "I do not find that neglect or improper treatment can be fairly charged against the surgeon." In the same year the *Garland Grove* arrived at Hobart with eight deaths to report—a mortality rate of one death to every 23·3 convicts embarked—and the *Margaret*, which made a protracted voyage by way of the Cape, lost four women on the passage, but her mortality rate was only one death to every 39 convicts embarked. In 1844 the *Greenlaw*, with five deaths, had a mortality rate of one death to every 24 prisoners embarked, and the rate for the *Emma Eugenia* in 1846 and the *Kinnear* in 1848 was approximately one death to every 28 women embarked[7].

The cause of the higher mortality rate in female transports eludes us, but it must be remembered that larger numbers of women were despatched to Tasmania in the final days of transportation to that colony. Between 1841 and 1853 some 50 shiploads of female convicts reached Hobart so that about a third of the convict ships in that period conveyed women prisoners. This was a much higher proportion than had been the case to either Sydney or Hobart prior to 1840. Moreover, the complements of the individual female transports were larger than they had been in previous years. Instead of carrying from 110 to 130 prisoners the roomier ships of the 1840's were mostly able to accommodate between 170 and 200 women. There does not seem to have been overcrowding by the standards of the day, but with more women being transported, and with larger numbers in each vessel, it was perhaps inevitable that there should be occasional instances of a high mortality rate. In the majority of the female transports the deaths were by no means excessive.

The Last Ship to Tasmania.

The last convict ship to reach Tasmania was the *St. Vincent*. She was an old ship, having been built at London in 1829, and was making her third voyage. She first entered the convict service in 1836, and early the following year arrived at Port Jackson, after a passage of 114 days from Cork. Her tonnage was then recorded as 410 tons register, but in 1844 she was lengthened and given thorough repairs, and in that year her A1 classification was restored for eight years. She was now computed as being of 497 tons by old measurement and of 630 tons by new measurement. Five years later she re-entered the convict service, and arrived at Hobart on April 4, 1850, 106 days out from the Downs.

Her last voyage was without incident. She left Spithead on January 17, 1853, and called at Gibraltar, where she landed 100 of her 210 prisoners from England and embarked in their stead 102. For some years it had become a regular practice for certain convict ships to take out prisoners to Gibraltar, and to embark others there for Tasmania. The *St. Vincent* did not reach Hobart until May 26, 1853. Five of her prisoners died on the passage, and she disembarked 207 convicts[8].

The First Ships to Western Australia.

In 1848 the *Ameer* was despatched to Western Australia, and she was followed in 1849 by the *Mary*. Both of these vessels, however, carried what were euphemistically termed "juvenile government immigrants", and consequently they did not officially rank in Australia as convict ships, although English records indiscreetly list them in that category.

The first convict ship proper to Western Australia was the *Scindian*. A barque of 535 tons old measurement and of 650 tons new measurement, she had been launched at Sunderland in 1844, and had been classed A1 for 12 years. Commanded by James Cammell, she left Portsmouth on March 4, 1850, and arrived at Fremantle, then known as Swan River, on June 1, having made a passage of 89 days. The *Hashemy*, a 33-years-old, Calcutta-built vessel which had carried exiles to Sydney the previous year, arrived later in 1850, after a passage of 95 days from Portland.

The *Scindian* landed 75 prisoners and the *Hashemy* 100. By previous standards, these were small shiploads. Most of the later West Australian transports each carried from 250 to 300 convicts but the stream of prisoners to Western Australia never reached the proportions it had attained to New South Wales and Tasmania. The greatest number of ships to arrive in a single year, excluding those which brought a few prisoners from India, was four in 1853. In most years only two or three transports arrived, and in some years but one.

More Modern Vessels.

The ships employed were in every respect superior to the majority of those that had carried prisoners to New South Wales and Tasmania. Half-a-dozen old vessels were chartered between 1850 and 1855, but from the latter year until the last convict ship arrived in 1868, the transports were large, modern vessels, all possessing an A1 classification and the majority launched in the '50's.

As during the last years of transportation to Tasmania, Sunderland-built frigates predominated. Out of the 33 transports which carried convicts to Western Australia, no fewer than 17 had been launched from Sunderland yards. They were splendid, frigate-built ships, larger than those of similar design which had been built at Sunderland in the '40's and which had engaged in the Tasmanian convict service in the final years of transportation to that colony.

Between them, these vessels made 21 of the 37 convict ship passages to Western Australia between 1850 and 1868.

Of the remaining 16 transports, half were Indian-built, five of them having come from Calcutta and three from Moulmein yards. Four of these were old ships, two of them dating back to 1817, but the other four were modern vessels launched during the '50's and compared favourably with the smart Sunderland frigates.

The *Dudbrook* (1848) and the *Corona* (1866) came from Dundee yards. The *William Jardine,* which previously had made one voyage to Port Jackson and two to Hobart with convicts, had been launched at Liverpool in 1836, and the *Robert Small* at Newcastle the previous year. The remaining four ships were modern. The *Lord Raglan* was built at Cardiff in 1854, the *Sea Park* at Shields in 1845, the *Clyde* at Glasgow in 1860, and the *Racehorse* at Jersey in 1853.

As illustrating the progress which had been achieved in the art of shipbuilding, and the increase which had occurred in the size of the convict ships over the years since the First Fleet had set forth on its adventurous voyage, it is interesting to compare the dimensions of typical convict ships of the earlier years with the beautiful frigate-built ships which were chartered for the Western Australian convict service:

Built	*Vessel*	*Ton*	*Length*	*Breadth*	*Depth*
1783	*Alexander*	452	114·3/10	31·0	
1786	*Prince of Wales*	333	103·0	29·3/10	
1810	*Minstrel*	351	104·5	28·9	
1811	*Surrey*	443	117·6	29·6	
1810	*Guildford*	521	123·8	31·0	5·10
1802	*Mangles*	574	121·2	32·3	5·6
1847	*Lord Dalhousie*	912	146·9	33·6	23·7
1851	*Vimiera*	941	165·7	33·6	22·9
1852	*Merchantman*	1018	175·0	34·0	22·0
1852	*Hougoumont*	875	167·5	34·0	23·0
1853	*Clara*	708	144·5	30·0	20·0
1853	*Racehorse*	1077	209·3	36·1	20·0
1854	*York*	940	172·0	32·5	21·6
1854	*Norwood*	786	160·0	31·2	20·5
1860	*Clyde*	1151	214·1	33·1	22·6
1862	*Belgravia*	889	169·0	34·5	21·2
1866	*Corona*	1199	209·6	35·0	22·0

The *Alexander* and the *Guildford* had 3·6 and 3·9 beams to length respectively, and these figures were typical of all the early ships. In the *Lord Dalhousie,* the first frigate-built ship mentioned above, the ratio of beams per length was 4·3, and in the next earliest built, the *Vimiera,* 4·9. The later ships, however, averaged between five and six beams per length. The ratio of beams to length in the two largest in point of tonnage, the *Corona* and the *Clyde,* both clippers, was respectively 5·9 and 6·4. The latter was an iron ship, built at Glasgow in 1860; the *Corona,* built at Dundee six years later, had an iron frame planked. So far as the frigate-built merchantmen are concerned, their hull design was very similar to that of the clippers of the period, and the number of beams per length was almost identical in both types.

Regarding rig, no comparison between the early and the late ships is possible; for while we have a great deal of information for the frigates and clippers, we have none for such early convict ships as the *Alexander,* the *Prince of Wales,* the *Surrey,* the *Guildford* and the *Mangles.* The latter, of course, were not nearly as lofty, and they did not spread anything like as much canvas.

Duncan Dunbar's Fleet.

The predominant position of Sunderland-built vessels during the last years of transportation to Tasmania, and in the West Australian convict trade throughout its existence, was due primarily to the immense growth from the '40's onwards of the Sunderland shipbuilding industry. But a subsidiary factor was the entry of Duncan Dunbar into the convict trade.

This highly successful shipowner, who had succeeded his father in 1825, was a comparatively latecomer to the convict service. One or two of his ships may have been chartered to carry convicts in the 1830's. He owned, for instance, the *Earl Grey,* which first reached Australia as a convict ship in 1837, and the London-built *Isabella* was another of his large fleet, although I do not know whether he owned her when she arrived on her fourth and fifth voyages in 1832 and 1833 respectively. But it was not until the '40's that he supplied any considerable number of ships to the convict service.

Dunbar was a great believer in Indian-built ships, and many of the vessels which flew his house-flag were built of teak at his own yard at Brema, Moulmein. He was also, however, one of the first shipowners to patronise the Sunderland yards, where Laing turned out a number of ships for him in the '40's. The *Cressy*, the *Aboukir*, the *Rodney* and the *Hyderabad* were among his Sunderland-built ships which conveyed prisoners to Hobart, and, as we have seen, these frigates performed particularly well in that trade.

His interest in the convict service continued when transportation to Western Australia was inaugurated in 1850, and until his death in 1862 vessels flying his house-flag conveyed prisoners to Swan River. At least 10 of his vessels—nearly a third of the total convict ships to Western Australia—were chartered by the Admiralty for the conveyance of prisoners. Six of these were Sunderland-built: the ships *Pyrenees*, *Minden*, *Nile*, *Phoebe Dunbar* and *Sultana*, and the barque *Ramillies*. The first three and the last-named illustrate his penchant for naming his vessels after famous British victories by land and sea. The *Pyrenees* made two voyages to Western Australia before she was taken up as a transport for the Crimean War in 1854, while the *Sultana* served in a similar capacity before visiting Swan River.

The frigate-built *Ramillies*, turned out by Laing for Dunbar in 1845, made the best passage of these six vessels. In 1854 she went out to Swan River from London in 79 days. This was not a record, but as she called both at Plymouth and Gibraltar it was an excellent passage. Indeed, only five convict ships to Western Australia bettered her time, and all five made their passages direct.

Of Dunbar's other four vessels in this trade, the *Sea Park*, which ran out from London in 94 days in the same year as the *Ramillies*, was built at Shields in 1845, and the *Lord Raglan*, which took 88 days from Plymouth in 1858, at Cardiff in 1854. The *Marion* and the *Lincelles* were both Indian-built.

The *Marion*, launched at Calcutta in 1834, reached Swan River early in 1852 after a passage of 89 days from Portland. It was her fourth voyage in the convict service, her three previous passages with prisoners having been to Hobart in the '40's. On the second of these, in 1845, she had gone out from London in 94 days. A teak-built ship, she had, like so many Indian ships, a particularly long life, finally being wrecked off Newfoundland in 1877.

The *Lincelles* lasted even longer. She was launched from Dunbar's yard at Moulmein in 1858, and made her only voyage in the convict service in 1861-2, when she had a protracted passage of 115 days from Portland. She disembarked 306 prisoners. On Dunbar's death, the *Lincelles* was purchased by the London shipowner, John Allan, whose fleet included the Sunderland-built *York*. The latter went out to Swan River with convicts in 1862, making a passage of 84 days from Portland. Both the *Lincelles* and the *York* were employed by Allan in the India-Mauritius coolie trade, in which the former normally carried 400 coolies at a time. She was later sold to Genoese owners, and did not disappear from the register until 1906-7, nearly half a century after her launching.

The Somes Ships.

Duncan Dunbar's participation in the convict trade was never on the same scale as that of another highly successful shipowner, Joseph Somes, who had first entered the shipping world as an India husband. Somes built up a very large fleet, and traded to all parts of the world. From an early date he furnished transports for the convict service, and over a long period of years no individual shipowner engaged so extensively in the conveyance of prisoners to New South Wales and Tasmania. His only rival in this regard was probably Thomas Ward, but the latter never furnished anything like the number of convict ships provided by Somes.

The latter's house-flag differed from the White Ensign only in that it displayed an anchor instead of the Union Jack in the canton, and tradition asserts that it was granted in recognition of the assitance to the government in the provision of troop and convict transports. I am uncertain as to when his ships first flew this flag, but there is no doubt that it was a familiar sight at both Sydney and Hobart. In later years he was assisted in the management of his fleet by his sons, who, trading as Somes Brothers, were the registered owners of many of the ships. After the death of Joseph Somes, the firm changed its name to the Merchant Shipping Company.

The best-known of the ships to carry the Somes house-flag in the Western Australian convict service was the ship *Merchantman* which was launched from Laing's yard at Sunderland in 1852. If we except some of the warships which conveyed prisoners to Australia, she was the first vessel of over 1000 tons register to be employed as a convict ship. She made her first passage to Swan

River in 1862-3. Leaving London on October 28, 1862, she carried prisoners to Bermuda. Having disembarked the whole or part of her convicts there, she filled up their berths with prisoners previously transported to Bermuda, and then sailed for Swan River, where she arrived the following February, 110 days out from London.

She made a second voyage in 1864, her master, as on her previous voyage, being William Gardiner. Leaving Portland on July 1, the *Merchantman* made a direct passage to Fremantle of 73 days. This was at that time a record passage for a convict ship to Swan River, beating by two days the record set the previous year by the Glasgow-built clipper *Clyde*, a larger ship than the *Merchantman*. The *Clyde* was also owned by Somes.

Another of the firm's ships to carry prisoners to Swan River was the *Belgravia*, a ship of 889 tons registered in the ownership of the Merchant Shipping Company. She went out from Portland in 1866 in 88 days.

The "Racehorse's" Voyage.

Probably the best account extant of a West Australian convict ship's voyage was written by Captain A. J. A. Mann, who had spent 45 years at sea in sail and steam. As a 14-years-old apprentice, he went out in the Jersey-built clipper *Racehorse* when she carried prisoners to Swan River in 1860. Captain Mann's account was written many years after the events he describes, and, due no doubt to the lapse of time, it contains some minor errors. He states, for instance, that the *Racehorse* made a record passage of 61 days from Portland, but official Western Australian records prove that she took 76 days.

The *Racehorse* was a ship of 1077 tons register, "a beautiful, long, yacht-like craft", as Captain Mann describes her. Her cutwater, he adds, was "adorned with a shield supported on each side by a well-carved figure of a racehorse". She carried a crew of 105 officers and men, with a guard of about 50 pensioners under the command of a sergeant-major. These men were accompanied by their wives and children, and, as was the custom in the West Australian convict ships, they received free passages in return for their services in guarding the prisoners.

The arrangements for the security of the convicts differed very little from those which always had operated in the convict ships. The 'tween deck was divided into four large sections, with a heavy oak bulkhead running from side to side where the mainmast came through the deck. The space forward of the bulkhead was reserved for the prisoners, whose sole means of entry or egress was through a small iron-studded door in the bulkhead. It would allow the passage of but one man at a time, and to pass through it he had to stoop and almost crawl. The hospital was situated on the starboard side abaft the bulkhead, with the corresponding space on the port side serving as the quarters of the eight warders and their families. These warders seem to have been found only in the West Australian transports, and presumably were sent out to maintain order among the prisoners, to serve as religious instructors and teachers to them, and to assist generally the guard of pensioned soldiers. Then came the crew's quarters, with the guard and their families quartered aft.

A stairway led from the soldiers' quarters up through the cuddy, which served also as the arms room, and thence to the poop. This arrangement was designed to enable the poop to be manned within a matter of seconds in the event of an alarm, so that it could be converted into a citadel for the defence of the ship. The officers, soldiers and crew were armed with rifles, revolvers, cutlasses, and boarding-pikes. A strong barricade, extending from bulwark to bulwark, stood on the main deck, dividing it into two sections; at each end of this barricade was a small door, guarded day and night by a sentry. On each side of the quarter-deck was placed a cannon, loaded with grapeshot and pointing forward.

The *Racehorse* cleared Portland on May 26, 1861, according to Captain Mann, but actually she sailed on May 26, 1865. The prisoners had all been assigned individual numbers, which were stencilled in "great white figures" on the back and each breast of each man's coat. Those with odd numbers were allowed on deck at one time, to be followed for the next period by those with even numbers. The men were divided into messes, as had been the custom in the New South Wales and Tasmanian ships. They were awakened daily by bugle call at 5.30 a.m., and locked up for the night at 6.30 p.m. Breakfast, according to Captain Mann, consisted of a basin of gruel, half a pint of cocoa, and six ounces of biscuit, and was served at 7.45 a.m. Dinner was at noon, and comprised soup, four ounces of salt beef and pork on alternate days, and six ounces of biscuit, with half a pound of "duff" on Thursdays and Sundays. For supper, served at 5.30 p.m., there was a half a pint of tea and four ounces of biscuit. The water allowance was three quarts daily.

To avoid the frequent quarrels between individual prisoners, the surgeon permitted disputants who were fairly evenly matched to fight it out on the upper deck, provided the permission of the head warder was first obtained. "On these occasions," says Captain Mann, "a ring was quickly formed, seconds duly appointed and a regular mill ensued, with fair play until the better man won." One tragedy resulted in consequence of this practice. The victor in one mill was savagely attacked in the prison during the night with an iron belaying-pin, and died some weeks later of his wounds, when the ship was within a week's sail of her destination.

There was no evidence as to the identity of this man's assailant. The prisoners were therefore told that until they gave the attacker up, or he surrendered voluntarily, the ventilating fans of the prison would be kept stopped. As the *Racehorse* was then in the doldrums, and the weather was excessively hot, this punishment was sheer torture, especially as at the same time the convicts were placed on half allowance of food and water. At the end of 24 hours a man surrendered and confessed to the assault. He was punished with three dozen lashes, and thereafter was segregated from his companions, being kept on the poop, but it was later rumoured that he was not the real culprit and had surrendered so that the remainder of the prisoners would not have to bear the stifling heat of the unventilated prison in the tropics.

One morning after crossing the Equator, when the *Racehorse* was creeping down the north-east coast of Brazil, a convict on the forecastle-head ran out along the cathead and sprang overboard. At the cry of "Man Overboard", the convicts on deck ran to the side, and flung the ends of ropes to the man in the water. As he drifted aft, the prisoners crowded in a mass towards the bulkhead. "The sentry ordered them off," says Captain Mann, "but with shouts and curses they still kept coming on in apparent efforts to throw the man in the water another rope." At this moment the captain, his speaking trumpet in one hand and a revolver in the other, appeared on the poop, and quickly took command. Captain Seward called out the guard, had the cannon manned, and backed the main-yard. Order was almost instantly restored, the starboard cutter lowered, and the man picked up. "I think, and the captain told me years afterwards that it was his firm opinion, the whole thing was part of a pre-arranged plan to rush the poop and in the confusion capture the ship," wrote Captain Mann. "If so, the moment was well chosen; for the chief mate had gone down into the afterhold along with the carpenter on some business, leaving the deck in temporary charge of the third mate who was not equal to the occasion." The man who had jumped overboard was punished by being placed in the sweat-box. Captain Mann describes it as "a wooden erection, something like a sentry-box, only much smaller . . . about six and a half feet in height with just enough room inside for a man to stand upright". Half-a-dozen augur holes allowed the man to see and breathe when the door was closed on him. He could only stand in this contraption. It was a severe punishment, and Captain Mann states that six hours in the box was as much as a strong man could endure. The hapless convict who had flung himself overboard spent six hours daily in the box for a week.

After this incident, the remainder of the *Racehorse's* passage was uneventful. Although Captain Mann says she conveyed 350 prisoners, she actually embarked 280 and disembarked 278, one man having died during the passage and a second after arrival[9].

The "Corona's" Record Passage.

The fastest passage to Swan River by a convict ship was made by the ship *Corona* in 1866. She was a new vessel, launched that year at Dundee, and was making her maiden voyage. She was also the largest merchantman ever employed in the Australian convict service, being of 1199 tons register, 48 tons more than the *Clyde*.

Commanded by William S. Crudace, she left Portland on October 16, and anchored in Swan River on December 22, disembarking 306 convicts, the full complement she had embarked. The *Corona* thus made a passage of 67 days, clipping six days off the *Merchantman's* record. The *Corona's* later history I have not been able to trace, but Crudace, of course, became a prominent Dundee shipowner in later years.

Few Changes in Routine.

The shipment of convicts to Western Australia varied little from the system which previously had been in force in the despatch of prisoners to New South Wales and Tasmania. The surgeons-superintendent, mostly, if not all, selected from the ranks of naval surgeons, reported on taking up their appointment to the Captain-Superintendent of the Deptford Victualling Yard and the ships were still inspected and passed by the Agent for Transports. The fitting-out, although usually done at the Deptford Naval Dockyard, was sometimes carried out elsewhere. In 1864, for instance, the *Clara* was fitted out in the West India Dock at London, as was the *Racehorse* the following year, and the *Vimeira* in 1865 was altered in the East India Dock. In the administrative arrangements, however, the office of the Directors of Convict Prisons now had a part. This department not only selected the prisoners for despatch, but provided discipline officers to accompany the convicts until the ships' last port of call in England and appointed assistant warders and a religious instructor to sail in the ship to Fremantle. As these officials were often accompanied by their wives and families, they presumably were selected because they wished to emigrate to Western Australia. The pensioners who formed the guards on the West Australian ships were selected for the same reason, receiving free passages for their wives and children[10].

The ships, at least at the beginning, were fitted out in much the same way, and in 1850 we find the surgeon-superintendent, John W. Bowler, complaining of the enormously heavy fittings and thick wooden stanchions of the prison in the *Hashemy* and urging that such heavy, clumsy construction should be replaced by light iron framework, so that both light and ventilation might be improved. The routine aboard ship was almost unchanged. The cooks were the first prisoners to appear on deck in the mornings, usually at five o'clock or half-past, but in the *Norwood* in 1862 as early as four o'clock. At daylight or at either six o'clock or half-past the convicts began to wash after stowing their hammocks. Sick rounds by the surgeon followed the issue of the daily ration of water and biscuit, and at eight o'clock breakfast was served. Morning school began at either ten o'clock or half-past, and in most ships the daily allowance of lime juice was served before, and the allowance of wine after, dinner, which seems to have been almost always timed for one o'clock, although in the *Clyde* in 1863 it was served at noon. Afternoon school in this ship lasted from half-past one until three o'clock, but in most ships did not assemble until two or half-past. There was a good deal of variation in the hour for supper and in the time by which all prisoners had to be below. In the earlier vessels the prisoners seem to have been sent below at five o'clock or half-past and supper served at 6.30, but in the later ships it seems to have been usually served at four-thirty or five o'clock and the prisoners sent below at eight o'clock[11].

The Lash Less Used.

Although flogging was still a legal punishment, the lash was not used with the same frequency or severity in the West Australian ships as it had been in those despatched to New South Wales and Tasmania. However, William Smith, the surgeon of the *Merchantman* in 1864, seems to have been a strict disciplinarian and a believer in the efficacy of the cat-o'-nine-tails. Before the ship's departure from England a convict received 36 lashes for an unnatural offence, but his flogging was inflicted by an authorised officer from Portland Prison and, as he was relanded after punishment, the penalty may not have been imposed by the surgeon. During the passage two men each received 48 lashes for assault, and two other prisoners, for other offences, each received 36. In other West Australian ships, however, the maximum number of lashes usually imposed seems to have been 24, and most of the men flogged received no more than 12 or 18 strokes of the cat[12].

The most common punishment was solitary confinement in the "Black Box" on bread and water. The convict was sometimes kept there for a few hours only, but confinement for one, two or three days was common and in the *Clyde* in 1863 one man was confined for eight days. An hour daily for exercise was usually allowed to the prisoner sentenced to confinement. The "Black Box" does not seem to have been the small punishment box found on some of the early convict ships to the eastern States, but a dark and narrow cell erected under the forecastle. Other forms of punishment included handcuffing, leg-ironing, ironing on the poop, and the stopping of a man's wine or lime juice allowance[13].

Prisoners Better Educated.

Practically the only evidence we possess regarding the state of education of the convicts shipped to Australia is contained in the surgeons' journals and the few reports by the schoolmasters which have survived. These tell us little more than the numbers who could both read and write, read only or neither read nor write, and the numbers who had received some sort of an education at Sunday schools only, day schools or other schools. The reports on the work of the schools aboard ship have to be accepted cautiously, as the surgeon or schoolmaster naturally desired to place his own work in the most favourable light, and those included in the total of the prisoners who learnt to read or write on the passage out probably included men and women who had mastered only a short religious passage or could write but a few words. Nevertheless, there is no doubt the schools did good and imparted to convicts some rudimentary knowledge.

The little evidence we have shows that more convicts sent to Western Australia could both read and write when they came aboard than had been the case with the men sent to New South Wales and Tasmania. It would seem that rarely in the ships to New South Wales and Tasmania did more than 50 per cent of the convicts read and write and often the percentage was lower. In the West

N.S.W. and Tasmania

Year	*Ship*	*Total*	*Read and Write*	*Read Only*	*Neither Read Nor Write*
1826	*England*	148	68	26	54
1827	*Asia*	200	89	39	72
1833	*Captain Cook*	230	110	52	68
1846	*Lord Auckland*	180	82	25	69

West Australian

1858	*Lord Raglan*	270	238	20	12
1860–1	*Lincelles*	304	204	61	39
1862–3	*Merchantman*	191	166	25	—
1864	*Merchantman*	259	186	61	10
1865	*Racehorse*	280	163	72	45
1867	*Norwood*	254	183	64	7

Australian ships the percentage was sometimes as high as 75 and not often greatly below. The above table, while by no means conclusive, is instructive and probably is not far wide of the mark as illustrating the proportion of illiterates among the convicts.[14]

We are told that only one of the 320 convicts in the *Clyde* in 1863 was uneducated, and that in the *Clara* in 1864, 25 of the 301 prisoners were in that category. No details of female transports have been included, since no women were shipped to West Australia.

The Last Convict Ship.

Considering the part which Indian and Sunderland vessels had played in the transportation of prisoners to Australia, it was fitting that the last convict ship should have come from a Moulmein yard, and the second last have been a Sunderland-built ship. The latter was the *Norwood*, launched in 1854. She first went out to Swan River with convicts in 1862, and on her second passage arrived on July 13, 1867. She took 85 days from Portland on the first occasion, and 86 from the same port on the second.

The last convict ship to Australia was the *Hougoumont*, which arrived at Fremantle on January 9, 1868, after a passage of 89 days from London. A ship of 875 tons, she had been launched at Moulmein in 1852, and had originally been one of Duncan Dunbar's fleet, named after Hougoumont Farm at the battle of Waterloo. When she carried convicts to Western Australia, however, she had passed into the ownership of Luscombe of London.

The *Hougoumont* is remembered, not only as the last convict ship, but as the transport aboard which John Boyle O'Reilly, the Irish political prisoner who escaped to America and wrote *Moondyne*, was brought to Australia. His pen-picture of life in a convict ship has already been recorded in these pages. It was not strictly accurate of the *Hougoumont's* voyage; for the last of the convict ships, of course, carried no women prisoners and only one convict died on her passage to Fremantle. She landed safely 279 of the 280 convicts she had embarked, 63 Irish political prisoners being numbered among them.

As with some of the other West Australian convict ships, a ship's newspaper was produced aboard the *Hougoumont* by the prisoners. It was called *The Wild Geese*, and was the work of the Irish prisoners, who used paper and writing materials furnished them by their chaplain, Father Delaney. Several copies were presumably made, but the content was principally circulated by the paper being read aloud to groups of the convicts. There is no mention of manuscript newspapers of this kind having been produced on any of the Tasmanian or New South Wales convict ships, but several of the Western Australian transports published them. In the *Lord Raglan* in 1858 the weekly paper was called *Life Boat*, and was edited by a convict, Stephen Stout, a man of 29 who had been educated at a Sunday and day school in France and who was, in the surgeon's opinion, a "good scholar". Stout delivered lectures to the prisoners during the passage, his subjects varying from Eclipses, with special reference to an eclipse of the sun, to Australia and Australian employment. *The Belgravean Weekly Journal* was issued in the *Belgravia* in 1866, *Norwoodiana or Sayings and Doings on Route to Western Australia*, in the *Norwood* the following year, and *A Voice of our Exiles or the Clara Weekly Journal* in the *Clara* in 1864. Doubtless there were also others[15].

And so, with the *Hougoumont's* arrival at Fremantle, the long history of the convict ships comes to an end—a story of human misery and suffering, but a story also of nautical achievement, and of the development and evolution of the humble merchantman. It began with the blunt-nosed, pot-bellied craft of Phillip's little fleet; it ended with the splendid frigates and sleek clippers of the golden age of sail.

NOTES AND REFERENCES

ABBREVIATIONS IN THE NOTES AND REFERENCES

To conserve space, the following abbreviations have been used in the Notes and References:

Accts. & Pap.	=	Accounts and Papers relating to convicts on board the hulks and those transported to N.S.W. Ordered to be printed 10 and 26 Mar., 1792.
Aust. Dict. Biog.	=	*Australian Dictionary of Biography*, i, 1788–1850, A–H (Melbourne, 1966); ii, 1788–1850, I—Z (Melbourne, 1967).
Aust. Ency.	=	*Australian Encyclopaedia*, 10 vols. (Sydney, 1958).
Bradley, *Jour.*	=	Lieut. William Bradley, MS. Journal, Mitchell Library, Sydney, N.S.W.
Collins	=	David Collins, *An Account of the English Colony in N.S.W.* (London, 1798).
Col. Sec. Pap.	=	Colonial Secretary's Papers.
HRA	=	*Historical Records of Australia*, 27 vols. (Government Printer, 1914–1924).
JRAHS	=	*Journal of the Royal Australian Historical Society.*
Lloyd & Coulter	=	Christopher Lloyd and Jack L. S. Coulter, *Medicine and the Navy*, iii, 1714–1815 (Edinburgh, 1961) and iv, 1815–1900 (Edinburgh, 1963).
NSW Arch.	=	Archives Office of N.S.W., Public Library of N.S.W., Sydney.
NSWHR	=	*Historical Records of N.S.W.*, 8 vols. (Sydney, 1893–1901).
Tas. Arch.	=	Archives Office of Tasmania, The State Library of Tasmania, Hobart.
Tench	=	Watkin Tench, *Sydney's First Four Years* (Sydney, 1961).
Vic. Hist. Mag.	=	*Victorian Historical Magazine*, published by the Victorian Historical Society, Melbourne.
White	=	John White, *Journal of a Voyage to N.S.W.* (Sydney, 1962).

NOTES AND REFERENCES

CHAPTER ONE

1. **Instructions to Capt.** Cook for his Three Voyages, *The Naval Miscellany*, v. iii (Navy Records Society, v. 63, London, 1928), 347.
2. *Aust. Ency.*, i (Sydney, 1958), 438-9; JRAHS, xvi (Sydney, 1930), 51 sq.; *Aust. Dict. Biog.*, i, 62-3.
3. On the history of transportation see George Ives, *A History of Penal Methods* (London, 1914), 107 sq.; L. O. Pike, *A History of Crime in England*, v. ii (London, 1876), 349 sq.; Leon Radzinowicz, *A History of English Criminal Law and its Administration from* 1750, v. i (London, 1948), 108-10; Sir James Fitzjames Stephen, *A History of the Criminal Law of England*, v. i (London, 1883), 480 sq.: A. G. L. Shaw, *Convicts and the Colonies* (London, 1966), 30-7. Sir Charles Middleton, Comptroller of of the Navy, to Nepean, 11 Dec., 1786 (NSWHR, I, ii, 35-6), indicates the differences between the old and new systems of transportation were realised.
4. Shaw, *Convicts*, 33 and n. 2, 34.
5. For petitions for and against transportation see *Copies of all Petitions on the subject of Convict Discipline and Transportation . . . from Australia or Van Diemen's Land since* 1838 . . . Ordered to be printed 20 Mar., 1851; *Copies of all Memorials or Reports on the subject of Convict Discipline and Transportation* . . . Ordered to be printed 6 May, 1851; *Do. from Australia or Van Diemen's Land since* 1838 . . . Ordered to be printed 8 May, 1851; *Copies of Extracts of desptaches . . . from the Governors of the Australian Colonies with petitions against the continuation of Transportation.* Presented to both Houses of Parliament, June, 1864. Contemporary newspapers report fully the proceedings of meetings of protest and of demonstrations against transportation on the arrival of exiles.
6. E. Scott, "The Resistance to Convict Transportation in Victoria, 1844-53," *Vic. Hist. Mag.*, v. i (1911), 101-42; "The Australasian League, 1851-4", *Pacific History Review* (Dec., 1939), 385-400, and contemporary newspapers, *passim.*
7. J. S. Battye, *Western Australia: A history from its discovery to the inauguration of the Commonwealth* (London, 1924), *passim.*
8. *Ibid., passim.* For petitions to make West Australia a penal colony see *Copies of all Memorials or Reports on . . . Convict Discipline and Transportation, etc.* Order to be printed 6 May, 1851, 35-45.

CHAPTER TWO

1. Sydney to Treasury, 18 Aug., 1786, to Adm., 31 Aug., 1786; Adm. to Sydney, 12 Oct. and 21 Nov., 1786 (NSWHR I, ii, 14-20, 20-2, 23-4, 29); Bradley, *Jour.*, 2.
2. Rose to Stephens, 21 Oct., 1786; Stephens to Nepean, 18 Jan., 1787; Sydney to Phillip, 20 Apr., 1787 (NSWHR I, ii, 25-6, 47, 82).
3. Jour., Lt. P. G. King (NSWHR, ii, 514); Court Directors, East India Co., 9 Feb. and 4 Apr., 1787. (*Ibid.*, I, ii, 48.)

4. Macaulay and Gregory to Nepean, 21 Aug., 1786 (NSWHR, I, ii, 20). Cf. Long to East India Co., 17 Jan., 1792, and East India Co. to Treasury, 2 Feb., 1792 (*Accts. & Pap.*, 104-5.)
5. Contract 20 Feb., 1792 with Geo. Whitlock (*Accts. & Pap.*, 53-7); Charter of Affreightment with Brown, Welbank & Petyt, 27 Oct., 1801 (HRA I, iii, 358-363); *Do.* with Joseph Lachlan, 1 June, 1827 (Col. Sec. Pap., N.S.W. Arch., 28/1946); *Do.* with Joseph Lachlan, 6 July, 1829 (*Ibid.*, 30/495).
6. J. A. Nixon, "Health and Sickness", in C. Northcote Parkinson (Ed.), *The Trade Winds* (London, 1948), 122, citing Sir Gilbert Blane.
7. Deputy Librarian, Admiralty, to the author, 27 Oct., 1953; William Laird Clowes, *The Royal Navy*, 7 vols. (London, 1897-1903), chapters on civil history of Royal Navy, *passim*; John Ehrman, *The Navy in the War of William II*, 1689-1697 (Cambridge, 1953), 174. A history of the Transport Service, as far as I am aware, has not been written.
8. Jours., A. Watson, surgeon-supt. *Racehorse*, 1865, M/T 32/9 (Microfilm 3181) and Wm. Crauford, surgeon-supt. *Vimeira*, 1865-6, M/T 32/10 (*Ibid.*).
9. Journ., John Smith, surgeon-supt. *Clyde*, 1838, Adm. 101/17 (Microfilm 3192).
10. Charter of affreightment, Brown, Welbank & Petyt, 27 Oct., 1801 (HRA I, iii, 360). I have unfortunately mislaid the reference to the Navy Board's decision of 1831.
11. Stephens to Navy Board, 4 Jan., 1787 (NSWHR I, ii, 44-5).
12. Lloyd and Coulter, iv, 1, 2.
13. King to Transport Cmmrs., 9 Nov., 1802; Transport Cmmrs. to King, 14 Nov., 1803, with encl. Bray to Cmmrs., 9 June, 1803 (HRA I, iii, 719; iv, 425-7); Post, pp. 186 (mulct of contractors) and pp. 207 (*Chapman*); Bathurst to Macquarie, 12 Apr., 1819, with encls. (HRA I, x, 143-5).
14. Heads of a plan for removing and employing convicts both in the hulks and in Botany Bay, by Lord Pelham, 13 Dec., 1801 (NSWHR, iv., 635-8); Pelham to Adm., 9 Mar., 1802 (HRA I, iii, 570).
15. Memo. of *Lady Juliana's* charter, 27 Dec., 1790 (NSWHR I, ii, 423).
16. Contract with Geo. Whitlock, 27 Aug., 1789 (*Accts. & Pap.*, 53-7); Memo. of contract with W. Richards (NSWHR I, ii, 671); Transport Cmmrs. to Portland, 11 June, 1800 (NSWHR iv, 91-2); Charter, Brown, Welbank & Petyt, 27 Oct., 1801 (HRA I, iii, 358-363).
17. Navy Bd. to Grose, 5 Mar., 1794 (HRA I, i, 467); *Rep. Select Cmtte.* on *Transportation*, 1812, 28.
18. Charters of affreightment (Col. Sec. Pap., N.S.W. Arch.), *passim*. At the time I examined these there was a bundle of miscellaneous charter parties grouped together, but others were scattered through this correspondence.

CHAPTER THREE

1. Professor Michael Lewis, Royal Naval College, Greenwich, to author, undated, in reply to letter of 21 Oct., 1953.
2. Warrants of 27 Aug. and 17 Nov., 1789, from Navy Board to Lieut. Shapcote (*Accts. & Pap.*, 64-5).
3. Surgeons' Jours. (Microfilms 3187-3216), *passim*; Transport Cmmrs. to Portland, 11 June, 1800 (NSWHR, iv, 92).
4. Transport Cmmrs. to Portland, 11 June, 1800 (NSWHR, iv, 92); Charter, Brown, Welbank & Petyt, 27 Oct., 1801 (HRA I, iii, 363); Surgeons' Jours., *passim*; J. S. Battye, *Western Australia* (London, 1924), 208; Grey to Fitzgerald, 20 Dec., 1850; *Perth Gazette*, 19 Dec., 1851.

5. Macquarie to Bathurst, 18 Mar., 1819, and 24 Mar., 1819 (HRA I, x, 46, 87-8).
6. Tench, 173.
7. Professor Michael Lewis, Royal Naval College, Greenwich, undated letter in reply to author's letter of 21 Oct., 1953; Deputy Librarian, Admiralty, to author, 27 Oct., 1953; Surgeons' Jours., *passim*.
8. Relevant Navy Lists; Shapcote to Navy Cmmrs., 24 Apr., 1790 (NSWHR I, ii, 334); Post, pp. 126-31. Shapcote died on or about May 12, 1790. Navy Cmmrs'. Rep., 15 Feb., 1792, (*Accts. & Pap.*, 62).
9. *Annual Register*, 1792, Chronicle 23; King to Phillip, 10 Jan., 1792 (HRA I, i, 332); Remarks and Statement of the Proceedings of Donald Trail, n.d. (*Accts. & Pap.*, 73-77).
10. Hill to Wathen, 26 July, 1790 (NSWHR I, ii, 367-8).
11. Nelson to Jervis, 27 July, 1797 (W. H. Nicolas, *Dispatches and Letters of Nelson*, v. ii (London, 1845), 423); *Private Papers of George, 2nd Earl Spencer*, 1794-1801 (Navy Rec. Soc. v. 48, London, 1914), 415 n.; relevant Navy Lists (*Steel's, Sea Officers* and *Hamilton's New*).
12. Relevant Navy Lists; Stephens to Navy Bd., 4 Jan., 1787 (NSWHR I, ii, 44-5).
13. John Marshall, *Royal Naval Biography*, v. ii pt. ii (London, 1825), 540-44; relevant Navy Lists. Cf. D. C. Tilghman, "Captain Daniel Woodriff, C.B., R.N., a brief biography compiled from original sources", (*Vic. Hist. Mag.*, v. 32, 141-61).
14. Jours., J. W. Hallion, *Isabella*, 1818, and A. Montgomery, *Elizabeth*, 1820-1, Adm. 101/36, 101/24 (Microfilms 3198, 3194).
15. Jours., Morgan Price (*Hadlow*), 1820, T. C. Roylance (*Lord Sidmouth*), 1820-1, James Scott (*Castle Forbes*), 1819-20 (Adm. 101/32, 101/44, 101/16 (3197, 3201, 3191).
16. Jour., J. J. W. Roberts (*Lord Auckland*), 1846 (Adm. 101/43 (3200)); Surgeons' Jours., *passim*.

CHAPTER FOUR

1. *Rep. Select Cmtte. on Transportation*, 1812, 10; *Letters and Papers of Lord Barham*, iii (Navy Rec. Soc., v. xxxix, London, 1911), 120 sq.; Lloyd and Coulter, iii, 3 sq.
2. *Ibid.*; St. Vincent to Spencer, 30 June, 1797, encl., *Private Papers of 2nd Earl Spencer*, 1794-1801, v. ii (Navy Rec. Soc., v. 48, London, 1914), 212.
3. Instructions to masters and surgeons, 10 June, 1801 (NSWHR, iv, 399-400).
4. Lloyd and Coulter, iv, 2-3; Surgeons' Jours., *passim*.
5. Redfern to Macquarie, 30 Sept., 1814 (HRA I, viii, 290-2).
6. *Ibid.*; Norman J. Dunlop, "William Redfern, the First Australian Medical Graduate, and His Times", JRAHS, xiv (1928), 57 sq.
7. J. A. Nixon, "Health and Sickness", *op. cit.*, 136-7.
8. Nepean to Kent, 12 Dec., 1792 (NSWHR I, ii, 678-9); HRA I, i, 783 n.
9. Cmmrs. Navy to Phillip, 17 May, 1792 (HRA, I, i, 356); *Do.* to *Do.*, 25 July, 1792 (*Ibid.*, 370); Nepean to Kent, 12 Dec., 1792 (NSWHR, I, ii, 678); Bowen to Nepean, 28 Jan., 1793 (*Ibid.*, ii, 5).
10. Post, 145-7; Phillip to Dundas, 11 Oct., 1792, Grose to Dundas, 12 Oct., 1793 (HRA I, i, 397, 454).
11. Nepean to Kent, 12 Dec., 1792 (NSWHR I, ii, 678-9).

12. Michael Lewis, ***England's Sea Officers*** (London, 1948), 256, 257; Michael Lewis, *A Social History of the Navy*, 1793-1815 (London, 1960), 235, 245; Lloyd & Coulter, iii, 10 sq.; iv., 11 sq. and *passim*.

13. Kent to ? – – –, 2 Sept., 1793, Thomson, Baker and Pattullo to King, 21 Apr., 1794, Campbell to Cmmrs. Navy, 2 Aug., 1794, Evidence of Matthew Austin, 21 Mar., 1796 (NSWHR, ii, 61-2, 854-5, 856; iii, 108); *Rep. Select Cmmtte. on Transportation*, 1812, evidence of Alexander McLeay, 28.

14. Post, 144, 145, 147, 151, 171.

15. Hunter to Portland, 25 June, 1797 (HRA I, ii, 31-2); Decision in Proceedings of a Bench of Magistrates (*Ibid.*, 67-8).

16. Navy Bd. to Grose, 5 Mar., 1794 (HRA I, i, 467); *Rep. Select Cmmtte. on Transportation*, 1812, evidence of Alex. McLeay, 28.

17. Transport Cmmrs. to surgeons of *Minorca*, *Canada* and *Nile*, 8 June, 1801 (HRA I, iii, 98); to masters (*Ibid.*, 97-8).

18. Redfern to Macquarie, 30 Sept., 1814 (HRA I, viii, 290-2).

19. Macquarie to Transport Cmmrs., 1 Oct., 1814, and to Bathurst, 7 Oct., 1814, Bathurst to Macquarie, 4 Dec., 1815 (HRA I, viii, 274, 293, 638).

20. Macquarie to Bathurst, 18 Mar., 1816, and 4 Apr., 1817 (HRA I, ix, 56-7, 344); Macquarie to Bathurst, 18 Mar., 1819 (*Ibid.*, x, 344), to which no reply, apparently, was ever made.

21. Queade to Governor, n.d., enclosing Queade to Lieut. Franklin, 23 Jan., 1817, to master of *Pilot*, 23 Jan., 10 Mar. and 4 May, 1817, and to prisoners, 24 Jan., 1817; (NSW Arch., Col. Sec. Pap., 4/1738.)

22. Many surgeons included in their journals copies of their regulations governing the prisoners, e.g. *Eliza*, 1822, Adm. 101/23 (Microfilm 3194), *Canton*, 1839-40, Adm. 101/15 (3191), *Lincelles*, 1860-1, M.T. 32/2 (3181).

23. *Copies of Instructions to the surgeons-superintendent and masters of convict ships during their Voyage to Foreign Settlements*, 23 June, 1832, ordered to be printed 4 Mar., 1834. *Cf. Instructions for the Surgeons-superintendent on board Convict Ships proceeding to N.S.W. or V.D.L. and for the masters of those ships*. (London, 1838). War Office Regulations.

24. Kent to ? – – –, 2 Sept., 1793, and to Nepean, 7 Mar., 1795 (NSWHR, ii, 62, 285).

25. Macquarie to Bathurst, 24 June, 1815, Bathurst to Macquarie, 1 Apr., 1816, with encls., incldg. Arnold to Transport Bd., 5 Nov., 1815; Macquarie to Bathurst, 1 Apr., 1817 (HRA I, viii, 554; ix, 102-5, 270-1); Instructions to Surgeons-superintendent, 23 June, 1832, *op. cit.*, cl. 41. Cf. Bathurst to Macquarie, 4 July, 1818 (HRA I, ix, 811-2).

26. Instructions to surgeons-superintendent, 23 June, 1832, *op. cit.*, cl. 40.

27. Geo. Thomson to Col. Sec., 16 Jan., 1829 (Col. Sec. Pap., NSW Arch., 4/2013); Certificate to David Watson, 28 Mar., 1838 (*Ibid.*, 4/4532); Richard Lewis to *do.*, 26 and 29 Dec., 1829 (*Ibid.*, 4/2057); Col. Sec. to Wm. Anderson, 12 Mar., 1829 (*Ibid.*, 4/2022); Geo. Fairfowl to Col. Sec., 9 Feb., 1830 (*Ibid.*, 4/2066). Other examples of the practices referred to in the text will be found in the Col. Sec. Pap.

28. NSW Arch., 4/2115.

29. Surgeons' Jours., *passim*. For information about disease and sickness at sea consult Lloyd & Coulter, iii and iv, *passim.*; J. A. Nixon, "Health and Sickness", *op. cit.*, 121-138.

CHAPTER FIVE

1. Jours., Thos., Prosser, *Maria*, 1818-9 (Adm. 101/49, Microfilm 3203), Harman Cochrane, *Mary*, 1823 (*Ibid.*, 101/51, 3203, 3204), W. C. Watt, *Roslin Castle* (*Ibid.*, 101/64, 3208), Joseph Steret, *Edward*, 1834 (*Ibid.*, 101/22, 3193).

2. Jours., James Scott, *Castle Forbes*, 1819-20 (Adm. 101/16, 3191), A. Taylor, *Prince Regent*, 1820 (*Ibid.*, 101/60, 3207), J. Alexander, *Almorah*, 1820-21 (*Ibid.*, 101/2, 3187), Chas. Inches, *Portland*, 1832-3 (*Ibid.*, 101/60, 3207).

3. Jours., H. Morris, *Bangalore*, 1848 (Adm. 101/7, 3189), C. R. Kinnear, *Cadet*, 1847-8 (*Ibid.*, 101/15, 3191), C. A. Browning, *Margaret*, 1840 (*Ibid.*, 101/48, 3202), C. Smith, *Duke of Cornwall*, 1850 (*Ibid.*, 101/20, 3192).

4. Jours., J. Rutherford, *Pyramus*, 1831-2 (Adm. 101/62, 3208), W. S. B. Jones, *Aurora*, 1851 (*Ibid.*, 101/6, 3189), J. Steret, *Camden*, 1832-3 (*Ibid.*, 101/15, 3191), T. Galloway, *Asia*, 1832-3 (*Ibid.*, 101/5, 3188), I. Noott, *Layton*, 1839 (*Ibid.*, 101/42, 3200), A. Cross, *Equestrian*, 1852-3 (*Ibid.*, 101/26, 3195). A specimen of the medical certificate is given in Jour., S. Sinclair, *Mary*, 1831 (*Ibid.*, 101/51, 3204).

5. Jours., J. Gilchrist, *Bussorah Merchant*, 1831 (Adm. 101/14, 3190), B. Bynoe. *Aboukir*, 1851-2 (*Ibid.*, 101/3187), J. Hamilton, *Adamant*, 1821 (*Ibid.*), I. Noott, *Layton*, 1839, (*Ibid.*, 101/42, 3200), R. Wylie, *Arabian* 1846-7 (*Ibid.*, 101/4, 3188).

6. Jours., G. Birnie, *Asia*, 1831 (Adm. 101/5, 3188), A. D. Wilson, *Asia*, 1831-2 (*Ibid.*), C. A. Browning, *Arab*, 1834 (*Ibid*), W. McDowell, *Blenheim*, 1839 (*Ibid.*, 101/12, 3190), J. G. Stewart, *British Sovereign*, 1840-1 (*Ibid.*, 101/13, 3190).

7. Jours., J. Edward, *Charles Kerr*, 1837 (Adm. 101/16, 3191), A. Lang, *Lord Sidmouth*, 1818-9 (*Ibid.*, 101/44, 3201), T. C. Roylance, *Lord Sidmouth*, 1820-1 (*Ibid.*), G. Birnie, *Asia*, 1831 (*Ibid.*, 101/5, 3188), A. Henderson, *Lord William Bentinck*, 1832 (*Ibid.*, 101/45, 3201).

8. Jours., C. A. Browning, *Arab*, 1834 (Adm. 101/4, 3188), M. Goodsir, *Countess of Harcourt*, 1826-7 (*Ibid.*, 101/18, 3192), J. C. Bowman, *Cadet*, 1847-8 (*Ibid.*, 101/15, 3191).

9. Jours., G. Fairfowl, *Hive*, 1833-4 (Adm. 101/34, 3198), D. Deas, *Lord Petre*, 1843 (*Ibid.*, 101/44, 3201), T. Clarke, *Kains*, 1830-1 (*Ibid.*, 101/40, 3199), P. Jones, *Prince Regent*, 1841-2 (*Ibid.*, 101/61, 3207), J. Steret, *Edward*, 1834 (*Ibid.*, 101/22, 3193).

10. Patton to Transport Office, 6 June, 1800, Rains to *do.*, 9 June, 1800, Transport Cmmrs. to Portland, 11 June, 1800, Fitzpatrick to Hobart, 30 Jan., 1802, List of convict ships attended by Fitzpatrick, 1795-1802 (NSWHR, iv, 89-94, 681-3, 787).

11. Jour., H. Kelsall, *Margaret*, 1836-7 (Adm. 101/48, 3202). Details of clothing and hospital comforts will be found in *Instructions to surgeons-superintendent*, ordered to be printed 4 Mar., 1834, and in documents attached to charter-parties in NSW Archives, Col. Sec. Pap. (e.g. 4/1869, 4/2021). Jours., J. Lawrence, *John*, 1832 (Adm. 101/37, 3199) and J. Rutherford, *Mangles*, 1832-3 (*Ibid.*, 101/47, 3202) mention the change from flannels before embarking.

12. Jours., A. Montgomery, *Elizabeth*, 1820-1 (Adm. 101/24, 3194), P. McTernan, *Manlius*, 1828 (*Ibid.*, 101/48, 3202), A. Henderson, *Aurora*, 1835 (*Ibid.*, 101/6, 3189).

13. C. France, *Isabella*, 1841-2 (Adm. 101/36, 3198), J. O. McWilliam, *Forfarshire*, 1843 (*Ibid.*, 101/28, 3198), A. Kilroy, *Australasian*, 1849 (*Ibid.*, 101/6, 3189), D. Deas, *Lord Petre*, 1843 (*Ibid.*, 101/44, 3201), A. Donoghoe, *City of Edinburgh*, 1832 (*Ibid.*, 101/17, 3191), W. Hamilton, *Elizabeth*, 1818 (*Ibid.*, 101/24, 3194).
14. *Instructions to Surgeons-superintendent*, ordered to be printed 4 Mar., 1834, Charters *Sovereign* and *Harmony* (NSW Arch., 4/1869, 4/2021).
15. *Sydney Gazette*, 1 July, 1820, p. 1.
16. Jours., P. McTernan, *Mariner*, 1826-7 (Adm. 101/49, 3203) and W. Rae, *Marquis of Hastings*, 1828 (*Ibid.*, 101/50, 3203) for hospital diets; W. West, *Equestrian*, 1843-4 (*Ibid.*, 101/26, 3195), J. Clarke, *Greenlaw*, 1844 (*Ibid.*, 101/30, 3196), R. W. Clarke, *Barretto Junior*, 1850 (*Ibid.*, 101/7, 3189), C. H. Fuller, *Blenheim*, 1850 (*Ibid.*, 101/12, 3190).
17. Peter Cunningham, *Two Years in NSW*, 2 v. (London, 1827), ii, 216-7.
18. Jours., W. Evans, *Earl Grey*, 1836 (Adm. 101/21, 3193), W. Leyson, *Augusta Jessie*, 1838 (*Ibid.*, 101/6, 3189), A. Cross, *Equestrian*, 1852-3 (*Ibid.*, 101/26, 3195), C. H. Fuller, *Agincourt*, 1844 (*Ibid.*, 101/1, 3187), W. McDowell, *Blenheim*, 1839 (*Ibid.*, 101/12).
19. Jours., W. Evans, *Bencoolen*, 1819 (Adm. 101/7, 3189), G. Fairfowl, *Asia*, 1847 (*Ibid.*, 101/4, 3188), J. W. Johnston, *Asia*, 1840 (*Ibid.*, 101/5, 3188), J. Rutherford, *Hooghly*, 1834 (*Ibid.*, 101/35, 3198), A. Millar, *Anson*, 1843-4 (*Ibid.*, 101/3, 3187).
20. Jours., G. Thomson, *England* (Adm. 101/26, 3195), J. Alexander, *Almorah*, 1820-1 (*Ibid.*, 101/2, 3187), T. R. Dunn, *Augusta Jessie*, 1839-40 (*Ibid.*, 101/6, 3189), G. Fairfowl, *Asia*, 1827 (*Ibid.*, 101/4, 3188).
21. *Dublin Chronicle*, 12 Jan., 1792 (NSWHR, ii, 792-3).
22. Macquarie to Bathurst, 16 and 30 May, 1818 (HRA I, ix, 792-3, 807); Peter Cunningham, *op. cit.*, ii, 215-6; Charles Wilkes, *Narrative of the U.S. Exploring Expedition*, 1838-42, 5 v. (Philadelphia, 1850), ii, 208-9.
23. Jours., G. Birnie, *Asia*, 1831 (Adm. 101/5, 3188), J. G. Stewart, *Nautilus*, 1838 (*Ibid.*, 101/56, 3205), J. W. Bowler, *Hashemy*, 1850 (*Ibid.*, 101/32, 3197).
24. Jours., J. G. Stewart, *Nautilus*, 1838 (Adm. 101/56, 3205), W. Gregor, *Medina*, 1825 (*Ibid.*, 101/52, 3205), Joseph Cook, *Forth*, 1830 (*Ibid.*, 101/28, 3195), T. Galloway, *Isabella*, 1832 (*Ibid.*, 101/36, 3198), A. McLaren, *Maitland*, 1843-4 (*Ibid.*, 101/46, 3202), G. Fairfowl, *Hive*, 1833-4 (*Ibid.*, 101/34, 3198), Morgan Price, *Almorah*, 1824 (*Ibid.*, 101/2, 3187), Wm. Crauford, *Clyde*, 1863 (MT 32/6, 3181).
25. J. B. O'Reilly, *Moondyne, A Story of Life in West Australia* (Melbourne, 1880), 186, 189.
26. Jours., Robert Bower, *Cadet*, 1844 (Adm. 101/15, 3191), J. O. McWilliam, *Hydrabad*, 1844-5 (*Ibid.*, 101/35, 3198), J. Inches, *Lady Harewood*, 1832 (*Ibid.*, 101/41, 3200), A. Nisbet, *Earl Grey*, 1838 (*Ibid.*, 101/21, 3193), W. West, *Equestrian*, 1843-4 (*Ibid.*, 101/26, 3195), O. Sproule, *Isabella*, 1833 (*Ibid.*, 101/36, 3198), J. Bower, *Emma Eugenia*, 1850-1 (*Ibid.*, 101/25, 3195), J. Ellis, *Diana*, 1833 (*Ibid.*, 101/19, 3192).
27. Jour., W. Rae, *Eliza*, 1822 (Adm. 101/23, 3194).
28. Hill to Wathen, 26 July, 1790 (NSWHR I, ii, 367), Documents attached to charter party of *Layton* (NSW Arch, 4/1869), *Proportion of stores for* 100 *convicts*, *Instructions to Masters*, ordered to be printed 4 Mar., 1834.
29. Jours., A. Donoghoe, *City of Edinburgh*, 1832 (Adm. 101/17, 3191), J. Syme, *Gilmore*, 1843 (*Ibid.*, 101/29, 3196), T. C. Roylance, *Hadlow*, 1818-9 (*Ibid.*, 101/32, 3197), John Bower, *Lord Raglan*, 1858 (MT 32/1, 3181). J. Bowman, *John Barry*, 1819 (Adm. 101/38, 3199), C. Queade, *Minerva*,

1821 (*Ibid.*, 101/54, 3205), W. Smith, *Merchantman*, 1864 (MT 32/7, 3181), A. Watson, *Racehorse*, 1865 (*Ibid.*, 32/9, 3181), P. Cunningham, *Grenada*, 1821 (Adm., 101/30, 3196), G. Thomson, *England*, 1826 (*Ibid.*, 101/26, 3195).

30. For ironing, surgeons' jours., *passim*; Charles Wilkes, *op. cit.* ii, 209; Jours., J. Bower, *Lord Raglan*, 1858 (MT 32/1, 3181), W. Smith, *Merchantman*, 1864 (*Ibid.*, 32/7, ib.), W. Crawford, *Corona*, 1866 (*Ibid.*, 32/11, ib.).

31. J. L. Clarke, *Navarino*, 1840-1 (Adm. 101/56, 3205), R. Espie, *Elizabeth*, 1836 (*Ibid.*, 101/24, 3194), R. Espie, *Lord Sidmouth*, 1822-3 (*Ibid.*, 101/44, 3201), J. Ellis, *Diana*, 1833 (*Ibid.*, 101/19, 3192), W. Elyard, *John Bull*, 1821-2 (*Ibid.*, 101/38, 3199), R. Espie, *Lord Sidmouth*, 1822-3 (*Ibid.*, 101/44, 3201), J. Patton, *Persian*, 1827 (*Ibid.*, 101/58, 3206), O. Pineo, *Pyramus*, 1836 (*Ibid.*, 101/62, 3208).

32. Jours., J. Ellis, *Diana*, 1833 (Adm. 101/19, 3192), J. A. Mercer, *Asia*, 1824-5 (*Ibid.*, 101/4, 3188), J. Lardner, *Asia* (*Ibid.*, 101/5, 3188), C. H. Fuller, *Blenheim*, 1850 (*Ibid.*, 101/12, 3190), Cmmrs. Navy to Governor, 31 Aug., 1826, NSW Arch., Col. Sec. Pap., 4/1921, and similar documents in same collection, C. Carter (*Arab*) to Goulburn, 23 Nov., 1822, *Ibid.*, 4/1753, and similar reports in same collection.

33. C. A. Browning, *The Convict Ship and England's Exiles*, 3rd ed. (London, 1848), 22; P. Cunningham, *op. cit.* ii, 216-7; Jours., E. Johnston, *Captain Cook*, 1831-2 (Adm. 101/16, 3191), J. Syme, *Gilmore*, 1843 (*Ibid.*, 101/29, 3196).

34. J. Gilchrist, *Bussorah Merchant*, 1831 (Adm. 101/14, 3190), T. E. Ring, *John Renwick*, 1842-3 (*Ibid.*, 101/39, 3199), G. Thomson, *England*, 1826 (*Ibid.*, 101/26, 3195), J. Andrews, *Marion*, 1847-8 (*Ibid.*, 101/49, 3203), H. Kelsall, *John Calvin*, 1846 (*Ibid.*, 101/39, 3199), W. West, *Equestrian* (*Ibid.*, 101/26, 3195), G. T. Moxey, *Mount Stuart Elphinstone*, 1849 (*Ibid.*, 101/55, 3205), J. L. Clarke, *Navarino*, 1840-1 (*Ibid.*, 101/56, 3205), J. Donovan, *Rajah*, 1841 (*Ib.*, 101/63, 3208), H. Cochrane, *Mariner*, 1824-5 (*Ibid.*, 101/49, 3203).

35. Jours., T. Clarke, *Kains*, 1830-1 (Adm. 101/40, 3199), R. Espie, *Lord Sidmouth*, 1822-3 (*Ibid.*, 101/44, 3201), T. Clarke, *op. cit.*, A. McLaren, *Hydery*, 1832 (*Ibid.*, 101/35, 3198).

36. *Return of number of persons . . . transported to N.S.W. . . .* since 1 Jan., 1812. Ordered to be printed 16 May, 1817.

37. Col. Sec. Pap., NSW Arch.

38. Middleton to Nepean, 11 Dec., 1786 (NSWHR I, ii, 35).

39. For descriptions of the routine on male ships see Jours., J. A. Mercer, *Albion*, 1823 (Adm. 101/1, 3187), P. Cunningham, *Recovery*, 1819 (*Ibid.*, 101/63, 3208), J. Mitchell, *Neptune*, 1820 (*Ibid.*, 101/56, 3205), W. Lawrance, *Randolph*, 1849 (*Ibid.*, 101/63, 3208), and for West Australian ships Jours., J. Bower, *Lord Raglan*, 1858 (MT 32/1), A. Watson, *Norwood*, 1862 (*Ibid.*, 32/3), W. Smith, *Merchantman*, 1862-3 (*Ibid.*, 32/5), W. Crawford, *Clyde*, 1863 (*Ibid.*, 32/6, all 3181). For female ships, Jours., P. Leonard, *Atwick*, 1837-8 (Adm. 101/6, 3189), S. Sinclair, *Mary*, 1831 (*Ibid.*, 101/51, 3204), W. Bland, *Mary Ann*, 1839 (*Ibid.*, 101/52, 3204), J. S. Hampton, *Mexborough*, 1841-2 (*Ibid.*, 101/53, 3204), J. G. Stewart, *Nautilus*, 1838, (*Ibid.*, 101/56, 3205), D. Thomson, *New Grove*, 1834-5 (*Ibid.*, 101/56, 3206). W. S. B. Jones, *Aurora*, 1851 (*Ibid.*, 101/6, 3189) and P. Hill, *Earl St. Vincent*, 1820 (*Ibid.*, 101/21, 3193) give details of bathing, and W. Evans, *Bencoolen*, 1819 (*Ibid.*, 101/7, 3189) and A. Hume, *Guildford*, 1817-8 (*Ibid.*, 101/31, 3196) deal with shaving and hair-cutting. For laundry arrangements see also T. R. Dunn, *Augusta Jessie*, 1839-40 (*Ibid.*, 101/6, 3189).

40. Surgeons' Jours., *passim*, Port Regulations for Port Jackson and Instructions for the guidance of surgeons-superintendent arriving in the Derwent with prisoners, both attached to charter, *James Pattison*, NSW Arch. Col. Sec. Pap. 4/2064, Navy Cmmrs. instructions re return of stores, 2 Mar., 1830, referred to in their letters of 20 and 25 June, 1831, *Ibid.*, 4/2121.

41. Assignments and Indents, *passim*; P. R. Eldershaw, *Guide to the Public Records of Tasmania*, Section 3: *Convict Department Record Group* (Hobart, 1965), Introduction, 4 sq.

CHAPTER SIX

1. For tonnages see the lists included in the text, 97 (First Fleet) and 120-71 (1789-1800) and Appendices I to VI (1801-1868), 336-75.
2. Frank C. Bowen, *Sailing Ships of the London River* (London, n.d.), 32.
3. Freight rates are given in a return of the Transport Dept., 19 Mar., 1822, ordered to be printed 27 Mar., 1822, covering the period 5 Jan., 1816-5 Jan., 1822, and, for 1828-29, in *Accounts of the number of Convicts sent from England and Ireland*, ordered to be printed 5 July, 1830. Individual charters in Col. Sec. Pap., NSW Arch. and in Tas. Arch., will also be found to include the charter rate for the particular ship.
4. Navy Cmmrs. Authority, enclosed Raine to Col. Sec., 14 Nov., 1828, NSW Arch., Col. Sec. Pap., 4/2000.
5. H. Moyse-Bartlett, *A History of the Merchant Navy* (London, 1937), R. J. Cornewall-Jones, *The British Merchant Service* (London, 1898), W. S. Lindsay, *History of Merchant Shipping*, 4 vols. (London, 1874-6), C. Northcote Parkinson (Ed.), *The Trade Winds* (London, 1948), Sir Evan Cotton, *East Indiamen* (London, 1949), E. Keble Chatterton, *The Old East Indiamen* (London, n.d.), Ralph Davis, *The Rise of the English Shipping Industry in the 17th and 18th Centuries* (London, 1962), P. G. Parkhurst, *Ships of Peace*, v. i., A Record of Some Problems which came before the Board of Trade . . . from early days to 1885 (New Malden, 1962). The musters are scattered through the Col. Sec. Pap., in NSW Arch., usually attached to the ship's charter (e.g. 4/2064, 2073, 2080, 2085, etc.).
6. Correspondence Librarian, *Lloyd's Register of Shipping*, to the author and relevant regulations in the registers.
7. Dundas to Phillip, 15 May, 1792 (HRA I, i, 354), Bonwick Transcripts, (Mit. Lib.), East India Co., especially 25 Aug., 29 Sept. and 15 Oct., 1790, 9 Feb. and 16 Mar., 1791, 4 May, 1796, 9 May and 18 July, 1798, 11 Nov., 1801.
8. Hobart to King, 29 Aug., 1802, Pelham to Admiralty, 9 Mar., 1802, Adm, to Pelham, 4 Apr., 1802, King to Hobart, 9 May, 1803 (HRA I, iii, 565, 570-1; iv, 83); King to Banks, 9 May, 1803 (Mit. Lib., Banks Pap.. Brabourne Coll., vii, 191-2).
9. Grenville to Phillip, 19 Feb., 1791, Phillip to Grenville, 5 Nov., 1791, Glenelg to Bourke, 31 Jan., 1836, Phillipps to Hay, 13 Jan., 1836, Phillipps to Wood, 6 Jan., 1836, Wood to Phillipps, 9 Jan., 1836 (HRA I, i, 215, 267; xviii, 274, 281-2).
10. The rigs and tonnages given in the text and appendices have been obtained, as far as possible, from charter parties, ship registers, Australian official records of shipping inwards and outwards, and other official documents and records, discrepancies being reconciled in accordance with what has seemed to the author the weight of evidence. *Lloyd's Register*

and its predecessors have been freely consulted, and in the absence of satisfactory official evidence non-official sources, such as letters of ship-owners and masters, advertisements, and the shipping reports of contemporary newspapers, have been utilized. On methods of tonnage measurement consult *The Mariner's Mirror* (London: Society for Nautical Research), v. 52, 173, 329, articles by William Salisbury.

CHAPTER SEVEN

1. Sydney to Treasury, 18 Aug., 1786, to Admiralty, 31 Aug., 1886 (NSWHR I, ii, 14-22), Collins, Introduction, i.
2. Bradley, *Jour.* (Mit. Lib.); Secretary, *Lloyd's Register of Shipping*, London, to author, 1 Oct., 1953, with extracts from registers; Librarian, H.M. Customs & Excise, London, to author, 19 Mar. and 27 May, 1955; Registrar-General of Shipping & Seamen, Cardiff, to author, 19 Apr., 1955, with transcripts of registers.
3. King, Jour. (NSWHR, ii, 514); Register of Transports, Adm. 49/127.
4. King, Jour. (NSWHR, ii, 513), Collins, Introduction, ii; *The Mariner's Mirror*, xxi, 210.
5. Particulars of the *Great Britain* and her 1852 voyage are from Dickson Gregory, *Australian Steamships, Past and Present* (London, 1928), 146, 147.
6. The evidence as to the number of convicts in the First Fleet is analysed by E. O'Brien, *The Foundation of Australia*, 1786-1800 (London, 1937), Appendix B, 374-80.
7. Teer to Nepean, 9 Dec., 1786, Middleton to Nepean, 11 Dec., 1786, Stephens to Navy Bd., 4 Jan., 1787, King, *Jour.*, logbooks *Alexander*, *Lady Penrhyn*, *Prince of Wales*, *passim* (NSWHR I, ii, 33-4, 36, 45-6; ii, 515, 399, 406, 403), Bradley, *Jour.*, 10, O'Brien, *op. cit.*, for deaths; Phillip to Nepean, 18 Mar., 1787 (NSWHR I, ii, 59).
8. Jour., Bowes, 13.
9. Phillip to Sydney, 5 June, 1787 (NSWHR I, ii, 106-7), John White, *Journal of a Voyage to NSW* (Sydney, 1962), 51, King, *Jour.* (NSWHR ii, 515).
10. O'Brien, *op. cit.*, Appendix B. Although he signed himself "Dennis Conssiden", I have followed the more usual spelling and which he himself seems to have later adopted. The account of the First Fleet's voyage is based on the logbooks of the *Sirius* and other vessels (NSWHR ii, 395 sq.), Jours., King (*Ibid.*, 515-543), Arthur Bowes or Bowes-Smyth, Lieut. William Bradley, Lieut. Ralph Clark (MSS., Mit. Lib.), Phillip's despatches, with their official returns, the reports and returns of Major Robert Ross, commanding the marines, and of Surgeon White, Collins, White, *op. cit.*, Sergt. James Scott, *Remarks on a Passage to Botany Bay*, 1787-1792 (Sydney, 1963), Private John Easty, *Memorandum of the Transactions of a Voyage from England to Botany Bay*, 1787-1793 (Sydney, 1965), the two latter being William Dixson Foundation reproductions of manuscripts in the Dixson Library, and other sources. I have not thought it necessary to exhaustively "source" my narrative, since most of the authorities mentioned are well known and easily accessible.
11. Clark, *Jour.*, 22 July, 1787.
12. White, *Jour.*, 63.
13. Clark *Jour.*, *passim*, particularly 19 June, 3, 18, 19, 20, 26 July, 1 Aug.
14. Scott, 4, White, *Jour.*, 60, Bradley, *Jour.*, 19 June, King, *Jour.* (NSWHR ii, 520).
15. Scott, 17.

16. Scott, 8, 6, 13; White, *Jour.*, 73-4, 76; Easty, 5, 12, 31, 32.
17. Clark, *Jour.*, *passim.*
18. Daniel Southwell to Mrs. Southwell, 11 Nov., 1787 (NSWHR, ii, 675).
19. Clark, *Jour.*, 8 Nov., 28 Oct., 1 Nov., 1787.
20. Bowes, *Jour.*, 73; Scott, 28; Logbook, *Prince of Wales*, 17 and 18 Dec., 1787 and 9 Jan., 1788 (NSWHR, ii, 405).
21. Southwell to Mrs. Southwell, 5 May, 1788 (NSWHR, ii, 678).
22. A Return of the Sick, etc., 30 June, 1788 (HRA I, i, 53-4).
23. Bowes, *Jour.*, 57-8.
24. Clark to Kempster, 8 Nov., 1787, with MS. Jour., Mit. Lib.
25. Bowes, *Jour.*, 61-2.
26. *The Voyage of Governor Phillip to Botany Bay* (London, 1790), 185 sq. with Appendix 10, Tables VI-IX, dealing with the return voyages. The ships' subsequent histories are from Secretary, *Lloyd's Register of Shipping*, London, to author, 1 Oct., 1953, and Registrar-General of Shipping and Seamen, Cardiff, to author, 19 Apr., 1955, with their relevant enclosures.

CHAPTER EIGHT

1. Memorandum, 27 Dec., 1790, Navy Office Accts., 5 June, 1793 (NSWHR I, ii, 423; ii, 38), Bonwick Transcripts (Mit. Lib.).
2. John Nicol, *The Life and Adventures of John Nicol, Mariner* (Edinburgh, 1822), 108-33. A modern edition, edited by Gordon Grant and with a foreword and afterword by Alexander Laing, was published in America in 1936 (pp. 115-28) and in London in 1937 (pp. 127-44). A reproduction of Nicol's narrative in *The Sea, the Ship and the Sailor: Tales of Adventure from Log Books and Original Narratives*, Marine Research Society, v. 7 (Salem, Mass., 1925), 105 sq., is abridged, but without any indication of the fact. Stephens to Treasury, 12 and 26 May, 1789 (NSWHR I, ii, 231-2, 235-6.)
3. Christopher Lloyd, *Captain Cook* (London, 1952), 151-2; *Recollections of James Anthony Gardner, Commander R.N.*, 1775-1814 (Navy Rec. Soc., v. 31, London, 1906), 159-60, 170; Nicol, *op. cit.*, 113.
4. Alley to Nepean, 29 Mar., 1790 and Riou to Stephens, 20 May, 1790 (NSWHR I, ii, 323-4, 338); Alley to ? – – –, 22 Mar., 1790, in *Dublin Chron.*, 28 Aug., 1790, letter from female convict, 24 July, 1790, in *Morning Chron.*, 4 Aug., 1791, and letter from Sydney, 24 Mar., 1791, in *The Bee*, 15 May, 1792 (*Ibid.*, ii, 755-6, 767, 772-3); Phillip to Nepean, 16 June and 6 Aug., 1790 (HRA I, i, 178, 204); Collins, 114-6, 118-9, 123; Tench, 169; Scott, 51-2; O'Brien, 385.
5. Nicol, *op. cit.*, 112-4, 117.
6. *Ibid.*, 136-7, 111-2, 114-5, 118, 119.
7. *Ibid.*, 120-2, 128-9.
8. *Ibid.*, 128; Collins, 123, 127; King to Nepean, 3 July, 1791 (NSWHR I, ii, 493).
9. The story of the *Guardian* is based on "The Log of the *Guardian*, 1789-90", edited from the Journal of Capt. Riou by Ludovic Kennedy, in *The Naval Miscellany*, iv (Navy Rec. Soc., xcii, London, 1952), 296-358; Riou to Stephens, 25 Nov., 1789, 22 and 25 Feb., 7 and 15 Mar., 20 May and 19 Oct. (NSWHR I, ii, 283, 310, 311, 317, 318, 336-9, 408); Riou to Adm., 25 Dec., 1789 (*Ibid.*, 286-7); Stephens to Riou, 9 Oct., 1790 (*Ibid.*, 405-7); John Williams, boatswain, to his agents, 27 Mar., 1790, in *Public*

Advertiser, 6 Aug., 1790 (*Ibid.*, ii, 757-8), *Public Advertiser*, 30 Apr., 1790 (*Ibid.*, ii, 765-7); Letter from a gentleman at the Cape, in *Dublin Chron.*, 31 July, 1790 (*Ibid.*, 754-5); *Annual Register*, 1790, 254-262. A list of convicts embarked in the *Guardian* is in HO 11/1 (Microfilm 87).

10. Letter of Surgeon Alley, 22 Mar., 1790, in *Dublin Chron.*, 28 Aug., 1790; John Williams to agents, 27 Mar., 1790, in *Public Advertiser*, 6 Aug., 1790; *Public Advertiser*, 30 Apr., 1790; Newton to Johnson, 27 May, 1790; *London Chron.*, 28 Apr., 1790 (NSWHR, ii, 756, 757, 766, 438-9, 763-4); *Annual Register*, 1790, 258-62; Riou to Stephens, 20 May, 1790 (*Ibid.*, I, ii, 339); Grenville to Phillip, 16 Nov., 1790, Phillip to Grenville, 7 Nov., 1791, and Warrants of Conditional Emancipation, 16 Dec., 1791 (HRA I, i, 213, 289, 325-6).

11. Contract with George Whitlock, of Crutched Friars, London, for owners of *Surprize*, *Neptune* and *Scarborough*, 27 Aug., 1789 (*Acct. & Pap.*, 53-7); Entries in 1791-2 *Registers* (*Neptune*, *Surprize*), 1787 (*Scarborough*); Navy Bd. to Shapcote, 27 Aug. and 17 Nov., 1789 (*Acct. & Pap.*, 64-5); Hill to Wathen, 26 July, 1790 (NSWHR I, ii, 367); Bonwick Transcripts (Mit. Lib.), East India Co., Court of Directors, 4 Nov. and 2 Dec., 1789.

12. Hill to Wathen, 26 July, 1790, Riou to Stephens, 20 May, 1790 (NSWHR I, ii, 366-7, 338); Collins, 121-2; O'Brien, *Foundation of Australia* (London, 1937), 381-2, 385; cf. Tench, 314, n. 10; Phillip to Grenville, 13 July, 1790, with undated Return relating to Second Fleet (HRA I, i, 188-9); Shapcote to Navy Cmmrs., 24 Apr., 1790, with reports from Gray, Waters, Beyer and Harris (*Accts. & Pap.*, 66-8); Johnson to Thornton, n.d., (NSWHR I, ii, 387); Tench, 173; Collins, 123; Indents (NSW Arch.) 4/3998.

13. Hill to Wathen, 26 July, 1790 (NSWHR I, ii, 367-8).

14. Letter from Samuel Burt, in *Dublin Chron.*, 23 Oct., 1790 (NSWHR ii, 762-3); Collins, 123.

15. Johnson to Thornton, n.d. (NSWHR I, ii, 387, 388).

16. *Ibid.* (*Ibid.*, 387); Collins 122; Phillip to Grenville, 13 July, 1790 (HRA I, i, 188-9).

17. Dundas to Phillip, 10 Jan., 1792 (HRA I, i, 330-1); correspondence regarding address concerning conditions in the *Neptune* to Colonial Office by Thomas Evans (NSWHR, ii, 460-4); Remarks and statement of the proceedings of Donald Trail, n.d., in *The Diary, or Woodfall's Register*, 4 Aug., 1792, Owners' instructions to Trail, 19 Dec., 1789, Proceedings at Guildhall, *Dublin Chron.*, 1 Dec., 1791 (NSWHR ii, 802-6, 750-2, 791); King to Phillip, 10 Jan., 1792, Dundas to Phillip, 15 May, 1792 (HRA I, i, 334, 353); *Annual Register*, 1792, Chronicle, 8 June; Certificate of service from Nelson, 3 July, 1783 (*Accts. & Pap.*, 78); Elphinstone to Admiralty, 25 June, 1796, *The Keith Papers*, i (Navy Rec. Soc., lxii, London, 1927), 429.

18. *Lloyd's Register of Shipping* to author, 20 Jan., 1954, with entry from 1791-2 register; Indent, NSW Arch. 4/3998; Phillip to Grenville, 5 Nov., 1791; List of Transports, 1 Feb., 1791; Return of Transports, 9 July–16 Oct., 1791 (HRA I, i, 267, 225, 275); Collins, 187-8; Tench, 240; Scott, 63; Easty, 129; Calvert to Nepean, 23 Dec., 1790 (NSWHR I, ii, 422).

19. Phillip to Grenville, 5 Nov., 1791 (HRA I, i, 267, 273); Collins, 178-9, 182; Scott, 67; Easty, 131-2; Indent, NSW Arch. 4/3998.

20. *Lloyd's Register of Shipping* to author, 1 Oct., 1953 and 20 Jan., 1954, with relevant register entries. I have not thought it necessary to indicate the sources from which the names of masters and surgeons have been obtained, as these are so varied. Bench of Magistrates, Court of Criminal Judicature, Vice-Admiralty Court and other legal papers in NSW Arch.

(1/296, 1152, 1163, 1162), as well as many letters and reports in Col. Sec. Pap., together with despatches and enclosures printed in NSWHR and HRA, have yielded information on these points, as also have charters of affreightment for individual ships in NSW Arch.

21. Bowen to Navy Cmmrs., n.d. (*Accts. & Pap.*, 92-3); Thomson to King, 11 Nov., 1793 (NSWHR, ii, 80-1); Return of Transports, 9 July–16 Oct., 1791, Phillip to Grenville, 5 Nov., and to Nepean, 18 Nov., 1791 (HRA I, i, 275, 269, 307); Indents, NSW Arch. 4/3998; Collins, 173-4, 175; Scott, 66; Easty, 131; O'Brien, *Foundation Aust.*, 382-3, 385.

22. Unaddressed, unsigned letter (almost certainly from Young) from Madeira, 24 Apr., 1791, King to Nepean, 4 May, 1791, Cock to Duke of Leeds, 13 May, 1791, Private letter from Madeira, 25 Apr., 1791, in *Dublin Chron.*, 14 July, 1791 (NSWHR I, ii, 487-8, 489; ii, 447-9, 781); Phillip to Stephens, 18 Nov., 1791 (HRA I, i, 313); Collins, 171, 181-2; Scott, 64-5.

23. Return of Transports Arrived, 9 July–16 Oct., 1791 (HRA I, i, 275)· Collins, 171, 172; Tench, 242-3, 326 n. 12; Scott, 64-5; Easty, 130; Indent, NSW Arch. 4/3998; O' Brien, *op. cit.*, 385.

24. Return of Transports, *op. cit.*; Phillip to Grenville, 5 Nov., 1791, and Magisterial Proceedings (HRA I, i, 274, 283-8); King to Nepean, 29 July, 1791 (NSWHR I, ii, 508); Indents, NSW Arch., 4/3998; Collins, 179-80; Scott, 67; Easty, 132; O'Brien, *op. cit.*, 383, 385.

25. Unaddressed, unsigned letter from Madeira, 24 Apr., 1791 ,King to Nepean; 3 May and 17 and 29 July, 1791 (NSWHR I, ii, 487-8, 489, 505, 508); Return of Lt. Young, 9 Aug., 1791 (*Accts. & Pap.*, 107); Collins, 181-2, Easty, 132, 133; Scott, 67; O'Brien, *op. cit.*, 385; Return of Transports, *op. cit.* (HRA I, i, 275); *Lloyd's Register of Shipping* to author, 1 Oct., 1953, with entry for *Admiral Barrington*.

26. Phillip to Grenville, 5 Nov., 1791 (HRA I, i, 274); O'Brien, *op. cit.*, 385; Indents, NSW Arch. 4/3998, 4/4002; Return by Lt. Young, 9 Aug., 1791 (*Accts. & Pap.*, 107); Collins, 182.

27. Phillip to Nepean, and to Stephens, 18 Nov., 1791 (HRA I, i, 307-8, 312); Collins, 182, 187, 190; Bonwick Transcripts (Mit. Lib.), East India Company, Court of Directors, 9 Feb., 1791; Vancouver to Hanson, 29 Dec., 1792 (NSWHR I, ii, 682 and n.); F. Rhodes, *Pageant of the Pacific* (Sydney n.d.), i, 112.

28. Bonwick Transcripts, *op. cit.*, 7 and 21 Sept., 1791, 29 Mar., 1796; *Lloyd's Register of Shipping* to author, 20 Jan., 1954, with relevant register extracts.

29. Treasury to Cmmrs. Navy, 20 May, 1791, Dundas to Treasury, 23 June, 1791, Reports of naval officers, 25 and 30 June, 1791, Treasury to Navy Cmmrs., 7 July, 1791 (*Accts. & Pap.*, 82-4, 87-8, 90-1); Dundas to Phillip, 5 July, 1791 (HRA I, i, 266).

30. Phillip to Dundas, 19 Mar., 1792 (HRA I, i, 336); Manning to Macaulay, 24 Oct., 1791, Grose to Nepean, 22 Oct., 1791 (NSWHR I, ii, 525-8); Bligh to Stephens, attachment to letter of 26 Nov., and second letter of 18 Dec., 1791; *Dublin Chron.*, 12 Jan., 1792; Jour., Geo. Thompson; Soldier's letter, 13 Dec., 1794, in *Saunders's News-Letter*, 31 July, 1795 (*Ibid.*, ii, 459-60, 792, 795, 815); Collins, 201-2, 237; Indent, NSW Arch., 4/3998; O'Brien, *op. cit.*, 385.

31. Log of *Royal Admiral* (Log 338F, Commonwealth Relations Office, London); Navy Cmmrs. to Phillip, 17 May, 1792, Phillip to Dundas, 11 Oct., 1792 (HRA I, i, 356, 397); Collins, 236-8, 240; Indent, NSW Arch., 4/3998, 4/4002; O'Brien, *op. cit.*, 385.

32. Woodriff to Phillip, 19 Nov., 1792, Transportation Statistics, 13 June, 1794 (NSWHR, ii, 483-4, 222-3); Dundas to Phillip, 10 Feb., 1792 (HRA I, i, 336); Indent, NSW Arch. 4/3998, 4/4002; O'Brien, *op. cit.*, 385; Collins, 223, 245-6; Protest of Geo. Ramsay, NSW Arch. 1162.

33. *Lloyd's Register of Shipping* to author, 20 Jan., 1954, with register entries; Protest of Matthew Boyd, 6 Feb., 1793, NSW Arch. 1162; Collins, 261-2, 263-4; Indent, NSW Arch. 4/3998, 4/4002; O'Brien, *op. cit.*, 385.

34. *Lloyd's Register of Shipping* to author, 20 Jan., 1954, with register entries; Kent to Nepean, 6 Feb., 1793, Musgrave to Nepean, 10 Feb. and n.d., 1793, Fox to Musgrave, 5 Feb., 1793, Bell to Nepean, 18 Feb., 11 Mar. and 12 July, 1793, Bell to Dundas, 12 July, 1793, Kent to ? – – –, 2 Sept., 1793, Chalmers to ? – – –, 3 Sept., 1793 (NSWHR, ii, 6-7, 8-9, 17-18, 57, 56, 61-2); Grose to Dundas, 3 Sept. and 12 Oct., 1793, and to Nepean, 12 Oct., 1793 (HRA I, i, 446, 454-5); Transportation Statistics, 13 June, 1794 (NSWHR, ii, 223); Collins, 304-5, 311-2; Indents, NSW Arch. 4/3998, 4/4002; O'Brien, *op. cit.*, 385.

35. *Lloyd's Register of Shipping* to author, 20 Jan., 1954, with register entries; Indents, NSW Arch. 4/4002, 4/3998; Campbell to Navy Cmmrs, 2 Aug., 1794, Baker to *do.*—Aug., 1794, Campbell to Camden, Calvert and King, n.d. and encl., Petition of Palmer & Skirving, with encls., to Grose and other correspondence (NSWHR, ii, 857-872); Mutiny on *Surprise*, in *Saunders's News-Letter*, 5 Mar. and 14 July, 1795 (*Ibid.*, 874-7, 879); T. F. Palmer, *Narrative of the Sufferings of T. F. Palmer and W. Skirving* (London, 1797), *passim*; O'Brien, *op. cit.*, 385.

36. *Lloyd's Register of Shipping* to author, 20 Jan., 1954, with register entry; Collins and Balmain to Hunter, 3 Apr., 1796, with encl., 21 Mar., 1796, and Statement by Capt. Hogan, 10 Sept., 1795 (HRA I, i, 653-661); Hunter to Portland, 3 Mar. and 2 May, 1796 (*Ibid.*, 555-6, 569); Protest by Michael Hogan and ors., n.d. (NSW Arch. 1162); Letter from St. Helena, 22 Oct., 1795, in *True Briton*, 18 June, 1796, and *Edinburgh Advertiser*, 15 Jan., 1796 (NSWHR, ii, 819-20; iii, 4); Austin, Certificate of Victualling, 10 Mar., 1796 (*Ibid.*, iii, 34); Collins, 455-6, 478-9; Indent, NSW Arch. 4/3998; O'Brien, *op. cit.*, 385.

37. *Lloyd's Register* to author, 20 Jan., 1954, with register entry; Bonwick Transcripts (Mit. Lib.), 8 Feb., 1797; Elphinstone to Adm., 30 July and 3 Aug., 1796, *The Keith Papers*, i (Navy Rec. Soc. v. lxii, London, 1927), 435, 437.

38. Murchison to Campbell, 21 Jan., 1798 (NSWHR, iii, 413-4); Report of Talleyrand-Perigord, in *Moniteur*, 27 Mar., 1798 (Bibliotheque Nationale); Convict Transport Registers, PRO, H.O. 11/1 (Microfilm 87); *Dict. Nat. Biog.*, xvii (London, 1909), 1179. The statement that Knowles was in the *Lady Shore* rests on Dore to Fleming, 5 Feb., 1798 (NSWHR, iii, 356), but as he makes Semple one of the chief instigators of the mutiny he is scarcely to be relied upon, although O'Brien, *op. cit.*, 385, says she carried two male and 66 female convicts.

39. J. Black, *An Authentic Narrative of the Mutiny on board the ship Lady Shore* (Ipswich, 1798); Murchison to Duncan, 22 May, 1798, and encl. giving account of the mutiny, Murchison to Campbell, 21 Jan., 1798; *Saunders's News-Letter*, 21 July, 1801 (NSWHR, iii, 391-7, 413-5; iv, 443); *Annual Register*, v. 40 (1798), 60; v. 41, 41; Ministere des affaires Etrangeres, Paris, Archives Diplomatique et de la Documentation, Correspondances Politiques, Espagne, v. 651, f. 121, 218, 328, 329, 352, 353; v. 654, f. 5; Report of Talleyrand-Perigord, *op. cit.*

40. *Lloyd's Register* to author, *op. cit.*, with register entries; Bonwick Transcripts (Mit. Lib.), 9 May and 18 July, 1798; Log of *Minerva* (Log 14F, Commonwealth Relations Office, London); Transport Cmmrs. to King,

23 July, 1798, Castlereagh to King, 8 Sept., 1798, Transport Cmmrs. to King, 18 Jan., 1799, and Duncan to Cmmrs. 15 Jan., 1799, Cmmrs. to King, 23 July, 1799, and Charnock to Duncan, 16 July, 1799 (NSWHR, iii, 417, 480, 529, 696-7); T. C. Croker (Ed.), *Memoirs of Joseph Holt* (London, 1838), *passim*; Indent, NSW Arch. 4/3999; O'Brien, *op. cit.*, 293, 385.

41. Vessels Inwards, 3 Nov., 1799–13 May, 1800 (HRA I, ii, 572); Patrickson to King, 11 Aug., 1796, Fitzpatrick to King, 23 Oct., 1796 (NSWHR, iii, 67, 161-3); Hunter to Portland, 25 June, 1797 (HRA I, ii, 32); Indents, NSW Arch. 4/3999, 4/3998, 4/4000; O'Brien, *op. cit.*, 385.

42. Proceedings of Bench of Magistrates (HRA I, ii, 36-68); Hunter to Portland, 25 June and 6 July, 1797 (*Ibid.*, 31, 33-4); Fitzpatrick to King, 23 Oct., 1796, Castlereagh to King, 18 Sept., 1798 (NSWHR iii, 163-4, 488); Return of Male Convicts Landed, 1 Jan., 1793–1 Jan., 1800 (HRA I, ii, 563); Indents, NSW Arch. 4/3998; O'Brien, *op. cit.*, 385.

43. Log of *Barwell* (Log 420G, Commonwealth Relations Office, London); Hunter to Portland, 12 Sept., 1798, Portland to Hunter, 5 Nov., 1799 (HRA I, ii, 224-5, 391); King to Calvert, 24 Oct., 1799, Proceedings of Vice-Admiralty Court, Aug., 1798, Dore to Fleming, 5 Feb., 1798 (NSWHR iii, 726, 453-72, 355-6); Vice-Admiralty Ct., NSW Arch. 1163; Indents, NSW Arch. 4/3998, 4/4000, 4/4001; O'Brien, *op. cit.*, 385.

44. William Noah, *Diary* (Dixson Library MS.); Hunter to Portland, 27 July, 1799, to King, 28 July, 1799 (HRA I, ii, 376-7, 378); Portland to Transport Cmmrs., 4 June, 1800, Patton to Transport Office, 6 June, 1800, Rains to *do.*, 9 June, 1800, Transport Cmmrs. to Portland, 11 June, 1800 (NSWHR, iv, 88-94); Return of Convicts Landed, *op. cit.*; Indents, NSW Arch. 4/3998, 4/4000, 4/4001; O'Brien, *op. cit.*, 385.

45. Journal of the Missionaries from Portsmouth to Rio de Janeiro in *Royal Admiral* (Haweis Pap., Mit. Lib., MS. A 1963); Log of *Royal Admiral* (Log 338I, Commonwealth Relations Office, London); King to Portland, 30 Nov., 1800 and 10 Mar., 1801, to Hobart, 30 Oct., 1802 (HRA I, ii, 697; iii, 5, 583); *Parramatta Hist. Soc. Jour.*, iii, 99-101, 108n.; Indents, NSW Arch. 4/3999; O'Brien, *op. cit.*, 385.

CHAPTER NINE

1. *Report of Select Committee on Transportation*, 1812, evidence of Alexander McLeay. See Appendices, post, 336-75, for tonnage details of transports.

2. Classification details for transports, wherever ascertainable, have been included in the Appendices, post, 336-75.

3. Charters of affreightment, NSW Arch., Col. Sec. Pap., *passim*, which specify the size and type of the guns, and reports of Vessels Inwards and Outwards (HRA, *passim*), which record simply the total guns in each ship.

4. Jour., D. Reid, *Baring*, 1819 (Adm. 101/7, 3189), S. Sinclair, *Mary*, 1831 (*Ibid.*, 101/51, 3204).

5. Vessels Inwards, 30 Sept., 1800–31 Mar., 1801, Outwards 1 July–31 Dec., 1801 (HRA I, iii, 127, 453); Transport Board to Hunter, 29 Mar., 1799 (*Ibid.*, ii, 340); Jour. of the Missionaries in the *Royal Admiral* (Haweis Pap., Mit. Lib., MS. A1963).

6. Jour., *Royal Admiral* missionaries, *op. cit.*; King to Portland, 30 Nov., 1800 and 10 Mar., 1801, and to Transport Cmmrs., 10 Mar., 1801 (HRA I, ii, 697; iii, 9, 15, 84); Stewart to ? – – –, 26 Aug., 1800, in *Portsmouth Telegraph*, 9 Feb., 1801 (NSWHR, iv, 326n.).

7. Curtis to King, 12 Dec., 1800 (NSWHR, iv, 264); Bathurst to Macquarie, 14 Oct., 1819, and Hobhouse to Goulburn, 29 Sept., 1819 (HRA I, x, 203-4); Indent, NSW Arch. 4/4004.

8. Log of *Coromandel* (Log 206 A, Commonwealth Relations Office, London); *Lloyd's Register of Shipping* to author, 20 Jan., 1954, with register details; Inwards Shipping, 1 Jan.–30 June, 1802 (HRA I, iii, 637); Charter of *Coromandel* and *Perseus*, 27 Oct., 1801 (*Ibid.*, 358 sq.); King to Hobart, 23 July, 1802, and to Transport Cmmrs., 9 Aug., 1802 (*Ibid.*, 531, 552-3); King to Sterling, 30 June, 1802 (NSWHR, iv, 808); Indent, NSW Arch. 4/4004; *Aust. Dict. Biog.*, ii, 530.

9. Log of *Hercules* (Log 77A, Commonwealth Relations Office, London); Betts to King, 26 June, 1802 (HRA I, iii, 556-7); Trial of Betts (*Ibid.*, 536-49); King to Hobart, 23 July, 19 Aug. and 30 Oct., 1802 (*Ibid.*, 531, 535, 584); Remission of sentence on Betts, 20 July, 1802 (*Ibid.*, 549-50); Trial of Wm. Stow and ors. (*Ibid.*, 550-1); Examination into conduct of Betts (*Ibid.*, 558-9); NSW Arch., Vice-Admiralty Court, 1163; Transport Cmmrs. to King, 26 Aug., 1801 (HRA I, iii, 269); Indent, NSW Arch. 4/4004.

10. Log of *Atlas* (Log 27E, Commonwealth Relations Office, London); Walker to Transport Cmmrs., 8 July, 1802 (NSWHR, iv, 798-9); Jamison to Hobart, 8 Nov., 1802 (HRA I, iii, 701-5); Brooks to King, 6 July, 1802 (*Ibid.*, 554); King to Transport Cmmrs., 9 Aug and 9 Nov., 1802 (*Ibid.*, 553-4, 719;) Jamison to King, 12 Nov., 1802, and encls. (*Ibid.*, 706-10); Examination into conduct of Brooks, 11 July 1802 (*Ibid.*, 555-6); King to Hobart, 30 Oct. and 9 Nov., 1802 (*Ibid.*, 584, 648); Brooks to Transport Cmmrs., 14 Apr., 1802 (NSWHR, iv, 739-40), Transport Cmmrs. to King, 14 Nov., 1803, with encl., Bray to Transport Cmmrs., 9 June, 1803 (*Ibid.*, iv, 425-7); King to Brooks, 3 Aug., 1802 (*Ibid.*, 806-7); Indent, NSW Arch., 4/4004; Return relating to convicts on *Atlas*, (HRA, iii, 554); *Aust. Dict. Biog.*, i, 156 (Brooks), 526 (Hayes).

11. Colnett to Nepean, 14 Sept., 1803 (NSWHR, v, 207); King to Nepean, 9 May, 1803 (HRA I, iv, 247-8); *Sydney Gazette*, 19 Mar., 1803; J. H. Tuckey, *An Account of a Voyage to Establish a Colony at Port Phillip in Bass's Strait* (London, 1805), *passim*; Hobart to Collins, 7 Feb., 1803 (HRA I, iv, 10-16); Collins to Sullivan, 31 May and 16 July, 1803 (*Ibid.*, III, i, 21, 23-4); Collins to Hobart, 15 July, 22 Aug., 5 and 14 Nov., 1803 (*Ibid.*, 21-4, 24-5, 26-31, 34-8); Trades and occupations of convicts landed at Port Phillip (*Ibid.*, 32); Indents, NSW Arch. 4/4004.

12. Relevant registers; Vessels Inwards, 5 Jan.–31 Mar., 1810 (HRA I, vii, 320); Paterson to Castlereagh, 9 July, 1809 (*Ibid.*, 166); *Sydney Gazette*, 2 July, 1809; Indent, NSW Arch. 4/4004; Vessels Inwards, 1 Jan.–14 Aug., 1804 (HRA I, v, 120); *Sydney Gazette*, 24 June and 1 July, 1804; Indent, NSW Arch. 4/4004. Unless otherwise stated, ship details, such as date and place of build, given in the text are from relevant registers at *Lloyd's Register of Shipping*, extracted by Miss J. March, and I have not felt it necessary henceforth to give the source of this information in the notes.

13. Log of *William Pitt* (Log 184G, Commonwealth Relations Office, London); Vessels Inwards, 1 Jan.–12 Aug., 1806 (HRA I, v. 767); King to Transport Commissioners, 18 June, 1806 (*Ibid.*, v, 716-7); Indent, NSW Arch. 4/4004; *Sydney Gazette*, 13 and 20 Apr., 1806.

14. Librarian, H.M. Customs & Excise, London, to author, 19 Mar., 1955, with extracts from *Minstrel's* register (Hull, 5/1811). For details of passages see Appendices, 2 post, 288-324.

15. Vessels Inwards and Outwards, 1 Jan.–12 Aug., 1806 (HRA I, v, 767-8); King to Transport Cmmrs., 18 June, 1806 (*Ibid.*, 716); HRA I, vi, 712, n. 30.

16. Paterson to Castlereagh, 14 Oct. and 7 Nov., 1809 (HRA I, vii, 175, 179); Macquarie to Castlereagh, 12 Mar., 1810 (*Ibid.*, 240-1); Memorial of George Bruce, 4 June, 1813 (*Ibid.*, viii, 93-4); Marsden to Macquarie, 30 May 1815 (*Ibid.*, 577-8).

17. Goulburn to Macquarie and to Davey, 19 Oct., 1812, Bathurst to Macquarie, 23 Nov., 1812, Macquarie to Bathurst, 28 June, 1813; Bathurst to Macquarie, 30 Apr., 1813 (HRA I, vii, 524, 668, 728, 700); Department of the Navy, Division of Naval History, Washington, to author, 17 Feb., 1955.

18. Macquarie to Bathurst, 18 Mar., 1816 (HRA I, ix, 55, 57, 59); Department of the Navy, Division of Naval History, Washington, to author, 17 Feb., 1955; Vessels Inwards, 1 July–30 Sept., 1815, and Outwards, 1 Oct.–31 Dec., 1815 (HRA I, ix, 81, 86); *Sydney Gazette*, 5 and 12 Aug., 1815; Bathurst to Macquarie, 25 May, 1817, and Beckett to Goulburn, 5 May, 1817 (HRA I, ix, 414-5).

19. Appendices, post, 336-75 sq.; Grahame E. Farr (Ed.), *Records of Bristol Ships*, 1800-1838 (Bristol Rec. Soc., xv, Bristol, 1950), 230; Grahame E. Farr, *Chepstow Ships* (Chepstow, 1954), 178; Richard Weatherill, *The Ancient Port of Whitby and its Shipping* (Whitby, 1908), 116.

20. Redfern to Macquarie, 30 Sept., 1814 (HRA I, viii, 275-293); Macquarie to Transport Cmmrs., 1 Oct., 1814, and to Bathurst, 7 Oct, 1814 (*Ibid.*, 274-6, 295); Indent, NSW Arch., 4/4005; *Sydney Gazette*, 30 July, 1814.

21. Wm. S. Edwardson, *Jour. of Voyage in the ship Surrey*, 1816 (Mit. Lib. MS.); Macquarie to Bathurst, 4 Apr., 1817 (HRA I, ix, 343); Bayley to Macquarie, 2 Jan., 1817, NSW Arch., 29/1817; Indent, *Ibid.*, 4/4005; *Sydney Gazette*, 31 Dec., 1816.

22. Vessels Inwards, 1 Jan.–15 Feb., 1814 (HRA I, viii, 201); Medical Officers to Campbell, 24 Mar., 1814, with encl. Proceedings of Medical Court of Inquiry, 16 Mar., 1814 (*Ibid.*, 244-8); Redfern to Macquarie, 30 Sept., 1814 (*Ibid.*, 275-293); Macquarie to Bathurst, 7 Feb. and 28 Apr., 1814 (*Ibid.*, 138 140); Indent, NSW Arch. 4/4004; *Sydney Gazette*, 12 Feb., 1814. Harris's praise of the surgeon was given in his evidence before the inquiry and will be found in the Proceedings mentioned in the note.

23. Redfern to Macquarie, 30 Sept., 1814 (HRA I, viii, 275-293); Macquarie to Bathurst, 24 May, 1814 (*Ibid.*, 253-5); Indent, NSW Arch., 4/4004; *Sydney Gazette*, 7, 14 and 21 May, 1814.

24. Log of *Indefatigable* (Log 786 A, Commonwealth Relations Office, London); Macquarie to Liverpool, 18 Oct., 1811 (HRA I, vii, 382-3); Liverpool to Macquarie and to Murray, 19 May, 1812 (*Ibid.*, 488, 489-90); Macquarie to Bathurst, 28 June, 1813 (*Ibid.*, 728); Assignment of Convicts, 9 May, 1812 (*Ibid.*, 490-2); Tas. Arch., 2/58; NSW Arch. Convict Ships—Musters and other papers; *Sydney Gazette*, 24 Oct. and 12 Dec., 1812.

25. Macquarie to Bathurst, 16 May, 1818 (HRA I, ix, 792, 794); Sorell to Macquarie, 29 June, 1818 (*Ibid.*, III, ii, 332-3); Indents sent to Bigge (*Ibid.*, iii, 512); Statement of Prisoners (*Ibid.*, 554); Macquarie to Bathurst, 4 Apr., 1817 (*Ibid.*, I, ix, 343-4); *Do.* to *do.*, 20 July, 1819 (*Ibid.*, x, 190); Sorell to Macquarie, 21 May, 1819, and to Goulburn, 3 June, 1819 (*Ibid.*, III, ii, 398-9, 403); Indents, NSW Arch., Convict Ships—Musters and other papers; Tas. Arch., 2/58; CSO (A), 9107; Macquarie to Bathurst, 23 Mar., 1819 and 7 Feb., 1821 (HRA I, x, 83, 401); Jour., Joseph Arnold, 22 Oct., 1815 (Mit. Lib. MS.).

26. Weatherill, *op. cit.*, 42; *Colonial Times*, 20 Oct., 1826; Reports of Wylde & Wentworth, and of Campbell, 15 Nov., 1817 (HRA I, ix, 613-45, 645-9); Macquarie to Bathurst, 12 Sept., 12 and 20 Dec., 1817, with encls. (*Ibid.*, 484-5, 561-612, 649-707, 741-7); Bethurst to Macquarie, 12 Apr., 1819, Hobhouse to Goulburn, 29 Jan., 1819, and Maule to Hobhouse, 19 Jan., 1819 (*Ibid.*, x, 143-5); Return of Sick, Killed and Wounded, 14 Mar.–26 July,. 1817 (*Ibid.*, ix, 654); NSW Arch., Indent 4/4005, and Convict Ships—Musters and other papers.

27. Macquarie to Bathurst, 3 Mar., 1818 (HRA I, ix, 749-52); Cosgreave to Macquarie, 14 Jan., 1818 (*Ibid.*, 752-4); Depositions and Report by Bench of Magistrates, 26 Feb., 1818 (*Ibid.*, 754-9); Indent, NSW Arch., 4/4005, and Convict Ships—Musters and other papers.
28. Macquarie to Bathurst, 1 Sept., 1820 (HRA I, x, 365); Report of Bench of Magistrates, 24 June, 1820 (*Ibid.*, 322); Sorell to Macquarie, 25 June, 1820 (*Ibid.*, III, iii, 37); NSW Arch., Indent 4/4007, and Convict Ships—Musters and other papers; *Sydney Gazette*, 6 May, 3 June and 29 July, 1820.
29. Field to Macquarie, 1 Dec., 1817 (HRA I, ix, 510).
30. Jour., Robert Armstrong (Adm. 101/72, 3212); Macquarie to Bathurst, 24 Mar., 1819 (HRA I, x, 85); Indent, NSW Arch., 4/4006, and Convict Ships—Musters and other papers.
31. Jour., David Reid (Adm. 101/7, 3189); Sorell to Macquarie, 19 June, 1819 (HRA III, ii, 405); Macquarie to Bathurst, 20 July, 1819 (*Ibid.*, I, x, 190-1); Queade to Brisbane, 28 Jan., 1822 (*Ibid.*, 618); NSW Arch., Indent 4/4006, and Convict Ships—Musters and other papers; *Hobart Gazette, Supplement*, 19 June, 1819.
32. For details see Appendices, post, 336-75.
33. Jour., James Scott (Adm. 101/16, 3191); Macquarie to Bathurst, 28 Feb., 1820, and to Sorell, 14 Feb., 1820 (HRA I, x, 278; III, iii, 7); Sorell to Macquarie, 8 Mar., 1820 (*Ibid.*, III, iii, 9); Examination of James Kelly before Bigge, 29 Jan., 1820 (*Ibid.*, 460); NSW Arch., Indent 4/4007, and Convict Ships—Musters and other papers.
34. *Aust. Dict. Biog.*, i, 137-8 (Bowman); 155-6 (Bromley).
35. *Sydney Gazette*, 23 Sept., 1820; Macquarie to Bathurst, 7 Feb. and 21 July, 1821 (HRA I, x, 381, 531); Macquarie to Bathurst, 18 Mar., 1816 (*Ibid.*, ix, 59); Bathurst to Macquarie, 30 Jan., 1817 (*Ibid.* 203); Darling to Bathurst, 2 Mar., 1826, and encl. (*Ibid.*, xii, 197-203); Bathurst to Darling, 13 July, 1826 (*Ibid.*, 359); *Aust. Dict. Biog.*, ii, 427-8 (Scott).

CHAPTER TEN

1. Jour., William Elyard, 5 June–21 Oct., 1821 (Mit. Lib. MS. A2884; Adm. 101/38, 3199); Brisbane to Bathurst, 4 Feb., 1822 (HRA I, x, 612); Indent, NSW Arch., 4/4007.
2. *Sydney Gazette*, 31 June and 5 July, 1832 (*Burrell*); 24 Mar. and 17 Apr., 1832 (*Isabella*); Indents, NSW Arch. 4/4017, 4/4016.
3. McTernan to Governor, 27 Aug., 1823 (NSW Arch., Col. Sec. Pap., 4/1765, p. 55); J. McTernan, Jour. (Adm. 101/57, 3206); Indent, NSW Arch., 4/4009.
4. Dalrymple to Thornton, 19 Aug., 1824, and Court of Inquiry, same date (NSW Arch., Col. Sec. Pap., 4/1782, p. 5); Jour., John Crocket (Adm. 101/47, 3202); Indent, etc., NSW Arch., 4/4010, 4/4565.
5. Rae to Col. Sec., 17 Dec., 1823 (NSW Arch., Col. Sec. Pap., 4/1765, p. 76); Jour., Wm. Rae (Adm. 101/36, 3198); Indent, NSW Arch., 4/4009, X33.
6. Fairfowl to Governor, Apr., 1825 (NSW Arch., 4/1782, p. 21); Jour., Geo. Fairfowl (Adm. 101/65, 3209); Indent, NSW Arch., 4/4010, 4/4567.
7. NSW Arch., Col. Sec. In-letters, 32/4441 and Box No. 4/2145; Jour., James Lawrence (Adm. 101/37, 3199); Indents, NSW Arch., 4/4017, 4/4563.
8. Jour., D. Macnamara (Adm. 101/38, 3199); Indent, etc., NSW Arch., 4/4007, 4/4563.
9. Jour., And. Henderson (Adm. 101/27, 3195); Indent, NSW Arch., 4/4016, 4/4561, Printed p. 127.

10. Brisbane to Bathurst, 24 June, 1824, and magisterial proceedings, 27 and 29 May and 1 June, 1824 (HRA I, xi, 283-301); Hall to Governor and other papers, NSW Arch., 4/1774, p. 21; Jours., Jas. Hall, *Brothers* (Adm. 101/12, 3190), *Georgiana* (*Ibid.*, 101/29, 3196), Indents, NSW Arch., 4/4009, 4/4558.

11. Darling to Cmmrs. Navy, 26 July, 1826 (HRA I, xii, 451); Arthur to Hay, 20 June, 1826, and Cmmrs. Navy to Hay, 2 Mar., 1827 (*Ibid.*, III, v, 285-6, 533); Tas. Arch. 2/60, CSO (A) 3546; Mit. Lib. MS. A1059, i, 205; ii, 124; Jour., M. Burnside, 1825-6, (Adm. 101/62, 3208).

12. Arthur to Horton, 14 May, 1825 (HRA III, iv, 266); Tas. Arch., Board of Inquiry, CSO (A) 3387; 2/60; Mit. Lib. MS. A1059, i, 19, 51, 102, 152; Jour., Wm. McDowell, 1824-5 (Adm. 101/41, 3200); NSW Arch., 4/4564.

13. Darling to Cmmrs. Navy, 4 Nov., 1827 (HRA I, xiii, 593); McDowell to Governor, 30 Oct., 1827, and Navy Cmmrs. to Governor, 5 May, 1828 (NSW Arch. Col. Sec. Pap., 4/1952, 4/1999); Jour., Wm. McDowell, 1827 (Adm. 101/32, 3197).

14. Darling to Bathurst, 4 Feb., 1826, and Bathurst to Darling, 12 July, 1826 (HRA I, xii, 158-9, 358); Indents, *Hibernia*, Tas. Arch., 2/58, CSO (A) 9107; NSW Arch., 4/4563; *Henry Porcher*, NSW Arch., 4/4010.

15. Proceedings against Ebsworthy, 1821, NSW Arch., Col. Sec. Pap., 4/1749, No. 68.

16. List of Ships in Sydney Cove, 1828, NSW Arch., Col. Sec. Pap., 4/2001; *Sydney Gazette*, 12 Aug., 16 Sept. and 9 Dec., 1824; *The Australian*, 13 Jan. and 17 Feb., 1825; P. R. Stephensen, *The History and Description of Sydney Harbour* (Adelaide, 1966), 360-1.

17. *Sydney Monitor*, 26 July, 1827; NSW Arch. Col. Sec. Pap., 4/1945; Indent, NSW Arch., 4/4012.

18. *Sydney Gazette*, 11 Mar., 1824; *Sydney Monitor*, 30 Mar., 1827; Registrar-General of Shipping and Seamen to author, with transcripts of registers, London, 364/1810, 65/1825, 152/1829; Indents, NSW Arch., 4/4009, 4/4562 (1824), 4/4014, X32, 4/4562 (1829).

19. Jour., E. Evans (Adm. 101/59, 3207).

20. Registrar-General of Shipping and Seamen to author, 9 July, 1955, with transcripts of registers, London 187/1804, 320/1813, 80/1816, 53/1820, 5/1825, 131/1829, 310/1832, 334/1839, 383/1841; *Sydney Gazette*, 17 Feb. and 24 Feb., 1825; Medical Certificate, filed with Vessels Arrived, 1833 (NSW Arch., 4/5204).

21. Hughes to Arthur, 7 Oct., 1826, and Report of Committee of Inquiry into escape of prisoners, 12 Oct., 1826 (HRA III, v, 381, 383); Indents, etc., Tas. Arch. 2/60, CSO (A) 403; Mit. Lib., MS. A1059, ii, 98; NSW Arch., 4/4559.

22. Darling to Huskisson, 28 Aug., 1828 (HRA I, xiv, 347-8); Indents, etc., NSW Arch. 4/4005, 4/4566 (1817); 4/4006 (1818); 4/4007 (1820); 4/4013, X34, 4/4566 (1828), 4/4014, 4/4566 (1829); Tas. Arch., 2/59, CSO (A) 7161, NSW Arch., 4/4566 (1823).

23. *The Blue Peter*, 1930, 136-143.

24. *Sydney Gazette*, 7 June, 16 and 23 July, 3 Nov., 24 Dec., 1831; Vessels Arrived, 1831 (NSW Arch. 4/5202); Tas. Arch., CSO 1/707/15466; *Sydney Gazette*, 12 Jan., 1832 (Supplement); Indents, NSW Arch., 4/4016, 4/4564; printed, p. 137.

25. Bourke to Stanley, 16 Apr., 1834, Hay to Bourke, 20 Nov., 1834 (HRA I, xvii, 410, 588; *Hobart Town Courier*, 10 Jan., 1834.

26. Montagu to MacLeay, 4 July, 1835, *Do.* to *Do.*, 27 Aug., 1835, *Do.* to Commandant, Launceston, 30 June, 1835, Report, correspondence and examinations of Board of Inquiry, 6 July, 1836, etc., Glenelg to Bourke, 31 Jan., 1836, with encls. (HRA I, xviii, 37-8, 136, 137-150, 273-82); Letters of Col. Arthur, Mit. Lib. MS. A1962, 152-3; Hull, *Chronology of Tasmania, Ibid.*, A588, 97; *Full and Horrifying Account of the Wreck of the Neva, Ibid.*, An 7. For map illustrating her loss see Governor's Despatches, Mit. Lib. MS. A1214, 327.

27. Report, 11 Feb., 1836, Evidence and Account of Expenses, Governors' Despatches (Mit. Lib. MS. A1267, v. iv, 1645-1656); Bourke to Glenelg, 20 Dec., 1835 and 18 Mar., 1836 (HRA I, xviii, 232-3, 360); Papers regarding the *Hive*, 14 Dec., 1835 (NSW Arch., 35/10071 in 4/2282.2); Ant. Donoghue, Jour. (Adm. 101/34, 3198).

28. *Hobart Town Courier*, 17 Apr., 1835; Tas. Arch. CSO (A) 17014.

29. Tas. Arch. CSO (A) 10651 and 14864.

30. Brisbane to Bathurst, 4 Feb., 1822, Bowman to Goulburn, 6 Jan., 1822, Queade to Brisbane, 28 Jan., 1822 (HRA I, x, 612, 613-5, 615-9); Indent, etc., NSW Arch., 4/4007, 4/566.

31. Bowman to Goulburn, 29 Sept., 1823 (HRA I, xi, 155); McTernan to Governor, 27 Aug., 1823 (NSW Arch., Col. Sec. Pap., 4/1765, p. 55); Jour., Jas. McTernan (Adm. 101/57, 3206); Indent, NSW Arch., 4/4009, 4/4565.

32. Gipps to Glenelg, 17 Aug. and 24 Sept., 1838 and 8 Mar., 1839 (HRA I, xix, 547, 591-2; xx, 57); Health Officer's Report, filed with Vessels Arrived, 1838 (NSW Arch., 4/5213); Jour., O. Pineo (Adm. 101/44, 3201); Indent, NSW Arch., Printed p. 94, 4/4564.

33. Jours., Robt. Tainsh, Wm. Gregor (*Medina*), Wm. West, Jas. Ellis (*Bengal Merchant*) (Adm. 101/21, 3193; 101/52, 3204; 101/14, 3190; 101/8, 3189); Indents, etc., NSW Arch., 4/4009, X31 (*Earl St. Vincent*); 4/4016, Printed p. 149, 4/4558 (*Burrell*); 4/4019, Printed p. 28, 4/4558 (*Bengal Merchant*); Tas. Arch., 2/60, CSO (A) 3348; Mit. Lib. MS. A1059, ii, 325 (*Medina*).

34. Jour., Jas. Patton (Adm. 101/23, 3194); Patton to Col. Sec., 18 Nov., 1828 (NSW Arch., 28/9359 in 4/5001); Indent, etc., 4/4013, 4/4561; Dan Macleod to Col. Sec., 20 Aug., 1829, Stewart to Col. Sec., n.d., Montgomery to Col. Sec., 19 Aug., 1829, etc. (NSW Arch., 4/2043); Indent, *Ibid.*, 4/4014.

35. J. A. Nixon, "Health and Sickness", in C. Northcote Parkinson, (Ed.), *The Trade Winds* (London: 1948), 121; Lloyd & Coulter, iv; 84; Jour., T. Galloway (Adm. 101/58, 3206).

36. Jour., Alex. Stewart (Adm. 101/2, 3187).

37. Health Officer's Report, filed with Vessels Arrived, 1840 (NSW Arch., 4/5216); Gipps to Russell, 20 Mar., 1840 (HRA I, xx, 575); Jour., John Baird (Adm. 101/54, 3205); Indent, etc., NSW Arch., 4/7077, Printed p. 6, 8, 4/4565.

38. Jours., Geo. Fairfowl and Geo. Birnie (Adm. 101/2, 3187, 101/5, 3188).

39. Tas. Arch., CSO (A) 16764; Acc. No. 1/24; GO 2/10; Mit. Lib. MS. A1059, vii, 371; Indent, etc., NSW Arch., 4/4018, Printed p. 54.

40. Jour., F. Logan (Adm. 101/27, 3195); Goderich to Bourke, 19 July, 1832 (HRA I, xvi, 678-9); Indent, etc., NSW Arch., 4/4017, Printed p. 211, 4/4561.

41. Jours., John Osborne, Oliver Sproule, Thos. Galloway (Adm. 101/28, 3196, 101/36, 3198, 101/5, 3188); Tas. Arch., CSO (A) 15081; Mit. Lib. MS. F143, A1059, vii, 269; NSW Arch., 4/4017, Printed p. 69.

42. Jour., John Stephenson (Adm., 101/40, 3199); Tas. Arch., CSO (A) 13784, 14776; Mit. Lib. MS. A1059, vii, 195; Jour., Allan McLaren (Adm. 101/35, 3198); Tas. Arch., CSO (A) 13881; Mit. Lib. MS. A1059, ix, 511.

43. Jour., Robt. Dunn (Adm. 101/14, 3190); Report of Robt. Dunn, 26 July, 1828, Minute of Proceedings of Executive Council, 29 July, 1828, Darling to Huskisson, 28 Aug., 1828 (HRA I, xiv, 350, 348, 347); *Sydney Gazette*, 28 July and 30 Aug., 1828; Indent, etc., NSW Arch., 4/4013, 4/4558.

44. D. B. Wilson, of Hobart, Tas., to author, 16 Nov., 1959; Jour., A. D. Wilson (Adm. 101/5, 3188); *Aust. Dict. Biog.*, ii, 612.

45. Vessels Arrived, 1840, with Health Officer's Report attached (NSW Arch., 4/5217); Jour., G. E. Forman (Adm. 101/22, 3193); Indents, etc., Printed p. 156, 4/4560.

CHAPTER ELEVEN

1. *Shipping Gazette*, 12 Feb., 1848; Register of Vessels Arrived, 20 Nov., 1848 (Hobart Marine Board); Biddle MS., i, 118-9 (Victorian Archives); *The Argus*, 4 Dec., 1852; W. A. Hall, "The Convict Hulk *Success*", (*Vic. Hist. Mag.*, xiv, 73); H. A. White, "The True History of the Hulk *Success*" (*Austral Light*, vii, 150-60, 205-12); Charles E. Planck to author in conversation.

2. Manuscript Narrative of the Wreck of the *Waterloo*, by Dr. Henry Kelsall, lent me by Miss Rose T. Kelsall, of Nedlands, W.A.; Ships *Abercrombie Robinson* and *Waterloo*, ordered to be printed by the House of Commons, 7 Mar., 1843; Tas. Arch. CSO (RB) 249.

3. Register of Vessels Arrived, 24 Nov., 1842 (Hobart Marine Board); Tas. Arch., Acc. No. 1/25; CSO (RB) 249.

4. Register of Vessels Arrived, 1842 (Hobart Marine Board); Tas. Arch. Acc. No. 1/25; CSO (RB) 52, 159, 193; Jour., Thos. Gibson (Adm. 101/68, 3210).

5. J. V. Barry, *Alexander Maconochie of Norfolk Island: A Study of a Pioneer in Penal Reform* (Melbourne, 1958), 167.

6. N.S.W. Arch., 4/4566 (*Mount Stewart Elphinstone*); Grey to Fitzroy, 5 June, 1849, Governor's Despatches (Mit. Lib. MS. A1308); *Do.* to *Do.*, 24 Nov., 1849 and 21 Dec., 1850 (*Ibid.*), Fitzroy to Grey, 5 July, 1850, with Report of Principal Superintendent of Convicts and of Brisbane Magistrate, 4 May, 1850 (*Bangalore*). Much information will be found in the Despatches to and from the Governors and the Superintendent of Port Phillip (Mit. Lib. MS. Collections) regarding the "exile" ships.

7. Jour., Edw. Caldwell, 1843 (Adm. 101/22, 3193); Tas. Arch., CSO (RB) 52; Jour., William Bland (*Garland Grove*), 1843 (Adm. 101/29, 3196); CSO (RB) 343, Jours., J. A. Mould (*Margaret*), 1843 (Adm. 101/48, 3203); James Clarke (*Greenlaw*), 1844 (*Ibid.*, 101/30, 3196); John Wilson (*Emma Eugenia*), 1844 (*Ibid.*, 101/25, 3195); J. G. Williams (*Kinnear*), 1848 (*Ibid.*, 101/40, 3200).

8. Vessels Arrived, 27 May, 1853 (Hobart Marine Board); Jour., Thos. Somerville, 1852-3 (Adm. 101/66, 3209).

9. "A Boy's Voyage in a Convict Ship", by Comdr. B. Wemyss-Gorman, *Blackwood's Magazine*, v. 273 (No. 1649, Mar., 1953), 242-52; Jour., A. Watson (M.T. 32/9, 3181); Shipping Lists, Col. Sec. Office, 1865 (W. A. Archives).

10. Jours., John Bower (*Lord Raglan*), 1858 (M.T. 32/1, 3181); *Clara* 1864 (*Ibid.*, 32/7, 3181); A. Watson (*Racehorse*), 1865 (*Ibid.*, 32/9, 3181); Wm. Crauford (*Vimeria*), 1865-6 (*Ibid.*, 32/10, 3181); and other surgeons' journals, *passim*.

11. Jours., J. W. Bowler (*Hashemy*), 1850 (Adm. 101/32, 3197); J. Bower (*Lord Raglan*), 1858 (M.T. 32/1, 3181); *Lincelles*, 1860-1 (*Ibid.*, 32/2, 3181); A. Watson (*Norwood*), 1862 (*Ibid.*, 32/3, 3181); Wm. Smith (*Merchantman*) 1862-3 (*Ibid.*, 32/5, 3181); Wm. Crauford (*Clyde*), 1863 (*Ibid.* 32/6, 3181); *Clara*, 1864 (*Ibid.*, 32/7, 3181); A. Watson (*Racehorse*), 1865 (*Ibid.*, 32/9, 3181).

12. Jours., Wm. Smith (*Merchantman*), 1864 (M.T. 32/8, 3181); J. Bower (*Lord Raglan*), 1858 (*Ibid.*, 32/1, 3181); Wm. Crauford (*Corona*), 1866 (*Ibid.*, 32/11, 3181).

13. Jours., J. Bower (*Lord Raglan*), 1858 (M.T. 32/1, 3181); Wm. Smith (*Merchantman*), 1862-3 and 1864 (*Ibid.*, 32/5, 32/8, 3181); Wm. Crauford (*Corona*), 1866, and (*Clyde*), 1863 (*Ibid.*, 32/11, 32/6, 3181).

14. Jours., G. Thomson (*England*), G. Fairfowl (*Asia*), J. Morgan (*Captain Cook*), J. W. Roberts (*Lord Auckland*) (Adm. 101/26, 3195; 101/4, 3188; 101/16, 3191; 101/43, 3201); *Lord Raglan, Lincelles, Merchantman* (1862-3) and (1864), *Racehorse, Norwood, Clyde* and *Clara* (M.T. 32/1, 32/2, 32/5, 32/8, 32/9, 32/12, 32/6, 32/7, 3181).

15. Shipping Returns, Col. Sec. Office (W. A. Archives); Jour., John Bower (*Lord Raglan*), 1858 (M.T. 32/1, 3181); Capt. C. E. Parkes, of St. Austell, Cornwall, to author, 28 June, 1859, regarding his purchase of *A Voice of our Exiles or the Clara Weekly Journal*; Francis Edwards, Ltd., Catalogue of Books about the Sea and Shipping, 1938, offering a number of these convict ship newspapers for sale. Some were preserved in the Mitchell Library, but have disappeared: being hand-written, they may have been mislaid or inadvertently thrown out. According to the Francis Edwards catalogue, several were illustrated with water-colour drawings.

APPENDICES

NOTE TO APPENDICES, I—VI.

THE appendices have been compiled primarily from Australian sources. *Dates of Arrival* These are as given in governors' despatches, customs returns, tide waiters' or harbourmasters' reports of arrival, surgeons' journals, or other official returns, and only in the absence of such records, from newspaper reports. Where it is obvious that a date officially recorded is wrong, I have not hesitated to correct it; where conflicting dates are recorded, I have adopted that which seems most probably correct, after weighing the value of the evidence. *Rig*: This is given as recorded in official reports, but after 1837 I have followed Lloyd's Register, although I do not believe this source to be always reliable. *Tonnage*: Preference has been given to the tonnages recorded in the following sources in the order given: (*a*) charters of affreightment; (*b*) Port Jackson ships' musters, where the tonnage is recorded for the computation of harbour dues; (*c*) tide waiters' and harbourmasters' reports of ships' arrivals; (*d*) health officers' reports. After 1837, tonnages are as recorded in Lloyd's Register; where two tonnages are given, that by new measurement is incorporated in the appendices. *Masters and Surgeons*: wherever possible, Christian and surnames have been taken from the individuals' signatures, when decipherable; otherwise names are as given in surgeons' journals, ships' musters, health officers' reports, or returns of arrivals by tide waiters or harbourmasters. Christian names have had to be abbreviated. Masters and surgeons who died on the passage are marked with an asterisk (*), ships which were wrecked with a dagger (†). *Sailing dates*: The following sources have been preferred in the order indicated: (*a*) surgeons' journals, surgeons' or masters' reports of arrival; (*b*) masters' letters re lay days; (*c*) health officers' reports; (*d*) tide waiters' or harbourmasters' reports of arrivals; (*e*) P.R.O. H.O. 11/20 list of sailing dates. The latter has been used only when other official returns have not been available: the P.R.O. sailing dates are almost always embarkation dates. Where log books, journals, or narratives of voyages have been available, dates as recorded therein have been adopted in preference to all other sources. *Route*: From log books, journals, narratives of voyage, or, in absence of these, from health officers' reports and tide waiters' or harbourmasters' returns. Vessels have been marked as making direct passages only when such information is specifically recorded, but it will be obvious that many other vessels made direct passages, although I have never assumed a direct passage without evidence.

Abbreviations: S.=Ship. Bk.=Barque. Bg.=Brig. Cp.=Cape. C. Vde=Cape Verde Is. Gib.=Gibraltar. Hob.=Hobart. KGS=King George's Sound. Mad.=Madeira. Mrs.=Mauritius. Pt. Py.=Port Praya. Pt. P.=Port Phillip. St.H.=St. Helena. S.L.=Sierra Leone. St. P. Is.=St. Pierre Island. T. d'A.=Tristan D'Acunha. Ten.=Teneriffe.

I. CONVICT SHIPS TO NEW

Date of Arrival	Vessel	R.	Ton	Built at	Year	C	D
1801							
21 Feb.	*Anne I* (or *Luz St. Anna*)	S.	384	Foreign			
12 June	*Earl Cornwallis*	S.	784	London	1783	2	3
14 Dec.	*Canada* (1)	S.	393	Shields	1800	1	2
14 Dec.	*Minorca*	S.	407	Newcastle	1799		
14 Dec.	*Nile I*	S.	322	Newcastle	1799	1	2
1802							
13 June	*Coromandel I* (1)	S.	522	Chittagong	1793	1	2
26 June	*Hercules I*	S.	406	Shields	1801	1	2
7 July	*Atlas I* (1)	S.	437	Shields	1801	1	2
4 Aug.	*Perseus*	S.	362	Stockton	1789	1	1
30 Oct.	*Atlas II*	S.	547	Quebec	1801	1	2
1803							
11 Mar.	*Glatton*	HMS.					
12 May	*Rolla*	S.	438	Shields	1800	1	2
1804							
7 May	*Coromandel I* (2)	S.	522	Chittagong	1793	1	2
24 June	*Experiment I*	S.	568	Stockton	1798	1	3
1806							
15 Feb.	*Tellicherry*	S.	467	Thames	1796	1	2
11 Apr.	*William Pitt*	S.	604	Liverpool	1804	1	2
12 July	*Fortune* (1)	S.	620	Spain		2	2
20 Aug.	*Alexander I*	S.	278	Quebec	1801		
1807							
18 June	*Sydney Cove*	S.	282	Rotterdam	1803	1	2
27 July	*Duke of Portland* (1)	S.	523	Bordeaux	1790	2	2
1808							
16 Nov.	*Speke I* (1)	S.	473	Calcutta	1790	2	2
20 Dec.	*Admiral Gambier* (1)	S.	501	Newcastle	1808	1	2
1809							
26 Jan.	*Aeolus*	S.	289	Denmark		2	2
25 June	*Experiment II*	Bg.	146	Georgia	1802	1	1
14 Aug.	*Boyd*	S.	392	Thames	1793	2	3
18 Aug.	*Indispensable*	Bg.	350	Foreign			
1810							
27 Feb.	*Anne II*	S.	627	Foreign			
8 Sept.	*Canada* (2)	S.	393	Shields	1800	1	2
16 Dec.	*Indian*	S.	522	Whitby	1809	1	2
1811							
2 July	*Providence I*	S.	649	Calcutta	1808	1	2
29 Sept.	*Admiral Gambier* (2)	S.	501	Newcastle	1808	1	2

SOUTH WALES, 1801-1849

Master	*Surgeon*	*Sailed*	*From*	*Route*	*Days*
Jas. Stewart		26 6 00	Cork	Rio, Cape	240
Jas. Tennent		18 11 00	England		206
Wm. Wilkinson	Jn. Kelly	21 6 01	Spithead	Rio	176
Jn. Leith	Geo. Longstaff	21 6 01	Spithead	Rio	176
Jas. Sunter	Jos. Hislop	21 6 01	Spithead	Rio	176
Alex. Sterling	Chas. Throsby	12 2 02	Spithead	Direct	121
Luckyn Betts	J. J. W. Kunst	29 11 01	Ireland	Rio, Cape	209
Rchd. Brooks	Elph. Walker	29 11 01	Ireland	Rio, Cape	220
Jn. Davison	W. S. Fielding	12 2 02	Spithead	Rio, Cape	173
Thos. Musgrave	Thos. Davie	30 5 02	Cork	Rio	153
Capt. Jas. Colnett, R.N.	Jb. Mountgarrett	23 9 02	England	Mad., Rio	169
Rbt. Cumming	Jn. Buist	4 11 02	Cork	Rio	189
(*a*) Jn. Robinson*		4 12 03	England		154
(*b*) Geo. Blakey					
Fran. J. Withers		2 1 04	Cowes	Rio	174
Thos. Cuzens	Jn. Connellan	31 8 05	Cork	Madeira	168
Jn. Boyce	Jos. Blyer	31 8 05	Cork	Mad., S. Salvadore, Cape	223
Hy. Moore		28 1 06	England		165
Rchd. Brooks					
Wm. Edwards		11 1 07	Falmouth	Direct	158
Jn. C. Spence					
Jn. Hingston	J. Macmillan	18 5 08	Falmouth	Rio, Cape	182
Ed. Harrison		2 7 08	P'smouth		171
Rbt. Addie	Rchd. Hughes				
Jos. Dodds		21 1 09	Cork	Rio	155
Jn. Thompson		10 3 09	Cork	Cape	157
Hy. Best	William Evans	2 3 09	England	Rio	169
Chas. Clarke					
Jn. B. Ward		23 3 10	England	Rio	169
And. Barclay	Maine	18 7 10	England		151
And. Barclay	Rchd. Hughes	21 1 11	Falmouth	Rio	162
Ed. Sindrey		12 5 11	England	Rio	140

Date of Arrival	Vessel	R.	Ton	Built at	Year	C	D
10 Oct.	*Friends*	S.	339	Foreign	1799	2	2
1812							
18 Jan.	*Guildford* (1)	S.	521	Thames	1810	1	2
25 Oct.	*Minstrel* (1)	S.	351	Hull	1810	1	2
	**Emu*	Bg.					
1813							
16 Feb.	*Archduke Charles*	S.	525	Newcastle	1809	1	2
11 June	*Fortune* (2)	S.	620	Spain		2	2
9 Oct.	*Earl Spencer*	S.	672	Thames	1803	1	2
1814							
9 Jan.	*Wanstead*	S.	253	America	1811	1	2
7 Feb.	*General Hewart*	S.	973	Bengal	1812	1	3
4 May	*Catherine*	S.	325	New Bedford	1811	1	2
6 May	*Three Bees*	S.	459	Bridgewater	1813	1	2
28 July	*Broxbornebury*	S.	720	Thames	1812	1	2
28 July	*Surrey I* (1)	S.	443	Harwich	1811	1	2
16 Oct.	*Somersetshire* (1)	S.	450	Thames	1810	1	2
1815							
27 Jan.	*Marquis of Wellington*	S.	653	Calcutta	1801	2	2
26 Apr.	*Indefatigable* (2)	S.	549	Whitby	1799	2	3
18 June	*Northampton*	S.	548	Thames	1801	2	3
5 Aug.	*Canada* (3)	S.	393	Shields	1800	2	2
8 Aug.	*Francis and Eliza*	S.	345	Thames	1782	2	2
7 Sept.	*Baring* (1)	S.	842	Thames	1801	2	3
1816							
18 Jan.	*Fanny I*	S.	432	Thames	1810	1	2
19 Jan.	*Mary Anne I* (1)	S.	479	Batavia	1807	2	2
30 Jan.	*Ocean I*	S.	560	Quebec	1800	2	2
4 Apr.	*Alexander II*	Bg.	227	America	1811	1	1
8 Apr.	*Guildford* (2)	S.	521	Thames	1810	1	2
22 July	*Atlas III*	S.	501	Whitby	1812	1	2
5 Oct.	*Elizabeth I* (1)	S.	481	Chepstow	1809	1	2
11 Oct.	*Mariner* (1)	S.	449	Whitby	1807	2	2
20 Dec.	*Surrey I* (2)	S.	443	Harwich	1811	1	2
1817							
24 Feb.	*Lord Melville I* (1)	S.	412	Shields	1805	1	2
8 Mar.	*Fame*	S.	464	Quebec	1812	1	1
10 Mar.	*Sir William Bensley*	S.	584	Ipswich	1802	2	2
10 Apr.	*Morley* (1)	S.	480	Thames	1811	1	2
24 Apr.	*Shipley* (1)	S.	381	Whitby	1805	2	2
26 July	*Chapman* (1)	S.	558	Whitby	1777	2	2
29 July	*Pilot*	S.	392	Newcastle	1813	1	2
6 Aug.	*Canada* (4)	S.	393	Shields	1800	2	2
29 Aug.	*Almorah* (1)	S.	416	Selby	1817	1	2
30 Sept.	*Lord Eldon*	S.	583	Shields	1802	2	3
22 Nov.	*Larkins* (1)	S.	676	Calcutta	1808	1	2
1818							
10 Jan.	*Ocean II* (1)	S.	437	Whitby	1808	1	2
14 Jan.	*Friendship*	S.	441	Thames	1793	2	3

* Captured by the American privateer *Holkar* on 30-11-12 and taken into New York as a prize.

Master	*Surgeon*	*Sailed*	*From*	*Route*	*Days*
Jas. Ralph			England	Rio	
Magnus Johnson		3 9 11	London	Rio	137
Jn. Reid	Alex. Noble	4 6 12	England	Rio	143
Lt. Alex. Bissett, R.N.					
J. P. Jeffries	Jn. Pawson	15 5 12	Cork	Rio, Cape	277
Thos. Walker		3 12 12	England	Rio	190
Wm. Mitchell	D. Mackenzie	2 6 13	England	Madeira	129
Hy. Moore		24 8 13	Spithead		138
Percy Earl	Rchd. Hughes	26 8 13	England	Rio	165
Wm. Simmonds	Palmer	8 12 13	Falmouth		147
Jn. Wallis		8 12 13	Falmouth		149
Thos. Pitcher, Jr.	Colin McLachlan	22 2 14	England		156
Jas. Patterson		22 2 14	England	Rio	156
Alex. Scott		10 5 14	Spithead	Mad., Rio	159
Geo. Betham	Thos. Leighton	1 9 14	England	Mad., Rio	148
Matthew Bowles			England	Rio	
Jn. O. Tween	Jos. Arnold	1 1 15	P'smouth	Rio	169
Jn. Grigg	Rbt. Browne	5 12 14	Cork	Ten., Sene-	243
Wm. Harrison	Major West	5 12 14	Cork	gal, S.L. Cp.	246
Jn. Lamb	Dav. Reid	20 4 15	England	Mad., Rio	140
Jn. Wallis	Wm. McDonald	25 8 15	Downs	Rio	146
Jn. R. Arbuthnot	Jas. Bowman				
Alex. L. Johnson	Ed. F. Bromley			Rio	
Wm. Hamilton	Jn. W. Hallion	4 11 15	Ireland	Rio	152
Magnus Johnson	Alex. Tayler		Ireland		
Walter Meriton	Pat. Hill	23 1 16	P'smouth	Rio	181
Wm. Ostler	Caryer Vickery	4 6 16	England		123
Jn. Herbert	Jn. Haslam	? 6 16	England	Cape	
Thos. Raine	Jn. F. Bayley	14 7 16	Cork	Rio	159
Thackray Wetherell	Dan. McNamara	15 9 16	England		162
Hy. Dale	Jn. Mortimer	9 10 16	Spithead		150
Lew. E. Williams	Wm. Evans		England	Cape	
Rbt. R. Brown	Rbt. Espie	18 12 16	England	Cape	113
Lew. W. Moncrief	Geo. W. Clayton	18 12 16	England	Direct	127
Jn. Drake	Alex. Dewar	14 3 17	Cork		134
Wm. Pexton	Chas. Queade	9 3 17	Cork	Rio	142
Jn. Grigg	Jas. Allan	21 3 17	Cork	Rio	138
Wm. McKissock	Ed. F. Bromley	26 4 17	Downs	Rio	125
Jas. T. Lamb	Jas. Bowman	9 4 17	England	Mad., Rio	174
Hy. R. Wilkinson	Wm. McDonald	20 7 17	P'smouth	Direct	125
Sam. Remmington	Geo. Fairfowl	21 8 17	Spithead	St. H.	142
And. Armet	Ptr. Cosgreave	3 7 17	England		195

Date of Arrival	*Vessel*	*R.*	*Ton*	*Built at*	*Year*	*C*	*D*
1 Apr.	*Guildford* (3)	S.	521	Thames	1810	1	2
5 Apr.	*Batavia*	S.	566	Topsham	1802	2	3
30 Apr.	*Lady Castlereagh*	S.	842	Thames	1802	2	2
30 Apr.	*Minerva I* (1)	S.	530	Lancaster	1804	2	3
5 May	*Neptune I* (1)	S.	477	Whitby	1810	2	2
14 Sept.	*Glory*	S.	399	Quebec	1811	1	2
14 Sept.	*Isabella I* (1)	S.	579	Thames	1818	1	2
17 Sept.	*Maria I*(1)	S.	427	Gainsborough	1798	2	2
14 Oct.	*Tottenham*	S.	557	Stockton	1802	2	3
7 Nov.	*Morley* (2)	S.	480	Thames	1811	1	2
18 Nov.	*Shipley* (2)	S.	381	Whitby	1805	2	2
19 Nov.	*Elizabeth I* (2)	S.	482	Chepstow	1809	1	2
16 Dec.	*Earl St. Vincent* (1)	S.	412	Topsham	1800	2	2
24 Dec.	*Hadlow* (1)	S.	372	Quebec	1813	1	2
24 Dec.	*Martha*	S.	410	Quebec	1810	1	2
31 Dec.	*General Stewart*	S.	635	Thames	1801	2	2
1819							
4 Jan.	*Tyne*	S.	486	Thames	1806	2	2
8 Jan.	*Globe*	S.	363	Scarborough	1810	1	2
4 Mar.	*Surrey I* (3)	S.	443	Harwich	1811	1	3
11 Mar.	*Lord Sidmouth* (1)	S.	411	Shields	1817	1	2
26 June	*Baring* (2)	S.	842	Thames	1801	2	3
25 Aug.	*Bencoolen*	S.	416	Liverpool	1818	1	3
26 Aug.	*Mary I*	S.	405	Bideford	1811	1	
1 Sept.	*Canada* (5)	S.	393	Shields	1800	2	2
21 Sept.	*Daphne*	S.	553	Topsham	1806	2	2
26 Sept.	*John Barry* (1)	S.	520	Whitby	1814	1	2
19 Oct.	*Atlas I* (2)	S.	437	Shields	1801	2	2
21 Oct.	*Grenada* (1)	S.	408	Hull	1810	2	2
30 Oct.	*Malabar* (1)	S.	525	Shields	1804	2	2
18 Dec.	*Recovery* (1)	S.	493	Batavia	1799	2	2
17 Dec.	*Minerva I* (2)	S.	530	Lancaster	1804	2	3
1820							
20 Jan.	*Lord Wellington*	S.	399	Chatham	1810	1	2
21 Jan.	*Eliza I* (1)	S.	511	India	1806	2	2
27 Jan.	*Prince Regent I* (1)	S.	527	Shields	1810	1	2
27 Jan.	*Castle Forbes* (1)	S.	439	Aberdeen	1818	1	2
28 Jan.	*Dromedary*	HMSt.					
4 Apr.	*Coromandel*	HMSt.					
3 May	*Janus*	S.	308	New York	1810	1	2
16 July	*Neptune I* (2)	S.	477	Whitby	1810	2	2
5 Aug.	*Hadlow* (2)	S.	372	Quebec	1813	1	2
7 Aug.	*Mangles* (1)	S.	594	Bengal	1802	2	2
16 Aug.	*Earl St. Vincent* (2)	S.	412	Topsham	1800	2	2
19 Sept.	*Dorothy*	S.	416	Liverpool	1815	1	3
22 Sept.	*Agamemnon*	S.	542	Sunderland	1811	1	
26 Sept.	*Shipley* (3)	S.	381	Whitby	1805	2	2
30 Sept.	*Guildford* (4)	S.	521	Thames	1810	1	2
30 Sept.	*Morley* (3)	S.	492	Thames	1811	1	2
22 Dec.	*Almorah* (2)	S.	416	Selby	1817	1	2
28 Dec.	*Asia I* (1)	S.	532	Aberdeen	1819	1	2

Master	Surgeon	Sailed	From	Route	Days
Magnus Johnson	Arch. Hume	14 11 17	Cork	Rio	138
Wm. B. Lamb	Jas. Billing	1 11 17	Plymouth	Madeira	155
Geo. Weltden	Jas. Craigie	22 12 17	England		129
Jn. Bell	Jas. Hunter	1 1 18	Ireland		119
Rbt. Carns	Thos. Reid	20 12 17	Downs	Cape	136
Ed. Pounder	Wm. Stewart		England	Direct	
Rbt. Berry	Jn. W. Hallion	3 4 18	Spithead	Rio	164
Hy. Williams	Thos. Prosser	15 5 18	Deal	Direct	125
Dugald McDougall	Rbt. Armstrong	27 3 18	Spithead		201
Rbt. R. Brown	Jn. Whitmarsh	18 7 18	Downs	Direct	112
Lew. W. Moncrief	Rbt. Espie	18 7 18	Woolwich	Direct	123
Wm. Ostler	Wm. Hamilton	26 7 18	Cork		116
Sam. Simpson	Jn. Johnston	7 8 18	Cork	Direct	131
Jn. Craigie	Thos. C. Roylance		England	Cape	
Jn. Apsey	Morgan Price	18 8 18	Cork		128
Rbt. Granger	And. Smith	19 7 18	P'smouth	St. H.	165
Cassey Bell	Hy. Ryan		Ireland		
Jos. Blyth	Geo. Clayton		P'smouth	Madeira	
Thos. Raine	Matt. Anderson	29 9 18	Sheerness	Rio	156
Wm. Gunner	Arch. Lang	20 9 18	Sheerness	Rio	172
Jn. Lamb	Dav. Reid	27 1 19	Downs	Mad., Hobt.	150
Jos. B. Anstice	Wm. Evans	24 4 19	Cork		123
Jn. Lusk	J. Morgan	25 5 19	Cork		123
Alex. Spain	Dan. McNamara	23 4 19	London	Rio	131
Hugh Mattison	Rbt. Armstrong	28 5 19	Cork	Ten.	116
Stephenson Ellerby	Jas. Bowman	30 4 19	P'smouth	Rio	149
Jos. Short	Jn. Duke	10 6 19	Gravesend	Cape	131
And. Donald	Eman. Lazzaretto	8 5 19	England	Rio	166
Wm. Ascough	Evan Evans	17 6 19	Spithead	Rio	135
Wm. Fotherly	Ptr. Cunningham	31 7 19	Woolwich	Direct	139
Jn. Bell	Chas. Queade	26 8 19	Cork	Direct	113
Lew. Hill	Ed. F. Bromley		Ireland	Rio	
Fran. Hunt	Jas. M. Brydone	15 or 16 10 19	England	Direct	97 or 98
Wm. Anderson	Jas. Hunter		England		
Thos. Reid	Jas. Scott	3 10 19	Cork		116
Capt. Rchd. Skinner, R.N.	Geo. Fairfowl	11 9 19	England	Hobart	139
Capt. Jas. Downie, R.N.	Arch. Hume	1 11 19	Spithead	Hobart	154
Thos. J. Mowat	Jas. Creagh*	5 12 19	Cork	Rio	150
Wm. McKissock	Jas. Mitchell	23 3 20	Downs	Direct	114
Jn. Craigie	Morgan Price	2 4 20	Cork		125
Jn. Cogill	Matt. Anderson	11 4 20	Falmouth	Direct	118
Sam Simpson	Pat. Hill	12 4 20	P'smouth		126
Jn. Hargraves	Rbt. Espie	5 5 20	Cork	Rio	137
Rbt. Surtees	Jas. Hall	3 5 20	P'smouth	Rio	142
Lew. W. Moncrief	Hy. Ryan	5 6 20	Downs		113
Magnus Johnson	Hugh Walker	14 5 20	P'smouth	Cape	139
Rbt. R. Brown	Thos. Reid	22 5 20	London	Hobart	131
Thos. Winter	Sam. Alexander	22 8 20	Waterford		122
Jas. Morice	Wm. B. Carlyle	3 9 20	England		116

Date of Arrival	*Vessel*	*R.*	*Ton*	*Built at*	*Year*	*C*	*D*
31 Dec.	*Elizabeth I* (3)	S.	482	Chepstow	1809	2	2
31 Dec.	*Hebe*	S.	434	Hull	1809	2	2
1821							
9 Jan.	*Prince Regent II* (1)	S.	383	Rochester	1811	1	2
12 Feb.	*Prince of Orange* (1)	S.	359	Sunderland	1813	1	2
19 Feb.	*Lord Sidmouth* (2)	S.	411	Shields	1817	1	2
12 Mar.	*Dick*	S.	398	Thames	1788	2	3
18 May	*Speke* (2)	S.	473	Calcutta	1790	2	2
8 Sept.	*Adamant*	S.	427	Blythe	1811	1	2
16 Sept.	*Grenada* (2)	S.	408	Hull	1810	2	2
7 Nov.	*John Barry* (2)	S.	520	Whitby	1814	1	2
24 Nov.	*Hindostan* (1)	S.	424	Whitby	1819	1	2
16 Dec.	*Minerva I* (3)	S.	530	Lancaster	1804	2	3
18 Dec.	*John Bull*	S.	464	Liverpool	1799	2	3
1822							
7 Jan.	*Providence II* (1)	S.	380	Lynn	1812	1	1
23 Jan.	*Mary II*	S.	547	Calcutta	1813	1	2
9 Mar.	*Southworth* (1)	S.	350	Chester	1821	1	2
9 Mar.	*Isabella I* (2)	S.	579	Thames	1818	1	2
11 Mar.	*Shipley* (4)	S.	381	Whitby	1805	1	2
20 May	*Mary Anne I* (2)	S.	479	Batavia	1807	2	2
15 July	*Guildford* (5)	S.	521	Thames	1810	1	2
24 July	*Asia I* (2)	S.	532	Aberdeen	1819	1	2
8 Nov.	*Mangles* (2)	S.	594	Bengal	1802	2	2
22 Nov.	*Eliza I* (2)	S.	511	India	1806	2	2
21 Dec.	*Countess of Harcourt* (2)	S.	517	India	1811	1	2
1823							
27 Feb.	*Lord Sidmouth* (3)	S.	411	Shields	1817	1	2
4 Mar.	*Surrey I* (4)	S.	443	Harwich	1811	1	3
9 Mar.	*Princess Royal* (1)	S.	402	Yarmouth	1794	2	1
22 Apr.	*Brampton*	S.	432	Lynn	1817	1	3
25 June	*Woodman* (1)	S.	419	Gainsborough	1808	2	2
30 July	*Recovery* (2)	S.	493	Batavia	1799	2	2
26 Aug.	*Henry* (1)	S.	386	Quebec	1819	1	1
27 Aug.	*Ocean II* (2)	S.	437	Whitby	1808		2
9 Sept.	*Earl St. Vincent* (3)	S.	412	Topsham	1800	2	2
18 Oct.	*Mary III* (1)	S.	361	Ipswich	1811	2	2
16 Dec.	*Isabella I* (3)	S.	579	Thames	1818	1	2
29 Dec.	*Medina* (1)	S.	467	Topsham	1811	2	2
1824						*Class*	
15 Jan.	*Castle Forbes* (2)	S.	439	Aberdeen	1818		
5 Mar.	*Guildford* (6)	S.	521	Thames	1810		
7 May	*Brothers* (1)	S.	425	Whitby	1815	A1	
12 July	*Countess of Harcourt* (3)	S.	517	India	1811	E1	
15 July	*Prince Regent I* (2)	S.	527	Shields	1810		
20 Aug.	*Almorah* (3)	S.	416	Selby	1817		
27 Oct.	*Mangles* (3)	S.	594	Bengal	1802	E1	
19 Nov.	*Minerva I* (4)	S.	530	Lancaster	1804		
1825							
2 Jan.	*Ann and Amelia*	S.	553	India	1816	E1	

Master	*Surgeon*	*Sailed*	*From*	*Route*	*Days*
Wm. Ostler	And. Montgomery	18 8 20	Downs	Rio	135
Thackray Wetherell	Chas. Carter	31 7 20	England		153
Fran. Clifford	Alex. Tayler	19 9 20	Cork		112
Thos. Silk	Geo. S. Ruther				
	ford	8 10 20	Downs		127
Jas. Muddle	Thos. C. Roylance	4 11 20	Cork		107
Wm. Harrison	Rbt. Armstrong	4 11 20	England		128
Ptr. McPherson	Ed. Coates	22 12 20	England		147
Wm. Ebsworthy	Jas. Hamilton	29 3 21	England		163
And. Donald	Ptr. Cunningham	9 5 21	P'smouth	Ten.	130
Roger Dobson	Dan McNamara	16 6 21	Cork	Rio	144
Wm. Williamson	Wm. Evans	29 7 21	P'smouth		118
Jn. Bell	Chas. Queade	1 8 21	Downs	Direct	137
Wm. Corlett	Wm. Elyard	25 7 21	Cork	St. Jago	146
Jas. Herd	Dav. Reid	13 6 21	England	Pt. Py., Rio, Hobart	208
Chas. Arcoll	Jn. Rodmell	5 9 21	P'smouth		140
Dav. Sampson	Jos. Cook	18 11 21	Cork	Ten.	111
Jn. Wallis	W. Price	4 11 21	Cork	Direct	125
Lew. W. Moncrief	Geo. S. Ruther				
	ford	7 11 21	London	Direct	124
Hy. Warington	Jas. Hall	25 12 21	P'smouth	Rio, Hob.	146
Magnus Johnson	Jas. Mitchell	7 4 22	London	Ten.	99
Thos. L. Reid	Jas. A. Mercer	4 4 22	England	Direct	111
Jn. Cogill	Matt. Anderson	21 6 22	Cork	Rio	140
Jas. Hunt	Wm. Rae	20 7 22	Sheerness		125
Geo. Bunn	Rbt. Armstrong	3 9 22	Cork		109
Jas. Ferrier	Rbt. Espie	11 9 22	Woolwich	Rio, Hob.	169
Thos. Raine	Chas. Linton	5 10 22	P'smouth	Direct	150
Hy Sherwood	Jas. Hunter	5 11 22	England		124
Sam. Moore	Morgan Price	8 11 22	Cork	Cape	165
Hy. Ford	Geo. Fairfowl	25 1 23	Cork	Rio	151
Wm. Fotherly	Ptr. Cunningham	5 4 23	Cork		116
Thos. Thatcher	Thos. Davies	28 4 23	London		120
Wm. Harrison	Jas. McTernan	24 4 23	P'smouth		125
Ptr. John Reeves	Rbt. Tainsh	29 4 23	Cork	Rio	133
J. F. Steel	Harman Cochrane	10 6 23	London	Hobart	130
Jn. Wallis	Wm. Rae		Ireland		
Rbt. Brown	Jn. Rodmell	5 9 23	Cork		115
Jn. W. Ord	Matt. Anderson	28 9 23	Cork	Direct	109
Magnus Johnson	Jas. Mitchell	28 8 23	P'smouth	Ten., Rio	190
Chas. Motley	Jas. Hall	6 12 23	Downs	Hobart	153
Geo. Bunn	Jas. Dickson	23 3 24	Downs	Direct	111
Alex. Wales	Thos. B. Wilson	13 2 24	Cork	Rio	153
Geo. Hay Boyd	Morgan Price	6 4 24	Cork	Direct	136
Jn. Cogill	Jn. Crocket	13 7 24	P'smouth	Ten.	106
Jn. Bell	Alex. Nisbet	14 7 24	London	Cape	128
Wm. Ascough	Jas. Lawrence	8 9 24	Cork		116

Date of Arrival	Vessel	R.	Ton	Built at	Year	Class
23 Jan.	*Grenada* (3)	S.	408	Hull	1810	E1
22 Feb.	*Asia I* (3)	S.	532	Aberdeen	1819	A1
27 Feb.	*Henry* (2)	S.	386	Quebec	1819	A1
22 Apr.	*Hooghly* (1)	S.	466	London	1819	A1
29 Apr.	*Royal Charlotte*	S.	471			
29 Apr.	*Asia III*	S.	492	Bombay		E1
7 May	*Hercules II* (1)	S.	482	Whitby	1822	A1
10 July	*Mariner* (2)	S.	449	Whitby	1807	E1
18 Aug.	*Norfolk* (1)	S.	537	Littlehampton	1814	
22 Aug.	*Minstrel* (2)	S.	351	Hull	1810	E1
4 Sept.	*Lonach*	S.	391	Littlehampton	1817	
3 Dec.	*Henry Porcher* (1)	S.	485	Bristol	1817	A1
17 Dec.	*Midas* (1)	S.	430	Hull	1809	E1
1826						
3 Jan.	*Marquis of Hastings* (1)	S.	452	London	1819	A1
3 Jan.	*Sir Godfrey Webster* (2)	S.	548	Thames	1799	E1
18 Feb.	*Mangles* (4)	S.	594	Bengal	1802	E1
21 Mar.	*Sesostris*	S.	487	Hull	1817	A1
17 May	*Lady Rowena*	S.	320	Montreal	1825	A1
5 Aug.	*Regalia*	S.		Sunderland		
13 Sept.	*Marquis of Huntley* (1)	S.	564	Aberdeen	1804	E1
18 Sept.	*England* (1)	S.	425	Chepstow	1814	E1
28 Oct.	*Boyne*	S.	620	Calcutta	1816	
26 Nov.	*Speke II*	S.	473	Calcutta	1790	E1
25 Dec.	*Phoenix III*	S.	500	Topsham	1810	E1
1827						
23 Jan.	*Grenada* (4)	S.	408	Hull	1810	E1
2 Feb.	*Brothers* (2)	S.	425	Whitby	1815	E1
14 Feb.	*Albion* (2)	S.	479	Bristol	1813	E1
15 Feb.	*Midas* (2)	S.	430	Hull	1809	E1
23 May	*Mariner* (3)	S.	449	Whitby	1807	E1
28 June	*Countess of Harcourt* (4)	S.	517	India	1811	E1
25 July	*Guildford* (7)	S.	533	Thames	1810	E1
31 July	*Marquis of Hastings* (2)	S.	452	London	1819	A1
6 Aug.	*Princess Charlotte* 2)	S.	400	Sunderland	1812	E1
11 Aug.	*Manlius* (1)	S.	479	Quebec	1825	A1
17 Sept.	*Cambridge*	S.	533	Pr. Edw. Is.	1824	A1
27 Sept.	*Harmony* (1)	S.	373	St. John's	1818	E1
27 Sept.	*Prince Regent I* (3)	S.	527	Shields	1810	E
17 Oct.	*Champion*	S.	394	New Brunsw'k	1824	A1
8 Nov.	*Eliza II* (1)	S.	538	India	1806	E
25 Nov.	*John I* (1)	S.	464	Chester	1810	E1
3 Dec.	*Louisa*	S.	407	Workington	1810	E1
1828						
3 Jan.	*Florentia* (1)	S.	453	Newcastle	1821	A1
12 Jan.	*Elizabeth II*	S.	527	Calcutta	1816	
30 Jan.	*Marquis of Huntley* (2)	S.	564	Aberdeen	1804	E1
24 Feb.	*Hooghly* (2)	S.	466	London	1819	A1
3 Mar.	*Morley* (5)	S.	492	Thames	1811	E1
13 Mar.	*Asia I* (4)	S.	536	Aberdeen	1819	A1

Master	*Surgeon*	*Sailed*	*From*	*Route*	*Days*
Alex. Anderson	Ptr. Cunningham	2 10 24	London	Ten.	113
Thos. F. Stead	Jas. A. Mercer	29 10 24	Cork	Direct	116
Jas. Ferrier	Wm. B. Carlyle	12 10 24	London	St. Jago, Hobart	138
Ptr. J. Reeves	Rbt. Tainsh	5 1 25	Cork	Rio	107
Corbyn	Geo. Fairfowl	5 1 25	P'smouth	Ten.	114
Wm. L. Pope	Thos. Davies	6 1 25	P'smouth		113
Wm. Vaughan	Michael Goodsir	29 12 24	P'smouth		129
Wm. Fotherly	Harman Cochrane	12 3 25	Cork		120
Alex. Greig	Wm. Hamilton	17 4 25	P'smouth	Direct	123
Chas. Arcoll	Hugh Walker	17 4 25	P'smouth	Direct	127
Wm. H. Driscoll	Alick Osborne	16 5 25	Cork		111
Jn. Thomson	Chas. Carter	5 8 25	Dublin		120
Jas. Baigrie	Chas. Cameron	24 7 25	London	St. Jago, Hobart	146
Wm. Ostler	Geo. S. Rutherford	22 8 25	P'smouth	Rio	134
Jn. Rennoldson	Wm. Evans	11 7 25	Cork	Ten., Cape	176
Jn. Cogill	Thos. B. Wilson	23 10 25	Cork		118
J. T. Drake	Jn. Dulhunty	30 11 25	P'smouth	Direct	111
Boum Russell	Rbt. Espie	19 1 26	Cork	Direct	118
Rbt. Burt	Jas. Rutherford	16 3 26	Dublin	Rio	142
Wm. Ascough	Wm. Rae	16 5 26	Sheerness		120
Jn. Reay	Geo. Thomson	6 5 26	Downs	Direct	135
Wm. L. Pope	Harman Cochrane	29 6 26	Cork		121
Rbt. Harrison	Alick Osborne	8 8 26	Sheerness	Direct	110
Alex. Anderson	Jos. Cook	27 8 26	Dublin		120
Jn. Tracy	Alex. Nisbet	8 9 26	Downs	Hobart	137
Chas. Motley	Jas. Forrester	3 10 26	Cork		122
Jas. Ralph	Walk	4 10 26	Plymouth		133
Jas. Baigrie	Jas. Morice	16 10 26	Plymouth		122
Rbt. Nosworthy	Pat. McTernan	14 1 27	Cork	Cape	129
Wm. Harrison	Michael Goodsir	14 2 27	Dublin	St. Jago	134
Magnus Johnson	Chas. Linton	31 3 27	Plymouth	Ten.	116
Jn. Jeffrey Drake	Gilbert King	18 4 27	P'smouth	Ten.	104
Dan. Stephenson	Chas. Cameron	31 3 27	Woolwich		128
Wm. Johnson	Dav. B. Conway	17 4 27	Downs		116
Rchd. Pearce	Wm. Gregor	2 6 27	Dublin		107
Rchd. D. Middleton	Wm. McDowell	4 6 27	London		115
Wm. Richards	Wm. Rae	11 6 27	Deal	Ten.	108
Hy. Lock	Fran. Logan	3 6 27	London	Cape	136
Dan. Leary	Geo. S. Rutherford	19 7 27	Cork	Direct	112
Wm. Jn. Moncrief	Jas. McKerrow*	22 7 27	London	Direct	126
Aaron Smith	Jos. Cook	24 8 27	Woolwich		101
J. T. Billett	Jas. Dickson	15 9 27	England		110
Walt. Cock	Jos. H. Hughes	27 8 27	Cork		138
Wm. Ascough	Jn. Smith	27 9 27	Cork	Cape	125
Ptr. J. Reeves	Alex. Nisbet	5 11 27	London		111
Hy. Williams	Ptr. Cunningham	3 11 27	Dublin	Ten.	121
Thos. F. Stead	Jas. McTernan	23 11 27	London		111

Date of Arrival	*Vessel*	*R.*	*Ton*	*Built at*	*Year*	*Class*
2 June	*Mangles* (5)	S.	594	Bengal	1802	E1
12 July	*Borodino*	S.	615	Thames	1810	E1
14 July	*Phoenix I* (2)	S.	493	Topsham	1810	E1
26 July	*Bussorah Merchant* (1)	S.	530	Calcutta	1818	A1
8 Sept.	*Countess of Harcourt* (5)	S.	517	India	1811	E1
10 Oct.	*Competitor* (2)	S.	425	Whitby	1813	E1
12 Oct.	*Marquis of Hastings* (3)	S.	452	London	1819	A1
3 Nov.	*Albion* (3)	S.	479	Bristol	1813	E
12 Nov.	*City of Edinburgh* (1)	S.	366	Corina	1813	E1
18 Nov.	*Eliza III* (1)	S.	391	Java	1815	E1
24 Dec.	*Royal George* (1)	S.	486	Hull	1820	E1
1829						
16 Jan.	*Governor Ready* (2)	S.	512	Pr. Edw. Is.	1825	
17 Jan.	*Vittoria*	S.	395	Gnsbr.	1813	E1
17 Jan.	*Sophia*	S.	537	Calcutta	1819	E1
26 Mar.	*Fergusson*	S.	554	Calcutta	1821	A1
18 Apr.	*Mellish* (1)	S.	424	Calcutta	1820	A1
26 Apr.	*Edward* (1)	Bk.	406	Bristol	1806	E1
6 May	*Lord Melville II* (1)	S.	425	Quebec	1825	A1
9 May	*Princess Royal* (2)	S.	402	Yarmouth	1794	E1
20 June	*Eliza II* (2)	S.	538	India	1806	E1
9 July	*Waterloo* (1)	S.	414	Bristol	1815	E1
3 Aug.	*Sovereign* (2)	S.	398	Hull	1814	E1
18 Aug.	*America* (1)	S.	391	Quebec	1827	
27 Aug.	*Norfolk* (2)	Bk.	537	Littlehampton	1814	E1
13 Sept.	*John I* (2)	S.	464	Chester	1810	
4 Nov.	*Guildford* (8)	S.	553	Thames	1810	E1
8 Nov.	*Layton I* (2)	S.	490	Lancaster	1814	E1
29 Nov.	*Lucy Davidson*	S.	363	Southampton	1818	E1
3 Dec.	*Morley* (6)	S.	492	Thames	1811	E1
6 Dec.	*Claudine* (2)	S.	452	Calcutta	1811	E1
7 Dec.	*Sarah* (1)	S.	488	London	1819	E1
12 Dec.	*Larkins* (2)	S.	647	Calcutta	1808	E1
1830						
13 Jan.	*Asia I* (5)	S.	536	Aberdeen	1819	E1
20 Jan.	*James Pattison* (1)	S.	513	London	1828	A1
18 Feb.	*Katherine Stewart Forbes* (1)	S.	457	Northfleet	1818	E1
30 Mar.	*Dunvegan Castle* (1)	S.	446	Chittagong	1819	E
26 Apr.	*Forth I*	S.	397	Calcutta	1814	E1
6 May	*Mermaid* (2)	S.	472	Calcutta	1817	E1
12 May	*Nithsdale*	S.	414	St. John's	1826	E1
29 June	*Roslin Castle* (2)	S.	450	Bristol	1819	E1
29 July	*Lady Feversham*	S.	430	Whitby	1826	A1
20 Aug.	*Adrian*	Bk.	373	Newcastle	1818	E1
21 Aug.	*Marquis of Huntley* (3)	Bk.	564	Aberdeen	1804	E1
12 Oct.	*Forth II*	Bk.	369	Leith	1826	A1
21 Oct.	*Lord Melville* (2)	S.	425	Quebec	1825	A1
1 Nov.	*Hercules II* (2)	S.	482	Whitby	1822	A1
8 Nov.	*Royal Admiral* (1)	S.	414	Lynn	1828	A1
15 Dec.	*Florentia* (2)	S.	453	Newcastle	1821	E1
18 Dec.	*Andromeda II* (1)	S.	408	Sunderland	1819	E

Master	Surgeon	Sailed	From	Route	Days
Wm. Carr	Harman Cochrane	23 2 28	Dublin		100
Rchd. Mentrup	Geo. Thomson	11 2 28	Cork	Lisbon	152
Thos. Cuzens	Wm. B. Carlyle	7 3 28	Spithead		129
Jas. Baigrie	Rbt. Dunn	27 3 28	London		121
Wm. Harrison	Jn. Drummond	3 5 28	London	St. Jago	128
Jn. Steward	Thos. Hunter	13 6 28	London		119
Jn. Jeffrey Drake	Wm. Rae	30 6 28	London	Ten.	104
Jas. Ralph	Thos. Logan	1 6 28	Sheerness	Cape	155
Jas. R. Clendon	Wm. Anderson	23 6 28	Cork	Direct	142
Wm. Doutty	Jas. Patton	29 6 28	London	Ten.	142
Rbt. Embledon	Wm. Gregor	26 8 28	Spithead		120
Jn. Young	Thos. B. Wilson	21 9 28	Cork		117
Jn. Smith	Jas. Dickson	1 9 28	Devonport	Ten.	138
Thos. A. Elley	Alick Osborne	15 9 28	Dublin		124
Jn. S. Groves	Chas. Cameron	16 11 28	Dublin		130
Arthur Vincent	Jos. Cook	2 1 29	Falmouth	Ten.	106
Jas. Gilbert	Wm. C. Watt	1 1 29	Cork	St. Jago	115
Rbt. Brown	Geo. S. Rutherford	5 1 29	London		121
Hy. Sherwood	And. D. Wilson	6 1 29	London		123
Wm. Nicholas	Jas. McTernan	2 3 29	Cork		110
Steph. Addison	Michael Goodsir	14 3 29	London		117
Wm. McKellar	Geo. Fairfowl	23 4 29	Downs		102
Rbt. S. Donal	Alex. Stewart	8 4 29	Woolwich		132
Alex. Greig	Jas. Dickson	22 5 29	Spithead		97
Rbt. B. Norsworthy	Jn. Love	27 5 29	Sheerness		109
Rbt. Harrison	Jn. Stephenson	12 7 29	Dublin		115
Jn. W. Hurst	Jas. Osborne	23 6 29	London		138
Wm. Wiseman	Jn. Osborne	20 7 29	London		132
Wm. Harrison	Rchd. Lewis	11 8 29	London		114
Wm. Heathorn	Wm. H. Trotman	24 8 29	London		104
Hy. C. Columbine	Alick Osborne	29 8 29	London	T. d'A., St. P. Is.	100
Wm. Campbell	Oliver Sproule	16 8 29	Cork		128
Thos. F. Stead	Alex. Nisbet	10 9 29	Cork		125
Jos. Grote	Jas. Gilchrist	2 10 29	Dublin		110
Thos. Canney	Pat. McTernan	14 10 29	Spithead		127
Wm. T. Walmsley	Rbt. Dunn	30 9 29	Sheerness	Hobart	181
Dav. Proodfoot	Wm. Clifford	1 1 30	Cork		115
Wm. Henniker	Dav. Boyter	5 12 29	Sheerness	Bahia	152
Thos. Christian	Rbt. Malcolm	1 1 30	Sheerness		131
Hy. Ferguson	Wm. C. Watt	3 3 30	Downs		118
Stephenson Ellerby	And. D. Wilson	8 4 30	P'smouth		112
Wm. Sadler	G. H. Weatherhead	27 4 30	P'smouth	Ten.	115
Wm. Ascough	Wm. B. Carlyle	9 4 30	Sheerness		134
Jas. Robertson	Jos. Cook	3 6 30	Cork	Direct	131
Rbt. Brown	Geo. Roberts	6 6 30	Downs		137
Wm. Vaughan	Wm. Martin	3 7 30	Dublin		121
Dav. Fotheringham	Geo. S. Rutherford	5 7 30	P'smouth		126
Jn. Jeffrey Drake	And. Henderson	16 8 30	Ireland		121
Rbt. Parkin	Geo. Fairfowl	28 8 30	Cork		112

Date of Arrival	*Vessel*	*R.*	*Ton*	*Built at*	*Year*	*Class*
19 Dec.	*Burrell* (1)	S.	402	Newcastle	1825	A1
1831						
7 Feb.	*York I* (2)	S.	429	Southwick	1819	E1
22 Feb.	*Edward* (2)	S.	406	Bristol	1806	E1
4 Mar.	*Lady Harewood* (2)	S.	429	Thames	1791	E1
11 Mar.	*Kains*	S.	353	Shields	1818	E1
5 Apr.	*Earl of Liverpool*	Bg.	229	Lynn	1826	A1
30 Apr.	*Waterloo* (2)	S.	414	Bristol	1815	E1
25 June	*Eleanor*	Bk.	301	Calcutta	1821	
25 July	*Camden* (1)	S.	450	Thames	1799	E1
27 July	*Georgiana I* (2)	S.	404	Quebec	1826	A1
28 July	*Exmouth*	S.	723	Calcutta	1815	E1
31 July	*Palambam*	S.	394	Shields	1821	
27 Sept.	*Hooghly* (3)	S.	466	London	1819	
5 Nov.	*Jane I*	S.	350	Calcutta	1822	A1
26 Nov.	*Surrey I* (6)	S.	461	Harwich	1811	E1
2 Dec.	*Asia V* (2)	S.	523	Calcutta	1814	E1
14 Dec.	*Bussorah Merchant* (3)	S.	530	Calcutta	1818	E1
1832						
9 Feb.	*Norfolk* (3)	Bk.	537	Littlehampton	1814	E1
13 Feb.	*Asia I* (6)	S.	536	Aberdeen	1819	E1
5 Mar.	*Pyramus* (1)	Bk.	362	Sunderland	1822	A1
15 Mar.	*Isabella I* (4)	S.	579	London	1818	E1
26 Mar.	*Portland* (1)	S.	385	Bristol	1822	E1
2 Apr.	*Captain Cook* (1)	S.	452	Whitby	1826	A1
20 May	*Burrell* (2)	S.	402	Newcastle	1825	A1
8 June	*John I* (4)	S.	464	Chester	1810	E1
14 June	*Southworth* (3)	S.	350	Chester	1821	E1
27 June	*City of Edinburgh* (2)	Bk.	366	Corina	1813	E1
5 Aug.	*Lady Harewood* (3)	S.	429	Thames	1791	E1
27 Aug.	*Clyde I* (2)	S.	490	Greenock	1819	E1
6 Sept.	*Eliza II* (4)	S.	538	India	1806	E1
15 Oct.	*Planter* (1)	S.	367	Lynn	1829	A1
16 Oct.	*Hercules II* (3)	S.	482	Whitby	1822	E1
16 Oct.	*Dunvegan Castle* (2)	S.	446	Chittagong	1819	E1
16 Nov.	*Parmelia* (1)	Bk.	443	Quebec	1825	A1
1833						
5 Jan.	*Mary III* (4)	Bk.	370	Ipswich	1811	E1
2 Feb.	*Fanny II*	Bk.	275	Calcutta	1829	A1
5 Feb.	*Roslin Castle* (3)	Bk.	450	Bristol	1819	E1
18 Feb.	*Camden* (2)	S.	450	Thames	1799	E1
9 Mar.	*Surrey II*	Bk.	363	Quebec	1825	A1
11 Mar.	*Andromeda II* (2)	S.	408	Sunderland	1819	E1
19 Apr.	*Mangles* (6)	S.	594	Bengal	1802	E1
25 May	*Diana*	Bk.	320	Whitby	1824	A1
26 June	*Portland* (2)	S.	385	Bristol	1822	E1
27 June	*Asia I* (7)	S.	536	Aberdeen	1819	E1
3 Aug.	*Waterloo* (3)	S.	414	Bristol	1815	E1
6 Aug.	*Caroline*	S.	329	Cochin	1825	A1
26 Aug.	*Captain Cook* (2)	S.	452	Whitby	1826	A1
19 Sept.	*Heroine*	S.	599	Calcutta	1817	E1

Master	*Surgeon*	*Sailed*	*From*	*Route*	*Days*
Jn. Metcalf	Wm. West	27 7 30	Plymouth		145
Dan. Leary	Campbell France	4 9 30	Sheerness	Ten.	156
Jas. Gilbert	Thos. Bell	17 10 30	Cork	St. Jago	128
Rchd. W. Stonehouse	Jas. McTernan	17 10 30	Sheerness	Pt. Py.	138
Wm. L. Goodwin	Thrasycles Clarke	8 7 30	London	Ten., Cape	246
F. B. Manning	Dav. Thomson	3 12 30	London		123
Steph. Addison	Wm. H. Trotman	18 12 30	Dublin		133
Rbt. Cock	Jn. Stephenson	19 2 31	P'smouth	Cape	126
Wm. Fulcher	Dav. Boyter	28 3 31	London		119
Jn. S. Thompson	Jn. Tarn	1 4 31	London		117
Dan. Warren	Wm. C. Watt	2 3 31	Woolwich		148
Geo. Willis	Jas. Osborne	23 3 31	Cork		130
Ptr. J. Reeves	Jas. Ellis	24 6 31	Cork	Direct	95
Jas. Baigrie	Oliver Sproule	29 4 31	Cork	Cape	190
Chas. Kemp	Colin A. Browning	17 7 31	P'smouth		132
Hy. Ager	Geo. Birnie	6 8 31	Cork		118
Jn. Moncrief	Jas. Gilchrist	16 8 31	Dublin	Direct	120
Wm. Henniker	Will Clifford	15 10 31	Cork		117
Thos. F. Stead	And. D. Wilson	16 10 31	P'smouth		120
Alex. Wilson	Jas. Rutherford	10 11 31	Cork		116
Wm. Wiseman	Thos. Galloway	27 11 31	Plymouth		109
Wm. Ascough	Jos. Cook	27 11 31	P'smouth		120
Wm. Steward	Eben. Johnston	5 11 31	Dublin		154
Jn. Metcalf	Geo. Williams	8 1 32	Woolwich		133
Sam. J. Lowe	Jas. Lawrence	7 2 32	Downs		122
Jn. J. Coombes	Jas. Forrester	6 2 32	Cork		129
Giles Wade	Ant. Donoghoe	18 3 32	Cork	Direct	101
Rchd. W. Stonehouse	Jn. Inches	15 3 32	P'smouth	St. Jago	143
Dan. N. Munro	Geo. Fairfowl	9 5 32	P'smouth	Direct	110
Jn. S. Groves	Thos. Bell	10 5 32	Cork		119
R. L. Fraser	Alick Osborne	16 6 32	P'smouth		121
Wm. Vaughan	Jn. Edwards	19 6 32	Downs	Direct	119
Jn. Duff	Pat. McTernan	1 7 32	Dublin	Direct	107
Jas. Gilbert	Rchd. Allen	28 7 32	Sheerness	Direct	111
Alex. Jamieson	Wm. C. Watt	4 9 32	London	Direct	123
Hy. Sherwood	Fran. Logan and Wm. B. Marshall	29 7 32	Downs	Cape	188
Wm. Richards	Geo. Imlay	8 10 32	Cork	Direct	120
Geo. T. Clayton	Jos. Steret	22 9 32	Sheerness	Direct	149
Wm. Veale	Ed. F. Bromley	5 11 32	Cork	Direct	124
Ben. Gales	Dav. Boyter	17 11 32	P'smouth	Direct	114
Wm. Carr	Jas. Rutherford	14 12 32	London	Direct	126
Geo. Brathwaite	Jas. Ellis	11 12 32	Woolwich	Cape	165
Wm. Ascough	Chas. Inches	21 2 33	Cork	Lisbon	125
Thos. F. Stead	Thos. Galloway	21 2 33	Downs		126
Jn. Cow	Jn. Stephenson	12 3 33	Sheerness		144
Alex. McDonald	Geo. Birnie	15 4 33	Cork		113
Wm. Thompson	Jn. Morgan	5 5 33	P'smouth	Direct	113
Rbt. McCarthy	Geo. Roberts	14 5 33	P'smouth		128

Date of Arrival	Vessel	R.	Ton	Built at	Year	Class
5 Oct.	*Buffalo*	H.M.S.	600			
18 Oct.	*Lord Lyndoch* (2)	S.	638	Calcutta	1815	E1
26 Oct.	*Royal Admiral* (2)	S.	414	Lynn	1828	A1
3 Nov.	*Aurora I* (1)	S.	550	Chittagong	1817	E1
18 Nov.	*Java*	Bk.	411	Calcutta	1813	
21 Nov.	*Neva* (1)	Bk.	331	Hull	1814	E1
18 Dec.	*Lloyds* (1)	Bk.	403	London	1830	A1
†	*Amphitrite*					
1834						
19 Jan.	*Royal Sovereign* (1)	Bk.	336	Whitby	1829	A1
15 Feb.	*Fairlie* (1)	S.	756	Calcutta	1812	
2 Mar.	*Parmelia* (2)	Bk.	443	Quebec	1825	AE1
11 June	*Hive* (1)	S.	485			
13 June	*Numa*	Bk.	323	Sunderland	1811	
29 June	*James Laing*	Bk.	418	Stockton	1818	
8 July	*Susan* (1)	S.	573	Calcutta	1813	AE1
17 Aug.	*Surrey I* (8)	S.	461	Harwich	1811	AE1
15 Sept.	*Roslin Castle* (4)	S.	450	Bristol	1819	AE1
17 Sept.	*Andromeda II* (3)	S.	408	Sunderland	1819	AE1
26 Oct.	*Henry Tanner*	Bk.	388	Sunderland	1834	A1
14 Nov.	*Blenheim I* (1)	S.	375	Jarrow	1834	A1
18 Nov.	*Hooghly* (4)	S.	466	London	1819	AE1
1 Dec.	*George Hibbert*	Bk.	328	London	1804	AE1
1835						
1 Jan.	*Henry Porcher* (2)	Bk.	485	Bristol	1817	
22 Jan.	*Royal Admiral* (3)	S.	414	Lynn	1828	A1
30 Jan.	*Bengal Merchant* (2)	S.	503	Calcutta	1812	AE1
3 Feb.	*Forth*					
9 Apr.	*Lady Nugent* (1)	S.	535	Bombay	1813	AE1
5 July	*Marquis of Huntley*	Bk.	563	Aberdeen	1804	AE1
15 July	*Westmorland* (1)	Bk.	405	Lynn	1832	A1
31 Aug.	*Hero*	S.	402	Bristol	1823	A1
6 Sept.	*Mary III* (5)	Bk.	365	Ipswich	1811	AE1
28 Sept.	*England* (3)	S.	425	Chepstow	1814	AE1
29 Sept.	*Blackwell*	Bk.	346			
26 Oct.	*Mary Anne II*	S.	587	Calcutta	1817	AE1
26 Oct.	*Lady Macnaghten*	S.	558	Calcutta	1825	A1
12 Dec.	*Royal Sovereign* (2)	Bk.	336	Whitby	1829	A1
†	*Neva* (2)	Bk.	331	Hull	1814	AE1
†	*Hive* (2)	S.	485			
1836						
17 Jan.	*John Barry* (4)	S.	520	Whitby	1814	AE1
7 Feb.	*Susan* (2)	Bk.	573	Calcutta	1813	AE1
7 Feb.	*Henry Wellesley* (1)	Bk.	304	India	1804	AE1
25 Feb.	*Roslin Castle* (5)	S.	450	Bristol	1819	AE1
25 Feb.	*Recovery* (3)	S.	493	Batavia	1799	AE1
17 May	*Surrey I* (9)	S.	461	Harwich	1811	AE1
9 June	*Thomas Harrison*	Bk.	355	Sunderland	1834	A1

Master	*Surgeon*	*Sailed*	*From*	*Route*	*Days*
Cmdr. F. W. N. Sadler	J. M. Hamilton	12 5 33	P'smouth	Rio and K.G.S.	146
Wm. Johnston	Dav. Watson	? 6 33	Sheerness	Rio	
Dav. Fotheringham	And. Henderson	4 6 33	Dublin	Direct	144
Dalrymple Dowson	Alex. Stewart	4 7 33	P'smouth	Direct	122
Jn. Todd	Rbt. Dickson	24 7 33	Cork		117
Ben. H. Peck	Morgan Price	29 7 33	Plymouth	Direct	115
Ed. Garrett	Jn. Inches	25 8 33	Downs		115
*Jn. Hunter	*Jas. Forrester	25 8 33	London		
Jn. Henderson	Ptr. Leonard	6 9 33	Dublin	Direct	135
Hy. Ager	Alick Osborne	27 10 33	England	Direct	111
Jas. Gilbert	Ant. Donoghoe	29 10 33	Cork	Direct	124
Jn. H. Luscombe	Geo. Fairfowl	29 1 34	P'smouth		133
Jn. Baker	Ed. F. Bromley	29 1 34	P'smouth	Cape	135
Geo. Tomlin	*Rchd. Allen	16 2 34	Dublin		133
Steph. Addison	(i) *Jn. Isatt (ii) Arch. G. Ross	10 3 34	London	Madeira	120
Chas. Kemp	Jn. Smith	7 4 34	Plymouth		132
Wm. Richards	Rbt. Espie	27 5 34	London		111
Ben. Gales	Hy. Kelsall	25 5 34	Cork	Direct	115
Hy. Ferguson	Jn. Edwards	1 7 34	London		117
Jas. Temple Brown	Jas. Wilson	27 7 34	Cork		110
Geo. Bayly	Jas. Rutherford	28 7 34	P'smouth		113
Geo. N. Livesay	Jn. Tarn	27 7 34	Downs		127
Jn. Hart	Thos. Galloway	4 9 34	Downs	Direct	119
Dav. Fotheringham	Jas. Osborne	27 9 34	Dublin	Direct	117
Wm. Campbell	Jas. Ellis	1 10 34	London	Direct	121
Hy. Hutton	Thos. Robertson	21 10 34	Cork	Direct	105
Jos. H. Fawcett	Oliver Sproule	4 12 34	Sheerness	Direct	126
A. L. Molison	Alick Osborne	27 3 35	Downs	Direct	100
Jn. Brigstock	Chas. Inches	9 3 35	London	St. Jago	128
Hy. C. Dowson	Dav. Boyter	15 3 35	Dublin	Rio and K.G.S.	169
Wm. Ascough	Jn. Inches	16 4 35	London	Direct	143
Thos. Bacon	Obediah Pineo	8 6 35	P'smouth		112
Dalrymple Dowson	Jn. Love	12 6 35	Cork	Direct	109
Aaron Smith	Campbell France	9 7 35	Sheerness		109
Geo. Hustwick	Geo. E. Forman	23 6 35	Dublin		125
Jn. Moncrief	Fran. Logan	29 7 35	England	Ascension	136
Ben. H. Peck	*Jn. Stephenson	8 1 35	Cork		
Jn. T. Nutting	Ant. Donoghoe		Ireland		
Jn. Robson	Jas. McTernan	21 9 35	Torbay	Ten.	118
Hy. Neatby	Thos. Galloway	16 10 35	P'smouth		114
Ben. Freeman	Rbt. Wylie	7 10 35	P'smouth	Direct	123
Wm. Richards	Jn. Edwards	28 10 35	Cork	Direct	120
Thos. Johnson	Alex. Neill	30 10 35	London		118
Geo. Sinclair	Thos. Robertson	9 1 36	Cork		129
Thos. O. Harrison	Hy. G. Brock	19 2 36	Cork		111

Date of Arrival	*Vessel*	*R.*	*Ton*	*Built at*	*Year*	*Class*
15 June	*Strathfieldsay* (2)	Bk.	476	Chepstow	1829	A1
31 Aug.	*Moffatt* (2)	S.	820	Bengal	1807	AE1
6 Sept.	*Waterloo* (5)	S.	414	Bristol	1815	AE1
12 Oct.	*Elizabeth IV*	Bk.	392	Dartmouth	1805	AE1
12 Oct.	*Lady Kennaway* (2)	S.	584	Calcutta	1817	AE1
13 Nov.	*Captain Cook* (3)	S.	451	Whitby	1826	AE1
9 Dec.	*Bengal Merchant* (3)	S.	503	Calcutta	1812	AE1
14 Dec.	*Pyramus* (2)	Bk.	362	Sunderland	1822	AE1
31 Dec.	*Earl Grey* (1)	S.	571	Newcastle	1835	A1
1837						
5 Jan.	*St. Vincent* (1)	S.	410	London	1829	A1
7 Feb.	*John II*	S.	473	London	1811	AE1
12 Feb.	*Norfolk* (5)	Bk.	537	Littlehampton	1814	AE1
23 Apr.	*Sarah and Elizabeth*	Bk.	270	Yarmouth	1830	A1
8 May	*Prince George*	S.	482	Bristol	1830	A1
30 May	*Margaret* (1)	S.	365	Chepstow	1829	A1
10 July	*Mangles* (8)	S.	594	Calcutta	1802	AE1
12 July	*Heber*	S.	443	Whitby	1835	A1
17 July	*Lloyds* (2)	Bk.	403	London	1830	A1
5 Aug.	*Calcutta II*	S.	706	Quebec	1835	A1
9 Oct.	*Charles Kerr*	S.	463	Sunderland	1826	AE1
25 Oct.	*James Pattison* (2)	S.	513	London	1828	A1
2 Dec.	*Asia V* (3)	S.	523	Calcutta	1814	AE1
22 Dec.	*Henry Wellesley* (2)	Bk.	304	India	1804	AE1
25 Dec.	*Sir Charles Forbes* (4)	S.	364	Aberdeen	1824	A1
1838						
2 Jan.	*Neptune II*	S.	499	Chepstow	1836	A1
8 Feb.	*Waterloo* (6)	S.	414	Bristol	1815	AE1
9 Feb.	*Emma Eugenia* (1)	Bk.	383	Whitby	1833	A1
28 Mar.	*Diamond*	S.	573	Isle of Man	1835	A1
11 Apr.	*William Jardine* (1)	S.	693	Liverpool	1836	A1
21 July	*Bengal Merchant* (4)	S.	503	Calcutta	1812	AE1
8 Aug.	*Lord Lyndoch* (4)	S.	638	Calcutta	1815	AE1
22 Aug.	*Westmoreland* (3)	Bk.	405	Lynn	1832	A1
27 Aug.	*John Renwick* (1)	Bk.	403	Newcastle	1826	A1
10 Sept.	*Clyde I* (3)	Bk.	490	Greenock	1819	AE1
21 Nov.	*Earl Grey* (2)	S.	571	Newcastle	1835	A1
18 Dec.	*Portsea*	Bk.	451	Calcutta	1808	AE1
29 Dec.	*Elphinstone* (3)	S.	425	Bristol	1825	AE1
1839						
5 Jan.	*Margaret* (2)	S.	365	Chepstow	1829	A1
31 Jan.	*Theresa* (1)	Bk.	497	Calcutta	1834	A1
9 Mar.	*Planter* (2)	Bk.	367	Lynn	1829	AE1
22 Mar.	*John Barry* (5)	S.	520	Whitby	1814	AE1
17 June	*Waverley* (1)	Bk.	436	Whitby	1838	A1
23 June	*Whitby*	Bk.	437	Whitby	1837	A1
1 Sept.	*Parkfield*	S.	496	Isle of Man	1833	A1
27 Sept.	*Blenheim I* (3)	Bk.	375	Jarrow	1834	A1
10 Nov.	*Mary Anne III* (1)	Bk.	394	Yarmouth	1835	A1
8 Dec.	*Barossa* (1)	Bk.	730	Bengal	1811	AE1
26 Dec.	*Minerva II* (2)	Bk.				
1840						
25 Jan.	*Middlesex*	Bk.	578	Sunderland	1839	A1

Master	Surgeon	Sailed	From	Route	Days
Plp. Jones	Thos. B. Wilson	18 2 36	P'smouth	Rio	118
Thos. Bolton	Jn. Smith	7 5 36	P'smouth		116
Jn. Cow	Geo. Roberts	21 5 36	Cork		108
Jn. Austin	Rbt. Espie	26 6 36	London		108
Rbt. P. Davidson	Jas. Wilson	11 6 36	Downs		123
Geo. W. Brown	Art. Savage	5 7 36	Cork		131
Wm. Campbell	Jn. Tarn	8 8 36	Downs	Ten.	123
Geo. N. Livesay	Obediah Pineo	20 8 36	Cork		116
Jas. Talbert	Wm. Evans	27 8 36	Cork	Cape	126
Jas. Muddle	And. Henderson	13 9 36	Cork	Direct	114
Adam Dixon	Chas. Inches	30 9 36	Sheerness		130
Jn. Gatenby	Jn. Inches	30 10 36	P'smouth		105
Jn. Davison	Jn. Rankine	1 1 37	Woolwich		112
Adolphus Holton	Thos. Bell	14 1 37	Torbay		114
Ed. Canney	Hy. Kelsall	24 1 37	Cork		126
Wm. Carr	Fran. Logan	23 3 37	P'smouth	Direct	109
Jn. Campbell	Alex. Neill	16 3 37	Dublin		118
Ed. Garrett	Dav. Watson	29 3 37	Downs	Direct	110
Jos. Brown	Ant. Donoghoe	19 4 37	Dublin	Direct	108
Harford Arnold	Jn. Edwards	8 6 37	Spithead	Direct	123
Jas. Cromarty	Thos. Robertson	16 7 37	Sheerness		101
Ben. Freeman	Jn. Gannon	4 8 37	Torbay	Direct	120
Ed. Williams	Wm. Leyson	20 7 37	Woolwich	Cape	155
Jas. Leslie	Wm. Clifford	11 8 37	Dublin		136
Jos. Nagle	Pat. Martyn	27 8 37	Dublin		128
Jn. Cow	Jas. Ellis	4 10 37	Sheerness	Cape	127
Giles Wade	Rbt. Wylie	6 11 37	P'smouth		95
Jas. F. Bisset	Wm. McDowell	29 11 37	Cork		114
Jn. Crosbie	Rchd. Lewis	28 11 37	Dublin		139
Wm. Campbell	Isaac Noott	28 3 38	Sheerness	Ten.	115
Wm. Stead	Obediah Pineo	4 4 38	England	Direct	126
Jn. Brigstock	Geo. McClure	27 4 38	Dublin	Direct	117
Jn. Byron	And. Smith	3 5 38	Downs	Direct	116
Jn. Matches	Jn. Smith	11 5 38	Dublin	Cape	122
Jas. Talbert	Alex. Nisbet	8 8 38	P'smouth	Direct	105
Sam. John Lowe	Thos. Bell	31 7 38	P'smouth	Hobart	140
Thos. Fremlin	Alick Osborne	8 9 38	Dublin		112
Ed. Canney	Geo. T. Moxey	1 9 38	Dublin	Cape	126
Walt. Young	Ed. Hilditch	10 10 38	Sheerness	Direct	113
F. B. Manning	Thos. Robertson	10 11 38	Portland	Cape	119
Jn. Robson	Campbell France	? 11 38	Sheerness	Ten.	
Jas. Morgan	Jas. Barr	22 2 39	Dublin		115
Thos. Wellbank	Jn. Kidd	18 2 39	Dublin		125
J. T. Whiteside	Alex. Neill	15 5 39	Sheerness		109
Jn. Gray	Wm. McDowell	19 5 39	Dublin	Cape	131
J. C. Hillman	Wm. Bland	18 7 39	Woolwich	Ten.	115
Jn. Austin	Rbt. Wylie	3 8 39	Sheerness	Direct	127
Geo. Brown	Pat. Magovern	18 8 39	Dublin	Cape	130
Chas. Munro	Jn. Baird	6 7 39	Dublin	Mauritius	203

Date of Arrival	*Vessel*	*R.*	*Ton*	*Built at*	*Year*	*Class*
9 Feb.	*Nautilus* (2)	Bk.	400	Shields	1833	A1
26 Feb.	*Woodbridge* (1)	S.	516	Calcutta	1809	AE1
27 Apr.	*Mangles* (9)	S.	594	Calcutta	1802	AE1
13 July	*Surrey I* (10)	S.	461	Harwich	1811	AE1
14 July	*Maitland* (1)	S.	648	Calcutta	1810	AE1
24 July	*Isabella II*	Bk.	323	Whitby	1827	A1
17 Aug.	*King William*	S.	380	Whitby	1831	A1
17 Aug.	*Margaret* (3)	S.	365	Chepstow	1829	A1
6 Nov.	*Pekoe*	S.	379	Dundee	1834	A1
18 Nov.	*Eden I* (2)	S.	513	London	1826	A1
1849						
9 June	*Hashemy*	Bk.	523	Calcutta	1817	AE1
20 Aug.	*Randolph*	S.	761			
8 Nov.	*Havering*	S.	906			
24 Dec.	*Adelaide* (1)	S.	640	Calcutta	1832	AE1

II. CONVICT SHIPS TO VAN

						C	*D*
1812							
19 Oct.	*Indefatigable* (1)	S.	549	Whitby	1799	1	3
1818							
7 June	*Minerva I* (1)	S.	530	Lancaster	1804	2	3
11 June	*Lady Castlereagh*	S.	842	Thames	1802	2	2
17 Dec.	*Lord Melville I* (2)	S.	412	Shields	1805	2	2
1819							
18 Mar.	*Surrey I* (3)	S.	443	Harwich	1811	1	3
11 May	*Hibernia* (1)	S.	430	Cowes	1810	1	2
14 June	*Baring* (2)	S.	842	Thames	1801	2	3
1820							
10 Jan.	*Dromedary*	HMSt.					
1 Mar.	*Castle Forbes* (1)	S.	439	Aberdeen	1818	1	2
12 Mar.	*Coromandel II*	HMSt.					
29 Aug.	*Morley* (3)	S.	480	Thames	1811	1	2
28 Oct.	*Guildford* (4)	S.	521	Thames	1810	1	2
17 Nov.	*Caledonia* (1)	S.	412	Sunderland	1815	1	2
1 Dec.	*Maria I* (2)	S.	427	Gainsborough	1798	2	2
28 Dec.	*Juliana*	S.	516	India	1798	2	1
1821							
13 Mar.	*Medway* (1)	S.	435	Rochester	1810	1	2
27 June	*Lady Ridley*	S.	373	Blythe	1813	1	1
27 July	*Countess of Harcourt* (1)	S.	517	India	1811	1	2

Master	*Surgeon*	*Sailed*	*From*	*Route*	*Days*
H. F. Alloway	Geo. McClure	17 9 39	Dublin	Direct	145
Wm. B. Dobson	Geo. T. Moxey	16 10 39	London	Cape	133
Wm. Carr	Alex. Nisbet	29 11 39	P'smouth	Ten., Cape	150
Geo. Sinclair	Ed. Leah	2 4 40	Downs	Direct	102
Geo. or Jn. Baker	Plp. Toms	22 3 40	Sheerness	Ten.	114
Alex. McAusland	Hy. W. Mahon	5 3 40	Dublin	Cape	141
Geo. Thomas	Campbell France	28 4 40	Dublin	Direct	111
Ed. Canney	Col. A. Browning	30 4 40	Dublin		109
Sampson Keen	Rbt. Bower	10 7 40	Dublin	Cape	119
Hy. J. Naylor	Geo. E. Forman	10 7 40	Sheerness	Ten.	131
Jn. Ross	Col. A. Browning and Edmonston	11 2 49	P'smouth	Cape, Pt. P.	118
Wm. Dale	(i) H. Goldney* (ii) Walt. Lawrance	28 4 49	London	Cape, Pt. P.	114
Jn. Fenwick	Thos. Bellott	4 8 49	Dublin	Direct	96
Steph. Wharton	Wm. F. Le Grand	17 8 49	London	Hob., Pt. P.	129

DIEMEN'S LAND, 1812-1853

Jn. Cross		4 6 12	England	Rio	137
Jn. Bell	Jas. Hunter	1 1 18	Ireland	Sydney	157
Geo. Weltden	Jas. Craigie	22 12 17	England	Sydney	171
Thackray Wetherell	Jn. McMillan	? 7 18			
Thos. Raine	Matt. Anderson	17 10 18	England	Rio, Syd.	152
Jn. Lennon	Chas. Carter	20 11 18	P'smouth		172
Jn. Lamb	Dav. Reid	27 1 19	Downs	Mad.	138
Cpt. Rchd. Skinner, R.N.	Geo. Fairfowl	11 9 19	England	Direct	121
Thos. Reid	Jas. Scott		Ireland	Sydney	
Capt. Jas. Downie, R.N.	Arch. Hume	1 11 19	Spithead	Rio	132
Rbt. R. Brown	Thos. Reid	22 5 20	London	Direct	99
Magnus Johnson	Hugh Walker	14 5 20	P'smouth	Sydney	167
Rbt. Carns	Alex. Jack	10 7 20	P'smouth	Direct	130
Harris Walker	Wm. Hamilton	28 7 20	England	Direct	126
Dav. Ogilvie	Wm. Graham	3 9 20	England	Direct	116
Borthwick Wight	Thos. Davis	13 11 20	England	Direct	120
Rbt. Weir	Jas. Wilson	14 1 21	P'smouth	Rio	164
Geo. Bunn	Morgan Price	19 4 21	P'smouth		99

Date of Arrival	Vessel	R.	Ton	Built at	Year	C	D
21 Oct.	*Malabar* (2)	S.	525	Shields	1804	2	2
15 Dec.	*Claudine* (1)	S.	452	Calcutta	1811	1	3
18 Dec.	*Providence II* (1)	S.	380	Lynn	1812	1	1
26 Dec.	*Lord Hungerford*	S.	707				
1822							
30 Apr.	*Richmond*	S.	466				
2 May	*Mary Anne I* (2)	S.	479	Batavia	1807	2	2
20 May	*Phoenix I* (1)	S.	493	Topsham	1810	2	2
23 July	*Prince of Orange* (2)	S.	359	Sunderland	1813	1	2
6 Nov.	*Caledonia* (2)	S.	412	Sunderland	1815	1	2
6 Nov.	*Arab I* (1)	S.	403	Greenock	1820	1	2
1823							
11 Jan.	*Morley* (4)	S.	480	Thames	1811	2	2
10 Feb.	*Lord Sidmouth* (3)	S.	411	Shields	1817	1	2
3 Aug.	*Competitor* (1)	S.	425	Whitby	1813	2	1
16 Aug.	*Commodore Hayes*	S.	678	Calcutta	1817	1	2
5 Oct.	*Mary III* (1)	S.	361	Ipswich	1811	2	2
21 Oct.	*Albion* (1)	S.	479	Bristol	1813	1	1
30 Dec.	*Sir Godfrey Webster* (1)	S.	548	Thames	1799	2	3
1824						*Class*	
19 Jan.	*Asia II*	S.	401	Shields	1816		
15 Apr.	*Brothers* (1)	S.	425	Whitby	1815	A1	
21 July	*Phoenix II*	S.	589	Thames	1798	E1	
27 July	*Chapman* (2)	S.	558	Whitby	1777		
9 Nov.	*Princess Charlotte* (1)	S.	400	Sunderland	1812	E1	
1825							
8 Feb.	*Henry* (2)	S.	386	Quebec	1819		
9 Apr.	*Lady East*	S.	590	Calcutta	1818		
18 Apr.	*Sir Charles Forbes* (1)	S.	364	Aberdeen	1824	A1	
14 Sept.	*Medina* (2)	S.	467	Topsham	1811	E1	
23 Nov.	*Midas* (1)	S.	430	Hull	1809	E1	
14 Dec.	*Medway* (2)	S.	435	Rochester	1810		
1826							
29 Apr.	*Woodman* (2)	S.	419	Gainsborough	1808	E1	
16 May	*Providence II* (2)	S.	380	Lynn	1812		
13 Aug.	*Earl St. Vincent* (4)	S.	412	Topsham	1800		
7 Oct.	*Chapman* (3)	S.	558	Whitby	1777		
22 Nov.	*Woodford* (1)	S.	522	Bristol	1819		
1827							
3 Jan.	*Sir Charles Forbes* (2)	S.	364	Aberdeen	1824	A1	
9 Jan.	*Grenada* (4)	S.	408	Hull	1810		
23 Feb.	*Andromeda I*	S.	383	Sunderland			
31 July	*Governor Ready* (1)	S.	512	Pr. Edw. Is.	1825		
5 Aug.	*Persian* (1)	S.	399	Quebec	1826	A1	
9 Oct.	*Layton I* (1)	S.	490	Lancaster	1814	E1	
20 Nov.	*Sovereign* (1)	S.	398	Hull	1814	E1	
30 Nov.	*Asia IV*	Bk.	455	Whitby	1813		
7 Dec.	*Asia V* (1)	S.	523	Calcutta	1814		

Master	*Surgeon*	*Sailed*	*From*	*Route*	*Days*
Wm. Ascough	Jn. Thompson	22 6 21	Gravesend		121
Jn. Crabtree	Hy. Ryan	24 8 21	Woolwich	Ten.	113
Jas. Herd	Dav. Reid	13 6 21	England	P. Py., Rio	188
Michael O'Brien	Michael Dorke	? 7 21	England		
Jas. Kay	Thos. B. Wilson	27 11 21	Sheerness	St. Jago	154
Hy. Warington	Jas. Hall	25 12 21	P'smouth	Rio	128
Thos. Wetherhead	Evan Evans	20 12 21	P'smouth	Rio	151
Jn. Moncrief	Jn. Crocket	1 4 22	England	Direct	113
Rbt. Carns	Williamson	19 6 22	P'smouth	Rio	140
Rbt. R. Brown	Chas. Carter	13 7 22	England	Direct	116
Geo. Holliday	Wm. B. Carlyle	25 9 22	Downs	Direct	108
Jas. Ferrier	Rbt. Espie	11 9 22	Woolwich	Rio	152
Wm. Ascough	Geo. Clayton	18 3 23	England	Cape	138
Lewis W. Moncrief	Geo. S. Rutherford	26 4 23	England		112
J. F. Steel	Harman Cochrane	10 6 23	London	Direct	117
W. R. Best	Jas. A. Mercer	20 5 23	Spithead	Cape	154
Jn. Rennoldson	Chas. Carter	1 9 23	London	Ten.	120
Jas. Lindsay	Wm. Evans	9 8 23	Downs	Cape	163
Chas. Motley	Jas. Hall	6 12 23	Downs	Direct	131
Rbt. White	Chas. Queade	29 3 24	P'smouth	Ten.	114
Jn. Milbank	Jas. Hamilton	6 4 24	England	St. Jago	112
Jos. Blyth	Jn. Dobie	9 7 24	Downs	Rio	123
Jas. Ferrier	Wm. B. Carlyle	12 10 24	London	St. Jago	119
And. Talbert	Wm. McDowell	16 12 24	England	St. Jago	114
Thos. Fullarton	Jos. Cook	5 1 25	P'smouth	Direct	103
Jn. Briggs	Wm. Gregor	26 4 25	Downs		141
Jas. Baigrie	Chas. Cameron	24 7 25	London	St. Jago	124
Borthwick Wight	Gilbert King	2 8 25	Downs	Direct	132
Dan. Leary	(i) *Jn. Rodmell (ii) Cornelius Kelly	6 12 25	London	Cape	144
Jn. Wauchope	Matt. Burnside	24 12 25	Downs	Ten.	143
Josiah Middleton	Jas. McKerrow	25 4 26	P'smouth	Direct	110
Jn. Milbank	Jos. H. Hughes	10 4 26	London	St. Jago, Rio	180
Ed. Chapman	Jas. Dickson	5 8 26	London		109
Alex. Duthie	Jas. McTernan	16 9 26	London	Direct	109
Jn. Tracy	Alex. Nisbet	10 9 26	London		121
Jas. Muddle	Wm. B. Carlyle	14 10 26	London		132
Jn. Young	Thos. B. Wilson	3 4 27	P'smouth		119
Rbt. Plunkett	Jas. Patton	14 4 27	London		113
Jn. H. Luscombe	Wm. Evans	17 6 27	Plymouth	St. Jago	114
Wm. McKellar	Rbt. Malcolm	14 7 27	London		129
Jn. Edman	Campbell France	1 8 27	London		121
Hy. Ager	Geo Fairfowl	17 8 27	P'smouth		112

Date of Arrival	Vessel	R.	Ton	Built at	Year	Class
1828						
6 Mar.	*Marmion*	S.	411	Quebec	1826	A1
27 June	*Mermaid* (1)	S.	472	Calcutta	1817	A1
29 July	*William Miles*	Bk.	581	Bristol	1808	E1
10 Aug.	*Bengal Merchant* (1)	S.	503	Calcutta	1812	
25 Aug.	*Woodford* (2)	S.	522	Bristol	1819	
8 Oct.	*Borneo*	S.	428	Borneo	1817	E1
9 Nov.	*Manlius* (2)	S.	479	Quebec	1825	E1
16 Dec.	*Roslin Castle* (1)	S.	450	Bristol	1819	
1829						
14 Jan.	*Harmony* (2)	S.	373	St. John's	1818	E1
20 Apr.	*Georgiana I* (1)	S.	404	Quebec	1826	A1
28 July	*Lady Harewood* (1)	S.	429	Thames	1791	E1
28 Aug.	*York I* (1)	S.	429	Southwick	1819	E1
1 Nov.	*Lady of the Lake*	Bk.	243	Chittagong	1820	A1
21 Nov.	*Thames*	S.	366	London		
14 Dec.	*Surrey I* (5)	S.	461	Harwich	1811	E1
1830						
10 Jan.	*Prince Regent I* (4)	S.	527	Shields	1810	E1
18 Jan.	*Bussorah Merchant* (2)	S.	530	Calcutta	1818	E1
24 Feb.	*Eliza III* (2)	S.	391	Java	1815	E1
10 Apr.	*Mary III* (2)	S.	361	Ipswich	1811	E1
27 July	*Sir Charles Forbes* (3)	S.	364	Aberdeen	1824	A1
12 Aug.	*Manlius* (3)	S.	479	Quebec	1825	E1
18 Aug.	*David Lyon*	S.	476	Ipswich	1819	E1
22 Sept.	*Mellish* (2)	S.	424	Calcutta	1820	A1
18 Oct.	*Royal George* (2)	S.	486	Hull	1820	E1
19 Oct.	*Southworth* (2)	S.	350	Chester	1821	E1
7 Nov.	*Persian* (2)	S.	399	Quebec	1826	A1
18 Dec.	*Clyde I* (1)	S.	490	Greenock	1819	
1831						
28 Jan.	*John I* (3)	S.	464	Chester	1810	E1
26 Mar.	*Red Rover*	S.	372	Yarmouth	1830	A1
9 May	*America* (2)	S.	391	Quebec	1827	
29 May	*Eliza II* (3)	S.	538	India	1806	E1
3 Aug.	*Argyle*	S.	597	Chittagong	1817	E1
3 Aug.	*Proteus*	Bk.	254	Java	1815	E1
19 Oct.	*Mary III* (3)	S.	361	Ipswich	1811	E1
19 Oct.	*Larkins* (3)	S.	647	Calcutta	1808	E1
1 Nov.	*Wm. Glen Anderson*	Bk.	389	Rochbert	1827	
15 Nov.	*Strathfieldsay* (1)	Bk.	476	Chepstow	1829	A1
18 Nov.	*Lord Lyndoch* (1)	S.	638	Calcutta	1815	E1
1832						
14 Feb.	*Elizabeth III*	S.	506	Calcutta		E1
22 Mar.	*Gilmore* (1)	S.	500	Calcutta	1824	A1
16 July	*Katherine Stewart Forbes* (2)	S.	457	Northfleet	1818	E1
18 July	*England* (2)	S.	425	Chepstow	1814	E1
10 Aug.	*Hydery*	S.	345	Calcutta	1822	
28 Aug.	*Lord William Bentinck I*	S.	443	Yarmouth	1828	
29 Dec.	*York I* (3)	S.	429	Southwick	1819	E1
1833						
10 Jan.	*Frances Charlotte* (1)	Bk.	296	Chittagong	1817	E1

Master	*Surgeon*	*Sailed*	*From*	*Route*	*Days*
W. Wright	Hy. G. Brock	7 11 27	P'smouth	Cape	120
Wm. Henniker	Jas. Gilchrist	17 2 28	Woolwich		131
Jn. G. Sampson	E. Johnston	24 3 28	Downs		127
Alex. Duthie	Jas. Skeoch	25 3 28	Plymouth	Rio	138
Jn. Milbank	Wm. Petrie	2 5 28	P'smouth		115
Rchd. M. Whichelo	Oliver Sproule	11 5 28	London	Mad., Cp.	150
Wm. Johnston	Pat. McTernan	20 7 28	London		112
Jn. T. Duff	Jas. A. Anderson	19 8 28	Downs		119
Bennett Ireland	Wm. Clifford	13 9 28	Downs		123
Jn. S. Thompson	(i) Coleman* (ii) D. B. Conway	15 12 28	Plymouth	Cape	126
Rchd. Limon	Campbell France	26 3 29	London		124
Jn. Moncrief	And. Henderson	11 5 29	London		109
Jas. Pearson	Wm. Evans	12 6 29	Woolwich	Ten.	142
Wm. Anderson	Thos. Bell	31 7 29	London		113
Chas. Kemp	Hy. G. Brock	11 8 29	London		125
Geo. Hustwick	Jn. Drummond	21 8 29	Sheerness		142
Geo. Johnston	Wm. Henderson	6 10 29	Downs		104
Wm. Doutty	Dav. Thomson	7 11 29	London		109
Alex. Jamieson	Rbt. Espie	18 12 29	London		113
Jas. Leslie	Wm. Petrie	5 4 30	Plymouth		113
Wm. Johnston	Eben Johnston	27 4 30	Sheerness		107
Jas. Berry	Chas. Cameron	2 5 30	Sheerness		108
Colin G. Cowley	Jn. Love	6 6 30	Spithead		108
Rbt. Embledon	Michael Goodsir	27 6 30	P'smouth		113
Jn. Coombs	Alex. Stewart	26 6 30	Sheerness		115
Rbt. Plunkett	Thos. Galloway	4 7 30	Falmouth		126
Dan N. Munro	Morgan Price	30 8 30	P'smouth		110
Jn. R. Norsworthy	Thos. B. Wilson	14 10 30	Spithead		106
Rbt. C. Chrystie	Jn. Osborne	24 10 30	Sheerness		152
Rbt. Donal	Rchd. Lewis	6 1 31	Downs		123
Jn. S. Groves	Wm. Anderson	6 2 31	P'smouth		112
Ptr. M. Stavers	Hy. G. Brock	18 3 31	Plymouth	Rio	138
Sylvester J. Brown	Thos. Logan	14 4 31	P'smouth		111
Alex. Jamieson	Sam. Sinclair	11 6 31	Woolwich		130
Wm. Campbell	Wm. Evans	18 6 31	Downs	Direct	123
Jas. Fawthrop	Chas. Inches	2 6 31	P'smouth	Cape	152
Wm. Harrison	Dav. Ross	2 8 31	Plymouth	Direct	105
Jn. H. Luscombe	Gilbert King	25 7 31	Sheerness		116
Jn. Craigie	Wm. Martin	7 10 31	London		130
Jas. Berry	Geo. Roberts	27 11 31	London		116
Jn. Anderson	Jn. Stephenson	27 2 32	Woolwich		140
Jas. Blyth	Thos. B. Wilson	4 4 32	Sheerness	Direct	105
Alex. McDonald	Allan McLaren	11 4 32	Plymouth		121
Wm. Doutty	And. Henderson	7 5 32	P'smouth		113
Rchd. Spratley	Jas. McTernan	1 9 32	Plymouth		119
A. Smith	Jn. Osborne	15 9 32	Downs		117

Date of Arrival	*Vessel*	*R.*	*Ton*	*Built at*	*Year*	*Class*
1 Feb.	*Georgiana II*	Bk.	406	Calcutta	1820	
16 Feb.	*Circassian*	Bk.	401	Newcastle	1822	
7 Apr.	*Surrey I* (7)	S.	461	Harwich	1811	E1
16 May	*Lotus*	S.	397	Whitby	1826	A1
28 May	*Jupiter*	Bk.	347	Chepstow	1827	
30 June	*Jane II*	S.	272	Calcutta	1825	A1
31 July	*Enchantress*	S.	401			
12 Aug.	*Emperor Alexander*	Bk.	366	Chepstow	1814	E1
24 Aug.	*Atlas IV*	S.	412	London	1820	A1
4 Sept.	*Stakesby*	Bk.	438	Whitby	1814	
23 Oct.	*William Bryan*	Bk.	302	Southampton	1816	E1
14 Nov.	*Isabella I* (5)	S.	579	London	1818	E1
1 Dec.	*John I* (5)	S.	464	Chester	1810	E1
1834						
14 Jan.	*Southworth* (4)	S.	350	Chester	1821	
9 May	*Moffatt* (1)	S.	820	Bengal	1807	AE1
30 June	*Arab I* (2)	S.	403	Greenock	1820	
11 Aug.	*John Barry* (3)	S.	520	Whitby	1814	AE1
4 Sept.	*Edward* (3)	S.	406	Bristol	1806	AE1
4 Sept.	*William Metcalfe*	S.	447	Sunderland	1834	A1
1835						
22 Jan.	*Augusta Jessie* (1)	Bk.	380	Sunderland	1834	A1
13 Feb.	*Lady Kennaway* (1)	S.	584	Calcutta	1817	AE1
3 Mar.	*Waterloo* (4)	S.	414	Bristol	1815	AE1
27 Mar.	*New Grove*	Bk.	385	Jarrow	1833	A1
†	*George Third*	S.	394	Thames	1810	
1 Aug.	*Mangles* (7)	S.	594	Calcutta	1802	AE1
28 Aug.	*Norfolk* (4)	Bk.	537	Littlehampton	1814	AE1
7 Oct.	*Aurora I* (2)	S.	550	Chittagong	1817	AE1
20 Oct.	*Hector*	Bk.	325	Newcastle	1819	
10 Dec.	*Layton II* (1)	Bk.	513	Lancaster	1814	
1836						
13 Jan.	*Bardaster*	S.	435	N. Brunswick	1833	A1
21 Feb.	*Asia I* (8)	S.	536	Aberdeen	1819	
25 Apr.	*Arab II*	Bk.	291	Southampton	1827	
24 May	*Elphinstone* (1)	S.	425	Bristol	1825	AE1
20 Aug.	*Lord Lyndoch* (3)	S.	638	Calcutta	1815	AE1
12 Nov.	*Lady Nugent* (2)	S.	535	Bombay	1813	AE1
15 Nov.	*Henry Porcher* (3)	Bk.	485	Bristol	1817	A1
3 Dec.	*Westmoreland* (2)	Bk.	405	Lynn	1832	A1
22 Dec.	*Eden I* (1)	S.	513	London	1826	A1
1837						
29 Mar.	*Sarah* (2)	S.	488	London	1819	AE1
15 May	*Frances Charlotte* (2)	Bk.	296	Chittagong	1817	AE1
16 July	*Blenheim I* (2)	Bk.	375	Jarrow	1834	A1
2 Oct.	*Elphinstone* (2)	S.	425	Bristol	1825	AE1
8 Oct.	*Recovery* (4)	S.	493	Batavia	1799	AE1
22 Oct.	*Platina*	Bk.	303	Sunderland	1830	A1
21 Nov.	*Susan* (3)	S.	573	Calcutta	1813	AE1
1838						
9 Jan.	*Royal Sovereign* (3)	Bk.	336	Whitby	1829	A1
18 Jan.	*Neptune III* (1)	S.	644	Calcutta	1814	AE1

Master	*Surgeon*	*Sailed*	*From*	*Route*	*Days*
Jn. S. Thompson	Jas. Hall	16 10 32	P'smouth	T. d'A.	108
Geo. Douthwaite	Wm. Porteous	14 10 32	Plymouth		125
Chas. Kemp	Dav. Wyse	4 12 32	Downs		124
Jn. Summerson	Hy. G. Brock	13 12 32	P'smouth	Rio	154
W. J. Clarke	Arch. Ferguson	7 1 33	Downs	Cape	141
F. Tupper	Rbt. Dunn	22 2 33	Torbay		128
Thos. Canney	Jas. Osborne	13 4 33	P'smouth		109
Jn. Hurst	Wm. Donnelly	10 4 33	Sheerness		124
Geo. Hustwick	Jn. Love	30 4 33	Plymouth		116
Miles Corner	Dav. Thomson	22 5 33	Spithead		105
J. Roman	Thos. Robertson	4 7 33	London		111
Dav. Brown	Oliver Sproule	28 7 33	Plymouth		109
Sam. J. Lowe	Art. Savage	6 8 33	Spithead		117
Wm. Maltby	Wm. Evans	25 9 33	Sheerness		111
Jas. Cromarty	Thos. B. Wilson	29 1 34	Plymouth		100
Geo. Binnie	Colin A. Browning	26 2 34	P'smouth		124
Jn. Robson	Jn. Osborne	4 4 34	London		129
E. A. Lindsay	Jos. Steret	5 5 34	Woolwich		122
Ed. Philipson	Hy. G. Brock	25 5 34	P'smouth	Direct	102
Hy. Edenborough	Jas. McTernan	29 9 34	P'smouth		115
Thos. Bolton	Thos. Bell	27 10 34	Cork		109
Jn. Cow	Geo. Roberts	20 11 34	P'smouth		103
Rbt. Brown	(i) Geo. Rowe[1] (ii) Dav. Thomson	25 11 34	Scilly Is.		122
Wm. H. Moxey	Dav. Wyse	12 12 34	Downs		
Wm. Carr	Ptr. J. Suther	21 4 35	London		102
Jn. Gatenby	Art. Savage	14 5 35	Sheerness		106
Jas. Gilbert	And. Henderson	27 6 35	Downs	Direct	102
G. M. Smith	Morgan Price	13 6 35	London		129
Giles Wade	Geo. Birnie	29 8 35	Sheerness		103
Alex. McDonald	Jos. Steret	16 9 35	P'smouth		119
Thos. F. Stead	Ptr. Leonard	8 11 35	Sheerness		105
Jas. Ferrier	Wm. Rogers	30 12 35	London		117
Thos. Fremlin	Colin A. Browning	30 1 36	Downs		115
Jn. Baker	Jas. Lawrence	24 4 36	London		118
Jas. Fawcett	Jn. Dobie	14 7 36	Sheerness	Cape	121
Jn. Hart	Jn. Smith	4 8 36	P'smouth		103
Jn. Brigstock	Jas. Ellis	12 8 36	Woolwich		113
Alex. L. Mollison	Gilbert King	31 8 36	P'smouth	Cape	113
J. T. Whiteside	Jas. McTernan	22 12 36	Spithead		97
Thos. Welbank	Alex. Nisbet	1 1 37	P'smouth	Rio, Cp.	134
T. (or J.) L. Spence	Geo Birnie	15 3 37	Woolwich	Direct	123
Thos. Fremlin	Campbell France	1 6 37	Downs	Direct	123
Thos. Johnson	Ed. Jeffery	1 6 37	Downs	Direct	129
Robson Coltish	Geo. E. Forman	3 5 37	London	Cape	172
Hy. Neatby	Ed. Hilditch	5 8 37	Spithead		108
Jn. Moncrief	And. Henderson	31 8 37	Sheerness	Ten.	131
W. J. Ferris	Jos. Steret	7 10 37	Sheerness		103

[1] Landed at Scilly Isles because of illness and succeeded by David Thomson.

Date of Arrival	Vessel	R.	Ton	Built at	Year	Class
23 Jan.	*Atwick*	Bk.	341	Sunderland	1827	AE1
1 Apr.	*Moffatt* (3)	S.	820	Bengal	1807	AE1
26 Aug.	*Lord Wm. Bentinck II*	Bk.	564	Bristol	1828	A1
29 Aug.	*Nautilus* (1)	Bk.	400	Shields	1833	A1
28 Sept.	*Minerva II* (1)	Bk.				
26 Oct.	*Coromandel III*	S.	639	London	1820	A1
6 Dec.	*Augusta Jessie* (2)	Bk.	380	Sunderland	1834	A1
1839						
22 Jan.	*Majestic*	S.	345	Aberdeen	1829	A1
24 Jan.	*Gilmore* (2)	S.	500	Calcutta	1824	AE1
24 Mar.	*Pyramus* (3)	Bk.	362	Sunderland	1822	AE1
23 July	*Marquis of Hastings* (4)	S.	452	London	1819	AE1
23 Aug.	*Egyptian* (1)	Bk.	359	Shields	1825	AE1
12 Sept.	*Hindostan* (2)	S.	445	Whitby	1819	A1
7 Dec.	*Layton II* (2)	Bk.	513	Lancaster	1814	AE1
1840						
12 Jan.	*Canton*	S.	507	Sunderland	1834	A1
28 Mar.	*Runnymede I*	Bk.	389	London	1825	A1
24 Apr.	*Gilbert Henderson*	Bk.	517	Sunderland	1837	A1
30 June	*Mandarin*	S.	425	Holton	1834	A1
6 Aug.	*Asia I* (9)	S.	536	Aberdeen	1819	AE1
12 Dec.	*Egyptian* (2)	Bk.	359	Shields	1825	AE1
1841						
17 Jan.	*Navarino* (1)	Bk.	493	Cochin	1808	AE1
19 Jan.	*Hindostan* (3)	S.	545	Whitby	1819	A1
5 Feb.	*Lord Lyndoch* (5)	S.	638	Calcutta	1815	AE1
17 Mar.	*Lady Raffles*	S.	648	London	1817	AE1
18 Mar.	*British Sovereign*	Bk.	493	Sunderland	1840	A1
19 Mar.	*Mary Anne III* (2)	Bk.	394	Yarmouth	1835	A1
18 Apr.	*Duncan*	S.	644	Isle of Man		
19 July	*Rajah*	Bk.	352	Whitby	1835	A1
21 Aug.	*Asia V* (4)	S.	523	Calcutta	1815	AE1
1 Sept.	*Layton II* (3)	Bk.	513	Lancaster	1814	AE1
12 Sept.	*Westmoreland* (4)	Bk.	405	Lynn	1832	A1
12 Sept.	*Waverley* (2)	Bk.	436	Whitby	1838	A1
4 Oct.	*David Clarke*	Bk.	608	Calcutta	1817	AE1
10 Oct.	*Garland Grove* (1)	Bk.	483	I. of Wight	1820	A1
18 Nov.	*Lord Goderich*	S.	361	Hull	1828	AE1
26 Dec.	*Mexborough*	Bk.	376			
1842						
3 Jan.	*Prince Regent II* (2)	S.	395	Rochester	1811	AE1
13 Jan.	*Barossa* (2)	Bk.	730	Bengal	1811	AE1
19 Feb.	*Tortoise*	HMS.	1000			
4 Mar.	*Richard Webb*	Bk.	486	Redbridge	1840	A1
6 Apr.	*John Brewer*	Bk.	549	Redbridge		
9 Apr.	*Emma Eugenia* (2)	Bk.	383	Whitby	1833	A1
19 May	*Isabella I* (6)	S.	579	London	1818	AE1
30 May	*Somersetshire* (2)	S.	449	London	1810	AE1
5 July	*Eden I*	S.	522	London	1826	

Master	*Surgeon*	*Sailed*	*From*	*Route*	*Days*
H. Mackay	Ptr. Leonard	30 9 37	London		115
Thos. W. Bolton	Gilbert King	9 11 37	Sheerness	Cape	143
Wm. S. Stockley	Jn. Rankine	14 4 38	P'smouth	Cape	134
J. Newcombe	Jn. G. Stewart	29 4 38	Woolwich	Direct	122
Geo. Brown	Jas. Wilson	28 5 38	Sheerness	Cape	123
Wm. Loader	J. Tweeddale	27 6 38	Sheerness	Direct	121
J. C. Edenborough	Wm. Leyson	14 8 38	London		114
G. Williamson	Ptr. Fisher	3 10 38	London	Cape	111
J. Theaker	Jos. Steret	5 10 38	Spithead		111
Geo. N. Livesay	Geo. E. Forman	22 11 38	Sheerness	Ten.	122
Hy. I. Naylor	Ed. Jeffery	17 3 39	P'smouth		128
Jn. Skelton	Jn. G. Stewart	9 4 39	Sheerness		136
Geo. Lambe	Thos. W. McDonald	9 5 39	London		126
Simon Cuddy	Isaac Noott	13 7 39	P'smouth	Ten.	147
Jn. Mordaunt	Jn. Irvine	22 9 39	Spithead		112
W. B. Forward	Ptr. Fisher	20 12 39	London		99
J. Tweedie	Sir Jn. Hamett	14 12 39	London	Ten., Cape	132
Jas. Muddle	Alex. McKechnie	25 2 40	Spithead	Cape	126
Jas. Fawcett	J. W. Johnston	27 4 40	Sheerness		101
Jn. Skelton	Jn. Kidd	19 8 40	Dublin		115
Chris. A. Warning	Jas. L. Clarke	12 10 40	Downs		107
Geo. Lamb	And. Henderson	7 10 40	Sheerness	Direct	104
Jn. Humble	Thos. W. McDonald	11 9 40	Plymouth	Cape	147
Ed. Hight	Rbt. Wylie	2 12 40	P'smouth	Cape	105
Jn. Cow	Jn. G. Stewart	16 12 40	Dublin	Direct	92
Adolphus Holton	Jas. Barr	27 11 40	Dublin	Cape	112
Thos. Grieves	Wm. McDowell	16 12 40	Sheerness	Cape	123
Chas. Ferguson	Jas. Donovan	5 4 41	Woolwich		105
Jn. Davison	And. Sinclair	17 4 41	P'smouth	Direct	126
Dan. W. Stephens	Alex. McKechnie	9 4 41	Sheerness	Ten., Cape	145
Jn. Brigstock	Jn. Gibson	19 5 41	Sheerness		116
Jas. Morgan	Thos. R. Dunn	25 4 41	Dublin	Bahia	140
Wm. B. Mills	Ed. Jeffery	7 6 41	Plymouth	Direct	119
Wm. B. Forward	Rbt. Dobie	23 6 41	London		109
Wm. Mills	Jas. Baird	29 6 41	Sheerness	Cape	142
Jn. H. Bridgman	Jn. S. Hampton	12 8 41	Dublin	Cape	136
Jn. T. Barclay	Plp. Jones	7 8 41	Dublin	Cape	149
Jn. Austin	Hy. W. Mahon	30 8 41	Sheerness	Ten.	136
Capt. J. Hood, R.N.	Thos. Brownrigg	26 10 41	Plymouth		116
Rbt. McLachlan	Wm. Rogers	15 11 41	Dublin		109
Rbt. Brown	Geo. E. Forman	5 12 41	Sheerness	Ten.	122
Geo. Kettlewell	Jn. Kidd	24 11 41	Woolwich	Cape	136
Geo. Sinclair	Campbell France	19 1 42	P'smouth	Direct	120
Chas. Motley	Thos. Gibson	20 12 41	Plymouth	Cape	161
Jn. Jones	Alex. Neill	22 3 42	Woolwich	Direct	105

Date of Arrival	Vessel	R.	Ton	Built at	Year	Class
20 July	*Candahar*	Bk.	642	Shields	1840	A1
25 July	*Susan* (4)	S.	573	Calcutta	1813	AE1
28 July	*Elphinstone* (4)	S.	425	Bristol	1825	AE1
3 Aug.	*Isabella Watson*	S.	514	Leith	1840	A1
11 Aug.	*Surrey I* (11)	S.	461	Harwich	1811	AE1
17 Aug.	*Hope*	S.	377	Bristol	1827	AE1
24 Sept.	*Royal Admiral* (4)	Bk.	414	Lynn	1828	AE1
23 Oct.	*Kinnear* (1)	Bk.	369	Yarmouth	1834	A1
7 Nov.	*Marquis of Hastings* (5)	Bk.	452	London	1819	AE1
23 Nov.	*Cape Packet*	Bk.	349	Sunderland	1838	A1
24 Nov.	*Emily I*	Bk.	461	Calcutta	1836	A1
†	*Waterloo* (7)	S.	414	Bristol	1815	AE1
28 Nov.	*Moffatt* (4)	Bk.	820	Bengal	1807	AE1
15 Dec.	*Waverley* (3)	Bk.	436	Whitby	1838	A1
19 Dec.	*Triton*	Bk.	492	Hull	1805	A1
1843						
10 Jan.	*Navarino* (2)	Bk.	493	Cochin	1808	AE1
14 Jan.	*Earl Grey* (3)	Bk.	571	Newcastle	1835	A1
18 Jan.	*Duchess of Northumberland* (1)	S.	541	Sunderland	1834	A1
20 Jan.	*Garland Grove* (2)	Bk.	483	I. of Wight	1820	A1
4 Apr.	*North Briton*	Bk.	402	Chepstow	1823	AE1
10 Apr.	*John Renwick* (2)	Bk.	403	Newcastle	1826	A1
19 July	*Margaret* (4)	Bk.	365	Chepstow	1829	A1
19 Aug.	*Gilmore* (3)	S.	500	Calcutta	1824	AE1
20 Aug.	*Cressy*	S.	720	Sunderland	1843	A1
29 Aug.	*Constant*	Bk.	535	Holton	1842	A1
21 Sept.	*East London*	Bk.	409	Sunderland	1839	A1
23 Sept.	*Asiatic*	Bk.	503	Sunderland	1841	A1
12 Oct.	*Emerald Isle*	S.	501	Moulmein	1836	A1
12 Oct.	*Forfarshire*	S.	614	Moulmein	1840	A1
15 Oct.	*Lord Petre*	Bk.	635	Whitby	1843	A1
19 Nov.	*Henrietta*	S.	560	Liverpool	1838	A1
21 Nov.	*Orator*	Bk.	440	Sunderland	1841	A1
25 Dec.	*Woodbridge* (2)	S.	516	Calcutta	1809	AE1
1844						
2 Jan.	*Duke of Richmond*	Bk.	470	Dysart	1842	A1
4 Feb.	*Anson*	HMS.	1870			
2 Apr.	*Emma Eugenia* (3)	Bk.	383	Whitby	1833	A1
3 Apr.	*Marion* (1)	S.	684	Calcutta	1834	A1
2 May	*Equestrian* (1)	S.	801	Hull	1842	A1
2 July	*Greenlaw*	Bk.	480	Moulmein	1839	A1
9 July	*London* (1)	S.	612	London	1833	A1
30 July	*Maria Somes* (1)	Bk.	786	Yarmouth	1841	A1
24 Aug.	*Cadet* (1)	Bk.	465	Isle of Man	1841	A1
24 Aug.	*Angelina*	Bk.	434	Hull	1842	A1
5 Sept.	*Barossa* (3)	Bk.	730	Bengal	1811	AE1
30 Oct.	*Emily II*	Bk.	580	Sunderland	1841	A1
15 Nov.	*Lord Auckland* (1)	S.	628	Calcutta	1836	A1
20 Nov.	*William Jardine* (2)	S.	693	Liverpool	1836	A1

Master	*Surgeon*	*Sailed*	*From*	*Route*	*Days*
Jn. P. Ridley	Ptr. Leonard	2 4 42	Spithead		109
Hy. Neatby	Geo. T. Moxey	24 4 42	Plymouth	Direct	92
Thos. Fremlin	W. H. B. Jones	10 4 42	Downs		109
Jn. A. McDonald	Rbt. Bower	1 5 42	Dublin		94
Hy. I. Naylor	Jn. Tarn	5 4 42	Downs	Cape	128
Jn. Goss	Rchd. Lewis	10 4 42	Dublin		129
Wm. T. Fell	Jn. R. Roberts	5 5 42	Woolwich	Cape	142
Wm. Liddesdale	Geo. I. Fox	10 7 42	Dublin	Direct	105
Jn. Biddle	Alex. Bryson	18 7 42	Spithead	Cape	112
Chris. Lamb	Hy. Kelsall	14 10 42	Cape		40
Jn. Humble	And. Henderson	28 6 42	Sheerness		149
Hy. Ager	Hy. Kelsall	1 6 42	Sheerness		
Jas. Gilbert	Jas. Smith	14 8 42	Plymouth	Direct	106
Jas. Morgan	Sam. Mackay	4 9 42	Dublin	Direct	102
Jos. Dare	Wm. McDowell	17 8 42	London	Cape	124
Chris. A. Warning	Jn. J. Lancaster	22 9 42	Dublin		110
Alex. S. Molison	Colin A. Browning	5 10 42	Plymouth	Direct	101
Chas. Scott	Wm. West	2 10 42	Sheerness	Direct	108
Wm. B. Forward	Wm. Bland	2 10 42	Woolwich	Direct	110
Thos. Fyall	Jas. L. Clarke	20 12 42	Dublin		105
Wm. Morgan	Thos. E. Ring	7 12 42	Spithead	Cape	124
Jn. F. Dye	(i) McAvoy (ii) Jn. A. Mould	5 2 43	London	Cape	164
Wm. M. Maw	Jas. Syme	14 4 43	Sheerness	C. Vde.	127
Jas. Molison	Jas. Lawrence	30 4 43	Plymouth	Cape	112
Jn. Hemery	Jn. S. Hampton	9 5 43	Dublin	Direct	112
Jas. Parley	Ed. Caldwell	10 5 43	Dublin	Mad.	133
Geo. Barlow	And. Sinclair	28 5 43	Sheerness	Cape	118
Rbt. Curling	Alick Osborne	30 6 43	Sheerness		104
Jn. Symons	J. O. McWilliam	27 6 43	Spithead		107
Jos. Luckley or Thos. Barker	Dav. Deas	7 7 43	London		100
Geo. Longford	Abraham R. Bradford	13 7 43	London		129
Wm. Tayt	Jas. Booth	12 8 43	Dublin		101
Wm. B. Dobson	Jason Lardner	3 9 43	London		113
Dav. Clark	Jn. W. Elliott	21 9 43	Dublin		103
Capt. Coglin, R.N.	And. Miller	1 10 43	Plymouth	Rio	126
Geo. Kettlewell	Jn. Wilson	30 11 43	London		124
Rbt. D. Guthrie	W. H. B. Jones	29 11 43	Deptford		126
Jas. Cromarty	Wm. West	20 1 44	Woolwich		95
Jn. Edgar	Jas. Clarke	5 3 44	Dublin		119
Jn. T. Attwood	Chas. Inches	23 3 44	P'smouth		108
Jn. Baker	Jas. Osborne	25 4 44	London		96
Jn. C. Hillman	Rbt. Bower	9 4 44	Dublin		137
Jn. Gray	Thos. E. Ring	28 4 44	Woolwich	Ten.	118
Jn. Austin	Jn. Gannon	17 5 44	Downs	Ten.	111
Hy. H. Greaves	Jn. Munro	14 7 44	Dublin		108
Rbt. Brown	Jn. J. Lancaster	16 7 44	London	Direct	122
Fran. Wilkins Lodge	Jn. Robertson	11 8 44	London		101

Date of Arrival	Vessel	R.	Ton	Built at	Year	Class
20 Dec.	*Tasmania* (1)	Bk.	502	Sunderland	1841	A1
26 Dec.	*Sir Robert Peel*	S.	724	Sunderland	1841	A1
1845						
2 Jan.	*Phoebe*	Bk.	578	Sunderland	1842	A1
27 Feb.	*Sir George Seymour*	S.	580			
9 June	*Elizabeth and Henry* (1)	Bk.	534	Sunderland	1845	A1
19 June	*Mount Stewart Elphinstone* (1)	S.	611	Bombay	1826	AE1
3 July	*Theresa* (2)	Bk.	497	Calcutta	1834	A1
4 July	*Tory* (1)	Bk.	512	Sunderland	1842	A1
30 Aug.	*Ratcliffe* (1)	S.	739	Whitby	1842	A1
16 Sept.	*Marion* (2)	S.	684	Calcutta	1834	A1
15 Oct.	*Equestrian* (2)	S.	801	Hull	1842	A1
7 Nov.	*Lloyds* (3)	Bk.	403	London	1830	A1
4 Dec.	*Tasmania* (2)	Bk.	502	Sunderland	1841	A1
25 Dec.	*Stratheden*	S.	429	Yarmouth	1834	A1
30 Dec.	*Pestonjee Bomanjee* (1)	S.	595	Dumbarton	1835	A1
1846						
18 Jan.	*Samuel Boddington*	Bk.	669	Whitby	1841	A1
19 May	*Joseph Somes* (1)	S.	780	London	1845	A1
5 June	*Emma Eugenia* (4)	Bk.	383	Whitby	1835	A1
22 Aug.	*Palmyra*	Bk.	602	Calcutta	1820	AE1
26 Aug.	*Lord Auckland* (2)	Bk.	628	Calcutta	1836	A1
29 Aug.	*Sea Queen*	Bk.	415	Calcutta	1841	A1
27 Oct.	*Maitland* (3)	S.	648	Calcutta	1810	AE1
1847						
4 Jan.	*Elizabeth and Henry* (2)	Bk.	534	Sunderland	1845	A1
17 Feb.	*Pestonjee Bomanjee* (2)	S.	595	Dumbarton	1835	
25 Feb.	*Arabian*	Bk.	391	Liverpool	1825	AE1
18 Mar.	*Tory* (2)	Bk.	512	Sunderland	1842	A1
21 July	*Asia V* (5)	Bk.	523	Calcutta	1814	AE1
25 Oct.	*Waverley* (4)	Bk.	436	Whitby	1838	A1
1848						
2 Jan.	*Cadet* (2)	Bk.	465	Isle of Man	1841	A1
9 Jan.	*Marion* (3)	S.	684	Calcutta	1834	A1
18 May	*John Calvin* (2)	Bk.	510	Greenock	1839	A1
18 May	*Mount Stewart Elphinstone* (2)	Bk.	611	Bombay	1826	AE1
7 June	*Anna Maria* (1)	Bk.	421	Calcutta	1836	A1
30 June	*Elizabeth and Henry* (3)	Bk.	534	Sunderland	1845	A1
14 July	*Bangalore* (1)	Bk.	877	Jersey	1843	A1
6 Aug.	*Tory* (3)	Bk.	512	Sunderland	1842	A1
7 Oct.	*Kinnear* (2)	Bk.	369	Yarmouth	1834	AE1
12 Nov.	*Ratcliffe* (2)	S.	739	Whitby	1842	A1
1849						
2 Jan.	*Pestonjee Bomanjee* (3)	Bk.	595	Dumbarton	1835	
20 Jan.	*Lord Auckland* (3)	Bk.	628	Calcutta	1836	A1
21 Jan.	*Eden* (4)	S.	513	London	1826	A1
2 Feb.	*Blenheim II* (1)	S.	808	Shields	1845	A1
12 Apr.	*Cadet* (3)	Bk.	465	Isle of Man	1841	A1
23 July	*Maria II*	Bk.	460	Yarmouth	1836	A1

Master	Surgeon	Sailed	From	Route	Days
Wm. Black	Thos. Seaton	8 9 44	London		103
Wm. Champion	Jn. A. Mould	9 9 44	London	Cape	108
Wm. Dale	Alex. C. Macleroy	25 9 44	Dublin		99
Jn. Young	Jn. S. Hampton	9 11 44	Woolwich	Direct	110
Clarke	T. W. Jewell	15 2 45	Dublin		114
Adolphus Holton	Jas. A. Gordon	7 3 45	London		104
Thos. Bacon	Colin A. Browning	1 4 45	London		93
Jn. P. Mills	Jn. Sloan	22 3 45	Woolwich	Ten.	104
Jas. Gilbert	Rbt. Dobie	19 5 45	Dublin		103
Kettlewell	Jn. W. Elliott	14 6 45	Woolwich		94
Jos. L. Spence	Thos. Robertson	5 7 45	London		102
Dav. Lewis	Chas. K. Nutt	26 7 45	Woolwich		104
Wm. Black	Jason Lardner	2 9 45	Dublin		93
Jn. Bruton	Hy. Baker	3 8 45	London		144
Jn. Austin	J. W. Johnston	10 9 45	Woolwich		111
Hy. Tamott	Jas. Carmichael	23 9 45	Dublin	Cape	117
Geo. Thompson	Jas. L. Clarke	22 12 45	Woolwich	Ten.	148
Wilfd. Beech	Jn. Wilson	10 2 46	P'smouth		115
Dan. W. Stephens	Dav. Geddes	8 3 46	Woolwich		167
Rbt. Brown	(i) Ben. Bynoe[1], (ii) J. J. W. Roberts	19 4 46	Dublin	Cape	120
Geo. W. Wood	T. W. Jewell	12 5 46	Woolwich		109
Jn. Gray	John Robertson	29 6 46	London		129
Wm. J. S. Clark	Harvey Morris	17 9 46	London		109
Jn. Austin	Col. A. Browning	25 10 46	London		115
Jn. Robertson	Rbt. Wylie	22 11 46	Dublin		95
Jn. Young	Rbt. McLean	11 11 46	Dublin		127
Jn. Roskell	Jason Lardner	23 3 47	Woolwich	Direct	120
Jas. Morgan	Plp. Jones	18 7 47	Dublin		99
Wm. Forsayth	Chas. R. Kinnear	9 9 47	London	Direct	115
Chas. W. M. S. McKerlie	Jn. Andrews	29 9 47	London		102
Jn. Davison	Jn. W. Bowler	24 1 48	Dublin	Direct	115
Adolphus Holton	Thos. H. Keown	6 2 48	Gibraltar		102
Ed. M. Smith	Rbt. Stephenson	9 3 48	Woolwich		90
Wm. J. S. Clark	Jn. Smith	13 2 48	London	Cape	138
———	Martyn Harvey Morris	——	——	Bermuda	—
Smith	Chas. Smith	30 4 48	London		98
Rbt. Heard	Jn. G. Williams	16 6 48	Dublin		113
Phillipson	Jn. Gibson	29 7 48	Spithead		106
Jn. Baker	Jn. Tarn	20 9 48	Dublin		104
Thos. Bacon	Jn. Moodie	11 10 48	Dublin		101
Murdoch	(i) Rbt. McCrea* (ii) Rbt. Beith	5 10 48	Plymouth	Mad.	108
A. S. Watson	Thos. R. Thomson		Dublin		
R. Pratt	Jn. C. Bowman	1 11 48	Woolwich		151
F. W. Plank	Ed. Nolloth	5 4 49	Dublin	Direct	109

[1] Superseded at Cape of Good Hope because of illness.

Date of Arrival	Vessel	R.	Ton	Built at	Year	Class
26 Aug.	*Hyderabad* (2)	S.	815	Sunderland	1841	A1
2 Sept.	*Stately*	Bk.	565	Sunderland	1847	A1
29 Sept.	*Australasia*	Bk.	500	Sunderland	1847	A1
29 Nov.	*Adelaide*	S.	640	Calcutta	1832	AE1
1850						
3 Apr.	*Eliza IV*	S.	682	Calcutta	1815	AE1
4 Apr.	*St. Vincent* (2)	S.	630	London	1829	A1
5 Apr.	*Neptune III* (2)	S.	644	Calcutta	1814	AE1
9 May	*Earl Grey* (4)	Bk.	571	Newcastle	1835	AE1
24 July	*Blenheim II* (2)	S.	808	Shields	1845	A1
25 July	*Baretto Junior*	Bk.	522	Calcutta	1818	AE1
9 Aug.	*Maria Somes* (2)	Bk.	786	Yarmouth	1841	A1
3 Oct.	*Nile II* (1)	S.	763	Sunderland	1849	A1
27 Oct.	*Duke of Cornwall*	S.	580	Bristol	1843	A1
14 Nov.	*William Jardine* (3)	S.	671	Liverpool	1836	A1
28 Nov.	*Rodney* (1)	S.	877	Sunderland	1850	A1
13 Dec.	*Hyderabad* (3)	S.	815	Sunderland	1842	A1
1851						
7 Mar.	*Emma Eugenia* (5)	Bk.	383	Whitby	1833	AE1
19 Mar.	*London* (2)	S.	612	London	1833	A1
28 May	*Lady Kennaway* (3)	Bk.	584	Calcutta	1817	AE1
29 May	*Blackfriar*	Bk.	621	Sunderland	1848	A1
11 June	*Cornwall*	Bk.	872	Calcutta	1811	AE1
10 Aug.	*Aurora II*	Bk.	536	Sunderland	1843	A1
31 Oct.	*Blenheim II* (3)	S.	808	Shields	1845	A1
20 Dec.	*Rodney* (2)	S.	877	Sunderland	1850	A1
1852						
26 Jan.	*Anna Maria* (2)	Bk.	421	Calcutta	1836	A1
20 Mar.	*Aboukir*	Bk.	816	Sunderland	1846	A1
22 May	*John William Dare*	Bk.	291	Cringa	1832	
3 July	*Fairlie* (2)	Bk.	756	Calcutta	1812	AE1
8 July	*Sir Robert Seppings*	S.	628	Moulmein	1844	A1
31 July	*Pestonjee Bomanjee* (4)	Bk.	595	Dumbarton	1835	
14 Aug.	*Lord Dalhousie* (1)	S.	912	Sunderland	1847	A1
1 Sept.	*Martin Luther*	Bk.	450	Greenock	1840	A1
9 Dec.	*Lady Montagu*	S.	763	Southampton	1848	A1
16 Dec.	*Equestrian* (3)	S.	801	Hull	1842	A1
1853						
29 Jan.	*Lord Auckland* (4)	Bk.	628	Calcutta	1836	AE1
12 Feb.	*Rodney* (3)	S.	877	Sunderland	1850	A1
19 Feb.	*Oriental Queen*	S.	645	Cork	1842	AE1
24 Feb.	*Midlothian*	Bk.	414	Sunderland	1835	AE1
21 Apr.	*Duchess of Northumberland* (2)	Bk.	541	Sunderland	1834	AE1
26 May	*St. Vincent* (3)	S.	630	London	1829	AE1

III. CONVICT SHIPS TO

1803						
9 Oct.	*Calcutta*	HMS.				
1844						
11 Nov.	*Royal George* (3)	S.	486	Hull	1820	A1

Master	Surgeon	Sailed	From	Route	Days
T. A. Castle	L. S. Cunningham	23 5 49	Dublin		95
Thos. Ginder	Jn. W. Elliott	16 5 49	Woolwich		109
Jas. Connell	Alex. Kilroy	26 6 49	Dublin		95
Steph. Wharton	Fred. W. Le Grand	17 8 49	Portland		104
Daniel	Jn. Andrews	24 12 49	London		100
Jn. Young	Sam. Donnelly	19 12 49	Downs	Direct	106
Henderson	Thos. Gibson			Cape	
H. E. Landsdowne	Jn. Ferrier	17 12 49	Dublin	Direct	143
Alex. S. Molison	Chas. Hy. Fuller	10 4 50	Plymouth		105
J. Huggins	R. Whitmore Clarke	13 4 50	Downs		103
Hy. I. Naylor	J. G. Williams	6 5 50	P'smouth		95
Geo. N. Livesay	Jn. Kidd	5 7 50	Portland		90
Jn. Whitehead	Chas. Smith		Dublin		
Jas. Raitte	Jn. Campbell	12 8 50	Portland		94
Alex. Maclean	Fred. W. Le Grand	23 8 50	Portland		07
T. A. Castle	T. H. Keown	13 9 50	Q'stown		91
F. T. Davies	Jn. Bower	30 10 50	London		128
J. Sceales	Jas. Booth	20 12 50	Dublin		89
J. Santry	J. Caldwell	5 2 51	P'smouth		112
T. Greeves	Jn. Moody	24 1 51	Dublin		125
Maundrell	Dav. Geddes	24 2 51	P'smouth	Gib.	107
Valentine Ryan	W. B. Jones	26 4 51	London		106
Alex. S. Molison	Jn. Smith	29 7 51	Cork		94
Alex. Maclean	Harvey Morris	24 9 51	Q'stown	Gib.	87
Ed. M. Smith	W. McCrea	6 10 51	Woolwich	Direct	112
Jn. Cowell	Ben. Bynoe	28 12 51	Plymouth		83
Thos. Walters	Rbt. W. Clarke	28 12 51	Dublin	Cape	146
Ed. Pavey	Ed. Nolloth	11 3 52	Plymouth		114
R. S. Stewart	L. S. Cunningham	18 3 52	Woolwich		112
Ed. Montgomery	Dan. Ritchie	18 4 52	Plymouth		104
W. T. Ferris	Chas. Anderson	30 4 52	Cork		106
Ken. Ross	Thos. Crawford	8 6 52	Dublin		85
And. Cheyne	Sam. Donnelly	9 8 52	Plymouth		122
M. C. Loney	Alex. Cross	1 9 52	Plymouth		106
Geo. Thompson	J. Davison	29 9 52	Cork		122
Alex. Maclean	Joseph Caldwell	24 11 52	Cork		80
S. R. Thomas	Dav. Geddes	4 11 52	Plymouth		107
J. Gibson	Dav. Thomas	17 11 52	Dublin		99
Geo. Mitchell	Chas. Smith	28 11 52	Woolwich		144
Jn. Young	Thos. Sommerville	17 1 53	Spithead	Gib.	128

PORT PHILLIP, 1803-1849

Capt. Dan. Woodriff R.N.		24 4 03	Spithead	Ten., Rio, Cape	168

Date of Arrival	Vessel	R.	Ton	Built at	Year	Class
1845						
20 Mar.	*Sir George Seymour* (*a*)	S.	580			
1846						
27 Jan.	*Stratheden*	S.	429	Yarmouth	1834	A1
9 Nov.	*Maitland* (3)	S.	648	Calcutta	1810	AE1
1847						
4 May	*Thomas Arbuthnot*	S.	621	Aberdeen	1841	A1
24 Sept.	*Joseph Somes* (2) (*a*)	S.	780	London	1845	A1
1848						
25 Jan.	*Marion* (3)	S.	684	Calcutta	1834	A1
22 June	*Anna Maria* (1) (*a*)	Bk.	421	Calcutta	1836	A1
1849						
4 Feb.	*Eden I* (3) (*a*)	S.	513	London	1826	A1
May	*Hashemy* (1) (*b*)	Bk.	523	Calcutta	1817	AE1
8 Aug.	*Randolph* (*b*)	S.	761			
13 Dec.	*Adelaide* (1) (*b*)	S.	640	Calcutta	1832	AE1

a Landed Port Phillip proportion of prisoners at Geelong.
b Prisoners did not disembark at Port Phillip, but were sent on to Sydney.

IV. CONVICT SHIPS TO

1840						
	Nautilus (2)	Bk.	400	Shields	1833	A1
27 Mar.	*Augusta Jessie* (3)	Bk.	385	Sunderland	1834	A1
	Mangles (9)	S.	594	Calcutta	1802	AE1
1844						
7 Feb.	*Maitland* (2)	S.	648	Calcutta	1810	AE1
12 July	*Blundell*	Bk.	573	Moulmein	1839	A1
9 Nov.	*Agincourt*	S.	958	London	1841	A1
1845						
19 Feb.	*Hydrabad*	S.	695	Shields	1843	A1
25 Aug.	*David Malcolm*	Bk.	495	Moulmein	1839	A1
2 Sept.	*Hyderabad* (1)	S.	815	Sunderland	1842	A1
1846						
8 Jan.	*Mayda*	Bk.	582	Sunderland	1845	A1
16 May	*China*	S.	524	Hull	1837	A1
21 Sept.	*John Calvin* (1)	Bk.	510	Greenock	1839	A1
1847						
	Tory (2)	Bk.	512	Sunderland	1842	A1
1850						
30 Apr.	*Eliza IV*	S.	682	Calcutta	1815	AE1

V. CONVICT SHIPS TO

1849						
1 Nov.	*Mount Stewart Elphinstone* (3)	S.	611	Bombay	1826	AE1
1850						
30 Apr.	*Bangalore* (2)	Bk.	877	Jersey	1843	A1

Master	*Surgeon*	*Sailed*	*From*	*Route*	*Days*
Jn. Young	Jn. S. Hampton	9 11 44	Woolwich	Hobart	132
Jn. Bruton	Hy. Baker	3 8 45	London	Hobart	177
Jn. Gray	Jn. Robertson	29 6 46	Spithead	Hobart	133
Thomson	Hy. Baker	10 1 47	Portland		114
Geo. Thompson	Jn. W. Elliott	4 6 47	Spithead		112
Chas. W. M. S. McKerlie	Jn. Andrews	29 9 47	Spithead	Ten., Hob.	128
Ed. M. Smith	Rbt. Stephenson	9 3 48	Woolwich	Hobart	106
Murdoch	(i) Rbt. McCrea* (ii) Rbt. Beith	5 10 48	Plymouth	Mad., Hob.	122
Jn. Ross	Col. A. Browning and Edmonston	11 2 49	P'smouth	Cape	
Wm. Dale	W. Lawrence	28 4 49	London	Cape	102
Steph. Wharton	Fred. W. Le Grand	17 8 49	Portland	Hobart	118

NORFOLK ISLAND, 1840-1847

Master	*Surgeon*	*Sailed*	*From*	*Route*	*Days*
H. F. Alloway	Geo. McClure	17 9 39	Dublin	Sydney	
J. S. Sparke	Thos. R. Dunn	11 11 39	Dublin	Sydney	
Wm. Carr	Alex. Nisbet	28 11 39	Plymouth	Ten., Cape Sydney	
	Allan McLaren	1 9 43	Plymouth	Cape, Sydney	159
Rbt. L. Hunter	Ben. Bynoe				
Hy. Neatby	Chas. Hy. Fuller	9 7 44	Woolwich	Cape	123
Alex. Robertson	J. O. McWilliam	21 10 44	Downs	Cape	121
Jas. Cable	Harvey Morris	13 5 45	Downs		104
T. A. Castle					
May	Alex. Kilroy	29 8 45	Woolwich	Cape	132
Livesay	Geo. S. Rutherford	7 1 46	Woolwich	Ten.	129
	Hy. Kelsall	13 5 46	Woolwich		131
Lukey or Jn. Young	Rbt. Maclean	11 11 46	Dublin		
Daniel	Jn. Andrews	24 12 49	London	Hobart	127

MORETON BAY, 1849-1850

Master	*Surgeon*	*Sailed*	*From*	*Route*	*Days*
Hy. C. Loney	Geo. T. Moxey	31 5 49	Spithead	Cork, Sydney	154
Wm. Morgan	Wm. B. Jones	7 1 50	Spithead	Direct	113

VI. CONVICT SHIPS TO

Date of Arrival	*Vessel*	*R.*	*Ton*	*Built at*	*Year*	*Class*
1850						
1 June	*Scindian*	Bk.	650	Sunderland	1844	A1
25 Oct.	*Hashemy* (2)	Bk.	523	Calcutta	1817	AE1
1851						
13 May	*Mermaid* (3)	Bk.	473	Calcutta	1817	AE1
28 June	*Pyrenees* (1)	S.	832	Sunderland	1851	A1
14 Oct.	*Minden*	S.	916	Sunderland	1848	A1
1852						
30 Jan.	*Marion* (4)	S.	684	Calcutta	1834	AE1
1 Aug.	*William Jardine* (4)	S.	671	Liverpool	1836	AE1
1853						
7 Feb.	*Dudbrook*	Bk.	601	Dundee	1848	A1
30 Apr.	*Pyrenees* (2)	S.	832	Sunderland	1851	A1
19 Aug.	*Robert Small*	S.	655	Newcastle	1835	AE1
30 Aug.	*Phoebe Dunbar*	S.	704	Sunderland	1850	A1
1854						
5 Apr.	*Sea Park*	S.	835	Shields	1845	A1
7 Aug.	*Ramillies*	Bk.	757	Sunderland	1845	A1
1855						
23 May	*Stag*	Bk.	678	Sunderland	1842	A1
18 July	*Adelaide* (2)	S.	640	Calcutta	1832	AE1
1856						
29 Mar.	*William Hammond*	S.	683	Sunderland	1853	A1
7 Sept.	*Runnymede*	S.	720	Sunderland	1854	A1
1857						
3 July	*Clara* (1)	S.	708	Sunderland	1853	A1
1858						
1 Jan.	*Nile II* (2)	S.	763	Sunderland	1849	A1
1 June	*Lord Raglan*	S.	756	Cardiff	1854	A1
20 Nov.	*Edwin Fox*	S.	892	Calcutta	1853	A1
1859						
19 Aug.	*Sultana*	S.	775	Sunderland	1854	A1
1861						
11 Feb.	*Palmerston*	S.	978	Moulmein	1853	A1
1862						
28 Jan.	*Lincelles*	S.	904	Moulmein	1858	A1
9 June	*Norwood* (1)	S.	849	Sunderland	1854	A1
31 Dec.	*York II*	S.	940	Sunderland	1854	A1
1863						
14 Feb.	*Merchantman* (1) (*a*)	S.	1018	Sunderland	1852	A1
29 May	*Clyde II*	S.	1151	Glasgow	1860	A1
28 Dec.	*Lord Dalhousie* (2)	S.	912	Sunderland	1847	A1

(*a*) Strictly speaking the *Merchantman* should not be included, as her convicts did not come from England, but Bermuda.

WESTERN AUSTRALIA, 1850-1868

Master	*Surgeon*	*Sailed*	*From*	*Route*	*Days*
Jas. Cammell	Jn. Gibson	4 3 50	P'smouth		89
Jn. Ross	Jn. W. Bowler	22 7 50	Portland		95
J. P. Anderson	Alex. Kilroy	9 1 51	P'smouth		123
Thos. Eagles	Alex. C. Macleroy	30 3 51	Torbay	Direct	90
R. D. Crawford	John Gibson	21 7 51	Plymouth		85
Alex. Bissett	Fred. W. Le Grand	2 11 51	Portland		89
Jas. Raiff	Jas. Donnet	3 5 52	Plymouth		88
Jn. Innes	Chas. W. Keveru	22 11 52	Plymouth		77
B. Freeman	Jn. Bower	2 2 53	England		87
J. H. Walker	Harvey Morris	1 5 53	London		110
T. Michie	Jn. W. Bowler	2 6 53	K'stown		89
Thos. Spedding	Josiah Caldwell	1 1 54	London		94
Chas. Hodder	Daniel Ritchie	20 5 54	London	Ply., Gib.	79
H. N. Clarke		5 2 55	London		107
M. Longman	S. Donnelly	19 4 55	Portland		90
Horatio Edwards	Geo. D. MacLaren	5 1 56	Plymouth		84
Wm. Burrows		15 6 56	Plymouth		84
Hy. Peachey		19 3 57	London		106
W. Johnson		23 9 57	Plymouth		100
Thos. Hybert	Jn. Bower	5 3 58	Plymouth		88
Jos. Ferguson		26 8 58	Plymouth		86
Art. Sharp		29 5 59	Plymouth		82
J. N. Seagrove		10 11 60	Portland		93
Edwin Gooch	Wm. Crawford	5 10 61	Portland	Cape	115
Frank Bristow	A. Watson	16 3 62	Portland		85
C. Breacey		8 10 62	Portland		84
Wm. Gardiner	Wm. Smith	12 10 62	London	Bermuda	125
Hy. Stephens	Wm. Crauford	15 3 63	Portland		75
Geo. Harvey		25 9 63	Portland		90

Date of Arrival	*Vessel*	*R.*	*Ton*	*Built at*	*Year*	*Class*
1864						
13 Apr.	*Clara* (2)	S.	708	Sunderland	1853	A1
12 Sept.	*Merchantman* (2)	S.	1018	Sunderland	1852	A1
1865						
10 Aug.	*Racehorse*	S.	1077	Jersey	1853	A1
22 Dec.	*Vimeira*	S.	941	Sunderland	1851	A1
1866						
4 July	*Belgravia*	S.	889	Sunderland	1862	A1
22 Dec.	*Corona*	S.	1199	Dundee	1866	A1
1867						
13 July	*Norwood* (2)	S.	786	Sunderland	1854	A1
1868						
9 Jan.	*Hougoumont*	S.	875	Moulmein	1852	A1

Master	Surgeon	Sailed	From	Route	Days
R. Burrows		11 1 64	London	Direct	93
Wm. Gardiner	Wm. Smith	1 7 64	Portland	Direct	73
M. H. Seward	A. Watson	26 5 65	Portland		76
Malcolm Green	Wm. Crauford	30 9 65	Portland	Direct	83
Jn. E. W. Jackson		7 4 66	Portland		88
Wm. S. Crudace	Wm. Crauford	16 10 66	Portland		67
Frank Bristow	W. M. Saunders	18 4 67	Portland	Direct	86
Wm. Cozens		12 10 67	London		89

NOTES TO APPENDIX VII

Prisoners: It is almost impossible to compile accurate convict statistics. The figures in official returns frequently differ, and there are discrepancies as between the papers relating to an individual ship. Apart from the mistakes made by the clerks who compiled or copied the returns, there is ample room for error by a modern historian in the interpretation of these documents. For example, in those ships which carried both men and women it is not always obvious whether a prisoner's name is that of a man or a woman, nor is it always possible to tell whether a convict relanded before sailing was replaced by another or not. The figures in this appendix are as accurate as is possible in the circumstances. They have in most instances been obtained by individually counting the names in the documents. The Indents, Muster Lists and surgeons' journals and reports are, in my opinion, the most reliable of these documents, to which, for a later period, have to be added the certificates given to surgeons and masters recording the number of convicts landed. In addition to these documents in Australian archives, I have also used a wide range of figures in the P.R.O. (HO 10/1, 11/1, etc., CO 207, etc.), as well as Assignment Lists and other official returns. *Figures* for which no definite evidence has been found, or which are arrived at from two established figures (e.g. where embarkation and disembarkation figures are proved and it has been assumed, after allowance for relanded and escaped, that the difference between the two is due to deaths on the passage) are preceded by a query mark (?). Figures not so marked have been established by evidence. Ships marked with an asterisk were wrecked. Ships which disembarked convicts at Sydney or Hobart *and* Norfok Island are included in Appendix VII (*c*) and those which disembarked prisoners at Hobart or Sydney *and* Port Phillip are included in Appendix VII (*d*).

On the question of the number of convicts transported to Australia, *see* L. L. Robson, *The Convict Settlers of Australia* (Melbourne, 1965), A. G. L. Shaw, *Convicts and the Colonies* (London, 1966), and P. R. Eldershaw, *Guide to the Public Records of Tasmania*, Section Three: Convict Department Record Group (Hobart, 1965), 62-63.

VII (a) STATISTICS OF MALE AND FEMALE CONVICTS FROM ENGLAND AND IRELAND, 1788-1886

(i) Male Convicts.

	Embarked	*Relanded, Probably Relanded or Escaped before Sailing*	*Probably Sailed*
1788-1800	6041	19	6022
1801-1810	3528	53	3475
1811-1820	15,438	46	15,392
1821-1830	28,753	60	28,693
1831-1840	43,515	259	43,257
1841-1850	26,106	74	26,032
1851-1853 (*a*)	4317	16	4301
1850-1868 (*b*)	9700	9	9691
Totals	137,398	535	136,863

	Deaths	*Should have Landed*	*Landed*	*Difference of Landed over Should have Landed*
1788-1800	705	5317	5304	−13
1801-1810	188	3287	3287	+1
1811-1820	201	15,191	15,192	+1
1821-1830	261	28,432	28,434	+2
1831-1840	583	42,674	42,506	−168
1841-1850	349	25,683	25,642	−41
1851-1853 (*a*)	42	4259	4260	+1
1850-1868 (*b*)	53	9638	9636	−2
Totals	2382	134,481	134,262	−219

(ii) Female Convicts.

	Embarked	*Relanded or Escaped before Sailing*	*Probably Sailed*
1788-1800	1441	—	1441
1801-1810	1304	2	1302
1811-1820	1933	6	1927
1821-1830	4144	4	4140
1831-1840	7719	64	7655
1841-1850	6954	17	6937
1851-1853	1856	2	1854
Totals	25,351	95	25,256
Males	137,398	535	136,863
Grand Totals	162,749	630	162,119

(*a*) Excluding Western Australia.
(*b*) Western Australia only.

	Deaths	Should have Landed	Landed	Difference
1788-1800	51	1390	1330	−60 (*c*)
1801-1810	30	1272	1271	−1
1811-1820	28	1899	1858	−41 (*d*)
1821-1830	41	4099	4099	—
1831-1840	321	7334	7337	+3
1841-1850	102	6835	6835	—
1851-1853	16	1838	1838	—
Totals	589	24,667	24,568	−99
Males	2382	134,481	134,262	−219
Grand Totals	2971	159,148	158,830	−318
Other Colonies			1321 (*e*)	
Grand total of convict arrivals			160,151 (*f*)	

(*c*) Sixty-six women on the *Lady Shore* did not arrive. As there were six unexplained arrivals on the *Albemarle* (*see* text, p. 122), embarkations and arrivals balance when these facts are taken into account, assuming that the six women in the *Albemarle* were originally embarked in the *Mary Ann*.

(*d*) The discrepancy is mainly explained by the capture of the *Emu*, which was carrying 40 women.

(*e*) This figure comes from A. G. L. Shaw, *Convicts and the Colonies*, 363-368.

(*f*) Shaw's appendix gives a grand total of 146,949 convicts disembarked in Australia, excluding Western Australia, where he says 9635 men arrived (p. 356). If we add these, his grand total becomes 156,584—2246 fewer than my grand total. His figures give 145,628 prisoners—120,950 men and 24,678 women—arriving in the eastern states and Norfolk Island as compared with my totals, excluding Western Australia, of 149,194—124,626 men and 24,568 women. He gives the number of deaths as 2378—2058 men and 320 women—as against my total of 2971—2382 men and 589 women. My deaths exceed Shaw's total by 593—324 men and 269 women —but it would seem he excludes deaths between embarkation and sailing (e.g. his total of 20 male and three female deaths for the First Fleet omits the 16 men and one woman who died before the fleet sailed). My total of 9636 male convicts arriving in Western Australia exceeds his by one. The fact that we have used the same sources but arrived at different figures indicates the difficulty of interpreting the conflicting official figures, apart altogether from errors in arithmetic. I should point out I have treated deaths before sailing as deaths on the voyage and have not deducted these in arriving at my figures of *Probably Sailed*.

VII (b) PRISONERS DISEMBARKED AT SYDNEY AND HOBART

In the relanding figures a ? denotes probable relanding, E signifies escapes, 1/1E signifies 1 relanded, 1 escaped.

		Embarked		Relanded	Deaths		Landed: Sydney		Landed: Hobart	
Year	*Vessel*	*M.*	*F.*		*M.*	*F.*	*M.*	*F.*	*M.*	*F.*
1801	*Anne* (or *Luz St. Anna*)	147	24	17	3	—	127	24	—	—
1801	*Earl Cornwallis*	193	95	—	27	8	166	87	—	—
1801	*Canada*	104	—	3?	—	—	101	—	—	—
1801	*Minorca*	104	—	3?	2	—	99	—	—	—
1801	*Nile*	—	96	—	—	—	—	96	—	—
1802	*Coromandel*	138	—	—	1	—	?137	—	—	—
1802	*Hercules*	140	25	—	44	—	96	25	—	—
1802	*Atlas* (Brooks)	151	28	3E	63	2	85	26	—	—
1802	*Perseus*	113	—	1	—	—	112	—	—	—
1802	*Atlas* (Musgrave)	208	—	15	?4	—	188	—	—	—
1803	*Glatton*	271	130	1/1E	7	5	262	125	—	—
1803	*Rolla*	127	37	5?	3	—	119	37	—	—
1804	*Coromandel*	200	—	—	—	—	200	—	—	—
1804	*Experiment*	2	136	—	—	6	2	130	—	—
1806	*Tellicherry*	130	36	—	5	1	125	35	—	—
1806	*William Pitt*	1	120	1	—	2	1	116	—	—
1806	*Fortune* }	260	—	—	4	—	256	—	—	—
1806	*Alexander* }	—	42	—	—	—	—	42	—	—
1807	*Sydney Cove*	4	113	—	—	3	4	110	—	—
1807	*Duke of Portland*	189	—	—	?	—	?189	—	—	—
1808	*Speke*	—	99	1	—	1	—	97	—	—
1808	*Admiral Gambier*	200	—	—	?3	—	197	—	—	—
1809	*Aeolus*	—	79	—	—	—	—	79	—	—
1809	*Experiment*	—	60	—	—	—	—	60	—	—
1809	*Boyd*	139	—	—	5	—	134	—	—	—
1809	*Indispensable*	—	62	—	—	1	—	61	—	—
1810	*Anne*	200	—	2?	1	—	197	—	—	—
1810	*Canada*	—	122	—	—	1	—	121	—	—
1810	*Indian*	200	—	—	8	—	192	—	—	—
1811	*Providence*	140	41	1M1F	3	2	136	38	—	—
1811	*Admiral Gambier*	200	—	—	3	—	197	—	—	—
1811	*Friends*	—	100	—	—	—	—	100	—	—
1812	*Guildford*	200	—	—	1	—	199	—	—	—
1812	*Indefatigable*	200	—	—	1	—	—	—	199	—
1812	*Minstrel*	—	127	1	—	1	—	125	—	—
1812	*Emu*	—	?40	—	—	—	—	—	—	—
1813	*Archduke Charles*	147	54	—	2	—	145	54	—	—
1813	*Fortune*	201	—	1	4	—	196	—	—	—
1813	*Earl Spencer*	200	—	—	4	—	196	—	—	—
1814	*Wanstead*	—	120	1	—	2	—	117	—	—
1814	*General Hewart*	300	—	—	34	—	266	—	—	—
1814	*Catherine*	—	98	—	—	1	—	97	—	—

(*N.B.*—Men were embarked both on the *Fortune* and *Alexander*, but separate figures for each ship are not available; women were embarked on the *Alexander* only.)

Year	Vessel	Embarked M.	Embarked F.	Relanded	Deaths M.	Deaths F.	Landed: Sydney M.	Landed: Sydney F.	Landed: Hobart M.	Landed: Hobart F.
1814	*Three Bees*	219	—	—	9	—	210	—	—	—
1814	*Broxbornebury*	—	120	—	—	2	—	118	—	—
1814	*Surrey*	200	—	—	36	—	164	—	—	—
1814	*Somersetshire*	200	—	—	1	—	199	—	—	—
1815	*Marquis of Wellington*	200	—	1	1	—	198	—	—	—
1815	*Indefatigable*	200	—	—	2	—	198	—	—	—
1815	*Northampton*	—	110	—	—	4	—	106	—	—
1815	*Canada*	160	—	4?	—	—	156	—	—	—
1815	*Francis and Eliza*	54	69	—	2	4	52	65	—	—
1815	*Baring*	300	—	—	2	—	298	—	—	—
1816	*Fanny*	174	—	—	3	—	171	—	—	—
1816	*Mary Anne*	—	103	1?	—	1	—	101	—	—
1816	*Ocean*	220	—	1	1	—	218	—	—	—
1816	*Alexander*	—	84	—	—	3	—	81	—	—
1816	*Guildford*	228	—	7?	1	—	?220	—	—	—
1816	*Atlas*	194	—	3/3?	1	—	187	—	—	—
1816	*Elizabeth*	155	—	2	2	—	151	—	—	—
1816	*Mariner*	145	—	—	—	—	145	—	—	—
1816	*Surrey*	150	—	—	—	—	150	—	—	—
1817	*Lord Melville*	—	103	2	—	2	—	99	—	—
1817	*Fame*	200	—	—	2	—	198	—	—	—
1817	*Sir William Bensley*	200	—	—	1	—	199	—	—	—
1817	*Morley*	175	—	—	—	—	175	—	—	—
1817	*Shipley*	125	—	—	—	—	125	—	—	—
1817	*Chapman*	200	—	2	12	—	186	—	—	—
1817	*Pilot*	119	—	2	—	—	117	—	—	—
1817	*Canada*	—	89	—	—	—	—	89	—	—
1817	*Almorah*	180	—	—	—	—	180	—	—	—
1817	*Lord Eldon*	221	—	1/1E	4	—	215	—	—	—
1817	*Larkins*	250	—	1E	2	—	247	—	—	—
1818	*Ocean*	180	—	—	—	—	180	—	—	—
1818	*Friendship*	—	101	—	—	4	—	97	—	—
1818	*Guildford*	204	—	5	1	—	198	—	—	—
1818	*Batavia*	221	—	1	—	—	220	—	—	—
1818	*Lady Castlereagh*	300	—	—	—	—	39	—	261	—
1818	*Minerva*	160	—	—	3	—	—	—	157	—
1818	*Neptune*	173	—	3	—	—	170	—	—	—
1818	*Glory*	170	—	—	—	—	170	—	—	—
1818	*Isabella*	230	—	—	3	—	227	—	—	—
1818	*Maria*	—	126	—	—	2	—	94	—	30
1818	*Tottenham*	200	—	—	10	—	190	—	—	—
1818	*Morley*	164	—	—	1	—	163	—	—	—
1818	*Shipley*	150	—	—	4(*a*)	—	146	—	—	—
1818	*Elizabeth*	—	101	—	—	—	—	101	—	—
1818	*Earl St. Vincent*	160	—	—	3	—	157	—	—	—
1818	*Lord Melville*	148	—	—	1	—	—	—	147	—
1818	*Hadlow*	150	—	—	1	—	149	—	—	—
1818	*Martha*	170	—	—	—	—	170	—	—	—
1818	*General Stewart*	250	—	—	4	—	246	—	—	—
1819	*Tyne*	180	—	—	1	—	179	—	—	—
1819	*Globe*	140	—	—	1	—	139	—	—	—
1819	*Surrey*	160	—	—	3	—	7	—	150	—

(*a*) One death after arrival and before convicts landed.

Year	Vessel	Embarked M.	Embarked F.	Relanded	Deaths M.	Deaths F.	Landed: Sydney M.	Landed: Sydney F.	Landed: Hobart M.	Landed: Hobart F.
1819	*Lord Sidmouth*	160	—	—	2	—	158	—	—	—
1819	*Hibernia*	160	—	—	3	—	—	—	157	—
1819	*Baring*	300	—	—	5	—	290	—	5	—
1819	*Bencoolen*	150	—	—	—	—	150	—	—	—
1819	*Mary*	160	—	—	1	—	159	—	—	—
1819	*Canada*	135	—	—	2	—	133	—	—	—
1819	*Daphne*	180	—	—	2	—	178	—	—	—
1819	*John Barry*	142	—	—	—	—	142	—	—	—
1819	*Atlas*	156	—	—	1	—	155	—	—	—
1819	*Grenada*	152	—	—	—	—	152	—	—	—
1819	*Malabar*	173	—	3	—	—	170	—	—	—
1819	*Recovery*	188	—	—	—	—	188	—	—	—
1819	*Minerva*	172	—	—	1	—	171	—	—	—
1820	*Dromedary*	370	—	1	—	—	22	—	347	—
1820	*Lord Wellington*	—	121	—	—	—	—	121	—	—
1820	*Eliza*	160	—	—	1	—	159	—	—	—
1820	*Prince Regent*	160	—	—	—	—	160	—	—	—
1820	*Castle Forbes*	140	—	—	—	—	4	—	136	—
1820	*Coromandel*	300	—	—	—	—	150	—	150	—
1820	*Janus*	—	105	1	—	—	—	104	—	—
1820	*Neptune*	156	—	—	—	—	156	—	—	—
1820	*Hadlow*	150	—	—	2	—	148	—	—	—
1820	*Mangles*	190	—	—	1	—	189	—	—	—
1820	*Earl St. Vincent*	160	—	—	1	—	159	—	—	—
1820	*Morley*	—	121	—	—	—	—	71	—	50
1820	*Dorothy*	190	—	—	—	—	190	—	—	—
1820	*Agamemnon*	179	—	—	1	—	178	—	—	—
1820	*Shipley*	150	—	1?	4	—	85	—	61	—
1820	*Guildford*	190	—	—	—	—	1	—	189	—
1820	*Caledonia*	150	—	—	—	—	—	—	150	—
1820	*Maria*	156	—	—	—	—	—	—	156	—
1820	*Almorah*	160	—	—	1	—	159	—	—	—
1820	*Asia*	190	—	—	1	—	189	—	—	—
1820	*Juliana*	160	—	—	1	—	—	—	159	—
1820	*Elizabeth*	172	—	1	1	—	170	—	—	—
1820	*Hebe*	160	—	1	—	—	159	—	—	—
1821	*Prince Regent*	144	—	—	—	—	144	—	—	—
1821	*Prince of Orange*	136	—	—	1	—	135	—	—	—
1821	*Lord Sidmouth*	175	—	15	—	—	160	—	—	—
1821	*Dick*	140	—	—	—	—	140	—	—	—
1821	*Medway*	156	—	—	—	—	—	—	156	—
1821	*Speke*	156	—	—	2	—	154	—	—	—
1821	*Lady Ridley*	141	—	3	1	—	—	—	137	—
1821	*Countess of Harcourt*	172	—	—	—	—	—	—	172	—
1821	*Adamant*	144	—	—	2	—	142	—	—	—
1821	*Grenada*	152	—	—	—	—	152	—	—	—
1821	*Malabar*	172	—	1	—	—	—	—	171	—
1821	*John Barry*	180	—	—	—	—	180	—	—	—
1821	*Hindostan*	152	—	—	—	—	152	—	—	—
1821	*Claudine*	160	—	—	1	—	—	—	159	—
1821	*Minerva*	172	—	—	3	—	169	—	—	—
1821	*Providence*	—	103	—	—	—	—	50	—	53
1821	*John Bull*	—	80	—	—	—	—	80	—	—
1821	*Lord Hungerford*	228	—	—	—	—	—	—	228	—

Year	Vessel	Embarked M.	Embarked F.	Relanded	Deaths M.	Deaths F.	Landed: Sydney M.	Landed: Sydney F.	Landed: Hobart M.	Landed: Hobart F.
1822	*Mary*	176	—	—	—	—	176	—	—	—
1822	*Southworth*	101	—	—	1	—	100	—	—	—
1822	*Isabella*	200	—	—	—	—	200	—	—	—
1822	*Shipley*	150	—	—	1	—	149	—	—	—
1822	*Richmond*	161	—	1	1	—	—	—	159	—
1822	*Mary Anne*	—	108	—	—	1	—	62	—	45
1822	*Phoenix*	184	—	—	2	—	—	—	182	—
1822	*Guildford*	190	—	—	1	—	189	—	—	—
1822	*Prince of Orange*	136	—	1?	4	—	—	—	132	—
1822	*Asia*	190	—	—	?1	—	189	—	—	—
1822	*Caledonia*	150	—	—	6	—	—	—	144	—
1822	*Arab*	157	—	1	3	—	—	—	153	—
1822	*Mangles*	191	—	1	—	—	190	—	—	—
1822	*Eliza*	160	—	—	—	—	160	—	—	—
1822	*Countess of Harcourt*	172	—	—	1	—	171	—	—	—
1823	*Morley*	172	—	—	2	—	—	—	170	—
1823	*Lord Sidmouth*	—	97	—	—	1	—	46	—	50
1823	*Surrey*	160	—	—	?3	—	157	—	—	—
1823	*Princess Royal*	156	—	—	?2	—	154	—	—	—
1823	*Brampton*	172	—	—	—	—	172	—	—	—
1823	*Woodman*	—	97	—	—	3	—	94	—	—
1823	*Recovery*	180	—	—	—	—	180	—	—	—
1823	*Competitor*	160	—	—	3	—	—	—	157	—
1823	*Commodore Hayes*	219	—	—	3	—	—	—	216	—
1823	*Henry*	160	—	—	—	—	160	—	—	—
1823	*Ocean*	173	—	2	6	—	165	—	—	—
1823	*Earl St. Vincent*	157	—	—	1	—	156	—	—	—
1823	*Mary*	—	127	1	—	—	—	59	—	67
1823	*Albion*	200	—	—	—	—	—	—	200	—
1823	*Isabella*	201	—	1?	5	—	195	—	—	—
1823	*Medina*	180	—	3	1	—	176	—	—	—
1823	*Sir Godfrey Webster*	180	—	—	—	—	—	—	180	—
1824	*Castle Forbes*	140	—	—	1	—	139	—	—	—
1824	*Asia*	150	—	—	—	—	—	—	150	—
1824	*Guildford*	160	—	—	1	—	159	—	—	—
1824	*Brothers*	—	89	—	—	—	—	39	—	50
1824	*Countess of Harcourt*	174	—	2	?1	—	171	—	—	—
1824	*Phoenix*	204	—	—	2	—	—	—	202	—
1824	*Prince Regent*	180	—	—	3	—	177	—	—	—
1824	*Chapman*	180	—	—	—	—	—	—	180	—
1824	*Almorah*	—	109	—	—	1	—	108	—	—
1824	*Mangles*	190	—	—	—	—	190	—	—	—
1824	*Princess Charlotte*	140	—	—	—	—	—	—	140	—
1824	*Minerva*	172	—	—	2	—	170	—	—	—
1825	*Ann and Amelia*	?200	—	—	—	—	200	—	—	—
1825	*Grenada*	—	82	1	—	—	—	81	—	—
1825	*Henry*	—	79	—	—	—	—	2	—	77
1825	*Asia* (Stead)	190	—	1?	—	—	190	—	—	—
1825	*Lady East*	210	—	—	2	—	—	—	208	—
1825	*Sir Charles Forbes*	130	—	—	2	—	—	—	128	—
1825	*Hooghly*	195	—	—	2	—	193	—	—	—
1825	*Royal Charlotte*	136	—	—	1	—	135	—	—	—
1825	*Asia* (Pope)	200	—	—	2	—	197	—	—	—
1825	*Hercules*	135	—	1	1	—	133	—	—	—

Year	Vessel	Embarked		Relanded	Deaths		Landed: Sydney		Hobart	
		M.	F.		M.	F.	M.	F.	M.	F.
1825	*Mariner*	—	?113	—	—	1	—	112	—	—
1825	*Norfolk*	180	—	—	2	—	178	—	—	—
1825	*Minstrel*	—	121	—	—	—	—	121	—	—
1825	*Lonach*	?144	—	—	1	—	143	—	—	—
1825	*Medina*	180	—	—	2	—	—	—	178	—
1825	*Midas*	—	109	—	—	1	—	50	—	58
1825	*Henry Porcher* ..	?176	—	—	1	—	175	—	—	—
1825	*Medway*	?175	—	—	3	—	—	—	172	—
1826	*Marquis of Hastings* ..	152	—	—	—	—	152	—	—	—
1826	*Sir Godfrey Webster* ..	196	—	2	3	—	191	—	—	—
1826	*Mangles*	190	—	—	—	—	190	—	—	—
1826	*Sesostris*	150	—	—	3	—	147	—	—	—
1826	*Woodman*	150	—	—	4	—	—	—	146	—
1826	*Providence*	—	100	—	—	1	—	—	—	99
1826	*Lady Rowena*	—	100	—	—	—	—	100	—	—
1826	*Regalia*	130	—	1	—	—	129	—	—	—
1826	*Earl St. Vincent* ..	160	—	—	—	—	—	—	160	—
1826	*Marquis of Huntley* ..	200	—	—	2	—	198	—	—	—
1826	*England*	148	—	—	—	—	148	—	—	—
1826	*Chapman*	100	—	2E	—	—	—	—	98	—
1826	*Boyne*	200	—	1	—	—	199	—	—	—
1826	*Woodford*	100	—	—	1	—	—	—	99	—
1826	*Speke*	156	—	—	—	—	156	—	—	—
1826	*Phoenix*	190	—	—	1	—	189	—	—	—
1827	*Sir Charles Forbes* ..	—	73	—	—	4	—	—	—	69
1827	*Grenada*	—	88	—	—	4	—	84	—	—
1827	*Brothers*	—	161	—	—	3	—	158	—	—
1827	*Albion*	192	—	—	—	—	192	—	—	—
1827	*Midas*	148	—	—	3	—	145	—	—	—
1827	*Andromeda*	146	—	—	3	—	—	—	143	—
1827	*Mariner*	161	—	1	2	—	158	—	—	—
1827	*Countess of Harcourt* ..	194	—	—	2	—	192	—	—	—
1827	*Guildford*	190	—	—	1	—	189	—	—	—
1827	*Marquis of Hastings* ..	168	—	—	—	—	168	—	—	—
1827	*Governor Ready* ..	191	—	—	1	—	—	—	190	—
1827	*Persian*	—	60	—	—	—	—	—	—	60
1827	*Princess Charlotte* ..	—	91	1?	—	1	—	?89	—	—
1827	*Manlius*	176	—	—	2	—	174	—	—	—
1827	*Cambridge*	200	—	—	2	—	198	—	—	—
1827	*Harmony*	—	80	—	—	—	—	80	—	—
1827	*Prince Regent*	180	—	—	—	—	180	—	—	—
1827	*Layton*	160	—	—	1	—	4	—	155	—
1827	*Champion*	128	—	1	1	—	126	—	—	—
1827	*Eliza*	192	—	—	—	—	192	—	—	—
1827	*Sovereign*	—	81	—	—	—	—	—	—	81
1827	*John*	188	—	—	3	—	185	—	—	—
1827	*Asia* (Edman)	160	—	2	1	—	—	—	157	—
1827	*Lousia*	—	90	—	—	—	—	90	—	—
1827	*Asia* (Ager)	200	—	—	2	—	—	—	198	—
1828	*Florentia*	172	—	6	1	—	165	—	—	—
1828	*Elizabeth*	—	194	—	—	2	—	192	—	—
1828	*Marquis of Huntley* ..	160	—	—	—	—	160	—	—	—
1828	*Hooghly*	100	—	1?	—	—	99	—	—	—
1828	*Morley*	195	—	—	3	—	192	—	—	—

Year	Vessel	Embarked		Relanded	Deaths		Landed: Sydney		Landed: Hobart	
		M.	F.		M.	F.	M.	F.	M.	F.
1828	*Marmion*	130	—	—	4	—	—	—	126	—
1828	*Asia*	100	—	—	—	—	100	—	—	—
1828	*Mangles*	200	—	—	3	—	197	—	—	—
1828	*Mermaid*	—	99	—	—	—	—	—	—	99
1828	*Borodino*	200	—	—	—	—	200	—	—	—
1828	*Phoenix*	190	—	—	—	—	190	—	—	—
1828	*Bussorah Merchant* ..	170	—	—	4	—	166	—	—	—
1828	*William Miles* ..	192	—	—	7	—	—	—	185	—
1828	*Bengal Merchant* ..	170	—	—	4	—	—	—	166	—
1828	*Woodford*	184	—	—	1	—	—	—	183	—
1828	*Countess of Harcourt* ..	184	—	—	—	—	184	—	—	—
1828	*Borneo*	—	73	—	—	3	—	—	—	70
1828	*Competitor*	—	99	—	—	—	—	99	—	—
1828	*Marquis of Hastings* ..	178	—	—	—	—	178	—	—	—
1828	*Albion*	192	—	—	4	—	188	—	—	—
1828	*Manlius*	176	—	—	1	—	—	—	175	—
1828	*City of Edinburgh* ..	—	80	—	—	—	—	80	—	—
1828	*Eliza*	158	—	—	8	—	150	—	—	—
1828	*Roslin Castle*	176	—	—	2	—	—	—	174	—
1828	*Royal George*	160	—	—	2	—	158	—	—	—
1829	*Harmony*	—	100	—	—	—	—	—	—	100
1829	*Governor Ready* ..	200	—	—	—	—	200	—	—	—
1829	*Vittoria*	160	—	—	9	—	151	—	—	—
1829	*Sophia*	192	—	—	2	—	190	—	—	—
1829	*Fergusson*	216	—	—	2	—	214	—	—	—
1829	*Mellish*	170	—	1	1	—	168	—	—	—
1829	*Georgiana*	170	—	—	3	—	—	—	167	—
1829	*Edward*	—	177	—	—	3	—	174	—	—
1829	*Lord Melville*	170	—	—	—	—	170	—	—	—
1829	*Princess Royal* ..	—	100	—	—	—	—	100	—	—
1829	*Eliza*	171	—	1	3	—	167	—	—	—
1829	*Waterloo*	180	—	—	2	—	178	—	—	—
1829	*Lady Harewood* ..	208	—	—	1	—	—	—	207	—
1829	*Sovereign*	—	119	—	—	—	—	119	—	—
1829	*America*	176	—	—	8	—	168	—	—	—
1829	*Norfolk*	200	—	—	—	—	200	—	—	—
1829	*York*	192	—	—	—	—	—	—	192	—
1829	*John*	188	—	—	—	—	188	—	—	—
1829	*Lady of the Lake* ..	—	81	—	—	2	—	—	—	79
1829	*Guildford*	200	—	—	4	—	196	—	—	—
1829	*Layton*	190	—	—	2	—	188	—	—	—
1829	*Thames*	160	—	—	2	—	—	—	158	—
1829	*Lucy Davidson* ..	—	101	—	—	2	—	99	—	—
1829	*Morley*	200	—	—	—	—	200	—	—	—
1829	*Claudine*	180	—	—	2	—	178	—	—	—
1829	*Sarah*	200	—	—	1	—	199	—	—	—
1829	*Surrey*	200	—	—	1	—	—	—	199	—
1829	*Larkins*	200	—	1	3	—	196	—	—	—
1830	*Prince Regent*	200	—	1?	1	—	—	—	198	—
1830	*Asia*	—	200	1	—	3	—	196	—	—
1830	*Bussorah Merchant* ..	200	—	—	2	—	—	—	198	—
1830	*James Pattison* ..	200	—	—	1	—	199	—	—	—
1830	*Katherine Stewart Forbes*	200	—	—	1	—	199	—	—	—
1830	*Eliza*	—	117	—	—	2	—	—	—	115

Year	*Vessel*	*Embarked*		*Relanded*	*Deaths*		*Landed: Sydney*		*Landed: Hobart*	
		M.	*F.*		*M.*	*F.*	*M.*	*F.*	*M.*	*F.*
1830	*Dunvegan Castle*	180	—	—	5	—	175	—	—	—
1830	*Mary*	168	—	—	1	—	—	—	167	—
1830	*Forth*	118	—	—	3	—	115	—	—	—
1830	*Mermaid*	200	—	—	2	—	198	—	—	—
1830	*Nithsdale*	184	—	—	1	—	183	—	—	—
1830	*Roslin Castle*	—	128	—	—	—	—	128	—	—
1830	*Sir Charles Forbes*	160	—	—	2	—	—	—	158	—
1830	*Lady Feversham*	180	—	—	2	—	178	—	—	—
1830	*Manlius*	200	—	—	—	—	—	—	200	—
1830	*David Lyon*	220	—	—	3	—	—	—	217	—
1830	*Adrian*	169	—	1	—	—	168	—	—	—
1830	*Marquis of Huntley*	228	—	—	1	—	227	—	—	—
1830	*Mellish*	—	118	—	—	3	—	—	—	115
1830	*Forth*	—	120	—	—	—	—	120	—	—
1830	*Royal George*	215	—	—	4	—	—	—	211	—
1830	*Southworth*	160	—	—	1	—	—	—	159	—
1830	*Lord Melville*	176	—	—	—	—	176	—	—	—
1830	*Hercules*	200	—	—	1	—	199	—	—	—
1830	*Persian*	198	—	—	1	—	—	—	197	—
1830	*Royal Admiral*	193	—	—	—	—	193	—	—	—
1830	*Florentia*	200	—	—	4	—	196	—	—	—
1830	*Andromeda*	181	—	1	8	—	172	—	—	—
1830	*Clyde*	216	—	—	—	—	—	—	216	—
1830	*Burrell*	192	—	—	3	—	189	—	—	—
1831	*John*	200	—	—	—	—	—	—	200	—
1831	*York*	200	—	—	2	—	198	—	—	—
1831	*Edward*	158	—	—	5	—	153	—	—	—
1831	*Lady Harewood*	216	—	1	1	—	214	—	—	—
1831	*Kains*	—	120	—	—	2	—	118	—	—
1831	*Red Rover*	168	—	—	2	—	—	—	166	—
1831	*Earl of Liverpool*	—	90	1	—	1	—	88	—	—
1831	*Waterloo*	200	—	—	1	—	199	—	—	—
1831	*America*	—	189	—	—	3	—	—	—	186
1831	*Eliza*	224	—	—	—	—	—	—	224	—
1831	*Eleanor*	140	—	7	—	—	133	—	—	—
1831	*Camden*	198	—	—	—	—	198	—	—	—
1831	*Georgiana*	182	—	—	2	—	180	—	—	—
1831	*Exmouth*	290	—	—	1	—	289	—	—	—
1831	*Palambam*	—	116	—	—	2	—	114	—	—
1831	*Argyle*	250	—	1	5	—	—	—	244	—
1831	*Proteus*	112	—	—	—	—	—	—	112	—
1831	*Hooghly*	—	186	2	—	—	—	184	—	—
1831	*Mary*	—	151	—	—	2	—	—	—	149
1831	*Larkins*	280	—	—	—	—	—	—	280	—
1831	*William Glen Anderson*	166	—	—	—	—	—	—	166	—
1831	*Jane*	130	—	—	2	—	128	—	—	—
1831	*Strathfieldsay*	224	—	—	3	—	—	—	221	—
1831	*Lord Lyndoch*	266	—	—	—	—	—	—	266	—
1831	*Surrey*	200	—	—	1	—	199	—	—	—
1831	*Asia*	220	—	3	11	—	206	—	—	—
1831	*Bussorah Merchant*	200	—	2	—	—	198	—	—	—
1832	*Norfolk*	200	—	1	4	—	195	—	—	—
1832	*Asia*	200	—	—	—	—	200	—	—	—
1832	*Elizabeth*	220	—	—	—	—	—	—	220	—

Year	Vessel	Embarked M.	Embarked F.	Relanded	Deaths M.	Deaths F.	Landed: Sydney M.	Landed: Sydney F.	Landed: Hobart M.	Landed: Hobart F.
1832	*Pyramus*	—	151	2	—	2	—	147	—	—
1832	*Isabella*	224	—	—	—	—	224	—	—	—
1832	*Gilmore*	224	—	—	1	—	—	—	223	—
1832	*Portland*	178	—	—	—	—	178	—	—	—
1832	*Captain Cook*	200	—	—	2	—	198	—	—	—
1832	*Burrell*	—	101	—	—	—	—	101	—	—
1832	*John*	200	—	1	2	—	198	—	—	—
1832	*Southworth*	—	134	—	—	1	—	133	—	—
1832	*City of Edinburgh*	145	—	6	—	—	139	—	—	—
1832	*Katherine Stewart Forbes*	222	—	—	13	—	—	—	209	—
1832	*England*	200	—	—	2	—	—	—	198	—
1832	*Lady Harewood*	200	—	—	1	—	199	—	—	—
1832	*Hydery*	—	150	1	—	3	—	—	—	146
1832	*Clyde*	200	—	—	1	—	199	—	—	—
1832	*Lord William Bentinck*	186	—	—	1	—	—	—	185	—
1832	*Eliza*	198	—	—	2	—	196	—	—	—
1832	*Planter*	200	—	—	—	—	200	—	—	—
1832	*Hercules*	200	—	—	2	—	198	—	—	—
1832	*Dunvegan Castle*	200	—	—	—	—	200	—	—	—
1832	*Parmelia*	200	—	—	4	—	196	—	—	—
1832	*York*	200	—	—	—	—	—	—	200	—
1833	*Mary*	170	—	—	2	—	168	—	—	—
1833	*Frances Charlotte*	—	?100	—	—	7	—	—	—	95
1833	*Georgiana*	184	—	—	—	—	—	—	184	—
1833	*Fanny*	—	106	—	—	8	—	98	—	—
1833	*Roslin Castle*	199	—	4	1	—	194	—	—	—
1833	*Circassian*	186	—	—	—	—	—	—	186	—
1833	*Camden*	200	—	—	2	—	198	—	—	—
1833	*Surrey* (Veale)	—	142	3	—	—	—	141	—	—
1833	*Andromeda*	186	—	—	4	—	182	—	—	—
1833	*Surrey* (Kemp)	?204	—	—	1	—	—	—	204	—
1833	*Mangles*	236	—	—	1	—	235	—	—	—
1833	*Lotus*	216	—	—	—	—	—	—	216	—
1833	*Diana*	—	100	—	—	1	—	99	—	—
1833	*Jupiter*	167	—	—	4	—	—	—	163	—
1833	*Portland*	193	—	1	8	—	184	—	—	—
1833	*Asia*	?230	—	—	10	—	?225	—	—	—
1833	*Jane*	—	115	—	—	2	—	—	—	113
1833	*Enchantress*	200	—	—	1	—	—	—	199	—
1833	*Waterloo*	214	—	—	11	—	203	—	—	—
1833	*Caroline*	—	120	—	—	—	—	120	—	—
1833	*Emperor Alexander*	210	—	—	2	—	—	—	208	—
1833	*Atlas*	200	—	—	—	—	—	—	200	—
1833	*Captain Cook*	230	—	—	4	—	226	—	—	—
1833	*Stakesby*	216	—	—	—	—	—	—	216	—
1833	*Heroine*	260	—	—	4	—	256	—	—	—
1833	*Buffalo*	—	180	1	—	1	—	178	—	—
1833	*Lord Lyndoch*	330	—	1	4	—	325	—	—	—
1833	*William Bryan*	—	130	—	—	7	—	—	—	123
1833	*Royal Admiral*	221	—	1	5	—	215	—	—	—
1833	*Aurora*	300	—	—	—	—	300	—	—	—
1833	*Isabella*	306	—	—	6	—	—	—	300	—
1833	*Java*	206	—	—	5	—	201	—	—	—
1833	*Neva*	170	—	—	1	—	169	—	—	—

Year	Vessel	Embarked M.	Embarked F.	Relanded	Deaths M.	Deaths F.	Landed: Sydney M.	Landed: Sydney F.	Landed: Hobart M.	Landed: Hobart F.
1833	*John*	260	—	—	3	—	—	—	257	—
1833	*Lloyds*	201	—	2	1	—	198	—	—	—
1833	*Amphitrite**	—	101	—	—	101	—	—	—	—
1834	*Southworth*	190	—	—	2	—	—	—	188	—
1834	*Royal Sovereign*	170	—	—	2	—	168	—	—	—
1834	*Fairlie*	376	—	—	4	—	372	—	—	—
1834	*Parmetlia*	220	—	—	2	—	218	—	—	—
1834	*Moffat*	400	—	1E	6	—	—	—	393	—
1834	*Hive*	250	—	—	2	—	248	—	—	—
1834	*Numa*	—	140	—	—	2	—	138	—	—
1834	*James Laing*	201	—	1	3	—	197	—	—	—
1834	*Arab*	230	—	—	2	—	—	—	228	—
1834	*Susan*	300	—	—	8	—	292	—	—	—
1834	*John Barry*	320	—	—	2	—	—	—	318	—
1834	*Surrey*	260	—	—	—	—	260	—	—	—
1834	*Edward*	—	151	—	—	—	—	—	—	151
1834	*William Metcalfe*	240	—	—	—	—	—	—	240	—
1834	*Roslin Castle*	230	—	—	3	—	227	—	—	—
1834	*Andromeda*	—	176	1	—	2	—	173	—	—
1834	*Henry Tanner*	220	—	—	2	—	218	—	—	—
1834	*Blenheim*	200	—	—	2	—	198	—	—	—
1834	*Hooghly*	260	—	—	—	—	260	—	—	—
1834	*George Hibbert*	—	144	—	—	—	—	144	—	—
1835	*Henry Porcher*	260	—	—	8	—	252	—	—	—
1835	*Royal Admiral*	203	—	—	2	—	201	—	—	—
1835	*Augusta Jessie*	210	—	—	3	—	—	—	207	—
1835	*Bengal Merchant*	270	—	—	3	—	267	—	—	—
1835	*Lady Kennaway*	311	—	18	19	—	—	—	274(*a*)	—
1835	*Waterloo*	224	—	—	—	—	—	—	224	—
1835	*New Grove*	—	165	—	—	—	—	—	—	165
1835	*Lady Nugent*	286	—	—	2	—	284	—	—	—
1835	*Forth*	196	—	—	1	—	195	—	—	—
1835	*George III**	220	—	—	139	—	—	—	81	—
1835	*Marquis of Huntley*	320	—	—	1	—	319	—	—	—
1835	*Westmoreland*	220	—	—	2	—	218	—	—	—
1835	*Mangles*	310	—	—	—	—	—	—	310	—
1835	*Norfolk*	280	—	—	—	—	—	—	280	—
1835	*Hero*	202	—	3	2	—	197	—	—	—
1835	*Mary*	—	180	2	—	1	—	177	—	—
1835	*England*	230	—	—	—	—	230	—	—	—
1835	*Blackwell*	152	—	2	—	—	150	—	—	—
1835	*Aurora*	300	—	—	1	—	—	—	299	—
1835	*Hector*	—	134	—	—	—	—	—	—	134
1835	*Mary Anne*	306	—	—	1	—	305	—	—	—
1835	*Lady MacNaghten*	305	—	5	2	—	298	—	—	—
1835	*Neva**	—	151	—	—	145	—	6	—	—
1835	*Hive**	252	—	2	2	—	248	—	—	—
1835	*Layton*	270	—	1	2	—	—	—	267	—
1835	*Royal Sovereign*	170	—	—	1	—	169	—	—	—
1836	*Bardaster*	240	—	—	5	—	—	—	235	—

(*a*) The military prisoners embarked at Cork were not landed at Hobart; presumably some of the deaths occurred among them, and, apparently, 18 were landed at Sydney.

Year	*Vessel*	*Embarked* M.	F.	*Relanded*	*Deaths* M.	F.	*Landed: Sydney* M.	F.	*Hobart* M.	F.
1836	*John Barry*	320	—	2	2	—	318	—	—	—
1836	*Susan*	300	—	—	6	—	294	—	—	—
1836	*Henry Wellesley*	—	118	—	—	5	—	113	—	—
1836	*Asia*	290	—	—	2	—	—	—	288	—
1836	*Roslin Castle*	—	165	—	—	3	—	162	—	—
1836	*Recovery*	284	—	4	—	—	280	—	—	—
1836	*Arab*	—	132	—	—	1	—	—	—	131
1836	*Surrey*	229	—	2	5	—	222	—	—	—
1836	*Elphinstone*	240	—	—	2	—	—	—	238	—
1836	*Thomas Harrison*	—	112	—	—	—	—	112	—	—
1836	*Strathfieldsay*	270	—	—	1	—	269	—	—	—
1836	*Lord Lyndoch*	330	—	—	5	—	—	—	325	—
1836	*Moffatt*	400	—	1	3	—	396	—	—	—
1836	*Waterloo*	224	—	—	2	—	222	—	—	—
1836	*Elizabeth*	—	161	—	—	—	—	161	—	—
1836	*Lady Kennaway*	300	—	—	2	—	298	—	—	—
1836	*Lady Nugent*	286	—	—	—	—	—	—	286	—
1836	*Captain Cook*	236	—	7	1	—	228	—	—	—
1836	*Henry Porcher*	260	—	—	2	—	—	—	258	—
1836	*Westmoreland*	—	185	—	—	1	—	—	—	184
1836	*Bengal Merchant*	270	—	—	1	—	269	—	—	—
1836	*Pyramus*	—	121	1	—	—	—	120	—	—
1836	*Eden*	280	—	—	3	—	—	—	277	—
1836	*Earl Grey*	297	—	6	3	—	288	—	—	—
1837	*St. Vincent*	193	—	2	1	—	190	—	—	—
1837	*John*	260	—	—	5	—	255	—	—	—
1837	*Norfolk*	280	—	—	2	—	278	—	—	—
1837	*Sarah*	255	—	1	9	—	—	—	245	—
1837	*Sarah and Elizabeth*	—	100	2	—	2	—	96	—	—
1837	*Prince George*	250	—	—	6	—	244	—	—	—
1837	*Frances Charlotte*	150	—	—	—	—	—	—	150	—
1837	*Margaret*	—	162	9	—	2	—	151	—	—
1837	*Mangles*	310	—	—	2	—	308	—	—	—
1837	*Heber*	243	—	25	1	—	217	—	—	—
1837	*Blenheim*	210	—	—	6	—	—	—	204	—
1837	*Lloyds*	200	—	—	—	—	200	—	—	—
1837	*Calcutta*	360	—	20	10	—	330	—	—	—
1837	*Elphinstone*	240	—	—	1	—	—	—	239	—
1837	*Recovery*	280	—	—	5	—	—	—	275	—
1837	*Charles Kerr*	250	—	—	4	—	246	—	—	—
1837	*Platina*	—	?116	2	—	—	—	—	—	113
1837	*James Pattison*	270	—	—	—	—	270	—	—	—
1837	*Susan*	300	—	1	6	—	—	—	293	—
1837	*Asia*	280	—	—	3	—	277	—	—	—
1837	*Henry Wellesley*	—	140	1	—	—	—	139	—	—
1837	*Sir Charles Forbes*	—	150	2	—	1	—	147	—	—
1838	*Neptune*	200	—	—	3	—	197	—	—	—
1838	*Royal Sovereign*	150	—	—	—	—	—	—	150	—
1838	*Neptune* (Ferris)	350	—	—	2	—	—	—	348	—
1838	*Atwick*	—	151	—	—	1	—	—	—	150
1838	*Waterloo*	224	—	—	—	—	224	—	—	—
1838	*Emma Eugenia*	200	—	—	1	—	199	—	—	—
1838	*Diamond*	—	162	—	—	1	—	161	—	—
1838	*Moffatt*	400	—	—	3	—	—	—	397	—

Year	Vessel	Embarked M.	Embarked F.	Relanded	Deaths M.	Deaths F.	Landed: Sydney M.	Landed: Sydney F.	Landed: Hobart M.	Landed: Hobart F.
1838	*William Jardine*	224	—	12	2	—	210	—	—	—
1838	*Bengal Merchant*	270	—	—	3	—	267	—	—	—
1838	*Lord Lyndoch*	330	—	—	19	—	311	—	—	—
1838	*Westmoreland*	254	—	37	4	—	213	—	—	—
1838	*Lord William Bentinck*	320	—	—	3	—	—	—	317	—
1838	*John Renwick*	—	174	1	—	1	—	172	—	—
1838	*Clyde*	216	—	26	—	—	215	—	—	—
1838	*Nautilus*	—	137	4	—	1	—	—	—	132
1838	*Minerva*	160	—	—	1	—	—	—	159	—
1838	*Coromandel*	350	—	—	2	—	—	—	348	—
1838	*Earl Grey*	290	—	—	2	—	288	—	—	—
1838	*Augusta Jessie*	210	—	—	1	—	—	—	209	—
1838	*Portsea*	240	—	—	1	—	239	—	—	—
1838	*Elphinstone*	255	—	23	—	—	232	—	—	—
1839	*Margaret*	—	189	22	—	1	—	166	—	—
1839	*Majestic*	—	126	3	—	—	—	—	—	123
1839	*Gilmore*	280	—	1	1	—	—	—	278	—
1839	*Theresa*	266	—	—	2	—	264	—	—	—
1839	*Planter*	—	171	—	—	—	—	171	—	—
1839	*John Barry*	320	—	—	1	—	319	—	—	—
1839	*Pyramus*	170	—	—	—	—	—	—	170(*a*)	—
1839	*Waverley*	176	—	—	—	—	176	—	—	—
1839	*Whitby*	—	133	—	—	1	—	132	—	—
1839	*Marquis of Hastings*	240	—	—	7	—	—	—	233	—
1839	*Egyptian*	190	—	—	1	—	—	—	189	—
1839	*Parkfield*	240	—	—	—	—	240	—	—	—
1839	*Hindostan*	—	179	—	—	1	—	—	—	178
1839	*Blenheim*	207	—	7	4	—	196	—	—	—
1839	*Mary Anne*	—	143	—	—	1	—	142	—	—
1839	*Barossa*	336	—	—	2	—	334	—	—	—
1839	*Layton*	263	—	3	4	—	—	—	256	—
1839	*Minerva*	—	119	1	—	2	—	116	—	—
1840	*Canton*	240	—	—	?10	—	—	—	230	—
1840	*Middlesex*	200	—	—	8	—	192	—	—	—
1840	*Woodbridge*	230	—	—	1	—	229(*b*)	—	—	—
1840	*Runnymede*	200	—	—	—	—	—	—	200	—
1840	*Gilbert Henderson*	—	185	1	—	1	—	—	—	183
1840	*Mandarin*	212	—	1	1	—	—	—	210	—
1840	*Surrey*	—	213	—	—	1	—	212	—	—
1840	*Maitland*	310	—	5	3	—	302	—	—	—
1840	*Isabella*	—	119	—	—	—	—	119	—	—
1840	*Asia*	276	—	—	2	—	—	—	274	—
1840	*King William*	180	—	—	—	—	180	—	—	—
1840	*Margaret*	—	133	2	—	1	—	130	—	—
1840	*Pekoe*	184	—	4	3	—	177	—	—	—
1840	*Eden*	270	—	—	1	—	269	—	—	—
1840	*Egyptian*	170	—	—	—	—	—	—	170	—
1841	*Navarino*	—	183	3	—	2	—	—	—	178
1841	*Hindostan*	210	—	1	—	—	—	—	209	—
1841	*Lord Lyndoch*	321	—	1	6	—	—	—	314	—

(*a*) Landed 76 at Hobart and 94 at Port Arthur.
(*b*) Eighty of these prisoners were transhipped in *Augusta Jessie* to Norfolk Island, the remainder disembarking at Sydney.

Year	Vessel	Embarked M.	Embarked F.	Relanded	Deaths M.	Deaths F.	Landed: Sydney M.	Landed: Sydney F.	Landed: Hobart M.	Landed: Hobart F.
1841	*British Sovereign* ..	180	—	—	—	—	—	—	180	—
1841	*Lady Raffles*	330	—	—	3	—	—	—	327	—
1841	*Mary Anne*	—	125	—	—	1	—	—	—	124
1841	*Duncan*	259	—	—	—	—	—	—	259	—
1841	*Rajah*	—	190	10	—	1	—	—	—	179
1841	*Asia*	260	—	—	2	—	—	—	258	—
1841	*Layton*	250	—	—	5	—	—	—	245	—
1841	*Westmoreland*	202	—	—	2	—	—	—	200	—
1841	*Waverley*	176	—	—	2	—	—	—	174	—
1841	*David Clarke*	308	—	—	1	—	—	—	307	—
1841	*Garland Grove* ..	—	180	—	—	1	—	—	—	179
1841	*Lord Goderich*	186	—	—	—	—	—	—	186	—
1841	*Mexborough*	—	145	—	—	2	—	—	—	143
1842	*Prince Regent*	181	—	—	3	—	—	—	178	—
1842	*Barossa*	350	—	—	2	—	—	—	348	—
1842	*Tortoise*	400	—	3	3	—	—	—	394	—
1842	*Richard Webb*	193	—	—	4	—	—	—	189	—
1842	*John Brewer*	200	—	1	1	—	—	—	198	—
1842	*Emma Eugenia* ..	—	191	—	—	1	—	—	—	190
1842	*Isabella*	267	—	—	1	—	—	—	266	—
1842	*Somersetshire*	219	—	—	1	—	—	—	218	—
1842	*Eden*	280	—	2	5	—	—	—	275	—
1842	*Candahar*	250	—	—	1	—	—	—	249	—
1842	*Susan*	299	—	—	2	—	—	—	297	—
1842	*Elphinstone*	230	—	—	1	—	—	—	229	—
1842	*Isabella Watson* ..	201	—	4	2	—	—	—	195	—
1842	*Surrey*	250	—	—	3	—	—	—	247	—
1842	*Hope*	—	139	—	—	2	—	—	—	137
1842	*Royal Admiral* ..	—	204	—	—	2	—	—	—	202(*c*)
1842	*Kinnear*	174	—	—	2	—	—	—	172	—
1842	*Marquis of Hastings* ..	240	—	—	2	—	—	—	238	—
1842	*Emily*	240	—	—	2	—	—	—	238	—
1842	*Waterloo**	220	—	1	144	—	—	—	72(*d*)	—
1842	*Moffat*	390	—	1	2	—	—	—	387	—
1842	*Waverley*	—	149	—	—	—	—	—	—	149
1842	*Triton*	256	—	—	3	—	—	—	253	—
1843	*Navarino*	180	—	—	2	—	—	—	178	—
1843	*Earl Grey*	264	—	—	3	—	—	—	261	—
1843	*Duchess of Northumberl'd*	270	—	—	3	—	—	—	267	—
1843	*Garland Grove*	—	191	1	—	8	—	—	—	182
1843	*North Briton*	179	—	—	1	—	—	—	178	—
1843	*John Renwick*	161	—	1	—	—	—	—	160	—
1843	*Margaret*	—	156	—	—	4	—	—	—	152
1843	*Cressy*	296	—	—	1	—	—	—	295	—
1843	*Gilmore*	?254	—	—	3	—	—	—	249	—
1843	*Constant*	204	—	—	3	—	—	—	201	—
1843	*East London*	—	?133	—	—	17	—	—	—	116
1843	*Asiatic*	188	—	—	2	—	—	—	186	—
1843	*Emerald Isle*	214	—	—	1	—	—	—	213	—
1843	*Forfarshire*	240	—	—	1	—	—	—	239	—
1843	*Lord Petre*	238	—	—	1	—	—	—	237	—

(*c*) Eighty were landed at Launceston, the balance at Hobart.
(*d*) Landed by *Cape Packet*, from the Cape.

Year	Vessel	Embarked M.	Embarked F.	Relanded	Deaths M.	Deaths F.	Landed: Sydney M.	Landed: Sydney F.	Landed: Hobart M.	Landed: Hobart F.
1843	*Henrietta*	190	—	—	—	—	—	—	190	—
1843	*Orator*	170	—	—	1	—	—	—	169	—
1843	*Woodbridge*	—	204	—	—	—	—	—	—	204
1844	*Duke of Richmond*	111	—	—	—	—	—	—	111	—
1844	*Anson*	506	—	6	1	—	—	—	499	—
1844	*Marion*	301	—	1	5	—	—	—	295	—
1844	*Emma Eugenia*	—	170	—	—	—	—	—	—	170
1844	*Equestrian*	290	—	—	2	—	—	—	288	—
1844	*Greenlaw*	—	120	—	—	5	—	—	—	115
1844	*London*	250	—	—	—	—	—	—	250	—
1844	*Maria Somes*	264	—	—	2	—	—	—	262	—
1844	*Cadet*	?164	—	—	—	—	—	—	164	—
1844	*Angelina*	—	170	—	—	3	—	—	—	167
1844	*Barossa*	324	—	3	2	—	—	—	319	—
1844	*Emily*	205	—	—	—	—	—	—	205	—
1844	*Lord Auckland*	238	—	—	2	—	—	—	236	—
1844	*William Jardine*	270	—	—	3	—	—	—	267	—
1844	*Tasmania*	—	191	—	—	2	—	—	—	189
1844	*Sir Robert Peel*	254	—	—	1	—	—	—	253	—
1845	*Phoebe*	—	129	—	—	1	—	—	—	128
1845	*Elizabeth and Henry*	200	—	—	1	—	—	—	199	—
1845	*Mt. Stewart Elphinstone*	266	—	6	1	—	—	—	259	—
1845	*Theresa*	220	—	—	—	—	—	—	220	—
1845	*Tory*	—	170	—	—	—	—	—	—	170
1845	*Ratcliffe*	215	—	—	—	—	—	—	215	—
1845	*Marion*	301	—	1	—	—	—	—	300	—
1845	*Equestrian*	300	—	1	1	—	—	—	298	—
1845	*Lloyds*	—	170	—	—	—	—	—	—	170
1845	*Tasmania*	—	140	—	—	1	—	—	—	139
1845	*Pestonjee Bomanjee*	300	—	1	1	—	—	—	298	—
1846	*Samuel Boddington*	143	—	—	—	—	—	—	143	—
1846	*Joseph Somes*	?250	—	—	7	—	—	—	243	—
1846	*Emma Eugenia*	—	170	—	—	6	—	—	—	164
1846	*Palmyra*	300	—	6	2	—	—	—	292	—
1846	*Lord Auckland*	180	—	—	4	—	—	—	176	—
1846	*Sea Queen*	—	170	—	—	1	—	—	—	169
1847	*Elizabeth and Henry*	—	170	1	—	—	—	—	—	169
1847	*Pestonjee Bomanjee*	200	—	4	4	—	—	—	174(a)	—
1847	*Arabian*	—	150	—	—	1	—	—	—	149
1847	*Asia*	—	169	—	—	—	—	—	—	169
1847	*Waverley*	—	134	—	—	5	—	—	—	129
1848	*Cadet*	—	164	—	—	1	—	—	—	163
1848	*John Calvin*	—	171	—	—	1	—	—	—	170
1848	*Mt. Stewart Elphinstone*	240	—	—	—	—	—	—	240	—
1848	*Elizabeth and Henry*	—	170	—	—	1	—	—	—	169
1848	*Bangalore*	204	—	—	2	—	—	—	222	—
1848	*Tory*	—	170	—	—	—	—	—	—	170
1848	*Kinnear*	—	144	—	—	5	—	—	—	139
1848	*Ratcliffe*	250	—	—	? 2	—	—	—	248	—
1849	*Pestonjee Bomanjee*	304	—	4	2	—	—	—	298	—
1849	*Lord Auckland*	—	200	—	—	1	—	—	—	199
1849	*Blenheim*	300	—	—	1	—	—	—	299	—

(*a*) Disembarked at Maria Island.

Year	Vessel	Embarked M.	Embarked F.	Relanded	Deaths M.	Deaths F.	Landed: Sydney M.	Landed: Sydney F.	Landed: Hobart M.	Landed: Hobart F.
1849	*Cadet*	—	150	—	—	7	—	—	—	143
1849	*Hashemy*	239	—	11	16	—	212	—	—	—
1849	*Maria*	—	166	—	—	1	—	—	—	165
1849	*Randolph*	300	—	—	5	—	295	—	—	—
1849	*Hyderabad*	300	—	—	3	—	—	—	297	—
1849	*Stately*	—	169	2	—	4	—	—	—	163
1849	*Australasia*	—	200	—	—	3	—	—	—	197
1849	*Havering*	336	—	—	2	—	334	—	—	—
1849	*Adelaide*	303	—	3	1	—	259	—	40	—
1850	*Eliza*	60	—	—	—	—	—	—	60	—
1850	*St. Vincent*	—	207	—	—	2	—	—	—	205
1850	*Neptune*	300	—	—	?	—	—	—	282	—
1850	*Earl Grey*	—	240	—	—	4	—	—	—	236
1850	*Blenheim*	300	—	7?	4	—	—	—	289	—
1850	*Baretto Junior* ..	—	190	—	—	4	—	—	—	186
1850	*Maria Somes*	257	—	—	2	—	—	—	255	—
1850	*Nile*	300	—	—	1	—	—	—	299	—
1850	*Duke of Cornwall* ..	—	200	—	—	2	—	—	—	198
1850	*William Jardine* ..	261	—	—	? 1	—	—	—	260	—
1850	*Rodney*	312	—	—	4	—	—	—	308	—
1850	*Hyderabad*	287	—	—	—	—	—	—	287	—
1851	*Emma Eugenia* ..	—	170	—	—	—	—	—	—	170
1851	*London*	288	—	—	3	—	—	—	285	—
1851	*Lady Kennaway* ..	250	—	—	1	—	—	—	249	—
1851	*Blackfriar*	—	261	—	—	1	—	—	—	260
1851	*Cornwall*	300	—	—	1	—	—	—	299	—
1851	*Aurora*	—	232	—	—	3	—	—	—	229
1851	*Blenheim*	310	—	—	2	—	—	—	308	—
1851	*Rodney*	312	—	12?	—	—	—	—	300	—
1852	*Anna Maria*	—	200	—	—	4	—	—	—	196
1852	*Aboukir*	280	—	—	1	—	—	—	279	—
1852	*John William Dare* ..	—	172	—	—	3	—	—	—	169
1852	*Fairlie*	294	—	—	2	—	—	—	292	—
1852	*Sir Robert Seppings* ..	—	220	—	—	1	—	—	—	219
1852	*Pestonjee Bomanjee* ..	292	—	1	3	—	—	—	287	—
1852	*Lord Dalhousie* ..	325	—	1	2	—	—	—	322	—
1852	*Martin Luther* ..	—	212	—	—	—	—	—	—	212
1852	*Lady Montagu* ..	290	—	—	?10	—	—	—	280	—
1852	*Equestrian*	294	—	—	? 4	—	—	—	290	—
1853	*Lord Auckland* ..	248	—	—	2	—	—	—	246	—
1853	*Rodney*	342	—	—	3	—	—	—	339	—
1853	*Oriental Queen* ..	280	—	—	3	—	—	—	277	—
1853	*Midlothian*	—	170	2	—	1	—	—	—	167
1853	*Duchess of Northumberl'd*	—	219	—	—	3	—	—	—	216
1853	*St. Vincent*	212	—	—	5	—	—	—	207	—

VII(c). CONVICTS DISEMBARKED AT NORFOLK ISLAND AND SYDNEY OR HOBART

Year	Vessel	Embarked M.	Embarked F.	Relanded	Deaths M.	Deaths F	Landed: Norfolk Is. M.	Landed: Norfolk Is. F.	Landed: Sydney M.	Landed: Sydney F.
1840	*Nautilus*	200	—	—	1	—	178	—	21	—
1840	*Augusta Jessie* ..	161	—	—	1	—	120	—	34	—
1840	*Mangles*	290	—	—	1	—	236	—	53	—
1844	*Maitland*	200	—	1	5	—	195	—	—	—
1844	*Blundell*	210	—	—	—	—	210	—	—	—
1844	*Agincourt*	224	—	—	4	—	220	—	—	—
1845	*Hydrabad*	260	—	—	1	—	259	—	—	—
1845	*David Malcolm* ..	220	—	—	—	—	220	—	—	—
1845	*Hyderabad*	250	—	—	—	—	250	—	—	—
1846	*Mayda*	199	—	—	4	—	195	—	—	—
1846	*China*	200	—	—	1	—	199	—	—	—
1846	*John Calvin*	199	—	—	—	—	199	—	—	—
1847	*Tory*	200	—	—	5	—	195	—	—	—
1850	*Eliza*	60	—	—	—	—	56	—	4(*a*)	—

(*a*) Landed at Hobart.

VII(d). CONVICTS DISEMBARKED AT PORT PHILLIP AND HOBART OR SYDNEY

Year	Vessel	Embarked M.	Embarked F.	Relanded	Deaths M.	Deaths F.	Landed: Pt. Phillip M.	Landed: Pt. Phillip F.	Landed: Hobart M.	Landed: Hobart F.
1803	*Calcutta*	307	—	—	8	—	299	—	—	—
1844	*Royal George*	21	—	—	—	—	21	—	—	—
1845	*Sir George Seymour* ..	345	—	—	1	—	175(*a*)	—	169	—
1845	*Stratheden*	155	—	1	—	—	51	—	103	—
1846	*Maitland*	299	—	—	3	—	291	—	6	—
1847	*Thomas Arbuthnot* ..	289	—	—	1	—	288	—	—	—
1847	*Joseph Somes*	249	—	—	—	—	248(*a*)	—	1	—
1848	*Marion*	299	—	—	2	—	292	—	?	—
1848	*Anna Maria*	190	—	—	—	—	163(*a*)	—	27	—
1849	*Eden*	237	—	—	5	—	198(*a*)	—	35	—

(*a*) Landed at Geelong.

VII(e). CONVICTS DISEMBARKED AT MORETON BAY

Year	Vessel	Embarked M.	Embarked F.	Relanded	Deaths M.	Deaths F.	Landed: M.	Landed: F.
1849	*Mt. Stewart Elphinstone*	232	—	2	3	—	225(*a*)	—
1850	*Bangalore*	297	—	1	4	—	292	—

(*a*) In addition disembarked two prisoners at Sydney, who were forwarded to Tasmania.

VII(f). CONVICTS DISEMBARKED AT WESTERN AUSTRALIA

Year	*Vessel*	*Embarked* M.	F.	*Relanded*	*Deaths* M.	F.	*Landed* M.	F.
1850	*Scindian*	75	—	—	—	—	75	—
1850	*Hashemy*	100	—	—	—	—	100	—
1851	*Mermaid*	209	—	—	1	—	208	—
1851	*Pyrenees*	296	—	—	3	—	293	—
1851	*Minden*	302	—	—	1	—	301	—
1852	*Marion*	280	—	—	1	—	279	—
1852	*William Jardine* ..	212	—	—	—	—	212	—
1853	*Dudbrook*	230	—	1	1	—	228	—
1853	*Pyrenees*	296	—	—	3	—	293	—
1853	*Robert Small*	?312	—	—	9	—	303	—
1853	*Phoebe Dunbar* ..	295	—	—	10	—	285	—
1854	*Sea Park*	304	—	—	—	—	304	—
1854	*Ramillies*	280(*a*)	—	1	2	—	277	—
1855	*Stag*	225	—	—	1	—	224	—
1855	*Adelaide*	260	—	—	1	—	259	—
1856	*William Hammond* ..	250	—	—	1	—	249	—
1856	*Runnymede*	248	—	—	—	—	248	—
1857	*Clara*	262	—	—	—	—	262	—
1858	*Nile*	270	—	—	—	—	270	—
1858	*Lord Raglan*	270	—	—	2	—	268	—
1858	*Edwin Fox*	280	—	—	—	—	280	—
1859	*Sultana*	224	—	—	—	—	224	—
1861	*Palmerston*	296	—	—	3	—	293	—
1862	*Lincelles*	306	—	—	2	—	304	—
1862	*Norwood*	293	—	3	—	—	290	—
1862	*York*	300	—	—	1	—	299	—
1863	*Merchantman*	191	—	—	—	—	191	—
1863	*Clyde*	321	—	1	—	—	320	—
1863	*Lord Dalhousie* ..	270	—	—	—	—	270	—
1864	*Clara*	301	—	—	—	—	301	—
1864	*Merchantman*	260	—	1	2	—	257	—
1865	*Racehorse*	280	—	—	2	—	278	—
1865	*Vimiera*	281	—	—	1	—	278	—
1866	*Belgravia*	277	—	—	1	—	276	—
1866	*Corona*	310	—	2	3	—	305	—
1867	*Norwood*	254	—	—	1	—	253	—
1868	*Hougoumont*	280	—	—	1	—	279	—

(*a*) Embarked 280 in England, of whom 160 landed at Gibraltar, where she embarked 157 prisoners. This made her complement on leaving Gibraltar 277. The surgeon's journal mentions only one convict death, leaving a discrepancy of one. It seems clear no deaths occurred between Gibraltar and Australia.

INDEX

INDEX